The American West

Interactions, Intersections, and Injunctions

Series Editors

Gordon Morris Bakken
California State University, Fullerton
and

Brenda Farrington
Long Beach City College

Series Contents

Law in the West

Edited with introductions by

Gordon Morris Bakken
California State University, Fullerton
and
Brenda Farrington
Long Beach City College

Routledge
Taylor & Francis Group

NEW YORK AND LONDON

First published by Garland Publishing, Inc.

This edition published 2013 by Routledge

Routledge   Routledge
Taylor & Francis Group   Taylor & Francis Group
711 Third Avenue   2 Park Square
New York, NY 10017   Milton Park, Abingdon
                             Oxon OX14 4RN

Routledge is an imprint of the Taylor & Francis Group, an informa business

10 9 8 7 6 5 4 3 2 1

The Library of Congress Cataloging-in-Publication Data

Environmental problems in America's garden of Eden / edited with
  Introduction by Gordon Morris Bakken and Brenda Farrington.
      p. cm. — (Liberty, property, and the law ; 1)
  ISBN 0-8153-3459-1 (alk. paper)
  1.   Human ecology—West (U.S.)—History. 2. Environmental
  law—West (U.S.)—History. 3. Environmental policy—West (U.S.)—
  History. I. Bakken, Gordon Morris. II Farrington, Brenda. III.
  American West (Garland Publishing, Inc.) ; no. 4.

  GF504.W35 E58 2000
  333.7'0978—dc21   00-063591

SET ISBN 9780815334620
POD ISBN 9780415643016
VOL1 9780815334569
VOL2 9780815334576
VOL3 9780815334583
VOL4 9780815334590
VOL5 9780815334606
VOL6 9780815334613

Contents

To Erika Lyn Herderson
Yorba Linda, California

Series Introduction

This anthology of western history articles emphasizes the New Western History that emerged in the 1980s and adds to it a heavy dose of legal history, a field frequently ignored or misunderstood by the New Western historians. The New Western History rejects the "Frontier Thesis" of Frederick Jackson Turner announced in 1893 and replaces it with a new set of questions. Because the New Western historians believe that place more than process facilitates historical analysis, the question of where the West can be located is an on-going debate. Because the New Western historians reject a Euro-centric process orientation of waves of pioneers civilizing western peoples red and brown in successive frontier experiences, we favor multi-cultural historical approach. We recognize that gender is a category of analysis necessary for any western history inquiry. Looking from the West at these issues we see multi-cultural interactions, and intersections of significant meaning. Further, we accord the legal system a far more important role than do most New Western historians. In legal conflict we find gender, race, and place. In the urban West with its unique environment dependent upon limited water supplies for all phases of economic life, the law of place changed as did the peoples that populated this dynamic landscape.

When Frederick Jackson Turner announced his frontier thesis in 1893, most Americans had no doubt where the West was. It was simply all of the land west of the Mississippi River. It was simply the "Wild West" of Indians and cowboys riding horses and you could see those Indians and cowboys when the Wild West show came to town. But that Wild West was not part of San Francisco in 1893 or Denver. Those instant cities had acquired the degree of civilization based on wealth, commerce, and culture to make them part of a greater American urban landscape.

Turner's frontier thesis positing that the process of civilizing the West from the colonial period until 1890 produced both American democracy and the American character started historians down the path of proof to find evidence supporting or debunking Turner's thesis. The debate continues. Early supporters of Turner found settlers from the East finding greater democracy in the West. Detractors found evidence that eastern urban factory workers did not migrate to the West in any great numbers and the West was not a safety value for labor unrest. So it went. Books and articles offered proof on both sides until the New Western Historians arrived with publication of Patricia Nelson Limerick's *The Legacy of Conquest: The Unbroken Past of the American West*

(New York: Oxford University Press, 1987). Limerick shifted the debate by noting Turner's Euro-centric focus on an east to west process whose vision was strictly limited to that of the pioneers, not those experiencing the process and seeing the pioneers as conquerors from their perspective of looking to the east from the west.

Limerick's call for inclusion in western history was not the first, but clearly the most noticed. Herbert Eugene Bolton already had suggested the utility of borderland studies noting the richness of cultural interaction in New Spain's northern territories in several books including *The Colonization of North America, 1492–1783* (New York: Macmillan Co., 1920), *Coronado, Knight of Pueblos and Plains* (Albuquerque: University of New Mexico Press, 1949), and *Spain's Northern Frontier, 1763–1800* (Chicago: Denoyer-Geppert Co., 1967). Bolton appreciated the fact that Europeans and Indians had occupied lands together for generations in the American Southwest. Limerick's argument acknowledges the need for such studies, but rejects Bolton's emphasis on the opening and closing of Spanish and English empires in favor of the continuity of conquest. Further, Limerick tapped into the scholarly dissatisfaction of the 1960s with the political synthesis in American history and joined the legions of historians including women, persons of color, and maginalized classes in the general fabric of American history. Most importantly, Limerick called for studies of place. Here the West as a region needed recognition and definition.

Scholars more easily accepted the concept of the West as place or region than they were able to identify exactly what made any geographic area the "West." The most ambitious attempt to do so was William E. Riebsame's *Atlas of the New West: Portrait of a Changing Region* (New York: W.W. Norton and Co., 1997). This beautifully executed volume offers a variety of definitions of region noting that the West keeps moving around in time and space, if not the mind. Geographers, historians, artists, and writers have defined the West by certain marks. The West is characterized by its extractive industries such as mining, logging, ranching, and irrigated farming. It is rooted in natural resources and their exploitation. The West is more urbanized than the East. From space at night, it is clear to any observer that the East shimmers and the West has spots of brilliance. The West contains more public land administered by the federal government resulting in jurisdictional boundaries drawn by the Bureau of Reclamation and United States Forest Service gridding the mapscape. Huge portions of this mapscape represent American Indian reservation lands. Indian country in the West is recognizable and substantial in space. These lands were developed with capital from the East, by corporations housed in the East, and managed by executives living in the East but visiting the West. The West remains Turner's, but it is Ted rather than Frederick Jackson that now defines the present reality.

The *Atlas* has its critics because much of what many consider the West is hacked off, even the pacific coast and the Dakotas. But there is little to replace it excepting alternative concepts of how to define the West and where to fix its boundaries.

It is not difficult to start identifying regions and subregions. Earl Pomeroy's *The Pacific Slope: a History of California, Oregon, Washington, Idaho, Utah, and Nevada* (New York: Knopf, 1965) identified region crying out for analysis and demonstrated the utility of such analysis. But can the Pacific Northwest stand scrutiny as a region? What ties the states of Oregon, Washington, and Idaho together, much less California, Utah, and

Nevada? They all have extractive industries and logging clearly characterized Washington and Oregon. Idaho had logging, but mining and potato farming seem clearer markers of identity. Perhaps the salmon would be a better regional icon. The whiteness of the present population of Oregon and Idaho set them apart from the multi-racial West of the borderlands. The Great Basin Kingdom belongs to Leonard Arrington's *Great Basin Kingdom: An Economic History of the Latter-Day Saints, 1830–1900* (Cambridge: Harvard University Press, 1958), but his economic history of the Mormons in Utah gives religion a central part in identity. For Limerick, Mormon history was very much a part of the history of the West and today Mormon history has multiplied from many scholarly parents. But is the Great Basin a region? If we look to the people who live there, they thought so. If we look at it ecologically, it does have a hydraulic identity. What about the Rocky Mountains? Do the people of these majestic peaks see themselves linked to others? Would John Denver's calling upon the mountains for inspiration equally move people to see unity? Are they clearly not linked to the people of Omaha? Is the Great Plains different and if so how? These are the kinds of questions that flow from the issue of regional identity and their exploration will continue into the next century.

Western Legal history has come of age with the work of John Phillip Reid and others guiding a research agenda finding the familiar in American law in the West and identifying the unique flowing from water and mining law development. In addition, Professor Reid and others have identified a research agenda including multicultural legal analysis that should prove to illuminate the vitality of western legal history. Reid suggested that there were numerous layers of western legal history, most only partially explored. They included the development of law during the westward expansion, the law of Indian Territory, the law of cattle drives and the open range, the law of the Mormons, mining law, water law, the law of American Indian nations, violence and the law, and transboundary law. His observations in "The Layers of Western Legal History" contained in John McLaren, Harmar Foster, and Chet Orloff, eds., *Law for the Elephant, Law for the Beaver: Essay in the Legal History of North America* (Pasadena, CA.: Ninth Judicial Circuit Historical Society, 1992) clearly delineate a topical and conceptual agenda for research. The work in western legal history is extensive, but as Reid suggests a great deal of scholarly opportunity awaits researchers.

In addition to Reid's research agenda, the "New Western Historians" have offered some insights on law in the American West. Howard Lamar made the following observation in 1992 in "Westering in the Twenty-first Century: Speculations on the Future of the Western Past" in William Cronon, George Miles and Jay Gitlin, eds., *Under an Open Sky: Rethinking America's Western Past* (New York: W.W. Norton and Co., 1992): "Bureaucracy thrives on rules. Rules suggest laws, and laws lead to litigation. In the past fifty years both citizens and the state and federal governments have hired armies of lawyers to fight their battles in legislative halls or in courts. The current debate over water needs, pollution, the environment, and development has been cast in legal terms. In addition to studying the history of these endless litigations, we should ask why the debate has taken this form. Are we a legal-minded people, or, as one suspects, have Americans become so accustomed to using the law as a selfish manipulative tool — from the time of the first Indian treaty on through two centuries of abuse of public lands — that it is a fundamental part of our culture? The new bureaucracy itself now seems to be using the law, sometimes callously, to achieve its own ends. The point is not to condemn but to ask how we came to this litigiousness and why we continue it."[pp. 263–64] Lamar's formulation of the research question is confrontational. Are the American people, particularly those that people the West, law-minded as John Phillip Reid found on the overland trail, or is the law a tool of capitalistic oppression as the critical legal studies school would have us believe.

Patricia Nelson Limerick writing in the same volume finds the West a place of opportunity for legal history research. "Western history is full of . . . examples of words consulted and puzzled over as if they were Scripture. When mining law awarded ownership of all the "angles, dips, spurs, and variations" of a vein to the person who claimed the "apex" of that vein, lawyers took on the trying task of translating a verbal construction into a geological reality." Limerick also found lawyers representing "forests and rivers, antelope and coyotes." She offered that "when inarticulate nature found voice in legal proceedings, the world of words had reached its peak of inclusiveness." Further, "legal words provide abundant opportunities for cross-cultural comparisons." Finally, "written or oral, legal tradition is transmitted in words, by which power and influence flow toward the appointed custodians and interpreters of those words. The study of law and verbal behavior also provides important information on intergroup relations in the West."[pp. 181–82] The research opportunities according to Limerick and Reid are abundant.

In the recent past, historians have started the process of recovering the gendered past of the American West. The stereotypes of western women as civilizers in sunbonnets have yielded to the complexity of western women's history. First, historians have recognized that the West was the most multi-cultural region of the country. Ethnic and racial backgrounds played a significant part in the roles of women on the West's varied stages. Migration experiences were formative for many, but varied widely in time, place, and manner of migration. Women formed bonds with other women of like and dramatically different cultural heritages. The contributions of women to the success of families varied with time, place, and class as well as race. American Indian women were, for example, in charge of economic transactions and the means of production such as Navaho sheep. Women struggled for rights, but in the West we can see variation found in few other regions. While white women marched for the vote in California, they already had the vote in Wyoming Territory in 1869. American Indian women found it hard to contemplate the vote without citizenship and they would wait until 1924 to become citizens. Asian women would wait until World War II to gain rights to citizenship. Black women in Kansas would suffer the indignities of racial discrimination in public accommodations while women of color in the San Francisco Bay Area would be riding local street cars in the 1860s and attending desegregated schools thirty years later. The similarities as well as the differences in female experience because of race further complicate the West.

Race also impacted women's outlook on the future and the range of choice in the past. In many ways, these choices had to do with relationships with men. Men obviously wanted women in the West particularly when gender balances were out of center in the 1850s and 1860s. Henry Halleck stood on the floor of the 1849 California Constitutional convention advocating women's legal rights as a lure to bring them west.

Wyoming's female franchise found advocates because of another form of lure. When they arrived, women varied by marital status, sexual preference, religion, race, class, and culture. Some came from rural America, others the factories of the East. Some came west to escape religious persecution in the east and find Zion in Utah or Idaho. All of these factors molded a woman's perception of the West. While the men of the West looking for women frequently did not recognize these distinctions, historians have done so recognizing the diversity of the women of the West. Rather than marginalizing women because of a distinction, historians have found it necessary to account for difference in critically analyzing the experiences of western women.

The contact of peoples in the American West was a multi-cultural event with national implications. The contact was necessarily local or regional, but historians have found numerous issues of race and gender in this multi-cultural tapestry. This is a field of inquiry in the formative stage of development, but holding great promise for social and institutional history.

Contact among the tribes of the West was, in part, a product of contact among tribes in the East. Clearly, the tribes of the East jockeyed for hunting and planting territory, established migration patterns, and pushed others out of homelands onto new homelands. Most significant tribe for the West was the Sioux, a name given to them by those attacked, displaced, and slaughtered in their wake. To themselves, they were Lakota, the people. To other American Indians, they were the mobile troops of a tribe seeking increased hunting ground, their hunting ground. The Sioux were not the only tribe pushing their territorial limits. The West before settlement was a dynamic ground of contact.

Contact with the American Indian in the seventeenth and eighteenth centuries was bi-coastal. In the East, the English, Spanish, Dutch, and French would encounter the tribes, trade with them, make war, peace, and alliances. Some personal alliances, even formal marriage, cemented relationships of trade and cultures. In the West, the Spanish had the greatest impact settling much of the Southwest with missions and military fortifications. Missions and presidios would give way to pueblos and ranchos. New generations of American Indians and Spanish speaking residents would continue the process of contact in new economic and cultural circumstances. Both East and West, European diseases devastated native populations. Yet, Indians actively resisted the economic, military, and cultural assaults upon their persons and tribes. This resistance took many forms including female agency accepting trade goods that improved the lives of families yet refusing the cultural incursions of the Europeans. Other forms of resistance included graffiti on mission walls and the maintenance of tribal rituals despite church membership and attendance.

African American contact dates to 1528 when Esteban washed ashore on the Texas coast. As a slave of the Spanish, he had already encountered Europeans and with Indian contact, Esteban continued in slavery to the Indians. With the expansion of New Spain, the black-Indian and black-Spanish population rose to 369,790 by 1793. Quintard Taylor's *In Search of the Racial Frontier: African Americans in the American West, 1528–1990* (New York: W.W. Norton and Co., 1998) begins with this familiar tale and paints a detailed but nuanced portrait of a multi-cultural West. It was a West where Asian and Hispanic alliances played a critical role in the achievement of civil rights. Albert S.

Broussard's *Black San Francisco: The Struggle for Racial Equality in the West, 1900–1954* (Lawrence: University of Kansas Press, 1993) puts the personal and organizational puzzle together focusing upon political action, church oriented activity, and local politics as part of the black struggle in the West. The story of black San Francisco finds similarity across the Bay. Delores Nason McBroome's *Parallel Communities: African Americans in California's East Bay: 1850--1963* (New York: Garland Publishing, Inc., 1993) demonstrates how World War II changed the black community and moved its interests forward. Interestingly, all three authors note that Charlotte Brown's lawsuits in San Francisco resulted in the desegregation of the transit system in 1866. This common-law assault upon discrimination was separate from the Civil Rights Act of 1866 emerging from the United States Congress according black Americans equal access to property among other rights. While San Francisco would have desegregated transit in the 1860s and desegregated schools in the 1890s, this was not true for the West in general. The struggle of African Americans for civil rights would continue for a century.

Asians would find the struggle equally daunting, but their resolve unshaken. Charles J. McClain's *In Search of Equality: The Chinese Struggle against Discrimination in Nineteenth-Century America* (Berkeley: University of California Press, 1994) carefully documents and analyzes how the Chinese used law to achieve rights. Legislation dramatically restricting Asian access to property and outright de jure discrimination was prevalent from the 1850s. Yet the Chinese were remarkably successful in American courts overturning many of these statutes. The Chinese prevailed in court because they had resources. Many of the Chinese were employed and some were prosperous merchants. Their community was highly organized and had access to pooled resources to pay legal fees. After 1878 the Chinese consulate played an increasingly significant role in protecting rights and contributing funds for litigation. The Chinese were careful to employ competent counsel to represent them in court. Finally, the legal climate favored Chinese legal success. America was committed to the rule of law. The Civil Rights Act of 1870 contained specific provisions protecting the Chinese from state action hostile to their interests across the nation. Politicians in the West knew this and opposed the legislation. The Chinese had treaty rights under the Burlingame Treaty of 1868, and reconfirmed in 1880, that guaranteed them the same rights as citizens or subjects of any most favored nation. The Chinese also had the Fourteenth Amendment to the United States Constitution to argue in court. That amendment guaranteed them due process of law and equal protection just as it did all others in this nation. These were powerful arguments for rights and the Chinese used them. The African-American struggle for rights followed a similar path using the law to gain access to public transportation and accommodations. The civil rights campaigns in the West were often fought in courts.

The Chinese struggle had a markedly female dimension. Early female immigration to the West was for forced prostitution. Missionaries in San Francisco and across the West worked to rescue these women. Peggy Pascoe's *Relations of Rescue: The Search for Female Moral Authority in the American West, 1874–1939* (New York: Oxford University Press, 1990) provides an in-depth study of the work of Protestant missionary women in San Francisco's Chinatown. Judy Yung's *Unbound Feet: A Social History of Chinese Women in San Francisco* (Berkeley: University of California Press, 1995) explores female agency in the movement of Chinese women from the home and shop to the public sphere. The movement of the Chinese community in the West was not a singular one from courthouse to equality.

Several distinguished historians have given the Mexican-American community in the West a great deal of analytic attention. Albert Camarillo's *Chicanos in a Changing Society: From Mexican Pueblos to American Barrios in Santa Barbara and Southern California, 1848–1930* (Cambridge, Mass.: Harvard University Press, 1979) documented the impact of European migration, institutions, and politics upon Mexican-Americans and their reactions. Richard Griswold del Castillo's *The Los Angeles Barrio, 1850–1980* (Berkeley: University of California Press, 1982) provides a social history of a people in place focused upon economic and social conditions. His *La Familia: Chicano Families in the Urban Southwest* (Notre Dame: University of Notre Dame Press, 1984) expanded the analysis of social conditions to the urban Southwest. In *The Treaty of Guadalupe Hidalgo: A Legacy of Conflict* (Norman: University of Oklahoma Press, 1990) Professor Castillo analyzed the expectations of many Mexican-Americans under the treaty and the long-term conflict and animosity arising from the failure of its promise. Professor Castillo joined with Richard A. Garcia in *Cesar Chavez: A Triumph of Spirit* (Norman: University of Oklahoma Press, 1995) to produce an important biography of one of America's great labor leaders. Castillo and Arnoldo De Leon published *North to Azlan: A History of Mexican Americans in the United States* (New York: Twayne Publishers, 1997) chronicling the migrations of Mexicans to the Southwest, this borderland in transition, the impact of depression and World War II, and the politics of the Chicano movement. David Gregory Gutierrez's *Walls and Mirrors: Mexican Americans, Mexican Immigrants, and the Politics of Ethnicity* (Berkeley: University of California Press, 1995) focuses upon twentieth-century emigration and immigration in politics and government. His analysis includes consideration of the legacies of conquest of the American Southwest by the United States. George J. Sanchez's *Becoming Mexican American: Ethnicity, Culture and Identity in Chicano Los Angeles, 1900–1945* (New York: Oxford University Press, 1993) explores the impact of Mexican railroads upon the patterns of migration, the process of generational change and language facility in the barrio, and culture of urban Mexican-Americans. These important books are foundational to our understanding of Mexican-Americans and their interactions in the West.

Most recently, Elliott West's *The Contested Plains: Indians, Goldseekers, and the Rush to Colorado* (Lawrence: University Press of Kansas, 1998) takes contact history to another level of refinement. West paints a portrait of the plains as rich in pre-contact history with the tribes of the plains, woodlands, and pacific coast interacting through trade and warfare. Interaction of the Pueblo and plains tribes occurred because of the Spanish invasion from the south and west. From the east, fur trappers and traders reach the Cheyenne, now out of their settlements in Minnesota and mounted on horses courtesy of the Spanish. The Cheyenne decision to adopt a horse culture and to pursue the bison put them in contest with other tribes and white men moving onto the contested plains. In addition to contact by fur men and Overland Trail emigrants, the Cheyenne faced the onslaught of gold seekers in the Pike's Peak rush. Denver city builders contested for the land with Cheyenne dog soldiers. Aided by the strong arm of the federal government and territorial militia, the land was made safe for capital, land developers, and a hydraulic society. Choices made by all participants had consequences in pre-contact and contact phases of historical development. This second layer of analysis forms a new and exciting basis for the historical work that is sure to come from West's insights.

Looking at the West in the 1990s, we find the most urbanized region of America. Over eighty percent of the people live in cities and if we exclude Texas and the Plains states, the West contains almost half the American Indian and Hispanic population, and more than one half of the Asian population. The West is urban and diverse. Some of these cities were instant cities; that is, they were created by a boom, grew from nothing to city size in months, and took on the trappings of urban America within a few years. San Francisco, Denver, and Butte fit into this category. Many of the small cities and villages revolved around booms of another sort. The cattle trails out of Texas gave Kansas cities along the railroad instant business and instant economic distress when the herds no longer visited. Many of the cities reached out along routes of transportation for business and population. All sought to prosper and survive, some did not. The West also is a place for ghost towns like Bodie, California, now a tourist destination rather than a place of homes and families. The urban West was many things over time. It continues to change with population shifts and telecommuting.

San Francisco was a diverse community from its origins in the gold rush. The flood of humanity that docked there and stayed there produced a city with clear cultural and ethnic diversity. The Irish and the Chinese were the labor that built the Transcontinental Railroad and populated the city. The Irish moved into politics and the Chinese into Chinatown. Jews, Irish, and Italians moved into the imbedded mercantile elite. African-Americans formed a small but vibrant community. Chinese and blacks sought legal counsel when threatened within their communities and on the streets. Charlotte Brown's lawsuits in the 1860s would ultimately desegregate the San Francisco transit system in the 1890s. Mary Frances Ward's suit against Noah Flood in 1872 would lead to a California Supreme Court case requiring San Francisco to establish separate but equal schools for black children. In 1875 the San Francisco Board of Education would end segregation and allow black children to attend any public school. Anti-Chinese zoning ordinances would be challenged in court and overturned by the United States Supreme Court. Accommodations had rough spots, but diversity and accommodation became the mark of the city. Not so in Los Angeles or many other cities of the West that maintain segregated public facilities. Remember that *Brown v. Board of Education* (1954) was a Kansas case. *Sweatt v. Painter* (1950) was a decision attacking segregation in a Texas state law school. *McLaurin* v. *Oklahoma State Regents* (1950) outlawed the admission of blacks to graduate school but segregated them within classrooms and other facilities. The racial liberalism of San Francisco was not followed throughout the West.

On our southern borders, America has a clear Mexican-American West that is both very urban and very sparsely settled. El Paso and San Diego are examples of our binational borderland of intensive interaction with a large cultural region of Hispanic settlement and enterprise. But border cities and borders have a long reach due to cross border migration and economic and family ties. Los Angeles in the twentieth century was the designation of many Mexican workers. Beyond the factories in the fields that characterized agriculture in California's Imperial Valley, urban jobs constituted a substantial lure.

Cities in the West, in turn, have relationships with other western cities. Carl Abbott's *The Metropolitan Frontier: Cities in the Modern American West* (Tucson: University of Arizona Press, 1993) describes a nested hierarchy of smaller cities and towns with strong regional, economic linkages. Most large economic regions are subdivided with one or more of these cities controlling significant economic interests. Denver's junior economic partner is Salt Lake City. Stockton and Fresno serve the interests of San Francisco. Phoenix and El Paso share economic territory not gobbled up by Dallas on the east or Los Angeles on the west. Much of this territoriality is historical. Dallas, for example, retains a long-term commitment to serving as a comprehensive trading and financial center while its sister city, Fort Worth, early concentrated upon and continues to serve the West Texas cattle business. Beyond the reach of these trading and financial giants, smaller regional cities serve smaller markets. Lincoln, Nebraska, Bismark, North Dakota, and Billings, Montana are such centers of regional economic activity. The cities of the West live by these economic relationships that transportation made possible and the computer sustains with invisible speed.

Other western cities rose with industry and fell with industry. Butte, Montana is perhaps the most colorful example. Anyone visiting the World Mining Museum or the M & M Bar knows that you are not in Kansas anymore. Mary Murphy's *Mining Cultures: Men, Women, and Leisure in Butte, 1914-41* (Urbana: University of Illinois Press, 1997) is the most insightful book on the subject. Butte was another instant city growing from three thousand in 1880 to 90,000 in 1916 on the wealth of its copper deposit, the mining and milling operations, and the diversity of its people. Copper mining was the lifeblood of the city with three shifts of workers tramping from home to mine every eight hours and back again. By the 1920s, men continued to work in the mines but women dominated clerical work. Unions protected the interests of both. The prosperity of Butte rode on copper wires and the demands of World War I. When the war ended, Butte's economic fortunes turned sour and one-third of its population left by 1921. Prohibition and the crusade to save the world for democracy went hand in hand, but in Butte, the former opened new doors for women. In addition to jobs, the clandestine entertainment industry welcomed women with leisure time and money. Nightclubs encouraged women to attend. Roadhouses encouraged women to pass through their door and some women became owner/operators.

Butte was an ethnically diverse city. The Irish dominated the city and its union, but Finntown was the dominant ethnic neighborhood. The East Side of Butte also was home to Lebanese, Serbs, Croatians, Slovenes, Montenegrins, and Slavs. Further east in Meaderville and McQueen, Austro-Hungarians, Swedes, Norwegians, Germans, and French lived together. These diverse groups organized their social life around the complexities of class and ethnicity. A clear blue-collar normative behavior characterized these neighborhoods with the challenges of mining and the harsh environment of Montana pasting diverse peoples into a western pastiche.

Beyond the common law, western legislatures were busy dealing with some of the same problems. In 1852 the California legislature passed an "Act to prevent certain public nuisances." This statute declared it a public nuisance and a misdemeanor to pollute any creek, stream, pond, road, alley or highway. The same session passed a law to protect salmon runs. In 1862 the solons regulated trout fishing. The next year their legislative hands moved to protect seals and sea lions. In 1872 they banned the killing of Mocking Birds. Six years later they banned fishing on Lake Bigler. In 1877 the Montana Territorial Legislature outlawed the dumping of coal slack in the waters. As early as *Nelson* v. *O'Neal*, 1 Montana 284 (1871) the Montana Territorial Supreme Court would declare in a trespass case that there was "no right to fill the channel of a creek with tailings and debris." California's high Court would make a similar decision in *California* v. *Gold Run Ditch and Mining Company*, 66 California 318 (1884). As Robert Bunting points out in his *The Pacific Raincoast: Environment and Culture in an American Eden, 1778–1900* (Lawrence: University of Kansas Press, 1997), Washington and Oregon passed laws to forbid the dumping of sawdust in streams to protect fish. State lawmakers were busy providing piecemeal for environmental protection. Some of this legislation had environmental protection in mind to increase the profits of farmers. Mark Fiege's *Irrigated Eden: The Making of an Agricultural Landscape in the American West* (Seattle: University of Washington Press, 1999) surveys water law as well as Idaho seed purity law finding that the reach of law was not always as intended.

The federal government got into the pollution control business late in the century. In 1899 the Congress passed the Rivers and Harbors Appropriation Act that came to be known at the Refuse Act of 1899. This act facilitated the Corps of Engineers mission of keeping navigation channels free of obstructions. Section 407 forbade the dumping of refuse in any navigable stream or on the banks so as to be washed into the waters without a permit. Section 411 contained criminal penalties and a reward for informants who reported violations. The enforcement of this act federalized pollution control on our nation's waterways and made industry change its ways in part. The Clean Water Act of 1972 created tougher standards and a bureaucracy to put permitting into practice. The Clean Air Act of 1970 created modern federal regulatory control law, a bureaucracy to administer it, and continuing administrative law and congressional tinkering with emissions standards. The federal bureaucracies in the environmental field must follow the procedures set out in the Administrative Procedures Act of 1946. This statute sets out procedures for agency rulemaking and adjudication. Implicit in these procedures is public notice and citizen participation in many of the stages of rulemaking.

The biodiversity of the West was furthered by another federal statute, the Endangered Species Act of 1973. This legislation was in line with the Convention on International Trade in Endangered Species. The federal Fish and Wildlife Service and the Commerce Department's National Marine Fisheries Service administer the program. Under the statute, the Services place endangered and threatened species on the federal endangered species list. They also prepare recovery programs. Most importantly, the law forbids all federal agencies to act in a manner that would jeopardize the existence of a listed species or destroy critical habitat of a listed species. In 1978 the Congress created a cabinet-level "God Committee" with the power to issue exemptions after findings of necessity and lack of alternatives. An amendment in 1982 further weakened the statute by allowing petitioners to obtain "incidental take" permits from the Secretaries. These petitioners must go through an extensive labyrinth of procedures including Habitat Conservation Plans that can include strict controls of private projects. The statute includes civil penalties and criminal sanctions for violation. The success of the program can been seen by all Americans in the return of the Bald Eagle in our skies.

In the federal courts, the United States Supreme Court in a 1907 Georgia case involving interstate air pollution recognized that the states have a legally enforceable interest in stopping pollution. Copper heaps and smelting such as Montana witnessed in Butte was producing acid rain wiping out forests and crops. This doctrine was dormant until *Texas v. Pankey*, 441 F.2d 236 (1971). These cases recognized that states have a right to protect ecological interests from impairment by polluters. Because such pollution is interstate in nature and the federal government has exclusive jurisdiction over commerce under the commerce clause of the constitution, this judicial recognition of state authority to sue to abate pollution when other governmental entities have not was significant. Questions of federal pre-emption of state action were raised in *California Tahoe Regional Planning Agency v. Jennings*, 594 F. 2d 181 (1979). The court found that the Clean Air Act and the Federal Water Pollution Control Act did not preempt state action to protect the environment under the federal nuisance law doctrine.

Unfortunately, a comprehensive history of these legal developments has not seen print. The shear breadth of such a study and its technical nature may mean that another decade of articles will be needed to form a secondary source foundation for interpretation.

Although federal and state environmental law draws scholars to the public policy and politics aspects of history, other historians have found biodiversity and its science to be equally illuminating. Mark Fiege's *Irrigated Eden*, Peter Boag's *Environment and Experience: Settlement Culture in Nineteenth-Century Oregon* (Berkeley: University of California Press, 1992), and Robert Bunting's *Pacific Rainforest* demonstrate the limits of man's control of the environment through careful discussion of biodiversity and man's impact. Different kinds of grass, insects, rodents, and rabbits inhabit their pages and give readers basic ecology to nuance the narrative. Introduced species conflict with native plants and animals often to their detriment. Science produces insecticide, fungicide, and rodenticide to further alter nature's course. Again, the science that is applied to nature may have unintended consequences further diminishing nature's economy. The stories vary in time and place but the consequences frequently converge in human error.

Finally, historians have started the process of understanding that there is no more a singular West than there was an American Indian. Region and section in the Turnerian world of yesterday and the regional location of the West in the eyes of "New Western Historians" has been further refined by environmental historians who recognize micro-climates, watersheds, and arroyos. Again this is an interdisciplinary enterprise as Robert I. Rotberg and Theodore K. Rabb's *Climate and History: Studies in Interdisciplinary History* (Princeton: Princeton University Press, 1981) demonstrated. Beyond history, these scholars must include biology, chemistry, geography, and geology in their quiver of inquiry.

The best analytic work using law in the New West questions is Debra L. Donahue"s *The Western Range Revisited: Removing Livestock from Public Lands to Conserve Native Biodiversity* (Norman: University of Oklahoma Press, 1999). Professor Donahue brings extensive training and experience in rangeland science together with a law professor's analytic quiver of tools to suggest the "unthinkable": the removal of livestock from many western rangelands on the grounds that it make economic sense, is ecologically wise, and clearly is legally justifiable. In the process of arriving at this politically explosive suggestion, Professor Donahue analyzes why the cattle industry has been able to retain such political and bureaucratic clout despite clear evidence that their grazing practices are destroying the region's grasslands. It was most fitting that the press released this book in the last month of the millennium because it brings the New Western History into an analytic framework that both informs and convicts public policy.

The collection of articles that follow are designed to do the same: inform and convict. The impact of the New Western History is evident in many, yet grounded in what has come before in the literature. We hope that students of the American West will use these book in that spirit. We need to recognize a new point of view from West to East to see both process and place.

Gordon Morris Bakken
California State University, Fullerton

Brenda Farrington
Long Beach City College

To Richard "Rick" Henderson
Yorba Linda, California

Volume Introduction

Western Legal history has come of age with the work of John Phillip Reid and others guiding a research agenda finding the familiar in American law in the West and identifying the unique flowing from water and mining law development. In addition, Professor Reid and others have identified a research agenda including multicultural legal analysis that should prove to illuminate the vitality of western legal history. . Reid suggested that there were numerous layers of western legal history, most only partially explored. They included the development of law during the westward expansion, the law of Indian Territory, the law of cattle drives and the open range, the law of the Mormons, mining law, water law, the law of American Indian nations, violence and the law, and transboundary law. His observations in "The Layers of Western Legal History" contained in John McLaren, Harmar Foster, and Chet Orloff, eds., *Law for the Elephant, Law for the Beaver: Essay in the Legal History of North America* (Pasadena, CA.: Ninth Judicial Circuit Historical Society, 1992) clearly delineate a topical and conceptual agenda for research. The work in western legal history is extensive, but as Reid suggests a great deal of scholarly opportunity awaits researchers.

In addition to Reid's research agenda, the "New Western Historians" have offered some insights on law in the American West. Howard Lamar made the following observation in 1992 in "Westering in the Twenty-first Century: Speculations on the Future of the Western Past" in William Cronon, George Miles and Jay Gitlin, eds., *Under an Open Sky: Rethinking America's Western Past* (New York: W.W. Norton and Co., 1992): "Bureaucracy thrives on rules. Rules suggest laws, and laws lead to litigation. In the past fifty years both citizens and the state and federal governments have hired armies of lawyers to fight their battles in legislative halls or in courts. The current debate over water needs, pollution, the environment, and development has been cast in legal terms. In addition to studying the history of these endless litigations, we should ask why the debate has taken this form. Are we a legal-minded people, or, as one suspects, have Americans become so accustomed to using the law as a selfish manipulative tool — from the time of the first Indian treaty on through two centuries of abuse of public lands — that it is a fundamental part of our culture? The new bureaucracy itself now seems to be using the law, sometimes callously, to achieve its own ends. The point is not to condemn but to ask how we came to this litigiousness and why we continue it."[pp. 263–64] Lamar's formulation of the research question is confrontational. Are the

American people, particularly those that people the West, law-minded as John Phillip Reid found on the overland trail, or is the law a tool of capitalistic oppression as the critical legal studies school would have us believe.

Patricia Nelson Limerick writing in the same volume finds the West a place of opportunity for legal history research. "Western history is full of . . . examples of words consulted and puzzled over as if they were Scripture. When mining law awarded ownership of all the "angles, dips, spurs, and variations" of a vein to the person who claimed the "apex" of that vein, lawyers took on the trying task of translating a verbal construction into a geological reality." Limerick also found lawyers representing "forests and rivers, antelope and coyotes." She offered that "when inarticulate nature found voice in legal proceedings, the world of words had reached its peak of inclusiveness." Further, "legal words provide abundant opportunities for cross-cultural comparisons." Finally, "written or oral, legal tradition is transmitted in words, by which power and influence flow toward the appointed custodians and interpreters of those words. The study of law and verbal behavior also provides important information on intergroup relations in the West."[pp. 181–82] The research opportunities according to Limerick and Reid are abundant.

Looking at Richard White's *It's Your Misfortune and None of My own": A History of the American West* Norman: University of Oklahoma Press, 1991), it is clear that there is plenty of law in the New West, but a good deal of analysis and explanation regarding that law remains for close study. My conservative count of law references in this text yielded 107 citations. Many of these references should not be surprising to students of legal history or the American West. Numerous federal statutes pertained to the West or had substantial impact in the West such as the Trade and Intercourse Act of 1834, the Oregon Donation Act of 1850, the Dawes Act of 1887, American land law generally, the Northwest Ordinance of 1787, the Edmunds Acts of 1882 & 1887, the Chinese Exclusion Act of 1882, the California Land Act of 1851, the Sherman Anti-Trust Act, the Alien Land Law of 1887, the Boulder Canyon Act of 1928, the General Mining Law of 1872, the Coal Lands Act of 1873, the Mineral Leasing Act of 1920, the Carey Act of 1894, the Newland's National Reclamation Act of 1901, the Forest Management Act of 1897, the Yosemite Act of 1864, the Lacy Act of 1906, the Tydings-McDuffie Act of 1934, the 1917 Immigration Act, the 1917 Literacy Test Act, the 1921 and 1924 Immigration Quota Laws, the Emergency Relief and Construction Act of 1934, the Agricultural Marketing Act of 1924, the Silver Purchase Act of 1934, the Lanham Act, the Agricultural Act of 1956, Public Law 283 of 1952, the Sustained Yield Act of 1944, the Multiple Use-Sustained Yield Act of 1960. The U. S. Housing Act of 1949, the Collier-Burns Act of 1948, the Federal Interstate Highway Act of 1956, the Payments in Lieu of Taxes Act of 1976, the Federal Land Policy and Management Act of 1976, the Religious Freedom Act of 1978, the Indian Civil Rights Act of 1968, the Immigration and Naturalization Act of 1952, the Immigration Act of 1965, and the Simpson-Mazzoli Act of 1986. This is quite an impressive list.

The federal courts also are part of the New West legal landscape. White notes *Lone Wolf* v. *Hitchcock* (1903), *U.S.* v. *Reynolds* (1879), *Woodruff* v. *North Bloomfield* (1884), *Muller* v. *Oregon* (1908), the *Hernandez* decision of 1954, *U.S.* v. *Wheeler* (1978), *U. S.* v. *John* (1980) and the *Boldt* decision of 1974. Arizona also went to the federal courts to determine its water rights under the Colorado River Compact.

State and territorial law are included in the portrait. Women used Spanish law in New Mexico to manage their affairs and gain a great deal of independence, but the law of debt peonage forced Indians to work one year for a creditor. Americans in pre-Revolutionary Texas complained about the Mexican legal system. With the Mexican War, New Mexico had Kearny's Code as a base. In Utah, the Mormons used their probate courts against Gentile aggression. California passed a Foreign Miners Tax Act in 1850 to run the Californios off the diggings. California courts refused to uphold the communal land rights of Hispanics. Mexican and American law was in conflict in California regarding the law of heirship. Western railroad boosters wanted lawmakers to give railroads "breaks." Western miners and smelter workers got the 8-hour day by statute. A California statute of 1850 enabled the peonage of Indians. Western state law and federal statute, in sum, disfranchised western minorities by denying citizenship, imposing poll taxes, and creating white-only primaries. Western states passed prohibition statutes. California enacted a Railroad Commission law, but the Southern Pacific used legal procedures to frustrate or delay the law's impact. Oregon's Compulsory School Act of 1922 was unconstitutional. Texas statutes and court decisions prevented a Standard Oil monopoly in Texas. Western water law was the product of legislatures and courts. Tax law changes in Texas caused a civil war in South Texas, 1915-17. California's alien land laws, 1913, to bar Japanese land use was avoided and later declared unconstitutional. Texas and Oklahoma used executive orders, statutes and court actions to regulate the oil industry. State law after World War II made municipal annexation easier stimulating expansion of city boundaries. Since the 1960s, state law has attacked environmental pollution, taxed extractive industries, regulated land use, and expanded the tax base. The states of the New West were busy using law.

Law at the local level does not escape Professor White's extensive research net. Both elite and peasant women in New Mexico go to court to maintain their rights within marriage. The expansion of the bureaucratic state in the 19th century West brought with it the growth of administrative law before it was ever noticed in the nation. When it was discovered that trapping beaver violated Mexican law, the Hudson's Bay Company ordered it stopped. Restrictive covenants in deeds proved an effective way of segregating minority communities, particularly Asians. Stockmen often worked out law among themselves without resort to courts. Law at the operational level also is an important part of understanding the New West.

Acknowledging that Professor White has produced a very ambitious text for the New Western History relying heavily upon secondary works as well as his extensive scholarship, it is still fair to say that his work raises legal history questions more narrow than those asked by Professor Lamar regarding bureaucracy and legal culture. A few examples will make the point of my research agenda for western legal history.

On page 14 Professor White discusses the role of property in New Mexico society with no reference to the law governing property rights and the distribution of power. Rather he focuses upon race and caste as organizing factors. Yet three pages later he notes that New Mexico's 18th and 19th century women used Spanish law to manage their affairs and gain a great deal of independence. He notes that both peasant and elite women went to court to maintain rights within marriage. Why did law work benefits for women under certain circumstances and not for men caught up in debt peonage?

On page 71 Professor White observes that Americans violated Mexican law by trapping beaver, but Hudson's Bay Company ordered the practice stopped. Why? Is the difference a culture of law factor? A policy issue?

On page 91 Professor White calls the Oregon Donation Act of 1850 a violation of U. S. law. What is the basis for this legal conclusion?

On pages 141-2 Professor White refers to the "extralegal modification of land law" in claims clubs, the time-entry system, and the market in land scrip. Why extralegal? What are the legal values of each, if any? Are there traditional market protection mechanisms at work? Was the "law-in-action" observed by those claiming land an encouragement for private collective action to activate the "spirit" of the law?

On page 241 Professor White cites the uses of tax delinquency sales as examples of fraud. How so and on what legal basis? Tax title sales were common across the country and state statutes provided owners an opportunity to redeem their land upon payment of taxes, costs, and legal interest. Why should possessors of land go without paying taxes?

On page 262 Professor White notes that the Alien Land Law of 1887 never resulted in a single confiscation of land. Why not? Was the law a dead letter or did "aliens" use law to avoid confiscation?

On page 345 Professor White tells us that the "Texas Fence Cutting War of 1883-4" was ended by a statute. Does this mean that the rule of law was more powerful than the forces of violence referred to on the prior page—cattlemen using violence because their legal rights to land were unclear?

On page 421 Professor White cites municipal ownership and regulation of utilities with approval. There is a great deal of literature on "home rule" and regulation in general that demonstrates that law was an organizing tool to rationalize competition and provide municipal services.

On page 525 Professor White condemns the Army Corps of Engineers because they "condemned Indian lands in violation of treaty rights and offered inadequate compensation." What is the legal standard for this judgment? We need to know if these issues were litigated. If they were and the Indians received court-ordered compensation, how is that "inadequate"? Until page 580 when the Indians start winning in court, the law seems not to be approved regarding Professor White's Indians.

This last issue, like that of the "dispossession of the Californios" under the California Land Act of 1851, is a volatile one with a great deal of political baggage. From the legal historian's perspective, the analysis usually ends with the issue of due process, that fundamental principle of American constitutional right and liberty. While the Indians both won and lost cases in court, we must remember that the Chinese often used those same courts to win and lose. Perhaps when western historians ask legal history questions we will learn more about how to play the game, than who won and lost. Perhaps the best players were the winners with the best lawyers sitting at the Mad Hatter's Tea Party trying to make sense of western history.

The best analytic work using law in the New West questions is Debra L. Donahue"s *The Western Range Revisited: Removing Livestock from Public Lands to Conserve Native Biodiversity* (Norman: University of Oklahoma Press, 1999). Professor Donahue brings extensive training and experience in rangeland science together with a law professor's analytic quiver of tools to suggest the "unthinkable": the removal of livestock from many western rangelands on the grounds that it make economic sense, is ecologically wise, and clearly is legally justifiable. In the process of arriving at this politically explosive suggestion, Professor Donahue analyzes why the cattle industry has been able to retain such political and bureaucratic clout despite clear evidence that their grazing practices are destroying the region's grasslands. It was most fitting that the press released this book in the last month of the millennium because it brings the New Western History into an analytic framework that both informs and convicts public policy.

The articles that follow will likewise lead you to counter-intuitive conclusions about the West of film and the 1950s. As one country western lyricist wrote: "You're not in Kansas anymore." The New West is the true west of the new millennium and its questions convict much of public policy about the environment and the regional politics that created the legal landscape.

Gordon Morris Bakken   Brenda Farrington
California State University, Fullerton   Long Beach City College

WHAT'S OLD ABOUT THE NEW WESTERN HISTORY?

Part 3: LAW

JOHN R. WUNDER

Late on the sultry night of July 11, 1907, Ham Pak ambled to the back room of his Chinese restaurant, the Sing Hai Low, on Douglas Street in downtown Omaha. The restaurant had already closed, and he needed to count the receipts.[1] Two of his waiters suddenly burst in. These young African American men, who had only recently moved to Omaha, were with someone else, a white man Ham Pak had recently hired but did not really know. One of them attacked Ham Pak with a pickax, but he recovered from the impact and began a struggle for his life. The intruders also used a heavy club and a meat cleaver, and blood splattered all over the room. Nevertheless, before Ham Pak passed out he managed to injure at least one of his assailants. The three attackers limped away with more than two hundred dollars they had taken from a tin box.

Next morning the iceman, Edward Gardipee, went to the Sing Hai Low with his regular delivery and found Ham Pak barely alive on the floor. A doctor was called but could not save the victim, who died without regaining consciousness. The authorities were also called. A robbery had become a murder, and suspicion immediately turned to Ham Pak's employees Willie Almack, Basil Mullen, and Charles Pumphrey, when they failed to show up for work.[2]

John R. Wunder is professor of history at the University of Nebraska–Lincoln.

[1] *Omaha Bee,* July 12, 1907, quoted in Thomas Massey, "*Pumphrey v. State of Nebraska* (1907): Race and Law on the Great Plains," (honor's thesis, University of Nebraska-Lincoln, 1990) [hereafter cited as Massey, "*Pumphrey v. Nebraska*"], 12.

[2] Massey, "*Pumphrey v. Nebraska,*" supra note 1 at 1-2, 12-13; Ke Lu, "Asians, Race and Law in the American West: *Charles Pumphrey v. State of Nebraska*

Two had known each other for some time, and had probably moved to Omaha together. They sometimes referred to themselves as the Rogers brothers, an alias. Almack, who was only nineteen at the time of the murder, grew up in southeastern Iowa on a farm owned by his father just outside Melrose. Mullen, who was probably in his mid-twenties, was from Lenox, a town in the south-central region of Iowa, where coal mining and subsistence farming predominated. As a child he had been in trouble, and had spent time at the Iowa reform school for children at Eldora. The third man was Charles Pumphrey, a short, swarthy young white man born in St. Louis who had moved to Omaha to live with his brother, two sisters, and mother in an apartment not far from the Sing Hai Low. He also worked as a bellboy at a downtown hotel.[3]

After they robbed Ham Pak, all three boarded trains leaving Omaha for the east. They headed for Chicago, but whether they got there is not known. Petty criminals, even murderers, often return to familar ground, and that was exactly what Mullen and Pumphrey did. Mullen went back to the rural area around his home town in Iowa, and Pumphrey to St. Louis. He took Almack with him. Omaha police, meanwhile, were searching for Mullen and Almack.[4]

After ten days, Pumphrey made a mistake. He wrote to a woman from Omaha, one Anna Parr, who worked at the hotel with Pumphrey. She told her employer and then the police that Pumphrey was involved in the crime and that he was with Almack in St. Louis. The St. Louis authorities were notified, and Almack was arrested. Parr may have been in on the robbery, since at first she described herself as merely an acquaintance until it was discovered that she lived with the Pumphreys in their apartment.[5]

Almack was returned to Omaha to stand trial for murder and robbery charges, and began to lay the blame on the other two. Although Pumphrey was still at large, the manhunt next closed in on Mullen, who was arrested in Lenox. He, too, had a story for the Omaha police, explaining that he had not really participated in the murder, that it was Pumphrey's plan to commit the robbery, and that he had taken his share and immediately left town.[6]

(1909), A Case Study" (Ph.D. diss., University of Nebraska–Lincoln, 1997), 146-53.

[3]Ibid. at 13-14.

[4]Ibid. at 13-14. The *Omaha Bee* followed this case closely during the summer of 1907.

[5]Ibid. at 14-15.

[6]Ibid. at 15-16.

Almack and Mullen were charged with murder and robbery, convicted, and sentenced to life in prison. Pumphrey was captured and tried separately. During his trial there was a surprise, which eventually led to an important legal precedent. A witness, Jack Naoi, a Japanese laborer, knew Pak well and was able to identify a ring and watch found in Pumphrey's apartment as the victim's. Because Naoi's testimony would be particularly damaging, Pumphrey's attorneys challenged it on the basis that the court could not allow a person of Japanese descent to testify, as he was racially suspect and not a Christian.[7]

This amazing pattern of facts happened in the turn-of-the-century American West. Where else in the United States might Chinese, African American, white, and Japanese people be involved in a significant legal precedent but in the American West? The murder of Ham Pak involves circumstances that led to a test of American law and western American society, and its telling now is a direct result of the advance made in the New Western History.

Elsewhere I have articulated some of the essence of the New Western History with reference to discussions of race, gender, economics, and the environment. In those essays, new investigations of western history have been characterized more often than not as transitional. This is especially true of much of the new literature on race, most of it on gender, and some of it on the environmental history of the American West. New works on western economic history and some aspects of environmental history have represented a greater break from past historiography.[8] The basic question posed—What's old about the New Western History?—is particularly relevant to understanding the breadth, scope, and meaning of the new scholarship. Now that it has been applied to topics of race, gender, economics, and the environment, it is necessary to address the growing and developing field of the legal history of the American West. Is there, in fact, a New Western *Legal* History, and, if so, does it represent a clear break from the past? Have American legal historians and New Western History proponents collaborated, or are they on parallel paths? Further, might the New Western History as applied to law require additional considerations? And,

[7]Ibid. at 9-10, 22-24. For interracial legal relationships in the American West, see, for example, Sucheng Chan et al., eds., *Peoples of Color in the American West* (Lexington, Mass., 1994), esp. chs. 8 and 10.

[8]See John R. Wunder, "What's Old About the New Western History?: Race and Gender, Part 1," *Pacific Northwest Quarterly* 85 (April 1994), 50-58 [hereafter cited as Wunder, "What's Old About New Western History?: pt. 1"]; idem, "What's Old About the New Western History?: The Environment and the Economy, Part 2," *Pacific Northwest Quarterly*, forthcoming [hereafter cited as Wunder, "What's Old About New Western History?: pt. 2"].

finally, might there be something "old" about the new legal
history of the American West?

TURNER, WEBB, AND WESTERN LEGAL HISTORY

A number of historians have already commented on the relative strengths and weaknesses of the works of Frederick Jackson Turner and Walter Prescott Webb. Both sought to explain
the unique contribution of the frontier to American history and
the place of the American West within a process. New Western
historians reject the Turner frontier thesis and its related
Webb corollary for a variety of reasons. Turner, they point out,
viewed economic development as a forward-advancing process
with minimal hardship to those involved, and the environment
as an enemy to be conquered. Webb accepted these concepts
and further posited a more environmentally deterministic outlook with his notion that the Great Plains acted as an institutional fault line requiring adaptation as settlers passed it. As
for women and members of minority groups, both men either
ignored them or used stereotypical and pejorative references.
New Western historians reject these treatments.[9]

Turner and Webb differ, however, in their references to law.
Turner rarely directly addresses the role law and legal institutions might have played in his frontier process. True, he does
state that "free" land was crucial to the evolution of settlement
and by implication admits that land law had to adjust in order
for settlement to occur. He even hints at questions of regional
legal cultural development when he states that "Behind institutions, behind constitutional forms and modifications, lie the
vital forces that call these organs into life and shape them to
meet changing conditions."[10] For Turner, Americans adapted
and created new institutions, and that presumably meant legal
institutions for "winning a wilderness."[11]

In his description of successive frontiers, he seems on the
verge of articulating a central role for law. It was the Atlantic
frontier from which democratic institutions were kindled and
made complex from the simple, and it was this frontier that

[9]Frederick Jackson Turner,"The Significance of the Frontier in American
History," *Annual Report of the American Historical Association for the Year
1893* (Washington, D.C., 1894),199-227 [hereafter cited as Turner, "Significance
of Frontier"]; Walter Prescott Webb, *The Great Plains* (New York, 1931) [here-
after cited as Webb, *Great Plains*]. For recent criticism of the Turner thesis, see
Patricia Nelson Limerick, Clyde A. Milner II, and Charles E. Rankin, eds.,
Trails: Toward a New Western History (Lawrence, Kans., 1991).

[10]Turner, "Significance of Frontier," supra note 9 at 199.

[11]Ibid.

Frederick Jackson Turner put little emphasis on law in his frontier thesis. (Reproduced by permission of the Huntington Library, San Marino)

had to resolve the issues surrounding the distribution of land. Successive frontiers built upon these endeavors, and when new kinds of problems presented themselves, innovations in law were discovered and freshly applied. Turner cites the lead-mining experience in Wisconsin, Illinois, and Iowa, and how, after statutes had incorporated mining customs, the law assisted in the creation of the mining frontier so successfully that the same lead-mining laws were used in California's gold rush.[12] He leaves this idea undeveloped, however.

Later in his thesis, Turner does note that law played a critical role in the history of the frontier because legislation was conditioned by the frontier. Moreover, he claims that nationalism and political institutions were dependent upon frontier advances. He is quite direct when he states that slavery, in particular, is not nearly as important as these general political and, by implication, legal adaptations. Thus, it is in the West rather than the South that the American experience can more adequately be explained. He goes so far as to state that "The purchase of Louisiana was perhaps the constitutional turning point in the history of the Republic," a recognition of the importance of westward expansion to American legal history.[13] Still, he is dealing with law indirectly, and when the hunter, trader, miner, rancher, farmer, and urban builder parade across his frontier landscape, nowhere is the lawyer to be found. There is great irony and short-sightedness here, for if there were ever a place to find a lawyer, it is in social and economic movements and in disputes over land.

Webb, however, in his classic work, *The Great Plains*, directly addresses the role of law in the American West. He does so in a variety of ways, all within a Turnerian framework. For Webb, the Great Plains forever changed all those who lived on it or passed through it. This included notions of law and legal institutions. He wrote, "Practically every institution that was carried across it [the Great Plains] was either broken and remade or else greatly altered." His choice of words shows his respect for the implications behind legal change. He noted that "The ways of travel, the weapons, the method of tilling the soil, the plows and other agricultural implements, and *even* the law themselves were modified."[14]

What, then, did the Great Plains do to people and their relationships to law and legal institutions? Webb noted four fundamental alterations—what we might term aspects of western

[12]Ibid. at 204-6.
[13]Ibid. at 217-18.
[14]Webb, *Great Plains*, supra note 9 at 8-9. Emphasis added.

legal exceptionalism. First, he explained that because of the
environmental harshness of the Plains and the uniqueness of
the terrain, people who lived there developed a different approach to life from those in other regions. He singled out the
police and the criminals of the Plains, all of whom seemed
more courageous and self-reliant than those of other regions.
While he granted that such characteristics could occur in places
other than the American West, he emphasized that the method
and equipment Plains law enforcers and lawbreakers used with
their mental acuity were influenced by their environment. It
made them distinctive.[15]

Second, people's survival in the arid West meant, according
to Webb, that they were consistent lawbreakers. Why was this?
Social conditions were such that people frequently had to act
on their own volition, and the laws and legal institutions transported to the West were often not useful. Webb cites preexisting land law, federal Indian policy, water law, and fence legislation as being irrational in application to the West, and states
that as a result westerners either ignored them, broke them, or
forcibly changed them. Thus, for Webb, the "blame for a great
deal of Western lawlessness rests more with the lawmaker than
with the lawbreaker."[16]

Webb noted a third characteristic of westerners stemming
from either the absence of law or the presence of unsuitable
laws: Westerners worked out customs and extralegal ways for
dealing with the maintenance of order in society. Webb says an
"understanding" was reached among westerners; in essence, a
code of the West evolved. This legal mentality required fundamental fairness and class equity, and punishments that were
swift and that fit the nature of the crime in terms of surviving
in a difficult environment. Because of this "code," he surmises,
there was little petty thievery on the Plains. And the most severe crime, that of stealing a horse, met with the most severe of
punishments—death.[17]

Finally, he confronts what he calls the radical legal tradition
of the West. Given the spirit of self-reliance, the culture of law-
breaking, and the need to find extralegal solutions to problems,
it should not be surprising, he allows, that the Plains embraced
radical politics, particularly when confronted with threats to its
legal culture that had evolved. Moreover, Plains people just as
quickly cast aside radical solutions to problems if the threat
eased. According to Webb, "When men suffer, they become

[15]Ibid. at 496-98.
[16]Ibid. at 500.
[17]Ibid. at 497-98.

politically radical; when they cease to suffer, they favor the existing order."[18] Because this tradition culminated in the failed Populist movement, Webb, like Turner, ends the unique history of the West with the coming of the twentieth century. This time freeze, of course, New Western historians emphatically reject.

THE NEW WESTERN HISTORY AND LAW

Any study of New Western History and law requires an essential question to be addressed. Its mere asking makes some New Western historians and American legal historians nervous. The question legal historians of the American West are tackling is whether the West developed its own unique regional legal culture.[19] To some degree, Webb was attempting to answer this question, but he could not get beyond the strictures of the Turner frontier thesis and his own baggage as a scholar. This question places at the apex of any New Western Legal History the fundamental issue of exceptionalism.[20]

The intersection of the New Western History and legal studies has been anything but direct. Just as Turner danced around the subject of even an Old Western Legal History, so, too, have many modern American history scholars. One of the greatest myths in the writing and reading of American history is that legal history requires an understanding or training nearly impossible to attain. All too many historians of the American West have bought into this mythology, which consequently allows them to avoid the legal dimensions of human actions.

That few western history practitioners have sought to participate in an extensive evaluation of American legal history shows in the primary works devoted to the New Western

[18]Ibid. at 503.

[19]See Kermit L. Hall, "The Legal Culture of the Great Plains," *Great Plains Quarterly* 12 (Spring 1992), 86-98; John R. Wunder, "Toward a Legal History of the Great Plains," in *Law and the Great Plains: Essays on the Legal History of the Heartland*, ed. idem (Westport, Conn., 1996), 3-8, and "Persistence and Adaptation: The Emergence of a Legal Culture in the Northern Tier Territories, 1853-1890," in *Centennial West: Essays on the Northern Tier States*, ed. William L. Lang (Seattle, 1991), 104-21.

[20]For a recent discussion of exceptionalism, Turner, and the West, see David M. Wrobel, *The End of American Exceptionalism: Frontier Anxiety from the Old West to the New Deal* (Lawrence, Kans., 1993). See also Gregory M. Tobin, *The Making of a History: Walter Prescott Webb and "The Great Plains"* (Austin, 1976), and "Walter Prescott Webb," in *Historians of the American Frontier: A Bio-Bibliographical Sourcebook*, ed. John R. Wunder (Westport, Conn., 1988), 713-28.

History. Richard White and Patricia Nelson Limerick have
consulted little secondary material on western legal history,
either because it does not exist, as is often the case, or because
their training lacked a grounding in legal history or their own
interests have not found it conducive to consult. This means
that their seminal works do not address a fundamental issue,
that of the nature of a western legal culture, but they have not
completely ignored "the law."

White helped redefine western history with the publication
of his text, *"It's Your Misfortune and None of My Own": A
New History of the American West*, in 1991.[21] Look in the
table of contents or the index for a specific treatment of western law. You won't find it in a chapter, and in the index the
only singular reference to law is land law (a necessity for any
Vernon Carstensen student to consider); water law; and "L.A.
Law," the glamorous TV serial.[22]

That one cannot identify a specific "legal" chapter or specific
references under law in the index, however, does not mean that
law is not present in the text. It is there. For example, White
mentions fourteen court cases, twelve U.S. Supreme Court
decisions and two from the California State Supreme Court.
Of the California decisions, one, *Woodruff v. North Bloomfield*,
concerned mining dumping and environmental concerns, and
the other, *Lux v. Haggin*, dealt with water rights.[23] Of the U.S.
Supreme Court cases, eight of twelve concerned disputes over
Indian rights and federal and state laws, although three were
disputes not originating from the West. State and territorial
courts are ignored, as are local courts, traditional mining
courts, and Indian courts.

Law is most often involved in discussions of land policy,
federal Indian programs, and water law. Water law, in particular, is cogently and carefully presented, and this is important
because water and its shortage is crucial to any understanding
of the West's past. Extralegal violence is mentioned frequently
as social history, and here the inability of legal institutions to
function is addressed. Federal statutes are also added to discussions that involve almost every aspect of the West's development in the twentieth century.

Nevertheless, law is always supplementary or peripheral
to the historical subject at hand. Sometimes it is missing
altogether. How can one consider internment of the Japanese

[21]Richard White, *"It's Your Misfortune and None of My Own": A New History
of the American West* (Norman, 1991) [hereafter cited as White, *"It's Your
Misfortune"*].

[22]Ibid. at 636-44.

[23]Ibid. at 234, 402.

Patricia Nelson Limerick and other New Western historians have rarely integrated legal history into their syntheses of the West's past. (Photograph by Ken Abbott, courtesy Center of the American West)

without describing attempts by the Japanese to resist through state and federal courts? How does one evaluate the Chinese experience without a discussion of *Yick Wo v. Hopkins*? Is the treatment of Elizabeth Gurley Flynn, a cofounder of the American Civil Liberties Union, and labor unrest in the Pacific Northwest complete without a paragraph or two devoted to the free-speech movements or mention of the murder trial of Big Bill Haywood for the assassination of Idaho's governor, which dramatically pitted the lawyers William Borah and Clarence Darrow against each other?[24] One could continue to nitpick, which is inherently unfair, yet the point must be made that while law permeated the social and economic history of the American West, it has yet to infiltrate deeply into any synthesis of the West's past.

Limerick, in *The Legacy of Conquest*, also skirts the issue of a western legal culture.[25] Ironically, the question, if openly addressed, clearly assists with her paradigm. There are hints that she believes it is an integral part. For example, in her introduction, she explains how her conquest paradigm works. For her, "Conquest basically involved the drawing of lines on a map, the definition and allocation of ownership (personal, tribal, corporate, state, federal, and international), and the evolution of land from matter to property."[26] She sees these vital steps as a two-pronged process. First the lines had to be drawn, but second—and here is where law might aid her—the significance of the lines had to be backed up by power. To Limerick, western history is a distillation of what she calls a "competition for legitimacy," in which ethnic diversity and resource allocations clash. "The contest for property and profit," she observes, "has been accompanied by a contest for cultural dominance." She uses words such as "contest," "struggle," and "dispute" without ever mentioning "law."[27]

It is not as though Limerick has not thought about this. She has, and the evidence is in her book. She is especially perceptive in her discussions about mining and law.[28] She even addresses the question of how legal doctrines had to be changed in order for western mining technology to advance. However, more often than not, she either ignores or only indirectly considers it. Perhaps the best example in comparison with mining

[24]Ibid. at 293, 320-23, 510-13.

[25]Patricia Nelson Limerick, *The Legacy of Conquest: The Unbroken Past of the American West* (New York, 1987).

[26]Ibid. at 27.

[27]Ibid.

[28]Ibid. at 108-16.

11

is her treatment of farming, where law has a direct impact up to the present, or even prostitution, which by definition is a legal creation. To the latter she devotes four pages, but does not discuss how western legal systems, as distinct from those in other regions, reacted to it.[29] How does one explain this? As in White's book, questions surrounding a western legal culture are secondary to Limerick's general thesis.

Western Legal History AND THE NEW WESTERN HISTORY

To be fair to Limerick and White, one must emphasize that the integration of the New Western History and legal history is only just beginning. They should not be expected to have anticipated this development. What signs there have been of this integration are mixed. They may even be too underdeveloped to call transitional, yet, clearly, new approaches by western legalists fit into the New Western History.

The evolution of modern western legal history scholarship began in the late 1970s, with some talk among legal history scholars based in the West of forming a Pacific Coast branch of the American Society for Legal History patterned on the Pacific Coast Branch—American Historical Association. It resulted in the first conference devoted to legal history to be held in the West at Pepperdine University's School of Law. Although such a branch was never formed, legal historians who wrote western history or who lived in the American West resolved to continue a dialogue.

In 1988 a new journal, *Western Legal History*, was born.[30] The journal is the official organ of the Ninth Judicial Circuit Historical Society. Chet Orloff, its founding editor, wrote on its first page that the journal was to include contributions of more than just the study of courts. Embedded in it were to be the seeds of the New Western History, for Orloff included on his list "issues of natural resources and minorities."[31] The journal was to embrace the greater American West beyond the boundaries of the U.S. Courts for the Ninth Circuit.

John Phillip Reid wrote the first published essay, "Some Lessons of Western Legal History," in which he used David Langum's then path-breaking book, *Law and Community on*

---

[29]Ibid. at 49-52, 54, 124-33, 170.

[30]First printed in 1988, the journal was founded to encompass the legal history of the entire American West, and not be restricted to the states served by the United States Courts for the Ninth Circuit. It has also expanded into the Canadian West.

[31]Chet Orloff, Foreword, *Western Legal History* 1 (Winter/Spring 1988), 1.

the Mexican California Frontier (1987),[32] as a springboard to a discussion of why considerations of regional legal culture are so important. Reid observed that Langum's theme, "a clash of legal cultures," was unique to the American West. It could only have occurred in a place where competing legal cultures were forced to deal with each other. For Reid, who has also investigated the mobile legal life of the Oregon Trail in his pioneering work, *Law for the Elephant*,[33] there was more to be done: "Evidence of a nineteenth-century legal culture provided by the westward movement—by the behavior of emigrants on the overland trail and the conduct of expatriates in Mexican California—has raised issues about the nature of American law ways that require that more scholars begin to investigate western legal history. It is a neglected field awaiting its reapers and its gleaners."[34] He is not sure that the West as a place encompasses a unique regional culture, but he has an open mind to further investigations.

Western Legal History is now ten volumes old. It was created just when the New Western History was noticed not only within the West but beyond it. The eighty-one essays published up to, and including, the issue of Winter/Spring 1995 include twenty-six on race and law in the American West, or roughly 31 percent.[35] This can be broken down into topical essays as follows: fourteen devoted to Native Americans, four to Chinese, two to other Asian groups, four to Hispanics, and two to multiple racial topics. Western women's history has not been as likely to be found in print. Approximately 15 percent, or twelve articles, deal with western women's legal history, and of those, six appeared in a recent special issue on the topic.[36] Articles devoted to economic history and natural-resource topics are even scarcer, only six having been published in the period under review. This is somewhat surprising, considering that the modern age of American legal history is predicated upon economic and resource considerations, and that two of

---

[32]David J. Langum, *Law and Community on the Mexican California Frontier: Anglo-American Expatriates and the Clash of Legal Traditions, 1821-1846* (Norman, 1987).

[33]John Phillip Reid, *Law for the Elephant: Property and Social Behavior on the Overland Trail* (San Marino, Calif., 1980).

[34]John Phillip Reid, "Some Lessons of Western Legal History," *Western Legal History* 1 (Winter/Spring 1988), 17.

[35]Compilations are based upon all issues through vol. 8, no. 1.

[36]See *Western Legal History* 7(Summer/Fall 1994), "Women, Legal History, and the American West," special issue; guest editors, John R. Wunder and Paula Petrik; articles by Anne M. Butler, Margaret K. Holden, Donna C. Schuele, and James Muhn; interview by Carole Hicke.

the most prominent legal historians in this area—Lawrence
Friedman and Harry Scheiber—are based in California.

Although the initial charge said that the new journal would
not emphasize writings that dealt with courts, that has been
the pattern. The twenty-three essays about courts and judges
represent nearly 30 percent of all published contributions. This
is somewhat inflated because of the early policy of including
recollections from oral histories of prominent jurists and members of the bar. Legal doctrine is the subject of ten articles, the
second-highest demarcation of traditional legal history topics.
Thus it would appear that *Western Legal History* as a journal
has been receptive to New Western History topics, particularly
those dealing with race and law, while maintaining a balance
with Old Western Legal History approaches.

The evolution of western legal history scholarship has been
significantly advanced in the 1990s by the Ninth Judicial Circuit Historical Society's sponsorship of western legal history
sessions at the annual meeting of the Western History Association; the start of two new western legal history book series at
the two largest western academic presses, the University of
Nebraska Press and the University of Oklahoma Press;[37] and
the first transboundary legal history conference on the North
American West, at the University of Victoria in February 1991.
Entitled "Law for the Elephant, Law for the Beaver," the conference gathered together, for the first time, legal history scholars
of the American and Canadian Wests. Out of the symposium
came a volume of essays by seven Canadians and five Americans.[38] John Phillip Reid, in his provocative essay "The Layers
of Western Legal History," opens the book, and he issues a
warning. He is skeptical about any finding that there is a
unique western legal culture. Instead, he sees greater clarity
in pursuing comparative North American legal parallels. Although he notes a number of specific "western" contributions
to law, he prefers to stress continuities of continental law and

[37]The works published by 1995 include Christian G. Fritz, *Federal Justice in
California: The Court of Ogden Hoffman, 1851-1891* (Lincoln, 1991); Gordon
Morris Bakken, *Practicing Law in Frontier California* (Lincoln, 1991); Shelley
Bookspan, *A Germ of Goodness: The California State Prison System, 1851-
1944* (Lincoln, 1991); M. Catherine Miller, *Flooding the Courtrooms: Law and
Water in the Far West* (Lincoln, 1993) [hereafter cited as Miller, *Flooding the
Courtrooms*]; C. Blue Clark, *Lone Wolf v. Hitchcock: Treaty Rights and Indian
Law at the End of the Nineteenth Century* (Lincoln, 1994) [hereafter cited as
Clark, *Lone Wolf v. Hitchcock*]; and Jeffrey Burton, *Indian Territory and the
United States, 1866-1906: Courts, Government, and the Movement for
Oklahoma Statehood* (Norman, 1995).

[38]John McLaren, Hamar Foster, and Chet Orloff, eds., *Law for the Elephant,
Law for the Beaver: Essays in the Legal History of the North American West*
(Pasadena, 1992).

commonalities.[39] Nevertheless, the sympathy of those giving
papers at the conference and writing in the anthology was for
investigating thoroughly the notion of a distinct western legal
culture. Canadian West legal historians, unencumbered by
Turnerisms and frontier theses, have made substantial progress
in this area.[40]

In the fall of 1990 the annual meeting of the American Society for Legal History was to take a rare trip to the Far West. It
was scheduled to meet in San Francisco. The meeting was not
held in California, however, because the day before its conven-
ing a devastating earthquake struck the Bay Area. Instead, the
society met in Atlanta the following February. A session originally planned for San Francisco was held, entitled "Western
Legal History: Where Are We and Where Do We Go From
Here?" It featured a panel of western legal history scholars who
had been present at its modern creation: Lawrence M. Friedman, Christian G. Fritz, David J. Langum, Harry N. Scheiber,
and Gordon M. Bakken.[41]

Taken as a whole, in many ways the panel accurately sums
up the relationship of current western legal history scholarship
to the New Western History. Bakken was the only panelist
directly to embrace a legal history connection to the New
Western History. Addressing the notion of a western legal culture, he said, "Western legal history is distinctive because the
law of the East had to come to grips with the facts of the trans-
Mississippi West." Bakken sees western law as being directly
connected to the West as a unique place. Known for his work
on the reception of common law in the American West and the
history of western legal institutions, he reflects that during his
scholarly life he has sought to discover continuities in American legal and constitutional history. "My answers have been
mixed," he observes. "There has been continuity; there is some
uniqueness. Western legislatures and jurists drew upon American legal experience when they made law for unique situations." But what is important to Bakken—as in the study of
western water law—is that new law of such a distinctive nature was created to make the West an exceptional place.[42]

Friedman reversed the question of western legal exceptionalism, suggesting that after a century of legal distinctiveness

[39]John Phillip Reid, "The Layers of Western Legal History," in ibid., 23-73.
[40]See, for example, Tina Loo, *Making Law, Order, and Authority in British Columbia, 1821-1871* (Toronto, 1994), and Constance B. Backhouse, *Petticoats and Prejudice: Women and the Law in Nineteenth-Century Canada* (Toronto, 1991).
[41]*Western Legal History* 3 (Winter/Spring 1990), 115-43.
[42]Gordon M. Bakken, ibid. at 115-18; quotation, 117.

perhaps the West, like the South, is developing a legal history of convergence with the rest of the nation. But in addressing this concern, he notes the hallmarks of the New Western History. He believes that economic development, law and order, and the presence of minorities in the West must be investigated fully.[43]

Fritz carefully posited the dilemma of western legal exceptionalism in mainstream ideology. He sees the law of the American West as characterized by "some distinctive aspects," but considers those distinctions unimportant unless they are compared with the rest of the country. Fritz wants to understand western legal history through treatments of minority groups, histories of federal courts, and shared constitutional cultures, such as state constitution-making. Although he is taking a somewhat traditional approach, he recognizes that certain aspects of western history, such as the California gold rush, require highlighting. Might the gold rush immigrants, he asks, have developed a shared legal culture?[44]

Langum saw value in studying the history of western law comparatively. He rejects Limerick's fundamental notion about ethnicity and the West and does not believe that the West differs much from the East in terms of diversity. Rather, it is the West as "place"—its vastness and isolation—that makes it different. Nevertheless, he credits western ethnic diversity with creating exceptional alternative systems of law, but is uncomfortable with examinations of the treatment of western minorities before American legal systems as evidence of western legal exceptionalism.[45]

Scheiber issued a clarion call for adopting portions of the Turnerian concepts in the examination of western legal culture. He encouraged western legal historians to look into community building, territorial legal experiences, and constitution-making from a framework of successive regional frontiers. Having harkened back to the Old Western History, he then suggested that conquest as a paradigm can be addressed within this framework. Known for his work on law and the economy, he turned to an important link for law to the New Western History, anticipating notably the works of William Robbins and Donald Worster.[46] Scheiber connects law to the New

---

[43]Lawrence M. Friedman, ibid. at 118-19.

[44]Christian G. Fritz, ibid. at 119-23.

[45]David J. Langum, ibid. at 123-26.

[46]See William G. Robbins, *Colony and Empire: The Capitalist Transformation of the American West* (Lawrence, Kans., 1994); and Donald Worster, *Rivers of Empire: Water, Aridity, and the Growth of the American West* (New York and Oxford, 1985), and idem, *Under Western Skies: Nature and History in the American West* (New York and Oxford, 1992).

16

Western History focus on the environment and the economy when he notes that the West's relationship to world capitalism is a most fruitful area for scholars. Potential western legal exceptionalism is found where the West struggled to develop its natural resources. "The problem for western law," he observed, "was to accommodate large-scale capitalism and the latest, state-of-the-art technologies. . . . In some respects, the western states confronted some of the most difficult and intractable problems of modern capitalism even earlier than other parts of the country."[47]

There is thus no clear consensus on the direction of western legal history, but it is obvious that the New Western History has begun to penetrate the debate. This is especially true of those western legalists who have received both legal and history training and who conceptualize the history of the American West in regional terms. Nevertheless, as Scheiber noted during the panel discussion, "It's a mixed picture: regionalism is a slippery concept."[48]

RACE AND GENDER

The New Western History is especially persuasive when it considers questions of race and gender, areas previously ignored. Western legal historians have also begun to look into these topics, and they have done so through a variety of approaches. The result is a strong, original treatment in most instances.

Considerations of race and western law are most developed in new works on the history of American Indians. This should not be too surprising, because so much of the history of Native Americans relates to legal definition. Even how one becomes a member of a tribe requires significant legal considerations. Two recent works on this topic, Sidney L. Harring's *Crow Dog's Case: American Indian Sovereignty, Tribal Law, and United States Law in the Nineteenth Century*[49] and Blue Clark's *Lone Wolf v. Hitchcock: Treaty Rights and Indian Law at the End of the Nineteenth Century*[50]—both case biographies —deserve our attention.

---

[47]Harry N. Scheiber, *Western Legal History* 3 (Winter/Spring 1990), 127-32; quotation, 130.

[48]Ibid. at 131.

[49]Sidney L. Harring, *Crow Dog's Case: American Indian Sovereignty, Tribal Law, and United States Law in the Nineteenth Century* (New York and Cambridge, 1994) [hereafter cited as Harring, *Crow Dog's Case*].

[50]Clark, *Lone Wolf v. Hitchcock*, supra note 37.

Harring immediately establishes how the New Western History has had an impact on American legal history in his book about the U.S. Supreme Court case *Ex parte Crow Dog* (1883). He explains how classic legal histories have ignored American Indian legal history. In particular, he singles out J. Willard Hurst's *Law and Economic Growth: The Legal History of the Lumber Industry in Wisconsin, 1836-1915*, a book generally regarded as the origin of modern American legal history.[51] It should not be overlooked that Hurst taught at Turner's university, and that his modernization of American legal history dealt with economic legal aspects of an industry prominent in the West—that of timber.

Hurst's legal history left out Indians, even though Indians had a great deal to do with the legal history of Wisconsin's forests. Harring observes, "Omitted is any discussion of the forced removal of the Winnebago, fraudulent timber contracts on Chippewa and Menominee lands (there were hearings in Congress in 1889 they were so blatant), a lawsuit over state title to timber on school lands on the Menominee Reservation that reached the U.S. Supreme Court in 1877, deprivation of Indian hunting and fishing rights reserved by treaty, and an extensive legal conflict over basic issues of federalism as the state resisted federal jurisdiction over the tribes resulting in at least ten reported cases."[52] This is a serious and significant indictment. Harring precisely argues the need for a New Western *Legal* History, and does so around the issue of race.

What Harring has done is to take a traditional form—that of a biography—and use it in a nontraditional way. He demonstrates conclusively that the best approach to discussing Indian law is to explain and discover the two kinds of law at play. This is really a historical exercise in the conflict of laws. There are two legal traditions in conflict, and to explain the legal issues at hand one must uncover and understand all the cultural dimensions, not just one of several. Harring's book represents a call for ethnohistorical legal history.[53]

Harring proves that tribal law has not disappeared. It continued to function, not only in Crow Dog's case on the Rosebud

[51]James Willard Hurst, *Law and Economic Growth: The Legal History of the Lumber Industry in Wisconsin, 1836-1915* (Cambridge, Mass., 1964).

[52]Harring, *Crow Dog's Case,* supra note 49 at 9.

[53]Ibid. at 10. Thomas Biolsi eloquently argued recently that law is "a fundamental constituting axis of modern social life—not just a political resource or an institution but a constituent of all social relations, particularly relations of domination." Idem, "Bringing the Law Back In: Legal Rights and the Regulation of Indian-White Relations on Rosebud Reservation," *Current Anthropology* 36 (August-October 1995), 543.

Reservation, but in other instances. Crow Dog, or Kan-gi-shun-ca, shot and killed Sin-ta-ga-le-Scka, or Spotted Tail, a prominent Brulé Sioux chief. These are undisputed facts. When the event became known, the families of both men met and settled on a means of atonement: a case remuneration of six hundred dollars from Crow Dog's family to Spotted Tail's family, plus eight horses and one blanket. Under tribal law, harmony through restitution had been achieved.[54]

However, because the Bureau of Indian Affairs and other federal officials were anxious to establish legal control over tribal institutions, Crow Dog was indicted for murder and convicted in Dakota Territory courts. The BIA actually influenced the lawyers for both sides so as to guarantee an appeal. Crow Dog's attorney eventually appealed to the U.S. Supreme Court, and in *Ex parte Crow Dog*[55] the court ruled that Crow Dog must be released because U.S. federal courts had no criminal jurisdiction over Indian tribes in Indian country. This was ostensibly because Congress had not given them jurisdiction. The door was now open for legal attack, and the next several decades witnessed a frontal assault on tribal law and sovereignty, an era Harring describes as a period of legal genocide.[56]

As influential a book as *Crow Dog's Case* is, it includes at least one transitional element. Harring is sometimes less convincing because of what he does not consider. He thoroughly discusses *Crow Dog* and subsequent cases at both the U.S. Supreme Court and appellate and district court levels, and places much of this research impressively in his overall theme. The problem is that he does not observe that legal genocide, the war on tribal institutions, is essentially a place war. It is centered in the American West. The force may have been national, but its impact is overwhelmingly western.

For example, Harring accurately summarizes the dualism he is unraveling. "The contradiction between tribal sovereignty and a colonial mode of imposed law," he explains, "was nowhere more publicly debated than in U.S. policy toward the Indian nations in eastern Oklahoma."[57] This is a potentially powerful entry into a regional discussion, but it never happens. Instead, Harring ties these legal developments into a national framework and ignores regional legal ramifications. This one aspect, an approach used in virtually all studies of American

---

[54]Harring, *Crow Dog's Case*, supra note 49 at 1.

[55]*Ex parte Crow Dog*, 109 U.S. 556 (1883).

[56]Harring, *Crow Dog's Case*, supra note 49 at 251-52.

[57]Ibid. at 37.

Indian law, is the only strand that separates *Crow Dog's Case* from all aspects of the New Western History.[58]

The other recent Indian legal history, Clark's study, considers what is arguably the most important U.S. Supreme Court decision regarding Indian law in American history. In *Lone Wolf v. Hitchcock*, Clark explains why this challenge to the basic fabric of Indian culture occurred and what its legacy proved to be. The case grew out of the allotment policy designed to carve up Indian reservations and separate lands not assigned to individual tribal members so that they could be sold to non-Indians. Most Indians opposed this land grab, and the Kiowas residing on their reservation in southwestern Oklahoma were especially adamant.

Lone Wolf was one of several Kiowas who tried to adjust to reservation life by finding ways to preserve as much of their national culture as they could, and he realized that maintaining the Kiowa communal land base was crucial to cultural preservation. The federal government wanted to take as much land as possible from the reservations and force Indians onto individual allotments so that they might be more like whites. Despite the unfairness of these concepts, many whites could not resist attempting to take all the land by illegal means, and even when this was revealed, Congress accepted the allotment of the Kiowa land holdings. Lone Wolf and other Indians on the reservation challenged this action in U.S. courts, and eventually the Supreme Court ruled that Congress had plenary power over Indians and could exercise that power regardless of whether fraud had occurred or treaty provisions were violated. It was a devastating legal pronouncement for Indians whose reservations were at risk throughout the American West.[59]

In his treatment of *Lone Wolf*,[60] Clark successfully provides the dualistic approach that Harring so eloquently urges in *Crow Dog's Case*. Read together, these case biographies set the standard for new treatments of Indian law. Clark takes Kiowa

[58]One year later, *Zuni and the Courts* was published. This is a collection of essays and original testimony by those who have been most involved in Zuni Pueblo's attempts to obtain payment for lands taken by the United States without adequate compensation, restitution for environmental damage to Zuni lands caused by the U.S. government, and the retention of religious rights in the face of non-Zuni intimidation. E. Richard Hart, a public historian who directs the Institute of the North American West, a private research company headquartered in Seattle, edited the volume. This collection does not fit into either Sidney Harring's model for Native American legal history or the general direction of the New Western History. E. Richard Hart, ed., *Zuni and the Courts: A Struggle for Sovereign Land Rights* (Lawrence, Kans., 1995).

[59]Clark, *Lone Wolf v. Hitchcock*, supra note 37 at 95-106.

[60]*Lone Wolf v. Hitchcock*, 187 U.S. 553 (1903).

history seriously, and he outlines how this history and the individual role of Lone Wolf play essential parts in this seminal case's evolution. He treats the federal side and its myriad characters similarly, from the Jerome Commission and the fraudulent petitions it forced upon the Kiowas to a future Supreme Court justice, Willis Van Devanter, who argued the case before the Supreme Court.

Clark shows dramatically the duality of understanding. When he explains how the Treaty of Medicine Lodge, which was essential to the Kiowa defense, was negotiated, he tells us that federal government representatives called the Kiowas their children and asked that the children obey their father and cede their lands. The Kiowas, however, discussed the mutual responsibilities that were a part of every family. Thus, writes Clark, "one spoke of relationships; the other spoke of land transactions."[61]

These latest works in Native American legal history show the dynamics of the New Western History. There are a few transitional elements and some traditional methodological forms, but generally they represent considerable breakthroughs. Not only are many topics being addressed for the first time, but they are stretching the parameters of traditional American legal history.[62]

Although the treatment of women's and men's roles within western legal institutions has not received as much attention as race, what it has received is significant. The first systematic investigation of modern gender and law in the American West can be found in Paula Petrik's *No Step Backward: Women and Family on the Rocky Mountain Mining Frontier, 1865-1900* (1987).[63] In this book, Petrik explains in a case study of Helena, Montana, how an urban mining frontier transformed women,

[61]Clark, *Lone Wolf v. Hitchcock*, supra note 37 at 22.

[62]See, for example, a summary of questions concerning race and law in the American West, in John R. Wunder, "The Intersection of History, Race, and Law in the American West," *Universitas Helsingiensis (University of Helsinki Quarterly)* 4 (December 1995), 43-45, synopsis of inaugural address at the University of Helsinki, September 1995. See also "Rotu ja lainkäyttö," *Yliopisto* 16 (September 1995), 40.

See also recent works on Chinese and law in the American West, such as Charles J. McClain, *In Search of Equality: The Chinese Struggle against Discrimination in Nineteenth-Century America* (Berkeley and London, 1994); Lucy E. Salyer, *Laws Harsh as Tigers: Chinese Immigrants and the Shaping of Modern Immigration Law* (Chapel Hill, 1995); and John R. Wunder and Clare V. McKanna, Jr., "The Chinese and California: A Torturous Legal Relationship," *California Supreme Court Historical Society Yearbook*, vol. 2 (1995), 195-214.

[63]*No Step Backward: Women and Family on the Rocky Mountain Mining Frontier, 1865-1900* (Helena, 1987).

affording them increased economic opportunity and providing
them greater social equality. These developments were reinforced by the legal system. Is this not the making of a specific
legal culture? Possibly so, particularly in family law and suffrage, two topics Petrik addresses thoughtfully.[64]

Petrik's Helena is diverse. There are Christians and Jews,
whites and Chinese. Class is also important, and she investi-
gates several representative examples. Sex and age ratios fluc-
tuate, and considerably affect the legal environment.[65]

When Petrik considers the law, she looks at three major distinctions. The first of these, although not explicitly stated, is
defined by law and its selective enforcement. It is prostitution,
the largest female employment category outside the home.
Petrik approaches prostitution primarily from the perspective
of business history, and convincingly demonstrates how
women lost control over prostitution to men and how the
marketplace became much more dangerous as a result. What
is fascinating is the level of legal involvement of prostitutes in
Helena in property transactions (Petrik found that 44 percent of
Helena's prostitutes owned realty), in the movement of capital,
and in the use of civil and criminal law to control their businesses. In 1874 Montana Territory created this kind of legal
terrain by approving a law giving separate business identities
to women. Thus to Petrik the role of law in prostitution might
seem secondary to economic activity, but she does allow that
law inadvertently reshaped the profession.[66]

After a full discussion of prostitution, Petrik considers the
life of middle- and upper-class women. They, too, benefitted
from Montana's favorable business climate. By 1900, women in
Montana had made lives for themselves apart from marriage,
were frequently employed, and used the legal system to advance reforms and to obtain self-protection, primarily through
divorce. Middle-income women demonstrated significant community activism, and this took the form of advocating legal
change.[67]

Petrik's greatest contribution in terms of addressing gender
issues and the law comes in chapter 4, "Occasions of Unhappy
Differences: Divorce in Helena, 1865-1907."[68] Here she defini-
tively shows how Montana helped create distinctive family
law. Courts responded to women by broadly interpreting the

[64]Ibid. at xiii, xv.
[65]Ibid. at 5-9, 16, 21.
[66]Ibid. at 25-6, 29, 37.
[67]Ibid. at 71, 86.
[68]Ibid. at 97-114.

grounds of extreme physical and mental cruelty in divorce actions. Women used divorce courts. The Montana divorce rate from 1865 to 1870 was 33 percent of all marriages, and in one year—1867—the number of divorces actually exceeded marriages in the territory. Women successfully achieved severance of their marriages by pressing actions based upon abandonment; adultery; cruelty, including sexual abuse; and drunkenness. In addition, alimony and child-custody decisions in Montana allowed women to make a clean break from difficult marital relationships.[69]

Eventually Montana adopted the Domestic Law Code in 1895, and the effect of this action was to begin to tighten court interpretations and attempt to nationalize Montana family law. Whether this movement succeeded is not the subject of Petrik's book, but it remains an important question, for if Montana family law was nationalized, then a possible special legal culture had been altered.[70]

Petrik concludes (as have a number of scholars of western women's history) by trying to find something Turnerian to apply to the subject at hand. Perhaps if the conclusion were being written today she might alter it. Nevertheless, she provides a framework for looking carefully at gender in the American West and its relationship to American law. She states that "the frontier had shaped a new vision of what was necessary and possible for women."[71] It reordered social relationships of the sexes and provided alternatives under new pronouncements on domestic law, both within and outside family structures.[72] This was possible only in the American West.

Another recent development in western legal gender studies occurred with the publication of the Summer/Fall 1994 issue of *Western Legal History*.[73] Four historians present four separate, very promising areas of research: Anne Butler on work requirements of women in western prisons, Margaret Holden on white women's roles in the Oregon anti-Chinese extralegal movement, Donna Schuele on California's struggle with married women's property rights under community property legal traditions, and James Muhn on western women exercising their rights under the Homestead Act. These essays show that further studies may provide an opportunity to address questions pertaining to the western formation of a distinct legal

[69]Ibid. at 97-100, 108.

[70]Ibid. at 111.

[71]Ibid. at 136.

[72]Ibid. at 137-38, 140-41.

[73]John R. Wunder and Paula Petrik, guest eds., *Western Legal History* 7 (Summer/Fall 1994), 193-331.

culture.[74] Gender, law, and the American West await significant developments.

ECONOMICS AND THE ENVIRONMENT

It is not surprising to find new works in the legal history of
the American West that consider various aspects of western
economies and the environment. This is simply because of the
tradition of modern American legal history and the works of
Hurst, Friedman, Scheiber, and many others. Indeed, Scheiber's
location, first at the University of California, San Diego, and
then at the University of California, Berkeley, has assured the
profession of the evolution of new scholars whose interests lie
in regional economic and environmental legal studies. Among
them are Arthur F. McEvoy and M. Catherine Miller, the authors of *The Fisherman's Problem: Ecology and the Law in the
California Fisheries, 1850-1980*[75] and *Flooding the Courtrooms:
Law and Water in the Far West,*[76] respectively.

Perhaps McEvoy has taken western legal history furthest into
the domain of the New Western History. *The Fisherman's
Problem* avoids all the pitfalls of the Old Western History. It
does not set arbitrary time frames ending economic and environmental considerations in 1890. It does not ignore or dismiss
the contributions of nonwhite participants. It does not sugar-
coat the message of environmental despoliation and economic
sacrifice and disruption. It does not pretend there is no colonial
relationship between the West and outside economic forces.
In short, McEvoy's history of California's fishing industry is a
prototype of how New Western History concepts can be successfully adapted to legal economic and environmental topics.

McEvoy traces the history of ecological change affecting California's fish population in its rivers and offshore waters over a
130-year period. It is not a happy story, and it includes wanton
destruction of the most valuable fisheries, tremendous human
loss and bitter rivalries among diverse groups, and public
agency failure.[77] Through it all, McEvoy keeps in mind the
intersection of ecology with economic enterprise and the
legal processes involved. For him, in the history of California's

[74]See John R. Wunder and Paula Petrik, "Women, Legal History, and the
American West," in ibid. at 193-99.

[75]Arthur F. McEvoy, *The Fisherman's Problem: Ecology and the Law in the
California Fisheries, 1850-1980* (New York and Cambridge, 1986) [hereafter
cited as McEvoy, *Fisherman's Problem*].

[76]Miller, *Flooding the Courtrooms,* supra note 37.

[77]McEvoy, *Fisherman's Problem,* supra note 75 at xi.

fisheries, "It was simply not possible to maximize both environmental values and the satisfaction of human needs."[78]

McEvoy clearly enunciates what he believes is needed in any discussion of the environmental history of the American West. There must be a careful delineation of the ecology, an understanding of the complexities of production, and a thorough tracing of the role of legal process. From each change associated with each of these concepts may ensue a uniquely western legal culture. Hurst, as McEvoy sees it, understood intuitively that the law and the market were interrelated, but for McEvoy one must push beyond Hurst to factor in time, place, and culture to describe more fully the interrelationship of law with ecology and economy.[79]

In California, McEvoy finds that a story of conquest is at play. There is resource depletion and economic waste, and there are gross inequities among diverse peoples, including Native Americans and Chinese, Japanese, Italian, and Portuguese immigrant fishers, which McEvoy describes as "patterns of ethnic regulation."[80] As to the racial composition of the state's fishing industry, he observes that "Nowhere else in the United States, and possibly the world, has [it] ever been so ethnically diverse."[81]

The key to resource depletion was demand, and the demand for fish took a variety of turns. Agricultural expansion claimed swamps and floodplains, and farming necessitated vast quantities of fertilizer made from the fish. Motorized technology had an enormous effect on the industry, making fishing more effective and efficient. McEvoy echoes William Robbins when he observes that western capitalism promoted and facilitated the destruction of California's fisheries because it allowed for the open license of individual self-interest that could adapt quickly to a changing environment.[82]

Interestingly, it is the state (in this case California) that first recognizes the potential crisis. It tries to regulate the fishing industry, but is generally unsuccessful. McEvoy explains that the greatest hindrance to state regulation or anyone's intervention in this environmental destruction came from federalism. Control over California's fish became a matter of political economy, and federalism "encouraged a kind of competition in regulatory flaccidity" between states, and, in the case of

[78]Ibid. at 11-12.

[79]Ibid. at 13. McEvoy also directly distinguishes his work from that of Turner and Webb. Ibid. at 39.

[80]Ibid. at 15-16, 95.

[81]Ibid. at 65.

[82]Ibid. at 72-73. See also Robbins, *Colony and Empire*.

California's fishing industry, between the state and federal bureaucracy.[83] With the New Deal, federal regulatory agencies prevailed, but even the environmental consciousness of the 1970s and its natural legal outgrowth at both federal and state levels could not save California's fish.[84]

If there is any aspect of this book that seems related to the Old Western History, it is the lack of a personal dimension. The only profiles of participants are of fishing-industry lobbyists and scientists. Individual laborers, such as Chinese, Italians, or Yuroks, are not described in detail. True, the "other's" participation is interwoven throughout the book, much to the author's credit, but McEvoy's history of California's fisheries emanates a kind of antiseptic tragedy to it. This aside, *The Fisherman's Problem* represents one of the best works on the legal history of the West's environment and economy that has yet been produced.

A different approach, although no less effective, is found in M. Catherine Miller's chronicling of the legal web surrounding one western cattle company, Miller & Lux, and its fight for water in California, Oregon, and Nevada. Miller & Lux was no ordinary ranching operation. The company, formed in 1858 by two butchers in California, became synonymous with agricultural capitalism. Its first purchase was twelve thousand acres, a quarter of a Spanish land grant ranch in the San Joaquin Valley; this was followed by an "orgy of land and cattle buying" until Miller & Lux accumulated nearly a million acres in three states.[85]

Miller (not related to the founder of the company) notes that the key to profitability for Miller & Lux was water. In her legal study of this prominent land and cattle company, she ponders questions surrounding the role of law in the development of California and the American West. She shows how Miller & Lux fought to maintain its water rights, which it associated with riparian water law.

Flooding the Courtrooms takes issue with one of the key aspects of the New Western History, that of how water and its control is central to understanding the history of the American West. Miller sees Donald Worster's conceptualization of a hydraulic society for the American West as too one-dimensional. It was not simply a matter of physical control of water that formulated the basis for a hydraulic society, a social and economic concept Miller accepts, but also one of law and

[83]McEvoy, *Fisherman's Problem*, supra note 75, quotation at 182; 182-84.
[84]Ibid. at 228-47.
[85]Miller, *Flooding the Courtrooms*, supra note 37, quotation at 3; 1-3.

ideology.[86] To Miller, water was "an object of physical, ideological and legal contention," and Miller & Lux, as a western company, manipulated the legal system in order to retain physical control of vast amounts of water.[87] In short, Miller has built upon Worster with *Flooding the Courtrooms*.

Although she does not attempt to argue that a special legal culture was at play in Miller & Lux's legal world, she does note that western water law's evolution is differentiated from that in other regions and transcends in time any restrictive "frontier" processes. This is because of the advent of capitalism. Miller writes: "While its environment was unique, California was struggling with the implications of corporate capitalism for government, law, and society, and Miller & Lux, like many others in the legalistic culture of the United States, looked to law to mediate its place in these changing times."[88]

The story of Miller & Lux's early legal success is one of a struggle for power over resources. Competing legal doctrines gave courts choices, and, with Miller & Lux's help, judges adopted a doctrine that fit the land and the region. It was an issue of past settlement and its incumbent need to keep secure property rights versus future development and property risks. Miller says it was a legal contest pitting regional and local stability against national futuristic projections, and for the last half of the nineteenth century Miller & Lux and regional considerations prevailed.[89] This triumph of legal ideology was evident in the California Supreme Court's watershed case *Lux v. Haggin*,[90] decided in 1886.

Population growth and economic development repeatedly challenged Miller & Lux for control of water. Most threatening were power companies, so Miller & Lux simply joined them. Irrigation, by 1900, was marketed as "a new frontier for the expansion of family farming," and Miller & Lux co-opted it by building their own canal system and selling water. Still more legal struggles continued, pitting competing ideologies, that of water being available to all who needed it against the protection of private property rights in water that could be bought

[86]Ibid. at 5, 181-82.

[87]Ibid. at 5.

[88]Ibid. at 1. Miller also concludes, "While the lawyer's prism refracted the material conflicts over water into legal categories, the lens of ideology refocuses them. Ideology linked the private demands of Miller & Lux and the issues of *western water law* to broader changes in the capitalist economy and mediated the relationship between legal doctrine and material development." Ibid. at 178 (emphasis added).

[89]Ibid. at 7-16.

[90]Ibid. at 17. See *Lux v. Haggin*, 69 Cal. 255 (1886), and White, *"It's Your Misfortune,"* supra note 21 at 402.

and sold. Questions of water rates, water rights, water value, and taxation were fleshed out.[91]

Until the end of the Progressive Era, courts in California generally favored vested property rights. This had a strange side effect. Riparian rights made ownership of public utilities an effective means for private companies to retain cheap water. "Ironically," concludes Miller, "the commitment of the courts, of the state, to private property also rendered inoperative efficiency models of pricing and economic growth in the capitalist system."[92] This clearly places her within the debate of the New Western History and its recent discussions concerning the role of capitalism in the history of the American West.

Miller & Lux lost control of its exclusive water rights and its strength and viability as a corporate player in the 1920s. In the company's pursuit of profits, economic rivalry and class hostility generated notions of justice that sometimes overrode legal formalism, but the struggles that counted usually featured not the general public versus corporate interests, but intraclass, company versus company, legal interplay. Missing from Miller's description are not the individual winners and losers from the upper classes, but the losers from the small water users and the original owners of the lands under question. Miller is in a league with most other western historians in this aspect of her work.[93]

Thus *Flooding the Courtrooms* links the legal history of the American West with the modern scholarship of the New Western History. It focuses economic and environmental issues in a legal construct that has not been considered widely by most historians. As in *The Fisherman's Problem*, this particular kind of legal history extends the intellectual boundaries of the New Western History.

NEW WESTERN HISTORY CRITICS

To summarize, it should be clear at this point that a New Western Legal History exists. Proponents are asking new questions and uncovering new data about a neglected region. The break from Hurstian notions of modern American legal history may not be as pronounced as it is among anti- and neo-Turnerians, but there is a clear separation nevertheless. New Western Legal History has much to contribute to the New Western

[91]Miller, *Flooding the Courtrooms*, supra note 37 at 20, 26, 29-30, 33, 40, 50, 55, 59-61.

[92]Ibid. at 66.

[93]Ibid. at 67, 79, 118.

History, and it may be that both groups of scholars are travelling the same road, but recognition by non-legal New Western historians of this new dimension, particularly that of a distinct western legal culture debate, remains minimal.

Criticism of the New Western History by Turnerians and ascribers to the Old Western History has been loud and confrontational. It has been met by writers of the New Western History with vigor. These contests have been summarized previously in academic journals, newspapers, and popular magazines.[94] Yet somewhat remarkable and at the same time quite explainable is the lack of criticism or even recognition of new works in western legal history, or of what might be termed the New Western Legal History. Only reporters seem to appreciate the overriding significance of law to the new history of the American West.[95] Throughout the barrage, few have taken on, for example, preliminary notions of a distinct western legal culture.

At best there is a generalized criticism that the New Western History is too dark, that it emphasizes the down side in the story of the American West. This most certainly can be stated with reference to new revelations about the role of law in the history of the American West. The works of Harring, Clark, and McEvoy lend credence to this generalization. Still, a counter argument exists—that there are good and bad in history, and historians make choices about whether to present *all* of the facts or just some of the facts. If the information leads to "dark" conclusions, then a truthful recounting of the past demands that it be told.

One reason for the lack of debate over a New Western Legal History may be a more general deficiency. It is possible that only the people reading about water law, divorce in Montana,

---

[94]For critics, defenders, and observers, see Gerald D. Nash, "Point of View: One Hundred Years of Western History," *Journal of the West* 32 (January 1993), 3-4; William W. Savage, Jr., "The New Western History: Youngest Whore on the Block," *Bookman's Weekly* 92 (October 4, 1993), 1242-47; Larry McMurtry, "How the West Was Won or Lost," *New Republic* (October 22, 1990), 32-38; John Mack Faragher, "Gunslingers and Bureaucrats," *New Republic* (December 14, 1992), 29-36; and Wunder, "What's Old About New Western History? pt. 1," supra note 8 at 57-58, esp. nn. 24-27; and idem, "What's Old About New Western History?: pt. 2," supra note 8.

[95]Richard Bernstein, "Unsettling the Old West," *New York Times Magazine* (March 18, 1990), 34, 57, 59. Bernstein notes in a legal reference that one critic, William H. Goetzmann, "mingles skepticism over the supposed newness of some of the new historians' discoveries with a strong sense that the scales of judgment have tipped too far toward the negative." Ibid. at 57. Also see Dick Kreck, "Showdown in the New West," *Denver Post Magazine* (March 21, 1993), 6-8, and "New History of the West Fans Fiery Debate on Culture, Myth," *Omaha World Herald* (October 22, 1995), 12A.

and Indian Supreme Court decisions may be western legal historians themselves, not the general public or, in particular, nonlegal scholars of the history of the American West. This realization points toward an urgent challenge. If this new kind of message, this new kind of research about law and the American West is to have an impact, it must be explained to the general public and nonlegal historians in much the same way as New Western historians, such as White, Limerick, and Worster, have taken to film, popular news magazines, and other media. The myth of the law's complexity must be overcome in the minds of the audience.

There is, after all, drama to this story of law in the American West, and there is a general readership that wants to know about it. The year 1995 closed with a new book at the top of the best-selling fiction list. *Snow Falling on Cedars* is a historic dramatization of a 1950s murder trial on an island in Puget Sound that addresses issues of law, race, gender, war, environment, and economics with such power that most who begin to read the book cannot stop, and when they finish they feel compelled to talk about it.[96]

Such a historical recreation can easily be found in the nonfiction records of any local western courthouse, such as those in Douglas County, Nebraska, which revealed an important legal decision in 1907. And it is the New Western History that has opened these archives to the general public and has thrown light on such classic dramas as that facing Charles Pumphrey, Ham Pak, Jack Naoi, Anna Parr, Willie Almack, and Basil Mullen in early twentieth-century Omaha.

Pumphrey was found guilty of murdering Ham Pak, despite arguments made by his attorneys to try to keep out the damning testimony of the Japanese witness Jack Naoi. When their painting of Naoi as a "citizen of a heathen nation" who could not swear to tell the truth did not sway the judge, they appealed to the Nebraska Supreme Court, hoping to create new law for the American West.[97] Two years after the trial court in Omaha convicted Pumphrey for a brutal murder, his appeal was heard before Nebraska's seven supreme court justices.

In a unanimous opinion written by Justice Jesse Root, the Nebraska Supreme Court ruled that testimony by a Japanese against a white person in a Nebraska criminal court was constitutional. Pumphrey's lawyers, arguing that Naoi could not testify because he did not hold Christian beliefs and consequently could not swear to give truthful testimony, had sought to have him classified as an Indian, not unlike an 1854 determination

---

[96]David Guterson, *Snow Falling on Cedars* (New York, 1995).

[97]Massey, "*Pumphrey v. Nebraska*," supra note 1 at 18.

In separate trials held at the Douglas County Courthouse in Omaha, Willie Almack, Basil Mullen, and Charles Pumphrey were convicted of murdering Ham Pak. (Courtesy Nebraska State Historical Society)

by California's highest court that excluded Chinese testimony through a Native American evidentiary California exclusion statute. Justice Root and Nebraska's highest court, however, would have nothing of this argument and responded with a patronizing directness.[98]

One might think that justice had been served, and that racial and cultural prejudice had not been allowed to tarnish a legal decision. Testimony by Japanese in western courts was admissible. However, Pumphrey, who had been in prison since 1907 and, after this appeal was denied, was condemned to a life of imprisonment, was not to serve his full term. Unlike his African American counterparts, in 1909, shortly after the Nebraska Supreme Court decision, his sentence was reduced by Governor Ashton C. Shallenberger to seven years. With good time, on

[98]Ibid. at 32-33. See *Pumphrey v. State*, 84 Neb. 636 (1909). California precedents were not considered viable by Nebraska's highest court. See *People v. Hall*, 4 Cal. 399 (1854) and *Speer v. See Yup Co.*, 13 Cal. 73 (1859). See also John R. Wunder, "Chinese in Trouble: Criminal Law and Race on the Trans-Mississippi West Frontier," *Western Historical Quarterly* 17 (January 1986), 25-41, and idem, "*Territory of New Mexico v. Yee Shun*: A Turning Point in Chinese Legal Relationships in the Trans-Mississippi West," *New Mexico Historical Review* 65 (July 1990), 305-18.

January 21, 1913, Charles Pumphrey, the murderer of Ham Pak, was released from the Nebraska State Penitentiary, after which he drops from the historical record. As far as can be determined, Willie Almack and Basil Mullen died in prison.[99]

Thus race did play a role in this legal confrontation, but not in the way one might have surmised. Surprises like those found in tracing the history of *Pumphrey v. State of Nebraska* await all who search for answers to the questions raised by the New Western History and law in the American West.

---

[99]Massey, "*Pumphrey v. Nebraska*," supra note 1 at 37-41. These disparities in murder sentencing in the American West based upon racial variables have been researched by Clare V. McKanna, Jr., in *Homicide, Race, and Justice in the American West, 1880-1920* (Tucson, 1997).

SOME LESSONS OF WESTERN
LEGAL HISTORY

BY JOHN PHILLIP REID

Why western legal history? it may be asked. Surprisingly, western lawyers have sometimes given the wrong answers. Max Radin, a California law professor of much repute, has been quoted reminding lawyers that they "are necessarily historians, but for some absurd reason they do not seem to like to admit it although they work with precedents which are 'pure history.'"[1] Another Californian, sometime the state's attorney general and governor, said much the same when occupying the position of chief justice of the United States. "All lawyers are," he observed, "in some sense students of legal history. The knowledge of medieval law, which is essential to the most elementary understanding of our land law, is an obvious example."[2]

Radin and Warren were wrong to confuse precedent and history. Precedent is valued by lawyers not as evidence of the past, but as authority for the present. Historians, by contrast, read judicial opinions for evidence and do not think of an overruled decision as "wrong law." They value it as an interpretation and an explanation

John Phillip Reid is Professor of Law at New York University School of Law. Research for this article was supported by the Filomen D'Agostino Greenburg and Max E. Greenburg Faculty Research Fund at the School of Law.

[1] Frank W. Grinnell, "The Revival of Legal History," 42:1 *Massachusetts Law Quarterly* 68 (1957), quoting, without page attribution, Max Radin, *The Law and You* (New York, 1948).

[2] Earl Warren, "Introduction," *American Journal of Legal History* 1 (1957) 1. Californians and lawyers are not the only ones who have written such nonsense. A distinguished historian once claimed: "There is, after all, a fairly close relationship between the day-to-day methodology of the judicial process and that of historical scholarship. When a court ascertains the nature of a law to be applied to a case through an examination of a stream of judicial precedent, after the time-honored Anglo-American technique, it plays the role of historian. A historian might well say that in this process the court goes to the 'primary sources.'" Alfred H. Kelly, "Clio and the Court: An Illicit Love Affair," 1965 *Supreme Court Review* 119, 121.

In this July 27, 1849 James G. Bruff scene, a wagon train crosses two steep hills between the north and south forks of the Platte River. The man on horseback in the lower right hand corner stops to read a tombstone with the word "Chol." visible on it. (Huntington Library)

of a formerly valid rule. A lawyer has a different perspective. Consider a lawyer dealing with a matter of water rights that refers him back to an Oregon statute of 1888. That lawyer is not interested in the meaning of that legislation as it was understood or intended by the legislators who enacted it. Nor is today's lawyer interested in the historical evolution of water rights vested by authority of that statute. He is, rather, interested in the latest interpretation of the law, the "new wine" that Oregon judges have poured into the "old bottle" of the 1888 statute, an interpretation that historians would (with too much haste) label as a "perversion" of the original meaning.[3]

We should not be deterred. The conclusion that legal history can teach pseudo lessons does not mean that there are no lessons. Indeed, the question that this journal should pose before it becomes set in its ways, is not what lessons can be learned from

[3] Frederic William Maitland, the common law's leading historian, once explained: "A lawyer finds on his table a case about rights of common which sends him to the Statute of Merton. But is·it really the law of 1236 that he wants to know? No, it is the ultimate result of the interpretation set on the statute by the judges of twenty generations. The more modern the decision, the more valuable for his purpose. That process by which old principles and old phrases are charged with a new content is, from the lawyer's point of view, an evolution of the true intent and meaning of the old law; from the historian's point of view it is almost of necessity a process of perversion and misunderstanding." Robert Livingston Schuyler, *Frederic William Maitland, Historian* (1960) 11.

western legal history, but, rather, what are the lessons that are worth learning. It is too easy to say that we should look at the origin of doctrine and ask why the rules of today have developed as they have. It does not do to ignore the risk inherent in lawyer's history, that we may make history the handmaiden to serve today's law by providing apparent answers to today's problems, or to ignore the risk in lawyer's legal history, that, by asking how our present-day institutions evolved, we may become merely antiquarian.

What this journal is labelling "western legal history" is a relatively new discipline. Despite what they might think, the generalists among western historians have ignored matters of law. The leading series of books dealing with general western history, *The Histories of the American Frontier*, do not have a law volume. Indeed, one reason we need *Western Legal History* is because so little has been written. What work we have can loosely be divided into three categories. The first — which includes the books of John D. Guice,[4] John R. Wunder,[5] and, most notably, Gordon Morris Bakken[6] — asks questions about the law in the westward expansion that bear on general American legal history. That is, they cover developments in a western territory or state pertaining to such matters as torts, bar practice, court procedures, or judicial behavior, they extracted lessons that are related to and are not substantially different from mainstream American legal history.

The second category embraces subjects of law found only in the West —law of the Mexican borderlands,[7] law of the Indian Territory,[8] law on the California and Oregon trails,[9] law of the

---

[4] John D. Guice, *The Rocky Mountain Bench: The Territorial Supreme Courts of Colorado, Montana, and Wyoming, 1861-1890* (New Haven, 1972).

[5] John R. Wunder, *Inferior Courts, Superior Justice: A History of the Justices of the Peace on the Northwest Frontier, 1853-1889* (Westport, Conn., 1979).

[6] Gordon Morris Bakken, *Rocky Mountain Constitution Making, 1850-1912* (Westport, Conn., 1987); Gordon Morris Bakken, *The Development of Law in Frontier California: Civil Law and Society 1850-1890* (Westport, Conn., 1985); Gordon Morris Bakken, *The Development of Law in the Rocky Mountain Society, 1850-1912* (Westport, Conn., 1983).

[7] Hans W. Baade, "The Historical Background of Texas Water Law," 18 *St. Mary's Law Review* 1-98 (1986); Edwin W. Young, "The Adoption of the Common Law in California," *American Journal of Legal History* 4 (1960) 355-63; Joseph W. McKnight, "The Spanish Legacy to Texas Law," *American Journal of Legal History* 3 (1959) 222-41; Noel C. Stevenson, "Glorious Uncertainty of the Law, 1846-1851," 28 *California State Bar Journal* 374-80 (1953).

[8] Glenn Shirley, *Law West of Fort Smith* (New York, 1957); the articles on the courts of the Quapaw, Creek, Cherokee, and Chickasaw nations that were published in 4 *Indian Territory Bar Association Proceedings* (1903).

[9] John Phillip Reid, "Governance of the Elephant: Constitutional Theory on the Overland Trails," 5 *Hastings Constitutional Law Quarterly* 421-43 (1978); David J. Langum, "Pioneer Justice on the Overland Trails," *Western Historical Quarterly* 5 (1974) 421-39.

cattle drives, law in the gold mining camps,[10] the suppression of
Morman polygamy,[11] and (although not peculiar to the West it has
for too long been misinterpreted by western historians) water
law.[12] These subjects, if we can find historians with the compe-
tence to handle them, could teach us lessons of law we may not be
able to learn by studying eastern legal history alone.

There is yet a third category of exploration that deserves the
particular attention of western legal historians. Like the first
category, it concerns lessons that can be learned in the East as well
as in the West, but, because before white settlers moved onto the
Pacific slopes there had already been two centuries of the
American legal experience, the western evidence may teach
different, deeper lessons about the nature and strengths of
American law and institutions. One topic belonging to this
category has only recently been developed by historical
scholarship: the existence of a legal culture shaping the behavior
of ordinary people. It is the potential of that subject that provides
the questions raised in this article.

LESSONS OF GOEBEL

Recent historians of the overland trails to the Pacific and of the
Mexican borderlands seem to have been surprised when they
stumbled upon the existence of a legal culture determining the
behavior of ordinary nonlawyer Americans. The discovery should
have been expected. Julius Goebel, Jr., of the Columbus Law
School, anticipated it decades earlier when seeking the legal roots
of New England's first settlers: the origins of the law of the
Plymouth Plantation.

Before Goebel, historians of sixteenth-century Massachusetts
law had compared that law to contemporary English law and,
finding it markedly different from the common law of the
sixteenth-century King's Bench and the assize courts, had
concluded that the law of the Pilgrims and the Puritans was *sui
generis*, a new plant that first took root in American soil.[13] Goebel
exposed their error. It did not do, he knew, to equate sixteenth-
century common law with sixteenth-century "English law."
During the early decades of North American settlement, the term

[10] James G. Rogers, "The Mining District Governments of the West: Their
Interest and Literature," 28 *Law Library Journal* 247-59 (1935).

[11] Orma Linford, "The Mormons and the Law: The Polygamy Cases," 9 *Utah Law
Review* 308-69, 543-91 (1965).

[12] Donald J. Pisani, "Enterprise and Equity: A Critique of Western Water Law in
the Nineteenth Century," *Western Historical Quarterly* 18 (1987) 15-38.

[13] Charles Hilkey, *Legal Development in Colonial Massachusetts,* in *Columbia
University Studies in History, Economics & Public Law* 37 (1910) 159.

"common law" was not synonymous with English law. There were many English laws at that time, of which common law was but one among equals competing for survival.[14] Why not, Goebel asked, go back and look at the other laws to see if they contained the origins of early colonial law? The most promising source, he thought, at least for the settlers of Plymouth Colony and Massachusetts Bay, was local law: the law of the boroughs and the manors of sixteenth and seventeenth-century England. It was when exploring this question that he tripped over (but does not seem to have noticed) the possibility that the behavior of average men and women might owe much to their legal culture.

> It was inevitable that the local courts and the customary law would assume a position of transcendent importance in the life of the ordinary man. It was to these courts that the small farmer or artisan would turn if he wished to replevy his cows or to collect a bill, and that turned upon him if his hogs were unringed or if he put his garbage in the street. Except what these humble men may have known of the ecclesiastical courts, with their sompnours spying upon their amours, and the apparitors to take them to jail if they worshipped heretically, the workings of the county, manorial, or borough tribunals were the length and breadth of their knowledge of the administration of justice, the local customs the sum of their law. Since, it was men from these walks of life by which the Plymouth colony was established, we must seek the secular source from which their legislative inspiration flowed in the local institutions of their native land.[15]

By the ordinary course of historical scholarship, the revelation of the Goebel thesis would have been the death knell of what, up until he wrote in 1931, had been the dominant explanation of the origins of American Law: the "frontier theory."[16] If it was not the death knell of the frontier theory, one reason why may be that the Goebel thesis was not further tested against historical evidence

[14] See Mark De Wolfe Howe, "The Sources and Nature of Law in Colonial Massachusetts," in George Athan Billias, ed., *Law and Authority in Colonial America* (Barre, Mass., 1965) 1, 2-5.

[15] Julius Goebel, "King's Law and Local Custom in Seventeenth Century New England," 31 *Columbia Law Review* 416, 420-21 (1931), reprinted in David Flaherty, ed., *Essays in the History of Early American Law* (Chapel Hill, 1969) 83, 88-89.

[16] For the "frontier theory," see: Frederick Jackson Turner, *The Frontier in American History* (1920) 10; Roscoe Pound, *Criminal Justice in America* (1930) 122; Roscoe Pound, "The Pioneers and the Common Law," 27 *West Virginia Law Quarterly* 1 (1920). For a devastating rejection of the "pioneer theory" by Professor Goebel, see: Julius Goebel and T. Naughton, *Law Enforcement in Colonial New York* (New York, 1944) at xix-xx.

until thirty-two years after Goebel wrote. There were monographs on related issues demonstrating that the hypothesis had great promise. For instance, there was much evidence showing that, on constitutional as opposed to legal questions, the early settlers carried with them and maintained in the New World a culture of English rights and practices remembered from Westminster Hall and the county assizes.[17] In nonconstitutional and nonlegal history, there was much work, most notably by T.H. Breen, on the transfer of English local culture to North America.[18]

Sumner Chilton Powell was the first to test the validity of Goebel's thesis, asking many of the questions about English legal institutions that Goebel said should be asked. In *Puritan Village*, his 1963 prize-winning book, Powell traced the governmental customs and legal practices of the town of Sudbury, Massachusetts, back to the villages and communities of seventeenth-century England from whence came its original settlers.[19] Then, in 1981, David Grayson Allen gave the thesis about as wide a test as it is likely to receive. His research went beyond Powell's in at least three respects. First, he paid closer attention to rules of law and legal customs. Second, he studied the origins of five Massachusetts towns, not just one. And third, some of these towns had been settled almost exclusively by people from one small locality in England, rather than, as was Sudbury, by people from various, diverse regions, allowing Allen to trace specific customs and to demonstrate specific transferral of rules from the old to the new world. Allen's evidence led him to three further conclusions. First, that average people could understand seventeenth-century local English law. Second, that consciously or unconsciously the first settlers of Massachusetts Bay carried with them to the new world as part of their cultural values a remarkable amount of local law. And third, once settled on the shores of the Massachusetts Bay, they continued to behave according to the norms of English law ways.[20]

Goebel, Powell, and Allen were primarily concerned with the

---

[17] Mark De Wolfe Howe, "The Sources and Nature of Law in Colonial Massachusetts," supra note 14 at 15.

[18] T.H. Breen, *The Character of the Good Ruler* (New Haven, Conn., 1970); T.H. Breen, "Transfer of Culture: Change and Design in Shaping Massachusetts Bay, 1630-1660," *New England Historical & Genealogical Register* 132 (1978) 3; T.H. Breen, "Persistent Localism: English Social Change and the Shaping of New England Institutions," *William & Mary Quarterly* 32 (1975) 3; T.H. Breen and Stephen Foster, "Moving to the New World: The Character of Early Massachusetts Immigration," *William & Mary Quarterly* 30 (1973) 189-222.

[19] Sumner Powell, *Puritan Village: The Formation of a New England Town* (Middletown, Conn., 1963) 80-81.

[20] David Grayson Allen, *In English Ways: The Movement of Societies and the Transferal of English Local Law and Custom to Massachusetts in the Seventeenth Century* (Chapel Hill, N.C., 1981).

transferral of legal institutions and legal norms from an old to a new physical environment, the extension of English legal behavior to North America. They, therefore, only uncovered the existence, they did not explore the extent to which our earliest settlers were the products of a legal culture. Besides, their people came from a heritage of customary law, small-village communal life, in which daily activity was controlled by timeless practice, land and its uses were held by inherited standards, and personal rights were secured by the shared remembrance of past procedures. It was a quite different legal culture from that which we know. Our legal culture — of law by legislative command rather than custom, of rights secured by judicial direction rather than jury consensus, and of legal rules upheld by police enforcement rather than by community self-help — would be developed by their American descendants shortly after the Revolution against Great Britain. It thus has been the task for historians of the nineteenth century to seek lessons about the strengths of a legal culture in a law world of the type with which we are familiar.

It is on this matter, the legal culture contributing to the behavior of average Americans, that western legal history has made its first contribution to our knowledge of the history of American law. It was, after all, during the westward movement, the push onto the unoccupied frontier, that people were likely to find themselves beyond the reach of the formal institutions of law: of police, of courts, of the advice or direction of lawyers. It was then, during such nineteenth-century movements, that the nuances of an American legal culture can best be measured. One place that the measure has been taken is the overland trail to California and Oregon.

Studies of the emigrants who crossed the western half of the North American continent over the wagon trails to the Pacific Coast show that they were immersed in a legal culture. To a stunning extent, their behavior was determined by legal norms. The average emigrants said — and certainly believed — that they had tracked out onto a region where there was "no law," yet they continued to behave as if controlled by law. Contracts provide one example. Hundreds of overland travellers, even while claiming to be far out in lawless territory, made agreements to bail animals, transferred property on the promise of future payment, and sold their personal services on the reliance of executory obligations. It is clear from the evidence that the conception of the overland emigrants of the elements creating binding contracts was not precisely the same as that of contemporary American law during the late 1840s and the 1850s. That, however, is a matter of legal education not legal culture, and it is legal culture that is our concern. Emigrants who said there was no law on the overland trail, yet negotiated agreements expecting they would be honored, were doing more than creating moral obligations. They were relying on a tradition of shared legal notions: expecting that the other party shared the same values they did, that they understood a contract in the same sense they did, and believed that promises mutually exchanged created obligations for the same reason they did. In other words, supporting every exchange that was not barter, there were commonly shared values that surely owed as much to the emigrants' remembrance of legal principle enforced east of the Missouri River as to religious teachings or moral upbringing.[21]

The law of property furnishes a slightly different lesson. The emigrants understood the law of property much as it was practiced by lawyers in the eastern states. They not only understood but out on the trail they observed distinctions between personal property, mess property, partnership property, company property, and joint-stock property. Acting on these shared definitions, they avoided conflict and resolved quarrels. When concurrent ownership became too divisive, they converted it to personalty; when continued companionship became impossible, they divided provisions by the law of ownership, not the law of need.[22] Indeed, to an incredible degree, the law of property shaped human behavior on the overland trail. As will be discussed below, actions were judged not as our western novels or movies would lead us to expect, by Christian values, but by ownership. There was displayed on the overland trail a "habit of property," a "morality of law," that had never been appreciated or utilized by our judges and our legislators.[23]

Evidence from the overland trail not only reveals a legal culture of shared definitions, but a legal culture of shared procedures. The remembrance was not only of things experienced, but of institutions that had only been observed, or perhaps only described. An example is the criminal trial.

What we know about trials on the California and Oregon trails comes largely from accounts of prosecutions against men accused of deliberate homicide. One basic generality can be gleaned from these cases — the emigrants did not attempt to create *sui generis* institutions. Instead, they duplicated or imitated the courts and judicial procedures remembered from back home. If two lawyers were present, one might be appointed to prosecute, the other to defend. Someone served as prosecutor for minor as well as major

---

[21] John Phillip Reid, "Binding the Elephant: Contracts and Legal Obligations on the Overland Trail," *American Journal of Legal History* 21 (1977) 285, 314-15.

[22] John Phillip Reid, "Dividing the Elephant: The Separation of Mess and Joint Stock Property on the Overland Trail," 28 *Hastings Law Journal* 73-92 (1976); John Phillip Reid, "Sharing the Elephant: Partnership and Concurrent Property on the Overland Trail," 45 *UMKC Law Review* 209-22 (1976).

[23] John Phillip Reid, *Law For the Elephant: Property and Social Behavior on the Overland Trail* (San Marino, 1980).

offenses. A defendent might be permitted to hire a lawyer, even a stranger passing by in another train.[24]

Most telling of all was the emigrants' insistence that the triers of fact duplicate the function of the jury in American criminal law. To the untrained eye of the nonlawyer, it might on first glance appear that emigrants had a different model in mind. In noncapital

Courthouse Rock as drawn by James G. Bruff on July 3, 1849 while traveling by wagon train through the Nebraska Territory south of the Platte River. The geologic formation, a noted landmark on the wagon trail, was so named because of its resemblance to courthouses in the East, particularly the courthouse in St. Louis, which was the starting point of most western emigrants. (Huntington Library)

cases the whole company sometimes decided guilt or innocence, and it was not unknown for a murder prosecution to be settled by vote of every emigrant present — whether witnesses, companions, or strangers. In a sense these trials depart from the Anglo-American norm, but not as much as they might have, and the departure is not basic. The overland emigrants did not do what logic might have dictated — i.e., they did not go back to the early English pattern and entrust the decision to those who knew the facts. With a small population, no regular tribunals, no police, no rules of evidence, and an uncertain supply of lawyers, it would have made sense to have asked the truth of those possessing the truth. Instead, the general rule — especially in homicide situations — was to select a jury of twelve men and, after

[24] John Phillip Reid, "Prosecuting the Elephant: Trials and Judicial Behavior on the Overland Trail," 1977 *Brigham Young University Law Review* 327, 329.

presenting evidence through witnesses, entrust the decision to them.[25]

That overland juries were close copies of common-law juries should be greeted with surprise, not dismissed as inevitable. Not only were overland jurors not required to know the circumstances of the alleged crimes, they did not have to come from the company of the accused. Legal theory on the trail took for granted that "stranger emigrants" could render a fair verdict, much as in an established American court of law, by hearing evidence from witnesses, weighing arguments, and reaching decisions. Thus one caravan tried a homicide accusation with "a jury of men out of another train and witnesses out of our train." Another manslayer was tried by "[t]ribunal representatives of over 200 wagons in the neighborhood," while a third panel was selected from fifty men "collected from both front and rear trains."[26]

Of course, had the emigrants thought about the question, they should have adopted the medieval English model of the jury, with the triers of fact drawn from those with knowledge of the facts. But they were not thinking so much as behaving. They followed the nineteenth-century model of the uninformed, impartial jury because that was what their shared experience told them was "law." Behavior is the operative concept that teaches us our lesson of a nineteenth-century legal culture carried from the civilization of the eastern states to the wilderness of the Sierra Nevada. It is the taught, remembered, respected, and shared legal behavior that furnishes our lesson — not implementation of specific legal concepts. On the long, dangerous overland trail to California and Oregon, it was legal behavior that shaped conduct settling disputes without acts of violence,[27] allocated precious resources according to shared notions of property rights rather than by force, and, when crime occurred, dealt with offenses not by summary drumhead procedures, but with the trappings of a remembered judicial process.

LESSONS OF LANGUM

There is even more to be said about the culture of law than has been thought. The overland trail is an obvious place to look for legal behaviorism. It takes patience, not imagination, to find our lessons there. A less likely place, one offering both a greater historical and greater legal challange, is the "borderland" of Mexican California. David J. Langum, the premier legal historian

[25] Reid, "Prosecuting the Elephant," supra note 24 at 339-40.
[26] Ibid. at 340-41.
[27] John Phillip Reid, "Paying for the Elephant: Property Rights and Civil Order on the Overland Trail," Huntington Library Quarterly 41 (1977) 37-64.

at Cumberland School of Law, opened up a new field of historical scholarship in 1987 with the publication of his first book, *Law and Community on the Mexican California Frontier*. As with the travellers on the overland trail, the story of Americans, English, Scots, and Irish in preconquest California, is a story revealing a strong nineteenth-century common-law culture. Expatriates, he writes, "peacefully invaded California, bringing with them their preconceptions of the proper legal order." Langum's evidence is even more revealing than the evidence of the overland emigrants, for rather than clinging to their law ways in vast, open expanses, without police, lawyers, or courts, his people brought their legal ideas into conflict with an established, sovereign judicial system. "These Americans, and their British cousins as well," Langum discovered, "spoke, wrote, and thought in legal terms. The [common] law was deeply revered and was an ingrained and inextricable part of their culture."[28]

Langum's theme is of a clash of legal cultures that could never had occurred had not ordinary nineteenth-century Americans, even those with little formal education and no legal education, possessed an innate, shared, cultured sense of "law" and of how they expected "law" to operate. "When an expatriate [in Mexican California] wrote a contract or settled a dispute," Langum notes, "he did so without any lawyer to guide him. The extent to which the foreigners correctly used law suggests the degree to which legal norms had become a part of their general culture.[29]

The expatriates' knowledge of American and English law did more than provide a guide for conducting their own business affairs. It explains the basis for their hostility against Spanish-Mexican law. "The expatriates drew on the local law only to the extent absolutely necessary. Instead, they did their best to order their present circumstances in a manner harmonious with the remembered law of the eastern and midwestern states from which they had come."[30]

The reasons why Americans and their fellow common-law expatriates disliked Mexican law are clear. What is surprising is that the reasons were not due to prejudice or feelings of Anglo-Saxon superiority, but followed from innate expectations of how a legal system should operate and from expectations about the definitiveness of judgments. Americans simply did not like the Mexican judicial process,[31] which functioned largely without

[28] David J. Langum, *Law and Community on the Mexican California Frontier: Anglo-American Expatriates and the Clash of Legal Traditions, 1821-1846* (Norman, 1987) 3. [Hereafter cited as Langum, *Law.*]

[29] Ibid. at 7.

[30] Ibid. at 267.

[31] Langum explains the law of Mexican California — one hundred pages on civil and criminal substantive and adjective law. Some sections read like a procedure hornbook. Ibid. at 30-130.

lawyers,[32] and was presided over by lay judges often serving
reluctantly.[33] Although Mexican jurists were much more powerful
than their common-law counterparts,[34] it was an authority seldom
exercised, as civil procedure was geared toward reconciliation, not
adjudication.

"Mexican society believed that litigation was to be avoided —
almost at all costs," Langum observes.[35] It was a cost that put
Americans ill at ease. As lawsuits "were regarded as disruptive of
the community's functions,"[36] "the primary function of the
Mexican California courts was to prevent litigation, a startling
reversal of our normal expectations of the judicial process."[37]
Americans turned to that process seeking judgment and
enforcement of legal expectations. They were, instead, directed
toward conciliation[38] and told to depend not on lawyers but on
hombres buenos.[39] Even when judgments were rendered "[t]hey
were subject to defendants coming back into court with a tale of
woe that the crop was bad, the cattle were too thin to slaughter, or
some other excuse, and asking that the installment payments be
extended."[40]

Substantive law reflected adjective law and it may be wondered
whether, to Americans of the 1840s, it appeared to be "law" at all.
"For the law that did exist, very little use was made of it, either by
litigants or judges," Langum concludes. "Both relied instead on

[32] "The lack of trained lawyers was chronic throughout Mexico. In the early
Federalist period some Mexican states had as few as two or three attorneys
within their entire jurisdiction." Langum, *Law*, supra note 28 at 46.

[33] "[T]he judges were all lay personnel, thrust into their judgeships often against
their will by threats of fines if they refused to accept the appointment." Ibid at 70.
"Illiteracy was not a sufficient excuse" for not serving as a judge. Ibid. at 44.

[34] "[T]he alcalde's word was literally the law itself, unfettered by substantive
standards (legal rules) for the resolution of conflicts. He could decree as he
thought fit, confined only by the cultural and religious mores of the local village
in which he sat." Ibid at 30. Walter Colton, alcalde at Monterey, resolved
questions with which American law would not have dealt. Ibid. at 134.

[35] Ibid. at 133. "There was a Spanish tradition of compromise as early as the late
Middle Ages. Although Castile was reasonably litigious, its communities
emphasized the need for rapid and amicable resolution of disputes. Compromise
was the ideal, and a settlement arbitrated within the community was the
preferred method of dispute resolution." Ibid. at 132.

[36] Ibid.

[37] Ibid. at 131-32.

[38] "As a condition to commencement of a lawsuit the plaintiff had to show by a
certificate that an attempt at conciliation had first been attempted in an effort to
resolve the dispute." Ibid. at 38.

[39] Ibid. at 98-99.

[40] Ibid. at 113. And what of the payments? "Very few conciliation judgments,
whether accepted or not, called for an immediate payment of money. Almost all
California judgments called for payments at least partly in goods, usually hides."
Ibid. at 99.

vague appeals to 'rights' or the 'law' and seemed satisfied with
assertions or denials of 'rights' and 'laws' that were uninformed by
written substantive law that was available to them. Thus justice as
actually administered was largely of the curbstone variety."[41]

Even when Spanish-Mexican law was "law" rather than "justice,"
it was, by common-law standards, remarkably imprecise. An
example from the area of property rights was recently provided by
Michael C. Meyer in his 1984 history of Mexican water law. "There
were no riparian rights for agricultural or industrial uses in New
Spain," Meyer pointed out. "The grant of a piece of land fronting on
a river entitled the owner, without additional authorization, to use
the water for domestic purposes, but for nothing else."[42] Even so,
"nobody was to use more water than was absolutely necessary." An
official empowered by government authority "was to divide it in
such a way that all the land subject to irrigation (that portion
previously designated as subject to irrigation) would receive its
benefits."[43]

> Spanish law made special effort to guard the interests of
> those landowners whose property did not have a direct
> outlet to the water source. Through practice, custom, and
> law (jus aquoeductus), an individual was allowed to
> construct an acequia on another man's land if there was
> no other way to conduct the water to his own. A land-
> owner could drive his cattle through his neighbor's
> property to water them (jus aquoe hausius) if there were
> no watering holes on his own land. Even the foundations
> of houses and churches could be altered so that water
> could pass through them.[44]

At first glance these seem valuable property rights to water, in
many respects going beyond anything at common law (which
allowed individuals to patent water holds and exclude neighbors,
and — as it seldom compromised the tort of trespass except in the
mining districts — did not recognize a claim by a nonriparian
landowner to a share of the nearest source of water). But were
these what a nineteenth-century American, intent on capitalizing
property and on reaping profits from things in which he had

[41] Langum, Law, supra note 28 at 126. "The lack of significant use of substantive
law does not mean that the judges' decisions were capricious or that they lacked
common sense in the resolution of disputes." Ibid. at 127. But for nineteenth-
century Americans, legalism was a shield against arbitrariness.

[42] Michael C. Meyer, Water in the Hispanic Southwest: A Social and Legal History
1550-1850 (Tucson, 1984) 119-20. Although this book discusses neither common
nor American law, Meyer has written the best legal history of water in America.

[43] Ibid. at 36.

[44] Ibid. at 71.

invested his own time and resources, would have called property rights in water?

There is a second question to be asked. Why say that these different attitudes toward law and judicial process were due to cultural expectations rather than due to national antagonisms? One answer is that the Anglo-American complaint was not about Mexican law or that these were Mexican judges, but that they were law and judges functioning in the civilian rather than the common-law tradition. The articulated objections were directed against perceived institutional eccentricities and reflected the disappointment of unfulfilled expectations.[45] The expatriates may not have wanted "clear winners and clear losers," as Langum suggests,[46] but they did want the certainty and predictability of what they called "law," or what Langum describes as "the cultural expectations the expatriates brought with them."[47] A fact to be especially marked is that these expectations involved both substance and enforcement.

"In this Anglo-American legal expectation," Langum observes of specific rules and doctrine, "there was every demand for settled substantive law firmly applied, and no room at all for a quixotic judge varying the rules to achieve justice in a particular case. The California practices of installment judgments and modification deeply offended that principle."[48]

Perhaps even more revealing of cultural expectations was expatriate dissatisfaction with mesne and final process.

> Much of the expatriate criticism of the alcalde system was accurate. The courts were inefficient, at times unpredictable, and they lacked any semblance of effective enforcement techniques.... But the depth of the Anglo-American criticism reflected differing cultural norms of what was wanted and expected from a legal system. The expatriates wanted certainty, predictability, and efficiency in enforcement of judgments.[49]

[45] Significantly, Langum finds that Mexican criminal justice did not "victimize" expatriates; if anything, they were favored. Langum *Law.* supra note 28 at 89, 94, 96. Yet they distrusted the system because of some of its aspects that differed from common criminal law. Ibid. at 69. Among the most interesting complaints, one voiced not just by Americans but *by British* as well, was the joining of executive, legislative, and judicial functions in one official, the alcalde. Langum, *Law,* supra note 28 at 51, 52, 65, 7-, 121.

[46] Ibid. at 271.

[47] Ibid. at 139.

[48] Ibid. at 140.

[49] Ibid. at 273. "What common law judge would dare change the due date of an obligation, or the medium of payment, or issue an installment judgment? The purpose behind this accommodation was not to favor improvident borrowers or credit purchasers nor to relieve them of just debts, as many expatriate creditors

In their shared legal culture, the Anglo-American expatriates equated law with enforcement. For them, a "law of contract" had no substance if the stipulated obligation could not be enforced. Fair dealing, reasonable price, adjustment, compromise, and accommodation were not enough.[50]

CONCLUSION

David Langum's book must be read in full to be appreciated. The evidence is too rich and the findings too surprising to bear summary treatment. It is, of course, but one step in the writing of western legal history, uncovering the story of legal conflict in the Spanish borderlands, and, most important, taking the measure of legal culture in nineteenth-century North America.

There is much work yet to be done. Evidence of a nineteenth-century legal culture provided by the westward movement — by the behavior of emigrants on the overland trail and the conduct of expatriates in Mexican California —has raised issues about the nature of American law ways that require that more scholars begin to investigate western legal history. It is a neglected field awaiting its reapers and its gleaners.

It is not enough to agree that there was a legal culture directing, guiding, and even motivating nineteenth-century Americans. The next task is to evaluate and explain it. David Langum believes that he is describing a fundamental clash of legal values in Mexican-American California: a clash between the customary law ways and languid procedures of the preindustrial, pastoral Californios, and the atomistic, individualist energies of Yankees in the very throes of the Industrial Revolution.[51] That explanation may be plausible but there is much more to be said than that the industrial age developed different values than the preindustrial. The preindustrial, pastoral New Englanders of late colonial times would have been no more at home in the California of the 1840s than were their descendants. They may have, as William E. Nelson has shown, confused "law" with community values by entrusting judgment to juries who decided law as well as fact, but they still wanted decisions rendered and verdicts executed.[52] They may not have experienced the Industrial Revolution, but they had more in common with Langum's expatriates than they would have had

---

sincerely believed, but to resolve an unsettled and antagonistic condition by fashioning a decree that could rest easily on all concerned and resolve the dispute without exalting a winner or crushing a loser." Ibid.

[50] Ibid. at 184-86.

[51] Ibid. at 9.

[52] William E. Nelson, *Americanization of the Common Law: The Impact of Legal Change on Massachusetts Society, 1760-1830* (Cambridge, Mass., 1975).

with the preindustrial Californios. Of course, in the economics of
small-town, subsistence agriculture and in much of their way of
life, the colonial New Englanders had more in common with the
Californios. What seems to have counted most, however, with the
Anglo-American expatriates was a factor they shared with the
New Englanders: they had come to age in a common-law
jurisdiction.

A more convincing argument is procedural. Langum thinks the
mandatory conciliation process through the use of *hombres
buenos* was well suited to Mexican California where community
harmony was a high social value, but despised by the Anglo-
Americans who thought it a waste of time as it delayed the "more
appropriate clash of trial."[53] But again, there must be more to the
explanation. What was there about the legal culture of the
common-law expatriates that made a "clash of trial" more
appealing than social harmony? After all, as a distinct, alien
minority, one might think they would have sought the procedure
that avoided conflict and encouraged compromise.

Professor Langum attributes the contrasting attitudes to
different cultural values. Mexican adjective law, with its emphasis
upon reconciliation through adjustment of claims, taught the
value of community interest over individual interest. Common-
law procedure, he argues, taught people that "rights" were
"absolute," instilling respect for "adversarial combat" with the
expectation of determining "a clearly defined winner." As a result,
the interest of the individual was a higher value than either
communal interest or communal harmony.[54]

Langum's explanations are more evidence of effects than
discussion of causes. Further work remains to be done and by the
very nature of the problem we may expect that western legal
history will be utilized for a good portion of the answer. Langum
provides an important start (and on this point he may be on the
right track for finding answers) with his speculation about the role
of individualism in the common law. The Anglo-American
emigrant to California, he argues, came out of a legal culture that
fostered individualism,[55] a "rugged" individualism of let the chips
fall where they may, encouraged by a law that was fast ridding
itself of restrictions upon individual initiative such as the
medieval law of nuisance or the English rule of waste.[56]

[53] Langum, *Law*, supra note 28 at 272.

[54] Ibid. at 271.

[55] Ibid. at 29.

[56] Ibid. at 271. See also 142. It is interesting but not persuasive evidence that a
California Senate Committee in 1850 drew the same contrast: "[T]he Common
Law allows parties to make their own bargains, and when they are made, hold
them to a strict compliance; whilst the Civil Law looks upon man as incapable of
judging for himself, assumes the guardianship over him, and interpolates into a

The execution on June, 11, 1851 of John Jenkins by the San Francisco
Committee of Vigilance. Jenkins had stolen a safe and, when being chased
across San Francisco Bay, had dropped it in the water. He was captured by
the Committee's policemen and, after insulting and haranguing his
captors, was quickly found guilty and hanged before a crowd of several
thousand onlookers the same night as his trial. Drawing by James G.
Bruff. (Huntington Library)

If we accept for the sake of argument that the Mexican legal
system discouraged or suppressed individual assertiveness, we
still need to seek more evidence about the individualism fostered
by the common-law culture. After all, that same legal culture was
a major factor contributing to social harmony and the peaceful
resolution of disputes on the overland trail. There is an apparent
contradiction here, a paradox of a legal culture encouraging
accommodation in a situation without judicial tribunals, yet
discouraging it when encountering tribunals that mandated not
individual rights but reconciliation. We will have to encourage
much more research in western legal history before we can resolve
the puzzle. It may be that we already have an indication of how it
will be resolved, that David Langum points out at least one
solution when he observes that the Anglo-American expatriates
in nineteenth-century California were

> deeply imbued with the rugged, highly individualistic
> concepts of this period of the common law. Rights were
> absolute entitlements and duties their stern correlatives,
> owed unconditionally. No matter how onesided or unfair,
> a contract should be enforced strictly according to its

contract that which the parties never agreed to." California Senate Committee on
the Judiciary, Report on Civil and Common Law (1850), quoted in Ibid. at 140.
The report, dated 27 February 1850, is printed in 1 *California Reports* 588-604.

terms. Courts should not rewrite agreements. If debts
were owed or damages assessed, judgment should be
rendered for immediate payment in cash, with no
extensions and regardless of a defendant's personal needs
or ability to pay.[57]

Langum may be referring only to the legal perceptions of
nineteenth-century Americans. What he says would be an overstatement of the absoluteness of rights at common law, the law,
that is, of the eastern courts and the professional bar. He does not
overstate the impression of absolute property rights that the
average participant in the westward movement carried as part of
his innate, inherent legal culture. This same absolutism that
produced conflict when its cultural values clashed with the
judicial process of mandatory reconciliation in Mexican
California produced harmony when, on the "lawless" overland
trail, perceived legal cultural values furnished emigrants with
objective norms of behavior.
    There is more to the overland trail evidence than is mentioned
above. It was not just law and legal definitions that emigrants
shared as part of their cultural baggage. They also shared attitudes
about the role of law and important rights to society, and those
attitudes helped shape specific behavior on the roads to California
and Oregon. On this point — legal perceptions effecting conduct
— a striking illustration is provided by the manner in which
property rights were regarded on the overland trail: property rights
were treated as absolute.
    An emigrant with title to a wagon or a horse could do with "his
property" whatever whim and fancy dictated. Just the bare, single
fact that he "owned," that the material items "belonged" to him, was
determinative of the behavior of the overwhelming majority of his
fellow overlanders. Ownership silenced all objections they might
have raised about the manner in which he used, misused, or
hoarded "his property." There was no assertion of communal
sharing on the overland trail. One emigrant's desperation created
no demand right on another emigrant's surplus. When any surplus
was granted as gifts or sold rather than destroyed, the receiver
wrote of generosity and thankfulness, not of the fulfillment of just
expectations. Had the "owner" destroyed rather than granted or
sold, fellow emigrants might criticize his unchristian behavior, but
always acknowledged his unquestioned right. In a cultural perception of absolute privilege, that would not have been countenanced
in a nineteenth-century court of equity or common law, lay the
roots of the social harmony prevailing during the westward
movement.[58]

[57] Langum, *Law*, supra note 28 at 270.
[58] Reid, *Law for the Elephant*, supra note 23 at 289-304.

That there are questions to be resolved does not diminish the evidence that has been brought to light. David Langum pointed the way to one direction for western legal history to take when he uncovered some lessons from the experience of Anglo-American expatriates in preconquest California. A lesson for western historians to take to heart is the extent that nineteenth-century Americans "subconsciously adhered to common law legal concepts,"[59] and "the great extent to which the common law norms and concepts had ingrained themselves into the American and British psyches."[60] The lesson for judges and lawyers to puzzle over is why, "because of that successful acculturation to the common law," these expatriates were unable "to understand the procedures, purposes, and cultural assumptions of the Mexican legal system."[61] Is it possible that a culture of behaviorism instilling obedience to one law can be so strong it will produce disobedience to another law?

Permission to quote from David J. Langum, *Law and Community on the Mexican California Frontier: Anglo-American Expatriates and the Clash of Legal Traditions, 1821-1846* (Norman, Oklahoma, 1987) has been kindly granted by the University of Oklahoma Press, Norman, Oklahoma.

---

[59] Langum, *Law,* supra note 28 at 268.
[60] Ibid. at 269.
[61] Ibid.

Outlaw Gangs of the Middle Border: American Social Bandits

RICHARD WHITE

Americans have often regarded western outlaws as heroes. In popular culture—legend, folksongs, and movies—the American West might as well be Sherwood Forest; its plains and prairies teem with what E. J. Hobsbawm has called social bandits. Driven outside the law because of some act sanctioned by local conventions but regarded as criminal by the state or local authorities, the social bandit has been forced to become an outlaw. Members of his community, however, still consider him an honorable and admirable man. They protect him and are ready to reassimilate him if persecution by the state should stop. The social bandit is a man who violates the law but who still serves a higher justice. He robs from the rich and gives to the poor and only kills in self-defense or just revenge. As long as he observes this code, he is, in myth and legend, invulnerable to his enemies; he can die or be captured only when betrayed by friends.[1]

In the American West, stories of this kind have gathered around many historical outlaws: Jesse James, Billy the Kid, Cole Younger, Sam Bass, John Wesley Hardin, Bob Dalton, Bill Dalton, Bill Doolin, and more. These men exert a surprising fascination on a nation that takes some pride in due process and the rule of law and where the standard version of western settlement is the subordination of "savagery" to law and civilization. These bandits, however, exist in more than legend; as actual outlaws many enjoyed substantial amounts of local support. Such outlaws must be taken seriously as social bandits. Their appeal, while complex, is not mysterious, and it provides insights not only into certain kinds of western settlement and social conditions but also into basic paradoxes of American culture itself.[2]

Richard White is associate professor of history, Michigan State University, East Lansing.

[1] E. J. Hobsbawm, *Primitive Rebels: Studies in Archaic Forms of Social Movement in the 19th and 20th Centuries* (New York, 1965), 13-29.

[2] There is much popular literature on these bandits, but scholars have usually ignored them. Two important exceptions are: William A. Settle, Jr., *Jesse James Was His Name or, Fact and Fiction Concerning the Careers of the Notorious James Brothers*

The tendency to justify certain outlaws as decent, honorable men despite their violation of the law is, in a sense, unique only because these men openly were bandits. In other ways social bandits fit into a continuum of extralegal organizations, such as claims clubs, vigilantes, and whitecaps—prevalent throughout the United States but most common in the West.[3] In certain situations the differences between social bandits (criminals) and vigilantes (law enforcers) were not great, and although this may offend certain modern law and order sensibilities, it is a mistake to impose such contemporary distinctions on nineteenth-century conditions.

In the American West during this period, concepts of legality, extralegality, and illegality became quite confusing. Well into the late nineteenth century public law enforcement remained weak, particularly in rural areas where a variety of extralegal organizations supplemented or replaced the constituted authorities. Members of claims clubs, vigilantes, and whitecaps, of course, proclaimed their allegiance to community norms and saw themselves as establishing order, not contributing to disorder. On many occasions they were probably correct. Often, however, the line between extralegal organizations who claimed to preserve order and extralegal gangs accused of creating disorder was a fine one indeed. Claims clubs using threats of violence or actual violence to gain additional public land for their members, even when this involved driving off legitimate claimants, vigilante committees whose targets might only be economic or political rivals, or whitecaps who chose to upgrade the moral tone of the community through beatings and whippings may not be outlaws, but distinguishing them from criminals on moral or legal grounds is not very compelling.[4] In the West, *criminal* could be an ambiguous term, and vigilantes often became the armed force of one racial, class, or cultural group moving against other groups with opposing interests. In such cases vigilantes often provoked retaliation, and local civil war resulted. American history is full of such encounters, ranging from the Regulator/Moderator conflicts of the colonial Carolina backcountry, through the anti-Mormon movements of the American frontier, to the Johnson County War of 1892.

of *Missouri* (Columbia, Missouri, 1966); and Kent Ladd Steckmesser, *The Western Hero in History and Legend* (Norman, 1965), 57–102.

[3] Richard Maxwell Brown, *Strain of Violence: Historical Studies of American Violence and Vigilantism* (New York, 1975), 91–179. See also William F. Holmes, "Moonshining and Collective Violence: Georgia, 1889–1895," *Journal of American History*, 67 (December 1980), 589–611.

[4] Allan G. Bogue, "The Iowa Claim Clubs: Symbol and Substance," *Mississippi Valley Historical Review*, XLV (September 1958), 231–53; Brown, *Strain of Violence*, 24–25, 128, 150–51.

Social bandits, however, did not represent this kind of organized opposition to vigilantes. They, too, arose where law enforcement was distrusted, where criminal was an ambiguous category, and where the legitimacy of vigilantism was questioned. Where social banditry occurred, however, the vigilantes and their opponents did not form two coherent groups, but instead consisted of numerous, mutually hostile factions. Regulator/Moderator struggles represented broad social divisions; social bandits thrived amidst personal feuds and vendettas.

Three gangs that seem most clearly part of a western social bandit tradition are the James-Younger gang of western Missouri and its lineal successors led by Jesse James (1866[?]–1882), the Dalton gang of Oklahoma Territory (1890–1892), and the Doolin-Dalton gang of Oklahoma Territory (1892–1896).[5] Such a list is purposefully narrow and is not meant to be exclusive. These are only the most famous gangs, but an examination of them can establish both the reality of social banditry and the nature of its appeal.[6]

Social bandits are almost by definition creations of their supporters, but this support must be carefully defined. Virtually all criminals have some people who aid them, since there will always be those who find profit and advantage in doing so. Social bandits, too, may have supporters who are essentially confederates. What separates social bandits from ordinary criminals, however, is the existence of large numbers of other people who aid them but who are only technically implicated in their crimes. Such people are not themselves criminals and are willing to justify their own actions in supporting outlaws on grounds other than fear, profit, or expediency. When such people exist in large enough numbers to make an area a haven for a particular group of outlaws, then social banditry exists. For the James-Younger, Dalton, and Doolin-Dalton gangs, this support had three major components: the kinship networks so important to western settlement in general, active supporters, and those people who can be termed passive sympathizers.

That two of these three gangs organized themselves around sets of brothers—the James brothers, the Younger brothers, and the Dalton brothers—is perhaps the most striking illustration of the importance of kinship in social banditry. Centered on blood relations, the James-Younger

[5] The initial robberies of the James-Younger gang are hard to verify. Settle, *Jesse James Was His Name*, 34–38. The Doolin-Dalton gang fragmented before 1896, but the killing of Bill Doolin seems the best date for its demise.

[6] Others who might qualify as legitimate social bandits are Billy the Kid, John Wesley Hardin, Sam Bass, and the various Mexican-American outlaws whose real activities served as the basis for the Joaquin Murieta stories. Such additions would extend the realm of social banditry to central Texas and the Mexican-American communities of the Southwest.

gang and, to a much lesser extent, the Dalton gang depended on relatives to hide them, feed them, warn them of danger, and provide them with alabis. The James brothers recruited two of their cousins—Wood and Clarence Hite—into the gang, and even the Ford brothers, who eventually murdered Jesse, were recruited because they were related by marriage to Jim Cummins, another gang member.[7] Only the Doolin-Dalton gang lacked widespread kin connections, and this forced them to rely more heavily on other forms of support, which were, however, common to all the gangs.

Besides kinspeople, the gangs drew on a larger group of active supporters who knew the outlaws personally and who duplicated many of the services provided by relatives of the bandits. The James-Younger gang recruited such supporters largely from among neighbors and the ex-Confederate guerrillas who had ridden with them in the Civil War. Such "friends of the outlaws" were, according to the man who broke the gang —William Wallace—"thick in the country portions of Jackson County," and many people in the region believed that no local jury would ever convict members of the James gang.[8]

Similar support existed in Oklahoma. The Daltons—Bob, Emmett and Grat—had possessed "many friends in the territory" and had found aid not only among farmers but also on the ranches along the Cimarron River, in the Creek Nation, and in the Cheyenne-Arapaho country.[9] The Doolin-Dalton gang apparently built on this earlier network of support. Frank Canton, who as undersheriff of Pawnee County pursued the Doolin-Dalton gang, distinguished their active sympathizers from the twenty-five to thirty confederates who fenced stolen goods for the outlaws.

[7] For the family connections of the Jesse-Younger gang see Settle, *Jesse James Was His Name*, 6–9, 23; Robertus Love, *The Rise and Fall of Jesse James* (New York, 1926), 53. Jesse James, Jr., *Jesse James Was My Father* (Independence, Missouri, 1899), 76–77. Jim Cummins, *Jim Cummins' Book* (Denver, 1903), 107–8. For the Daltons see Glenn Shirley, *West of Hell's Fringe: Crime, Criminals, and the Federal Peace Officer in Oklahoma Territory, 1889–1907* (Norman, 1978), 43–44, 47, 60; *The Dalton Brothers and Their Astounding Career of Crime by an Eye Witness* (Chicago, 1892), 86–87; Evan Barnard, *A Rider of the Cherokee Strip* (New York, 1936), 198.

[8] William H. Wallace, *Speeches and Writings of William H. Wallace with Autobiography* (Kansas City, 1914), 264, 273, 278; Settle, *Jesse James Was His Name*, 42, 59, 94, 114. Cummins, *Jim Cummins' Book*, 33, 37–38, 49, 106, 113–15, 142; and George Miller, Jr., ed., *The Trial of Frank James for Murder with Confessions of Dick Liddil and Clarence Hite* (New York, 1977), 312–13, 319.

[9] W. F. Jones, *The Experiences of Deputy U.S. Marshal of the Indian Territory* (Tulsa, 1937), 25; Zoe Tilghman, *Outlaw Days: A True History of Early-Day Oklahoma Characters* (Oklahoma City, 1936), 33, 39, 58; Emmett Dalton, "Beyond the Law: First True Account of the Exploits of the World's Most Noted Outlaws," *Wide World Magazine*, 41 (May, June, July, August 1918), 92, 194; Harriet P. Gilstrap, "Memoir of a Pioneer Teacher," *Chronicles of Oklahoma*, 39 (Spring 1960), 21; Lon Stansbery, *The Passing of the 3-D Ranch* (Tulsa, n.d.), 18.

The Dalton gang and especially Bill Doolin had many friends among the settlers south of Pawnee along the Cimarron River, and along the line of Pawnee County. There is no doubt that Doolin furnished many of them money to buy groceries to live upon when they first settled in that country and had a hard struggle for existence. They appreciated his kindness even though he was an outlaw with a price upon his head, and there were plenty of people who would get up at the hour of midnight if necessary to ride to Bill Doolin to warn him of the approach of officers when they were seen in that vicinity.[10]

U.S. Marshal Evett Nix, too, complained that "protectors and friends" of the Doolin-Dalton gang "were numerous."[11] The small town of Ingalls in Payne County became a particularly notorious center of sympathy for the gang. Three deputy marshals died in the disastrous raid officers made on the town in 1893, and when a posse pursued the bandits into the surrounding countryside, local farmers misdirected the deputies. The frustrated officers retaliated by arresting a number of local citizens for aiding the outlaws.[12] Probandit sentiment persisted in the region into 1894 when a local newspaper reported that Bill Doolin was openly "circulating among his many friends in the Sooner Valley" and pointedly remarked that deputy marshals had been absent from the area as usual.[13] Years later, when the state erected a monument to the deputies who fell at Ingalls, at least one old local resident complained that it had been erected to the "wrong bunch."[14] In the case of all three gangs, the network of primary supporters remained localized. The James-Younger gang in its prime drew largely on Clay, Jackson, and Ray counties in Missouri, while the Daltons and the Doolin-Dalton gang relied heavily on people in Payne, Kingfisher, and Pawnee counties, as well as ranchers in the neighboring sections of the Indian nations and the Cherokee strip.

The final category of popular sympathy for outlaws was probably at once the largest, the least important in terms of the bandits' day-to-day activities, and yet the most critical in the transformation of the outlaws into local heroes. This third group consisted of passive sympathizers

[10] Edward Everett Dale, ed., *Frontier Trails: The Autobiography of Frank M. Canton* (Norman, 1966), 113.

[11] Shirley, *West of Hell's Fringe*, 185.

[12] For an account of the gunfight see Shirley, *West of Hell's Fringe*, 151–66. For sympathy and misdirection see *Payne County Populist* [Stillwater, Oklahoma], September 7, 1893; *Oklahoma State Capital* [Guthrie, Oklahoma], July 15, 1893. For the arrests see *Oklahoma State Capital*, September 7, 1893.

[13] *Payne County Populist*, November 23, 1894.

[14] Leslie McRill, "Old Ingalls: The Story of a Town that Will Not Die," *Chronicles of Oklahoma*, 36 (Winter 1958–1959), 445.

—people who probably had never seen an actual outlaw, let alone ever aided one. Their sympathy, however, was quite real, and given a chance they publicly demonstrated it. They mourned Jesse James, "lionized" Bill Doolin after his capture, flocked to see Frank James after his surrender, packed his trial, and applauded his acquittal. Such sympathizers appeared even in Coffeeville, Kansas, where the Dalton gang tried to outdo the James-Younger gang by robbing two banks at once. The result was a bloody debacle—the death of most of the gang and the killing of numerous citizens. Yet within days of the fight, some people openly sympathized with the outlaws on the streets of Coffeeville.[15]

The mere existence of support, however, does not explain the reasons for it. The simplest explanation, and one advanced by many anti-outlaw writers, was that the bandits' supporters acted from fear. This is not very persuasive. While arguing that fear brought support, many popular writers have often simultaneously incorporated major elements of the bandits' legends into their own writings. They paradoxically argue against a sympathy that they themselves reflect.[16] Such sympathy seems an unlikely product of fear, and there is little evidence for the reign of terror by these gangs reported by outside newspapers for Missouri in the 1870s and Oklahoma in the 1890s.[17] Both Dalton and Doolin-Dalton gang members were welcomed to the country dances and other community affairs in Oklahoma that they attended.[18] Certainly they had become locally notorious, but fear was not the dominant note in their notoriety. In Payne County, for example, a Stillwater grocer fortuitously named Bill Dalton capitalized on outlaw Bill Dalton's fame in an advertisement with banner headlines proclaiming that:

Bill Dalton's Gang Are (sic) After You And If You Can Give Them A Trial You Will Be Convinced That They Keep The Freshest & Best Goods In The City At The Lowest Prices.[19]

Feared killers are not usually relied on to promote the sale of groceries. Finally, if fear was the only cause of the bandits' support, it is hard to

[15] Tilghman, *Outlaw Days*, 99; *The Dalton Brothers*, 194, 198, 211, 221; *St. Joseph Gazette,* September 7, 1883; August 23, 1883; Henry Huston Crittenden, *The Crittenden Memoirs* (New York, 1936), 262, 270–71, 317.

[16] Tilghman, *Outlaw Days*, 58–59, 84–85, 86; J. A. Newson, *The Life and Practice of the Wild and Modern Indian* (Oklahoma City, 1923), 186–88.

[17] See, for example, letter in *Payne County Populist,* November 23, 1894; also see Settle, *Jesse James Was His Name,* 66–67, 109–10.

[18] Barnard, *Rider of the Cherokee Strip,* 198; McRill, "Old Ingalls," 430, 437; Shirley, *West of Hell's Fringe,* 305–6.

[19] *Payne County Populist,* January 5, 1894.

explain the continued expression of public sympathy after the outlaws were dead or imprisoned and no one had much to fear from them anymore.

A social bandit cannot survive through terror alone, and these bandits did not. They had ties to the local community predating their life of crime, and during their criminal careers social bandits reinforced those local ties. Gangs that did not have such connections or did not maintain them remained parasites whose lack of shelter and aid condemned them to destruction. The social bandits needed popular support; they could not undercut it by indiscriminately robbing the inhabitants of the regions in which they lived and operated. Those outlaws who simply preyed on local communities were hunted down like the stock thieves of Indian Territory. No one romanticized, and rarely even remembered, Dock Bishop and Frank Latham, or the more notorious Zip Wyatt-Ike Black gang, for example. The social bandits avoided such a fate by concentrating their robberies on railroads and banks. Thus, they not only avoided directly harming local people, but they also preyed upon institutions that many farmers believed were preying on them.

Beyond this, social bandits often did assist their supporters in at least small ways. There is no need to accept the numerous romantic stories of gallant outlaws paying the mortgages on the farms of poor widows to grant them an economic role in their local communities. Bill Doolin may very well have helped poor settlers through some hard times with groceries and small gifts; the Dalton and Doolin-Dalton gangs certainly did provide oysters and refreshments for local dances, and such small kindnesses were also probably practiced by the James-Younger gang. What was probably more significant to their supporters in chronically cash-short economies, however, was that all these gangs paid very well for the horses, feed, and supplies they needed. Their largess won them friends.[20]

If fear fails as an explanation for what appears to be legitimate social banditry, then the next logical recourse is to the interpretation E. J. Hobsbawm offered to explain European bandits. According to Hobsbawm, social banditry is a premodern social revolt—a protest against either excessive exploitation from above or against the overturn of traditional norms by modernizing elements in a society. It is quintessentially a peasant protest. Hobsbawm mentioned Jesse James himself as following in this European tradition. The shortcomings of a literal reading of

---

[20] Canton, *Frontier Trails,* 113. Jones, *Experiences of Deputy U.S. Marshal,* 28; Robert McReynolds, *Thirty Years on the Frontier* (Colorado Springs, Colorado, 1906), 121; McRill, "Old Ingalls," 430, 437; Dalton, "Beyond the Law," 194, 379.

Hobsbawm are obvious. Jesse James could not be a peasant champion because there were no American peasants to champion.[21] Yet Hobsbawm's analysis might be retrieved by reinterpreting the western outlaws more generally as champions of a "traditional" society against a "modern" society.

Such evidence as can be recovered, however, indicates that this interpretation, too, is badly flawed. Both the outlaws and their supporters came from modern, market-oriented groups and not from poor, traditional groups. The James-Younger gang had its origins in the Confederate guerrillas of the Civil War who were recruited from the economic and social elite of Jackson and neighboring counties. Usually guerrillas were the "elder offspring of well-to-do, slave holding farmers."[22] The chief members of the James-Younger gang were ex-guerrillas with similar origins. Colonel Henry Younger, the father of the Younger brothers, owned 3,500 acres of land in Jackson and Cass counties before the Civil War. His wife was a daughter of a member of the Missouri legislature. The father of Jesse and Frank James was a Baptist minister who in 1850 owned a 275-acre farm. Their stepfather was a physician who resided with their mother on a Missouri farm worth $10,000 in 1870, and their uncle, George Hite, Sr., was said, probably with some exaggeration, to have been worth $100,000 before losing heavily in the tobacco speculation that forced him into bankruptcy in 1877.[23]

Many of the gang's other supporters enjoyed similar social standing. Joseph Shelby, the Confederate cavalry leader, and members of the large Hudspeth family all aided the James-Younger gang, and all were prosperous farmers with sizable landholdings.[24] The jury that acquitted Frank James of murder was composed of twelve "well-to-do thrifty farmers," and Clay County, in the heart of the bandit country, was "one of the richest counties in the state," inhabited by a people who were "well-dressed, well-to-do, and hospitable."[25] These substantial farmers and

[21] Hobsbawm, Primitive Rebels, 25.

[22] Don R. Bowen, "Guerilla War in Western Missouri, 1862–65: Historical Extensions of the Relative Deprivation Hypothesis," Comparative Studies in History and Society, 19 (January 1977), 49.

[23] Love, Jesse James, 53; Settle, Jesse James Was His Name, 7–9, 23. Crittenden, Crittenden Memoirs, 152.

[24] Manuscript Census of Population, Jackson County, Missouri, Ninth Census, 1870. [W. Hickman], The History of Jackson County, Missouri (Topeka, Kansas, 1920), 554–55, 725–26, 624–28; Crittenden, Crittenden Memoirs, 238–39, 271; Manuscript Census of Population, Clay County, Missouri, Ninth Census, 1870; Manuscript Census, Jackson County, Missouri, Tenth Census, 1880.

[25] Crittenden, Crittenden Memoirs, 210–11; St. Joseph Gazette, August 23, 1883.

speculators seem an unlikely source for premodern rebels or as leaders of a revolt of the rural poor.

Members and supporters of the Dalton and Doolin-Dalton gangs were not so prosperous, but then these gangs did not have such a firmly established rural region to draw upon. The Daltons were, by most accounts, an ordinary midwestern farm family. Three Dalton brothers became farmers; one was a deputy marshal killed in the line of duty; the other four eventually became outlaws.[26] Bill Doolin was a ranch foreman and, according to local residents, a "respected citizen" before becoming a bandit.[27] Bitter Creek Newcomb, Little Bill Raidler, and Dick Broadwell all had middle-class origins in families of merchants and farmers, and Raidler had supposedly attended college. The remainder of these two gangs included equal numbers of previously honest cowboys and small-time thugs and drifters without close family connections.[28] Supporters of the Oklahoma gangs also apparently spanned class lines, ranging from small-scale farmers to large-scale ranchers like Jim Riley, who was locally considered well-to-do.[29]

Neither class nor traditional values seem to be significant factors in the support of bandits, but the tendency of supporters to live in rural rather than urban regions suggest a third possible explanation of social banditry as an exotic appendage of the agrarian revolt of post-Civil War America.[30] Some evidence, taken in isolation, seems to support such a

[26] For the background of the Daltons see *The Dalton Brothers*, 20–26; Richard Graves, *Oklahoma Outlaws: A Graphic History of the Early Days in Oklahoma* (Oklahoma City, 1915), 34–36; and Shirley, *West of Hell's Fringe*, 38–39.

[27] Graves, *Oklahoma Outlaws*, 56; Shirley, *West of Hell's Fringe*, 115–16; E. Bee Guthrie, "Early Days in Payne County," *Chronicles of Oklahoma*, 3 (April 1925), 77.

[28] For Bitter Creek Newcomb see Shirley, *West of Hell's Fringe*, 42; for Dick Broadwell see Shirley, *West of Hell's Fringe*, 41. For Little Bill Raidler see Shirley, *West of Hell's Fringe*, 186. For Tulsa Jack Blake see Shirley, *West of Hell's Fringe*, 116, 276; for Roy Daugherty see Shirley, *West of Hell's Fringe*, 142–43, and McRill, "Old Ingalls," 436–37; for Black-faced Charley Bryant see Barnard, *Rider of the Cherokee Strip*, 193; for Bill Powers see Stansbery, *3-D Ranch*, 50; for Ol Yantis see *Oklahoma State Capital*, November 19, 1892. These were the "honest" outlaws. Red Buck Waightman, a villain in many Dalton-Doolin gang stories, was a hired killer, "one of the most dangerous men ever in Oklahoma" according to Barnard, *Rider of the Cherokee Strip*, 197. Charley Pierce and Dynamite Dick Clifton also seem to have had criminal records before joining the gang. See Shirley, *West of Hell's Fringe*, 40, 42, 139.

[29] Shirley, *West of Hell's Fringe*, 54.

[30] Wallace, *Speeches and Writings*, 275; *St. Joseph Daily Gazette*, June 17, 1883. Village and urban businessmen were the most prominent opponents of the James gang. See *St. Joseph Gazette*, June 17, 1883. This same tendency seems to have operated in Oklahoma, where supporters were usually specified as rural people. Canton, *Frontier Trails*, 113; *Payne County Populist*, November 23, 1894, Dalton, "Beyond the Law," 194.

connection with rural radicalism. Both local boosters and government officials interested in attracting capital attacked the gangs. They blamed them for discouraging investment and immigration. Governor Crittenden and Senator Carl Schurz of Missouri, for example, defended the assassination of Jesse James in ridding the state of "a great hindrance to its prosperity and as likely to give an important stimulus to real estate speculation, railroad enterprise, and foreign immigration."[31]

On the other side, positions taken by some of the bandits after their careers were over make them appear to be radicals. Frank James credited his robberies with maintaining local prosperity because they had frightened eastern capital out of Jackson County and thus kept it free of mortgages.[32] And in 1897 he declared: "If there is ever another war in this country, which may happen, it will be between capital and labor, I mean between greed and manhood, and I'm as ready to march now in defense of American manhood as I was when a boy in the defense of the South. Unless we can stop this government by injunction that's what we are coming to."[33] Frank James was not alone in his swing to the left. James Younger became a socialist while in prison.[34]

Put in context, however, all of this is considerably less compelling. While active criminals, none of the bandits took radical political positions. Nor did agrarian groups show much sympathy for the bandits. Contemporary writers pointed out that politicians and capitalists stole far more than bandits, and individual farmers aided the gangs, but organized agrarians did not confuse banditry with political action. The leading agrarian party in Missouri in the 1870s—the People's party—although it attacked banks and monopolies, also denounced lawlessness, particularly that of the James-Younger gang.[35] It is also instructive to remember that the Farmers Alliance, which eventually spawned the Populist party, started out as a group to combat horse theft.[36] The Populists themselves showed no more interest in banditry as a variant of political action than

[31] The Carl Schurz quote is in Frank Triplett, *The Life, Times and Treacherous Death of Jesse James* (St. Louis, 1882), 335. Schurz himself had previously expressed similar sentiments. See Settle, *Jesse James Was His Name*, 66–67, and William Wallace, *Speeches and Writings*, 265. The railroads, needless to say, were quite active in breaking up the gang. *St. Joseph Gazette*, June 17, 1883; September 7, 1883; September 2, 1883; September 5, 1883; and Crittenden, *Crittenden Memoirs*, 188.

[32] Crittenden, *Crittenden Memoirs*, 270–71.

[33] Ibid.

[34] Cole Younger, *The Story of Cole Younger by Himself* (Houston, 1955), 101–3.

[35] Nick Aldzick, "Agrarian Discontent in Missouri, 1865–1880: The Political and Economic Manifestations of Agrarian Unrest" (doctoral dissertations, St. Louis University, 1977), 132–35, 140; Settle, *Jesse James Was His Name*, 64–66.

[36] Brown, *Strain of Violence*, 278–79.

had the People's party of Missouri. In any case, if banditry were political in nature and inspired by agrarian resentment against banks and railroads, it is hard to explain why support for bandits was largely confined to Oklahoma in the 1890s while Populism spread all over the South and West.[37]

A better explanation of social banditry is possible. It begins with the peculiar social conditions of western Missouri in the 1860s and 1870s and Oklahoma in the 1890s that allowed social bandits to emerge as variants of the widespread extralegal organizations already common in the West. The exceptional situations prevailing in both Missouri and Oklahoma encouraged popular identification with the outlaws whom local people supported not because of their crimes but rather because of certain culturally defined masculine virtues the outlaws embodied. In each locale there were good reasons to value such virtues. This emphasis on the bandits as symbols of masculinity, in turn, made them accessible to the larger culture at a time when masculinity itself was being widely worried over and glorified. The bandit's virtues made him a cultural hero and embarked him on a posthumous career (of a very conservative sort) which is far from over yet. All of this requires considerable explanation.

Public support of bandits can obviously exist only in areas where belief in the honesty and competency of public law enforcement has been seriously eroded. This was the case in both postwar Missouri and Oklahoma in the 1890s. In the Missouri countryside, ex-Confederates hated and feared Union sheriffs, who they believed used their offices to settle old scores from the war, and they regarded the state militia, called up to maintain order, as plunderers and freebooters. Wartime antagonisms and turmoil faded in time, but when the Pinkertons attacked the home of Zerelda Samuel, mother of the James boys, blowing off her arm and killing her young son—the half-brother of Jesse and Frank—they rekindled hatred of the authorities. Governor Crittenden's subsequent solicitation of assassins to kill Jesse only deepened the prevailing distrust of the equity and honesty of law enforcement.[38]

In Oklahoma settlers similarly distrusted U.S. deputy marshals, whom they often regarded as little better than criminals themselves. During the land rush, deputies used their office unfairly to secure the best lands and later spent much of their time arresting farmers who cut timber on the public domain or on Indian lands and prosecuting settlers who happened to be found with small amounts of whiskey in the Indian

[37] A reading of the extant numbers of the *Payne County Populist* of 1893–1895 shows constant attacks on railroads, banks, federal monetary policies, and deputy marshals, but at no time does the paper identify itself with the outlaws or praise their robberies.

[38] Settle, *Jesse James Was His Name*, 32, 76–80.

nations.[39] Farmers believed that deputies sought only the fees they collected by persecuting "poor defenseless claim holders."[40] On at least two occasions in the late winter and spring of 1893, resentment ran high enough for armed groups to attempt to attack deputy marshals and free their prisoners.[41]

Although newspapers praised their bravery when they died in the line of duty, living marshals merited much less sympathy.[42] Local newspapers rarely praised crimes social bandits committed, but they commonly ridiculed and denounced the lawmen who pursued them.[43] In April of 1894, for example, the *Pond Creek Voice* reported that deputy marshals riding past the garden of an old woman who lived near the Cimarron River had mistaken her scarecrow for an outlaw and had riddled it with bullets before riding off in panic to report their ambush by the Doolin-Dalton gang.[44] When Bill Dalton was actually killed, the *Stillwater Gazette* reported that it would come as a great relief to the deputy marshals "who have made it a practice to ride in the opposite direction from where he was every time they got him located."[45] In the eyes of many people, the deputy marshals were simply another group of armed men, distinguished mainly by their cowardice, who rode around the territory posing a threat to life and property. The transition of the Dalton brothers from deputy marshals and possemen to open criminals was no fall from grace. Indeed, it may have gained the brothers support in some areas.[46]

This distrust of law enforcement is particularly significant in the light of the widespread disorder existing in both areas. Following the Civil War, robbery and murder continued to occur in northwestern

[39] Solon J. Buck, "The Settlement of Oklahoma," *Transactions of the Wisconsin Academy of Sciences, Arts and Letters,* XV (September 1907), 352.

[40] *Stillwater Gazette,* February 28, 1895 (quote). Also see ibid., March 2, 1894; May 17, 1894; *Payne County Populist,* August 10, 1894; *Oklahoma State Capital,* February 18, 1893; April 1, 1893; Shirley, *West of Hell's Fringe,* 253–58.

[41] *Oklahoma State Capital,* February 18, 1893; April 1, 1893.

[42] *Oklahoma State Capital,* August 29, 1891; *Payne County Populist,* September 7, 1893.

[43] *Payne County Populist,* January 4, 25, 1895; March 3, 1894; May 11, 1894; April 27, 1894.

[44] Article from *Pond Creek Voice,* reprinted in *Payne County Populist,* April 27, 1894.

[45] *Stillwater Gazette,* June 14, 1894.

[46] *Stillwater Eagle-Gazette,* February 28, 1895; January 30, 1896. Even when Doolin was captured, some newspapers asserted he had merely agreed to surrender in exchange for part of the reward. His subsequent escape probably did little to dampen such stories. *Stillwater Eagle-Gazette,* January 23, 1896. For the early career of the Daltons see Shirley, *West of Hell's Fringe,* 39–46.

Missouri with appalling frequency. Gangs of ex-guerrillas from both sides pillaged and sought revenge for wartime acts; committees of public safety organized, and vigilantes remained active until the mid-1870s.[47] Numerous armed bands, each protecting its own interests, clashed in the countryside. Legal protection was often unavailable. All this was not merely the last gasp of the Lost Cause; it was not a simple reflection of Union/Confederate divisions. Many local ex-Confederates, for example, opposed the James-Younger gang.[48] The Confederate background of the outlaws certainly won them some sympathy, but only within the local context of chaotic, factional disorder.

The situation in Oklahoma in the 1890s was a remarkably similar mixture of predation, personal vengeance, and vigilantism. With the demand for Oklahoma land exceeding its availability, the government resorted to one of the most astonishing systems of distributing resources ever attempted by a modern state. Settlers in Oklahoma raced for their land. The races were spectacular, colorful, and virtually impossible to police. Numerous people—the "sooners"—stole over the line ahead of the starting time to stake claims. Sooners only increased the inevitable conflicts among people who claimed to have arrived first at a desirable plot of land. In the end the land rushes sowed a crop of litigation and violence. Even if nothing else divided a community, bitter factional struggles for land were sure to persist for years. In Payne County, the center of support for the Doolin-Dalton gang, the county attorney claimed, perhaps with some exaggeration, that there were fifty murders as the direct result of land claim cases in the early years. Such murders involved the leading citizens of Payne County. The first representative of Payne County to the Oklahoma legislature and speaker of the assembly, I. N. Terrill, terminated his political career in 1891 by murdering a man in a land dispute.[49]

Given the distrust of local law enforcement, protection in such disputes often demanded organization and violence. In 1893, for example, the *Oklahoma State Capital* reported the presumed lynching of three sooners by a local vigilante committee. Apparently both sides—the alleged

[47] Settle, *Jesse James Was His Name*, 32, 34–35; Cummins, *Jim Cummins' Book*, 115–17.

[48] Settle, *Jesse James Was His Name*, 53–56, 31–32; Wallace, *Speeches and Writings*, 264.

[49] For accounts of the Oklahoma land rush see Shirley, *West of Hell's Fringe*, 3–10, 171–78; and Buck, "The Settlement of Oklahoma," 343–60. For murders see Berlin Chapman, *Founding of Stillwater: A Case Study in Oklahoma History* (Oklahoma City, 1948), 182. For the Terrill case see *Oklahoma State Capital*, January 10, 1891; October 29, 1892; February 11, 1893. *Payne County Populist*, January 4, 1895.

sooners and the vigilante committee—were armed and resorting to violence. Such actions, the reporter contended, were common: "Reports are coming in every day of white cap whippings and terrorizing and it is nothing to see the sooner pulling out every day, claiming that they have been threatened with hanging by vigilant committees if they did not go."[50] The large numbers of horses and cattle thieves who had long existed in a sort of parasitic relationship with the large cattle operations and who now turned to stealing from settlers only increased the level of private violence.[51]

The situation in Oklahoma was, however, more complicated than extralegal groups enforcing the laws against thieves and sooners. There was some ambiguity about what constituted theft. For example, Evan Barnard, an ex-cowboy and settler in Oklahoma who wrote one of the best of western memoirs, defended stock theft by his friend, Ranicky Bill: "He was generous and big-hearted . . . if he knew any settler who was hungry, he did not hesitate to rustle beef, and give it to the starving people. In the early days of Oklahoma, a man who did that was not such a bad person after all."[52] According to Barnard, such attitudes were shared by many settlers. When it became clear that the large ranchers would lose their leases on Indian lands, the homesteaders moved in to steal wood, fencing, and stock. All the old-time cattlemen, Barnard contended, would admit that the "settlers were good rustlers."[53] In practice *sooner, rustler, vigilante,* and *outlaw* were ambiguous terms; very often they were only pejorative names for those whose interests were not the same as other citizens.

In both Missouri and Oklahoma, pervasive lawlessness and widespread distrust of public law enforcement divided the countryside not into two clearly opposing groups, but rather into innumerable local factions. Conditions were ripe for factional violence and social banditry. A rather detailed example from Oklahoma is perhaps the best way to illustrate how tangled the relationship of gangs, vigilantes, and other armed groups could become; how supposed, and even demonstrated, criminal behavior might not cost people public sympathy; how private violence could be deemed not only necessary but admirable; and how social bandits garnered support in such situations.

[50] *Oklahoma State Capital,* December 2, 1893.

[51] Tilghman, *Outlaw Days,* 22; Barnard, *Rider of the Cherokee Strip,* 78; Jones, *Experiences of Deputy U.S. Marshal,* 16. *Oklahoma State Capital,* November 18, 25, 1893; January 2, 1891; *Stillwater Eagle-Gazette,* November 29, 1894.

[52] Barnard, *Rider of the Cherokee Strip,* 191.

[53] Ibid., 213.

In 1889, Evan Barnard, his friend Ranicky Bill, and other ex-cowboys banded together before the run for Oklahoma Territory to secure and protect land claims. It was a necessary precaution because "just staking a claim did not hold it."[54] Barnard drove one man from his claim by flourishing a winchester and a six-shooter and telling him it was "a hundred and sixty acres or six feet, and I did not give a damn which it was."[55] Bravado was not sufficient to drive off two other challengers, however; for them, Barnard had to demonstrate "the backing I had among the cowboys."[56] This backing was available regardless of the merits of any specific case. One of Barnard's friends failed to secure a claim, but visits from Barnard's associates persuaded the legitimate claimant to sell out to him for $75. The claimant left but declared: " 'If I had half the backing that you have, I would stay with you until hell froze over'. . . . He left the claim and Ranicky Bill remarked, 'hits sure hell to get things regulated in a new country.' "[57] Ranicky Bill himself had to stop a contest on his claim by shooting up his opponent's camp.[58] Private force clearly was both a necessary supplement to, and a substitute for, legal right.

Such bullying understandably stirred up resentment against Barnard and his friends, and some regarded them as sooners, which they were not. When these accusations were compounded by charges that Ranicky Bill was a horse thief, the vigilantes struck. They attacked Ranicky Bill's cabin, and although he escaped, the vigilantes threatened to hang Barnard and another neighbor. Ranicky Bill surrendered to authorities to clear himself, but his real protection came from thirty cowboys who gathered a day after the incident and offered to help him. Later, vigilantes seized another neighbor and twice hoisted him off the ground with a rope that cut into his neck. He refused to confess and was released, but now the entire neighborhood armed against the vigilantes, who ceased their operations.[59]

According to Barnard, none of those accused by the vigilantes were thieves, but other incidents narrated in his book indicate how thoroughly such accusations were tied up in land disputes and factional quarrels. Friends and neighbors of Barnard apparently did steal a team of horses and other property from a claim jumper named Sniderwine during a

[54] Ibid., 141.
[55] Ibid., 192.
[56] Ibid., 142–43, 153.
[57] Ibid., 146.
[58] Ibid., 149.
[59] Ibid., 173–79.

land dispute. They considered this a legitimate means of driving him from his claim and probably perjured themselves to protect each other.[60]

In such an atmosphere, the organization of settlers into armed groups or gangs for protection seems to have been common. The argument made by an actual stock thief to a new settler that in Oklahoma a man's legal rights and property were worthless without friends sometimes led to the corollary that if you were going to be denounced and attacked for supposed crimes, then you might as well have the "game as the name."[61] And in practice, personal quarrels with each side denouncing the other as sooners and thieves sometimes left local newspapers totally unable to sort out the merits of the case.[62] Personal loyalties and personal qualities in these situations took on larger than normal significance. Law, theft, and even murder became ambiguous categories; strong men who protected themselves and aided their friends could gain local respect transcending their separate criminal activities.

This respect for strong men who could protect and revenge themselves is the real heart of the social bandits' appeal. It is precisely this personal element that gang members and their supporters chose to emphasize. What distinguished social bandits and their supporters (as it distinguished peasant social bandits and theirs) from radicals and revolutionaries was their stubborn refusal to envision the social problems enmeshing them in anything but personal terms. The James and Younger brothers claimed they were hounded into banditry by vindictive Union men who would not leave them alone after the war.[63] They fought only for self-preservation and revenge, not for a social cause. Supporters of Jesse James justified each of his murders as an act of vengeance against men who had attacked his comrades or family.[64] Indeed, the chief propagandist for the James brothers, Missouri newspaper editor John Edwards,

[60] Ibid., 161–65.

[61] Ibid., 200–204.

[62] For an example of such a feud in which the Doolin-Dalton gang was supposedly involved see *Stillwater Eagle-Gazette*, April 13, 20, 27, 1894; May 2, 1895; June 6, 13, 1895. George McElroy, one of the leaders of this feud, may have been connected with the murders of Pierce and Newcomb by the Dunn brothers. Dale, ed., *Frontier Trails*, 114–15.

[63] Younger, *Story of Cole Younger*, 53–55; Settle, *Jesse James Was His Name*, 53–56; John N. Edwards, *Noted Guerillas, or the Warfare of the Border* (St. Louis, 1877), 448–51.

[64] For instance, the murder of Captain John W. Sheets, cashier and principal owner of the Daviess County Savings Bank in Gallatin, Missouri, in a robbery sometimes attributed to the James brothers is explained as a revenge killing for his complicity in the killing of the Confederate guerrilla leader, Bloody Bill Anderson, during the war. Likewise, the James brothers supposedly either murdered or arranged the murder of Daniel Askew for his complicity in the Pinkerton attack, which cost their mother her arm and killed their half-brother. Finally, the murder of the conductor, William West-

made personal vengeance the underlying theme of all their actions from the Civil War onward. Edwards distinguished the guerrillas from regular soldiers by saying these men fought not for a cause but to avenge assaults against themselves and their families. Personal defense and revenge, he claimed, dominated the entire career of the James and Younger brothers.[65] Whether such a claim is accurate or not matters less than that it was credible. When John Edwards claimed these brothers were merely strong men seeking to defend their rights, the appeal could be felt deeply by those who knew that neither they nor the authorities could protect their own rights and property.

The Daltons' grievances, like those of the James and Younger brothers, were personal. They said they became outlaws because the federal government would not pay them for their services as deputy marshals and the express companies had falsely accused them of robbery.[66] They were not radicals who fought against the system itself; they fought against what they regarded as its corruption by their enemies. Emmett Dalton declared that "our fights were not so much against the law, but rather against the law as it was then enforced." At least two members of the Dalton gang asserted that their criminal careers began with land problems, and Bill Doolin, like Cole Younger before him, claimed it was only the personal vindictiveness of his enemies and the corruption of the authorities that stopped him from surrendering. Many of the supporters of the outlaws agreed with these assertions of persecution, and movements for full or partial amnesty for the gangs were common.[67]

Given social conditions in Oklahoma and Missouri, there was a decisive allure in strong men who defended themselves, righted their own wrongs, and took vengeance on their enemies despite the corruption of the existing order. Such virtues were of more than nostalgic interest. In praising bandits, supporters admired them more for their attributes than their acts. Bandits were brave, daring, free, shrewd, and tough, yet also loyal, gentle, generous, and polite. They were not common criminals.

fall, in the Winston train robbery was supposedly a revenge slaying for Westfall's role in aiding the Pinkertons. In this last case, however, Clarence Hite testified that Jesse only learned of Westfall's identity after the killing when he read it in a newspaper. He then expressed satisfaction at having killed him. See Settle, *Jesse James Was His Name*, 39–40, 85, 108; Miller, *Trial of Frank James*, 311–13.

[65] Edwards, *Noted Guerillas*, 21–22, 199, 448–51.

[66] Dalton, "Beyond the Law," 3–4, 95, 315.

[67] Dalton, "Beyond the Law," 3; Younger, *Story of Cole Younger*, 53–55; *Payne County Populist*, January 25, 1895; Shirley, *West of Hell's Fringe*, 40–41, 87, 321–22; Stansbery, *3-D Ranch*, 50. For the amnesty controversy over the James-Younger gang see Settle, *Jesse James Was His Name*, 74, 80–84.

Lon Stansbery, who knew Bill Doolin from the 3-D ranch, was, for instance, forthright about the bandits' heroic stature and masculine virtue:

> The outlaws of that day were not hijackers or petty thieves, and some of them had hearts, even though they were outlaws. They always treated women with respect and no rancher was ever afraid to leave his family on the ranch on account of outlaws. While they would stand up and shoot it out with men, when women were around, they were the first to take off their Stetsons and act like real men.[68]

And Red Orrington, a deputy marshal, called the Daltons "four of as fine fellows as I ever knew," brave men who went on the scout (the local term for banditry) for "love of adventure."[69]

From the initial exploits of the James-Younger gang until the death of Bill Doolin, appraisals of the outlaws' character by their supporters, while sometimes allowing for an understandable laxity in regard to the sixth and eighth commandments, remained strong and consistent in their praise. The James and Younger brothers were "brilliant, bold, indefatigable roughriders," and in the words of an amnesty resolution introduced in the Missouri legislature, "brave . . . generous . . . gallant . . . honorable" men.[70] The Daltons were "big hearted and generous" in every way, "like the average western man," while Bill Doolin was a "naturally . . . kind-hearted, sympathetic man."[71] A contemporary diary from Ingalls comments that the Doolin-Dalton gang was "as a rule quite (sic) and peaceable," even though they moved about heavily armed, and residents later remembered them as "well behaved . . . quiet and friendly," a description close to an Oklahoma schoolteacher's memory of the Daltons as "nice and polite."[72] Some supporters proclaimed them innocent of their crimes, others merely excused them, but all demanded sympathy not so much for the crime as for the criminal. Again it must be emphasized that what is being praised here is not lawlessness per se. Outlaw stories go out of their way to detach the social bandit from the ordinary criminal. Thus, in one story Bill Doolin turns a common thief who tried to join

[68] Stansbery, *3-D Ranch*, 22.

[69] Jones, *Experiences of Deputy U.S. Marshal*, 26.

[70] Settle, *Jesse James Was His Name*, 71, 81. Settle's book contains numerous similar descriptions.

[71] For quote on Daltons see Barnard, *Rider of the Cherokee Strip*, 198. For Doolin see *Payne County Populist*, January 25, 1895.

[72] Shirley quotes the same diary, that of Dr. Pickering, to show the outlaws were feared, but omits Pickering's assertion in a paragraph he otherwise quotes completely that "as a rule they were quite (sic) & peaceable." McRill, "Old Ingalls," 433, 430, 437; Shirley, *West of Hell's Fringe*, 153; Gilstrap, "Memoir of a Pioneer Teacher," 21.

his gang over to a deputy marshal, since "they would have no men in their outfit who would rob a poor man or any individual."[73] John Edwards also took pains to distinguish the James-Younger gang from common criminals.

> There are men in Jackson, Cass, and Clay—a few there are left— who learned to dare when there was no such word as quarter in the dictionary of the Border. Men who have carried their lives in their hands so long that they do not know how to commit them over into the keeping of the laws and regulations that exist now, and those men sometimes rob. But it is always in the glare of day and in the teeth of multitude. With them booty is but the second thought; the wild drama of the adventure first. These men never go upon the highway in lonesome places to plunder the pilgrim. That they leave to the ignobler pack of jackals. But they ride at midday into the county seat, while court is sitting, take the cash out of the vault and put the cashier in and ride out of town to the music of cracking pistols.[74]

And the *Ardmore [Oklahoma] State Herald* made the connections between the Doolin-Dalton gang and Robin Hood explicit:

> Their life is made up of daring. Their courage is always with them and their rifles as well. They are kind to the benighted traveler, and it is not a fiction that when robbing a train they refuse to take from a woman.
> It is said that Bill Doolin, at present the reigning highwayman, is friendly to the people in one neighborhood, bestowing all sorts of presents upon the children. It is his boast that he never killed a man.
> This is as fully a romantic figure as Robin Hood ever cut.[75]

Such Robin Hood descriptions only echoed those of the James-Younger gang twenty years before.[76]

By the 1890s, in Oklahoma at least, the standards of how proper social bandits should behave seemed clear enough for the *Oklahoma State Capital,* a paper with little sympathy for outlaws, to lecture Bill Dalton on his duties as the heir of a great tradition. Bill Dalton, in an interview with a local reporter only the week before, had claimed he was consid-

---

[73] Stansbery, *3-D Ranch,* 22.

[74] *Kansas City Times,* September 29, 1872, quoted in Settle, *Jesse James Was His Name,* 45.

[75] *Ardmore State Herald,* March 14, 1895, quoted in Shirley, *West of Hell's Fringe,* 265.

[76] Settle, *Jesse James Was His Name,* 45–46, 72.

ering teaming up with Frank James to open a saloon in Chicago to take advantage of their fame and the World's Fair. The saloon never materialized, and Bill Dalton had left Guthrie without paying his board bill. The *State Capital* had complained:

> There is supposed to be honor among thieves. Men who presume to be great in any calling avoid the common faults of men. There is a heroism even in desperadoes, and the people admire an ideal type of that class. The James and Younger brothers are remembered as never having robbed a poor family or assaulted an unarmed man. Even the "Dalton boys"—they who really stood up to their "knitten" and looked down the muzzles of Winchesters—did brave and not ignoble deeds. But Bill Dalton—"Board Bill" Dalton —has besmirched the family escutcheon. The brothers, dead, when they hear what he has done, will turn over in their graves and groan—"Oh, Bill."[77]

Bill Dalton's future specialization in bank and train robbery and his violent death presumably redeemed the family honor.

Social bandits thus did exist in a meaningful sense in the American West, yet their actual social impact, confined as it was to small areas with extreme conditions, was minor. They never sought social change, and the actual social evolution of Missouri and Oklahoma owes little to them. Nevertheless, their impact on American culture has been immense. The social bandits who metaphorically rode out of Missouri and Oklahoma into America at large quickly transcended the specific economic and political conditions of the areas that produced them and became national cultural symbols. The outlaws were ready-made cultural heroes —their local supporters had already presented them in terms accessible to the nation as a whole. The portrait of the outlaw as a strong man righting his own wrongs and taking his own revenge had a deep appeal to a society concerned with the place of masculinity and masculine virtues in a newly industrialized and seemingly effete order.[78]

Practically, of course, the outlaw as a model of male conduct was hopeless, and early popularizers of the outlaws stressed that although their virtues and qualities were admirable, their actions were inappropriate. Edwards portrayed the James and Younger brothers as men born out of their time, and Zoe Tilghman (whose book ostensibly denied the

---

[77] *Oklahoma State Capital,* April 29, June 10, 1893.

[78] For popular concern with masculine virtue at the turn of the century see Gerald F. Roberts, "The Strenuous Life: The Cult of Manliness in the Era of Theodore Roosevelt" (doctoral dissertation, Michigan State University, 1970), 134–62.

outlaws were heroic) claimed the Oklahoma bandits were cowboys "who could not bring their natures to the subjection of such a change from the wild free life to that kind that came to surround them. They were the venturesome spirits of the old Southwest and could not be tamed."[79]

Those who seriously worried about masculine virtue in the late nineteenth and early twentieth centuries romanticized toughness, loyalty, bravery, generosity, honor, and daring, but sought to channel it into muscular Christianity or college football, not into robbing banks and trains. The outlaws' virtues were cherished, but their actions were archaic and antisocial. In this paradox of accepted virtue without an appropriate arena in which to exist lay the real power of the outlaws' appeal. The outlaw legend, rather than the childish solutions of reformers who sought to provide for the development of "masculine" virtues through organized sports or the dangerous solutions of chauvinists who praised war, retained the complexity, ambivalence, and paradoxes of a personal experience in which accepted male virtue had little relevance to an industrialized, bureaucratized world.

Ambivalence saved Jesse James and the mythical western hero that sprang from his legends from becoming Frank Merriwell on a horse. The position of the western hero reflects the paradoxical position most Americans occupy in an industrialized capitalist society. The traits and acts of the outlaw become symbols of the larger, structural oppositions—oppositions of law and justice, individualism and community, nature and civilization—never adequately reconciled in American life. Assimilated into the classic western, the social bandit becomes the western hero —a figure of great appeal. The western is not the simple-minded celebration of the triumph of American virtue over evil that it is so often ignorantly and unjustly presumed to be; instead it is the opposite. It plays on the unresolved contradictions and oppositions of America itself.

The entire structure of the classic western film poses the hero between contrasting values both of which are very attractive: private justice and the order provided by law, individualism and community, nature and civilization. The hero, posed between the oppositions, remains ambivalent. Like the actual social bandit, the western hero never attempts to change the structure itself, but rather tries to achieve a reconciliation through his own courage and virtue. Western heroes personify culturally defined masculine virtues of strength, self-reliance, and honor in a world where they have ceased to be effective. More often than not the hero fails or only partially succeeds in his task and like the epitome of the classic western hero, Shane, is left wounded and out of place in a world he has

---

[79] Tilghman, *Outlaw Days*, 22-23; Settle, *Jesse James Was His Name*, 45.

himself helped to create. In the hero's dilemma, viewers recognize their own struggle to reconcile the cultural irreconcilables that society demands of them—individualism and community responsibility, personal dominance and cooperation, maximum productivity and respect for nature.[80] The bandit and the western hero are social failures, and this paradoxically guarantees them their cultural success. It is as a cultural symbol that Jesse James would survive and thrive even though "that dirty little coward, that shot Mr. Howard [had] laid poor Jesse in his grave."[81]

[80] This general view of the western at once owes much to, and differs substantially from, the best scholarly study of westerns; Will Wright, *SixGuns and Society: A Structural Study of the Western* (Berkeley, California, 1975). The legends emphasize male roles because the active world was assumed to be inherently masculine. That there is nothing inherently masculine about honor, self-reliance, or bravery is obvious. It is a sign of the conservatism of the legends that thus far the increasing emergence of women into the previously culturally defined "masculine" world has received little reflection in the western with the exception of the 1954 film *Johnny Guitar,* starring Joan Crawford.

[81] This version of the most famous James ballad is taken from Settle, *Jesse James Was His Name,* 115; other versions are available in E. C. Perrow, "Songs and Rhymes from the South," *Journal of American Folk-lore,* XXV (April–June 1912), 145–50; John A. Lomax, "Some Types of American Folk-Song," *Journal of American Folk-lore,* XXVIII (January–March 1915), 15.

Chinese in Trouble:
Criminal Law and Race on the
Trans-Mississippi West Frontier

JOHN R. WUNDER

On the evening of February 24, 1882, at dusk, six Chinese men gathered at the John Lee Laundry in East Las Vegas, New Mexico.[1] This was not an uncommon event for New Town, as the recent addition to Las Vegas was known. The Chinese began settling in this north-central New Mexico community since 1879. Many came to work on railroads, in laundries, and at restaurants.[2]

The Chinese reception by non-Chinese had not been gracious in Las Vegas, in New Mexico Territory, or throughout the trans-Mississippi West. The tone of comment was frequently pejorative. The *Las Vegas Optic* noted in October 1883 that "a new gang of Chinese struck the city today. They will find it pretty hard to catch on as our Yu-Lis and Wun Lungs have a corner on the Washee Business."[3] Two years later the same newspaper reported that three Chinese truck farmers who worked a vegetable farm on Nimbrio Creek were massacred, probably by Apaches, on their way to market. This event "created as much alarm and indignation as if the unfortunate victims were white."[4] Perhaps miners at Black Hawk best expressed the feelings of non-Chinese in their formal invitation to the women of Silver City, New Mexico Territory, to attend a dance in the winter of 1884:

'Soy, young ladies are y' wid us?
It's our Ball next Toosdie night
   We're de jolly Black Hawk miners,
And our mimbers is all white.
   We ain't much as doods, us snoozers,
But y'betcha coldest Chink
   Da no flies don't die on us, much —

John R. Wunder is professor of history, Clemson University, Clemson, South Carolina.

[1] *Territory of New Mexico v. Yee Shun* (1882), trial transcript, 27, 51-53, 87, San Miguel County District Court Records, New Mexico State Archives, Santa Fe.

[2] F. Stanley, *The Las Vegas Story* (Denver, 1951), 179.

[3] *Las Vegas Optic* (of New Mexico Territory, hereafter cited *LVO*), October 9, 1883.

[4] *LVO*, November 1885, as reported in *Silver City* (New Mexico Territory) *Enterprise*, November 27, 1885.

I should almost blush to blink.
  Well, young ladies, are y' wid us?
Oh! de boys they're all right
  As I said, no crooks ain't comin'
To our Ball next Toosdie night.[5]

Anti-Chinese feeling took various forms throughout the trans-Mississippi West in the late nineteenth and earliest portion of the twentieth century. Racial insults dotted editors' perorations and politicians' speeches. Physical violence punctuated the rhetoric; vigilante actions resulted in shootings and lootings, lynchings and massacres. Courts in the West were inevitably called upon to prevent, mediate, or sanction the treatment of the minority Chinese by a majority non-Chinese society.

Here the ambiguities of procedure and process prevailed, representing a significant failure of justice. Even the law proved not to be immune from cultural pressures, and it was in criminal law where anti-Chinese treatment found a firm hold. By providing special circumstances that required the examination of Chinese cultural values against Anglo-American tradition or denying direct access to the Chinese to a fair trial, the rules of evidence were reshaped to discourage or prevent Chinese from using the criminal justice system in the trans-Mississippi West.[6]

Specific attention was drawn to Chinese differences in several evidentiary ways. Challenges to oath taking, testimony against whites, witness in-

[5] *LVO*, February 1, 1884.

[6] Law and race in nineteenth-century America have been the subject of recent scholarly scrutiny, most effectively concerning blacks and Native Americans. See John R. Wunder, "The Chinese and the Courts in the Pacific Northwest: Justice Denied?" *Pacific Historical Review*, LII (May 1983), 191-211, for a brief listing of relevant significant works.

However, it is important that research on the Chinese and law be governed not exclusively by comparative models. There will be useful common elements, but the Chinese experience must be considered on its own merits.

Chinese and the law in the American West have been discussed in far fewer sources. Overviews are limited to indirect treatments in Elmer C. Sandmeyer, *The Anti-Chinese Movement in California* (Urbana, 1939); Alexander P. Saxton, *The Indispensable Enemy: Labor and the Anti-Chinese Movement in California* (Berkeley, 1971); Milton R. Konvitz, *The Alien and the Asiatic in American Law* (Ithaca, NY, 1946); and Stan Steiner, *Fusang: The Chinese Who Built America* (New York, 1979).

For more specific coverage, see also *The Chinese Texans* (San Antonio, 1978); William J. Courtney, "San Francisco Anti-Chinese Ordinances, 1850-1900" (doctoral dissertation, University of San Francisco, 1956); Susan W. Book, *The Chinese in Butte County, California, 1860-1920* (San Francisco, 1976); Gary P. BeDunnah, "A History of the Chinese in Nevada, 1855-1904" (master's thesis, University of Nevada, Reno, 1966); Christopher H. Edson, *The Chinese of Eastern Oregon, 1860-1890* (San Francisco, 1974); Edward C. Lydon, *The Anti-Chinese Movement in the Hawaiian Kingdom, 1852-1886* (San Francisco, 1975); John R. Wunder, "Law and Chinese in Frontier Montana," *Montana the Magazine of Western History*, 30 (Summer 1980), 18-31; M. Alfreda Elsensohn, *Idaho Chinese Lore* (Cottonwood, ID, 1970); Robert Edward Wynne, "Reaction to the Chinese in the Pacific Northwest and British Columbia, 1850 to 1910" (doctoral dissertation, University of Washington, 1964); and Roger Daniels, ed., *Anti-Chinese Violence in North America* (New York, 1978).

competency, and dying declarations either denied Chinese full opportunities to use western criminal justice or, more often, clouded trial proceedings with cultural insults and accusations. Western law became infused with racial and cultural requirements; legal doctrine eschewed color-blindness or cultural neutrality as a goal for fundamental fairness.

The question of whether a Chinese witness could be bound by an oath was one of several issues that predominated in criminal law in the trans-Mississippi West during the Gilded Age and oftentimes prevented Chinese defendants and witnesses from achieving equal treatment from the Anglo-American legal system. The establishment of precedents in non-Chinese cases created a context for Chinese litigants, and the focus upon religion and faith made oath-taking a particularly sensitive issue. At common law the ability to take an oath was crucial to the admission of any testimony. The oath—a promise to tell the truth or face God's wrath—was dependent upon the witness's religious beliefs. It gained its strength in Protestant England. Very early it was held that non-Protestant witnesses, in this instance Roman Catholics, could not be excluded. Still, witnesses whose religion— cacotheism—sanctioned false testimony might be refused and certainly such charges could be used to discredit witnesses.[7] Non-Christian adherents and nonwhite litigants were especially susceptible to this challenge.

The first significant court challenge concerning the issue of oath-taking and religious beliefs in the American West occurred between Anglo litigants in civil cases over the testimony of non-Chinese. In California in 1861 the California Supreme Court heard a divorce case on appeal. Silas Fuller had sued his wife Jane Fuller for divorce on the grounds of extreme cruelty and adultery. Silas offered testimony that Jane had beat him over the head with a shovel, scratched his face, tore his clothes, assaulted him with a hatchet and a fence rail, called him a dog, bastard, and viper, spat in his face, poured hot tea on him, stole all his papers including valuable credit notes, chased him all over Telegraph Hill, and threatened to kill him with a loaded pistol— all incidents that occurred on different occasions. He further produced his fourteen-year-old Chilean servant, James Cruz. Cruz testified, after he denied understanding the meaning of an obligation to an oath to tell the truth and it was explained to him by the trial court judge, that he had seen Jane in bed at the Fuller ranch with Silas's attorney, M. S. Chase. All was denied, but the defendant still lost.[8]

[7] Whitebread's Trial, 7 How. St. Tr. 311, 361, 379 (1679); and John Henry Wigmore, *A Treatise on the System of Evidence in Trials at Common Law* (Boston, 1904), 646-47. Cacotheism in seventeenth-century England was interpreted by the courts to mean a heretical or "harsh" theology. Cacotheists are not religiously prevented from taking oaths; inability to swear to an oath because of one's religious belief is a separate evidential problem.

[8] *Fuller* v. *Fuller*, 17 Cal 605 at 606-607 (1861).

On appeal the testimony of Cruz was attacked as not admissible because Cruz was from Chile and did not have a common religious belief. The appellant alleged that any person swearing to an oath needed to believe in a state of future rewards and punishments. Justices Joseph G. Baldwin and Stephen J. Field were not persuaded. They did not believe that the lower court had erred. Wrote Baldwin, "The witness seems to have been a foreigner. He was not disqualified by the mere act that he did not, when first produced, understand the meaning of the word obligation, as applied to an oath . . . a witness is competent without any respect to his religious sentiments or convictions; the law leaving the matter of *competency* to legal sanctions, or, at least, to considerations independent of religious sentiments or convictions."[9]

Ten years later in Kansas, Jacob Smith sued James H. Brown and eighteen other defendants in an action for ejectment on property known as the "Kansas Half-Breed Indian Lands." Title depended upon testimony given by "a certain Indian" who did not understand the nature of the oath.[10] He stated that he did not know what perjury was, but that he knew it was bad to lie. This was sufficient for the trial court to allow Indian testimony and for the Kansas Supreme Court. Chief Justice Samuel A. Kingman in upholding the lower court decision allowing the Indian testimony observed, "He was an uneducated Indian, not deficient in understanding, but uninstructed as to the nature of an oath . . . ; yet he knew that it was wrong to speak falsely. . . . Whether he believed that he would be punished in another life was a matter that could not be inquired into under our constitution." Besides, reasoned Kingman, "His evidence afterwards given is such as confirms the opinion we have expressed as to his competency."[11] Thus, from *Fuller* and *Smith*, two jurisdictions in the trans-Mississippi West had withstood a strict common law challenge to testimonial competency.

The first state appellate case to consider the Chinese within the framework of the witness oath issue was *Green v. State of Georgia* (1883).[12] Tom Green was convicted of burglary—he had stolen eighty-five cents that had been left in a store owned by Dorsey Lee, a Chinese resident of Augusta. Lee had testified at Green's trial, but before Lee was sworn he was challenged for competency. Lee stated he "believe the Bible, and believe the God of my religion," that if "man tell lies go to the bad place; go to devil; can't go to heaven, if tell lies." He further stated he did not know about oaths in China. The Georgia high court found that the examination of Lee was acceptable and that this Chinese witness, because he demonstrated an understanding of Christianity and life after death, was competent to testify.[13]

[9] Ibid., 612.
[10] *Smith v. Brown et al.*, 8 Kan 409 (1871).
[11] Ibid., 415.
[12] *Green v. State of Georgia*, 71 Ga 487 (1883).

Thus far, it would appear that oath-taking for Chinese litigants would involve only a quiz on fundamental religious beliefs.

Just one year later the *Yee Shun* case was decided. Here a Chinese, non-Christian witness who merely took an oath to bind his conscience was deemed competent to testify.[14] This landmark case at least allowed Chinese witnesses and defendants onto the witness stands in criminal trials, but there would be human costs involved in the mere establishment of competency.

Returning to John Lee's Laundry in East Las Vegas, New Mexico Territory, on the night of February 24, 1882, the six Chinese men—John Lee, Joe Chinaman, Sam Lee, Ah Locke, Yee Shun, and Jim Lee (also known as Sam Ling King or Frank)—became involved in a legally significant murder trial. During that night Jim Lee was shot twice, receiving a fatal wound to the upper chest. The witnesses agreed that Ah Locke and Sam Lee had come to visit John Lee to encourage him to sell his laundry to them. John Lee throughout the bargaining had remained on the floor in a corner smoking opium. Joe Chinaman was an ironer, and Jim Lee had merely dropped by to talk. All were known to each other except Yee Shun, who had arrived in Las Vegas from Denver that evening and had entered the laundry to ask the whereabouts of a friend, Gum Fing.[15] Yee Shun was twenty years old, 5′ 3½″ tall, with a "lightish brown yellow" complexion, "straight black" hair, and black eyes. A laborer with no property, he had been born in China and only recently had emigrated to the United States.[16]

A shot was fired, and then another, and Yee Shun, Ah Locke, and Sam Lee ran out the front door. On the floor lay Jim Lee dead. Non-Chinese on the street heard the shots and pursued Yee Shun. He was captured and placed under arrest.[17] On March 10, 1882, Yee Shun was taken before Judge Lebaron Bradford Prince, chief justice of the New Mexico Territory Supreme Court, who was holding district court in San Miguel County, and charged with murder. The next day John Lee was added to the indictment, the first one being dismissed. On March 13, attorneys for Yee Shun and John Lee and the defendants appeared and pleaded not guilty. Sidney Barnes, counsel for John Lee, asked for separate trials, a request that Judge Prince granted. Then the next day the defendants' attorneys asked for a change of venue, but this motion was denied. One day later the defendants requested a postponement, and the court, after argument, agreed to reschedule the separate trials for the fall term.[18]

[13] Ibid., 489-90, 492-93.

[14] *Territory v. Yee Shun*, 3 NM 100 (1884).

[15] *Yee Shun*, District Court Records, 133-35, 143-68.

[16] Prisoner Ledgers A & E, Number 2763, Kansas State Penitentiary Records, Kansas State Archives, Topeka.

[17] *Yee Shun*, District Court Records, 1-15.

[18] Criminal Record Book A, United States District Court of New Mexico Territory, San

On August 16, 1882, *Territory of New Mexico* v. *Yee Shun* began, but with a new judge, recently appointed Chief Justice Samuel B. Axtell. His first order of business was to deny the defendant's request for a continuance. A jury was chosen that consisted of twelve Mexican-Americans.[19] The actual trial with testimony began on August 17 and lasted until August 21. The next day the jury found Yee Shun guilty of second-degree murder and recommended life imprisonment. Judge Axtell followed the jury's recommendation. Yee Shun's attorney, T. A. Green, moved for a new trial, which was denied. He then filed notice of appeal to the New Mexico Territory Supreme Court.[20] Meanwhile young Yee Shun was transported to the Kansas State Penitentiary, arriving there on September 28, 1882, to await a hopefully favorable appeal.[21]

At Yee Shun's criminal trial, the key witness for the prosecution proved to be Joe Chinaman. He identified Yee Shun as the killer. Joe Chinaman was a laborer who had come to Las Vegas one year earlier from El Paso, where he had worked on the railroad; prior to his moving to El Paso he had mined gold in California.[22] When Joe Chinaman was sworn, the following exchange occurred between T. A. Green, Yee Shun's attorney; William Breeden, New Mexico Territory attorney general and prosecutor; and Joe Chinaman, aided by an interpreter:

By Mr. Green:

Q. I will ask you if you believe in Chinese worship: their Joss houses do believe in Chinese Joss?

A. I live in a Chinese house.

Q. I will ask you if you believe in the Chinese Joss house where they worship, where they have their religious services? Do you ever go with Chinamen in this country where they worship? Do you understand what a God is?

A. I don't know what it is. Yes, I believe the Chinese religion.

Q. Have you ever changed from Chinese to Christian religion since you came to this country?

Miguel County, New Mexico State Archives, 88, 90, 91, 95, 99, 101, 115. See also Walter J. Donlon, "LeBaron Bradford Prince, Chief Justice and Governor of New Mexico Territory, 1879-1893" (doctoral dissertation, University of New Mexico, 1967).

[19] Criminal Record Book A, 115-16, 145, 160-61. The jurors were Blas Martinez, Manuel Tagaija, Runaldo Archibeque, Alsolinario Almanzar, Jose Leon Martinez, Hijinio Garcia, Marcos Tagoya, Ysidro Torres, Manuel Jimenes, Manuel Urioste, Juan Chavez, and Juan E. Sena.

[20] Ibid., 163-64, 166, 170, 172-73, 176-77. See also Civil/Criminal Court Index, District Court, San Miguel County, 1847-1882, New Mexico State Archives.

[21] Prisoner, Kansas Penitentiary Records. New Mexico Territory transported felons to Kansas to house for a fee. This agreement preceded adequate and secure prison facilities in New Mexico.

[22] *Yee Shun*, District Court Records, 49-50.

A. I am a Chinaman, and believe in the Chinese religion.

Q. Was you ever a witness in Court before?

A. Yes.

Q. Do you know anything about the obligations of an oath under the Christian religion?

A. I don't know it.

By Mr. Breeden through Chinese interpreter:

Q. Ask him if he knows what he is required to do when he takes an oath here as a witness?

A. He come here for a witness to prove that a man got killed.

Q. Ask him what he is to do, or what his duty is in telling his story as a witness? If he knows what his duty is as to telling the truth?

A. I can tell the truth in this case.

Q. Do you know that you are sworn here so that you are to tell the truth?

A. Yes.[23]

Green then objected to the form of oath and the admissibility of any of the witness's testimony. He was overruled, but the incident formed the primary basis of his appeal in Yee Shun's behalf.

In his brief filed with the New Mexico Territory Supreme Court, Green listed six reversible errors, three of which were closely related substantive issues. Green argued that Joe Chinaman did not believe in God, that the witness was a pagan, and that the accuser was "idiotic" and "ignorant." All of these traits necessitated his testimony to be stricken, because the oath had no meaning to the witness.[24] The New Mexico Supreme Court was not persuaded to overrule the trial court. It found that the only question was whether the witness believed the oath to be "binding on his conscience" within the framework of his own religion. Thus, non-Christians could testify in New Mexico courts and take an oath certifying their truthfulness.[25]

What occurred in the Yee Shun case appeared on the surface to be a victory for Chinese litigants. In some ways it was. Chinese non-Christians could testify in criminal trials. However, the New Mexico courts and all other courts in the West required Chinese witnesses to explain their religion and their state of conscience. The Chinese as a group were not summarily allowed to take an oath; they had to accentuate their cultural distinctiveness first in order to testify. The ambiguity in the law encouraged

[23] Ibid., 50-51.

[24] T. A. Green, Appellant Brief, in *Territory of New Mexico v. Yee Shun* (1883), manuscript court records, Book 153-159, New Mexico Supreme Court Archives, Santa Fe.

[25] *Territory v. Yee Shun*, 3 NM 100, 2 Pac 84-85 (1884). See also Simon Greenleaf, *A Treatise on the Law of Evidence*, Sec. 370-371 (Boston, 1842), 414-17.

judges and juries to consider Chinese testimony as somehow different from non-Chinese testimony.

Even if a Chinese witness could pass the oath, other restrictions might be imposed. Several courts in the trans-Mississippi West moved toward the exclusion of Chinese testimony based upon the common law concept of infamy. If a witness had been convicted of treason or a crime involving deceit, any testimony would be stricken.[26] A crime of deceit, or the propensity to lie, was of special interest to Oregon courts and Chinese witnesses. Oregon law was interpreted to equate the Chinese with deceit. To allow Chinese testimony meant the witness had to prove he or she was *not* a liar.

In *State* v. *Mah Jim*, because the lower court allowed testimony from several Chinese witnesses to convict Mah Jim of murdering See Toy at a Tong meeting, the Oregon Supreme Court reversed the decision.[27] It reasoned that "experience convinces every one that the testimony of Chinese witnesses is very unreliable, and that they are apt to be actuated by motives that are not honest. The life of a human being should not be forfeited on that character of evidence without a full opportunity to sift it thoroughly."[28] As a point of law after 1886, Chinese witnesses in Oregon court proceedings were deemed belonging to a class whose testimony generally was presumed to be unreliable. Mah Jim received a new trial, but his supreme court decision placed in grave jeopardy any Chinese defendant accused of committing a crime who had only Chinese witnesses to use against the non-Chinese witnesses of the prosecution.

Two years later the Oregon Supreme Court further strengthened this rule in the case of *Ching Ling*. The defendant, along with Chee Gong, Fong Long Dick, Yee Gong, and Chee Son, stood accused of murdering one Lee Yick in the Portland Chinese Theater. All witnesses testifying to the event were Chinese, and they did not agree on who stabbed the mortal blow.[29] The lower court found Chin Ling guilty of murder, but the supreme court reversed. On the basis of testimony offered, the court took judicial notice of an inherent racial quality of the Chinese:

The object of this testimony evidently was to show that the appellant and other Chinamen charged with the offense bore such malice towards the deceased as to prompt them to commit the homicide. There could have been no other purpose for introducing it. The testimony was not sufficient to have had any weight whatever as against white persons. But very few of them at most could be found credu-

[26] Edward W. Cleary, ed., *McCormick's Handbook of the Law of Evidence* (St. Paul, 1972), 142.

[27] *State* v. *Mah Jim*, 13 Ore 235 (1886). For a further discussion of this case and *State of Oregon* v. *Ching Ling* within a regional context, see John R. Wunder, "The Chinese and the Courts in the Pacific Northwest: Justice Denied?" *Pacific Historical Review*, LII (May 1983), 204-5.

[28] *State* v. *Mah Jim*, 13 Ore 235 at 236-237 (1886).

[29] *State of Oregon* v. *Ching Ling*, 16 Ore 419 (1888).

lous enough to believe that *their* race, in consequence of such an occurrence as happened to Chee Gong and his friends, in the affair of their discharge from employment at the restaurant, would have been induced to plan and execute a murder.
As to Chinamen, however, it is different. Those among us have exhibited such a
peculiarity of temperament, that a circumstance of that character would incite a
strong suspicion against them.[30]

Given their infamous nature, a presumption against the innocence of
any Chinese person charged with a violent crime was given judicial sanction. One might assume that Ching Ling had no grounds for reversal, but
a greater truth remained to save him. All the prosecution witnesses were
Chinese and thereby suspect. The court espoused a higher law: "Juries should
be loath to convict a Chinaman of murder in the first degree upon Chinese
testimony; not wholly on account of a tender regard for the life of the accused, but also from a respect and reverence for truth and justice. If we
were disposed through a dislike of the race to consider the life of a Chinaman as a trivial matter, still we would have no right to immolate justice
upon the altar of our prejudice."[31]

In the summer of 1875, L. T. Townsend toured the West and observed
that all was not well between Chinese and non-Chinese. "Judging from the
present bitter complaints against the Chinaman," Townsend wrote, "it would
seem that our friends of the Pacific States are able to see under that 'rat-
and-tan complexion' merely an animal of 'sly' and 'peculiar ways.'"[32] Sly-
ness was interpreted by courts as a character flaw that jeopardized Chinese
participation in the criminal justice system.

Oregon had the harshest infamy evidential rules in the trans-Mississippi
West. Other states and territories modified the rote rules of the common
law. Nevertheless Chinese witnesses had to be examined with reference to
religious beliefs in all trans-Mississippi West jurisdictions before they were
allowed to testify,[33] and courts allowed admission into evidence the discussion of Chinese mythic propensities to be less than truthful.[34]

[30] Ibid., 423.

[31] Ibid., 425. See also *State of Oregon v. Chee Gong and Fong Long Dick*, 16 Ore 534 (1888).
Elmer Sandmeyer has observed, "In some cases the charge against the Chinese was simply
that they were dishonest and unreliable, and that the entire business life of China was permeated by the idea that every person who handled a transaction should take his share of
graft. More specifically, they were accused of having no regard for the sanctity of an oath."
Sandmeyer, *Anti-Chinese Movement*, 34.

[32] Luther Tracy Townsend, *The Chinese Problem* (Boston, 1876; rpt., San Francisco, 1970),
58. For black anti-Chinese attitudes, see Leigh Dana Johnsen, "Equal Rights and the 'Heathen Chinee': Black Activism in San Francisco, 1865-1875," *Western Historical Quarterly*, XI
(January 1980), 57-68.

[33] In the following trans-Mississippi states and territories, religious belief could not deny
testimonial oath-taking: Arizona, *Ari. Rev. Statutes*, Sec. 1866 and 2037 (1877); Colorado, *Colo.*

The admission of dying declarations into evidence at a trial probably began in early eighteenth-century Britain. The rule quickly traversed the Atlantic Ocean and was refined in the United States. Basically stated, a dying declaration was admitted because of the notion that a person about to die would tell the truth in order to entertain an afterlife and that a person near death may have been the only witness to the lethal assault. It followed that for a dying declaration to be admissible evidence, the declarant had to die and a public prosecution for the specific crime of homicide had to be commenced.[35] All jurisdictions treated the dying declaration as did California in *People* v. *Sanchez*. "Declarations," held the California Supreme Court in 1864, "of deceased persons, in cases of homicide, stand upon the same footing as the testimony of a witness sworn in the case."[36]

Given the circumstances surrounding dying declarations, Chinese and non-Chinese defendants charged with the murder of Chinese victims challenged the rule governing admissibility. Such defenses first alleged that a Chinese who made a dying declaration must have been a Christian or at least believed in some sort of afterlife in order for the statement to be admitted at a trial. At first it appeared Chinese dying declarations were free from cultural attack. In the case of *People* v. *Chin Mook Sow*, the defendant was found guilty of stabbing to death Yee Ah Chin. Before he died, Yee Ah Chin identified Chin Mook Sow as his assailant. On appeal the defendant asserted as reversible error the fact that Yee Ah Chin "did not entertain such a belief in a future state as rendered his dying declaration

Constitution, Art. II, Sec. 4 (1876), *Colo. Annot. Statutes*, Sec. 4821 (1891); Idaho, *Ida. Constitution*, Art. I, Sec. 4 (1899); Iowa, *Ia. Constitution*, Art. I, Sec. 4 (1857); Montana, *Mont. Constitution*, Art. III, Sec. 4 (1889); Nebraska, *Neb. Constitution*, Art. I, Sec. 4 (1875), *Neb. Comp. Statutes*, Sec. 5939 (1899); Nevada, *Nev. Constitution*, Art. I, Sec. 4 (1864), *Nev. Gen. Statutes*, Sec. 4578 (1885); New Mexico, *N.M. Comp. Laws*, Sec. 3015 (1897); North Dakota, *N.D. Constitution*, Art. I, Sec. 4 (1899); Oklahoma, *Okla. Statutes*, Sec. 4229 (1893); Oregon, *Ore. Constitution*, Art. I, Sec. 6, 7 (1859); South Dakota, *S.D. Constitution*, Sec. 86 (1889); Texas, *Tx. Constitution*, Art. I, Sec. 5 (1876), *Tx. P.C.*, Sec. 776 (1895); Utah, *Ut. Constitution*, Art. 1, Sec. 4 (1895); and Wyoming, *Wyo. Constitution*, Art. I, Sec. 18 (1889).

In the following trans-Mississippi West states, no witness could deny the being of God: Arkansas, *Ark. Constitution*, Art. XIX, Sec. 1 (1874); and Louisiana, *La. C. Pr.*, Sec. 478 (1894).

In the following trans-Mississippi West states, non-Christians such as many Chinese witnesses were to be sworn to oaths according to "peculiar ceremonies": Arkansas, *Ark. Statutes*, Sec. 2924 (1894); California, *Cal. C.C.P.*, Sec. 2096 (1872); Kansas, *Kan. Gen. Statutes*, Ch. 95, Sec. 351 (1897); Minnesota, *Minn. Gen. Statutes*, Sec. 5665 (1894); Missouri, *Mo. Rev. Statutes*, Sec. 8842 (1899); and Washington, *Wash. C. and Statutes*, Sec. 6057 (1897).

See also Wigmore, *Treatise Evidence*, III:2365-71.

[34] See also *State* v. *Lu Sing*, 34 Mont 31 (1906). In *Fernandez* v. *State*, 16 Ari 269 (1914), the testimony of an elderly Apache-Mohave was accepted by her merely promising not to tell a lie.

For exclusion of testimony in federal courts based upon tests of infamy, see *U.S.* v. *Biebusch*, 1 Fd 213 (1880), and particularly perjury, see *State* v. *Harras*, 22 Wash 57 (1900).

[35] Wigmore, *Treatise Evidence*, II:1798-819.

[36] *People* v. *Sanchez*, 24 Cal 17 at 26 (1864).

admissible."[37] The California Supreme Court did not agree with the contentions of the defense. It held that evidence of a declarant's lack of belief in Christianity or of a life thereafter would not affect the competency of the declaration. This information, however, was useful to a jury to help it determine the weight it wanted to give to such testimony.[38]

In spite of *Chin Mook Sow*, California continued to grapple with this issue. In *People v. Lim Foon*, the defendant was convicted by a San Joaquin County Court of murdering an elderly Chinese, Yip Suey. Upon arrest, the defendant had been placed in front of Yip Suey, who stated, "Yes, him man shoot me." Yip Suey then expired. After conviction Lim Foon appealed arguing that the declarant had no religious convictions and had specifically disdained any belief in a spiritual afterlife, thereby making the declaration inadmissible. The California Supreme Court did not agree, but it allowed that the lack of Christian beliefs made dying declarations greatly impaired and subject to incredulity.[39]

Again the cloudy nature of the law allowed for cultural and racial discussions in court. The need for the California court to make such a pronounced anti-Chinese statement in the *Lim Foon* case may have arisen from its own decision made just two years earlier in *People v. Dallen*. Here, on the late afternoon of June 8, 1913, in the small community of Sisson, the town marshal was informed that the "Greek pimp," one Theodore Dallen, had just arrived at a house of ill fame known as the "Buckskin." The marshal and his assistant, Andrew Dougherty, went to the bawdy house to arrest the Greek pimp. Dallen evidently heard them, so he jumped out a window and hid under the house. The marshal said he wanted to find the "son-of-a-bitch," and then Dougherty heard something, looked under the house, lit a candle, and was shot in the calf by the Greek pimp. The wounded Dougherty was taken to the home of his half-sister, and then on June 10 he was moved to a hospital where his condition was attended to by one Dr. Legge. He prescribed amputation of Dougherty's leg, but during the probing the physician decided that the gangrenous state was too advanced and halted the operation. Dougherty died on June 13.[40]

Dallen was convicted of murder, and he appealed upon many grounds, including the argument that Dougherty's statement implicating Dallen was not admissible because there had been time for the declarant to have been given an oath. The California court refused to adopt this contention saying that dying declarations require only basic standards for admissibility and that to require more interfered with the province of the jury.[41]

---

[37] *People v. Chin Mook Sow*, 51 Cal 597 at 599 (1877).
[38] Ibid., 599-600.
[39] *People v. Lim Foon*, 155 Pac 477 (1915).
[40] *People v. Dallen*, 132 Pac 1064 (1913).
[41] Ibid.

Other trans-Mississippi West jurisdictions also grappled with dying declarations and Chinese interests. The Supreme Court of Oregon in *State of Oregon* v. *Charley Lee Quong, Ah Lee, and Lee John* directly embraced the question of the religious condition of a dying declarant. This dispute involved the premeditated, malicious killing of Chin Sue Ying, a member of the Chinese Mission School in Portland and a recent Christian convert. Chin, the night before he was murdered, had gone to a Chinese joss house where he broke a Chinese "stink-pot" on the floor. A policeman was called who saw some dark-looking and foul-smelling liquid on the joss house floor, and he heard Lee Quang call Chin, according to court records, a "ki gi," meaning a "man who acts like a prostitute."[42] The officer inquired as to whether he should arrest Chin, but Lee Quong said he should wait until the next morning to swear out a warrant. The next day Chin once again went to the joss house and proceeded to attempt to throw a piece of raw meat on the joss statue, whereupon he was dealt two hatchet blows to the head and two pistol shots to the abdomen.[43]

After the trial of each defendant separately, Ah Lee was convicted and appealed to the Oregon Supreme Court alleging several points of error including an objection to the admission into evidence of Chin Sue Ying's dying declaration on the basis that Chin was an imperfect Christian and did not believe in the existence of a Supreme Being. In rejecting this contention, the court took judicial notice of the deceased probably being "a worshipper of Joss, and the heathenish religion of his race," but since he had been attending a Portland missionary school and since he had defaced the joss house, Oregon's general rule was modified to allow this dying declaration to remain as acceptable evidence.[44] A similar conclusion was reached in several cases by Idaho's highest court.[45]

Several years later this same issue was once again taken up by the Oregon Supreme Court. In *State* v. *Foot You* the defendant had been convicted of second-degree murder for shooting Ching Bo Qung at a Portland bar known as the "Temperance Saloon." At the trial the the district attorney presented as evidence two written statements signed by the deceased that identified Foot You as his murderer. These statements were sworn to by

---

[42] *State of Oregon* v. *Charley Lee* (indicted under the name of Charley Lee Quong), and *Ah Lee* (indicted under the name of Lee Jaw), jointly indicted with *Lee John*, 7 Ore 237 at 249 (1879). The invective was probably "k'ai-ai," meaning homosexual.

[43] Ibid., 258.

[44] *State of Oregon* v. *Ah Lee*, 8 Ore 214 at 217 (1880). For a further discussion of these cases, see Wunder, "Chinese in Pacific Northwest," 197-98.

[45] See *People* v. *Ah Too*, 2 Ida 47 (1884); Appellant's brief, *People* v. *Ah Too*, filed January 29, 1884, Respondent's brief, *People* v. *Ah Too*, filed January 31, 1884; Blaine County District Court trial transcript, *State* v. *Yee Wee*, June 29, 1899, all in Idaho State Archives, Boise; and *State* v. *Yee Wee*, 7 Ida 188 (1900). See also John R. Wunder, "The Courts and the Chinese in Frontier Idaho," *Idaho Yesterdays*, 25 (Spring 1981), 23-32.

an interpreter, and another attorney was present when they were signed. Defendant's counsel objected, claiming the dying declaration was orchestrated in a hearing-like setting without opposing counsel's presence. The court ruled that the possible pressure exerted by the prosecution during the dying declaration process was a jury consideration and did not prevent introduction of the dying declaration as valid evidence.[46]

The final Oregon word on Chinese dying declarations occurred in the case of *State v. Yee Gueng* (1910). Here Yee Gueng was convicted of murdering Lee Tai Hoy on a stairway outside an apartment building in downtown Portland. Lee Tai Hoy in a dying declaration identified the defendant as his killer. At the trial, defendant's counsel attempted to have the dying declaration rendered inadmissible because of Lee Tai Hoy's lack of religious belief and membership in a faction of the Bo On Tong Society, both of which affected his ability to be truthful. The judge refused and went one step further. He ordered the jury not to consider any testimony given as to the declarant's religious beliefs. The Oregon Supreme Court, in a significant departure from other jurisdictions, affirmed this position. Chinese religion could not be introduced as mitigating circumstances to dying declarations in Oregon trials. The question of trust and honesty did, however, remain for the jury to weigh.[47]

Where Oregon refused to go, Washington took the step to accept dying declarations from infamous or near-infamous declarants. On August 9, 1895, Edwin Baldwin, Ozro Perkins, and Ulysses Loop beat up Alonzo Wheeler. From these wounds Wheeler died, but before he died he declared the names of the three killers. At the trial where the three defendants were convicted of manslaughter, their counsel sought to expunge the dying declarations because the declarant had been convicted of cattle stealing and had not been pardoned. The trial court refused to sustain the objection and the Washington Supreme Court agreed. The high court strongly suggested that only for perjury could a dying declaration be denied admissibility.[48]

Thus, for nineteenth- and early twentieth-century courts in the trans-Mississippi West, the dying declaration provided significant legal comment and controversy. While justice was sometimes upheld, it provided yet another opportunity for evaluation of the Chinese by non-Chinese and a chance to question and impugn the role Chinese witnesses, defendants, and victims should play in the criminal justice system.

Nowhere would attempts be more concerted to deny Chinese direct access to criminal justice than in California under the development of its

[46] *State v. Foot You*, 24 Ore 61 (1893).

[47] *State v. Yee Gueng*, 57 Ore 509 (1910).

[48] *State v. Baldwin et al.*, 15 Wash 15 (1896).

racial exclusionary rule.[49] This occurred as a result of an 1854 California Supreme Court decision, *People* v. *Hall*.[50]

In this case the white defendant was convicted of murder on the basis of testimony from Chinese witnesses. He appealed, asserting that Chinese testimony against a white person was inadmissible per se because a Chinese was a person of color and thereby banned from testifying by criminal statute. This statute, Section 14 of California's 1850 Act Concerning Crimes and Punishments, read: "No black or mulatto person, or Indian shall be permitted to give evidence in favor of, or against, any white person."[51] The California Supreme Court agreed with Hall's contention and his conviction was reversed.

The language and reasoning employed by Chief Justice Hugh C. Murray reflected the extremes to which law and race fell in nineteenth-century America. Murray found as a point of law that Indian meant Chinese. He wrote:

> When Columbus first landed upon the shores of this continent, in his attempt to discover a western passage to the Indies, he imagined that he had accomplished the object of his expedition, and that the Island of San Salvador was one of those Islands of the Chinese sea, lying near the extremity of India, which had been described by navigators.
>
> Acting upon this hypothesis, and also perhaps from similarity of features and physical conformation, he gave to the Islanders the name of Indians, which appellation was universally adopted, and extended to the aboriginals of the New World, as well as of Asia.
>
> From that time, down to a very recent period, the American Indians and the Mongolian or Asiatic, were regarded as the same type of the human species.[52]

Having established the racial link, it remained for Murray to connect Chinese to the intention of the legislature. Murray reasoned: "The evident intention of the Act was to throw around the citizen a protection for life and property, which could only be secured by removing him above the corrupting influences of degraded castes. . . . [T]he apparent design was to protect the white from the influence of all testimony other than of persons of the same caste."[53] Murray then invoked Chancellor Kent's analysis of whether the Chinese could become citizens of the United States under existing federal statutes. Wrote Kent, "[T]he Act confines the description to 'white' citizens, and it is a matter of doubt, whether, under this provision,

---

[49] J. A. C. Grant, "Testimonial Exclusion Because of Race: A Chapter in the History of Intolerance in California," *UCLA Law Review*, 17 (November 1969), 192-201.

[50] *People* v. *Hall*, 4 Cal 399 (1854).

[51] California, *Cal. Statutes*, Ch. 99 (1850).

[52] *People* v. *Hall*, 4 Cal 399 at 400 (1854).

[53] Ibid., 403.

any of the tawny races of Asia can be admitted to the privileges of citizen-ship."[54] Murray then illogically applied this notion to California:

[T]he same rule that would admit [Chinese] to testify, would admit them to all the equal rights of citizenship, and we might soon see them at the polls, in the jury box, upon the bench, and in the legislative halls.

This is not a speculation which exists in the excited and over-heated imagina-tion of the patriot and statesman, but it is an actual and present danger.[55]

Hysteria then gripped the chief justice's pen. The Chinese, he con-cluded, are "a race of people marked as inferior, and who are incapable of progress or intellectual development beyond a certain point, as their his-tory has shown."[56] Thus, after *People* v. *Hall*, the Chinese were denied ac-cess to criminal trials strictly on account of their race if a white was a defendant.[57]

The rule in *People* v. *Hall* was extended to civil cases in 1859,[58] was in-voked to formulate a color test covering mixed-bloods, i.e., "Chinese Mes-tizoes,"[59] and was extended to cover specifically the injured party.[60] In this latter case, *People* v. *Howard*, Chief Justice Stephen J. Field wrote that "it is possible . . . that instances may arise where, upon this construction, crime may go unpunished. If this be so, it is only [a] matter for the consideration of the Legislature."[61]

Lest there be any doubt, the California legislature acted. In 1863, three years after *Howard*, an amended Section 14 expressly included the Chinese in the exclusionary rule, "No . . . Chinese [as well as mulattos and Indians] shall be permitted to give evidence in favor or against, any white man."[62]

There were limits to the testimonial exclusion. In *People* v. *Awa*, a Chi-nese man was convicted of manslaughter. At his first trial, he offered as evidence a Chinese witness. The testimony was disallowed on the basis of the exclusionary rule. On appeal the California Supreme Court reversed, concluding that the state—the People—were not exclusively white.[63] Then in *People* v. *Jones*, the defendant was convicted of stealing four ounces of gold

[54] Ibid., 404.

[55] Ibid., 404-5.

[56] Ibid., 405.

[57] Jack Chen, *The Chinese of America* (San Francisco, 1980), 45; and Daniel Chu and Samuel Chu, *Passage to the Golden Gate: A History of the Chinese in America to 1910* (Garden City, 1967), 84.

[58] *Speer* v. *See Yup Company*, 13 Cal 73 (1859).

[59] *Sanchez* v. *Stout*, 1 D.C.R. (Labatt) 241 (Cal App. 1857) as cited in Grant, "Testimonial Exclusion," 196; and *People* v. *Elyea*, 14 Cal. 145 (1859).

[60] *People* v. *Howard*, 17 Cal 64 (1860).

[61] Ibid., 65.

[62] California, *Cal. Statutes*, Ch. 70 (1863).

[63] *People* v. *Awa*, 27 Cal 639 (1865).

from Ah Po. There was no admissible evidence except from the victim. The trial court had instructed the jury: "If the best evidence cannot be produced, then secondary evidence is admissible. In the present case Ah Po [the victim] . . . would be the best witness to prove the robber. But the law precludes his testimony, and hence what would be secondary testimony in ordinary cases becomes the best evidence in the case at bar."[64]

On appeal the California Supreme Court reversed, but it urged a legislative reconsideration:

> It does not appear to us reasonable that a less measure of proof, or testimony of a less persuasive character, should be required to convict a man of the crime of robbery, when committed upon a Chinaman, than when committed upon a citizen of California, merely because a Chinaman is an incompetent witness; and for that reason it might be impossible to prove the body of the offense in accordance with the rules of evidence well established in the law.[65]

Relief appeared to be coming to Chinese criminal victims and defendants. In 1866 in an attempt to make it easier to prosecute prostitution, the legislature lifted the ban allowing Chinese testimony in such cases.[66] That same year the Civil Rights Act was passed, but in *People* v. *Washington* the California Supreme Court narrowly limited the act to apply only to blacks. In this case George Washington, a mulatto, was convicted of robbing Ah Wang on the testimony of Chinese witnesses. This conviction was reversed under the federal Civil Rights Act; black was now white, which disallowed Chinese testimony against blacks in California.[67] One year later Chinese testimony against a white, this time under the Fourteenth Amendment, was disallowed by the same California Supreme Court.[68]

The California Chinese exclusionary rule eventually was stricken during codification reforms of the 1870s. Section 1321 of the Penal Code of 1872 formally ended the racial exclusionary rule.[69] No other state or territory adopted the California position, although Nebraska, Minnesota, and Washington retained racial exclusions upon Native American testimony, and Nebraska in *Pumphrey* v. *State* was asked to adopt *People* v. *Hall* with reference to Japanese testimony, but it declined.[70] A foremost specialist on evidence, John Henry Wigmore, in 1904 attempted to understand the policy

[64] *People* v. *Jones*, 31 Cal 566 at 572 (1867).

[65] Ibid.

[66] Grant, "Testimonial Exclusion," 197.

[67] Ibid., 198-201; and *People* v. *Washington*, 36 Cal 568 (1869).

[68] *People* v. *Brady*, 40 Cal 198 (1870).

[69] Grant, "Testimonial Exclusion," 200-201. See also *People* v. *McGuire*, 45 Cal 56 (1872).

[70] Nebraska, *Nebr. Comp. Statutes*, Sec. 4734, 5902; Minnesota, *Minn. Gen. Statutes*, Sec. 2007; Washington, *Wash. Annot. Code & Statutes*, Sec. 6940, 7316; and *Pumphrey* v. *State*, 84 Neb. 636 (1909).

behind California's Chinese exclusionary rule. "The condition of public feeling in that community against the economic encroachments of Chinese laborers," wrote Wigmore, "explains and extenuates (while it may not excuse) this blunder in the policy of the testimonial law."[71]

In order for the Chinese to participate in the American criminal justice system, they clearly needed more than constitutional amendments and federal laws. Left to state and territorial legislatures and courts, they were indeed in trouble. Chinese willing to come to a trial or those unfortunate enough to be charged with a crime frequently risked cultural insults and, worse, legally sanctioned discrimination. Challenges to oath-taking abilities, questions of near-infamy disqualifications, erosions to legitimate dying declarations, and adherence to a racial testimonial exclusion discouraged Chinese cooperation in criminal cases and denied to the Chinese fundamental forms of fairness in criminal law. Ambiguities allowed non-Chinese to pass judgments upon the culture of the Chinese during an era of intolerance. The criminal justice system in the West became for Chinese what the criminal justice system of the South represented for blacks in immediate post-Civil War America.

But what happened to Yee Shun, the young Chinese involved in a murder in Las Vegas, New Mexico Territory? He had been transported to the Kansas State Penitentiary to await word of his appeal from the New Mexico Territory Supreme Court. Finally, during the January term, 1884, the court issued its opinion denying his appeal.[72] Yee Shun's attorney, T. A. Green, no doubt delayed sending the bad news to his client, who had already served two years in prison. Perhaps when Yee Shun heard the decision, it proved too much for the twenty-two-year-old. On September 11, 1884, Yee Shun took drastic action, which was recorded the next morning in the Leavenworth (Kansas) *Times:* "Yee Shun, a Chinaman, confined in the penitentiary on a life sentence from New Mexico, hanged himself yesterday morning in his cell. He committed the deed with a small cord that he had taken from his bed."[73]

[71] Wigmore, *Treatise Evidence*, 1:645-46.

[72] *Territory of New Mexico v. Yee Shun*, 3 NM 100 (1884).

[73] Prisoner, Kansas Penitentiary Records; and Leavenworth (Kansas) *Times*, September 12, 1884, p. 4, col. 2.

Popular Sovereignty, Vigilantism, and the Constitutional Right of Revolution

CHRISTIAN G. FRITZ

The author is a member of the school of law in the University of New Mexico.

The focus of this article is the interplay of an indigenous American idea—popular sovereignty—and two American traditions: vigilante justice and constitutional conventions during the nineteenth century. While the traditions may seem unconnected, they are linked by the doctrine of popular sovereignty, which was based on the notion that "the people" are the ultimate and only legitimate basis for government and that "the people" possess the right to reform, alter, or abolish their government at any time. What emerged in the debates over both the proposed California constitution of 1849 and the San Francisco vigilante activities of the 1850s were conflicting views about both the scope and means whereby the people could exercise this sovereignty.

It is a commonplace that the American legal and constitutional order rests on the idea of a government "of laws and not of men." The phrase implies the primary role that law plays in ordering and maintaining order in American society as well as the close identification of lawyers with that process. It would seem anomalous today to identify members of the legal profession with a vigilante movement that expressly denies the validity of the existing legal system. This reaction is a measure of the distance between our contemporary legal culture and

The author thanks Dean Leo Romero of the University of New Mexico for a summer research grant that made this article possible and Joseph Franaszek, Marlene Keller, and an anonymous *PHR* referee for their helpful comments on an earlier draft of the paper.

nineteenth-century America. While legal vigilantism seems oxy-moronic today, it was not the case in the nineteenth century. The explanation rests on a set of nineteenth-century assumptions common to lawyers and laymen and involves the evolution of how Americans perceived the doctrine of popular sovereignty.

Since the nineteenth-century debates in California over vigilantism and constitution making centered on the source of law—or the operation of processes outside the established legal order—it is particularly revealing to examine the roles and attitudes of members of the legal community towards popular sovereignty. By focusing on lawyers, the degree to which the terms popular sovereignty and vigilantism have shifted in con-notation is more easily observed. Lawyers would be more apt to draw on legal or constitutional arguments, if they felt such existed, to justify vigilantism. And lawyers formed a natural occupational link between vigilantism, which a good number of them supported, and the work of nineteenth-century constitu-tional conventions in which lawyers almost always played a significant if not dominant role.

From popular sovereignty's earliest appearance, its revolu-tionary potential frightened some people enough to prompt a redefinition of the nature of sovereign power and how it could be exercised within the evolving American republic. Eventually, private power would be constrained by public institutions of justice, and the almost limitless possibilities of constitutional conventions would be restricted by the ability of the people to amend existing constitutions. Ultimately, this limitation on the potential of popular sovereignty kept federal and state constitu-tional revision within a narrow channel.

At the national level, the revolutionary implications of popular sovereignty were clearly presaged by provisions that appeared in the earliest American state constitutions promul-gated in the 1770s. For example, Virginia's bill of rights asserted that "all power is vested in, and consequently derived from, the people; that magistrates are their trustees and servants, and at all times amenable to them," while Delaware's bill of rights provided that "whenever the Ends of Government are perverted, and public Liberty manifestly endangered...[,] the People may, and of Right ought to[,] establish a new, or reform[,] the old government."[1] It took little stretch of the imagination to see in such language the specter of political instability and rapid changes driven by the popular will. Indeed, during the revolutionary struggle itself, Americans had justified the use of mobs and popular uprisings as a legitimate means of resisting the British.[2]

The use of "extralegal" movements, combined with the constitutional expressions of popular sovereignty, prompted some American leaders in the course of the late eighteenth century to redefine the nature of sovereign power within republican governments. Between the American Revolution and the adoption of the federal Constitution in 1787, thinking about the nature of governments ultimately based on the people's will experienced a significant shift that tended to confine popular sovereignty.[3] Increasingly, leaders of the revolutionary movement addressed the question of how to balance involving the people in government against maintaining government they regarded as stable, sober, and right thinking.[4] The more revolutionary

---

1. William F. Swindler, *Sources and Documents of United States Constitutions* (11 vols., Dobbs Ferry, N.Y., 1973-1979), II, 198, X, 49. See also Willi Paul Adams, *The First American Constitutions: Republican Ideology and the Making of the State Constitutions in the Revolutionary Era* (Chapel Hill, N.C., 1980), 129-149.

2. Pauline Maier, "Popular Uprisings and Civil Authority in Eighteenth-Century America," *William and Mary Quarterly*, XXVII (1970), 3-35; John Phillip Reid, "In a Defensive Rage: The Uses of the Mob, the Justification in Law, and the Coming of the American Revolution," *New York University Law Review* XLIX (1974), 1043-1091.

3. For the dimensions of this shift in republican thought, see Gordon S. Wood, *The Creation of the American Republic, 1776-1787* (Chapel Hill, N.C., 1969); Daniel Elazar, ed., *Republicanism, Representation, and Consent: Views of the Founding Era* (New Brunswick, N.J., 1979); Donald S. Lutz, *Popular Consent and Popular Control: Whig Political Theory in the Early State Constitutions* (Baton Rouge, 1980); Joyce Appleby, "The American Heritage: The Heirs and the Disinherited," *Journal of American History*, LXXIV (1987), 798-813; Robert F. Williams, "'Experience Must Be Our Only Guide': The State Constitutional Experience of the Framers of the Federal Constitution," *Hastings Constitutional Law Quarterly*, XV (1988), 403-427; and John R. Vile, "American Views of the Constitutional Amending Process: An Intellectual History of Article V," *American Journal of Legal History*, XXXV (1991) 44-69. But compare James A. Gardner, "Consent, Legitimacy and Elections: Implementing Popular Sovereignty under the Lockean Constitution," *University of Pittsburgh Law Review*, LII (1990), esp. 192-213.

4. For such concerns affecting the thought of James Madison between the Revolution and the Constitutional Convention, see Charles F. Hobson, "The Negative on State Laws: James Madison, the Constitution, and the Crisis of Republican Government," *William and Mary Quarterly*, XXXVI (1979), 215-235.

ideas articulated in the first state constitutions and generated by the American Revolution did not, however, simply disappear. A political tradition emerged that essentially sought to convert the concept of "the people" from a passive source of constitutionalism into an active role in enforcing and amending the federal constitution. This vision included a state of affairs in which the government and the constitution would be continually reassessed by the people, epitomized by Thomas Jefferson's assertion that the federal constitution belonged only to the living generation.[5]

Ultimately, however, James Madison and other federalists argued successfully for limits to popular sovereignty by confining federal constitutional revision to the cumbersome procedures spelled out in Article Five or to judicial interpretation by the U.S. Supreme Court. In effect, what Madison and others accomplished for the national government was to relegate popular sovereignty to a theory that commanded universal assent while suppressing its actual revolutionary possibilities. The adoption of the Constitution in 1787 and John Marshall's assertion of the power of judicial review in *Marbury* v. *Madison* (1803) in large measure achieved the objectives of those who feared, with Madison, the political instability threatened by too much popular control.[6] Thus, the struggle between these two competing visions of federal constitutional revision was relatively quickly resolved by the early national period.

Nonetheless, the American struggle over the role of "the people" in the context of "altering, reforming or abolishing" their government did not come to an end with the mechanism adopted for constitutional change in the Constitution or by Marshall's assumption of judicial review. The debate instead shifted to the states and was largely conducted within state constitutional conventions during the nineteenth century. Indeed, the continuing debate over the meaning of popular

5. Edmond Cahn, "An American Contribution," in Edmond Cahn, ed., *Supreme Court and Supreme Law* (Bloomington, 1954), 1-25; Merrill D. Peterson, "Mr. Jefferson's 'Sovereignty of the Living Generation,'" Virginia Quarterly Review, LII (1976), 437-447; Peterson, "Thomas Jefferson, the Founders, and Constitutional Change," in J. Barlow, Leonard Levy, K. Masugi, eds., *The American Founding: Essays on the Formation of the Constitution* (New York, 1988), 275-293.

6. Kermit L. Hall, *The Supreme Court and Judicial Review in American History* (Washington, D.C., 1985), 1-25; *Marbury* v. *Madison*, 5 U.S. 137 (1803).

sovereignty in state constitutional conventions underscores the connection between vigilantism and constitutional revision. Moreover, the existence of that debate and the ideas it generated gave a legitimacy to proponents of vigilantism that is difficult to appreciate today. If vigilantism represented, in the eyes of its critics, a fearsome source of social disorder, it was equally true that assertions of direct and frequent changes in a constitution by the people represented a similar danger. On the other hand, those who favored a more direct role for the people in constitutional revision—based on a more active or dynamic definition of popular sovereignty—were inclined to acknowledge the justification of vigilantism. In essence, those who opposed vigilantism were quite uncomfortable with the notion that popular sovereignty contained a dimension that placed the right of revolution (and hence a higher authority than the written constitution) in the hands of "the people." By the same token, an overly active resort to the constitutional process of revision threatened to undermine the fundamental nature of constitutional law. This does not mean that those who championed popular sovereignty in state constitutional conventions necessarily favored vigilantism, but that their argument about the nature of popular sovereignty itself gave important theoretical legitimacy to vigilance activities. The issue of the existence of power remained separate from the question of its use.

Eventually it became constitutional orthodoxy to reject any literal attempt to invoke popular sovereignty.[7] Nonetheless, this position was hardly inevitable or clear in mid-nineteenth-century America. In fact, the debates over vigilantism and constitutional revision reflected a broader struggle over the role of the people in government that would only be resolved after the Civil War.

---

7. The most dramatic attempt to invoke popular sovereignty was the so-called Dorr Rebellion in Rhode Island in 1842, which has been called "the only revolutionary republican movement that occurred after the Revolution." Harold M. Hyman and William M. Wiecek, *Equal Justice under Law: Constitutional Development, 1835-1875* (New York, 1982), 3. On the Dorr Rebellion, see George M. Dennison, *The Dorr War: Republicanism on Trial. 1831-1861* (Lexington, Ky., 1976); and William M. Wiecek, "'A Peculiar Conservatism' and the Dorr Rebellion: Constitutional Clash in Jacksonian America," *American Journal of Legal History*, XXII (1978), 237-253.

Popular Sovereignty: Origins and Dynamism

The American Revolution generated considerable thought about the nature of the right of revolution and the wisdom of various means of political change. The Declaration of Independence had enunciated the right of the people "to alter or to abolish" government "whenever" it became "destructive" of the people's inalienable rights, such as to life, liberty, and the pursuit of happiness. Yet, while articulation of the theoretical right of popular sovereignty remained largely static, what simultaneously happened during the nineteenth century was a redefinition of "the people" and new understandings about the practical implications of their exercise of power.[8]

The theory of popular sovereignty justified the American Revolution and republican government, and established a basic premise in American political life: that political legitimacy ultimately rested with the consent of the people. England's constitutional tradition developed a notion of fundamental law, associated with the ancient heritage of the English common law, implying limits on governmental power.[9] While fundamental law originated as a means of checking kingly power, eventually constitutional arrangements in England gave Parliament supreme powers.[10] Even though English political theorists were familiar with the concept of popular sovereignty (in their search for a competing theory to the divine right of kings), it was left to the United States to invent the mechanism of the constitutional convention, the institution that conceptually permitted the exercise of popular sovereignty in the creation of American fundamental law.[11]

Growing tensions between those who held a more conservative view of republicanism and those who believed in majority rule stimulated this rethinking about the governed.

---

8. Lance Banning, *The Jeffersonian Persuasion: Evolution of a Party Ideology* (Ithaca, N.Y., 1978).

9. Wood, *Creation of the American Republic,* 306-389; J. W. Gough, *Fundamental Law in English Constitutional History* (Oxford, 1955); J. G. A. Pocock, *The Ancient Constitution and the Feudal Law* (Cambridge, Eng., 1957).

10. Geoffrey Marshall, *Constitutional Theory* (Oxford, Eng., 1971), 35-72. The classic treatment of the theory of parliamentary sovereignty remains A. V. Dicey, *Introduction to the Study of the Law of the Constitution* (10th ed., London, 1959).

11. Edmund S. Morgan, *Inventing the People: The Rise of Popular Sovereignty in England and America* (New York, 1988), esp. 55-93 and 239-287.

Indeed, an important division in nineteenth-century American political thought consisted of those who responded to the revolutionary implications of popular sovereignty with greater or lesser ease. This response did not necessarily conform to traditional political party divisions such as those between Whigs and Democrats.

The phrase "popular sovereignty" figured in the debate during the mid-1840s over the issue of slavery in the territories. In the context of that debate, popular sovereignty was used to imply "territorial sovereignty" or the right of the territories to decide whether or not slavery would be permitted within their boundaries.[12] Indeed, the invocation of popular sovereignty and, later, state sovereignty, in the context of the antebellum debates over slavery, had less to do with the basis of republican government than it did with the question of who exercised what specific power within the federal constitutional structure. To some extent the use of "popular sovereignty" by northern Democrats like Stephen A. Douglas gave the term the added weight it carried, just as the doctrine of state sovereignty would continue to be burdened by its association with the arguments for nullification and secession. Moreover, the association that developed between vigilante action and the doctrine of popular sovereignty tended to discredit "the people" as a legitimate basis of power, even as that doctrine remained the basis of republican institutions. Thus, by the end of the nineteenth-century, a more conservative version of popular sovereignty constrained both the practical political choices and the theoretical basis for action that popular sovereignty had implicitly made possible earlier in the country's history.

As popular government, majoritarianism, and democracy developed political meaning in the course of the nineteenth century, a natural connection emerged with vigilantism. Nineteenth-century citizens, more than those of the twentieth, asserted a closer relationship between the people and their government, including a greater expectation of political accountability and responsiveness. According to historian William C.

---

12. Arthur Bestor, in a now classic article, made this point in describing the "configurative" role that the federal constitution played in the events leading up to the Civil War. See Bestor, "The American Civil War as a Constitutional Crisis," *American Historical Review*, LXIX (1964), 327-352.

Culberson, they "accepted more completely...the concept that
government is the servant of the people, subject to their
immediate control," and that the people had a "right to shortcut
government and overrule officials."[13] Scholars studying violence
in America have identified a positive or constructive aspect to
nineteenth-century vigilantism: it sought to buttress weak institutions and establish law and order.[14] In one view, vigilantism was
"a communal desire and willingness to enforce existing law or
to precipitate a new 'necessary and proper' order by popular
rule, in order to meet social exigencies."[15]

The American practice of using vigilance committees sometimes originated in settings that were not frontiers and that faced
crises unrelated to the problem of frontier violence. These early
committees, as well as later ones, drew on the long-standing
American habit of vigilance: being watchful in regard to the
condition of the governed and the welfare of the nation. Such
vigilance on the part of the people, implied in American
republicanism, underlay the strength of the militia concept of
citizen soldiers and the claims to the right to bear arms. Not
surprisingly, some of the earliest vigilance committees were
composed of leaders of the community.[16] Only in the 1840s and
1850s would the doctrine of citizen vigilance merge with the
South Carolina regulator tradition resulting in the association

---

13. William C. Culberson, *Vigilantism: Political History of Private Power in America*
(New York, 1990), 3-4.
14. Richard Maxwell Brown, *Strain of Violence: Historical Studies of American
Violence and Vigilantism* (New York, 1975). Brown has located the origin of American
vigilantism in the violent activities of the South Carolina Regulators of 1767-1769.
This two-year extralegal movement sought to suppress frontier violence in the
South Carolina back country and initiated an American tradition. Although
eighteenth-century London had its "regulators" and Europe experienced some
similar episodes, for Brown the tradition of American vigilantism was "indigenous"
since it possessed the unique characteristics of regular (though illegal) organization
and existence for a definite (though possibly short) period of time. See Brown,
Strain of Violence, 96-98, and Brown, *The South Carolina Regulators* (Cambridge, Mass.,
1963).
15. Culberson, *Vigilantism*, 11.
16. *Ibid.*, 19; Brown, *Strain of Violence*, 114. For example, during the War of
1812, a Virginia Committee of Vigilance organized by the leading men of
Richmond and headed by Chief Justice John Marshall had as its purpose the
defense of the region from possible British attack. See "The Vigilance Committee:
Richmond during the War of 1812," *Virginia Magazine of History and Biography,* VII
(1899-1900), 225-241.

of vigilance committees with the control of frontier crime and violence.[17] Given the prevalence of guns on the frontier, this combination generated a good deal of western vigilantism. But as San Francisco's experience in the 1850s demonstrates, a frontier setting was unnecessary to produce two of the largest vigilance movements in American history.

Popular Sovereignty and State Constitutional Conventions

Americans in California agitated to establish their own civil government before the end of military hostilities between Mexico and the United States. Many were impatient by the time the American military governor of California, Bennett Riley, called for a constitutional convention in 1849 to establish "a more perfect political organization" and one "fully authorized by law." The convention's president, Robert Semple, also underscored the need for constitutional government by telling the delegates that they were engaged in "the preliminary movement for the organization of a civil government, and the establishment of social institutions.[18]

When Elisha Crosby, lawyer and delegate to the convention, looked back on conditions before the establishment of state government, he contended that

Every man carried his code of laws on his hip and administered it according to his own pleasure. There was no safety of life or property [and] so far as the intervention of law was concerned there was no police. Spanish law was in operation here then and the only way it could be enforced was through the Military Governor and the Prefects and Alcaldes holding office under him. It was an unknown system to our people and we were absolutely in a state of chaos, society was entirely unorganized....[19]

Crosby's memoirs reflected his desire to establish a familiar government based on common law. His views also captured the

---

17. Brown, *Strain of Violence*, 115.

18. William Henry Ellison, *A Self-Governing Dominion: California, 1849–1860* (Berkeley, 1950), 1-21; Neal Harlow, *California Conquered: War and Peace on the Pacific, 1849–1850* (Berkeley, 1982), 317-337; J. Ross Browne, *Report of the Debates in the Convention of California on the Formation of the State Constitution in September and October, 1849* (Washington, D.C., 1850), 5, 18.

19. Elisha Oscar Crosby, *Memoirs of Elisha Oscar Crosby: Reminiscences of California and Guatemala from 1849 to 1864*, edited by Charles A. Barker (San Marino, 1945), 42.

unwillingness, if not inability, of Anglo-American lawyers to understand the civil law-based Mexican-California law and legal institutions in operation before they arrived in California.[20] Failing to comprehend law rooted in a different legal tradition or misinterpreting what they did see, common law-trained lawyers, like Crosby, emphasized the need to create institutions of government and law that were like those in "the states." The Mexican-California system—characterized by a conciliatory, communal, and paternalistic approach to dispute resolution (lacking juries, clear winners and losers, and effective judgments)— seemed to them like an absence of justice. They wanted an adversarial, jury-based system that reflected their own concepts of legal certainty and predictability.

Despite the desire for an American-style civil government, some Anglo-Californians had doubts about proceeding without congressional approval. Congress, however, hesitated to upset the delicate balance between free and slave states. Military governor Riley justified the call for a convention on the grounds that since "Congress has failed to organize a new Territorial government, it becomes our imperative duty to take some active measures to provide for the existing wants of the country." The convention was to meet and "frame a State constitution or a Territorial organization, to be submitted to the people for their ratification," and then seek congressional approval.[21] Riley's plan did not meet with universal favor: San Francisco had already begun to organize a constitutional convention on the grounds that the people had a right to establish a government for their protection.[22] Eventually, the collective interest in securing a government overcame differences, and Riley's plan formed the basis for the convention that met in Monterey.

As the San Francisco movement suggested, there was broad agreement that the frame of government drew its legitimacy from the people and by implication required popular ratification. Riley's proclamation had called for ratification and the delegates

20. On the inability of Anglo-Americans to understand the indigenous California legal system, see David J. Langum, *Law and Community on the Mexican California Frontier: Anglo-American Expatriates and the Clash of Legal Traditions, 1821–1846* (Norman, 1987), 131-152.

21. Browne, *California Debates*, 3.

22. Ellison, *Self-Governing Dominion*, 24.

who assembled in Monterey clearly agreed. Indeed, the principle of popular sovereignty was expressly vindicated, and some proposed provisions for the new constitution came under criticism because they seemed incompatible with that principle. Early in the convention one delegate sought to place a provision in the bill of rights that proclaimed:

As constitutions are the instruments by which the powers of the people are delegated to their representatives, they ought to be construed strictly, and all powers, not expressly granted, should be taken to be reserved.[23]

Other delegates objected that this statement was unnecessary. It mistook the nature of state constitutions in which, by definition, all powers not granted were implicitly reserved to the people. Numerous delegates distinguished between the federal constitution, which represented a finite delegation of power from the sovereign authority of the people, and a state constitution, which represented plenary powers except as expressly limited, or which was, as one delegate put it, a "constitution of restrictions." Another delegate explained that the state legislature, "under the specified restrictions imposed upon it by the people themselves, is a direct emanation from the people."[24] Ultimately, the convention rejected the proposed language because it seemed obvious and was already covered in an earlier section of the state bill of rights: "all power is inherent in the people."[25] The defeated delegate persisted, and late in the convention introduced a provision with a similar objective, but it was rejected. As one delegate noted, popular sovereignty was "the fundamental principle" of "republican government" and the people "need hardly be reminded that they possess this power."[26]

The convention corollary to popular sovereignty was, of course, popular ratification of the constitution before it became fundamental law. This principle was likewise largely assumed by the delegates, although it prompted explicit discussion when some feared that the convention might take actions bypassing

---

23. Browne, *California Debates*, 51.
24. *Ibid.*, 52, 53.
25. *Ibid.*, 52.
26. *Ibid.*, 308-334.

the people. This occurred when a delegate proposed a resolution seeking the election of a three-person board to draft a code of laws that would be submitted to the legislature at its first session. The proposal triggered a debate over whether the convention had such authority. While many delegates wanted to facilitate the organization of California's government, they shared the reservations expressed by a fellow delegate:

If I understand the directions under which we come here, all our actions must be submitted to the people. I apprehend this resolution is not to go into the Constitution, nor is it to be inserted in the schedule. If so, I think it is clear and positive that it forms no part of our duty, and that we have no right to pass such a resolution.... If we deny that principle, I do not think we have a right to come here at all.[27]

The convention agreed and decided it lacked the power to establish such a committee.

The delegates were clear about their objectives as a constitutional convention even as they inflated their rightful claims for attention. The purpose of a constitution, stated one representative, was to "construct organization and form out of chaos" and "produce a good fundamental system of laws." Another declared that the delegates were "a new people, creating from chaos a government; left free as air to select what is good, from all republican forms of government." The essence of their "most solemn of trusts" was to secure the state's "prosperity and happiness." Their self-conscious charge as constitution-makers was to organize civil government and establish social institutions through fundamental law. "The object of a constitution," as still another delegate put it, was "to impose restrictions on the legislature, to form a state, and to provide a fundamental system of laws within its prescribed limits."[28]

Given such a momentous mandate, many delegates assumed their work would come under close examination. The "eyes not only of our sister and parent states are upon us, but the eyes of all Europe are now directed toward California," announced the convention president whose words were echoed by a delegate reminding those present that what they accomplished would be

27. *Ibid.*, 301.
28. *Ibid.*, 23, 27, 116, 184.

subjected to "the scrutiny of all the civilized nations of the earth."[29]

Though primarily concerned about the creation of the first organic law of a Pacific state, the delegates were also deeply interested in how that fundamental law, if ratified by the people, might be changed. At issue in the debate over the appropriate mechanism was the fear of instability versus a wish for a greater expression of popular sovereignty. The committee on constitutional revision originally proposed that amendments could be submitted to the people after two successive votes of the legislature (the first a simple majority and the second a two-thirds majority). One delegate protested that both votes of the legislature should be by a simple majority. To require otherwise, he argued, would be undemocratic and unrepublican. If a majority of the people were "dissatisfied with their constitution, let them, as they may deem fit, alter and amend it."[30] Many delegates agreed that if a simple majority of the people could create a constitution, a simple majority of them had the right to change the fundamental law.

But other delegates responded that a distinction should be made between how one changed ordinary law (statutes) and fundamental law (a constitution). Statutes, they argued, appropriately reflected "the will of the people" in the legislature to "make and unmake laws," but giving the legislature, which was "the mere transient majority of the people," the power to change the constitution would "greatly militate against the permanent prosperity of the people." The result, they predicted, would be "political excitement" running "wild" that would soon vindicate the need for the two-thirds rule. "[I]n amending the fundamental law of the land," they cautioned, "men should return to their sober second thought" and not put the constitution "at the mercy of the dominant political party of the state."[31] Despite such protests, the convention dropped the two-thirds voting requirement.

A similar example of the fears and concerns over popular sovereignty occurred in the Maryland constitutional convention

29. *Ibid.*, 18, 141.
30. *Ibid.*, 355.
31. *Ibid.*, 357-358.

of 1850–1851 that met just before San Francisco organized its first vigilance committee. There is no evidence that the constitution makers in Annapolis or the vigilantes of San Francisco took notice of one another, but both groups wrestled with the issue of legitimate powers and inalienable rights, with one group seeking to constrain and the other seeking to exercise popular sovereignty.

When the Maryland convention began discussing a bill of rights, one delegate proposed language acknowledging that the people "have at all times the inalienable right to alter, reform, or abolish their form of government, in such manner as they may think expedient." This declaration of popular sovereignty stimulated a long and vigorous debate during which delegates asked, as did one conservative Whig, whether "under any sudden impulse...the people might rise and by violence effect a change in the existing government?" After a thoughtful discussion, the convention delegates concluded that the stability and safety inherent in existing governmental structures precluded the need to add any expression to the constitution indicating that "the people" had rights that superseded constitutional procedures. This decision, as one delegate observed, reflected the fear of "any self-constituted body of men choosing to call themselves 'the people,' assuming the power to subvert, when...they please, the whole social and political fabric."[32] The additional language that had been suggested was considered inflammatory, but that language not only echoed the Declaration of Independence, but also had been a standard provision in most bills of rights in the first American state constitutions of the eighteenth century.[33]

The debates over the implications of popular sovereignty in California and Maryland, not to mention at other constitutional conventions of the day, raised the question of how to integrate the right of revolution into American constitutional thought and governmental form. Unable to deny the right of revolution as a legitimate and logical extension of popular sovereignty, nineteenth-century constitution-makers differed in how they described that right. The conventions in California and Maryland illustrated the range of positions and thought, and the

32. *Debates and Proceedings of the Maryland Reform Convention to Revise the State Constitution* (2 vols., Annapolis, 1851), I, 143.
33. Adams, *First American Constitutions*, 129-149.

more expansive understandings of popular sovereignty were hardly lost on the leaders and supporters of California's vigilance committees of the 1850s.

Popular Sovereignty and Vigilantism

Attitudes toward popular sovereignty did not necessarily dictate reactions to vigilantism. Put another way, not all vigilantes embraced a shared view of popular sovereignty. Still, those who accepted the more expansive aspects of that doctrine were more inclined to support vigilantism because they accepted the underlying rationale for extralegal action, although such a connection was not inevitable. Indeed, most of those who became the leaders of San Francisco's 1856 vigilance committee were conservatives who shied away from the destabilizing implications of popular forces reforming government and only later adopted an expansive theory of popular sovereignty as a justification for vigilantism.[34] These men—characterized by Josiah Royce as participants in a "Business Man's Revolution"—presented the irony of conservatives invoking constitutional theory to justify revolution.[35] Their control of the movement convinced them that the right of revolution could be exercised safely. In the mid-1850s, however, those who held a more expansive view of popular sovereignty tended to be the supporters of vigilantism.

This connection between popular sovereignty and vigilantism has been suggested by others, including Lawrence Friedman and Richard Maxwell Brown who have described a tilt in nineteenth-century criminal law toward crime control rather than due process.[36] Brown, in particular, has argued that lawyers in the late nineteenth and early twentieth century viewed justice

34. On the vigilante movements in San Francisco generally, see Robert M. Senkewicz, *Vigilantes in Gold Rush San Francisco* (Stanford, Calif., 1985); Kevin J. Mullen, *Let Justice Be Done: Crime and Politics in Early San Francisco* (Reno, 1989); Mary Floyd Williams, *History of the San Francisco Committee of Vigilance of 1851* (Berkeley, 1921); and Hubert H. Bancroft, *Popular Tribunals* (2 vols., San Francisco, 1887). Senkewicz provides a bibliographical essay on much of the San Francisco vigilance literature. *Vigilantes*, 203-231.

35. Josiah Royce, *California, from the Conquest in 1846 to the Second Vigilance Committee in San Francisco: A Study of American Character* (Boston, 1886), 346.

36. Richard Maxwell Brown, "Legal and Behavioral Perspectives on American Vigilantism," in Donald Fleming and Bernard Bailyn, eds., *Law in American History* (Boston, 1971), 95-144; Lawrence M. Friedman, "State Constitutions and Criminal Justice in the Late Nineteenth Century," *Albany Law Review*, LIII (1989), 265-281.

"as a continuum," with one end consisting of "due process legality" and the other of "crime repression extralegality."[37] Although lawyers supported the legal system, when it came to criminal activity they were more concerned with eliminating crime than observing due process. Consequently, they could support and even participate in extralegal activities when they felt there were weaknesses in the criminal justice system. For Brown, the legal community's involvement with vigilantism came only after a rational appraisal of the existing system of justice. Popular sovereignty played a role in their decision, he acknowledges, but it did not directly prompt their behavior. Closer examination of the evidence, however, suggests that popular sovereignty, rather than being one of a number of rationales for vigilantism, was the principal rationale for extralegal activities. The reason that many lawyers supported the vigilantes was because such a position found corroboration within the American constitutional tradition.

The constitutional contours of popular sovereignty by the mid-nineteenth century are illustrated in the positive, negative, and ambivalent reactions of lawyers to San Francisco vigilantism. Lawyers who sympathized with the 1851 and 1856 committees emphasized their concerns about the present state of affairs, thereby offering indirect evidence of the theoretical basis of their support for the extralegal activities. The perception of such lawyers formed the basis for action that paralleled the constitutional right to reform or even abolish government when it proved inimical to the public welfare. Lawyers who opposed vigilantism not only denied that the case for revolution had been made but also stressed the destabilizing potential of such popular action. The emphasis on this latter concern echoed worries expressed at nineteenth-century constitutional conventions over the implications of popular sovereignty and constitutional revision. Moreover, opposition to vigilantism also frequently reflected personal conservatism or a sense of duty rather than a rejection of the theoretical principles invoked by the vigilantes.

For some San Francisco lawyers, the presence of courts and government automatically eliminated any justification for the 1851 and 1856 vigilance movements. Moreover, the movements

---

37. Brown, "Legal and Behavioral Perspectives," 131.

posed an unacceptable challenge to order and opened the door to the possibility of mob control. If changes in the established order were necessary, they should be achieved within the existing legal framework. To recognize extralegal movements as legitimate was to court revolution by signaling that any group of "the people" could decide when revolutionary power could be exercised.

Those lawyers who sympathized with the vigilance movements accepted the practical consequences of popular sovereignty. For them, the right of popular action was a real option, not just a theory underlying the doctrine of popular sovereignty. If the established institutions in San Francisco were incapable of responding to the needs of the community, then resort to them to bring about changes was a futile and meaningless gesture. Under such circumstances, people's use of extralegal force to accomplish that which the existing government was designed to do, but temporarily unable to achieve, was justified.[38] For these lawyers, support for the vigilance movements seemed an extraordinary, but entirely defensible, choice, the more so because the movements were animated by public-spirited motives and led by leading members of the community.

Two local observers described to out-of-town correspondents the composition of San Francisco's vigilance committee of 1856 and the attitude of the legal community to that committee. According to William Norris, "most of the members of the bar took the unpopular side of law and order" and were being roundly castigated by the pro-vigilance newspaper, the *Bulletin*. He claimed objectivity for his assessment on the ground that his sympathies were with the committee, although "not identifying myself with it." A rather different view came from Thomas Larkin, one of the oldest and most successful merchants in California, who wrote a southern California friend: "there is much talk for and against the Committee," but a majority of the merchants were members and "half the best lawyers" supported the vigilantes.[39] The observers differed about the degree of support from the legal community but agreed that a significant number of lawyers,

38. *Ibid.*, 95-144.
39. William Norris to Montgomery Blair, Jan. 19, 1859, box 5, Blair Family Papers, Library of Congress; Thomas O. Larkin to Abel Stearns, May 31, 1856, box 40, Abel Stearns Papers, Huntington Library.

covertly if not openly, sympathized with the 1856 committee. Indeed, the personal papers of lawyers who practiced in San Francisco amply bear this out and also indicate that lawyers held pro-vigilante views even before the appearance of San Francisco's first major vigilance committee in 1851.

Support for Vigilance Activities

As early as 1849, a lawyer who became the acknowledged leader of the California bar sided with an extralegal movement to control crime. Hall McAllister became a "captain" in a group created to suppress a criminal element called the "Hounds."[40] After the vigilantes rounded up some of the chief offenders, they convened a meeting of "all the citizens who organized a "court." McAllister served as one of three prosecutors, who tried cases before three judges and a jury. After proceedings that "occupied many days," the defendants were convicted "according to the ordinary legal form."[41] Although some wished to hang the convicted Hounds, the extralegal group decided to banish them from San Francisco under penalty of death if they returned.

San Francisco's 1851 vigilance committee also found support among the legal community. In August 1851 Henry Haight, a San Francisco lawyer and graduate of Yale who became governor of California in 1867, wrote to his father in Missouri about the recent hangings carried out by the vigilance committee. Like McAllister, Haight emphasized the orderliness of the committee's activities. He also justified its existence because of governmental defects, namely the "inefficiency of the Courts, the imperfections of the laws and the corruption of public officers" that had "rendered the punishment of crime very uncertain and infrequent."[42]

Other lawyers were even more outspoken in their justification if not support for the vigilantes. John McCrackan wrote

40. For information on McAllister's life and career, see Oscar T. Shuck, *History of the Bench and Bar in California* (Los Angeles, 1901), 417; and Thomas Gamble, "The McAllisters, 1758–1888," articles printed in the *Savannah Morning News*, Oct. 5, Nov. 23 and 30, Dec. 14 and 28, 1930, Jan. 4, 11, and 25, 1931, and available in the Bancroft Library.

41. "Statement of Hall McAllister," 15, Vigilance Committee Miscellany, 1877, Bancroft Library.

42. Henry H. Haight to Samuel Haight, Aug. 29, 1851, Henry H. Haight Papers, Huntington Library.

detailed letters to his family in New Haven, Connecticut, between 1849 and 1853 describing his legal practice in San Francisco and the vagaries of the California justice system. In 1850 in a statement reflecting the city's fear of arson, he asserted: "If a person should be caught firing a building, he would be hung, without the least ceremony...." Nine months later the state of society and the level of crime had become "very bad."[43] This observation came a month after he had been mugged, an experience that inclined him to see the value of the 1851 committee. That committee, he told his sister Mary, was "composed of our first citizens, and men of wealth and standing." He then cited deficiencies in the punishment of crime, denying that a hanging by the committee was "cold blooded murder" and arguing that "none but the most severe punishment would terrify" the criminal element in the city.[44] Nonetheless, he acknowledged a tension between his support for the committee and a need to remain aloof from their actions. "[A]s the sworn defender and supporter of the law," he wrote another sister, Lottie, "I am precluded from acting a prominent part in the drama[;] I still I confess to a strong sympathy with the people, and feel inclined to justify their acts." Were he not a lawyer, however, he confessed to feeling "strongly enough to act with the most determined." He regretted that the committee had thus far executed only a minor offender, but even so it had provided a needed "terrible example." A month later he predicted that the "Law and Order" party opposing the vigilance movement would soon "see the folly" in combating "the favorable influence that is now being felt."[45] Indeed, his convictions had now reached the point that when a women's church group created a silk banner in honor of the committee, he and his law partner presented it to a crowd of three hundred vigilantes amid speeches and cheers. "A most happy affair," he recalled, noting as well that such public support of the committee benefitted his law practice, "even in these dull times."[46]

The strongest test of the San Francisco legal community's

43. John McCrackan to Lottie McCrackan, May 30, 1850, and Feb. 7, 1851, John McCrackan Papers, Bancroft Library.
44. John McCrackan to Mary McCrackan, June 12, 1851, *ibid.*
45. McCrackan to Lottie McCrackan, July 10, 1851, *ibid.*
46. McCrackan to his family, July 29 and Aug. 31, 1851, *ibid.*

attitude toward vigilantism came with the events of 1856. The
1856 committee—the largest and most influential vigilante group
in American history—triggered the strongest opposition and
generated federal court cases challenging its legitimacy. These
trials, involving San Francisco's resident federal judges Matthew
McAllister and Ogden Hoffman, best illustrate the tensions and
ambivalence lawyers felt about vigilantism. Opponents deliberately sought to involve McAllister and Hoffman as a means of
pitting federal authority against the vigilance committee, though
in fact, the committee's very existence challenged federal
authority.

As in 1851, lawyers who supported the vigilantes stressed
the conditions that gave rise to the movement and denied that
it had produced anarchy. James Crockett, later to sit on the
California supreme court, believed the committee was a response
to the "degraded classes" of people who had "caused so much
crime and vice." The trials were "conducted with the greatest
order and coolness," and he predicted that the vigilantes would
"purify the state thoroughly."[47]

Crockett soon found himself representing two committee
members accused of seizing weapons being transported to the
state militia. The trial, he told his wife, was an effort by enemies
of the committee to prompt a confrontation with the federal
government. Thus far, the vigilantes were acting "with great
forbearance," but he predicted "a revolution throughout the
State" if the federal government intervened. "Nine tenths of the
people will sustain the committee, even though it results in an
entire repudiation of the authority of the General government."
The "frivolous charges," he declared, were the result of "a few
restless and hot-brained men."[48]

Despite such bold statements, Crockett harbored the ambivalence common among lawyers who expressed sympathy for
the committee. He assured his worried wife that he was not a
member of the vigilance committee, but only its legal advocate,

47. Joseph B. Crockett to his wife, May 19, 1856, Joseph Bryant Crockett
Papers, Bancroft Library.
48. Crocket to his wife, Sept. 4, 1856, *ibid.* This episode and the federal
prosecution is well documented by John D. Gordan III, *Authorized by No Law: The
San Francisco Committee of Vigilance of 1856 and the United States Circuit Court for the
Districts of California* (Pasadena and San Francisco, 1987).

and he had advised his clients "to disband at once and restore peace." Still, he conceded that he had not "denounced and abused them, as some others have, because, however much they may have erred, I am satisfied they have acted from honest and upright motives." He described his own behavior as "neutral" and his role that of "a mediator and peacemaker" who was "on the most friendly terms with both sides." Crockett, as had John McCrackan in 1851, experienced the professional advantages of a sympathetic posture toward the committee. When the two committee members whom he was defending were acquitted, he noted that "business has largely increased and we are getting new clients daily, from the moderate and conservative course I have taken."[49] That Crockett could describe his actions as "conservative" reveals much about the range of reactions from other members of the bar.

An even more outspoken supporter of the 1856 vigilance committee belonged to San Francisco's leading law firm, Halleck, Peachy, and Billings. Frederick Billings delivered a speech defending the committee at the funeral of James King of William, the muckraking newspaperman whose murder proved the catalyst for the 1856 uprising. Those who "would call our revolutionary struggle a mob," declared Billings, deserve "the supreme contempt of every honest and high minded man in the state.... We can and do most fully endorse the actions and the measures of the vigilance committee of San Francisco."[50] With a member of one of the most respected legal firms taking such a public stand, it was not surprising that many other lawyers supported the committee, even if only in private.[51]

---

49. Crockett to his wife, Sept. 4 and 19, 1856, Crockett Papers.

50. Frederick Billings speech on the death of James King of William, p. 10, folder 695, box 7, Halleck, Peachy and Billings Papers, Bancroft Library. Henry Eno, another lawyer and eventual county judge for Calaveras and later Alpine counties, not only strongly supported the committee, but also urged that it take even more drastic action. Henry Eno to William Eno, Oct. 3, 1856, in W. Turrentine Jackson, ed., *Twenty Years on the Pacific Slope: Letters of Henry Eno from California and Nevada. 1848-1871* (New Haven, 1965), 125.

51. Lawyers not only supported the vigilante activities in 1856, but some of them also found the basis for invoking the constitutional right of revolution through the mechanism of the vigilance committee compelling, even after the passage of considerable time. See Annis Merrill, "Statement of Recollections on Early Days of San Francisco" (1878); William R. Wheaton, "Statement of Facts on Early California History" (1878), dictations for the Bancroft Library, Bancroft Library.

The extent of support for the 1856 committee can be seen in concerns expressed by a special agent for the U.S. Attorney General. Sent to San Francisco by Attorney General Caleb Cushing to deal with Mexican private land claims, the agent arrived as the vigilantes were organizing. Without prompt aid from the federal government, wrote Cushing, "there will not be left the shadow of constitutional authority within the state." Moreover, many federal officials were "giving open encouragement to the mob."[52] These observations and other complaints led Cushing's successor, Jeremiah S. Black, to remove the local U.S. district attorney for not being aggressive enough in his prosecution of the vigilantes accused of seizing weapons. The removed attorney conceded that he taken a more neutral approach because of a desire to "remove the impression created by the Vigilance Committee that the prosecution originated in angry party spirit and was without a shred of law or reason."[53]

Opposition to Vigilance Activities

As suggested earlier, those lawyers who opposed the vigilance committees did so out of a deep fear of anarchy. At the same time, however, they frequently expressed sympathy with vigilantes' objectives. William Shaw was one such person. After studying law in Cambridge, Massachusetts, and Ithaca, New York, and then practicing his profession in New York City, he left for California in 1849, serving briefly as a district attorney for San Francisco. Thirty years after the vigilante activities of 1856, he recalled that he had not only refused to join the committee but also "was earnestly and sincerely opposed to it from its start to its ending." Though he acknowledged that his "sympathies were more enlisted with them than I cared to express" and that he admired "the readiness of the people to suppress lawless outrages," he lamented the need to act out of anger.[54] Lawyer Peter Burnett, California's first civil governor, also recalled his opposi-

---

52. Lewis Worcester to Caleb Cushing, July 4, 1856, box 9, Correspondence on California Land Claims, Department of Justice, Record Group 60, National Archives, Washington, D.C.

53. William Blanding to Jeremiah S. Black, July 3 and 20, 1857, Attorney General's Letters Received, California, 1846–1870, ibid.

54. William J. Shaw, "Administration of Justice in the Early Days" (1886), 63, dictation for Hubert H. Bancroft, Bancroft Library.

tion to the 1856 committee on "the ground of principle": the movement was an "incipient rebellion and a fatal precedent." Still, he recognized that "the good people of San Francisco had great reason [not] to be satisfied with the administration of criminal justice."[55]

Judges, on the other hand, frequently took public stands against the extralegal committees, while privately harboring no approval or admiration for the vigilantes' goals. Their positions were in part a result of their being personally attacked or having the institutions they personified come under perceived dishonor, but what ultimately separated them from their fellow lawyers who privately or publicly supported the vigilantes was their fear that extralegal actions would cause society to break down entirely. In 1851 Ogden Hoffman, the federal district court judge for northern California, joined with several other San Francisco lawyers to wage a vigorous campaign on behalf of "the Supremacy of the Constitution and the Laws of [the] country."[56] His opposition to both the 1851 and 1856 committees derived from his strong commitment to maintaining order through institutions—values he shared in common with other conservative Whigs. During the events of 1856, a vigilante recalled Hoffman as "one of the most bitter opponents of the Vigilance Committee."[57]

Hoffman was hardly alone. Among the most strident opponents of the 1856 committee was an associate justice of the California supreme court, David Terry, who described the vigilantes as "a set of d___d pork-merchants."[58] Equally hostile was Matthew Hall McAllister, a special federal circuit judge for California, who presided over the trial of several 1856 committee members indicted for seizing the arms destined for the state

55. Oscar L. Shafter to his father, April 14, 1856, in Oscar L. Shafter, *Life, Diary, and Letters of Oscar L. Shafter,* edited by Flora Haines Loughead (San Francisco, 1915), 181; Peter H. Burnett, *Recollections and Opinions of an old Pioneer* (New York, 1880), 398.

56. San Francisco *Alta California,* March 6, 1851.

57. Thomas G. Cary, "The Vigilance Committee of San Francisco, 1856," Thomas G. Cary Notebooks, vol. 3, Library of Congress; Daniel Walker Howe, *The Political Culture of the American Whigs* (Chicago, 1979), 123-149, 181; *Gallagher* v. *"Yankee,"* 9 F.Case 1091 (D.C.N.D.Cal. 1859).

58. William Tecumseh Sherman, *Memoirs of General William T. Sherman* (2 vols., New York, 1875), I, 130.

militia. Those men were "authorized by no law," declared McAllister. William Tecumseh Sherman, a major-general in the state militia in 1856, shared these sentiments. While not a lawyer, he agreed with those judges appalled by the disrespect for institutions and threat to social stability. As a professionally trained soldier, he saw the movement as undermining his military authority to maintain order. To Sherman the 1856 committee was "an irresponsible organization claiming to be armed with absolute power by the people." It constituted "a personal as well as public threat" by encouraging "anarchy" and "the turbulent tendencies in democratic society." He later recalled that it had the support of "nearly all the best people," but he lamented that vigilantism had become "a fixed institution, and part of the common law of California." For Sherman, this was the ultimate regrettable legacy—one giving "great stimulus" to the "dangerous principle" that "would at any time justify the mob in seizing all the power of government." The principle was especially dangerous because future vigilance committees might "be composed of the worst, instead of the best, elements of a community."[59] Sherman had been prepared to use force to suppress the 1856 committee, but he found himself frustrated by the indecision of superior officers and the unwillingness of Washington to back such resistance with federal troops.

What Sherman, the judges, and other opponents of vigilantism feared most was the danger for extralegal action. Consequently, they sought to limit such action justified by the doctrine of popular sovereignty to the most dire circumstances in which unequivocal evidence existed that inalienable rights of citizens had been usurped. Many, like the future California Supreme Court Justice Oscar Shafter, found it "somewhat difficult to conceive a case where the doctrine of Revolution can have play."[60] A similar attitude echoed in Hoffman's opinion in *Gallagher* v. *The "Yankee*," a case brought by a victim of the 1856 committee who had been transported to Hawaii. According to Hoffman,

---

59. Sherman to Henry S. Turner, May 18, 1856, in Dwight L. Clarke, *William Tecumseh Sherman: Gold Rush Banker* (San Francisco, 1969), 213; Charles Royster, *The Destructive War: William Tecumseh Sherman, Stonewall Jackson, and the Americans* (New York, 1991), 89, 119-120, 137; Sherman, *Memoirs*, 119, 131.

60. Shafter, *Life, Diary, and Letters*, 181, 185.

So long as our country remains under the dominion of law, and so long as the great constitutional provisions which secure the citizen his life, liberty, and his property until deprived of them by due process of law...are prized by the American people, and are enforced by the courts, the deportation of a citizen to a foreign country in an American ship, commanded by an American master, in pursuance or execution of a sentence of an illegal and self-constituted body of men, must remain a marine tort of a most flagrant character.[61]

Similarly, for Judge McAllister, who heard the case on appeal, the critical issue was that the vigilantes were "a body of men authorized by no law, and who substituted their private judgments for the actions of those judicial tribunals to which the constitution and laws of their country had confided solely the distribution of justice."[62] This was precisely the point in dispute, for the vigilance committees most certainly rejected the idea that they were "authorized by no law." The principles on which they based their action were the natural right of self defense and especially the right of revolution that underlay the right of the people to reform their government at any time. The delegate who proposed language incorporating this idea into the Maryland constitution would have recognized this argument. So, too, would have most other constitution-makers in the nineteenth century. The real question is whether they would have agreed with the argument as a justification for the steps taken by the San Francisco committees or insisted, with opponents of the committees, that legitimate change could take place within the existing legal system.

This question resonated with the paradox inherent in *Luther v. Borden*, the United States Supreme Court's response in 1849 to the assertion that popular sovereignty justified the Dorr Rebellion in Rhode Island.[63] In rejecting that claim—that a group of people, even a majority, could place themselves in opposition to established state government—the court declared that the only remedy for disaffected persons was to work within the constraints of established law. The paradox was that the

---

61. *Gallagher* v. *"Yankee,"* 9 F.Case 1091 (D.C.N.D.Cal. 1859).
62. Quoted in Gordan, *Authorized by No Law*, 29.
63. *Luther* v. *Borden*, 48 U.S. 1 (1849).

existing system precluded the constitutional reforms long sought by Thomas Dorr's followers.

* * *

In the nineteenth century vigilantes and delegates to constitutional conventions shared a desire to reform government. For vigilantes, the goal was less to change the structure of government than to put better people into government. Delegates to constitutional conventions, on the other hand, focused primarily on changing the structure of government. Both groups, however, invoked the same fundamental right to justify their actions: popular sovereignty. In both contexts, the abstract doctrine of popular sovereignty could be formulated in ways and invoked for purposes that frequently made conservatives nervous. Delegates to constitutional conventions, such as those in California and Maryland, as well as the opponents of California vigilantism feared the danger to established order of extralegal activity. Their instincts were conservative in the true sense of the word—inclined to preserve existing institutions. A delegate to Ohio's constitutional convention reveled in the designation. He went so far as to declare "we are all conservatives," by which he meant that "no man, or any body of men in this country,...[is] willing that the law be violated—while the law exists."[64] The chief concern of such vigilante opponents as Hoffman, Terry, McAllister, and Sherman was the undermining of existing institutions. The judges stressed the responsibility imposed by their office on maintaining the legal system. As Terry told the members of the 1856 committee: "The difference between my position and yours is...that, being a judicial officer, it is my sworn duty to uphold the law." Sherman, a military officer, felt obligated by "the necessity of putting down this spirit of resistance to the Law."[65] How Americans—and particularly delegates to state constitutional conventions—felt about the invocation of extralegal means to attain change largely determined the role that popular sovereignty played in American political life. A delegate to California's constitutional convention of 1878–1879 expressed the

---

64. *Report of the Debates and Proceedings of the Convention for the Revision of the Constitution of the State of Ohio* (2 vols., Columbus, Oh., 1851), I, 686.

65. Gordan, *Authorized by No Law*, 33, 46.

continuing concern over the exercise of popular sovereignty when he described the powers of the convention.

We are representing the people, whose inherent rights are expressed through certain forms, imposed upon themselves by themselves. The people, with all these inherent rights, have found it necessary for their own safety to impose upon themselves rules which they cannot and will not violate....[66]

Another delegate to this convention reflected the same concern during debate over a provision in the bill of rights specifying the people's right to alter or reform their government. He sought to add the proviso that they could do so "only in accordance with previous established law," explaining that his proposed language sanctioned the right of revolution and thus placed in the constitution "the seeds of its own destruction."[67] His proviso was rejected, but it is revealing of the growing concern with instability that his proposed language was in the 1849 constitution and had provoked no comment during the convention when it was drafted.

Even more revealing of concern was the change incorporated into the 1878–1879 constitution for amending that document. The convention eliminated the old requirement of two successive simple majority votes by the legislature before a proposed amendment would be submitted to the people for ratification. Now, a single legislative vote was required, but it would take a two-thirds majority to approve the amendment. Significantly, when a delegate suggested requiring a simple majority vote, he ran into strong opposition on the grounds that such a change would make the constitution too susceptible to political majorities. Even the outspoken delegate representing the radical Workingman's party worried that "the legislature, by a majority vote, may very frequently submit propositions to the people under a temporary impulse; but if it requires a two-thirds vote, there will be more deliberation and care."[68] Convention

66. *Debates and Proceedings of the Constitutional Convention of the State of California, Convened at the City of Sacramento, Saturday, September 28, 1878* (3 vols., Sacramento, 1880–1881), III, 1221.

67. *Ibid.*, 1167.

68. *Ibid.*, 1277.

delegates spent less time debating the meaning of popular sovereignty than the procedures for revising the constitution.

By the end of the nineteenth century, the tradition of American vigilantism persisted, but it had lost much of its underlying justification.[69] Popular sovereignty continued into the twentieth century as an important political idea, but it no longer held the meaning that it did for nineteenth-century Americans. According to historian David Johnson, the demise of San Francisco vigilantism resulted from an acceptance of "the rule of *law* over the rule of *men*," a change that helped lead to "the modern state and its mechanisms of social control."[70] Thus, the process of developing a culture rooted in law inverted Jeffersonian notions of popular sovereignty that people and not forms (even of law) ought to control the direction of government. This more illusive meaning of popular sovereignty that envisioned the people occasionally retaking power into their own hands—articulated in the eighteenth century and enjoying a lively and legitimate life in state constitutional debates in the nineteenth century—is easily overlooked given the significance that the rule of law has today. To fully understand the American concept of popular rule, it is necessary to recapture the lost and very rich world of nineteenth-century state constitutionalism.

---

69. Brown, *Strain of Violence,* 144-179.
70. David A. Johnson, "Vigilance and the Law: The Moral Authority of Popular Justice in the Far West," *American Quarterly* XXXIII (1981), 562.

Crime and Punishment: Los Angeles County, 1850-1856

BY RONALD C. WOOLSEY

"Crime and Punishment" fittingly describes Los Angeles County in the early 1850s. Lawlessness was an important concern of the community during the formative years of statehood. More importantly, crime represented a loss of local control, ineffective government, and the inability of the community to establish a stable social order. This atmosphere of discontent with the legal system led to increased involvement by the local citizenry.

Public dissatisfaction was also an expression of Anglo prejudice. Many considered the Indian a primary reason for the community's plight. The belief that Indians were responsible for crime precipitated the use of severe legal measures against them. In many cases Indian treatment bordered on outright harassment.

Frontier justice in Los Angeles County involved more than citizen response to criminal activity. The courts and legislative bodies attempted to curb lawlessness. Increased prosecutions in court and the funding of a citizens' police force were specific responses to the problem of crime in Los Angeles. In addition, crime and citizen reaction forced government to re-examine its effectiveness in meeting the needs of the local populace. Educational reform and the internal improvement of county operation were specific measures designed to enhance the function of local government.

Criminal control was the important motivation behind any reform, either on the part of the government or the citizen. Thus, the friction within Los Angeles society not only stemmed from the criminal's presence, but from the methods needed for combating violence within the community.

The problem of crime in Los Angeles can first be traced to the varied economic and social changes that occurred in the early 1850s. It was a period of transition from a Mexican to a predominately Anglo-American community. More importantly, law enforcement and judicial procedures were affected by increasing violence in this changing society.

Between 1850 and 1852 American settlement in Los Angeles County rapidly increased. In 1850 the population totaled 3,530, including 1,598 whites and 336 Indians.' By 1852 the county's populace had dramatically increased to over 8,000. The white population had more than doubled to 3,991. The Indian community was even more significantly affected. Domesticated Indians accounted for over half the total population with an aggregate of 4,193.[2]

Natural migration accounted for only part of this population increase in Los Angeles County. In 1851 the county's boundaries were expanded to include the present county of San Bernardino.[3] The county lines extended to the Tehachapi Mountains, Death Valley, and also included the Mojave Desert.[4] This additional territory significantly altered the census figures and jurisdictional authority of the county.

The county's growth in the early years of the decade crystalized the importance of the Indian's role in the community. Indian manpower was an important factor in meeting the needs of a growing community and an increasing labor demand. Most Indians were employed as house or farm servants. Their willingness to work for low wages made them an important element in the domestic economy. Benjamin Wilson, who later became an Indian agent for the Southern District, observed:

> The common pay of Indian farm hands is from eight to ten dollars per month; and one dollar per day the highest in the towns—but few pay so much. No white man here, whether American, Sonoranian, or Californian, will work for such wages, nor anything like it.[5]

The growth of the population and territory of the county posed basic problems in the operation of local government, particularly in the area of law enforcement. The authority of the sheriff was frequently challenged. For example, during a six-week period in the summer of 1850, Sheriff G. Thompson Burrill was assaulted twice while attempting an arrest. In one instance a suspect refused to be taken to jail, and he then picked up two rocks and threatened to hit the officer while using "the most obscene language." A passerby helped Burrill arrest the belligerent.[6]

Law enforcement was generally unorganized and ineffective in dealing with local violence. This situation was in large part due to the lack of evening patrols. The local police were reluctant to investigate night crimes for fear of their own personal safety. For example, Los Angeles Marshall Alviron S. Beard responded to a brawl at a local bar after initially refusing to intervene in the matter. Beard then began to develop second thoughts about his sense of duty. He stated, "I started and after passing the Church I stopped for I did not like to go as far up that street by myself."[7]

The absence of effective law enforcement was duly noted in the local newspaper. The Los Angeles *Star* maintained that "the police must not relax any of the vigor with which they started out. A fatal result came very near being necessary last night solely for want of firmness at the outset."[8] The *Star* also noted that several murderers escaped arrest because of the lack of an effective night patrol. The newspaper cited a recommendation of a jury in a coroner's inquest that a night police be established "as a measure calculated to prevent the recurrence of similar crimes."[9]

The most frequent crimes brought to trial were assault and horse theft. In 1850 these two types of crimes comprised 58% of the total number of cases tried in Los Angeles.[10] The Indian, moreover, became the focal point of public indignation over the high crime rate. Indians were often accused of horse theft for lack of another suspect. Pío Pico filed a complaint of horses stolen "probably by Indians," although he presented no evidence to support his claim.[11]

Horse theft became such an alarming problem in the county that the Los Angeles Court of Sessions attempted to regulate horse branding procedures. In December 1851, the court delegated additional authority to outlying judges concerning the branding of cattle. The "judge of the plains" was to examine the brand to determine ownership. If the brand was not that of the present owner, a bill of sale had to be presented to verify ownership. If ownership could not be determined, the person whose brand the livestock bore could claim possession.[12]

In 1851 General Joshua Bean was given a military command to patrol the Cajon Pass and prevent Indian migration southward. The Los Angeles *Star* suggested that "the Indians find many ways to enter the valley besides the Cajon Pass, and they have taken horses over the mountains within a few miles of the Pass."[13]

Alcohol was often cited as the principal reason for the Indian's deterioration. One observer stated:

> Almost every other house is a grog-shop for Indians. They have, indeed, become sadly deteriorated, within the last two years; and it may be long, very long, before a sound public opinion will speak like the potent voice of the Mission Fathers.[14]

Yet, Indians were as much the recipients of violent activity as were the other segments of the community. Indian women were particularly vulnerable to assault and the local courts failed to impose adequate prosecution of their assailants. One Indian woman, Josefa, refused a proposition and was then attacked and beaten with a club. The court found the defendant guilty and fined him one dollar.[15] Another Indian woman, Rosa, was nearly drowned by her attacker. One witness testified:

> I heard the woman, Rosa, crying out and when looking up I saw Fernando Vacquites have Rosa in the water. He had his hand in her hair and was hitting her in the ribs and cursing her. Afterwards I saw him knock her down with his fist and then punch her with a stick about 18 inches long and 2 inches thick.[16]

The defendant, Fernando Vacquites, admitted that "it is all true that the witnesses have said with the exeception of striking with the stick."[17] The court dismissed the case and had Vacquites pay the court costs.

The judicial process not only neglected to protect Indian victims but furthermore, they imposed unwarranted verdicts against innocent Indians. For example, Judge White of San Gabriel overstepped his authority when he imprisoned an Indian who had committed no crime. The judge set bail at $5,000. The imprisoned Indian, Joaquín Machado, petitioned the Los Angeles Court of Sessions. He was eventually released after the court reprimanded White for misconduct in office.[18]

124

Indians were rarely protected under the California Penal Code and more often were the victims of American jurisprudence. In 1850 California enacted a severe Indian law that provided for the binding of Indians to labor contracts. A white man could give bond for the payment of the fine and costs of any Indian convicted before the justice of the peace. The Indian could then be required to work for the white man until the fine was paid.[19] This type of "indentured servitude" was implemented in Los Angeles during the early 1850s.

In 1850 Los Angeles passed a city ordinance that provided for the "hiring out" of Indians convicted of loitering, assaults, or disturbing the peace.[20] The law stipulated that if the chain gangs became overcrowded, the city could auction off Indians to the highest bidder.[21]

The crime of loitering was often interpreted by law enforcement officials in the most general terms, and Indians were arrested for no particular reason. For instance, Marshall A. S. Beard jailed José Antonio, an Indian, merely on general principles. Beard explained, "I found the within-named Indian at the jail and without asking any questions or without knowing cause, I put him in Jail."[22]

In the early 1850s the terms "Indian" and "crime" were synonymous. Most Los Angeles citizens argued that the Indian's presence in the community was the main cause of criminal activity. The Los Angeles *Star* proposed that a military garrison be established to insure the protection of the county against Indian raids. The newspaper suggested that at least "700 to 800 troops" be stationed in the vicinity.[23]

The county's frustration in coping with local violence managed to find expression in more "persuasive" terms. The *Star* hinted that in "the absence of an efficient police, our citizens must take measures to protect their property."[24] The extent of such measures was never fully articulated. Yet many Indians became the victims of various unsolved murders.

In February 1852, two Indians were found dead at a construction site. One of the victims was "stabbed and cut in various places." It was noted that "all inquiries were unsuccessful in ascertaining the perpetrators of the murder."[25] At Mission Viejo in August 1852, an Indian child was kidnapped while the parents were attending a local festival. A week later the infant was found drowned in a pond with "its throat cut."[26] Two months later the Tulare Indians presented a complaint to the Indian agent, stating that their white neighbors had encroached upon their grounds and had stolen "several of their children."[27]

Although the Indian was perceived as the cause of violence within the county, the basic reason for criminal activity appears to be the lack of judicial authority. The legal system was ineffective in prosecuting criminals. Of the twenty-three cases dealing with theft that occurred between June and November 1850, the Los Angeles Court of Sessions found fifteen defendants not guilty. Of the remaining eight cases, two defendants received fines of one dollar, and another suspect escaped from jail before a verdict could be reached.[28]

The crime of selling liquor to an Indian, the main reason why many citizens thought criminal activity so frequent, was cited only once by the court of sessions in the years 1850 to 1853. In that particular case, Charles Burrows was convicted of selling liquor to three Indians at his local bar. He was fined twenty cents for the violation.[29]

The legal system not only failed to impose stiff penalties for the convicted, but also failed to find anyone to convict. The number of actual crimes committed is difficult to determine. Yet, if one is to assume that growing public concern indicated an increase in crime, the same assumption should reveal an increase in the number of cases tried in court. The opposite is true.

Between 1850 and 1852 the number of cases tried by the court of sessions decreased significantly. In 1850 eighty-one cases were filed in the court. In 1851 the total number of cases fell to seventeen, and in the following year tallied only nineteen cases. Those figures are as follows:[30]

Crime	*No. of Cases:* 1850	1851	1852
Assault and Battery	32	4	3
Attempted Murder	3	4	7
Disturbing the Peace	7	0	0
False Imprisonment	0	1	0
Grand Larceny	15	5	1
Impersonation of an Officer	0	0	2
Indecent Exposure	1	0	0

Manslaughter	2	0	2
Murder	2	1	3
Petty Larceny	14	1	0
Rape	0	0	1
Selling Liquor to Indians	0	1	0
Wife Beating	1	0	0
Totals	77	17	19

The failure of the judicial process to prosecute effectively criminals was the result of many factors. The transition from Mexican to American rule created cultural obstacles that hampered effective court proceedings. Language barriers made it necessary for the court of sessions to appoint an interpreter. The first judge, Agustin Olvera, could not speak English and one of the justices of the peace could not speak Spanish.[31]

The lack of written law also contributed to judicial confusion. The scarcity of law books and formal court procedures posed problems in defining certain illegalities. In 1850 one merchant was charged with impersonating a justice of the peace. He attemped to have a dissatisfied customer arrested at his trading post. The court, however, exonerated him because no such law existed on the books.[32]

In addition, the absence of written law affected the performance of public officials. Doubt existed over the specific duties of those elected to public service. In April 1850, the county informed Governor Peter H. Burnett of the disorganized state of affairs in Los Angeles. The newly elected members of the county requested Burnett's advice on specific judicial and legislative responsibilities.[33]

In 1852 procedures in the local courts had deteriorated to an alarming degree. In March the district court annulled all criminal business taken by the court of sessions. This measure prompted the Los Angeles *Star* to remark:

> We understand that the decision of the District Court was not based on the want of a technical exactness in the proceedings of the inferior court, but from the fact that none of the most ordinary and necessary regulations of the law had been complied with. It is hoped that hereafter the Court of Sessions will pay more regard to the provisions of the Statutes of the State.[34]

The weakness of county government was best reflected by the absence of any permanent government structures. Most civic buildings were rented during the early 1850s. The first courthouse was a government building that existed during the Mexican period. The city rented this structure from Pío Pico, the last Mexican governor, who had used it as his residence.[35] In the following two years, the court was moved twice because of inadequate space or increased rent.[36]

The ineffectiveness of county operations was also evidenced by the poor sanitation conditions that existed in Los Angeles. One observer commented:

> No care was given to either the streets or sidewalks, and a daily evidence of this was the confusion in the neighborhood of John's shop, which, together with his yard, was one of the sights of the little town because the blacksmith had strewn the footway, and even part of the road, with all kinds of piled-up material; to say nothing of a lot of horses invariably waiting there to be shod.[37]

Crime was an important issue in Los Angeles County during the first three years of American control. The Indian was regarded as the principal cause of criminal activity. The county had experienced unusual growth in both population and geographic area, and the government's inability to meet the needs of this expanding community led to a growing sense of insecurity within the county. The weakness of government was evident in the poor operation of the police and the court system. A main reason for lawlessness, therefore, was the failure of judicial and law enforcement authorities to prosecute effectively the fugitive element within the county.

Public concern over lawlessness continued throughout the latter half of 1852 and into 1853. Local residents still considered the Indian a major cause of crime in the cummunity. Yet, public opinion seemingly intensified during this period as a result of a series of sensational crimes that occurred in the county.

In November 1852, General Joshua Bean, a prominent Indian fighter and local politician in San Gabriel, was fatally shot in his home following his return from a social function. Indians were immediately suspected of plotting the assasination. A town meeting was then arranged at the Los Angeles courthouse, and six suspects were promptly arrested.[38]

The murder of General Bean triggered renewed interest in finding a solution to the Indian problem. The first remedy discussed was to establish an Indian reservation in a remote part of the county. In January 1853, Benjamin D. Wilson, the Indian commissioner for the Southern District, proposed the development of a separate Indian community in the Tejon-San Gorgonio region.[39]

Attempts such as Wilson's proposal were not new to Los Angeles citizens. As early as March 1850, Thomas Butler King, a government surveyor, acknowledged the need "to collect the Indians together and to teach them in some degree the arts of civilization."[40] In December 1851, two reservations were established in southern California. This attempt, however, was a loosely organized venture that provided for little control of Indian affairs. Mounting hostility between white settlers and Indians necessitated the dispatching of a military unit in order to restore harmony in the area.[41]

Thus, the Wilson plan, coming only a few months after the Bean assassination, generated renewed enthusiasm within Los Angeles County. Although Wilson viewed the proposal as a philanthropic endeavor, most Angelenos considered the "Tejon plan" as a method of eliminating a malignancy from their society. The Los Angeles *Star* argued that the proposal would benefit "a people once more than half civilized, but now exhibiting such signs of retrogression and decay as must be deplored by every human heart."[42]

Yet enthusiasm over Wilson's plan waned as the months passed. In March 1853, an alleged Indian rape of a Mexican widow, Juana Ibarra, added to the frustration that was mounting within the community.[43] The *Star* asserted that the Indian's presence created widespread insecurity among the outlying farming communiy. The newspaper also suggested the use of violence by giving "them a whipping that they would remember."[44] Nor were Indian beatings beyond the realm of law enforcement procedures. The sheriff of Los Angeles, Alviron S. Beard, was described by one citizen as "the sheriff that always goes with a cane after Indians."[45]

The Los Angeles populace witnessed a series of "sensational" crimes during the spring and summer of 1853. Between May and June five cases of dueling were tried in the city's court of sessions. These incidents resulted from personal disputes among individuals in the Mexican community.[46] During the same period, ten criminals escaped from the county jail. The police were severely criticized for their dereliction in the matter.[47] In early June a robbery occurred at the store of Childs and Hicks. The theft netted $8,000 and no suspects were immediately apprehended.[48]

Violent activity also affected politics within the county. The infamous Roy Bean was a local agitator of unsavory reputation. In July 1853, he shot and seriously wounded a San Gabriel politician, Frank Carroll. Bean's party ticket had been defeated in a recent election and he apparently sought to avenge the loss. Following his arrest, Bean posted $500 bail, fled the city, and failed to appear for his arraignment in court.[49]

This sequence of events generated tremendous apprehension within the community. More importantly, these crimes altered the nature of public opinion. County residents suddenly realized the Indian was not the singular cause of crime. Race and nationality were no longer considered the only reasons for illegal activity. Miners, bandits, and fugitives were also perceived as a problem within the county.

Rumors of marauding bands of outlaws were reported in the local newspaper. The Los Angeles *Star* stated that a band of robbers were traveling through the neighboring Cahuenga rancho, stealing horses and creating havoc within the county. The publication further warned that citizens must "drive out this worthless scum of humanity, or they must give way before the pirates and be driven out themselves."[50]

Several factors contributed to the alarming rise in crime during this period. Law enforcement, both in the courts and on the streets, remained unsuccessful in effectively prosecuting the outlaw. The prison escape in May and the aborted effort to prosecute Roy Bean illustrate the ineffectiveness of local government. More importantly, the changing nature of the county's populace contributed to the rise in criminal activity.

By 1853 Los Angeles had become a "waystation" for migrant opportunists. Mining activity in outlying areas of the county attracted many people seeking fame and fortune. As early as May 1851, it was noted that "a company of men passed through this city on Friday on their way to the confluence of the Black and Gila rivers, where gold is represented to be very abundant."[51] In October 1852, talk of gold deposits located near San Buenaventura raised expectations within the county.[52]

Los Angeles County also became a refuge for surrounding communities that had experienced natural disasters. In the summer of 1853 the Four Creek region in Tulare County encountered severe flooding. Farmers suffered a total destruction of their crops and it was reported that "several families who have been engaged in farming, have left there and are now on their way to this community."[53]

Thus the influx of transients into the county may have created additional problems for the resident community. The lack of jobs and the failure to find gold generated a feeling of disillusionment, insecurity, and frustration within the area. In July 1853, the *Star* exclaimed that "this county is in a state of insurrection."[54] The newspaper focused its criticism on the miner as the principal cause of recent illegalities. It was stated that "a large gang of outlaws, many of them expelled for crime from the mines, are in open rebellion against the law."[55]

A series of sensational crimes, the failure to establish an Indian reservation, and the recognition of fugitive activity apart from the Indian, were factors that increased community concern. By the summer of 1853 public indignation had reached alarming proportions. The local populace sensed the only solution to widespread crime was to take matters into their own hands. It would mean the birth of vigilante activity in Los Angeles County.

In the summer of 1853 Los Angeles residents initiated drastic measures to combat criminal activity. In July a town meeting was held for the purpose of organizing a citizen's police force. A preamble was adopted that allowed for the arrest of "all suspicious persons wherever we may find them, and ridding the community of the same in such manner as may be advisable."[56]

In August the board of supervisors allocated $1,000 for the funding of a local police force, known as the Los Angeles Rangers.

Its membership consisted of a hundred citizens, twenty-five of which were active police.[57] During its first month of existence, the Rangers staged public "shooting drills" and parades in an attempt to gain local support and intimidate prospective criminals. In February 1854, the organization doubled its active enrollment to fifty members.[58]

The Rangers' immediate objective was to provide a sense of security for the local populace. This resulted in a swift apprehension of suspected criminals. The Rangers were frequently called upon to arrest alleged horse thiefs and murderers within the surrounding neighborhoods. In February 1854, they rode to San Gabriel and arrested three men suspected of horse theft after receiving "intelligence reports" of their whereabouts.[59] During the same month, the Rangers apprehended a suspected murderer while he was "trading off a watch" in Los Angeles.[60]

Indeed, the number of arrests for certain crimes did increase. In 1854 the total amount of murder and robbery cases brought to trial doubled over the previous year. Disturbing the peace and assault cases also multiplied during that year. The number of cases for these crimes are as follows:[61]

Crime	No. of Cases:	1853	1854
Assault and Battery		5	8
Disturbing the Peace		1	5
Murder		5	10
Robbery		2	5

The Los Angeles *Star* expressed enthusiastic support for the Rangers. The newspaper proudly noted the effectiveness of the police in arresting undesirables. The *Star* exclaimed: "Scarcely a day passes in which their assistance is not sought; and detachments are nearly all the time in the field. Wet or dry, they are always ready to start when called upon."[62]

The formation of the Rangers also signalled the beginning of extraordinary methods used in dealing with suspected culprits. Violence as a means of combating violence became an important mode of law enforcement. Lynchings occurred as a way of circumventing the judicial process. In October 1853, three men were sentenced to hang for horse theft. The convicted thieves were granted a reprieve by the local courts. As a result, the local authorities arranged for them to be shipped to San Luis Obispo where a "mob was assembled on the beach" waiting for their arrival. The three men were promptly taken "to the first tree and hung."[63]

In 1855 two convicted murderers were hanged in Los Angeles. Felipe Alvitre, a half-breed Indian, was sentenced to death for a murder he committed in El Monte. David Brown, reportedly a "good for nothing gambler," was also given the death penalty for shooting his companion, Pinckney Clifford.[64]

On January 12, 1855, Alvitre was finally hanged after the rope broke once, leaving him slumped on the ground near death. Brown, however, had received a stay of execution from the Supreme Court only two days earlier. Following Alvitre's execution, an angry crowd assembled at the county jail. The unruly mob broke into Brown's cell, dragged him across Spring Street, and hanged their victim from a corral gateway.[65]

Vigilante activity also had a profound effect on the prosecution of Indians. Individuals could apprehend Indians or confiscate their belongings merely because they suspected them of unscrupulous activity. One conscientous citizen, Charles Eschrecho, arrested an Indian and immediately took his horse, saddle, holster, and gun. According to Eschrecho, the Indian fled, leaving him with all the suspect's valuable possessions.[66]

By the middle of the decade Indians were being more severely prosecuted by the local courts. This was especially evident of crimes within the Indian community. One Indian, Enrique, was convicted of assaulting another Indian, Peniqro. The defendant was accused of stabbing his victim in the throat and ribs. The court of sessions sentenced him to three years in state prison.[67] Another Indian, Francisco, was sentenced to three years at hard labor for knifing his victim, Sediac, over a personal feud.[68]

Local concern over Indian crime crystalized the need for social reform within the community. Alcohol, prostitution, and gambling were cited as the vices responsible for Indian violence. More importantly, the white man was blamed for this unfortunate situation. The *Southern Californian* complained, "Every Sunday liquor is furnished these poor wretches by white men who ought to know better, and who should be held responsible to our laws for every crime committed by the Indian."[69]

Civic leaders did respond to the problems of vice during the mid-fifties. Prior to 1855 no cases of prostitution or gambling were tried in the local courts. In 1855 two gambling houses and one bordello were prosecuted in the court of sessions. In the following year the court conducted another five trials dealing with illegal gambling halls.[70]

In addition, selling liquor to Indians was increasingly monitored by law enforcement officials. The courts imposed harsher penalties and the number of prosecutions increased dramatically. In December 1854, George Walters, a proprietor of a local saloon, was convicted of selling liquor to an Indian woman and fined $42. Between 1854 and 1856 five such cases were tried in the court of sessions, a distinct change from previous years. Before 1854 only one case of selling liquor to an Indian was tried by the court.[71]

The community's direct involvement in law enforcement through the creation of the Rangers illustrated the need for reform within county administration. Crime reflected the ineffectiveness of local government in meeting the needs of its citizens. Thus, civic leaders initiated several plans to improve the operation of local affairs.

The county's first priority concerned the rental of government buildings. Increased expenditures and inadequate space were cause for concern among city officials. The board of supervisors addressed this problem by attempting to purchase a permanent city-county municipal building. In August 1853, Los Angeles acquired the home of a local resident, José Jorge Rocha, for $3,160. The supervisors also appropriated $1,000 for repair of the home, and the construction of the county jail on the adjacent lot.[72]

Public education was another important reform effort that generated local support. In the summer of 1853 Mayors John G. Nichols and Ygnacio Coronel led a joint effort to build a public school. Three prominent citizens, Lewis Granger, Stephen Foster, and J. Lancaster Brent, were appointed school commissioners.[73]

Yet, funding was a major obstacle to any educational reform. The expense of the new county buildings also meant that plans for a school system had to be curtailed. In August 1853, the board of supervisors levied new taxes in order to finance these innovations. On every $100 worth of property, a citizen was charged

$1.10 to provide a county surplus for a future school system. In addition, a 60c tax on every $100 of value was imposed on non-property owners.[74] By May 1854, the county had accumulated a $3,000 surplus. Mayor Stephen Foster began a renewed campaign to build a permanent school in Los Angeles. Finally, in early 1855 a brick schoolhouse was opened in the city.[75]

These limited reforms in education and the building of county facilities failed to change prevalent vigilante sentiment. Scandals contributed to the public mistrust of the local government. In March 1854, a justice of the peace, William G. Dryden, was reprimanded by the court of sessions for performing an autopsy in the absence of a coroner. What was particularly repugnant to the court was Dryden's failure to inter the body and it "decayed and was eaten by animals."[76] Two weeks later, the court tried A. S. Beard, marshall of Los Angeles, for embezzlement of $371. Beard alledgedly pocketed the money from taxes he collected within the community. Although there was insufficient evidence for a conviction, Beard was soon replaced as the city tax collector.[77]

A series of violent crimes also occurred that further discredited the county. In February 1854, two aborted attempts were made to set fire to the county jail. Both defendants in the case were exonerated and no further suspects were arrested.[78] In the same month, a Mexican woman, María Caneda, was raped more than nine times by four assailants. Although there were many witnesses to the attack, no law enforcement officials were available to aid the distraught victim.[79] Such activity tended to traduce the reputation of the Rangers, as well as the local authorities. The *Southern Californian* reiterated a familiar complaint that the community desperately needed a night police.[80]

The public hangings of Alvitre and Brown in January 1855 restored a temporary calm to the community. By the summer, however, public alarm over crime again surfaced as an important issue. The local newspapers reported on the unrestricted sale of liquor to Indians and the operation of a large counterfeit ring within the city. The *Southern Californian* pessimistically stated: "It smacks of old times to rise with the lark, go forth on the second day of the week and view the lifeless remains of humanity quietly sleeping by the wayside in the calm repose of death."[81]

Public discontent with the judicial process reached serious proportions by 1856. The murder of Antonio Ruiz triggered a bitter response from the Mexican populace. A white man, William Jenkins, was arrested for the murder.[62] While Jenkins was awaiting trial, one hundred angry citizens stormed the county jail hoping to capture him and hang him in the plaza. Marshal Getman was wounded in the affair while successfully protecting his prisoner. Several rioters including Francisco Carrergue and Vicente Guerro, the leaders of the raid, were brought to trial before the district court. Justice Benjamin Hayes reprimanded the disgruntled defendants and pleaded for co-operation in the legal process. Hayes stated:

> How long shall we labor through this anti-social distrust, and this painful sense of insecurity of property and life, now prevailing so generally? Shall the law be left nearly powerless, for want of adequate co-operation on the part of the people, in the efforts made by the officers for its enforcement? Must each man provide his own safety? This cannot be.[63]

Hayes' final plea was for reform rather than violence. He argued, "If they [laws] are bad, amend or repeal them. Let them never be overthrown for temporary ends that too often merely well a hasty vengeance under the pure form of Justice."[64]

The riot in the summer of 1856 epitomized a half-decade of local frustration. Despite the formation of the Rangers and the realization of certain social and governmental reforms, citizens still perceived the legal system as a failure. Although violence had created insecurity, it was violence the community had hoped would eliminate their fears.

In summation, crime was a persistent problem for Los Angeles County in the early 1850s. Local concern over lawlessness found expression in various forms. Reform in the operation of government and the establishment of a citizens' police were attempts to curb criminal activity and to assuage public apprehension. These efforts to reduce crime failed, at least in the mind of the public. Frustration resulted in more truculent attempts to combat illegal activity. Indian murders, lynchings, and mob violence were methods adopted to circumvent the judicial process.

Is it safe to describe these activities as a form of vigilantism? In the strict sense of the definition, yes. Vigilantism, at least in the context of the Los Angeles experience, was a viable response to crime during the formative years of statehood. Dissatisfaction with the ineffectiveness of county government led directly to extralegal activity. It has been correctly noted that even the Rangers, although they were under the auspices of the law, did not allow the judicial process to interfere with their mission.[85]

Yet, Los Angeles vigilantism was of an exclusive brand. In the broad context of the American experience, it would be unfair to label Los Angeles during this period as a center of vigilante activity. Certain ingredients were missing. There was no organized civic effort to work consciously against government in order to bring the criminal to justice. Unlike many cities, including San Francisco, Los Angeles did not experience a divisive battle to eliminate a political machine. In short, Los Angeles citizens attempted to reform the existing government, rather than to eliminate it.[86]

In reality, crime was the result of more complex factors than the community envisaged. As a frontier society, Los Angeles County experienced rapid change during the 1850s. Population and geographic increases led to an expanding community that government could not effectively manage. As a consequence, an effective judicial system developed slower than the community would tolerate.

The county did, however, attempt to meet its responsibilities to the local populace. Educational reform, the building of permanent government structures, and increased prosecution of illegal activity were specific responses to the community's needs.

Perhaps the failure of law enforcement was the result of inevitable circumstances. As a frontier society, Los Angeles County offered great expectations, hopes, and dreams for its people. Yet, opportunity was a two-way street. The noble ideas it may have tendered to one man could have been the greed and violence it provided to another. Thus, Los Angeles County was a society that enticed many types of emigrants, including the criminal. The problems created proved, temporarily at least, too much for the normal institutions to combat.

NOTES

Acknowledgement. The author wishes to express his thanks to Professors Gordon Bakken and Jackson K. Putman, California State University, Fullerton, for their critical comments which proved helpful in the development of this study.

¹ J. Max Bond, *The Negro in Los Angeles* (Ph.D. dissertation, University of Southern California, June 1936), pp. 7, 11.

² *California State Census of 1852*, Los Angeles County.

³ *Ibid.*, introductory remarks by Owen C. Coy.

⁴ Lynn Bowman, *Los Angeles: Epic of a City* (Berkeley: Howell-North Books, 1974), p. 145.

⁵ John Walton Caughey, ed., *The Indians of Southern California in 1852: The Benjamin D. Wilson Report and a Selection of Contemporary Comment* (Los Angeles: Plantin Press, 1952), pp. 21-22 (hereafter cited as Caughey, *The Wilson Report*).

⁶ Los Angeles Court of Sessions, *People vs. Refugio Guterriz*, July 8, 1850, transcript of case in longhand (hereafter only court, case title, and date will be cited).

⁷ Los Angeles Court of Sessions, *People vs. Alviron S. Beard*, testimony of Alviron Beard, November 11, 1853.

⁸ Los Angeles *Star*, August 16, 1851.

⁹ *Ibid.*, May 17, 1851.

¹⁰ Los Angeles Court of Sessions, *File Cabinet No. 1*, transcript of cases in longhand.

¹¹ Los Angeles Court of Sessions, *Complaint filed by Pio Pico and John Foster*, October 18, 1850.

¹² Los Angeles County, *Court of Sessions: Civil and Criminal Business*, Vol. 1, June 24, 1850 to February 16, 1852 longhand, December 3, 1851.

¹³ Los Angeles *Star*, May 24, 1851.

¹⁴ Caughey, *The Wilson Report*, p. 22.

¹⁵ Los Angeles Court of Sessions, *People vs. Juan de dios de Garcia*, testimony of Jesus Parado, September 10, 1850.

¹⁶ Los Angeles Court of Sessions, *People vs. Fernando Vacquites*, testimony of Samuel C. Won, July 11, 1850.

¹⁷ *Ibid.*, testimony of Fernando Vacquites.

¹⁸ Los Angeles Court of Sessions, *Reprimand of Michael White*, November 30, 1850.

¹⁹ Ferdinand F. Fernandez, "Except a California Indian: A Study in Legal Discrimination," *Southern California Quarterly*, L (1968), 163-164.

²⁰ Warren A. Beck and David A. Williams, *California: A History of the Golden State* (Garden City, N.Y.; Doubleday and Company, 1972), p. 241.

²¹ W. W. Robinson, "The Indians of Los Angeles and What Became of Them," *Quarterly Historical Society of Southern California*, (December 1938), p. 172.

²² Los Angeles Court of Sessions, *People vs. Alviron S. Beard*, November 21, 1853.

²³ Los Angeles *Star*, March 6, 1852.

²⁴ *Ibid.*, May 24, 1851.

²⁵ *Ibid.*, February 21, 1852.

²⁶ *Ibid.*, August 28, 1852.

²⁷ *Ibid.*, October 16, 1852.

²⁸ Los Angeles Court of Sessions, *File Cabinet No. 1*, longhand.

²⁹ Los Angeles Court of Sessions, *People vs. Charles Burrows*, March 20, 1851.

³⁰ Los Angeles Court of Sessions, *File Cabinet No. 1 &2*, longhand.

³¹ Los Angeles County Law Library, *The Courts in Early California*, Exhibit Notes, April, 1976, p. 2.

[32] Los Angeles Court of Sessions, *Jesus Luzan vs. Leopold Howard*, Case No. 99, 1852.

[33] Granville Arthur Waldron, "Courthouses of Los Angeles County," *Historical Society of Southern California Quarterly*, XLI (December 1959), 349-350.

[34] Los Angeles *Star*, March 6, 1852.

[35] Los Angeles County Law Library, *The Courts in Early California*, p. 3.

[36] Waldron, "Courthouses of Los Angeles County," pp. 351-353.

[37] Maurice H. and Marco R. Newmark, ed., *Sixty Years in Southern California 1853-1913: Containing the Reminiscences of Harris Newmark* (4th edition; Los Angeles: Zeitlin & Ver Bruge, 1970), p. 83.

[38] William B. Rice, *The Los Angeles Star 1851-1864* (Berkeley and Los Angeles: University of California Press, 1947, p. 45; Robert W. Blew, "Vigilantism in Los Angeles, 1835-1874," *Southern California Quarterly*, LIV (Spring 1972), 16-17.

[39] Los Angeles *Star*, January 15, 1853.

[40] William H. Ellison, "Indian Policy in California," *Mississippi Valley Historical Review*, IX (1922), 47.

[41] *Ibid.*, pp. 54-55; also, for a detailed account of the Indian uprising, see George H. Phillips, *Chiefs and Challengers* (Berkeley and Los Angeles: University of California Press, 1975), pp. 71-94.

[42] Los Angeles *Star*, January 15, 1853.

[43] Los Angeles Court of Sessions, *People vs. Juan*, April 7, 1853.

[44] Los Angeles *Star*, April 2, 1853.

[45] Los Angeles Court of Sessions, *People vs. Alviron S. Beard*, testimony of Ramon Figuaroa, November 11, 1853.

[46] Los Angeles Court of Sessions, *File Cabinet No. 2*, longhand.

[47] Rice, *The Los Angeles Star 1851-1864*, p. 46.

[48] Los Angeles *Star*, July 16, 1853.

[49] Los Angeles Corut of Sessions, *People vs. Roy Bean*, August 8, 1853.

[50] Los Angeles *Star*, July 16, 1853.

[51] *Ibid.*, May 17, 1851.

[52] *Ibid.*, October 16, 1852; Also, a shipload of prostitutes arrived from San Francisco in 1853, presumably to meet the needs of the miners. See Lynn Bowman, *Los Angeles: Epic of a City* (Berkeley: Howell-North Books, 1974), pp. 150-151.

[53] *Ibid.*, July 16, 1853.

[54] *Ibid.*, July 16, 1853.

[55] *Ibid.*, July 16, 1853; The friction between transients and native Californians also sparked violence within the community. See Blew, "Vigilantism in Los Angeles," pp. 11-12.

[56] Los Angeles *Star*, July 16, 1853.

[57] *Ibid.*, August 6, 1853.

[58] *Ibid.*, February 11, 1854.

[59] *Ibid.*

[60] *Ibid.*

[61] Los Angeles Court of Sessions, *File Cabinet No. 2 & 3*, longhand.

[62] Los Angeles *Star*, February 11, 1854.

[63] *Ibid.*, October 22, 1853.

[64] Newmarks, eds., *Sixty Years in Southern California 1853-1913*, p. 139.

[65] *Ibid.*, p. 140.

[66] Los Angeles Court of Sessions, *People vs. Miquel*, testimony of Charles Eschrecho, October 23, 1854.

[67] Los Angeles Court of Sessions *People vs. Enrique*, No. 218, February 14, 1855.

[66] Los Angeles Court of Sessions, *People vs. Francisco*, No. 281, August 16, 1856.

[69] *Southern Californian*, July 27, 1854.

[70] Los Angeles Court of Sessions, *File Cabinet No. 2, 3, & 4*, longhand.

[71] *Ibid.*, File Cabinet No. 1 and 2.

[72] Waldron, "Courthouses of Los Angeles County," pp. 360-361.

[73] Newmarks, eds., *Sixty Years in Southern California 1853-1913*, p. 105.

[74] Los Angeles County Board of Supervisors, *Minutes*, Book 1, 1852-1855, pp. 62-63 July 9, 1853 (longhand).

[75] Newmarks eds., *Sixty Years in Southern California 1853-1913*, p. 105.

[76] Los Angeles Court of Sessions, *People vs. William G. Dryden*, March 29, 1854.

[77] Los Angeles Court of Sessions, *People vs. Alviron S. Beard*, No. 166, April 14, 1854.

[78] Los Angeles Court of Sessions, *People vs. Jose A. Rodriguez*, February 22, 1854; *People vs. Manuel Garcia*, February 24, 1854.

[79] Los Angeles Court of Sessions, *Rape of Maria Caneda*, testimony filed in court, February 9, 1854.

[60] *Southern California*, August 31, 1854.

[81] *Ibid.*, May 30, 1850; Rice, *The Los Angeles Star 1851-1864*, p. 92.

[82] Apparently Jenkins, a deputy constable, shot Antonio Ruiz while attempting to repossess a guitar on which Ruiz owed a small debt. See Blew, "Vigilantism in Los Angeles," p. 21.

[83] Los Angeles Court of Sessions, *Special Hearing by Judge Hayes*, No. 272, July 22 1856.

[84] Los Angeles Court of Sessions, *Special Hearing by Judge Hayes*, No. 272, July 22, 1856.

[85] Blew assumes that most extralegal activity in Los Angeles, aside from the judicial process, can be considered vigilantism. Blew, "Vigilantism in Los Angeles," pp. 11-12.

[66] Article by Richard Maxwell Brown, "Pivot of American Vigilantism: The San Francisco Vigilance Committee of 1856," in Stephen Salsbury, ed., *Essays on the History of the American West* (Hinsdale, Ill.: The Dryden Press 1975), pp. 363-369. For a contrast of Blew's interpretation of vigilantism, see Richard Maxwell Brown, *Strain of Violence: Historical Studies of American Vigilantism* (New York: Oxford University Press, 1975), pp. 146-149; Herbert L. Packer, *The Limits of Criminal Sanction* (Stanford, Calif.: Stanford University Press 1968), pp. 154-173.

Rough Justice: Felony Crime and the Superior Court in San Luis Obispo County, 1880-1910

By Lyle A. Dale

SINCE THE MID-1970s, a growing number of scholars have researched and written on the subject of crime, disorder and criminal justice in the United States, especially in the nineteenth and early twentieth centuries. Much of this scholarship has consisted of case studies of a particular geographical area, usually through research of the records and files of the law enforcement organizations of that particular area.[1] The vast majority of these studies all share one interesting similarity: they are based upon the study of eastern or midwestern cities of some size.[2] Unfortunately, little attempt has been made to undertake a systematic study of public disorder, felony crime, and criminal justice in general for rural towns, and, especially, western rural towns.

One study that did break from the eastern-midwestern bias was *The Roots of Justice* by Lawrence M. Friedman and Robert V. Percival, which explores criminal justice in Alameda County, California, from 1870 to 1910.[3] Still, Alameda County, while a western community, is, again, a rather large, urban community. Furthermore, *The Roots of Justice* remains, again, essentially a case study. Friedman and Percival acknowledge that any claims they are to make can be attributed only to their immediate subject: Alameda County, 1870-1910. Furthermore, they admit that a larger question looms: how far beyond their case study can their data be pushed? Beyond Alameda County in 1870-1910, "What more can we claim? How many of our findings stop right there? How much is true of California, as a whole, at that time? Of the United States in general?"[4] The authors are not certain that they dare reach further. When they do, it is only to make "... a few wild stabs at further meaning."[5] Generally, these questions might apply to many of the other case studies in the field.

The question then must be asked: what will a detailed study of a rural community in the West, in roughly the same time period as other studies, show? Will another study reach essentially the same conclusions regarding felony crime and criminal justice? Or will such research demonstrate that criminal patterns were more localized, indicating that criminal justice was more parochial in nature, with little relationship to different, and larger, areas? Such a comparison with another place may help to validate other work and the conclusions of others, or to demonstrate that one such focused case study, while helpful, may not be greater than the sum of its parts; that many more such case studies remain to be completed if we are to reach broad conclusions about the history of criminal justice.

This article will explore these questions by examining felony crime and the Superior Court in San Luis Obispo County, California, in the general period of 1880-1910.[6] San Luis Obispo County was (and to some extent still is) a rural county. While California experienced enormous population and economic growth during the period, San Luis Obispo County was isolated for much of this time from the growth areas of northern and southern California. San Luis Obispo County lies midway between San Francisco and Los Angeles, along the central coast of the state, and is bordered to much of the north, east, and south by the Santa Lucia Mountains; the Pacific Ocean lies to the west. Until the arrival of the railroad at the end of the nineteenth century, travel to the north or south was difficult and the county remained relatively isolated and rural.[7] As a rural county, San Luis Obispo County had a more informal justice system, lacking the large court systems of Alameda County. As such, it offers a good juxtaposition for the Alameda County study; it may be possible to determine if the findings of Friedman and Percival in an urban setting transfer to the rural setting of San Luis Obispo County.

While Friedman and Percival began their study in 1870, the year 1880 is an equally sound starting point. In 1879 the new California constitution made radical changes in the judicial system of the state. A superior court replaced county and district courts for each county. From 1880 throughout our period of study, the Superior Court heard all felony cases. Since this system is still in operation today, it seems reasonable that comparisons between then and now will be valid, as will comparisons between the Superior Courts of San Luis Obispo and Alameda counties. Furthermore, the task is somewhat simplified by limiting analysis to essentially one (the present) judicial system.

The county Superior Courts kept felony trial records beginning in 1880. Friedman and Percival used two rich sources of information: the Register of Criminal Actions and the case files. The Register lists the defendant's name, the case number and charges and gives an outline of the proceedings of the case. The case file holds all of the documents relating to the case, including writs, warrants, transcripts and exhibits. Friedman and Percival drew a random sample of twenty-five percent of all felony cases from 1880 to 1910—696 cases in all—for close analysis of charges, dispositions and sentences.[8] Probably because the Superior Court system is still in operation today, the records of the San Luis Obispo County Superior Court are basically complete. Each case, beginning with number 1 in 1880, is listed in the Register of Criminal Actions and has its own case file. All papers relating to each case which remain are filed therein. As Friedman and Percival also discovered, the amount of information does vary from case to case. Sometimes the Register contains only sketchy data; sometimes the case file is incomplete. Together, however, they usually provide a rather complete picture.[9] Due to the number of cases in San Luis Obispo County (840 cases brought before the Superior Court from 1880 to 1910) a one hundred percent sampling is possible.

The ground rules for our analysis are established: the method of research will be the same, and the resources utilized will be similar. It is the results that now must be determined. Let us begin, then, with a brief look at felony crime in San Luis Obispo County, followed by a detailed study of the processing of the various criminal actions, including disposition and sentencing. Finally, we will end with our own conclusions. At all times we will keep an eye on the results of Friedman and Percival, as well as others where relevant, for similarities, discrepancies and questions unanswered.

The Superior Court for the County of San Luis Obispo first convened on Monday, January 5, 1880. Judge Louis McMurtry presented his commission from the governor and made several decrees regarding court record keeping. He then proceeded with court business by hearing cases.[10] Beginning in 1880, then, all felony criminal cases, as well as appeals from the lower court and writs of habeas corpus were heard by the Superior Court.[11]

Of the 744 total cases brought before the court during the period under study for which we can list a type of case represented, most, about 85 percent, were ordinary felony cases starting in Superior Court. Appeals from lower municipal courts accounted for 5.4 percent of cases, and the remainder, approximately 10 percent, were habeas corpus cases, really appeals also, whatever the technical term.[12]

The case load, in raw numbers, does not seem excessive, averaging approximately twenty-one felony cases per year. Indeed, throughout the period, the Superior Court in San Luis Obispo County consisted of only one superior court judge sitting at any one time. This contrasts with the more populous Alameda County where the Superior Court was divided into departments, with each department having its own judge and hearing only a particular type of case.[13] In San Luis Obispo County, one judge heard everything.[14]

As mentioned, the number of cases in the San Luis Obispo County Superior Court does not seem excessive. Still, we must ask what these raw numbers mean. That is, what type of criminal activity was represented in the cases heard by the court? A detailed examination of the crimes brought before the court, and the way in which the court dealt with those crimes should illustrate the nature and scope of the felony criminal situation.[15]

Of the types of felony crimes brought before the San Luis Obispo County Superior Court, the vast majority of offenses were against property and persons, with four types of crime accounting for the largest share—65 percent— of all criminal indictments: (1) assault with intent to kill; (2) assault with a deadly weapon; (3) grand larceny; and (4) burglary. On the face of it, these four crimes would seem to indicate that San Luis Obispo was a rather violent place. A closer examination however raises the question as to whether this was actually so. For instance, if the assault cases were indeed as serious as the indictments suggest (assault *to kill*, assault with *a deadly weapon*), then we should expect to see that the court dealt rather harshly with those individuals indicted for such crimes. However, as we shall see, this was not necessarily the case.

An examination of court records and testimony for various cases suggests the apparent answer: crime in San Luis Obispo was not particularly violent and aggravated, nor the result of hardened criminal activity. Furthermore, there were often extenuating circumstances involved, especially in assault cases. More often than not, assault cases involved an altercation that took place in the heat of the moment, many times as the result of alcohol; larceny cases consisted of the theft of rather minor property.

For example, in *People v. Jones* (Case No. 86) the court records indicate that the defendant hired a couple from San Francisco to work for him—the man as a hired hand and the woman as a cook.[16] Apparently, upon arriving in town the couple discovered that the arrangements were not as they had been led to believe, and so contrived to do their work poorly until, three days later, they were asked to leave. A question of compensation (not to mention complaints over the woman's poor cooking that precipitated the dismissal) soon erupted into a fight, and Jones was subsequently charged with assault with a deadly weapon. Obviously, this was not the result of hardened criminal activity, but more likely gastrointestinal discomfort. Still, the case was tried; however, the jury could not reach a verdict and the court dismissed the case.

Likewise, in *People v. Grady* (Case No. 14) the defendant, a San Luis Obispo policeman who was not on duty at the time, was charged with murder, the result of a barroom fight. As reported in the court transcript as well as the San Luis Obispo *Tribune,* the victim in the case, John Kith, met his end in a saloon called The People's Exchange in San Luis Obispo. As the *Tribune* reported, the victim, "under the influence of liquor... passed up to the bar, inviting two or three parties who were sitting in the saloon to drink, all of whom, it is needless to say, responded with promptness and dispatch."[17] Soon Kith was daring anyone to try to knock him down. According to the *Tribune,* defendant Grady smiled at this, which apparently Kith took as a challenge, for he said he would fight anyone in the house. Grady then advanced toward Kith, drew his pistol and fired three shots, two of which mortally wounded Kith. As it turned out, the *Tribune* told its readers, there had been bad blood between the two, the result of a previous encounter. Since then, as the *Tribune* reported, "a bitter enmity existed between the two men."[18] Although arrested and tried for murder, the jury found Grady not guilty.

Larceny crimes followed a similar pattern. Typically the theft consisted of such items as $90.00 in cash and one shirt (*People v. Lon Gin Wo*, No. 19), sacks of wheat and barley valued at $57.00 (*People v. Righetti*, No. 95), one bridle and saddle valued at $75.00 (*People v. Strand*, No. 280), and one cow (*People v. Salio*, No. 570). These crimes were certainly not the result of major criminal activity. Still the Superior Court had to deal with these crimes, and, remembering the type of crimes they were, the court records offer some interesting statistics.

As we might expect, most people appearing before the court initially pled "not guilty." Indeed, of the 594 total cases in which a plea is entered in the court records, 62 percent pled "not guilty." However, a sizeable number, 32 percent, also entered a "guilty" plea.

Interestingly, the figures differ significantly from those discovered by Friedman and Percival for Alameda County.[19] There, the incidence of "not guilty" pleas approached 80 percent compared with less than two-thirds of pleas in San Luis Obispo. Likewise, the incidence of "guilty" pleas was higher in San Luis Obispo; in fact, approximately double. What this might suggests is that, since the nature of the crime in San Luis Obispo was not particularly severe, or there were mitigating circumstances involved, it often simply made sense for the defendant to plead guilty, expecting the court to be lenient in its sentence. A look at pleas by indictment for each type of crime seems to bear this theory out. Guilty pleas were highest for the larceny and burglary crimes, as well as the assault cases, with guilty plea rates of 40 and 46 percent, respectively. The assault cases also had the highest incidence of pleading guilty to a lesser offense—in these cases to simple assault, with approximately 15 percent of defendants pleading guilty to a lesser offense. Perhaps when heads cooled later, and the court reviewed the facts, it was decided that the altercation warranted more limited charges.

We should consider also whether the higher incidences of

guilty pleas and pleas of guilty to a lesser offense might have represented some form of plea bargaining. Plea bargaining had become institutionalized as a standard feature of American urban criminal courts in the latter part of the nineteenth century.[20] Two major changes in criminal justice led to this development: (1) creation of a modern police force for apprehension of criminals, as well as a modern prosecutional staff; and (2) the development of prisons as the standard disposition in court.[21] The function of the court, then, became to determine who went to prison from among those eligible, since it was not possible to imprison all.[22] Plea bargaining became a sort of traffic management system; professionals would determine charges and sentences based upon the needs of the system.[23] San Luis Obispo County, however, does not appear to have reached the stage where criminal activity consumed such a significant share of the court's time, that such a management program would be warranted.

Still, can we be sure we know plea bargaining when we see it? Is there some sign to look for in the criminal records that would indicate plea bargaining? Friedman, for one, believes the signs are unambiguous: a plea change from "innocent" to "guilty of a lesser charge."[24] By this definition, there apparently was very little plea bargaining in San Luis Obispo for the instances of plea change are very rare indeed; no more than a dozen noted in the court register for our thirty year period.

Perhaps, however, there was implicit plea bargaining; that is, perhaps the plea bargaining took place away from court. The district attorney, for example, might have promised to put in a good word regarding sentencing if the defendant promised to plead guilty. Or the district attorney might have made such a promise in exchange for a plea of guilty to a lesser offense (especially, perhaps, if the evidence was not sound). Unfortunately, the records do not tell us if this was the case. Friedman and Percival, however, believe that such implicit plea bargaining was common in Alameda County.[25] Given the higher instances of guilty pleas and pleas of "guilty to a lesser offense" in San Luis Obispo County, implicit plea bargaining seems a rather good possibility.

When the case did finally come before the court, the court records again seem to suggest that the crimes themselves were not very serious, or at least that mitigating circumstances were involved. Of the 593 total cases during our period in which a disposition is listed in the court records, only 16 percent of defendants were convicted by a jury (with 4 percent being convicted of a lesser offense). This compares with a jury conviction rate of slightly over 20 percent for Alameda County as found by Friedman and Percival.[26]

What the figures also show is that a significant majority of the cases were taken out of the jury's hands—the celebrated trial by a jury of one's peers was not very common in San Luis Obispo.[27] In fact, cases were dismissed by the court only slightly less often than they were tried—27 percent were dismissed as opposed to 34 percent that were tried.[28] Interestingly, the dismissal rate in San Luis Obispo is approximately twice that found in Alameda County.[29] This apparently again demonstrates that when given time to reflect on the matter, the court decided the circumstances involved did not always warrant conviction of criminal charges.

Furthermore, a look at the disposition of cases as a function of type of crime by indictment helps to confirm that often the crime taking place or the circumstances involved did not warrant conviction of the defendant as indicted. Of all indictments brought before the Superior Court, only 14 percent of the defendants were found guilty at trial of the crime for which they were indicted; 6 percent were found guilty of a lesser crime. Approximately one quarter of all indictments were simply dismissed. The defendant stood a better chance of having his case dismissed than he did of being convicted.

Consider, for instance, the record of indictments for what surely must be considered the most serious crime of all — murder. The San Luis Obispo County Superior Court was surprisingly lenient. Close to half the cases tried resulted in a verdict of "not guilty" or "guilty of a lesser offense" (typically "manslaughter"). Another 14 percent were dismissed by the court. In fact in thirty years and forty-two murder indictments, only seventeen cases resulted in the court convicting the defendant of murder.

An examination of several murder cases indicates that mitigating circumstances often resulted in favorable court action for the defendant. We have already observed that this was so in *People v.*

Grady (Case No. 14). In the case of *People v. Dottie Luna* (Case No. 729), the defendant was charged with murder, having shot her father-in-law. According to the court records, the defendant's father-in-law believed that she was a "dirty tramp" who had tricked his son into marrying her. One night the deceased came to her front door, calling her "all kinds of a dirty tramp and a damn whore." The defendant testified that the deceased dared her to come out so that he could "slap my damn face." She testified that she believed the deceased had a gun, and so she got one. She then went to the door and shot the deceased. The testimony then went as follows:

Q. Why did you have a gun in your hands?

A. I wanted to scare him.

Q. Why did you shoot him?

A. I was afraid of him. He had his hand behind him. I was afraid he had something to kill me.

The court dismissed the case on a motion from the district attorney.

In *People v. Thomas Carrol* (Case No. 642), the court records indicate that the defendant had gone out to his barn to complete some chores. When he returned to the house, he found a man, the deceased, with his sister, and promptly ordered the man to leave. When the deceased struck Carrol, he took out a pistol and shot the deceased. At trial he claimed self-defense; the jury acquitted him of the murder charge.

Different circumstances, however, could result in a much less lenient decision from the court. In *People v. Thomas Loughlin* (Case No. 417), the defendant and the deceased got into an altercation over the sale of some chickens. The defendant testified that the deceased drew a gun and that he, the defendant, shot the deceased in self-defense. Unfortunately, there were no witnesses, and it was then that the defendant made his mistake. Concerned that no one would believe his story, he decided to destroy the body. He took the body into a remote area and burned it. The body, however, was discovered and soon the defendant found himself in court. His plea of self-defense was not considered very favorably by the court, and he received 30 years at Folsom State Prison. The San Luis Obispo *Tri-*

bune, in reporting the case, observed that "it was stated by certain parties that, had Loughlin made no effort to burn the body of his victim, his plea of self defense would have held good in any court."[30] The *Tribune* also reported that the 30 year sentence was equivalent to a life sentence since Loughlin "is past middle life and already broken down in health."[31]

Sentencing by the court, however, seems to refute the proposition that crime in San Luis Obispo County was not terribly aggravated. Of 335 total cases in which the court records indicate the sentence of the defendant, 75 percent of those defendants sentenced received a state prison term.

This is also a higher percentage than the approximately two-thirds rate Friedman and Percival observed for Alameda County.[32] However, if we consider sentencing according to the type of crime involved, the figures do seem to confirm our working hypothesis that crime or the circumstances involved were not usually aggravated in San Luis Obispo County.

Consider, for example, crimes against persons. Only 26 percent of those defendants indicted for these types of crimes were sentenced to state prison. Indeed, only 31 percent of those indicted for murder spent time at San Quentin or Folsom. Friedman and Percival found rates more than double that in Alameda County.[33] Assault cases resulted in even lower state prison sentencing, with only 17 percent of those indicted being sentenced to the state penitentiary. Again, the court apparently was not convinced of the seriousness of these types of crimes, when it considered the facts involved.

Crimes against property, however, brought on a much higher risk of incarceration in the state penitentiary. Fully 52 percent of those indicted for these crimes were sent to state prison. This may have been a function of the type of defendants involved. Perhaps the burglary and larceny defendants were transients or other persons with few ties to the community. With little reason to express leniency or concern over such a defendant, the court sent him off to be taken care of by the state, probably with the hope he would not return upon his subsequent release. Or perhaps the circumstances of the crime did not warrant much leniency. The defendant had either stolen or not; he could not very easily plead self-defense in a robbery case. In any event, expelling the offender from San Luis

Obispo for incarceration elsewhere was probably the greatest concern of the court. For instance in a robbery case, *People v. Alviso* (Case No. 419), the *Tribune,* in reporting on the sentencing, observed that the judge "considered that it was best for society to have such a man in safe keeping."[34] The judge gave him fifteen years at Folsom.

Fines were somewhat prevalent with 14 percent of sentences involving a fine. This is in sharp contrast to Alameda County where Friedman and Percival discovered that "fines for felonies were quite scarce."[35] Again, this seems to reflect the nature of San Luis Obispo County crime. For example, fines were most common among the various assault-type cases, where the result of the court action was often a plea or conviction on a lesser charge; close to one-third of those indicted for assault received a fine at sentencing. The court apparently felt that in such altercations as saloon brawls, and fights over a lady's attention, or other hot-headed battle, no one was totally at fault; the defendants were separated from some of their money as a reminder to be a little more civil the next time. Likewise, fines for property crimes were non-existent. As suggested earlier, the court did not want a defendant's money, it wanted him out of town.

The use of county jail as a sentencing option was not greatly utilized by the San Luis Obispo County Superior Court. Only 6 percent of sentences involved county jail — or approximately only a third the rate in Alameda County.[36] The use of county jail was utilized mainly for assault cases and morals cases, probably again demonstrating the court's view of the circumstances involved in these crimes. Property crimes did not bring a sentence to county jail. In 30 years, only two such defendants were sentenced to local incarceration. This seems to confirm that the court wanted these defendants gone. One final note about sentencing to county jail is worth noting. Those defendants indicted for injuring a jail (the local one) were uniformly sent to state prison. A defendant was not given a second opportunity to damage local government property.

Interestingly, in the period of 1880-1910, the San Luis Obispo County Superior Court handed down only two death sentences. The fact that the death sentence was even given by the court in these two cases, probably resulted from the circumstances in one case, and in the other case, the fact that the defendant was Chinese. In the first case, *People v. Ross* (Case No. 581), the twenty-four-year-old defendant in custody with a marshal was being transported by steamer from San Diego to San Francisco. The *Tribune,* in reporting on the crime, remarked that the defendant was on his way to San Quentin.[37] According to the trial testimony, the defendant hit the marshal over the head with a bottle four or five times and made his escape while the steamer was at Port Harford on the San Luis Obispo County coast. The defendant later surrendered when he heard that the victim had died. Although the defendant claimed that he never meant to kill the marshal, he was found guilty of murder and sentenced to die. Unfortunately, while the court records chronicle the appeal process for several years, there is no indication therein of whether or not the sentence was ever executed. The *Tribune* reported in 1903 on Ross' upcoming appeal before the United States Supreme Court.[38] Two months later, the *Tribune* reported that Ross "is sentenced to hang next Friday.[39] Unfortunately, that is the last mention of the case to be found in the *Tribune.*

The second death sentence case, *People v. Luis* (Case No. 808), involved a Chinese defendant. The court records indicate that the defendant shot and killed his step-mother in her sleep, apparently the result of a quarrel over some of her jewelry. According to the records, the defendant believed the jewelry should have belonged to him rather than to his father's new wife. Interestingly, the father, Ah Luis, was probably the most influential Chinese in San Luis Obispo. The *Tribune* had reported earlier on his business dealings, such as brick manufacturing and serving as a labor agent.[40] Ah Luis testified during the trial regarding the relationships in his family; his grief over his wife's death probably affected the jury. The jury convicted young Luis of murder, and he was sentenced to die. This time the records are more complete and we know from the warrant in the case file that the hanging took place at San Quentin on December 6, 1912.

Apparently, San Luis Obispo was not alone in its rather tolerant treatment of homicide cases. Hubert H. Bancroft, in his multi-volume *History of California,* complained of the laxity of the court in dealing with such crime. Citing evidence from San Francisco, he stated that "an average of 25 homicides have taken place yearly in the city for the last decade... and that out of 250 or more homicidal crimes, only four have been punished capitally and seventy-seven by imprisonment."[41] San Francisco's rate for capital punishment was even less than San Luis Obispo, while its rate of imprisonment in homicide cases was 30.8 percent; the rate in San Luis Obispo was 31 percent.

By contrast, in a study of Philadelphia during the period 1839 to 1901, Roger Lane found an imprisonment rate approaching 63 percent between 1895 and 1901, with the sentences becoming increasingly severe toward the end of the century.[42] Lane interpreted these changes as reflecting a lower tolerance for homicidal behavior and as a strengthening of social control. This may have been true of Philadelphia, a large eastern city, but it does not seem to have been true for cities and towns of the West.[43] Clearly Lane's observations do not hold up for all of America in the nineteenth century. As if to demonstrate this point further, a study of homicide in Sacramento County in the latter half of the nineteenth century showed a slightly declining rate of conviction for homicide crimes.[44] Furthermore, sentencing patterns were becoming less severe, not more, as in Philadelphia.[45] The Sacramento study also observed, as we have for San Luis Obispo, that most homicide events arose out of personal disputes and anger, not premeditated actions.[46]

One type of crime that was seldom prosecuted was morals crime. As has been observed in a previous study of the police and lower courts in San Luis Obispo, this type of crime surely existed, but the courts were rarely asked to deal with it.[47] Prosecutions for morals crimes were rare in San Luis Obispo County Superior Court. In our thirty year period of study, only twenty-three indictments were handed down. As was also observed in the study of the police and lower courts, prosecution for such crimes tended to be discriminatory in some manner; either the defendant's behavior had singled him out, or racial prejudice was involved. This prejudice seems clear, especially in the only two gambling cases to come before the Superior Court, since both of the defendants were Chinese (*People v. Ah Teng* and *People v. Ah Look*, Case No. 198), and both indictments were related. The court records are incomplete, but it seems safe to assume that the indictments in this instance were discriminatory in some sense. Likewise, the only two indictments for "keeping a house of ill-fame" were apparently related (*People v. Dennis*, Case No. 38 and *People v. Duarte*, Case No. 39). Again, the court records are incomplete, but we can speculate that these two defendants' actions must have been particularly notorious to attract the attention of the law. Both pled guilty and received a month in county jail. Similarly, the two unlucky Chinese pled guilty and were fined.

When the Superior Court was asked to deal with morals cases, the court was not inclined to convict the defendants; only 22 percent of those indicted were found guilty by the court. Close to one-third, 30 percent, of the cases were dismissed. Thirty-five percent of defendants did plead guilty; however, the defendants were typically the few indicted on prostitution and gambling charges. Perhaps indictments were meant only to make a statement: (1) cease such open or notorious behavior; or (2) show that the justice system was capable of protecting the good citizens of the county from such behavior when it felt warranted to do so. Otherwise, as we observed earlier, morals offenses were tolerated, unless action was forced by a particular conduct.

Even so, those morals crimes that were prosecuted often consumed a disproportionate share of the court's time and energy. The cases of seduction, adultery and others probably fascinated the rural citizens of that period (even as they seem to today). Court transcripts for morals cases typically ran to 100 pages (compared to ten or so for a typical case of a crime against persons or property). Furthermore, the trial typically went into the most intimate details of the crime, and the lives of those involved.

Typical is the case of *People v. Webster* (Case No. 546), the defendant being charged with adultery and "living in a state of open and notorious cohabitation." According to the trial testimony (a sixty-page transcript), the defendant owned a club housing a saloon, card room, and a dining room in Pismo Beach. He ran the saloon and card room while a woman ran the dining room. The defendant's living quarters were above the club and the woman also lived up there. Apparently this was too much for the good citizens of Pismo Beach, and adultery charges were brought. When witnesses at the trial were asked if they had ever seen the living quarters, and knew for a fact that the couple did not have separate quarters, the witnesses uniformly answered that they had, indeed, never seen the upstairs housing. But, when asked, then, how they knew that the two were in fact having a carnal relationship, the standard answer was, "Of course they were because everyone knows it." Ironically, the gossips who so loved the morals cases had, in fact, apparently created one. The defendant was found guilty, however, and paid a $100 fine.

Seduction cases also brought forth explicit sexual testimony. In *People v. Chaviel* (Case No. 470), the defendant was a twenty-six-year-old man who was staying with a forty-one-year-old woman and her nephew, the nephew and the defendant apparently being acquainted. At the trial the defendant testified that he and the woman had made love several times; it was only then that she said they must get married. The woman, however, testified that the defendant was the only man she had ever had a sexual relationship with; she had relied on his promise to marry her to have sex with him. The defendant did not want to marry her; hence, the prosecution. The most interesting part of the transcript, however, was in the judge's instructions to the jury:

> In this case the age, intelligence, experience and youthfulness of the defendant, and age, intelligence and mature womanhood of the prosecutrix should be considered. If you are not satisfied beyond a reasonable doubt that she yielded her person solely under promise to marry, as alleged, but that she consented thereto in order to satisfy her own sexual desires, you must find the defendant not guilty.... The act of intercourse by the parties, if induced simply by a mutual desire to gratify a lustful passion, would not constitute the crime charged.

The jury, however, found the defendant guilty as charged and he paid a $100 fine.

No doubt, these trials were providing a great source of public entertainment, indeed rather voyeuristic, titillating entertainment. Unfortunately, the court sometimes saw fit to conduct a case in private. As the *Tribune* reported on one such instance, "those who have been in the habit of whiling away an hour or two in grinning at the dubious stains upon family linen exposed to the general gaze in the legal laundry," found their occupation gone during a particular case.[48] According to the *Tribune*, "the excluded public stood around downtown and pretended not to care about being shut out of the circus, but the case, nevertheless, was a frequent subject of comment, and stories were numerous...."[49]

Throughout this article, the impression that has been created by our study of felony crime in San Luis Obispo County is that crime was not a serious problem. We did observe that the vast majority of felony offenses were against property and persons; over 65 percent of all such indictments, as brought before the San Luis Obispo County Superior Court, were either on assault or theft related charges. Typically, however, the assault cases involved some extenuating circumstances; many were alcohol related. The theft cases often consisted of the theft of rather minor property. Furthermore, when we consider the amount of felony crime, through an examination of felony rates, we see that felony crime was actually on the decrease throughout the period. Indeed, the rate of felony indictments that were brought before the San Luis Obispo County Superior Court went from a rate of 1.97 per 1,000 population in 1880 to a rate of 0.87 in 1910.

Friedman and Percival also observed a decline in felony rates, as demonstrated by their data; but they were unable to account for it, except to note it as a general trend elsewhere. Indeed, most researchers in the field have reached a consensus regarding the directional trend of nineteenth century felony crime: they assert with a reasonable certainty that offense rates declined from at least around 1850 to perhaps 1920.[50] There has been an argument, however, over the causes of this decline, and we should explore briefly certain of the theories that have been advanced.

The first theory, which has been most vigorously articulated by Roger Lane, argues that the social effects of urban, industrial growth, far from creating a chaotic breeding ground for crime, instead produced regimentation, regulation and increasing order.[51] Life became more sober and predictable. People became less reckless and shed their impulsive and violent ways. Another school, led by Ted R. Gurr, argues that the nineteenth century's newly created crime control organizations, especially the police, worked to deter crime.[52] Throughout the period of declining crime rates, then, this more active approach to crime control took its toll on offenders. A third approach as argued by Eric Monkkonen states that, along with the growth in crime control organization, other specialized control organizations grew.[53] These organizations cut into the broad behavioral spectrum that had originally fallen under the jurisdiction of the criminal justice system. Thus, criminal justice became focused more exclusively on criminal behavior. That is to say, by the early twentieth century, newly refined ideology was seeking to remove certain types of people and behavior (tramps, drunks) from the criminal justice system and place them into more appropriate treatment venues.

Unfortunately, these theories do not provide a very satisfactory answer to twentieth-century increases in crime rates. Gurr argued that increases in offenses, for reasons to be found in the larger political and social culture, simply overwhelmed the criminal justice system's real, but limited, deterrent capabilities. Lane saw the increase as a reflection of other post-industrial problems. Monkkonen, while effectively demonstrating that the system was no longer dealing with non-criminal urban disorders such as drunkenness and unemployment, still did not effectively address felony crime.

None of this seems particularly satisfying as a way of explaining the late nineteenth-century decline in felony crime rates, and the rise after the second decade of the twentieth century. At this point it seems pertinent to suggest an alternate theory, one that is demonstrated, if not universally, at least by the data in San Luis Obispo County. Simply put, felony crime rates were declining in the latter part of the nineteenth century because the felons were in jail. As we observed, crimes against property accounted for the largest number of felony indictments in San Luis Obispo throughout the period. Furthermore, as we observed, these criminals were much more likely to be sent to state prison, effectively removing them from the community for a number of years. Meanwhile, crimes against persons, especially assault cases, were more likely to have resulted from the particular circumstances of the moment (drinking, the heat of an argument), and did not typically represent hardened criminal activity. These criminals were not so likely to repeat their misdeeds, and therefore were not sent to state prison as frequently as were property offenders.

An interesting test of this theory is to investigate the rates of recidivism. If the criminals were removed from the community, then we would expect to see a low rate; they would not be able to repeat their deeds. This was certainly the case in San Luis Obispo, where the Superior Court register of felony indictments lists no more than six offenders a second time for criminal activity.[54] Clearly, San Luis Obispo was successful in removing those who the community believed were prone to criminal activity. Furthermore, anyone who demonstrated a propensity toward crime was severely dealt with. For example, the San Luis Obispo *Tribune,* in reporting on the sentencing of Fred Schiefferly, who was given five years in San Quentin for grand larceny, observed that the defendant had already gained much notoriety in the county for other offenses. Therefore, "his sentence was more severe than it otherwise would have been."[55]

This decline in recidivism rates has been observed elsewhere. In his study of Columbus, Ohio, Eric Monkkonen noted that recidivism rates were declining: in the period of 1877-1881, 25 percent of crime was committed by repeat offenders; in 1882-1885, the rate was 12 percent.[56] Monkkonen did speculate that this might mean the criminals were indeed in jail, but he was not certain. He also speculated that the criminal element might have been more transient, simply moving on to other areas to commit additional crime. Or, the lower rate of recidivism might have been due to the relative anonymity of the city, which made labeling less prevalent, and re-entry easier.[57]

As we have seen, there is no consensus among scholars concerning the reasons for the declining crime rate in the latter part of the nineteenth century. Still, as far as San Luis Obispo County is concerned, the theory that felony crime was declining because the criminals were in jail seems plausible. The rate of recidivism, as reflected in the Superior Court indictments, was quite low. Clearly, in San Luis Obispo anyway, if a person demonstrated any sort of criminal proclivity, especially in property crime, he was effectively removed from the community.

As if to confirm our observation that crime was not a serious problem in San Luis Obispo, another observation that our investigation suggests is the somewhat mechanical, almost perfunctory, manner in which the Superior Court worked. As Friedman and Percival also observed, the system, on balance, was more administrative than adjudicative.[58] In San Luis Obispo there was a significant number of guilty pleas or dismissals. Trials occurred in a distinct minority of the cases initially brought before the court. Still, the function of Superior Court was crime control, and from all available evidence, it does seem to have been efficient at this; felony crime rates were dropping. The process may have been rather routine, but the required results were produced: the effective elimination of crime perpetrators from the community.

Of course, there is, for the researcher, always the problem of whether most criminals were found out, arrested and punished. The relationship between recorded criminal activity and actual behavior remains unclear. Friedman and Percival formed an impression (and realized it could not be called more than that) that criminal defendants were a poor sample of the total criminals.[59] They believed that defendants were selected almost at random out of an oppressed class of citizens. Unfortunately, the types of demographic data that Friedman and Percival were able to utilize for such an impression were not available for San Luis Obispo. Still, from the sources that were available, the impression (and we can call it no more than that, also) one forms is that the majority of offenders, at least those that the public was aware of, were caught up into the justice system. For instance, the *Tribune* editorialized at one point on how orderly San Luis Obispo was, in spite of a reputation for rowdiness.[60] This may have been a bit of boosterism, but still, the sense, the impression, is that San Luis Obispo was a rather orderly community and that criminality was effectively controlled.

NOTES

[1]See for example Eric H. Monkkonen, *The Dangerous Class: Crime and Poverty in Columbus, Ohio, 1960-1988* (Cambridge, Mass: Harvard University Press, 1975); Roger Lane, *Violent Death in the City: Suicide, Accident and Murder in Nineteenth-Century Philadelphia* (Cambridge, Mass: Harvard University Press, 1979); John C. Schneider, *Detroit and the Problem of Order, 1830-1880: A Geography of Crime, Riot and Policing* (Lincoln: Nebraska Press, 1980); Eric H. Monkkonen, *Police in Urban America 1860-1920* (Harvard University Press, 1981); Eugene J. Watts, "Police Response to Crime and Disorder in Twentieth-Century St. Louis," *Journal of American History*, 70 (September 1983): 340-358.

[2]This bias in focus of study has been only briefly noted. Eugene Watts, for instance, noted that "All the world is not St. Louis," but expected basic similarities across the nation; "Police Response to Crime," p. 37. Eric Monkkonen observed that San Francisco did not conform to a national decline in public disorder, and suggested further city-level research; "A Disorderly People? Urban Order in the Nineteenth and Twentieth Century," *Journal of American History*, 68 (December 1981): 539-559.

[3]Lawrence M. Friedman and Robert V. Percival, *The Roots of Justice* (Chapel Hill, N.C.: University of North Carolina Press, 1981).

[4]Ibid., p. 311.

[5]Ibid.

[6]The author has previously looked at the work of the police department and the lower courts in San Luis Obispo for the same period, also exploring the difference between urban and rural responses to crime. See "The Police and Crime in Late-Nineteenth-and early Twentieth Century San Luis Obispo, California," *Western Legal History*, 4 (Summer/Fall 1991): 203-224.

[7]A brief look at population figures will confirm the lack of growth of San Luis Obispo County (population figures are from the *Census Reports of the United States:*

	1880	1890	1900	1910
San Luis Obispo County	9,142	16,072	16,637	19,383
State of California	864,694	1,208,130	1,585,053	2,377,549

A comparison of population density, in persons per square mile, further underscores the rural nature of San Luis Obispo County:

	1880	1890	1900	1910
San Luis Obispo County	2.74	4.82	4.99	5.87
State of California	5.54	7.75	9.52	15.30

[8]Friedman and Percival, *Roots of Justice* p. 17.

[9]Due to gaps in the San Luis Obispo County Superior Court records (*i.e.*, some cases listed contain no indictment listing, some contain no plea record and some are missing other portions of the court proceedings), the numbers discussed in this article do not always match. For example, we can state that there were 840 cases entered in the Superior Court Register in the period 1880-1910 but we can list only 624 cases according to indictments handed down. Similar discrepancies are found in plea and sentencing analysis.

[10]San Luis Obispo *Tribune*, January 10, 1880, p. 1.

[11]For a description of the proceedings of the Superior Court and methods of hearing cases, see Friedman and Percival, *Roots of Justice*, pp. 40-43.

[12]Ibid., p. 42.

[13]Ibid., p. 44.

[14]The judgeship of the San Luis Obispo County Superior Court was rather stable with only four justices sitting during our thirty year period of study, one judge served for 17 years: Louis McMurtry, 1880-1884; D. S. Gregory, 1885-1889; V. A. Gregg, 1890-1895; E. P. Unangst, 1896-1913.

[15]In accordance with the Friedman and Percival study, we will look at crimes that are divided into four main categories: (1) crimes against people; (2) crimes against property; (3) morals offenses; and (4) public order offenses. Friedman and Percival, *Roots of Justice*, p. 135.

[16]San Luis Obispo County Superior Court records are cited throughout by case number as filed in the Register of Criminal Actions.

[17]*Tribune*, July 24, 1880, p. 1.

[18]Ibid.

[19]Friedman and Percival, *Roots of Justice*, p. 174.

[20]Mark H. Haller, "Plea Bargaining: The Nineteenth Century Perspective," *Law and Society Review*, 13 (Winter 1979): 273. For more on plea bargaining, see also: Albert W. Alschuler, "Plea Bargaining and Its History," *Law and Society Review*, 13 (Winter 1979): 211-245, and Lynn M. Mather, "Comments on the History of Plea Bargaining," *Law and Society Review*, 13 (Winter 1979): 281-285.

[21]Haller, "Plea Bargaining," p. 275.

[22]Ibid.

[23]Ibid., p. 278.

[24]Laurence M. Friedman, "Plea Bargaining in Historical Perspective," *Law and Society Review*, 13 (Winter 1979): 247; Friedman and Percival, *Roots of Justice*, pp. 176, 180.

[25]Friedman and Percival, *Roots of Justice*, p. 180.

[26]Ibid., p. 173.

[27]Others have observed that trial by jury was on the decline by the end of the nineteenth century, apparently in response to reforms in court proceedings including the laws of evidence. These reforms made trial by jury an unwieldy method for adjudication. Case load pressure then led to plea bargaining and the adoption of bench trial. See: Susan C. Towne, "The Historical Origins of Bench Trial for Serious Crime," *American Journal of Legal History*, 26 (April 1982): 123-159. Friedman and Percival also observed that jury trials accounted for only 40 percent of all cases that were heard by the Alameda County Superior Court (*Roots of Justice*, p. 173). See also pp. 192-195 for a discussion of the decline of jury trials in Alameda County.)

[28]Trial in this period meant trial by jury; there were no bench trials. See Friedman and Percival, *Roots of Justice*, p. 173.

[29]Ibid.

[30]San Luis Obispo *Tribune*, December 13, 1895, p. 1.

[31]Ibid., December 15, 1895, p. 1.

[32]Friedman and Percival, *Roots of Justice*, p. 204.

[33]Ibid., p. 206.

[34]*Tribune*, December 15, 1895, p. 1.

[35]Ibid., p. 105.

[36]Ibid., p. 204.

[37]San Luis Obispo *Tribune*, November 12, 1899, p. 1.

[38]*Tribune*, December 16, 1903, p. 1.

[39]Ibid., December 16, 1903, p. 1.

[40]Ibid., April 11, 1903, p. 1.

[41]Hubert H. Bancroft, *History of California* (7 vols., San Francisco: The History Co., 1884-1890), VII: 216.

[42]Roger Lane, *Violent Death in the City: Suicide, Accident and Murder in Nineteenth Century Philadelphia* (Cambridge, Mass.: Harvard University Press, 1979), p. 120.

[43]See Robert R. Dykstra, *The Cattletowns* (New York: Alfred Knopf, 1968), p. 128. The author observes that court action in the West was lenient toward perpetrators of violence and homicide, and that there were few death penalties.

[44]Robert H. Tillman, "The Prosecution of Homicide in Sacramento County, California, 1853-1900," Southern California Quarterly, 68 (Summer 1986): 173.

[45]Ibid., p. 175.

[46]Ibid., p. 170.

[47]"Police and Crime," pp. 214-215.

[48]*Tribune*, October 21, 1891, p. 1.

[49]Ibid., Interestingly, the *Tribune* very rarely reported on morals cases to its readers. No more than five reports of such cases could be found in thirty years of newspaper records.

[50]Eric Monkkonen, "The Organized Response to Crime in Nineteenth- and Twentieth-Century America," *Journal of Interdisciplinary History*, 14 (Summer 1983): 116.

[51]Roger Lane, *Violent Death in the City: Suicide, Accident and Murder in Nineteenth-Cen-

tury Philadelphia (Cambridge, Mass.: Harvard University Press, 1979). See also John C. Schneider, *Detroit and the Problem of Order, 1830-1880: A Geography of Crime, Riot and Policing* (Lincoln: University of Nebraska Press, 1980). Schneider also considers the role of city in relationship to crime. However, his approach is concerned with where crime occurred, and how spatial arrangements structured criminal action. In his study, the differentiation of residences by ethnicity and class, the creation of a commercial downtown and the development of a vice area, all made the city free of the collective disorder and conflict it had known earlier.

[52]Ted R. Gurr, *The Politics of Crime and Conflict: A Comparative History of Four Cities* (Beverly Hills: Sage Publications, 1976).

[53]Eric Monkkonen, "The Organized Response to Crime," p. 116.

[54]From the records in San Luis Obispo, we cannot determine, of course, whether criminals from San Luis Obispo reverted to criminal activity in other locations once they were released from state prison. This suggests a subject for further research.

[55]San Luis Obispo *Tribune*, January 18, 1884, p. 1.

[56]Eric Monkkonen, *The Dangerous Class: Crime and Poverty in Columbus, Ohio, 1860-1885* (Cambridge, Mass.: Harvard University Press, 1975), p. 102.

[57]Ibid.

[58]Friedman and Percival, *Roots of Justice*, p. 312.

[59]Ibid., p. 317.

[60]San Luis Obispo *Tribune*, November 30, 1989, p. 1.

Historical Society of

Southern California

Bearers of the Burden: Justices of the Peace, Their Courts and the Law, in Orange County, California, 1870-1907

By John J. Stanley

Recent legal scholarship has made it clear that nineteenth-century Americans were extremely knowledgeable about the law. John Phillip Reid has shown us that they carried this knowledge with them on the overland trail, and exercised that law even when circumstances were desperate and when no conventional legal institutions existed.[1] Gold miners first reaching California found themselves in a virtual legal vacuum; laws passed in distant San Francisco hardly seemed relevant up some tributary of the Feather River. The miners demanded law, and in the absence of traditional offices frequently resorted to popular justice—swiftly, often brutally. The introduction of the office of justice of the peace reimposed legal order.

By the 1870s California's legal institutions had survived most of their significant challenges. In some incidents regular legal methods failed (the massacre of the Chinese in Los Angeles in 1872 was one of them), but by and large an eastern model of American law had fully taken root, supplanting Mexican civil law and mining-camp justice. Californians routinely turned to their courts for justice and the resolution of disputes. Since most of these issues were settled in lower justice or municipal courts, the justice of the peace was an important figure in most communities. Seldom a lawyer, it was he who enforced local mores and reflected local attitudes.

John J. Stanley is a deputy sheriff in Los Angeles County. He recently completed graduate work in legal history at California State University, Fullerton.

[1] See John Phillip Reid, *Law for the Elephant: Property and Social Behavior on the Overland Trail* (San Marino, 1980).

The justice court was often the furthest extent of the legal system as far as the average citizen was concerned. To determine the level of legal expertise Californians could expect at the end of the nineteenth century, and to consider the men who disseminated the law, this study will concentrate on the justices in Orange County from 1870 to 1907, bearing in mind that the region remained a part of Los Angeles County until 1889.

Wherever drifting emigrants lighted to the east of the Rockies, the seeds of American legal culture took root. These forces were unopposed everywhere except in Louisiana, where a strange hybrid of common and civil law grew. When migrants crossed the Rocky Mountains and reached California, however, they encountered a Mexican culture that thwarted their drive to extend American common-law tradition to the Pacific. Before the Treaty of Guadalupe Hidalgo in 1848, according to David Langum, Americans living in California "drew on local law only to the extent absolutely necessary," preferring instead "to order their ... circumstances in a manner harmonious with the remembered law of the eastern and midwestern states from which they had come."[2] Anglo-American expatriates' dislike for Mexican California's legal system quickly manifested itself when the Anglos assumed control of the region. They rejected many of the political and legal concessions established by the treaty and introduced more traditional American institutions.

The state constitution of 1849 further Americanized the region; remaining contentious matters were resolved in the courts.[3] The Mexican *alcalde* system was repudiated and the familiar American justice system was adopted. Article 1232 of the *General Law of California, 1850-1864*, stated that "the following shall be the courts of justice of this state: first, the supreme court; second, the district courts; third, the county courts; fourth, the probate courts; fifth, the justice courts; sixth, the recorder's and other inferior municipal courts." Articles 1278-1284 pertained specifically to the justice courts. Justices were responsible for minor civil cases, with the exception of probate, and were granted the power to marry people. They also had authority over certain criminal matters: petit larceny; assault and battery, except on a peace officer or when the assault was likely to produce great bodily injury; breaches of the peace; riots; affrays; vandalism, and all misdemeanors punishable by fines of less than

[2]David J. Langum, *Law and Community on the Mexican California Frontier: Anglo-American Expatriates and the Clash of Legal Traditions, 1821-1846* (Norman, 1987) 267.

[3]For the transition of law in California between the Mexican and American period, see Gordon M. Bakken, *The Development of Law in Frontier California, 1850-1890* (Westport, Conn., 1985) 21, 42, 93. The settlement of Mexican land-grant claims was the state's most troublesome early issue.

$500 or a maximum of six months in jail. This level of punishment was amended to $1,000 and one year by the legislature on April 1, 1870. In the absence of the county coroner, justices conducted formal examinations of the dead. Additionally, the justice courts were given authority over "proceedings respecting vagrancy and disorderly persons."

As in eastern communities, the justice of the peace was called on to reassure local inhabitants that all was well. The slow population growth at the southern end of the state retarded the development of justice courts, but once Americans settled in pockets of the region in any numbers the courts were quickly established.

As part of their study of the criminal-justice system in Alameda County, Lawrence Friedman and Robert Percival considered the composition of the justice courts.[4] The justices they studied held a wide range of occupations, from machinist to jack-of-all-trades. In 1880 the average age for a justice when he began his first tour on the bench was fifty-three. This age declined throughout the period, however, until in 1890 the average age was thirty-nine, and in 1900 Oakland city justices were, on average, twenty-eight when they heard their first case.[5] Unlike township justices of the peace, who could be laymen, Oakland city justices had to be lawyers. "This made the job less inviting" for those who were established, according to Friedman and Percival, than for "a young, up-and-coming lawyer," and probably explained the justices' increasingly young age.[6]

In John Wunder's study of justice courts in Washington Territory from 1853 to 1889, he found that justices averaged 40.6 years of age during their first term of service.[7] All of them were literate, at a time when 11.5% of the white population and 22.6% of the total population was not; most were men of more than average wealth and were politically active.[8] Twenty-two of the 197 justices Wunder studied practiced law, and 107 of them had access to law books. They were thus educated and legally qualified for the office they held.[9] Justices were highly respected in the Territory and, when called upon, were virtually always the court

[4] Lawrence M. Friedman and Robert V. Percival, *The Roots of Justice, Crime and Punishment in Alameda County, California, 1870-1910* (Chapel Hill, 1981) [hereafter cited as Friedman and Percival, *Roots of Justice*].

[5] Ibid. at 45.

[6] Ibid. at 46.

[7] John R. Wunder, *Inferior Courts, Superior Justice* (Westport, Conn., 1979) [hereafter cited as Wunder, *Inferior Courts*]. See also Francis S. Philbrick, *The Rise of the West, 1754-1830* (New York, 1965), and Robert M. Ireland, *The County Courts of Ante-bellum Kentucky* (Lexington, 1972).

[8] Wunder, *Inferior Courts*, supra note 7 at 26-28.

[9] Ibid. at 117.

of last resort. Only six vigilance committees were formed
throughout the history of Washington Territory, which Wunder
attributed in part to the quality of justice in the courts and
community. He concluded that "The justices of the peace of
Washington Territory dispensed a quality of justice generally
characterized by reason, accessibility, celerity, and community
acceptance."[10]

As they did in Alameda County and Washington Territory,
justices in the Santa Ana Valley played a vital role in the community.[11] Employing the same approach of collective biography to
twenty-one justices who served in the region from 1871 to 1907,
the author has found results that were both similar and dissimilar
to Wunder's and Friedman and Percival's studies (see Table 1).

Justices in the Santa Ana Valley averaged 45.8 years of age at
the beginning of their first term. This average dropped during the
decade of the 1890s, though it never reached as low a figure as in
Alameda County. With one exception, justices of the peace in
Orange County remained laymen throughout the period. Their
reasons for becoming justices appear to have varied and are
addressed below.

FLEDGLING JUSTICE TAKES WING

The lore and legend of Orange County states that Richard Egan
of San Juan Capistrano was the area's first justice of the peace. He
had migrated from Ireland to America in 1852, at the age of ten,
fought for the Confederacy during the Civil War as both a soldier
and sailor, and left for California in 1866. After trying his hand at
farming he went to work for a prominent landowner, Don Marco
Forster, first as a surveyor and afterward as Forster's adviser and
estate executor. When Egan arrived in San Juan he believed that
only he and two other men in the area spoke English. The local
community took to him immediately, however, and he became
first the traditional *alcalde* and then justice of the peace for the
newly formed San Juan/Silverado township. At the time he was in
his late twenties. In 1880 he was elected to the Los Angeles Board
of Supervisors; he was also an enumerator for the census that
year. In 1889 his reputation and experience made him a natural

---

[10]Ibid. at 167.

[11]Orange County's division from its parent county of Los Angeles was not
approved until March 1889 and did not take effect until August. Before that the
area was more commonly known as the Santa Ana Valley. The terms "Orange
County" and "Santa Ana Valley" are used interchangeably throughout this
study.

choice to arbitrate the disputes between the infant Orange
County and its former parent, Los Angeles County.[12]

Even to this day, Egan's reputation is prodigious. It seems
unlikely, however, that he was the first justice of the peace in
southern Los Angeles County. By 1870 San Juan was the lesser of
the two townships in the area. The other township, Santa Ana,
included on its rolls the 881 citizens of the town of Anaheim.
Santa Ana's total population of 1,445 numbered a thousand more
than that of the combined San Juan/Silverado township. Virtually
all of San Juan's population were Mexicans and Indians who
spoke no English. Their demands for a justice court would not
have been as pressing as those of the Anglos at Santa Ana. The
presence of this Anglo population in Santa Ana Township,
especially since it contained Anaheim within its borders, almost
certainly meant that at least one justice of the peace was in the
community before Egan's arrival in San Juan.

Unfortunately, none of Egan's docket books has survived, thus
making an assessment of his performance in office impossible.
The first extant docket books from the region come from the
court of Justice J.J. Johnson of San Joaquin (later Santa Ana)
Township. Little biographical information survives about Johnson. A forty-four-year-old farmer from North Carolina named
John J. Johnson is listed on the rolls of the Index to the Great
Register of Los Angeles County for 1876, and since justices were
all voters, that was probably the justice, but his common name
and the lack of any cross-references make verification impossible.[13] From scrutinizing his dockets it is clear that he was an
educated man and a competent writer. His dockets were detailed
and cited legal sources. His first docket book begins on February
13, 1871, and the first criminal case was recorded on April 4.[14]
Between February 1871 and June 1875 he heard 140 actions. Of
this total only nineteen were criminal cases: five felonies, twelve
misdemeanors, and two crimes of unknown type.[15] Justice courts

[12] Accounts of Egan's life were compiled from the *Santa Ana Register*, December
6, 1920, and February 9, 1923; Terry S. Stephensen's *Caminos Viejos* (Santa Ana,
1930) 92-95; Leo J. Friis's *The Village of Garden Grove, 1870-1905* (Santa Ana,
1959) 100, and 107; and Ellen K. Lee's "The Irish Alcalde," in *Orange Countiana,
A Journal of Local History* 1 (n.p., 1973) 30-37.

[13] Index to the Great Register of Los Angeles County, 1876, 70.

[14] A mayor's court was also operating at Anaheim during the same year. Mayor's
courts, recorder's courts, and police courts were all inferior courts that
constituted the sixth tier of the state judicial system as described in the *General
Law of California, 1850-1864*, vol. 1, Article 1232.

[15] Of the 121 civil actions, fifty were cases of estray involving horses, mules,
cattle, pigs and hogs. In seven cases in which the state was the plaintiff, six were
for failure to pay assessed school taxes. Amounts owed in school taxes ranged
from fifty cents to $62.50. The willingness of the state to pursue someone in
November 1872 for failing to pay half a dollar in school tax indicates how serious
the state was about supporting its schools.

could not try felony cases but they did conduct preliminary hearings (see Table 2). Of the five felony matters Johnson heard (three grand larceny, one assault with a deadly weapon, and one burglary), two were remanded to Los Angeles for trial, two were dismissed, and the fifth was never heard because the accused, a horse thief, escaped custody three days after his arraignment.[16]

By 1874 justice courts also existed at Anaheim and Orange, as we know from the cases Johnson both received and sent to these jurisdictions on change-of-venue motions. The presence of a justice court in Orange is particularly significant. Unlike Anaheim, which became a township at the beginning of the decade, Orange remained divided between Santa Ana and Silverado townships until 1889. Apparently, wherever citizens formed a distinct community, they insisted on a justice court of their own, even without the traditional sanction of an official judicial township.

There appears to be a direct correlation between the arrival of the railroad in the Santa Ana Valley and an increase in court activity that begins about the same time. The Southern Pacific's first line into the region reached Anaheim in 1875 and was extended to Santa Ana in 1877. Records for the San Joaquin Justice Court are missing for 1876, but when they resume again at the beginning of the next year, the new justice, Charles W. Humphreys, found himself far busier than his predecessor.

In the period beginning in January 1877 and ending in December 1880, Humphreys heard 69 criminal and 261 civil cases (see Table 2). Humphreys was a Kentucky native, the son of a sheriff in Mason County, and had arrived in the area with his wife and three children in 1874. He was employed as a real-estate broker, was quickly elected justice in 1875, and began service the following January. He served continuously until 1883, when he inexplicably left the bench, only to return at the beginning of 1885. A case entered in his docket book at the end of 1882 was completed by Justice Freeman, apparently because of Humphreys's sudden illness. After his return, Humphreys remained on the bench until the end of 1886. Three years later he was part of a syndicate that purchased the *Santa Ana Blade*. He was again elected justice in 1892 and served from January 1893 until January 1895. Before his return to the bench he became a lawyer. On his death in January 1896 he was lauded by members of the Orange County bar, whose obituary in the *Santa Ana Standard* remembered him as "a trusted counselor, [and] friend to the needy."[17] Like Egan, Humphreys had been new to the area and had used the bench to

[16] Docket Book of the San Joaquin Justice Court, J.J. Johnson, Justice, November 11, 1872.

[17] This brief biography of Humphreys was compiled from *An Illustrated History of Southern California* (Chicago, 1890) 857-58 [hereafter cited as *Illustrated*

forward his business career. His scholarly approach is reflected in the detail of his docket and his eventual membership of the bar.

The arrival of the railroad made the region much more accessible. Settlement in the Santa Ana Valley became easier and more attractive and local crops could be sent to distant markets. Between 1870 and 1880 the population of Los Angeles County more than doubled.[18] During the same period, the two townships in the Santa Ana Valley were divided into five and the population grew three and a half times. The increase in Humphreys's court reflected the region's expanded pool of potential litigants, although why so many citizens took their disputes to court is unclear.

The increase in criminal activity did not keep pace with the increase in civil actions, and what increases there were were not considered particularly alarming at the time. With the exception of 1877, felonies do not increase at all, and of the six felony cases that year one was dismissed, a second saw no action taken after the filing of the complaint, and a third was reduced from assault with a deadly weapon to disturbing the peace. Only three of the cases were remanded to higher court in Los Angeles for trial. The majority of criminal cases were for battery and disturbing the peace.

Lawyers also made their presence felt in criminal matters by the end of the decade. Only five of the nineteen defendants who stood before Justice Johnson (1871-75) did so with counsel, whereas between 1877 and 1880 nearly 54% of defendants were represented. Chinese defendants were almost always represented by counsel; Hispanic defendants rarely were.

If activity in Justice Humphreys's court is indicative of court activity throughout the region, the few lawyers who lived in the area did not want for employment at the end of the 1870s (see Table 2).[19] Matters appeared to change noticeably, however, in the early 1880s. A review of Santa Ana Justice Court records indicates a steady drop in civil litigation between 1879 and 1882. A similar

---

History]; the Index to the Great Register of Los Angeles County, 1880; the *Santa Ana Standard*, January 25, 1896; and Jim Sleeper's *Turn the Rascals Out!* (Trabuco Canyon, Calif., 1973) 122 [hereafter cited as Sleeper, *Turn the Rascals Out!*].

[18] The redivision of the townships was made in 1875.

[19] A possible explanation for the sudden flurry of participation by lawyers in the justice courts may have been the general business depression throughout California in the 1870s. Short on work, lawyers were eager to represent any clients who were willing to pay for their services. See Gordon M. Bakken's *Practicing Law in Frontier California* (Lincoln, 1991) for more on this hypothesis. Friedman and Percival noted that in some quarters lawyers who practiced in justice courts were not well thought of. Quoting from an 1892 *Yale Law Review* article, they noted that justice court lawyers were considered a "legal shark, a kind of tolerated legal vermin, devoid alike of honesty, learning and industry." Idem, *Roots of Justice*, supra note 4 at 64.

decrease may be observed in the justice courts at Westminster.
(The large, though declining, number of civil cases at the end of
the 1870s evidently reflects local circumstances rather than a
community that was suddenly more litigious. The railroad's
arrival brought new inhabitants to the area, and their presence
may have encouraged disputes of title and of minor debts.) An
explanation for the apparent wane in civil litigation might be
that, if the amount contested in individual suits exceeded the
limit imposed on justice courts by law, all actions were contested
in Los Angeles Superior Court. However, travelling the more than
thirty miles to Los Angeles was difficult by horse and buggy and
costly by train. Moreover, the lack of any noticeable increase in
the dollar amount of civil suits suggests that cases were unlikely
to exceed the justice court limit, and a review of the Los Angeles
County Superior Court plaintiff index from 1880 to 1889 reveals
no unusually high number of actions from the Santa Ana Valley.[20]

The drop in civil litigation appears to have affected criminal
actions in an interesting way. Beginning in 1881, fewer and fewer
criminal defendants were represented by counsel. In only five of
the twenty criminal cases that year was there counsel for the
defense. Except in 1883, when only two criminal cases were tried
before Justice Jacob Ross, attorneys represented criminal defendants only half, or less than half, the time.[21] By the end of the
decade such representation had declined even further. In 1888
only two of fifteen defendants were represented, and in Justice
Sam Craddick's court at Orange in 1889, defense counsel was
present in only one criminal case of forty-three. Contributing to
the situation in Craddick's court was the large number of vagrancy cases (see Table 3). In only one of the 212 vagrancy cases
studied from all courts was a defendant represented by an attorney.[22] Criminal representation by counsel was no better in

[20] The Los Angeles Superior Court system as it exists today was organized in
1880, before which the court was administered as a circuit court and its records
were maintained quite differently. Los Angeles County Archives' plaintiff and
defendant indexes date from 1880. Before that date it is virtually impossible to
ascertain official court records.

[21] Little is known about Ross, a farmer of limited judicial ability. He handled
only eleven cases in his two-year tenure on the bench. All three of his actions in
1883 came to him from another venue. His docket entries were brief and
tentative. Lawyers may have shifted litigation away from his court until
Humphreys's return in 1885.

[22] The docket book of the Anaheim Justice Court of James Howard for 1903
records that on February 19, 1903, Anaheim lawyer Will S. Tipton represented
accused vagrant George Ellis in a bench trial. Tipton demanded a jury trial for his
client but District Attorney Horace Head ordered that the matter continue
without one. Despite the presence of Tipton at his side, Ellis was found guilty
and sentenced to pay a fine of $60.00 or serve thirty days in county jail. Since
Ellis was accused of soliciting alms on the street, it was unlikely that he could
produce the fine, and he was remanded to the custody of the sheriff to serve his
sentence.

Westminster, where defense attorneys were present in only five of the twenty-six criminal cases between 1879 and 1889.

The justice courts of Westminster Township were ably manned when their first surviving docket books begin in 1879 and 1880 (see Table 4). Jonathan Wesley Aldridge was a fifty-one-year-old farmer from Indiana who, unlike Egan and Humphreys, had been in the region several years before becoming justice in 1880.[23] David Webster, who had been born in England and who lived in Garden Grove, began service as justice of the peace at Westminster Township's other justice court in 1879, two years after he had arrived from Ohio. In addition to his duties as justice, he served as postmaster, and was affectionately referred to as "Deacon" Webster because of his church activities. When he relinquished his office in 1893 at the age of 78 to the 26-year-old Luke Smith, he carefully listed in his docket the books he was transferring to the young man. They included "1 volume *Statutes of California, 1877-1888,* 1 volume *Amendments to the Codes, 1877-1878,* 1 volume *Statutes of California, 1880,* 1 volume *Amendments to the Codes, 1880,* 1 volume *Statutes & Amendments to the Codes, 1881,* 1 volume *Statutes & Amendments to the Codes, 1883.*"[24] His list indicated that, despite lacking formal legal training, justices had access to legal sources. The degree to which they scrutinized those sources depended on the justice.[25]

Practicing law in the southern precincts of Los Angeles County was a precarious business during the 1880s. Work in the justice courts was not sufficient to keep lawyers within the region when a superior court and a larger potential client pool was only thirty miles north in Los Angeles. Between the recording of the 1879 and 1886 Indexes to the Great Register of Los Angeles County, there was no change in the number of lawyers living in the Santa

[23] Aldridge served as justice until 1884. There are no further entries in the docket book from this court until 1888. When it resumed Thomas C. Hull, a forty-one-year-old merchant from Ohio, was the justice. Aldridge had moved to Westminster Colony in April, 1874, from Watsonville with his wife, Elizabeth. Thomas Hull and his wife, Emma, had arrived in the colony two months earlier. Hull was elected manager of the village store in November 1875 and in February 1878 purchased the store in partnership with F.A. Lund. Biographical information on Aldridge and Hull is from the Index to the Great Register of Los Angeles County, 1880, 1886 and 1888, and Ivana F. Bollman's *Westminster Colony, California: 1869-1879* (Santa Ana, 1983) 62, 90, 120, 124.

[24] Docket Book of the Westminster Justice Court, David Webster, Justice, 1893.

[25] Index to the Great Register of Los Angeles County, 1880; *History of Los Angeles County, 1880* (1880; reprint, Berkeley, 1959) 191 [hereafter cited as *History of Los Angeles County*]; Leo J. Doig, *The Village of Garden Grove, 1870-1905* (Santa Ana, 1959) 34, 63, 107-9. Doig makes no mention of Webster's tenure on the bench before 1893 and erroneously states that he was justice from 1901 to 1902. Webster died in 1896, however. The *Orange News* published his obituary on May 4 of that year.

Ana Valley. The index lists seven in 1879 and seven in 1886. Of the seven in 1886, however, only two were among the group from 1879.[26]

With two justice courts in each township, lawyers could exercise some choice as to which justices heard their civil cases. As we have seen, Humphreys was well regarded, and during his absence from the bench in 1883 and 1884 there was far less court activity during farmer Jacob Ross's tenure. Records from Santa Ana's other justice court have not survived, but it is likely that Justice George Freeman, who was seated there, was much busier than Ross during those years.

Freeman was a prominent fixture on Santa Ana's justice bench. He assumed the office in 1882 and remained in it until January 1903. Born in Hallowell, Maine, in 1829, he went to California by steamer in 1851, landing in San Francisco. He was occupied in mining and lumbering until he moved to Alameda County in 1869, where he changed occupations and became a carpenter and contractor. He continued to work as a contractor after arriving in the Santa Ana Valley in 1877. In April 1889, seven years after becoming a justice of the peace, he was elected recorder of the city of Santa Ana.[27]

During 1882, when Freeman completed some of Humphreys's cases, his entries in his colleague's docket were extensive and reflected an equal grasp of the law.[28] Throughout the eighties, Freeman enjoyed the full confidence of the community. This was clear in the election of 1890, when, despite not gaining the endorsement of any party ticket, he was reelected justice.[29] However, this confidence was somewhat shaken early in the next decade when Freeman, together with his colleague Isaiah Marks on the Santa Ana justice bench, and James Landell of Anaheim, were indicted by a grand jury for alleged irregularities over the collection of their fees.[30]

[26]Southern Township Attorneys, 1879 and 1886, compiled from the Index to the Great Register of Los Angeles County, 1880 and 1886. The name, place of birth, city of residence, and age at the time of the index are included.

[27]Illustrated History, supra note 17 at 886; Index to the Great Register of Los Angeles County, 1880.

[28]Docket Book of the Santa Ana Justice Court, Charles W. Humphreys, Justice, July 6, 1882.

[29]Santa Ana Standard, November 8, 1890.

[30]Freeman also bears the dubious distinction of conducting the 1892 preliminary hearing for accused murderer Francisco Torres before his lynching. To his credit, Freeman ordered that Torres be held to answer for the charge, and was considering a change-of-venue motion by Torres's attorneys. Torres's executioner noted this by leaving a sign around the hanged man's neck that read "Change of Venue."

George E. Freeman served on the Santa Ana justice bench between 1882 and 1903. (Santa Ana Public Library)

FEES, FINES, CRIMES, AND VAGRANTS

The office of justice of the peace was unsalaried. Justices received compensation from fees collected in civil and criminal matters. The front of Webster's docket book clearly lists the amounts set by the state legislature of 1870 that were to be assessed for each of the justice's functions. Los Angeles County officials convinced the state to attach a special provision to the law affecting justices within their boundaries.[31] By consequence,

[31] California, *Revised Statutes* (1870) 677. The most pertinent section of this law for this study was the one applying to justice fees for criminal actions in Los Angeles County, which stated: "For all services before a J.P. in a criminal action or proceeding, whether on examination or trial, $3.00. Provided in the county of Los Angeles the fees in a criminal action shall be collected from a defendant if convicted, but shall in no case become a county charge." State lawmakers had addressed the issue of justice fees as early as 1851, during the second session of the legislature (see the *Compiled Laws of California* [1851] 726, 733). It should be noted that the $3.00 fee for criminal matters was not increased between its imposition in 1870 and the end of this study in 1907.

justices' fees there were tightly regulated and protected against judicial abuse. The same law that specified justice fees also stipulated fees for constables, the justice's right arm. Constables acted as jailer, bailiff, and lawman and were also unsalaried.[32]

This system worked well through the 1870s and 1880s. Justices carefully sentenced convicted defendants to pay fines that covered court, constable, and any miscellaneous fees, such as those for witnesses and juries. Fines often exactly matched costs (Humphreys was well known for his precise match of fines to expenses.) The idea of using court fines to pay for other government services was obviously not a strong one at the end of the nineteenth century. The only reason the system worked as well as it did was because of the cooperation of convicted defendants, enough of whom paid fines and refused incarceration to maintain the system.[33] When things went well, justices and constables garnered the majority of their compensation from the civil side of the docket rather than the criminal. Problems began to arise at the end of the 1880s with an increase in criminal activity generally, the arrival of tramps specifically, and the creation of Orange County, which eliminated Los Angeles County's protection against unpaid criminal-justice fees' becoming a county charge.

The court of Anaheim justice A.V. Fox was the first to record a noticeable increase in criminal activity (see Table 5). Fox, a sixty-two-year-old hotel keeper from New Hampshire when he began his docket in November 1886, dealt with crimes that ranged from violating county licensing ordinances to robbery. In 1887 twenty of the fifty-nine crimes he handled concerned property—either theft, fraud, burglary, or robbery, an unusually high number. In 1888 only twelve crimes of the seventy handled involved property; in 1889, ten of forty-six; in 1890, eight of fifty-six. These figures are of interest since vagrants who flocked to the area in the 1890s were accused of being thieves and increasing the crime rate, yet property crimes peaked in Anaheim before tramps began to flood the local courts.

Fox handled eleven cases to do with vagrants in 1889, but in Orange thirty-nine of Craddick's forty-three criminal cases were

---

[32]Either one or two part-time constables maintained the peace throughout each township in addition to their duties in court. They were assisted in their law-enforcement duties by a number of other sources. Marshals (paid by the city) were responsible for law enforcement within Santa Ana, Anaheim, and Orange, although their primary duty was to collect city taxes. The sheriff and his deputies (paid by the county) also had jurisdiction over the unincorporated area of the county, but sheriff's personnel rarely dealt with non-felons. Other law enforcers were nightwatchmen, private citizens, and railroad employees, all of whom initiated complaints about criminal activity, especially vagrancy.

[33]Defendants who failed to pay their fines were generally ordered to serve one day in jail for each dollar of their fine. This decreased in the 1890s and 1900s to one day for each two dollars of a fine.

for vagrancy. Craddick, who was born in Iowa, had moved to the
Santa Ana valley for the sake of his wife's health after living in
the Middle West. He pursued an occupation in real estate and
quickly immersed himself in local politics. When he became an
Orange justice in 1889, he counted the establishment of Orange
County College as his greatest achievement.[34]

Of less distinction was Craddick's alleged proclivity for bringing vagrants before him. When he was bidding to return to the
bench in the election of 1894, the *Orange News* was quick to
remind its readers that, of Craddick's forty-three criminal cases
between August 1889 and the end of his first term of service in
January 1891, thirty-four were tramp or vagrancy cases. To the
News this meant that "he also was then engaged in a practice of
running his office largely for revenue only."[35] Surviving records of
his first term in office end in July 1890, therefore the paper's
statistics for the remainder of the year cannot be confirmed. If we
assume that they were accurate, however, and couple them with
Craddick's docket entries before August 1890, we learn that
during his first term as justice he actually heard sixty-seven
vagrancy cases out of a total of seventy-eight criminal cases. Thus
86% of his time on criminal matters was spent with vagrants.[36]
However, there is a problem with the *News*'s assertion about
Craddick's motivation for hearing vagrancy cases. Before the
division, his ability to garner fees for criminal cases was dictated
by the special Los Angeles County provision concerning the
collection of those fees. It is true that he listed his fees at three
dollars per defendant, but it is doubtful that he was able to collect
any of that money. In August 1890 the *Orange Post* printed with
pride that "Tramps give Orange a wide berth."[37] This was largely
attributed to the city's aggressive detention of suspicious persons,
in which activity Craddick had few rivals.

Despite Craddick's combative policy of prosecution, he was
somewhat more lenient when it came to sentencing. Of the sixty-
six accused vagrants whose names are recorded in his surviving
docket, only twenty ever saw jail time. No story was too implau-
sible to win the dismissal of a case. In February 1889 five vagrants,
found "penniless and . . . sleeping in a box car," asserted that they
were former employees of the Santa Fe and hoped to work for the
railroad again. This assertion created enough "reasonable doubt"
in the mind of the court "suffucient to earn their release."[38]

[34]*Illustrated History*, supra note 17 at 871.

[35]*Orange News*, October 24, 1894.

[36]Ibid.

[37]*Orange Post*, August 9, 1890.

[38]Docket Book of the Orange Justice Court, Sam M. Craddick, Justice, February
13, 1889. Their release did not prevent Craddick from charging a fee of $15.00 for
his time.

Those who were sentenced faced progressively longer stints in custody. On pleading guilty to a charge of vagrancy, William Brown was sentenced to fifteen days in jail on January 17, 1889.[39] Frank Eniges's guilty sentence at the end of the year, on the other hand, earned him thirty days' hard labor.[40] By 1890, however, even a guilty verdict did not necessarily mean jail time. Craddick routinely offered sentenced vagrants the option of leaving the county within several hours of their conviction in order to avoid the imposition of their jail sentences. This invitation, commonly referred to as a "floater," was always accepted, and no vagrant went to jail from Craddick's court between January and July of 1890. However, this did not deter the justice from filing his fees against the county coffers.

The questions that arise were whether justices of the peace in the county were attempting to take advantage of the homeless for their own monetary gain, and whether they were responding to the demands of the community. In the early 1890s the financial condition of the county was tenuous. A virtual flood of homeless people threatened the county's already stretched resources, and in 1895 the formation of a vigilance committee to address the problem was discussed at a meeting in Neill's Hall in Santa Ana. The gathering included some of that city's more prominent citizens, including the former district attorney, J.G. Scarborough.[41] The committee never came about, but one may ask whether the justices did not feel it incumbent upon themselves to maintain law and order by controlling the community's most visible reminder of its fear of economic failure. At the same time the justices had to balance their civic responsibilities as keepers of the law with their fiduciary responsibilities of not burdening the county treasury. With these opposing functions before them, conflict was inevitable.

When Orange County officially came into existence on August 5, 1889, it did so with justice courts already established within its five judicial townships, at Anaheim, Orange, San Juan, Santa Ana, and Westminster.[42] In fact, the region's justices of the peace played an integral part in the creation of the other layers of county government.[43] Justices of the peace and constables were the only elected officials to remain after the new county broke away from Los Angeles County.

[39] Ibid., January 17, 1889.

[40] Ibid., December 14, 1889.

[41] Santa Ana Standard, January 12, 1895.

[42] Supra note 26.

[43] Names of justices of the peace, past and present, lace the "Proceedings of the Board of Orange County Commissioners," the committee created on March 11, 1889, to organize the various offices of the new county and conduct a special election to confirm the new county's existence and elect its new officers. Justices of the peace were instrumental in calling the election on June 4 and establishing

While controversy did not characterize the office of justice of the peace in earlier years, the issue of fees and tramps was to change things. One of the justices affected was James Landell, of Anaheim, who was elected in November 1890 to succeed Fox. A longtime resident of the community, Landell appeared an excellent choice for justice. Like so many others, he had migrated to southern California (in 1874) for health reasons. He became a farmer and vineyardist, and also served as precinct clerk during the special election that chose the county's first officers in 1889.[44] Like Craddick, Landell spent a significant percentage of his court time on vagrancy cases between 1891 and 1893 (see Table 5). In 1894 controversy over the handling of his office arose, and it is regrettable that his docket is missing from October 1893 through December 1895.

Part of the problem between justices of the peace and county officials was the administration of the justice courts. While the region was part of Los Angeles County, justices worked without strict supervision from Los Angeles and were virtually autonomous. Local lawyers took turns being prosecution and defense counsel because assistant district attorneys did not travel south to prosecute cases. Justices' dockets were supposed to be reviewed annually by the Los Angeles grand jury, but one is hard-pressed to find many signatures from members of the grand jury who reviewed the records before the division.

With the advent of county offices in Orange County, the district attorney's office prosecuted significant cases and the grand jury scrutinized each justice's docket thoroughly. While the Santa Ana Valley was part of Los Angeles County, justices in the region routinely conducted their business without informing the distant district attorney's office. Orange County D.A.s wanted to review matters before justices adjudicated them. A justice's failure to consult the district attorney put a cloud on the fees he was claiming. Addressing the issue in 1894, the *Orange News* concluded that "The result of this practice was that many complaints were filed through spite, many improper cases and many wrong offenses and all tended to largely increase the expense to the county for criminal prosecution."[45] This was especially true when it came to vagrancy cases. The *News* continued that "in September 1893, it was also discovered that one or two justices and constables were making a business of

---

the voting place within each precinct. This information comes from *Orange County: From Birth to Metropolitan Status, 1889-1964* (Santa Ana, 1964), a photocopied, unpaginated compilation of original county documents assembled for Orange County's diamond jubilee by the county itself.

[44] For biographical information on Landell, see his obituary in the *Anaheim Gazette*, July 3, 1902, and the *History of Los Angeles County*, supra note 25 at 185.

[45] *Orange News*, October 24, 1894.

arresting tramps during the night in gangs of from 10 to 30, and prosecuting them without the knowledge of the district attorney, so that each tramp cost the county, in illegal fees to the officers, of from $5 to $6.50."[46]

The grand jury of 1893 responded to these alleged abuses in December, when it reviewed justices of the peace and constables for the previous year:

> The attention of this Grand Jury has been directed to the abuses of authority by Justices of the Peace and Constables, in their manner of handling the tramp and vagrant questions, by which their fees have been greatly increased beyond any contemplation of law, and thereby the taxpayers burdened with unnecessary expenses therein.
>
> It has been shown to the Grand Jury that these abuses have become extensive and flagrant, and that some restraint was absolutely necessary to be imposed, and we have accordingly taken such action and directed the attention of our efficient District Attorney to the same, and with a request to take such further steps as are necessary in the premises.[47]

The casualties from the grand jury's investigation were justices Freeman and Marks of Santa Ana, against whom indictments were returned.[48] Both indictments were dismissed at the beginning of 1894, but they served notice that the county would not tolerate any further excesses.[49] Because the dockets from both justices' courts are unavailable, it is not possible to know how many tramps were brought before them, but it may safely be assumed that it was Freeman and Marks to whom the *News* was referring. The only clue to the volume of vagrancy cases in their courts comes from Supervisor Samuel Armor's long article in the

[46]Ibid.

[47]Grand Jury Report, County of Orange, 1893, p. 7.

[48]This was not the first time that Freeman had found himself in court over the charges involved in the administration of a public office. In 1889 he had brought suit against the City of Santa Ana when it attempted to lower his salary as city recorder while he was in office. Freeman won his $20.00 suit, and the city was forced to pay another $80.00 to his attorney, Victor Montgomery. See Sleeper, *Turn the Rascals Out!*, supra note 17 at 131-32.

[49]Another county justice who had run afoul of the law was Luke E. Smith, of Westminster, who on February 22, 1893, faced charges of selling tobacco to a minor in the Westminster Justice Court of Josiah McCoy (see the Docket Book of the Westminster Justice Court, Josiah McCoy, Justice, February 23, 1893). A jury found Smith not guilty on March 1, but the scandal of the trial was apparently so great that he left the bench and was not replaced until 1895. There was so little court activity in Westminster that the absence of one court was no hardship, either to the community or to the other justice court.

Anaheim Gazette in February 1892.[50] Armor reported that fifty-three vagrants were brought before Freeman and one before Marks during January 1892 alone, which projects to a staggering number of vagrancy cases for the year—far more than in Landell's court, or in Craddick's during 1889 and 1890. Even if the "floater" was liberally applied in Santa Ana, the county was burdened with a huge population of tramps in its jails. Marks undoubtedly dealt with more such cases in other months to merit his indictment in 1893.

In addition to handing out indictments against Freeman and Marks, the county attacked the fee problem by refusing to honor the claims for fees made for vagrancy cases by constables. Constable C.F. Preble took his claim for fees owed to Superior Court Judge James Towner in March 1894. Preble asserted that he had filed a claim for $59.75 for bringing in tramps, but that the county had paid him only $25.75. Towner quickly dismissed the matter on the grounds that Preble had not followed the proper appeal process with the Board of Supervisors. Preble not only failed to collect his $34.00, but owed his attorney for bringing the unsuccessful action to court.[51]

By the end of 1894 the relationship between the district attorney and the county's justices of the peace had greatly improved. The district attorney now reviewed all cases that came before the justices, from whose courts fee claims went down as a consequence.[52] Not all accusations of abuse against justices were eliminated by improved relations with the district attorney's office, however. The *Anaheim Gazette* reported that the grand jury of 1894 narrowly failed to return indictments against "an officer and a Justice of the Peace of this township." The names of the justice and officer involved were not listed, but the two were under suspicion of "taking money from arrested parties and pocketing the same without bringing the accused to trial."[53] The grand jury expressed other concerns about practices in justice courts in 1894. Among them was the strange fact that the county treasurer received more money from justices than the justices claimed credit for.[54] The grand jurors also took exception to the practice of some justices of imposing fines "sufficient only to cover costs of the action, without any apparent regard to the gravity of the offense."[55]

[50] *Anaheim Gazette*, February 11, 1892.

[51] Ibid., March 22, 1894.

[52] The only justice courts whose docket books survived for 1894 and 1895 were in Westminster, but the volume of cases there was so small that it is impossible to notice any drop in caseload.

[53] *Anaheim Gazette*, December 13, 1894.

[54] *Los Angeles Times*, December 7, 1894.

[55] *Anaheim Gazette*, December 13, 1894.

Anaheim, ca. 1890, showing Center Street (where it intersected with Los Angeles Street), on which justices Pierce and Shanley had their business addresses. (Anaheim Public Library)

The last complaints leveled against justice courts by the grand jury came with the indictment of Justice Landell for misconduct in office in 1895. Like the previous indictments of Freeman and Marks, this action was dismissed early the following year.[56] If grand juries said anything about the work in justice courts after 1895, it was complimentary. A typical acknowledgment was made by the grand jury of 1900 to justices Frank Shanley of Anaheim and Romualdo Marquez of Yorba for the neatness of their docket books.[57]

After 1895 the tension surrounding the county's justice courts eased for other reasons. The tramp population began to decline, and the county's financial straits were less constricting. By the middle of the next decade, the county coffers were positively robust. Optimism was high, and individual wealth was sufficient for more than 250 men to list their occupation as "retired" when they filled out their application for the Great Register of 1906.[58] (Their average age was 56.8 years.)

[56] For Landell's indictment, see the Grand Jury Report, County of Orange, 1895, p. 7. Despite failing to name Landell as the justice involved, his indictment by the grand jury of 1895 suggests that it was he and not Justice Jason Pierce who was being criticized in 1894.

[57] Grand Jury Report, County of Orange, 1900, p. 5.

[58] Index to the Great Register of Orange County, 1906.

Justices of the peace once again settled into their familiar, anonymous role as maintainers of public order. Landell's docket resumes in 1896, for which year the docket for Anaheim's other justice court, under Jason B. Pierce, is also available. By 1896 Pierce had been justice in Anaheim for well over a decade. He was born in Vermont in 1821 and arrived in the Santa Ana Valley at the end of the 1860s. First president of the board of trustees of the local irrigation company,[59] in 1876 he became a commissioner of the Cajon Water District.[60] By 1880 he had 250 acres of wheat planted, the largest number of anyone in the region.[61] He became an agent of the Stearns Rancho,[62] and his interests continued to broaden. The *Orange County Directory* of 1895-96 listed among his occupations city recorder, notary public, insurance agent and real-estate broker, but did not bother to mention that he was also a justice of the peace.[63]

DIFFERENCES AND SIMILARITIES

With the records of both Anaheim justices available, it is possible to get an accurate picture of court activity within a busy township (see tables 6-11). Relying on numbers alone does not, of course, explain the differences between the two courts, which are quite striking in the sentencing patterns for vagrants. Landell and Pierce were both Republicans, with several years of court experience with vagrants by 1896. Like their colleagues in other courts, they had no doubt experimented with alternative sentencing, from "floaters" to hard labor. The economic and political constraints that had hampered their dealings with vagrants no longer pertained, and the justices could therefore sentence all defendants as they saw fit. Vagrancy defendants unlucky enough to be found guilty in Landell's court faced sentences ranging from ten days to several months in jail. A five-month sentence was given to Ah Foo, the only Chinese charged with vagrancy in the Anaheim records.[64] Pierce, on the other hand, dismissed some of the

[59] See the Docket Book of Anaheim Justice Court, Jason B. Pierce, Justice, October 25, 1870.

[60] Virginia L. Carpenter, *Placentia, A Pleasant Place* (Santa Ana, 1988), 42 [hereafter cited as Carpenter, *Placentia*].

[61] *History of Los Angeles County*, supra note 25 at 153.

[62] Carpenter, *Placentia*, supra note 60 at 87.

[63] *Orange County Directory, 1895-1896*, 102, 107.

[64] See the Docket Book of Anaheim Justice Court, James M. Landell, Justice, October 28, 1898. Ah Foo was again charged with vagrancy on May 8, 1899, in Justice Shanley's court, but no action was taken after the warrant of arrest was issued. See the Docket Book of Anaheim Justice Court, Frank Shanley, Justice, May 8, 1899.

James S. Howard served as justice of the peace in Anaheim from 1903 to 1921. (Anaheim Public Library)

vagrants who pled guilty before him, and his average sentence for vagrancy was less than ten days.

Neither the newspapers nor the justices themselves account for this disparity. Landell's harsh sentences reflected the county's growing capacity to fund its criminal-justice process, but his reasons for giving longer jail terms and Pierce's for giving shorter ones are not known. Earlier in the decade, Landell's sentences had not been unusually severe. Perhaps he was revenging himself for the accusations leveled against him, or was simply tired of playing the "floater" game.

Both Landell and Pierce, like Craddick before them, gave vagrants an audience and evaluated the merits of each case. Nothing that resembled a policy in such matters was ever in evidence. The vast majority of defendants charged with vagrancy pleaded guilty and were quickly dealt with, but just as many were set free after being admonished by the justices to choose better travelling companions and find employment.

Such an admonishment was delivered by Landell himself in 1892, before his sentencing habits changed. Vagrancy defendant E. Martin, who pled guilty as charged, was the recipient of this lecture. After considering Martin's sentence, Landell wrote: "On a due examination of the cause and finding that defendant had unwittingly and at a late moment become an associate of the company of the boxcar, and feeling satisfied that defendant was a well meaning young man, [I] discharge [the] defendant with the caution to avoid bad company in the future."[65] Though Landell later had a change of heart, Pierce continued this practice until he ended his years of service in January 1898.

In addition to a stronger economy and improved relations with the rest of the legal system, other considerations were affecting the justice courts at the end of the decade. A newspaper article pasted in both Pierce's and Landell's docket books reported passage of a state law permitting townships that contained a city with an elected recorder, not an appointed one, to have only one justice of the peace. The decision affected Anaheim, each of whose justices realized that one of them would soon be off the bench. Moreover, at the end of December 1896 a new judicial district was created in Fullerton. Court officers were appointed on January 18, 1897: two constables and two justices. The district comprised the Fullerton and Yorba voting precincts, reducing the jurisdiction of the Anaheim justices. This township would itself be divided in 1899, when Justice Romualdo Marquez moved over to the new township (see Table 12 for his workload, which was never heavy).[66]

On January 1, 1899, Pierce's and Landell's fears were realized when one of Anaheim's justice courts was abolished. Neither justice was around to see it, however, as both had stepped down from the bench when their terms expired at the end of 1898.

Frank Shanley, an insurance salesman as well as one of the founders of the First National Bank of Anaheim, became justice in 1899. He had arrived in the state three years earlier, and his service on the bench only solidified his already strong position in the community. His four-year tenure as justice was marked by a banker's precision in the keeping of his docket and stern jail sentences for the few vagrants who crossed his path. The twenty-nine vagrancy defendants before him faced sentences that averaged thirty days in length. They were never given the option of paying a fine (which might or might not have been possible for them), as they routinely would have been by his predecessors. (See Table 11 for Shanley's workload.)

When photographer James S. Howard became justice in January 1903, vagrants again had the choice of paying a fine, but the fines were so exorbitant that payment was unlikely, and Howard meted out the same lengthy jail sentences that Shanley had issued (see Table 11).

[65] Docket Book of Anaheim Justice Court, James M. Landell, Justice, November 17, 1892.

[66] By January 1, 1899, all townships in the county had only one justice of the peace except for Santa Ana, which, because of its size and population, retained two justices until January 1, 1903.

In 1905 Howard introduced an innovation to sentencing. On July 8, nine-year-old David Ruiz's thirty-day sentence for petit larceny was suspended on the condition that he report to probation officer S.O. Llewellyn every Saturday for six months.[67] A similar sentence was meted out to three juveniles accused of malicious mischief three weeks later.[68] Howard extended the practice to adults early the next year.[69]

The Santa Ana Valley passed through many phases during the years covered by this study. In the early 1870s the region was sparsely populated, with isolated pockets of new settlement. The large Mexican ranchos were just beginning to break apart, encouraging new settlement. The people who had staked a foothold by 1875 forced a rail line to link the region with Los Angeles. Coupled with the completion of the Southern Pacific's line through the Tehachapis to Los Angeles, this gave rise to a population boom at the end of the decade. The boom slowed in the early 1880s, but resumed again with the arrival of the Santa Fe. The major beneficiaries were the towns along the rail lines. Anaheim, Orange, and Santa Ana all grew as a result of their railroad connections, while towns like Tustin, which was unsuccessful in wooing a major rail route, declined. Other communities off the railroad's line of march remained isolated to transient outsiders who burdened the areas they visited. During the uncertain early years of Orange County, the region displayed a "hold-the-line" mentality against dangerous outsiders, unnecessary expenses, and anyone who threatened to overwhelm the area's tenuous economy.[70] This mentality was extended to justices of the peace who could not properly balance maintaining public order against holding down the cost of their offices. By 1896 the community's fears began to ease somewhat as economic conditions improved, and by the middle of the next decade conditions were so good that the concerns of the 1890s seemed merely a bad dream.

[67]Docket Book of the Anaheim Justice Court, James S. Howard, Justice, July 8, 1905.
[68]Ibid., *People v. A. Wirney, V. Lagourgue and D.A. Henrich*, July 31, 1905.
[69]Ibid., *People v. Ah Poy, Ah Sung, Ah Chuch, Ah Lung, and Ah Ching*, February 5, 1906. This was a gambling case.
[70]Lawrence M. Friedman, *A History of American Law* (New York, 1973) 296. Friedman asserts that American priorities shifted when the frontier was widely perceived as being closed. Before 1890 American law was driven by what Willard Hurst has called the "release of energy." Legal institutions had been shaped to promote the entrepreneur and encourage expansion into open territories, but closure of the frontier forced a rethinking of legal priorities. Consolidation and entrenchment began to replace unrestrained development, affecting both the civil and criminal side of law. In Orange County in the early 1890s, where the new government's foothold seemed tenuous in the face of a series of local and national economic setbacks, holding the line against external and internal threats through legal remedies seemed perfectly justifiable.

Throughout the period, justices of the peace went about their business. All of them were successful, civic-minded entrepreneurs. For some of them, including Richard Egan, Charles Humphreys, and Sam Craddick, assuming the position was a means of establishing their reputation in the community to help promote their other ambitions. Others were already established when they became justice, and their assumption of civic leadership was a response to their place in the community in the best tradition of republicanism. These included Thomas Hull, James Landell, and Jason Pierce. Given the positions they held before becoming justice, it seems unlikely that they entered the office motivated solely by the wages to be gained. The detail and reflection that went into their justice dockets indicated that they understood the importance of their role, endeavored to learn the law and dispense it properly, and in so doing attempted to serve their communities. The justices who did not display this capacity did not remain in the office for long.

This study of justice courts in the Santa Ana Valley also helps to dispel the myth that every new community in the West was a violent one. There was only one lynching during the period (that of Francisco Torres in 1892), and despite intimations that a vigilance committee was in operation at Orange in the 1870s, no solid evidence of it has materialized.[71] Santa Ana's influx of tramps was the cause of the meeting in Neill's Hall in January 1895 at which such a committee was discussed, but that was evidently the extent of it. The community was not without its rowdies, and fist fights and other batteries were common, but violent crime was virtually unknown. Table 13 shows that only 5% of a justice's time spent on criminal matters involved violent crime. Of these cases, nearly half were either dismissed or had no further action taken after filing. The odds on becoming a victim of a violent act were virtually nil for the average citizen of the community. Far more likely was an encounter with a vagrant.

The numbers in Table 14 confirm that vagrancy was a crime that followed railroads and concerned larger communities. The Fullerton/Yorba area was not heavily populated, but the main line of the Santa Fe passed through the region. Because no major rail line ran through Westminster and the community was dispersed and covered with farms, vagrants avoided the region. In Santa Ana they had not yet arrived during the years for which docket books have survived, but during the 1890s newspaper accounts suggest that it was the most heavily visited community by the associates of the company of the boxcar. Anaheim's numbers accurately reflected the extent of the problem in the larger railheads, while Orange showed a conspicuous zeal for prosecution. It is clear

[71] J.E. Pleasents, *History of Orange County, California* (Los Angeles, 1931) 402-6.

from a comparison of tables 13 and 14 that vagrancy was of
greater concern to the community than the threat of violent
assault. Evidence from the Santa Ana Valley may be added to that
gathered by Roger McGrath on Bodie, California, and Aurora,
Nevada, to show that the claim that new western communities
were unusually violent was inaccurate.[72]

In his analysis of justices of the peace in Washington Territory,
John Wunder concluded that they were educated, middle-aged,
politically active, land-owning men of considerable means.[73] This
analysis suggests that justices in the Santa Ana Valley were much
the same. They reflected the backbone of their society. They were
its leaders and reinforced its values. Politically conservative, they
appeared to deal with each case before them on its own merit.
The character, background, and ethnicity of a defendant did affect
sentencing, as did the year in which a case was heard and the
societal circumstances. Justices frequently lectured the defendants before them, especially vagrancy suspects, on proper living.
Cases were rarely appealed, and lawyers endorsed justices they
respected by bringing work to their courts.

Justices of the peace served an important social as well as legal
function. They bore the burden of the community's social ills.
The presence of large numbers of vagrants in the 1890s was the
greatest test of this function. Justices were called on to rid society
of this perceived menace while not overburdening the community
in the process. While the results of this undertaking were mixed,
a stricter definition of the relationship between justices and the
rest of the legal system was the most obvious result. Justices were
successful in holding the line against vagrants, however, until
economic conditions rebounded sufficiently for the vagrants
themselves to dwindle in number. In the end, justices performed
the function that they had since the days of their origin in England. As leaders of their communities, they assured their fellow
citizens that they would persevere by brandishing the shield of
law and wielding the staff of justice.

[72] Roger D. McGrath, *Gunfighters, Highwaymen and Vigilantes: Violence on the Frontier* (Berkeley and Los Angeles, 1984).

[73] Wunder, *Inferior Courts*, supra note 7.

APPENDIX: TABLES

TABLE 1
JUSTICES OF THE PEACE CONSIDERED IN THIS STUDY

	Age[1]	Place of Birth	Occupation	Terms Served
ANAHEIM				
Fox, A.V.[2,3]	62	New Hamp.	Hotelier	11/86?-10/90
Howard, James S.[2]	43	Iowa	Photographer	01/03-01/21
Landell, James W.[2]	53	Penn.	Farmer	11/90-01/99
Pierce, Jason B.[2,3]	63	Vermont	Farmer	0?/8?-01/99
Shanley, Frank[2]	56	Ireland	Insurance	01/99-01/03
FULLERTON/YORBA				
Marquez, Romualdo P.[2]	33	California	Merchant	F 01/97-01/99 Y 01/99-08/06
ORANGE				
Craddick, Sam M.[2]	35	Iowa	Real Est.	01/89-01/91 +01/95-01/99
SAN JOAQUIN/SANTA ANA				
Freeman, George E.	53	Maine	Contractor	01/82-03/03
Humphreys, Charles W.[2]	39	Kentucky	Real Est.	01/76-12/86 +01/93-01/95
Johnson, J.J.[2,3]	41	N. Carolina	Farmer	02/71?-06/75?
Marks, Isaiah G.	40	Penn.	Solicitor	01/91-01/93
Ross, Jacob[2]	35	Indiana	Farmer	02/83-01/85
Smith, C.F.[2]	32	Mass.	Surveyor	01/87-01/89
SAN JUAN				
Egan, Richard[3]	28	Ireland	Surveyor	00/7?-00/8?
WESTMINSTER				
Aldridge, Jon. W.[2,3]	51	Indiana	Farmer	01/80-02/84
Fawcett, Thomas W.[2]	70	Indiana	Farmer	01/91-01/93
Hull, Thomas C.[2]	41	Ohio	Clerk	01/88-12/88
Lane, John	25	Ohio	Farmer	06/95-12/96
McCoy, Josiah[2]	62	Penn.	Farmer	01/89-01/91 +01/93-01/07

TABLE 1 (continued)
JUSTICES OF THE PEACE CONSIDERED IN THIS STUDY

McKelvey,
  Sidney D.[2]   36   Rhode Is.   Groc. Mer.   02/97-01/99
Smith, Luke E.[2]   26   California   Clerk   01/93-07/93
Webster, David[2,3]   63   England   Postmaster   03/79?-01/93

Average age   45.76

[1]All ages are from the year the men were first elected justice.
[2]Indicates justices whose docket books were scrutinized.
[3]The first year of service as justice for Egan, Johnson, Fox, Aldridge, and
Webster is unknown. Egan was 28 in 1870. There is no way to
determine whether he was a justice before that year.

*   *   *

TABLE 2
ACTIONS IN SAN JOAQUIN/SANTA ANA JUSTICE COURT, 1871-1888

	CRIMINAL				CIVIL	Comb.
	Felony	Misd'm'r	Not Stated	Total		Total
1871	2	1	0	3	7[1]	10
1872	1	3	0	4	43[1]	47
1873	0	1	1	2	43[1]	45
1874	2	5	0	7	17[1]	24
1875[2]	0	1	2	3	9[1]	12
1877	6	12	0	18	61	79
1878	2	14	1	17	76	93
1879	2	12	1	15	74	89
1880	1	15	1	17	50	67
1881	5	15	0	20	25	50
1882	8[3]	4	0	12	8	20
1883[4]	0	2	0	2	1	3
1884[4]	0	3	0	3	5	8
1885	2	14	0	16	39	55
1886	2	13	0	15	22	37
1887	3	10	0	13	7	20
1888	0	15[5]	0	15	16	31
Total	36	142	6	184	486	670

[1]Of these 119 cases, 50 were for estray and no named defendant was
listed.
[2]The docket for this year ends in June.
[3]Four of these cases were for the same action.
[4]Humphreys was not on the bench in 1883 and 1884, when his place
was taken by Ross. The caseload increased on Humphreys's return.
[5]1 vagrancy.

*   *   *

TABLE 3
ACTIONS IN ORANGE JUSTICE COURT, JANUARY 1889–JULY 1890

| | | CRIMINAL | | | CIVIL | Comb. |
	Felony	Misd'm'r	Vagrancy	Total		Total
1889	0	4	39	43	21	64
1890	4	3	8	15	6	21
Total	4	7	47	58	27	85

*   *   *

TABLE 4
ACTIONS IN WESTMINSTER JUSTICE COURTS, 1879-1898

| | | CRIMINAL | | | CIVIL | Comb. |
	Felony	Misd'm'r	Not Stated	Total		Total
1879	0	0	0	0	18	18
1880[1]	0	1	0	1	20	21
1881	0	0	0	0	6	6
1882	2	13[2]	1	16	6	22
1883	0	1	0	1	2	3
1884	0	1	0	1	2	3
1885	0	1	0	1	1	2
1886	0	0	0	0	7	7
1887	0	0	0	0	2	2
1888	0	12	0	12	5	17
1889	0	1	0	1	11	12
1890	4	11	0	15	13	28
1891	1	2	1	4	4	8
1892	0	6	0	6	10	16
1893	0	11[3]	0	11	3	14
1894	0	1	0	1	6	7
1895	1	5	0	6	7	13
1896	0	0	0	0	3	3
1897	0	2	0	2	13	15
1898	1	2	3	6	16	22
Total	9	70	5	84	155	239

[1]Records are combined for both justice courts from this year until 1896.
Records for only one court survive from 1896 through 1898.
[2]Twelve of these cases were for only two actions.
[3]1 vagrancy.

*   *   *

TABLE 5

ACTIONS IN ANAHEIM JUSTICE COURT,
NOVEMBER 1886–SEPTEMBER 1893

| | CRIMINAL | | | | CIVIL | Comb. |
	Felony	Misd'm'r	Vagrancy	Total		Total
1886	1	7	0	8	1	9
1887	15	42	2	59	11	70
1888	5	61	4	70	10	80
1889	8	27	11	46	14	60
1890	6	36	14	56	16	72
1891	1	28	25	54	21	75
1892	3	17	22	42	24	66
1893	3	14	7	24	18	42
Total	42	232	84	359	115	474

*   *   *

TABLE 6

CASES HEARD IN JUSTICE LANDELL'S COURT,
JULY 1896–DECEMBER 1898

| | CRIMINAL | | | | CIVIL | Comb. |
	Felony	Misd'm'r	Vagrancy	Total		Total
1896	1	7	0	8	10	18
1897	6	22	7	35	31	66
1898	1	15	6	22	14	36
Total	8	44	13	65	55	130

*   *   *

TABLE 7

DEFENDANTS IN JUSTICE LANDELL'S COURT,
JULY 1896–DECEMBER 1898

	Vagrancy	Other Criminal	Total
1896	0	12	12
1897	12	47	59
1898	7	25	32
Total	19	84	103

*   *   *

TABLE 8
CASES HEARD IN JUSTICE PIERCE'S COURT,
JANUARY 1896–DECEMBER 1898

| | | CRIMINAL | | | CIVIL | Comb. |
	Felony	Misd'm'r	Vagrancy	Total		Total
1896	13	52	16	81	30	111
1897	7	30	6	43	27	70
1898	7	14	0	21	16	37
Total	27	96	22	135	73	218

*   *   *

TABLE 9
DEFENDANTS IN JUSTICE PIERCE'S COURT,
JANUARY 1896–DECEMBER 1898

	Vagrancy	Other Criminal	Total
1896	37	78	115
1897	20	39	59
1898	0	21	21
Total	57	138	195

*   *   *

TABLE 10
TOTAL DEFENDANTS FOR BOTH COURTS, 1896-1898

	Vagrancy	Other Criminal	Total
1896	37	90	127
1897	32	74	106
1898	7	39	46
Total	76	203	279

*   *   *

TABLE 11
ACTIONS IN ANAHEIM JUSTICE COURT,
JANUARY 1896–JANUARY 1907

		CRIMINAL			CIVIL	Comb.
	Felony	Misd'm'r	Vagrancy	Total		Total
1896	14	59	16	89	40	129
1897	13	52	13	78	58	136
1898	8	29	6	43	30	73
1899	1	14	3	18	20	38
1900	3	9	5	17	9	26
1901	4	12	6	22	11	33
1902	5	18	0	23	6	29
1903	2	23	6	31	16	47
1904	4	43	5	52	17	69
1905	3	20	10	33	33	66
1906	2[1]	25	4	31	47	78
1907	0	5	1	6	0	6
Total	59	309	75	443	287	730

[1]Same case, refiled.

*   *   *

TABLE 12
ACTIONS IN FULLERTON/YORBA JUSTICE COURT,
JULY 1897–NOVEMBER 1906

		CRIMINAL			CIVIL	Comb.
	Felony	Misd'm'r	Vagrancy	Total		Total
1897	2[1]	3	0	5	1	6
1898	3	0	3	6	1	7
1899	0	0	0	0	1	1
1900	0	2	2	4	0	4
1901	0	1	0	1	0	1
1902	1	2	1	4	0	4
1903	2	5	0	7	4	11
1904	0	5	0	5	2	7
1905	0	0	0	0	2	2
1906	0	1	0	1	0	1
Total	8	19	6	33	11	44

[1]Same case.

*   *   *

TABLE 13
VIOLENT CRIMES IN THE COURTS STUDIED,
FEBRUARY 1871–JANUARY 1907

	Violent Crimes[1]	Total Crim. Cases	Violent Crimes as % of Total Cases
Anaheim, 1886-1907	32	802	4
Fullerton/Yorba, 1897-1906	4	33	12
Orange, 1889-1890	2	58	3
Santa Ana, 1871-1888	13	184	7
Westminster, 1879-1898	8	84	10
Total	59	1,161	5

[1]Crimes considered in this table are: assault with a deadly weapon, murder, rape and assault to commit rape, and threatening to kill another.

*   *   *

TABLE 14
VAGRANCY IN THE COURTS STUDIED,
FEBRUARY 1871–JANUARY 1907

	Vagrancy Cases	Total Crim. Cases	Vagrancy as % of Total Cases
Anaheim, 1886-1907	159	802	20
Fullerton/Yorba, 1897-1906	6	33	18
Orange, 1889-1890	47	58	81
Santa Ana, 1871-1888	1	184	.05
Westminster, 1879-1898	1	84	1
Total	214	1,161	18

The Chinese and the Courts in the Pacific Northwest: Justice Denied?

John R. Wunder

The author is a member of the history department and the school of law in Texas Tech University.

> Chinaman clings to his idolatry and heathenism with the tenacity of life; lives upon less than the refuse from the table of a civilized man, and devotes his sister to the basest lusts of humanity, and makes her an unsexed prostitute to disseminate disease among the devotees of base passions.[1]

Such was the view in 1871 of a Montana editor toward the latest immigrants, the Chinese. His attitude was shared by many non-Asians in the United States during the nineteenth century, and it had been commonplace since the arrival of the first Chinese.

The Chinese began migrating to the U.S. in the 1840s during the California gold rush. Economic motives apparently prompted most to take the voyage, although a significant number in later periods came to the New World under duress. Population data available from the U.S. census indicate that the Chinese increased rapidly until 1890, the first count following enactment of national exclusionary legislation in 1882. The Chinese had never constituted more than 0.2 percent of the total population of the U.S., but their economic impact was considerably more significant than mere numbers indicate. Almost all were adult males who were concentrated in the West, especially in California and the Pacific Northwest (Washington, Oregon, Idaho, Montana,

---

[1]*Missoula and Cedar Creek Pioneer*, June 22, 1871.

and Wyoming). As early as 1870, 28.5 percent of all Idahoans and 9.5 percent of all Montanans were Chinese; in 1880, approximately one person out of every twenty in Oregon, Washington, and Wyoming was Chinese.[2]

In the late 1850s through the 1870s increased numbers of Chinese went to the Northwest in response primarily to mining discoveries in Idaho and Montana and jobs in railroad construction throughout the area. Oregon and Washington Territory greeted these new Americans with xenophobia and head taxes. In Wyoming Territory the hostility led to an outbreak on September 4, 1885, known as the Rock Springs Massacre. White coal miners, attempting to force all Chinese from the territory's mines, killed twenty-eight of them. Three days later, thirty-five Chinese hop workers in the Issaquah Valley of Washington Terri-

---

[2]Roger Daniels and Harry H. L. Kitano, *American Racism: Exploration of the Nature of Prejudice* (Englewood Cliffs, N.J., 1970), 35-45; U.S. Dept. of Commerce, Bureau of the Census, *Ninth Census of the United States, 1870: Population* (Washington, D.C., 1870), I, 8, 18; *Tenth Census of the United States, 1880: Population* (Washington, D.C., 1880), I, 38-39; *Eleventh Census of the United States, 1890: Population* (Washington, D.C., 1890), I, 468, 474.

THE CHINESE POPULATION IN THE UNITED STATES, 1860-1890

	Chinese Population by State			
	1860	1870	1880	1890
United States	34,933*	63,199	105,465	107,475
California	34,933*	49,277	75,132	72,472
Idaho	N.I.**	4,274	3,379	2,007
Montana	N.I.	1,949	1,765	2,532
Oregon	N.I.	3,330	9,510	9,540
Washington	N.I.	234	3,186	3,260
Wyoming	N.I.	143	914	465

*Figures available only for all Asians in U.S.
**No information available

	Chinese Percentage of Population			
	1860	1870	1880	1890
United States	0.1*	0.2	0.2	0.2
California	9.2*	8.8	9.8	6.0
Idaho	N.I.**	28.5	11.6	2.4
Montana	N.I.	9.5	5.0	1.9
Oregon	N.I.	3.7	5.8	3.0
Washington	N.I.	0.1	4.7	0.9
Wyoming	N.I.	1.5	4.7	0.8

*Figures available only for all Asians in U.S.
**No information available

tory were attacked; three were murdered. In September and October 1885, violence throughout northwestern rural areas forced the Chinese to flee to Washington port cities, north to British Columbia, and south to San Francisco. Anti-Chinese riots then occurred in Tacoma and Seattle which resulted in considerable property losses for Chinese residents and hasty evacuations.[3]

From the outset, the Chinese of the Pacific Northwest constituted a significant minority population, and they attracted and experienced some of the worst forms of legal and extralegal racism during the nineteenth century. Yet historical analysis of the legal issues involving the Chinese in the U.S. has been minimal.[4] Most treatments have dealt indirectly with such questions or have avoided them altogether. Only Milton Konvitz, in his *The Alien and the Asiatic in American Law*, has discussed the topic, but he concentrates on the federal level and ignores developments in the states and territories.[5]

What then of the courts of the Pacific Northwest? Were the Chinese afforded at least nominal legal equality? Could they go before a state

---

[3]Ore., Constitution, art. 15, sec. 8 (1857); Ore., *Stat.*, ch. 35, 815-817 (1862); W. P. Wilcox, "Anti-Chinese Riots in Washington," *Washington Historical Quarterly*, XX (1929), 204-211. For a survey of Chinese experiences in the Pacific Northwest, see Larry D. Quinn, " 'Chink Chink Chinaman': The Beginning of Nativism in Montana," *Pacific Northwest Quarterly*, LVIII (1967), 82-89; "The Japanese Problem in Oregon," *Oregon Law Review*, XXIV (1945), 208; Murray Morgan, *Skid Road: An Informal Portrait of Seattle* (New York, 1951), 63-102; Paul Crane and T. A. Larson, "The Chinese Massacre," *Annals of Wyoming*, XII (1940), 47-55, 153-161; John R. Wunder, "Law and Chinese in Frontier Montana," *Montana, the Magazine of Western History*, XXX (1980), 18-31, and "The Courts and the Chinese in Frontier Idaho," *Idaho Yesterdays*, XXV (1981), 23-32; M. Alfreda Elsensohn, *Idaho Chinese Lore* (Caldwell, Ida., 1971); Jules A. Karlin, "The Anti-Chinese Outbreaks in Seattle, 1885-1886," *Pacific Northwest Quarterly*, XXXIX (1948), 103-129, and "The Anti-Chinese Outbreak in Tacoma, 1885," *Pacific Northwest Quarterly*, XXIII (1954), 271-283; and Robert E. Wynne, *Reaction to the Chinese in the Pacific Northwest and British Columbia, 1850-1910* (New York, 1978).

[4]Historians have concentrated on social and economic issues within a federal or California framework. See B. Frank Dake, "The Chinaman before the Supreme Court," *Albany Law Journal*, LXVII (1905), 258-267; "Current Topics," *Central Law Journal*, XVII (1883), 261; "Status of the Chinese in the United States," *The Legal News*, 1 (1878), 373-374; Alexander Saxton, *The Indispensable Enemy: Labor and the Anti-Chinese Movement in California* (Berkeley, 1971); Gunther Barth, *Bitter Strength: A History of the Chinese in the United States, 1850-1870* (Cambridge, Mass., 1964); Cheng-Tsu Wu, ed., *"Chink"* (New York, 1972); Leigh Dana Johnsen, "Equal Rights and the 'Heathen Chinese': Black Activism in San Francisco," *Western Historical Quarterly*, XI (1980), 57-68; Elmer C. Sandmeyer, *The Anti-Chinese Movement in California* (Urbana, Ill., 1939); and Ping Chiu, *Chinese Labor in California, 1850-1880* (Madison, 1963).

[5]Konvitz, *The Alien and the Asiatic in American Law* (Ithaca, N.Y., 1946). Other minorities have begun to receive some attention from legal scholars. Most provocative is A. E. Keir Nash whose articles, among them "Fairness and Formalism in the Trials of Blacks in the State Supreme Courts of the Old South," *Virginia Law Review*, LVI (1970), 64-100, have examined the judicial treatment of blacks between 1830 and 1860.

or territorial court and obtain a fair hearing? To answer these questions, all decisions concerning Chinese litigants rendered by the territorial and state supreme courts of Oregon, Washington, Idaho, Montana, and Wyoming to 1902, when the third Chinese Exclusion Act permanently barred Chinese immigrants, have been reviewed. The following analysis discusses these cases under four general categories: civil cases appealed before passage of the first Chinese Exclusion Act (1882); criminal cases appealed before the passage of the same act; civil cases appealed between 1882 and 1902; and criminal cases appealed during the same period.[6]

In the Northwest prior to 1883, seven cases involving at least one Chinese litigant in a civil action reached state and territorial supreme courts.[7] In four of the seven civil cases, the highest courts ruled in favor of the Chinese party. Three of the four favorable decisions concerned such issues as child support, property rights obtained fraudulently, and misrepresentation of merchandise, and they all involved white litigants.[8] The fourth favorable decision dealt with a labor contract between Chinese and American Indian parties.

The Chinese-Indian dispute culminated in the 1871 decision of *Jack Gho* v. *Charley Julles* in Washington Territory. Gho, a Chinese, had been hired as a cook by Julles, a Snohomish who ran a logging camp. After Gho had performed his work as agreed, Julles refused to pay him. Gho then brought suit and won a lower court decision which Julles appealed to the territorial supreme court. Territorial courts, Julles argued, had no jurisdiction over Snohomish; in addition, he cited an 1847 congressional act that declared void all contracts made by Indians. The justices disagreed, finding that all persons, even Indians, could make binding agreements. The court looked more to the intent of Congress than to the letter of the law:

---

[6]The first U.S. restriction on Chinese immigration occurred in 1882 when Congress prohibited the entry of Chinese laborers for ten years. *U.S. Statutes at Large*, XXII, 58–61 (1882). Six years later the 1882 act was amended to prevent Chinese laborers, who had arrived in the U.S. prior to 1882, from regaining entry if they left the U.S. *U.S. Statutes at Large*, XXV, 476–479 (1888). In 1892 the first exclusionary law was renewed, and in 1902 the ban was made permanent. *U.S. Statutes at Large*, XXVII, 25–26 (1892); XXXII, 176–177 (1902).

[7]*Bridget Nine* v. *Lewis M. Starr*, 8 Ore 49 (1879); *First National Bank of Helena* v. *How et al.*, 1 Mont 604 (1872); *Hoy* v. *Smith*, 2 Wyo 459 (1878); *Jack Gho (A Chinaman)* v. *Charley Julles (An Indian)*, 1 Wash Terr 325 (1871); *Seattle and Walla Walla R. R. Co.* v. *Ah Kow et al.*, 2 Wash Terr 36 (1880); *City of Portland* v. *Lee Sam*, 7 Ore 397 (1879); *Wa Ching et al.* v. *Chris. Constantine*, 1 Ida 266 (1869).

[8]8 Ore 49 (1879); 1 Ida 266 (1869); 2 Wyo 459 (1878).

Does this law intend that the Indian, the moment he attempts to enter upon the pursuits that occupy the attention of our race, shall be stopped on the threshold, the door shut in his face? Is he to be walled up in barbarism? Is an insuperable obstacle to be thrust between him and all advance? ... [T]o forbid Indians to make executory contracts for money and goods only would be a derogation from natural right most hampering and injurious.[9]

It was a rarity when a western court sought to protect what Washington justices termed the "natural rights" of Native Americans, and in this instance such liberal reasoning benefited a Chinese plaintiff and many whites holding labor contracts with other Indians.

Not all pre-1883 civil cases resulted in favorable outcomes for Chinese litigants. Decisions reached in three instances by Northwest appellate tribunals favored over Chinese individuals such corporate interests as the First National Bank of Helena, the city of Portland, and the Seattle and Walla Walla Railroad.[10] The railroad case, in particular, represented a significant legal conflict for Chinese laborers.

The Seattle and Walla Walla Railroad, needing excavation and grading for its roadbed between Renton and Newcastle, negotiated a labor contract with L. D. Frank, who in turn made an agreement with three Chinese who promised to supply workers. The Chinese labor gangs toiled for several months, and when they received no wages, they sued the Seattle and Walla Walla Railroad. In a decision of far-reaching implications, the Washington territorial supreme court reversed the lower court which had held in favor of the Chinese laborers. In the opinion of the supreme court, only those Chinese specifically named in written contracts could collect (here, the three labor bosses only). The immediate result was that Chinese laborers

---

[9]1 Wash Terr 325, 327-328 (1871). On other occasions, the Chinese were considered Indians for bureaucratic or legal purposes. In 1877 when Roman Catholic priests desired to convert the Chinese in San Francisco, they found themselves without funds to set up a mission. To obtain the necessary financial support, they officially classified the Chinese as Native Americans thereby giving them access to the Pious Fund, money put aside by Rome for the express purpose of educating Indians. (James P. Gaffey, "Roman Catholic Efforts to Reach the Chinese in San Francisco, 1880-1925," paper presented at the annual meeting of the American Historical Association, Pacific Coast Branch, San Diego, Aug. 17, 1976.) Earlier in California, a statute prevented blacks, mulattos, and Indians from testifying in state courts for or against whites. When the question of whether the Chinese could so testify came before the California supreme court, it declared that because the Chinese came from Asia and Columbus thought he had discovered Asia, the Chinese were in fact American Indians and, therefore, no Chinese could testify in trials for or against white litigants. *California* v. *Hall*, 4 Cal 399 (1854).
[10]2 Wash Terr 36 (1880); 1 Mont 604 (1872); and 7 Ore 397 (1879).

could not be assured of their wages unless they signed agreements with the original procurer of their services. The long-term effect was more favorable since the decision helped inspire mechanics lien legislation and, more importantly for Chinese laborers, helped undermine the Chinese contract labor system.[11]

Just as with the majority of civil disputes involving Chinese, criminal cases decided in northwestern state and territorial supreme courts prior to 1883 indicated some effort by justices to protect Chinese defendants. Of the fifteen criminal appeals examined, nine resulted in reversals or affirmations favoring Chinese defendants. Appeals included convictions for rape, gambling, bribery, murder, and kidnapping.[12] Grounds for reversal usually were based upon gross violations of due process by local tribunals. In 1879 Tom, a Chinese, was indicted for allegedly raping a five-year-old Oregon girl, Ruby Sumption. At the circuit court level, two prospective jurors were seated even though they admitted having a "fixed opinion" about the guilt or innocence of the defendant. In addition, the testimony of the child was allowed into evidence even though she testified unsworn and was not subject to cross examination. The Oregon supreme court ordered a new trial because the lower court's process of selecting jurors and taking testimony had violated constitutional guarantees.[13]

Blatant disregard for court procedure was also apparent in *Oregon v. Gitt Lee et al.* (1877), *Deer Lodge County v. At* (1878), and *Oregon v. Charley Lee Quang, Lee Jaw, and Lee Jong* (1879). In the first case the defendants had been found innocent by the lower court of unlawfully playing a game for money. The grand jury had not been presented with physical evidence or even the name of the game. The Oregon statute covering gambling required evidence showing either the type of game played—such as poker, vintun, or faro—or the device used—such as cards or dice. Even so, the district attorney appealed the innocent verdict to the Oregon supreme court which curtly affirmed the lower court action because the indictment had not sufficiently described the offense.[14]

---

[11]2 Wash Terr 36, 40 (1880).

[12]*Oregon* v. *Gitt Lee et al.*, 6 Ore 425 (1877); *Oregon* v. *Moy Looke*, 7 Ore 54 (1879); *Oregon* v. *Charley Lee* [indicted under the name of Charley Lee Quong], *Ah Lee* [indicted under the name of Lee Jaw], *and Lee Jong*, 7 Ore 237 (1879); *Oregon* v. *Ah Sam*, 7 Ore 477 (1879); *Oregon* v. *Tom, A Chinaman*, 8 Ore 177 (1879); *Idaho* v. *Ah Ho*, (*Chinese Woman*), 1 Ida 691 (1878); *Montana* v. *Lee*, 2 Mont 124 (1874); *Deer Lodge County* v. *At*, 3 Mont 168 (1878); *Montana* v. *Ah Wah Yen*, 4 Mont 149 (1881).

[13]8 Ore 177-178 (1879).

[14]6 Ore 425 (1877).

In *Deer Lodge County* v. *At,* it was G. W. Irwin, a Montana justice of the peace, who violated due process. While Irwin was interrogating Ung Hah, who had been arrested for murder, Lee Sue, a friend of the defendant, twice interrupted the proceedings to offer Irwin money for bail. The judge became so agitated that he ordered the sheriff to arrest Lee Sue for attempting to bribe an officer and immediately convened a hearing on the charge. The baffled Lee Sue made no defense, and Irwin ordered him to jail until a grand jury could issue an indictment. Following the indictment and Sue's release on bail, he refused to appear and a default judgment was rendered although no complaint had been officially filed charging him with violating the law. The bail had been put up by a third Chinese named At, who now appealed to the Montana territorial supreme court for dismissal of the charges against Sue and the return of his bail money. The court agreed that Irwin had erred. Sue, declared the justices, had not waived

his statutory right to have a proper complaint containing a description of the offense with which he had been charged. Sue was arrested legally, and Irwin, as a justice of the peace, could take jurisdiction and proceed to judgment without issuing a warrant of arrest. But a written complaint against Sue, setting out his offense, was as necessary in his case as in any other.[15]

The supreme court of Oregon in the *Charley Lee Quang* case was also asked to scrutinize criminal trial procedures involving Chinese litigants. This dispute involved the murder of Chin Sue Ying, a recent Christian convert. Chin, the night before he was killed, had gone to a joss house, a building where Chinese cultural and religious activities were held, and smashed a Chinese "stink-pot" on the floor. A policeman was called, but Charley Lee Quang, the attendant, said he would wait until morning before swearing out a warrant. The next day Chin once again went to the joss house, and when he attempted to throw a piece of raw meat on a joss statue, he received two hatchet blows to the head and two pistol shots to the abdomen from Charley Lee Quang and two others.[16] At the ensuing trial the defendants were convicted of murder despite the testimony of two witnesses who stated in almost identical language that the deceased had attacked first thus necessitating self-defense on the part of the accused. The prosecutor urged the judge to instruct the jury to disregard any Chinese testimony on the grounds that it was "prejudicial" or untrue. The judge refused, but he

[15]3 Mont 168, 169–171 (1878).
[16]7 Ore 237, 249 (1879).

did tell the jury that the Chinese witnesses might be lying. The Oregon supreme court held that this instruction violated the defendants' right to a fair hearing and ordered a new trial.[17]

Two other decisions of northwestern supreme courts during this period resulted in favorable verdicts for Chinese, but they contained ominous implications. In *Oregon* v. *Moy Looke* (1879), the Chinese defendant was charged with kidnapping a Chinese woman, Wong Ho. During the trial, the legality of a marriage of Wong Ho to a Chinese national became crucial to the defense. Evidence concerning the customs of China was interpreted for the jury as a question of law by the judge. Upon conviction, Moy Looke appealed on the grounds that Chinese customs should be subject to cultural, not legal, interpretation. The Oregon supreme court reversed the lower court opinion, holding that as a "general rule . . . courts do not take judicial notice of the laws of a foreign country."[18] Moy Looke may have won, but now Oregon's frontier juries, noted for hostile attitudes toward Chinese customs, could interpret Chinese cultural values without judicial guidance.

A similar outcome emerged from a Montana dispute involving Chinese ownership of mining claims. The Montana territorial legislature in 1872 prohibited aliens from acquiring placer mine titles or profits and made alien claims subject to forfeiture to the territory. Fauk Lee challenged the validity of the statute by purchasing 3,000 feet of placer mining property. The district court found him guilty and confiscated his land; he appealed. In the landmark opinion of *Montana* v. *Lee* (1874), Justice Decius S. Wade, often called the "founder of Montana jurisprudence,"[19] focused upon two important issues: the rights of Chinese prior to the enactment of the forfeiture law and the power of the legislature to enact such legislation. Quoting liberally from such noted legal scholars as Coke, Blackstone, Marshall, and Kent, Wade observed that the Chinese had the power to own property against all the world except the sovereign "state," which he narrowly defined as Congress. Thus the Montana territorial legislature could neither prohibit Lee from owning property nor confiscate his property.[20] Justice Hiram Knowles, another outstanding figure in the

---

[17]*Ibid.*, 258.
[18]7 Ore 54, 56–58 (1879).
[19]John D. W. Guice, *The Rocky Mountain Bench* (New Haven, Conn., 1972), 75.
[20]2 Mont 124, 130–138 (1874).

early history of Montana, delivered a minority opinion that reflected the popular view. He believed sovereignty resided in both federal and territorial legislatures and that the denial of mining opportunities to the Chinese was a legitimate exercise of authority by the territorial legislature. "Time will fully demonstrate the benefits that would have accrued to this Territory had such legislation been sustained," he observed.[21] Although *Montana v. Lee* gave the Chinese defendant a significant victory over a hostile non-Asian community, it left the door ajar for the ouster of the Chinese from Montana's mines. By calling attention to the power of the federal government, the decision encouraged efforts to lobby Congress for a law barring alien ownership of real property. Such a proposal became law thirteen years later.

Though Chinese defendants prior to 1883 obtained favorable court decisions in such cases as *Lee* and *Moy Looke*, those decisions came grudgingly and rectified only flagrant violations. In other criminal decisions before 1883, appellate courts rejected Chinese efforts to assert their rights to due process of law. Tried and convicted of murdering John McGinness, Ah Hop appealed to the Idaho territorial supreme court, arguing that eight of the jurors at her trial had been summoned illegally, her counsel had not been permitted to give closing arguments, and the jury had not been instructed about the charges or her pleas. The Idaho court ruled in 1878 that she was raising "mere formalities" of the law which did not warrant the overruling of the lower court decision.[22]

Like Ah Hop, Lee Ping Bow, who was found guilty of larceny and sentenced to two years imprisonment in Oregon, failed to persuade the state supreme court to uphold his rights to due process. At his arraignment, the Chinese-speaking defendant had been refused an interpreter; at his trial his counsel had been absent when the verdict was announced and therefore unable to present necessary motions for appeal. However, the supreme court in 1881 reasoned that since Lee had appeared at all legal proceedings, he must have understood English, and since he understood English, absence of counsel did not constitute a reversible error.[23]

Courts arrived at such judgements by making considerations of due process secondary to certain broadly defined principles of common

[21]*Ibid.*, 156.
[22]*Idaho v. Ah Hop et al.*, 1 Ida 698 (1878).
[23]*Oregon v. Lee Ping Bow*, 10 Ore 27, 29–31 (1881).

law. A graphic illustration of this practice occurred in 1876 in Montana Territory. The supreme court allowed the successful prosecution of Ye Wan for gambling to stand even though the Montana gambling statute did not cover the defendant's actions. Instead, the common law doctrine of criminal nuisance was construed as being applicable. Justice Decius Wade dissented, noting tersely that "it was a work of folly to make a Criminal Code, if the common law system of crimes remains in force. . . ."[24] Behind such reliance on common law was antipathy toward the Chinese which became increasingly evident in the late 1870s. By the early 1880s some appellate courts did not even find it necessary to hide their prejudices behind common law. Symbolic of this change was the Oregon supreme court's hearing of the appeal that resulted from the retrial of the Chinese defendants in the Portland joss house murder. After the supreme court had reversed the initial conviction of the defendants, they had been retried separately. Ah Lee was the first to be reconvicted, and he appealed to the supreme court, alleging two lower court errors. He objected to the jury visiting the joss house without him or his counsel being present, but the court ruled he should have come along with the jury if he had wanted to be there. He also challenged the admission into evidence of Chin's dying declaration naming him as the killer on the grounds that Chin could not be believed because he was an "imperfect Christian" who did not believe in the existence of a Supreme Being. The court was not persuaded. Chin may have been "a worshiper of Joss, and the heathenish religion of his race," acknowledged the justices, but since he had been attending a Portland missionary school and since he had defaced the joss house, the common law rule—that the last words of a dying Christian were admissible testimony—prevailed.[25]

By 1883 appellate judges, such as those who decided the *Ah Lee* case, were becoming subject to the general anti-immigrant pressures of the late nineteenth century.[26] Their decisions reflected a changing United States western society which was forming strong attitudes of incomprehension or contempt for the Chinese and their culture. From 1883 to 1902, appellate courts heard twice as many civil disputes in-

---

[24]*Montana* v. *Ye Wan*, 2 Mont 478, 481 (1876).

[25]*Oregon* v. *Ah Lee*, 8 Ore 214, 218–219 (1880). Murder cases inevitably led to an examination of dying declarations and courts treated them with considerable caution if Chinese were involved. See *Idaho* v. *Yee Wee*, 57 Ida 188 (1900) and *Oregon* v. *Foot You*, 24 Ore 61 (1893).

[26]*Oregon* v. *Ah Lee*, 8 Ore 214, 221 (1880).

volving Chinese as in previous years, and most of the decisions had serious consequences for the Chinese community. Unlike before, a majority of the decisions—seventeen of twenty-nine—went against the Chinese, and represented justice denied. Of the twelve favorable rulings, most dealt with mining claims, one of the more popular occupations of Chinese in the Northwest.[27]

Idaho territorial supreme court justices defied these trends against Chinese when in 1893 they examined a mining dispute. A. C. McLean and his friends jumped a claim owned by James Witt and leased to Ah Kle and seven other Chinese miners; Witt, Kle, and the miners brought suit to regain the claim plus $7,000 damages. The Chinese lost in the lower court and appealed to Idaho's supreme court which found in their favor. The defendants had argued that Chinese could not work or lease mining claims since an 1887 act of Congress had denied aliens the right to own claims. The court ruled that the legislation was not applicable since holding title and leasing were separate legal rights. Ten months later Ah Kle was again before the supreme court in a suit he brought against the sheriff of Idaho County. The law officer had refused to enforce the previous supreme court decision because the sheriff demanded an unusually high bond that the plaintiff could not afford. Angered at the sheriff's recalcitrance, the court ordered him to honor Ah Kle's claim.[28]

Most civil decisions after 1882, however, went against the Chinese and often reflected ethnocentrism if not racism.[29] The Montana supreme court, for example, upheld state legislation that required a

---

[27]*Ah How* v. *Jacob Furth et al.*, 13 Wash 550 (1891); *Don Yook* v. *Washington Mill Co.*, 16 Wash 459 (1897); *Ah Kle et al.* v. *McLean et al.*, 2 Ida 812 (1891); *Ah Kle et al.* v. *McLean et al.*, 3 Ida 538 (1893); *Edward Rooney* v. *George H. Tong et al.*, 4 Mont 596 (1883); *Ah Kle* v. *Gregory*, 3 Ida 674 (1893); *Edward Rooney* v. *George H. Tong et al.*, 4 Mont 597 (1883); *Chung Yow* v. *Hop Chong et al.*, 11 Ore 220 (1884); *Ah Lep* v. *Gong Choy and Gong Wing*, 13 Ore 204 (1886); *Ah Lep* v. *Gong Choy et al.*, 13 Ore 429 (1886); *Oh Chow* v. *B. Brockway*, 21 Ore 440 (1891); *Marx* v. *Moy Ham*, 31 Ore 579 (1897).

[28]*Ah Kle et al.* v. *McLean et al.*, 3 Ida 538, 540, 544 (1893); *Ah Kle* v. *Gregory*, 3 Ida 674, 675–676 (1893); Wunder, "The Courts and the Chinese in Frontier Idaho," 30–32.

[29]*Riborado et al.* v. *Quang Pang Mining Co.*, 2 Ida 131 (1885); *Tibbitts* v. *Ah Tong*, 4 Mont 536 (1883); *Power et al.* v. *Gum*, 6 Mont 5 (1886); *Gum* v. *Murray et al.*, 6 Mont 5 (1886) and 6 Mont 10 (1886); *Montana* v. *Owsley et al.*, 17 Mont 94 (1895); *Woo Dan* v. *Seattle Electric Railway and Power Co.*, 5 Wash 466 (1893); *Sam Chong* v. *C. W. Fowler et al.*, 18 Wash 694 (1898); *Henry Weiner* v. *Lee Ching et al.*, 12 Ore 276 (1884); *Victor Guille* v. *Wong Fook*, 13 Ore 577 (1886); *Che Gong and Fong Long Dick* v. *L. B. Stearns*, 16 Ore 219 (1888); *In re North Pacific Presbyterian Board of Missions* v. *Ah Won and Ah Tie*, 18 Ore 339 (1890); *Yick Lee* v. *William Dunbar*, 20 Ore 416 (1891); *Ming Yue* v. *Coos Bay Railroad Co.*, 24 Ore 392 (1893); *Ah Doon* v. *Smith*, 25 Ore 89 (1893); *Alexander* v. *Ling*, 31 Ore 222 (1897); *Ah Foe* v. *Bennett*, 35 Ore 231 (1899); *Pot Lick* v. *Mason*, 37 Ore 629 (1900).

$500 bond from any employer of Chinese labor.[30] Similarly, the Oregon supreme court upheld lawyer J. W. Bennett who had been sued by his Chinese client, Ah Foe. Bennett had encouraged Ah Foe to sell some valuable land for much less than its market value to another person who was secretly in partnership with Bennett. Ah Foe claimed he had been deceived because of his inability to understand English, but the court ruled against him on the grounds that he had been a cook for twenty years around English-speaking people and should have understood English even if he claimed he did not.[31]

Some of the civil opinions revealed distinctly anti-Chinese prejudices of appellate judges. A graphic example occurred in Oregon in a custody dispute over two Chinese children—Ah Won, age eight, and her sister, Ah Tie, age ten. The issue arose in 1889 when the Portland Women's North Pacific Presbyterian Board of Missions petitioned the court to transfer custody of the children from their uncle, Yum Chung, to the Presbyterian women. The petition noted that the children's parents were dead and they were then living with their stepmother, who kept a house of ill-fame. Coming to the defense of the stepmother and Yum was Wong Chin Way, wealthy guardian of the estates of the children, who denied the allegations, accused the Presbyterians of trying to turn the children against Chinese ways, and promised to send the stepmother and children to China as soon as the father's estate was settled. When the lower court ordered the children placed in the custody of the Presbyterian women, Wong sought outside help and persuaded a ship captain, who was preparing to leave for Hong Kong, to take the children and deliver them to their relatives. The captain convinced the lower court judge to order the Presbyterians to give up the children, but rather than comply, the women appealed to the Oregon supreme court for a general review of all issues in the case.[32]

The court proceeded to ponder this classic example of cultural conflict in order to determine what was in the best interests of the chil-

[30]17 Mont 94 (1895).
[31]35 Ore 231, 235 (1899).
[32]18 Ore 339, 340–342 (1890). Similarly, in *Tape v. Hurley*, 66 Cal 473 (1885), the California supreme court ruled that Chinese must be allowed to enter public schools under existing California law. A teacher could not prevent a Chinese child from attending classes because the child was Chinese. However, the court invited the California legislature to make changes by classifying Chinese students as vicious or filthy. See also Charles M. Wollenberg, *All Deliberate Speed: Segregation in California Schools, 1855-1975* (Berkeley, 1977) and Irving G. Hendrick, *The Education of Non-Whites in California* (San Francisco, 1977).

dren. It promised to render a decision not "influenced by fanatical zeal on the one side or by morbid sentimentality on the other."[33] Despite such wishes, the justices reversed the lower court with an opinion that revealed blatant anti-Chinese bias:

The difficulty in such cases is to ascertain the truth. Chinamen such as we have among us can rarely be trusted in such matters, however bland and plausible they may appear. Those of the race who have come to this coast have generally exhibited a total disregard of virtue, candor and integrity, and have shown such a propensity to cunning, deception and perfidy, that if they were to engage in an effort to accomplish an apparently meritorious object a strong suspicion would arise that there was some covert, sinister scheme at the bottom of it. In this case their purpose may be to send these children to their grandmother for the sole benefit of the children; but we have no means of ascertaining whether or not such is their real motive. . . .[34]

So far as the court was concerned, sentimentality for these new Americans was misplaced and against the onrush of progress:

Our societies of today, whether in the church or out of it, are seldom engaged in any narrow sectarian schemes, but are endeavoring to elevate and improve the moral and physical condition of the lower strata of humanity. . . : Men and women who engage in such work,—who search in the dregs and scum of society, and find suffering and abused children, and relieve their wants and necessities, and train them in the path of rectitude, with a view to rendering them useful in the world, instead of being a burden and a nuisance,—are fit and proper to be the guardians of any child, whether of Christian or pagan extraction.[35]

Contemporaneous with such attacks upon Chinese social and cultural values were court efforts to restrain Asian economic interests. These came in cases involving agricultural disputes, railroad labor,[36] and especially mining. In 1883 the Montana territorial supreme court agreed to resolve a question being sharply debated in the mining areas: can an alien hold title to a mining claim, which had been conveyed to him by an American, against an American citizen who later filed on the location and demanded possession? In *Tibbitts* v. *Ah Tong* the court held that Congress in 1866 had opened mining lands to oc-

[33]18 Ore 339, 346.
[34]*Ibid.*, 348.
[35]*Ibid.*, 349.
[36]*Victor Guille* v. *Wong Fook*, 13 Ore 577 (1886); *Ming Yue* v. *Coos Bay Railroad Co.*, 24 Ore 392 (1893).

cupation and purchase by citizens and those intending to be citizens. Since Asians were aliens ineligible for citizenship, Ah Tong had to surrender his claim. But the court went further. It found the right to occupy contingent on the right to possess. In other words, Asians could not even work a mining claim because they had no potential to possess it. The practical effect of the decision was to overrule the earlier holding in *Montana* v. *Lee* and to ban Chinese in Montana from engaging in a major livelihood—placer mining.[37]

Civil suits in the Pacific Northwest after 1882 generally resulted in unfavorable verdicts for Chinese litigants, but even greater losses occurred as a result of criminal cases which produced rapid erosion of rights to due process. Of twenty-seven criminal decisions appealed, only eight led to reversals favorable for the Chinese, and some of these reversals came at the expense of basic rights.[38] In Oregon, two disputes decided by its supreme court were especially destructive for the Chinese. In *Oregon* v. *Mah Jim,* the supreme court reversed a lower court decision because Chinese witnesses had been allowed to offer testimony that convicted Mah Jim of murder. "Experience convinces everyone," declared the court, "that the testimony of Chinese witnesses is very unreliable, and that they are apt to be actuated by motives that are not honest. The life of a human being should not be forfeited on that character of evidence without a full opportunity to sift it thoroughly. . . . The witnesses referred to may have been attempting to carry out a diabolical design—no one can tell what that class of persons may have in view. Their practices are very peculiar and mysterious, and the court, in no such case, should adopt a refined, technical rule as to the admission of evidence tending to show what their motives may be."[39] Two years later, in 1888, the Oregon supreme court reaffirmed its earlier decision by voiding the murder conviction of a Chinese who had been found guilty on the basis of testimony of Chinese witnesses. "Juries should be loath," stated the court, "to convict a Chinaman of murder in the first degree upon Chi-

---

[37] 4 Mont 536, 540–541 (1883). See also Konvitz, *Asiatic in American Law,* 212–218, on the right of aliens to share in natural resources.

[38] *People* v. *Ah Too,* 2 Ida 47 (1884); *Montana* v. *Lee,* 13 Mont 248 (1893); *Oregon* v. *Mah Jim,* 13 Ore 235 (1886); *Oregon* v. *Ching Ling,* 16 Ore 419 (1888); *Oregon* v. *Chee Gong and Fong Long Dick,* 16 Ore 534 (1888); *Washington* v. *Hui and Sam Lee,* 3 Wash Terr 396 (1888); *Washington* v. *Lee Doon,* 7 Wash 308 (1893).

[39] 13 Ore 235, 236–237 (1886).

nese testimony; not wholly on account of a tender regard for the life of
the accused, but also from a respect and reverence for truth and justice."[40] The Oregon decisions produced new trials for the two Chinese
defendants, but at a heavy price.

Those Chinese whose appeals were rejected lost out entirely as the
courts made war on Chinese social and economic traditions. Of the
twenty-seven criminal appellate decisions delivered after 1882, nineteen (or over seventy percent) went against Chinese defendants.[41] One
such adverse decision that resulted in a major denial of due process
occurred in Washington as a result of Seattle's efforts to outlaw Chinese lotteries. Chin Let had been acquitted at the circuit court level on
the grounds that the Seattle ordinance had encroached on the police
power of the state.[42] The supreme court disagreed, asserting that the
Washington constitution gave municipalities the authority to legislate
on gambling. This decision went against Chin Let even though Seattle
was not represented by lawyers. The court regretted "that counsel for
the city have not seen fit to furnish us a brief or argument, or cite any
authorities upon any of the questions noticed in this opinion," but this
oversight proved no obstacle to the justices who rationalized their position in a five-page opinion.[43]

The lottery case was representative of other disputes involving what
the non-Chinese termed "Chinese crimes" against morality, but
which in reality were assaults on Chinese cultural practices. Ten of
the nineteen criminal cases going against Chinese defendants involved
cultural crimes, especially opium smoking and challenges to laundry
taxes. A typical example occurred in 1890 when Ah Lim was found
guilty of violating an 1883 Washington statute against opium smoking.[44] He appealed to the Washington supreme court, asserting that

---

[40]16 Ore 419, 425 (1888).

[41]*Idaho v. Kuok Wah Choi*, 2 Ida 85 (1885); *Idaho v. Yee Wee*, 7 Ida 188 (1900); *Idaho v. Quong*, 8 Ida 191 (1902); *Ah Lim v. Washington*, 1 Wash 156 (1890); *Washington v. Gin Pon*, 16 Wash 425 (1897); *Seattle v. Chin Let*, 19 Wash 38 (1898); *Montana v. Ah Jim*, 9 Mont 167 (1890); *Sam Toi v. French*, 17 Mont 54 (1895); *Montana v. Camp Sing*, 18 Mont 128 (1896); *Oregon v. Tom Louey and Loo Wan*, 11 Ore 326 (1884); *Jennie Wong v. Astoria*, 13 Ore 538 (1886); *Oregon v. Ah Sam*, 14 Ore 347 (1887); *Oregon v. Chee Gong*, 17 Ore 635 (1889); *Oregon v. Chew Muck You*, 20 Ore 215 (1890); *Ex parte Ah Hoy*, 23 Ore 89 (1892); *Oregon v. Foot You*, 24 Ore 61 (1893); *Ex parte Mon Luck*, 29 Ore 421 (1896); *Oregon v. Wong Gee*, 35 Ore 276 (1899).

[42]19 Wash 38 (1898).

[43]*Ibid.*, 43.

[44]Wash. Terr., *Statutes*, ch. 2073, sec. 30 (1883).

the statute violated his constitutional right to life and liberty and deprived him of his means of enjoyment without due process of law.[45] The court was completely unsympathetic. "It is common to indulge in a great deal of loose talk about natural rights and liberties, as if these were terms of well-defined and unchangeable meaning," declared all but one of the justices. "There is no such thing as an absolute or unqualified right or liberty guaranteed to any member of society."[46] The lone dissenter may have faced the issue more squarely than the majority. Justice Elmon Scott observed that under the Washington statute "a single inhalation of opium, even by a person in the seclusion of his own house, away from the sight and without the knowledge of any other person, constitutes a criminal offense under this statute. And this regardless of the actual effect of the particular act upon the individual, whether beneficial or injurious."[47] He also took cognizance of the majority opinion's speculative notions of legislative intent. To Scott, this holding was a dangerous precedent which violated not natural but constitutional rights. "Individual desires," proclaimed the dissenter, "are too sacred to be ruthlessly violated where only acts are involved which purely appertain to the person, and which do not clearly result in an injury to society."[48]

Oregon in 1887 also outlawed both the smoking and possession of opium. Convicted of illegal possession of the drug, Mon Luck appealed to the supreme court which turned him down. The statute infringed on personal liberties, acknowledged the court, but this was permissible because opium was "an active poison." When the defendant asserted that opium was no more harmful than alcohol and merited a similar legal treatment, the court distinguished between these two narcotic substances:

It is a matter of common knowledge that intoxicating liquors are produced principally for sale and consumption as a beverage, and so common has been their manufacture and use for this purpose that they are regarded by some courts as legitimate articles of property, the possession of which neither produces nor threatens any harm to the public. But the use of opium for any purpose other than as permitted in this act has no place in the common experience or habits of the people of this country, but is admitted by all to be an

---

[45] 1 Wash 156, 158 (1890).
[46] Ibid., 165.
[47] Ibid., 167.
[48] Ibid., 173.

insidious and demoralizing vice, injurious alike to the health, morals, and welfare of the public. . . .[49]

Judicial attitudes toward opium smoking clearly left no latitude for the Chinese. Any statute aimed at curbing the use of opium was permissible in the Northwest.

An even more blatant form of discrimination was the tax on laundries, a primary mode of occupation for many urban Chinese. The Montana legislature taxed three classes of laundries on a quarterly basis: steam laundry, $15; laundry operated by one male, $10; and laundry employing one or more persons, $25. Sam Loi challenged the constitutionality of this act by refusing to pay it. In his appeal to the Montana supreme court he relied on a twofold argument. First, he contended that the tax should be stricken because it was not a uniform tax as required by state law. The court reasoned that the levy was not a tax but a fee and constitutional provisions required uniformity for taxes only. Secondly, Loi claimed the law violated the Fourteenth Amendment of the U.S. Constitution by discriminating against Americans on the basis of race. "The fact that Chinamen are engaged in the hand laundry business," reported the court in 1895, "is purely fortuitous. The law, in its terms, applies to all male laundrymen, of every condition and nationality."[50] Montana courts ignored California[51] and United States Supreme Court decisions to the contrary. Nine years earlier in *Yick Wo* v. *Hopkins,* the U.S. Supreme Court had reviewed the constitutionality of a San Francisco ordinance requiring a license for operating a laundry in a wooden building. The ordinance appeared to be fire protection legislation, but the Board of Supervisors, which held administrative power under the act, issued eighty licenses, seventy-nine to white owners while denying licenses to some two hundred Chinese laundrymen. According to the U.S. Supreme Court, the administration of the ordinance reflected a flagrant violation of the equal protection clause of the Fourteenth Amendment.[52]

Extreme violations of due process did not go unchecked. The Mon-

---

[49]29 Ore 421, 427–428 (1896). See also 14 Ore 347 (1887).

[50]17 Mont 54, 60 (1895). See also 18 Mont 128 (1896) for further refinements of this concept.

[51]For laundry legislation and subsequent court interpretations in California, see *Ex parte Moynier,* 65 Cal 33 (1884) and *In re White,* 67 Cal 102 (1885).

[52]*Yick Wo* v. *Hopkins,* 188 US 356 (1886). The *Yick Wo* ruling was eroded and isolated by the court later in 1915 in *Truax* v. *Raich,* 239 US 33 (1915).

tana supreme court ruled that when the only prosecution witness in the grand larceny trial of a Chinese woman could not appear, her constitutional right to be confronted by her accuser had been violated.[53] The Washington supreme court found that even though a Chinese defendant's witness disobeyed a court order and stepped into the courtroom before being called to testify, he could not be prevented from testifying.[54] These decisions, however, were exceptions to the general trend of restricting Chinese civil liberties.

Statistically, two patterns can be identified in the disputes appealed to Pacific Northwest supreme courts between 1849 and 1902. Most cases decided prior to the Chinese Exclusion Act of 1882, whether criminal or civil, tended to favor Chinese litigants. From 1883 to 1902, however, the Chinese experienced a drastic turnabout in their success rates. They lost seventy percent of their appeals in criminal cases and fifty-nine percent of their civil actions. Put another way, they achieved favorable verdicts in only thirty-six percent of all their appeals. (See Table I.) Clearly Pacific Northwest supreme courts were joining in the wave of anti-Chinese sentiment following the Exclusion Act of 1882.

A further indication of this trend can be observed in Table II, which includes all criminal cases appealed to northwestern supreme courts.[55] Prior to 1883, 51 percent of the non-Chinese defendants and 60 percent of the Chinese defendants received favorable decisions. Between 1883 and 1902 the success rate for non-Chinese defendants fell ten percentage points while that for Chinese fell thirty percentage points. In every state and territory, a criminal defendant who was not Chinese had a better chance of vindication before a state or territorial supreme court than did a Chinese defendant.

The anti-Chinese juridical sentiment was doubtlessly aided by the collapse of the Reconstruction experiment. To the westerner, the end of Reconstruction in the South may have made it easier to justify op-

[53]*Montana* v. *Lee*, 13 Mont 248, 249–250 (1893).

[54]*Washington* v. *Lee Doon*, 7 Wash 308, 313 (1893).

[55]Information for criminal cases decided before 1883 was derived from *Idaho Reports*, vols. 1–2; *Wyoming Reports*, vols. 1–2; *Washington Territory Reports*, vols. 1–2; *Oregon Reports*, vols. 1–10; and *Montana Reports*, vols. 1–4.

Information for criminal cases decided from 1883 to 1902 was derived from *Idaho Reports*, vols. 2–8; *Wyoming Reports*, vols. 3–11; *Washington Territory Reports*, vols. 2–3; *Washington Reports*, vols. 1–30; *Oregon Reports*, vols. 10–42; and *Montana Reports*, vols. 5–27.

Table I
Chinese Litigants Before Pacific Northwest Supreme Courts, 1849 to 1902

	Cases Decided Before 1883					
	CIVIL			CRIMINAL		
State or Territory	For Chinese Litigants	Against Chinese Litigants	Total Civil Cases	For Chinese Defendants	Against Chinese Defendants	Total Criminal Cases
Idaho	1	0	(1)	1	2	(3)
Wyoming	1	0	(1)	0	0	(0)
Washington	1	1	(2)	0	0	(0)
Oregon	1	1	(2)	5	3	(8)
Montana	0	1	(1)	3	1	(4)
	4	3	(7)	9	6	(15)

	Cases Decided from 1883 to 1902					
State or Territory	For Chinese Litigants	Against Chinese Litigants	Total Civil Cases	For Chinese Defendants	Against Chinese Defendants	Total Criminal Cases
Idaho	3	1	(4)	1	3	(4)
Wyoming	0	0	(0)	0	0	(0)
Washington	2	2	(4)	2	4	(6)
Oregon	5	10	(15)	4	9	(13)
Montana	2	4	(6)	1	3	(4)
	12	17	(29)	8	19	(27)

pressing the Chinese—many had already been made the scapegoat for the severe depression in the West during the late 1870s, massive unemployment, the rise of labor unions, and the anxiety over conquering a new technological world. In addition, late nineteenth-century America was preparing to follow Rudyard Kipling's call to take up the white man's burden and to remake "alien" cultures.

The increasingly restive hostility held by a suspicious majority toward a minority coincided with major political developments in much of the Northwest. Washington, Montana, Idaho, and Wyoming entered the Union between 1889 and 1890, and their evolution from territory to state necessitated conventions, constitutions, elections, and, significantly, a new system of appellate courts staffed by local rather than national personnel. The new western jurists watched the federal government adopt its first of several discriminatory policies toward the Chinese in 1882 and observed how the U.S. Supreme Court undercut the Civil Rights Act of 1875. These developments doubtlessly pro-

Table II
Chinese and Non-Chinese Defendants Before
Northwestern Supreme Courts, 1849 to 1902

State or Territory	Criminal Cases Decided Before 1883			
	Decision Favoring Non-Chinese Defendant	Decision Favoring Government Prosecution	Decision Favoring Chinese Defendant	Decision Favoring Government Prosecution
Idaho	13 (38%)	21 (62%)	1 (33%)	2 (67%)
Wyoming	9 (56%)	7 (44%)	0 ——	0 ——
Washington	12 (80%)	3 (20%)	0 ——	0 ——
Oregon	34 (50%)	34 (50%)	5 (63%)	3 (37%)
Montana	12 (48%)	13 (52%)	3 (75%)	1 (25%)
	80 (51%)	78 (49%)	9 (60%)	6 (40%)

State or Territory	Criminal Cases Decided from 1883 to 1902			
	Decision Favoring Non-Chinese Defendant	Decision Favoring Government Prosecution	Decision Favoring Chinese Defendant	Decision Favoring Government Prosecution
Idaho	28 (29%)	68 (71%)	1 (25%)	3 (75%)
Wyoming	29 (60%)	19 (40%)	0 ——	0 ——
Washington	122 (38%)	198 (62%)	2 (33%)	4 (67%)
Oregon	97 (49%)	103 (51%)	4 (31%)	9 (69%)
Montana	78 (37%)	131 (63%)	1 (25%)	3 (75%)
	354 (41%)	519 (59%)	8 (30%)	19 (70%)

vided the fledgling appellate courts with the political security and legal precedents essential to deny the Chinese those constitutional guarantees non-Asian Americans regarded as sacrosanct. In 1905 B. Frank Dake wrote in the *Albany Law Journal* a rare article concerning the status of the Chinese under American law. It concluded with an impassioned plea for justice for all Americans:

The expulsion of the Moors by Spain, the expulsion of the Jews by every European nation but one, the revocation of the edict of Nantes, the expulsion of the Huguenots, the massacre of St. Bartholomew, the horrors of Ghetto life are some of the darker blots on the pages of history. The banishment and murder in recent years by a nation claiming to be a Christian people (Russia), of thousands of Jews, have been followed by swift and terrible retribution; and when the history of the dawn of the twentieth century shall be written, and we shall be judged by the standards by which we now judge other people and other times, shall it be said of us that, while claiming to be the greatest Christian country, proclaiming the principles of republican government and of universal freedom, to the pleas of the Chinaman for justice we have been deaf?[56]

These pleas, when taken to the appellate courts of the American Pacific Northwest during the late nineteenth century, met closed legal minds and considerable defective hearing.

---

[56]Dake, "Chinaman Before Supreme Court," 267.

Enterprise and Equity:
A Critique of Western Water Law in
the Nineteenth Century

DONALD J. PISANI

H alf a century ago, Walter Prescott Webb devoted twenty-one pages in *The Great Plains* to a discussion of western water law.[1] Webb became the first American historian to explore water law systematically. For all its flaws, some of which are mentioned in this paper, his work raised vital questions about the adaptation of institutions to the physical environment and the relationship of law to economic development. Unfortunately, historians of the western half of the nation have been slow to follow his lead. Most surveys of the nineteenth-century West pay scant attention to water and none at all to water law. Recently, a handful of scholars have provided good descriptions of many of the laws and have analyzed important legal conflicts. But they have paid inadequate attention to the antecedents, purposes, and economic consequences of western water rights as they evolved in the last century. They have neglected the critical relationship between the law and economic growth.[2]

Donald J. Pisani is an associate professor of history, Texas A & M University, College Station, Texas.

[1] Walter Prescott Webb, *The Great Plains* (Boston, 1931), 431-52.

[2] Several recent books deserve particular mention. Robert G. Dunbar's concise, lucid volume, *Forging New Rights in Western Waters* (Lincoln, 1983), is the only survey of western water law and has the great virtue of discussing twentieth- as well as nineteenth-century laws, and underground as well as surface water. It is a well-researched synthesis based on decades of work in western water law. (For a summary statement see Dunbar's "The Adaptability of Water Law to the Aridity of the West," *Journal of the West*, 24 [January 1985], 57-65.) Five chapters in my *From the Family Farm to Agribusiness: The Irrigation Crusade in California and the West, 1850-1931* (Berkeley, 1984), 30-53 and 129-282, treat the evolution of court and legislative water law in nineteenth-century California. Although Michael C. Meyer's *Water in the Hispanic Southwest: A Social and Legal History, 1550-1850* (Tuscon, 1984) does not discuss law in the American Southwest either before or after 1850, its thorough analysis of the nature of Spanish water law makes it required reading. Also see John D.W. Guice, *The Rocky Mountain Bench: the Territorial Supreme Courts of Colorado, Montana, and Wyoming, 1861-1890* (New Haven, 1972); Gordon Morris Bakken, *The Development of Law on the Rocky Mountain Frontier: Civil Law and Society, 1850-1912* (Westport, CT, 1983); Arthur Maass and Raymond L. Anderson, *. . . and the Desert Shall Rejoice: Conflict, Growth, and Justice in Arid Environments* (Cambridge, MA, 1978), 224-31; Norris Hundley, Jr., *Water and the West: the Colorado River Compact and the Politics of Water in the American West* (Berkeley, 1975), 66-73; Gordon R. Miller, "Shaping California Water Law, 1781-1928," *Southern California Quarterly*, 55 (Spring 1973),

This essay is not a systematic summary of western water law. It is built around five arguments rather than a central thesis. These are: first, that economic needs and conditions determined the shape of water law more than aridity or any other single physical factor; second, that prior appropriation[3] grew logically out of an adaptable common law and appeared in New England years before it developed in the West; third, that while the doctrine of prior appropriation stimulated economic development, it suffered from profound weaknesses and ultimately may have worked against the "common good;" fourth, that in many parts of the nineteenth-century West, riparian water rights[4] and Spanish or Mexican communal water laws offered viable legal alternatives to prior appropriation; and, fifth, that the desire of oldtimers to bolster their interests in competition with newcomers best explains water law reform in the late nineteenth century. At the heart of the paper are two assumptions: that the law is a conscious product of many discrete economic choices, not simply an elaboration of abstract legal principles; and that the initial dependence of the West on mining prevented greater legal consideration of the just and efficient allocation and distribution of water to agriculture. Not all these ideas are "revisionist" or original, nor can they be explored fully in one essay. But taken together, I hope they provide a useful overview and suggest a new, broader way of looking at the role of water law in western history.

In virtually every study of western water law statutes and court decisions appear in isolation, the product of immaculate conception, with no apparent kinship to law in the eastern half of the nation. The work of the nation's most prominent legal historians has had little influence on the study of water law even though it suggests that nineteenth-century property laws

9-42; Douglas R. Littlefield, "Water Rights during the California Gold Rush: Conflicts over Economic Points of View," *Western Historical Quarterly*, 14 (October 1983), 415-34; M. Catherine Miller, "Riparian Rights and the Control of Water in California, 1879-1928: The Relationship Between an Agricultural Enterprise and Legal Change," *Agricultural History*, 59 (January 1985), 1-24.

[3] In the arid West prior appropriation conferred an exclusive right to use water on the first claimant to a stream. The water could be used on any land, any distance from the water source. The amount was unlimited, save for the legal requirement that it be put to a "beneficial use." The first user enjoyed the only absolute grant. All other rights depended on the extent and priority of previous claims. In most states appropriative water rights were and are regarded as a species of property that can be sold in whole or in part.

[4] Riparian rights were part of title to land adjoining a stream. They did not exist independent of the land, nor were they absolute. In these two ways they differed markedly from appropriative rights. In theory, this system only served those whose land bordered a stream. A riparian user could divert water for any useful purpose, and the amount could vary from day to day, month to month, or year to year. Lack of use had no affect on the right. Except for the water they used for domestic needs and stock, riparian claimants could not substantially reduce the flow of a stream if downstream neighbors objected. In other words, riparian rights were "correlative," definable only as they related to other riparian claims.

developed from the same assumptions in all states. For years, James Willard Hurst, probably the nation's foremost legal historian, has called for a functional or "instrumental" approach to the law. Hurst maintains that in most state courts tradition, time-honored legal postulates, and dogma played little part in deciding how to allocate natural resources. As early as 1950, he declared that "[w]e shall get a more realistic grasp of the part law has played in United States history if we keep in mind the readiness of Americans to use it as a means to bring about immediate practical results." A decade and a half later, in his magisterial history of the nineteenth-century lumber industry in Wisconsin, he noted that Americans cherished the belief that "it was common sense and it was good, to use law to multiply the productive power of the economy." To the notion that Americans saw the law "more as an instrument for desired immediate results than as a statement of carefully legitimated, long-range values," what he called "the release of energy," Hurst added many ancillary ideas. He believed that nineteenth-century law promoted economic growth and did not just remove legal restrictions or limit the state's regulatory powers. Hurst asserted that the state used its power to affect the economy positively as much in the nineteenth-century heyday of laissez-faire as in the twentieth-century era of administrative regulation. He believed that trial and appellate court decisions revealed better the symbiotic relationship between the economy and legal system than U.S. Supreme Court judgments. And finally, Hurst recognized that government allocates property in many ways, not just through taxing and spending, but also through the distribution of public lands, the issuance of franchises, or the manipulation of the money system. Hurst worked "at the borderland of law and economic history," as one of his admirers aptly noted. His consideration of how government allocated resources through the operation of the law broke new ground for a generation of scholars.[5]

[5] James Willard Hurst, *Law and Markets in United States History: Different Modes of Bargaining Among Interests* (Madison, 1982); *The Growth of American Law: The Law Makers* (Boston, 1950), 4; *Law and Economic Growth: the Legal History of the Lumber Industry in Wisconsin, 1836-1915* (Cambridge, MA, 1964), 171-72; *Law and Social Order in the United States* (Ithaca, 1977), 23, 106; "The Release of Energy," in Lawrence M. Friedman and Harry N. Scheiber, eds., *American Law and the Constitutional Order: Historical Perspectives* (Cambridge, MA, 1978), 109-20, esp. 111, 112, and 114. See also Harry N. Scheiber, "At the Borderland of Law and Economic History: The Contributions of Willard Hurst," *American Historical Review*, 75 (February 1970), 744-56; David H. Flaherty, "An Approach to Legal History: Willard Hurst as Legal Historian," *American Journal of Legal History*, 14 (July 1970), 222-34; Earl Finbar Murphy, "The Jurisprudence of Legal History: Willard Hurst as a Legal Historian," *New York University Law Review*, 39 (November 1964), 900-943; Robert W. Gordon, J. Willard Hurst and the Common Law Tradition in American Legal Historiography," *Law and Society Review*, 10 (Fall 1975), 9-56; and Stephen Diamond, "Legal Realism and Historical Method: J. Willard Hurst and American Legal History," *Michigan Law Review*, 77 (January-March 1979), 784-94.

Other legal historians, including Harry Scheiber and Morton Horwitz have made significant contributions to Hurst's instrumentalist interpretation of property law.[6] Horwitz has described how the changing economy of New England in the early nineteenth century forced a redefinition of water rights in common law. After 1815 the proliferation of large scale integrated cotton mills dramatically increased the need for water power. The eighteenth-century assumption that the law was a fixed, unchanging standard that judges simply sought to discover and interpret, and that attention to legal precedent assured that judges would not stray from preexisting laws and principles, worked well in a stable, rural, agricultural society where nature limited wealth largely to profits derived directly from the land. But the dawn of a new economic order challenged old assumptions and, according to Horwitz, "the evolving law of water rights had greater impact than any other branch of the law on the effort to adapt private law doctrines to the movement for economic growth."[7]

The common law originally reflected the belief that rivers were part of God's plan as revealed in nature. God not only determined the course of streams, He dictated that, in Blackstone's words, water was "a moving, wandering thing," whose very nature defied conversion to property. Consequently, any attempt to dam or divert a stream was at the least an unnatural act. The construction of mills and factories produced several new kinds of legal conflict: actions by downstream riparian owners against landowners whose dams upstream interfered with the natural flow; suits by mill owners whose operations had been curtailed by downstream dams which, by backing up water, made the flow upstream sluggish and unpredictable; and, finally, riparian owners whose land had been flooded by dams. Between 1820 and 1831, the productive capacity of New England cotton mills increased six times. More water rights cases were decided in the decade between 1824 and 1833 than in the entire history of the common law. "By the middle of the nineteenth century," Horwitz concludes, "the legal system had been reshaped to the advantage of men of commerce and industry at the expense of farmers, workers, consumers, and other less powerful

[6] Much of Harry Scheiber's excellent work has focused on eminent-domain law. As a sample, see his "Property Law, Expropriation, and Resource Allocation by Government, 1789-1910," in Friedman and Scheiber, *American Law and the Constitutional Order*, 132-41; "The Road to *Munn*: Eminent Domain and the Concept of Public Purpose in the State Courts," *Perspectives in American History*, 5 (1971), 329-402; "Federalism and the American Economic Order, 1789-1910," *Law and Society Review*, 10 (Fall 1975), 57-118; and "Public Rights and the Rule of Law in American Legal History," *California Law Review*, 72 (March 1984), 217-51.

[7] Morton J. Horwitz, *The Transformation of American Law, 1780-1860* (Cambridge, MA, 1977) 34.

groups within the society." The law had "actively promoted a legal redistribution of wealth against the weakest groups in the society."[8]

The growth of factories in the East posed as much of a challenge to traditional riparian rights as the development of mining and irrigation in the West. In 1844 Massachusetts Chief Justice Lemuel Shaw declared that "[the] proprietor who first erects his dam for such a purpose has a right to maintain it, as against the proprietors above and below; and to this extent, a prior occupancy gives a prior title to such use." This decision, erected on the principle of "first in time, first in right," placed economic development ahead of equal access. Water had become property detached from the land, and prior appropriation offered businessmen a monopoly subsidy just as special franchises and charters did.[9]

Webb can be forgiven for declaring that there was "little occasion" to modify water rights in the East before 1850, but students of western water law have continued to suggest that common law water rights constituted a relatively changeless, static system.[10] Many western judges and legislators—cut off from adequate law libraries and a community of lawyers—did rely heavily on obsolete, traditional expositions of the law. They were simply unaware of how eastern courts modified the common law before the Civil War. Nevertheless, western courts often applauded the adaptability and sufficiency of common law principles. In an 1857 case, the California Supreme Court noted that in the absence of "direct precedent, as well as without specific legislation, we have been compelled to apply to this anomalous state of things the analogies of the common law and

---

[8] Horwitz, *The Transformation of American Law*, 253-54. Also see Horwitz's "The Transformation in the Conception of Property in American Law," in Friedman and Scheiber, *American Law and the Constitutional Order*, 148, and his "The Emergence of an Instrumental Conception of American Law, 1780-1820," in *Perspectives in American History*, 5 (1971), 287-326.

[9] Justice Shaw's quote is as printed in Horwitz, *The Transformation of American Law*, 41. Horwitz discusses the emergence of prior appropriation on pp. 34-42. He states that "[b]y mid-century it had outlived its usefulness and . . . was discarded," (p. 42) though he does not explain why it died out. Although not as concerned with changes in water rights, readers should also see William E. Nelson, *Americanization of the Common Law: The Impact of Legal Change on Massachusetts Society, 1760-1830* (Cambridge, MA, 1975); Leonard W. Levy, *The Law of the Commonwealth and Chief Justice Shaw*, (Cambridge, MA, 1957); and G. Edward White, *The American Judicial Tradition: Profiles of Leading American Judges* (New York, 1976), 42-43, 56, and 61. White notes that not all judges were as willing to use the power of the state to stimulate economic activity as Shaw and the Massachusetts court. Jurists such as Joseph Story and James Kent took a much more traditional view of the sanctity of private property.

[10] Webb, *The Great Plains*, 432; Miller, "Shaping California Water Law, 1781-1928," 23, 34; Dunbar, "The Adaptability of Water Law to the Aridity of the West," 57. Harry Scheiber and Charles W. McCurdy have observed, in "Eminent-Domain Law and Western Agriculture, 1849-1900," *Agricultural History*, 49 (January 1975), 113, that this narrow view has not been restricted to water law. "What both the romantic and pessimistic versions of early Far Western legal development have in common," the two men wrote, "is their emphasis on the alleged novelty and innovativeness that marked the early history of resource laws."

the more expanded principles of equitable justice."In an 1872 Colorado case upholding appropriation, the court maintained that the "principles of the [common] law are undoubtedly of universal application." And in 1907 the Arizona court proclaimed that "[t]he essence of the common law is flexibility and adaptability. It is not a body of fixed rules, but is the best product of human reason applied to the premises of the ordinary and extraordinary conditions of life. . . . Should the common law become so crystallized that its expressions take the same form, wherever the common-law system prevails, irrespective of physical, social, or other conditions peculiar to the locality, it would cease to be the common law of history, and would be but an inelastic and arbitrary code."[11] Not only did many court decisions proclaim the flexibility of the common law, but some early decisions freely mixed elements of riparian rights and appropriation.[12]

The failure to recognize the adaptability of common law has contributed to the assumption that nature dictated the evolution of western water law. Robert Dunbar, the foremost student of western water law, flatly declares: "Climate has been the determining factor in the development of western water law." And Gordon Bakken, who has written the best general surveys of law in the West, states: "Pioneer legislators and judges in the Rocky Mountain States created the law of prior appropriation to deal with this problem of aridity."[13] Certainly, many court decisions sustain this interpretation.[14] It is also reinforced by the fact that the driest states in the West—Nevada, Arizona, Utah, Colorado, Wyoming, Idaho, and New Mexico—recognize only prior appropriation, while the states with humid as well as arid and semiarid sections—California, Kansas, Montana, Nebraska, North and South Dakota, Oregon, Texas, Washington, and Oklahoma—recognize riparian as well as appropriative rights. Nevertheless, aridity is, at best,

[11]*Bear River and Auburn Water and Mining Co.* v. *New York Mining Co.*, 8 Cal. 327, 332 (1857); *Yunker* v. *Nichols*, 1 Colo. 551 (1872); *Boquillas Land & Cattle Co.* v. *Curtis*, 11 Ariz. 128, 140 (1907).

[12]*Crandall* v. *Woods*, 8 Cal. 136 (1857); *Bear River and Auburn Water and Mining Co.* v. *New York Mining Co.*, 8 Cal. 327, 333 (1857).

[13]Dunbar, "The Adaptability of Water Law to the Aridity of the West," 57; Gordon Morris Bakken, "The Influence of the West on the Development of Law," *Journal of the West*, 24 (January 1985), 67. Contemporary scholars have inherited this view of the rigidity of the common law from C.S. Kinney, the dean of western water lawyers, via Webb. They have absorbed without question the opinions and judgments of early twentieth-century scholars of water law, including Samuel Wiel, L. Ward Bannister, and, particularly, C. S. Kinney. See Clesson S. Kinney, *A Treatise on the Law of Irrigation and Water Rights and the Arid Region Doctrine of Appropriation of Waters* . . . , 4 vols. (San Francisco, 1912), 1: 871, 1011, and 1015, and Webb, *The Great Plains*, 448.

[14]For example, see *Yunker* v. *Nichols*, 1 Colo. 551, 553 (1872); *Coffin* v. *Left Hand Ditch Company*, 6 Colo. 443, 446 (1882); *Drake* v. *Earhart*, 2 Ida. 750, 753 (1890); *Stowell* v. *Johnson*, 7 Utah 215 (1891). Also see *Reno Smelting Works* v. *Stevenson*, 20 Nev. 269, 281-82 (1899); *Farm Investment Co.* v. *Carpenter*, 9 Wyo. 110, 136 (1900); and Dunbar, *Forging New Rights in Western Waters*, 78-82.

half an answer to why prior appropriation was embraced with such ardor in so many parts of the West.

The affection of western courts and legislatures for prior appropriation can only be understood in light of regional economic conditions in the last half of the nineteenth century. Aridity was a fundamental problem, but western agriculture was in its infancy in the 1850s and 1860s, and farmers had little influence in state or territorial legislatures. Moreover, most mining was conducted in the region's major mountain ranges where there was plenty of water, although not always in the right places. Lawmakers perceived the region primarily as an economic wilderness punctuated by oases of human activity. Transportation was poor, investment capital limited, and labor scarce. Obviously, most who went west in search of gold or silver saw the region's potential solely in economic terms, and many did not intend to stay. The West had its share of boosters from the beginning, but the golden dream of an empire on the Pacific must have seemed visionary to most residents of the region. If the West had any economic promise, it was in mining and perhaps stock-raising. Not surprisingly, in 1855 the California Supreme Court declared that "[t]he Legislature of our State in the wise exercise of its discretion has seen proper to foster and protect the mining interest as paramount to all others," a judgment it reiterated in 1875 when it declared that prior appropriation had been adopted "to distribute the bounty of the government among the greatest number of persons, so as most rapidly to develop the hidden resources of this region. . . ."[15]

Western courts and legislatures faced the fundamental problem of how to stimulate a fledgling industry whose activities were confined largely to the public domain. Here *was* a problem very different from those encountered by eastern courts. Initially, miners needed to turn away water to expose streambeds and get at placer deposits. But within a few years, especially in California, they began to divert water and transport it great distances to wash away topsoil in search of ancient streambeds. Virtually all water cases in the West before the 1870s pertained to mining and milling on government land, not to agriculture on private lands. Irrigation was very limited, and often used water provided by mining companies to raise crops sold in mining camps.

There could be no riparian rights where the federal government owned the land, and by the middle of the 1850s it still had not defined the rights of miners. Hence, all privileges were as between individuals, not absolute. Not only did prior appropriation allow water to be treated as private property, which the mining industry demanded, but it was the only possible

[15] *Fitzgerald v. Urton*, 5 Cal. 308, 309 (1855); *Bear River and Auburn Water and Mining Co. v. New York Mining Co.*, 8 Cal. 327, 334 (1857).

solution that followed the well-established precedent of *disseisin* rights, the right of a landholder to evict a trespasser when title to the land was held by a third party. In effect, since everyone on the public lands were disseisors of the United States, the earliest possession took priority, in both water and mineral claims.[16]

California courts warned repeatedly that prior appropriation had not and could not replace the riparian doctrine. In an 1859 case, the state supreme court declared that prior appropriation was "undoubtedly . . . a very convenient rule," but that the privilege did not constitute a grant from the federal government, which had never spoken on the water rights issue. In other words, prior appropriation was a makeshift which could be overturned by Congress at any time. Even more important, the court emphasized that "this exceptional privilege is, of course, confined to the public domain." The court reiterated this maxim in its 1884 *Lux* v. *Haggin* decision. "After carefully examining all the cases bearing on this question," it declared, "we are unable to find one in which it is held, or even suggested, that outside of the mining districts the common-law doctrine of riparian rights does not apply with the same force and effect in this state as elsewhere." Some states, led by Colorado and Wyoming, did not accept this premise. But California was not unique. The Montana Supreme Court maintained that "[i]t is not claimed that the decision of any court, either in this Territory or California, has pretended to establish the doctrine of prior appropriation . . . to agricultural lands."[17]

The mining legacy boxed Congress into a corner. Most of its members knew even less about water than they did about mining. State courts took the absence of Congressional legislation dealing with mining claims on the public domain as tacit acceptance of their judgments. Finally, in 1866, 1870, and 1877, Congress enacted measures recognizing the right of settlers to tap streams flowing through the public lands for mining, agriculture, and other purposes so long as water users conformed to local customs and procedures.[18] In fact, the 1877 legislation, the Desert Land Act, formally *restricted* water use to "bona-fide prior appropriation." Many legal scholars have assumed that Congress was, in effect, voting for appropriation as preferable to riparian rights, or rejecting riparian rights as inapplicable

[16] Charles N. McCurdy, "Stephen J. Field and Public Land Law Development in California, 1850-1866: A Case Study of Judicial Resource Allocation in Nineteenth Century America," *Law and Society Review*, 10 (Fall 1975), 256.

[17] *Boggs* v. *Merced Mining Co.*, 14 Cal. 279, 377 (1859); *Lux* v. *Haggin*, 69 Cal. 255, 4 Pac. Rep. 919, 923 (1884); *Thorp* v. *Freed*, 1 Mont. 651, 669, (1872). Also see *Irwin* v. *Phillips*, 5 Cal. 140 (1855); *Moore* v. *Smaw*, 17 Cal. 199 (1861); and *Drake* v. *Earhart*, 2 Ida. 750, 764 (1890).

[18] *U.S. Statutes at Large*, XIV: 253; XVI: 218; XIX: 377. For a discussion of the motives behind the 1866 law see Justice Stephen J. Field's reasoning in *Basey* v. *Gallagher*, 87 U.S. 670 at 683-84 (1874).

to the West. But since California and other states had encouraged appropriation, the lawmakers had little choice but to honor these rights.

State legislatures and courts extended prior appropriation to agriculture by applying questionable precedents culled from mining cases. This
process has never been adequately discussed by legal scholars. Nevertheless, since the 1870s, if not before, plenty of farmers, lawyers, and land
and water companies have preached the doctrine's virtues, and many students of the law have followed their lead. In 1911 a political scientist
proclaimed riparianism as "hopelessly inadequate," but dignified appropriation as "the only doctrine suited to an arid agriculture." Walter Prescott
Webb declared that "history. . . makes clear the necessity of . . . prior appropriation. . . ." In 1935 Carey McWilliams lauded appropriation as "the
fairest and most economical and the fullest use of an inadequate water supply," and in 1953 Wallace Stegner declared it "an essential criterion" in
an "irrigating country."[19]

Many nineteenth-century scientists and engineers did not share this
enthusiasm. By mandating prior appropriation on the public lands, the Desert Land Act touched off a mad scramble by speculative land and water
companies to claim water for new projects, many of which were chimeri-
cal. In his famous 1878 report on the arid lands, John Wesley Powell warned
that private ditch companies would be satisfied with nothing less than
monopolistic control over the region's water supply, and that once they
gained a foothold "evils will result therefrom that generations may not be
able to correct, and the very men who are now lauded as benefactors in
the [arid] country will, in the ungovernable reaction which is sure to come,
be denounced as oppressors of the people." This fear did not abate. When
Powell spoke to the constitutional convention of Dakota Territory in 1889,
he urged: "If you fail in making a constitution in any other respect, fail
not in this one. Fix it in your constitution that no corporation—no body
of men—no capital can get possession and right of your waters. . . . Such
a provision will prevent your agricultural resources from falling into the
hands of a few." Powell rejected both riparian rights and appropriation,
instead proposing the creation of autonomous water districts whose boundaries would conform to natural drainage basins rather than county or state
lines. Within such districts, farmers could tailor-make water laws to suit
their particular needs.[20]

[19] Katharine Coman, "Some Unsettled Problems of Irrigation," *American Economic Review*, 1 (March 1911), 4; Webb, *The Great Plains*, 448; Carey McWilliams, *Factories in the
Field: the Story of Migratory Farm Labor in California* (Santa Barbara, 1971); Wallace Stegner,
Beyond the Hundredth Meridian: John Wesley Powell and the Second Opening of the West (Boston,
1953), 226.

[20] John Wesley Powell, "Report on the Lands of the Arid Region of the United States,
with a More Detailed Account of the Lands of Utah," 45th Cong., 2d sess. House Executive Documents, no. 73, serial 1805 (Washington, DC, 1878), 41. The quote is from Howard

No state offered better examples of the dangers of prior appropriation than California. At the south end of the San Joaquin Valley, the Kern County Land and Water Company—the largest irrigation enterprise in the West—pieced together an empire of 300,000 acres and claimed about three times more water from the Kern River than the stream had ever carried. Control over the region's major water source allowed the company to buy up smaller ditches and build new canals until it established a water monopoly in the county. In the 1870s the company was hailed for making the desert blossom—though largely by farmers whose land dramatically appreciated in value as it was provided with water. But during the 1880s, the enterprise became increasingly unpopular. Irrigators who complained about the cost of water often had their supplies reduced or cut off. In addition, the company filed more than 100 suits against farmers who refused to sell their water rights, forcing many to give up their land and leave the county. It also used local officials, including judges, sheriffs, and tax assessors (who were owned or controlled by the company) to harass recalcitrant settlers. Little wonder that William Hammond Hall, California State Engineer from 1878 to 1889, advised his colleague, Elwood Mead of Wyoming: "I do not believe in the distribution or acquirement of water rights by *appropriation*. It is a word which should never have been admitted into Water Rights Legislation. . . . To 'appropriate' presupposes that the thing taken is without ownership, like a wild beast of the forest or of the plain . . . to be shot down and dragged out by the first brute that came in sight of it."[21]

Prior appropriation provided great economic incentives and opportunities for investors in irrigation projects, but it was grossly inefficient as a tool to parcel out a scarce resource. In most western states during the

R. Lamar, *Dakota Territory, 1861-1889: A Study of Frontier Politics* (New Haven, 1956), 279. Also see Lewis F. Crawford, *History of North Dakota* (Chicago, 1931), 327, 342. For additional examples of criticism of prior appropriation and water monopoly by scientists and federal officials see George Perkins Marsh, "Irrigation: Its Evils, the Remedies, and the Compensations," 43rd Cong., 1st sess., Senate Miscellaneous Document, no. 55, serial 1584 (Washington, DC, 1874), 16-19; the testimony of Powell's chief lieutenant on the Irrigation Survey, C. E. Dutton, in "Ceding the Arid Lands to the States and Territories," 51st Cong., 2nd sess., House of Representatives, no. 3767, serial 2888 (Washington, DC, 1891) 169, 170, 185, 186; Elwood Mead, head of the Office of Irrigation Investigations in the U.S. Department of Agriculture, in his *Irrigation Institutions: A Discussion of the Economic and Legal Questions created by Growth of Irrigated Agriculture in the West* (New York, 1903), 207; and University of Wisconsin economist and adviser to the Department of Agriculture Richard T. Ely to R.P. Teele, 27 July 1903, in "Correspondence of R.P. Teele, 1904-1909," Records Group 8, Records of the Bureau of Agricultural Engineering, Office of Irrigation Investigations, Federal Records Center, Suitland, Maryland.

[21] The Kern County Land and Water Company is discussed in Pisani, *From the Family Farm to Agribusiness*, 191-249. The quote is from William Hammond Hall to Elwood Mead, October 4, 1889, in "Elwood Mead, Territorial & State Engineer: Incoming Correspondence from Federal Government Officials, 1888-1890," Wyoming State Archives, Cheyenne. Also see Hall to J. DeBarth Shorb, 21 August 1886, in Incoming Business Correspondence, Shorb collection, the Huntington Library, San Marino, California.

nineteenth century, appropriators had to meet only one condition—put their diversion to a "beneficial use." Gordon Bakken has commented that without a "beneficial application the asset remained open to subsequent use by the numerous operatives vying for the valuable commodity." But this apparent limitation was largely ineffective because, as one legal scholar recently noted, "[p]ractically all of the farmers, miners, manufacturers, power companies, and cities of the West met this test when they took the water, since each had a practical wealth-producing use in mind. Each use advanced the development of the resources of the country. . . ."[22] Farmers routinely used far more water than they actually needed because benificial use did not mean either reasonable or economical use. Moreover, use varied year by year, so, of necessity, rights had an elastic quality in court. Farmers might not irrigate at all in wet years, and in dry years might leave a field fallow. Courts generally recognized claims for more water than was actually needed if an irrigator expected to expand his delivery system. The farmer who claimed water to irrigate 160 acres, but initially watered only 60 acres, usually received the full amount if he presented well-conceived plans to cultivate the entire acreage eventually. Until the water was needed, he could sell or lease the surplus. Moreover, "paper claims" could be maintained for years through minimal work on ditches. This was one reason the Salt River in Arizona had been appropriated 25 times over by 1900 and the San Joaquin River 172 times over.[23]

Unfortunately, the courts had neither the expertise nor revenue to gather stream flow data, check to see how much water was actually being used, or determine the quantity actually needed to raise different crops in different soils. Nor could they call on state officials to provide impartial information. So western courts relied almost exclusively on the testimony of interested witnesses, and extravagent claims often received the benefit of the doubt. For example, during the 1880s Colorado water decrees promised as much as five times the volume of water ditches were capable of carrying.[24] To make matters worse, decrees from different courts granted different amounts of water to irrigate the same kind of land and crops. Such allocations promoted expensive and inconclusive litigation. In 1893 John Norton Pomeroy, one of the few scholars of western water law sympathetic to riparian rights, concluded that prior appropriation had been "a most fruitful cause of litigation in California . . . but this is a feeble illustration

[22] The quotes are from Bakken, *The Development of Law on the Rocky Mountain Frontier*, 71, and Frank J. Trelease, "Uneasy Federalism-State Water Laws and National Water Uses," *Washington Law Review*, 55 (November 1980), 752-53.

[23] Pisani, *From the Family Farm to Agribusiness*, 339-40; Mead, *Irrigation Institutions*, 277.

[24] Dunbar, *Forging New Rights in Western Waters*, 101; Samuel Fortier, "The Agricultural Side of Irrigation," *Official Proceedings of the Eighteenth National Irrigation Congress Held at Pueblo, Colorado, Sept. 26-30, 1910* (Pueblo, n.d.), 335.

of the litigation and controversy which must arise from the statutes of Colorado and of the various territories when they come into full operation upon an increasing population." Pomeroy recognized that litigation had been created as much, if not more, by conflicts between rival appropriators as between appropriators and riparian owners.[25]

Comprehensive studies of the optimum amount of water required to raise different crops in different soils were not undertaken until the late 1890s; meanwhile, most farmers simply assumed that more was better. They encountered far more incentives to waste water than to save it. The courts recognized use as the basic criterion for determining how much water to award individual claimants, even if the amount used was excessive. By diverting the largest amount possible, farmers could, in effect, reserve water either for future use or sale. Moreover, companies often sold water by the number of acres irrigated rather than by the volume of water actually used, and farmers generally claimed far more water than they applied to the land because nineteenth-century irrigation systems were grossly inefficient and lost tremendous quantities of water to seepage and evaporation. The longer and smaller the canal, the greater the loss. In 1903 Secretary of Agriculture James Wilson estimated that canals which carried 100 cubic feet per second lost about 1 percent of their volume per mile while those carrying 25-50 c.f.s. lost over 5 percent per mile.[26]

Given these weaknesses in the doctrine of prior appropriation, what legal alternatives did westerners have to allocate the region's water? For decades historians have charged that riparian rights hindered western economic development.[27] Robert Dunbar maintained that riparian rights were "poorly suited to irrigation-based communities" because they "deprived millions of prospective farms of water."[28] Yet the riparian doctrine had many advantages over appropriation, particularly in the nineteenth century before massive reservoir projects dramatically increased the supply available for irrigation. The region's most productive land was the alluvial soil adjoining streams, and it was also the cheapest to irrigate. Riparian

[25] John Norton Pomeroy, *A Treatise on the Law of Water Rights* . . . (St. Paul, 1893), 328-29.

[26] James Wilson, untitled speech, *The Official Proceedings of the Eleventh National Irrigation Congress Held at Ogden, Utah, September 15-18, 1903* (Ogden, 1904), 164.

[27] For example, J.A. Alexander, in his *The Life of George Chaffey* (Melbourne, 1928), 35, called riparianism "a serious obstacle to the development of irrigation in the West," and in his survey of water resource development in California, *Aqueduct Empire: A Guide to Water in California, Its Turbulent History and Its Management Today* (Glendale, 1968), 409; Erwin Cooper charged that such rights were a "potential death sentence" on all other water claims. In a revised edition of his 1942 classic, *Our Landed Heritage: The Public Domain, 1776-1970* (Lincoln, 1976), 329, Roy M. Robbins declared that "[t]he heterogeneous [nineteenth century] medley of riparian laws and customs had led to chaos."

[28] Dunbar, *Forging New Rights in Western Waters*, 68. Also see Gordon R. Miller, "Shaping California Water Law, 1781-1928," 11, 23.

land did not require long canals, nor did riparian owners face the high cost of condemning land for canal rights-of-way. Moreover, the irrigation of riparian land permitted maximum "return flow," the water that seeped back into streams from saturated land. And since riparian titles permitted only the reasonable use of water, rather than an absolute property right, riparian rights easily expanded or contracted in response to seasonal fluctuations in the water supply. They were 'correlative' because they had no existence apart from each other. Riparian owners had an unquestionable right to sufficient water for domestic uses and stock; all other diversions existed at the sufferance of riparian neighbors.

Many early western courts recognized these virtues. Despite inconsistencies in its early decision, the California Supreme Court never completely lost sight of common-law principles. In 1853 it declared prior appropriation "impracticable in application." "The right of property in water is *usufructuary*, and consists not so much of the fluid itself as the advantage of its use. The owner of land through which a stream flows, merely transmits the water over its surface, having the right to its reasonable use during its passage. The right is not in the *corpus* of the water." In 1855 it proclaimed: "The right to water must be treated in this State as it has always been treated, as a right running with the land . . . and as such, [it] has none of the characteristics of mere personality." In the following year the court insisted that common law principles had "abundantly sufficed for the determination of all disputes which have come before us . . . we have neither modified its rules, nor have we attempted to legislate upon any pretended ground of their insufficiency." And in an 1865 case, the court summarily rejected "the notion, which has become quite prevalent, that the rules of the common law touching water rights have been materially modified in this state. . . . This notion is without substantial foundation."[29]

Nor was California unique. In 1871 the Nevada Supreme Court rejected the argument that in a hot, arid climate like Nevada's, riparian appropriators ought to be able to divert an entire stream for irrigation. It defended the rights of other riparian owners on the stream "who have an *equal need and an equal right*." In the following year the same court held that riparian rights gave "the greatest right to the greatest number, authorizing each to make a reasonable use of [the water], providing he does no injury to the others equally entitled to it with himself; whilst the rule of prior appropriation here advocated would authorize the first person who might choose to make use of or divert a stream to use or even waste the

---

[29] *Eddy* v. *Simpson*, Cal. 249, 252 (1853); *Hill* v. *Newman*, 5 Cal. 446 (1855); *Conger* v. *Weaver*, 6 Cal. 55 (1856); *Hoffman* v. *Stone*, 7 Cal. 46, 48 (1857), *Hill* v. *Smith*, 27 Cal. 432 (1865).

whole, to the utter ruin of others who might wish it.'' In 1890 a dissenting
Idaho opinion questioned whether it was fair to permit appropriators to
sell water to others and thereby prevent riparian owners from using water
that flowed by their property. And in 1903, Nebraska's Supreme Court
proclaimed: ''[W]e doubt whether a more equitable starting point for a
system of irrigation law may be found [than the riparian doctrine].'' John
Norton Pomeroy echoed this judgment in his survey of water law in the
Pacific Coast States. Pomeroy maintained that no law could ''tend to the
peace and prosperity of society which attempts to violate and override natural laws and natural rights, immutable truths which exist in the regular
order of nature.'' He urged that smaller streams be reserved entirely for
riparian irrigation, and that prior appropriation should be permitted on
larger streams only after the needs of riparian farmers had been satisfied.[30]

Virtually all the cases cited above were decided before the dramatic
growth of private irrigation projects in the late 1870s and 1880s. During
those decades, traditional riparian rights were abandoned in Nevada,
Colorado, and Idaho, and restricted in many other states. Nevertheless,
common law principles lived on. In Utah the Mormon church initially doled
out water, and the state did not formally acknowledge appropriation until
1880 or 1897.[31] There, mining played no part in the formulation of water
rights and water laws; irrigation took precedence from the beginning. Church
control over natural resources, and the dominance of agriculture in the state's
economy, permitted the attachment of water rights to the land. As the population of Utah grew, state courts recognized a form of prior appropriation,
but established two categories of rights, primary (early) and secondary (later).
Secondary claims were honored only when there was sufficient water to
serve all primary rights. And in each category, water was distributed equally,
not according to strict priority; in dry seasons each user's supply was cut
back. In effect, rights were correlative, and Robert Dunbar correctly observes that ''the Utah water rights was a blend of the appropriative and
the riparian.''[32]

[30] *Union Mill and Mining Co.* v. *Ferris*, 2 Saw. 176, 195 (1871); *Vansickle* v. *Haines*, 7 Nev.
249, 286 (1872); *Drake* v. *Earhart*, 2 Ida. 750, 763-64 (1890); *Crawford* v. *Hathaway*, 67 Neb.
365 (1903); Pomeroy, *A Treatise on the Law of Water Rights*, 346-47.

[31] Bakken, *The Development of Law on the Rocky Mountain Frontier*, 36-39. In 1880, in *Monroe*
v. *Ivri*, 2 Utah 535, the court proclaimed that land and water were open to appropriation
by all. Subsequently, the Utah legislature adopted an appropriation statute, but it was invalidated by the territorial supreme court. Appropriation was not formally recognized until
after statehood, in 1897.

[32] Dunbar, *Forging New Rights in Western Waters*, 82; Joseph F. Smith to William E. Smythe,
December. 14, 1901, Records Group 8, Records of the Bureau of Agricultural Engineering,
Office of Irrigation Investigations; General Correspondence, 1898-1912; Box 1, General Cor-
respondence, 1898-December. 31, 1902, Federal Records Center, Suitland, MD.

The Utah example is more evidence that the nature of the local economy, rather than aridity, did most to shape western water law. The early courts and legislatures of Utah, Idaho, Montana, Colorado, and Wyoming all tried to balance riparianism and appropriation. In 1861 Colorado's territorial legislature authorized diversions for irrigation, but limited irrigation to riparian land and provided for the appointment of water commissioners to divide the water "in a just and equitable proportion" during dry spells.[33] In the following year, the lawmakers declared that "there shall be at all times left sufficient water in said stream for the use of miners and farmers along said stream," suggesting once again that riparian users had the strongest rights.[34] The 1864 legislature acknowledged the preeminent needs of mining when it ordered that no stream could be diverted "to the detriment of any miner, millmen or others along the line of said stream, who may have a priority of right. . . ." However, it tempered this restriction by repeating that "there shall be at all times left sufficient water in said stream for the use of miners and agriculturists along said stream."[35]

The principles contained in the Colorado laws spread throughout the mountain West, but, as in Colorado, they were gradually debased and diluted. In 1865 Montana's first irrigation statute limited diversions to riparian landowners and provided for local commissions to apportion water in times of scarcity. Ten years later, Wyoming created commissions charged with dividing the water in lean years "as they may in their best judgement think best for the interests of all parties·concerned." However, the watermasters were required to observe "the legal rights of all" and nothing in the law could "impair the prior vested rights of any mill or ditch owner, or other person to use the water of any . . . water course." The nature of these "prior rights" was not explained or defined; neither prior appropriation nor riparian rights were mentioned directly. Local justices of the peace appointed Montana's commissioners, and the county courts selected Wyoming's. But when Idaho passed its first agricultural water law in 1881, it allowed private water companies to appoint the commissioners. No water could be diverted without permission from a watermaster or his deputy,

---

[33] *General Laws, Joint Resolutions, Memorials, and Private Acts, Passed at the First Session of the Legislative Assembly of the Territory of Colorado. . . .* (Denver, 1861), 67-69. The law made an exception for irrigators on Hardscrabble Creek, a tributary of the Arkansas River, by promising each of them enough water to serve 160 acres. However, even in this case it upheld riparian principles. In dry years, "the occupant nearest the source of said stream shall be first supplied."

[34] *General Laws, Joint Resolutions, Memorials, and Private Acts, Passed at the Second Session of the Legislative Assembly of the Territory of Colorado. . . .* (Denver, 1862), 48.

[35] *General Laws, Joint Resolutions, Memorials, and Private Acts, Passed at the Third Session of the Legislative Assembly of the Territory of Colorado. . . .* (Denver, 1864), 58. Also see Dunbar, *Forging New Rights in Western Waters*, 75-76. Dunbar does not consider the statutes passed by Montana, Wyoming, and Idaho.

but the law pledged to respect "the vested rights of individual companies or corporations . . . to the use and control of water which is or may be their private property." In the 1860s, when plenty of unclaimed water remained in most western streams, legislators could easily put community needs first. And at least a few jurists saw the implications of these laws. For example, Justice C.J. Wade of Montana maintained that the 1865 territorial law—which was overturned by the territorial supreme court in 1870 on grounds that only the courts could decide what was a "just and equitable" distribution of property—had been designed "to utterly abolish and annihilate the doctrine of prior appropriation, and to establish an equal distribution of the waters of any given stream in the agricultural districts of the Territory. . . ."[36]

Riparian rights were not the only casualty of the corporate irrigation boom of 1877-1893; laws inherited from Mexico suffered a similar fate. The nature of Spanish and Mexican water law has not been well understood. The Mexican government occasionally made exclusive water grants to individuals, but these carried no clear priority and were revocable by the government. Prior appropriation did not exist as a system, and community needs took precedence over individual rights, including the rights of riparian landowners.[37] The basic purpose of Mexican law was not to stimulate private enterprise but to irrigate the maximum acreage. "Legal rights, whether they be corporate or individual, did not constitute a single, over-bearing consideration in the adjudication of water disputes," Michael Meyer has written. "[J]udges were at pains to indicate to their superiors that their verdicts had been rendered with the common good in mind." Mexican water law derived from long-established principles inherited from Spain: that running water belonged to the king or state; that its use was common to all; that irrigation was permissible only with the approval of the government; that wherever possible irrigation should be a community endeavor; and that which lands to irrigate should be decided according to the feasibility of getting water to them, not on their date of settlement.[38]

---

[36] Irrigators made the choice themselves when not served by private companies. *Acts, Resolutions and Memorials, of the Territory of Montana, Passed by the First Legislative Assembly* (Virginia City, MT, 1866), 367-69; *The Compiled Laws of Wyoming. . . .* (Cheyenne, 1876), 377-79; *General Laws of the Territory of Idaho Including the Code of Civil Procedure, Passed at the Eleventh Session of the Territorial Legislature* (Boise City, 1881), 273-75. Justice Wade's quote is from his dissent in *Thorp* v. *Freed*, 1 Mont. 651 at 656 and 668 (1872). On the Montana law also see *Smith* v. *Denniff*, 24 Mont. 20, 22-23 (1900). *Basey* v. *Gallagher*, 87 U.S. 670, 675 (1874) reprinted an 1870 Montana law that extended the privilege of diversion to anyone who owned "agricultural lands within the limits of this Territory."

[37] A Mexican riparian grant carried the right to use water for domestic needs, but nothing more. Under both Spain and Mexico water was assumed to be a resource separate from the land, though ultimate ownership remained with the state.

[38] Meyer, *Water in the Hispanic Southwest*, 161, 163; Betty Eakle Dobkins, *The Spanish Element in Texas Water Law* (Austin, 1959), 143; Thomas F. Glick, *The Old World Background*

Surprisingly, major scholars of water law such as Kinney, Wiel, and Dunbar never discuss the Spanish and Mexican legacy, perhaps because it was so antagonistic to *both* riparian rights and prior appropriation. In 1854 the California legislature ratified a community control system that had prevailed in southern California since the Mexican period. It authorized the creation of water commissions in townships within the agricultural counties of San Diego, San Bernardino, Santa Barbara, Napa, Los Angeles, Solano, Contra Costa, Colusa, and Tulare. These commissions were required "to examine and direct such water courses, and apportion the water thereof among the inhabitants of their district, determine the time of using the same, and upon petition of a majority of persons liable to work upon ditches, lay out and construct ditches." The commissioners could condemn land for rights-of-way, levy taxes to pay for maintenance and construction, and apportion water. The law contained two significant restrictions: it did not apply to counties where mining was the major industry, and it prohibited diversions that interfered with the rights of downstream riparian owners.[39]

This law served community needs well. At the time, most irrigation works were inexpensive because they were constructed by groups of farmers, much as county roads had been laid out in the nineteenth century. All available capital poured into mining, so the 1854 statute provided a useful tool to develop California's agricultural resources. Not suprisingly, it did not sanction absolute individual rights to water. The legislature, or at least the Los Angeles legislator responsible for drafting the law, must have recognized that prior appropriation would serve no useful purpose.

Little is known about how the 1854 law operated, but it was promising enough to be amended and expanded many times as the legislature tried to tailor the public control principle to particular counties.[40] For example, in San Bernardino County, which had the largest community irrigation system outside Los Angeles, the law prohibited new settlers from taking up land along streams already fully committed to irrigation. Perhaps the most "revolutionary" aspect of the legislation, though it simply reaffirmed Mexican practices, was that it reserved all water in certain streams to public use. Unfortunately, after 1862, when the legislature granted private irrigation companies the right to condemn land for canal rights-of-way, these laws were emasculated. In 1866 the Tulare County water commission

of the Irrigation System of San Antonio, Texas (El Paso, 1972); Edwin P. Arneson, "Early Irrigation in Texas," *Southwestern Historical Quarterly*, 25 (October 1921), 121-30; Kinney, *A Treatise on the Law of Irrigation and Water Rights. . .*, v.1, 989-96; Webb, *The Great Plains*, 441.

[39] *California Statutes*, (1854), 76. For a full discussion of the 1854 law and its amendments see Pisani, *From the Family Farm to Agribusiness*, 39-45.

[40] *California Statutes* (1859), 217; (1862), 235 and 540; (1864), 87 and 375; (1866), 609 and 777.

233

lost the power to levy taxes and appoint independent watermasters to allocate water; now all appointees had to be drawn from nominees proposed by the county's private water companies. Two years later the legislature formally subordinated communal water rights to those acquired under prior appropriation.[41]

By the late 1870s, as corporate irrigation spread to nonriparian land, conflicts erupted between riparian owners and appropriators in many parts of the San Joaquin Valley, and the system of public control was all but forgotten. Its demise suggests that while California's courts took the lead in molding prior appropriation to fit mining, after 1862 the legislature took the lead in fitting appropriations to new uses on lands outside the public domain. One cardinal principle of constitutional law is that vested rights require protection even if the foundation of those rights is shaky. So the California Supreme Court accepted this species of legislated property rights even though it clearly preferred the riparian doctrine.

This same process occurred in New Mexico and Texas, though at a slower rate. Since few Anglo-American settlers entered New Mexico until the 1860s, the assembly blocked any change in the status quo and repassed many laws that prevailed before 1846.[42] In 1851 and 1852 it reaffirmed the system of community acequias. Statutes adopted in 1861, 1863, 1866, and 1880 reinforced and expanded these laws, even though the legislature also granted private companies the right to run irrigation ditches in 1874. The lawmakers proclaimed irrigation the primary use of water in the territory; for example, no mills could be constructed that reduced the value of a stream to farmers. All owners of tillable land were required to provide labor to maintain community water systems in proportion to the size of their farms, cultivated or not. Justices of the peace called landowners together each year to elect one or more overseers or watermasters. The watermasters were required to distribute water—in the words of the 1852 law—"with justice and impartiality," according to the acreage farmed and the crops cultivated by each settler. No one could tap into an acequia without permission, and those who wasted water, or shirked their responsibility to maintain the ditches, faced stiff fines.[43]

[41] *California Statutes* (1866), 313-14; (1868), 113; (1876), 547. The legislature formally recognized prior appropriation in 1872, when it first specified procedures for posting and filing water claims. The spread of riparian rights and perhaps even the exclusive "pueblo rights" to water enjoyed by such cities as Los Angeles and San Diego also helped undermine the 1854 law.

[42] Howard R. Lamar, *The Far Southwest, 1846-1912: A Territorial History* (New Haven, 1966), 91.

[43] *General Laws of New Mexico* (Albany, NY, 1880), 13-23. Also see Wells Hutchins, "The Community Acequia: Its Origin and Development," *The Southwestern Historical Quarterly*, 31 (January 1928), 261-84; and Bakken, *The Development of Law on the Rocky Mountain Frontier*, 34.

Texas differed from New Mexico, Arizona, and California in that mining played little part in its economy, the state contained no national public domain, and irrigation was unnecessary in the heavily settled, humid, eastern section.[44] Nevertheless, as in much of the American Southwest, traditional patterns of use persisted.[45] Lawmakers from San Antonio and El Paso, where most irrigation occurred in the nineteenth century, enacted a community irrigation statute in 1852. Because irrigation played only a small part in Texas agriculture during the nineteenth century, the legislature did not adopt appropriation until 1889, and the 1852 law was not repealed until 1913.[46]

The Mexican system eventually disappeared, but prior appropriation might still have been remodeled. In the late nineteenth century, critics of appropriation recommended that the western states grant more authority over the allocation of water to state administrative officials. They proposed the creation of state engineering offices to measure streams, administer the filing of claims, maintain centralized records of rights, and supervise diversions. They also asked that rights be attached to the land as an alternative to absolute ownership; that domestic use take precedence over all other water uses; that no water be diverted without formal permission from the state; that the amount granted be based on immediate rather than anticipated needs; and that, in times of scarcity, some provisions be made for rotation

[44] Arizona's first territorial legislature met in 1864 and borrowed most of its new irrigation law from New Mexico. Section 25 declared that [t]he regulations of acequias, which have been worked according to the laws and customs of Sonora and the usages of the people of Arizona, shall remain as they were made and used up to this day. . . ." The lawmakers also promised that "rights in acequias or irrigation canals heretofore established shall not be disturbed." Nominally, these provisions protected the Santa Cruz Valley's community ditch system, which served the territory's largest block of farmland. However, the law also reflected the preeminence of mining. It repeatedly emphasized that in case of conflicts over water, farmers had to give way. The law was inconsistent. While it sanctioned the traditional water systems, Section 17 specified that in dry times, the water supply of farmers would not be cut back equally—as in California, Texas, or New Mexico's communal systems— but "according to the dates of their respective titles or their occupation of the lands either by themselves or their grantors. The oldest titles shall have precedence always." Prior appropriation was grafted onto a completely antagonistic system. See *The Howell Code Adopted by the First Legislative Assembly of the Territory of Arizona* (Prescott, 1865), 422-26; and R. H. Forbes, "Irrigation in Arizona," U.S.D.A. Office of Experiment Stations, *Bulletin No. 235* (Washington DC, 1911), 57.

[45] Spanish and Mexican principles of water use were not restricted to the Southwest. The Colorado legislature initially recognized and accepted irrigation as practiced in the Rio Grande River's San Luis Valley. By limiting the law to Costilla and Conejos counties, the lawmakers were able to guarantee farmers the first claim on water during the growing season even though mining was the territory's dominant economic activity. See *General Laws, Joint Resolutions, Memorials, and Private Acts, Passed at the Fifth Session of the Legislative Assembly of the Territory of Colorado. . . .* (Central City, CO, 1866), 61-64.

[46] Dobkins, *The Spanish Element in Texas Water Law*, 136-39; Will Wilson, "A Reappraisal of Motl v. Boyd," *Proceedings, Water Law Conference, June 17-18, 1955* (Austin, 1955), 38-43; A. A. White, "The Flow and Underflow of Motl v. Boyd," *Proceedings, Water Law Conference, June 17-18, 1955*, 44-60.

of diversions. Reform first came to Colorado and Wyoming, then spread to Nebraska in 1892, Idaho in 1895, Utah in 1897, and by 1913 to virtually every other western state including California. However, the degree of reform varied. Colorado's constitution declared that all water not previously appropriated belonged to the state while Wyoming's provided that *all* water belonged to the state. Wyoming water laws also permitted administrative officials to reject water claims not deemed in the public interest, while in Colorado, and most western states, insufficient water was the only justification for turning down a claim. Only Wyoming and Nebraska successfully tied water rights to the land; in the other states water could be bought and sold independently. They were also the only two states to permit the adjudication of water rights by administrative commissions rather than the courts.[47]

Most legal scholars have seen the expansion of formal state administrative control over water as substantial reforms. Moses Lasky, one of the twentieth-century West's prominent water lawyers declared, "[T]he methods and machinery of administration adopted to enforce the doctrine of prior-appropriation were themselves an admission of the failure of the doctrine and resulted in a change from it." Unquestionably, these reforms were motivated in part by a quest for efficiency and a desire to limit the authority of the courts.

Gordon Bakken concludes that the "reconstruction" of prior appropriation symbolized the waning ethic of frontier individualism. "Lawmakers not only shifted legal direction away from first users but also acknowledged the wasteful practice born on the frontier and tried to maximize the efficient use of water." To use Bakken's phrases, "distributive administration" displaced "individual appropriation."[48]

Bakken's conclusion does not draw a careful enough distinction between the letter of the law and application of the law. In most states water law reform did not so much represent an assertion of power against "the interests" as an attempt by the interests to shore up their rights, especially against newcomers. This was particularly obvious in Colorado. There, most water laws enacted in the 1870s and early 1880s grew out of conflicts along the Cache La Poudre, a stream tapped first in 1865, then by the Greeley

[47] Dunbar's *Forging New Rights in Western Waters*, 99-132, provides a good overview of the new administrative systems, but does not devote enough attention to the implications of these reforms.

[48] Moses Lasky, "From Prior Appropriation to Economic Distribution of Water by the State—Via Irrigation Administration," *Rocky Mountain Law Review*, 1 (April 1929), 171; Bakken *The Development of Law on the Rocky Mountain Frontier*, 32; Dunbar acknowledges in his 1985 essay that increasing state control over water "did not displace the appropriative right, but rather subjected it to government control. The content remains, the freedom to appropriate without anybody's leave is gone." See "The Adaptability of Water Law to the Aridity of the West," 62.

Colony in 1870. A major drought in 1874 underscored the need for an orderly method to divide the water between farmers in the colony and more
recent settlers upstream. At the state constitutional convention in January
1876, a resolution was introduced calling for state ownership of water and
laws "to secure a just and equitable distribution of the water" and "promote the greatest good to the greatest number of citizens. . . ." The resolution said nothing about appropriation and received no support. As finally
adopted, Article XVI, Section 5, of the Colorado Constitution not only
confirmed and protected existing claims; it restricted all future rights to
appropriation.[49]

That Wyoming went far beyond other western states in drafting laws
that actually did put "public needs" first was partly due to Elwood Mead,
who wrote the provisions on water in the new state's constitution and served
as its first state engineer. But it was also the result of economic conditions
legal historians have largely ignored. First, Wyoming had a much larger
supply of unappropriated water than other western states and a relatively
small population. Second, unlike California and Colorado, mining had never
been extensive, so prior appropriation had not put down deep roots. Third,
the range cattle industry, upon which Wyoming was so dependent, suffered
a severe blow from the blizzard of 1886-1887 and drought of the late 1880s;
the state's future seemed bleak unless it could attract small farmers by
guaranteeing them an adequate, cheap water supply. Finally, Wyoming
did not have large, established communities of farmers with vested water
rights, such as those at Greeley in Colorado or Fresno in California. In
short, the whole economic context was different. That the "Wyoming
Idea"—which granted substantial quasi-judicial powers to the state engineer
and water commission—could be adopted enthusiastically in Wyoming but
win so little support elsewhere becomes understandable when we look at
the different economic conditions throughout the arid and semiarid West.
In states or territories with an established, flourishing irrigation industry,
comprehensive water law reform— even in the name of justice and
efficiency—posed more of an economic threat than opportunity. While many
states borrowed *parts* of the Wyoming system, only Nebraska, the Dakotas,
and Oklahoma adopted it whole. In none of these was irrigation a vital
part of agricultural development. The arid states created new administrative bureaucracies, but most left the ultimate power to allocate and distribute water in the hands of local courts and the water users themselves.

By 1900 prior appropriation was firmly fastened on the West, though
it coexisted with riparian rights in the Pacific Coast and Great Plains states.
Robert Dunbar has maintained that appropriation, "[f]orged as an adaption [sic] to the arid west, . . . continues to be shaped by western needs

[49] *Proceedings of the Constitutional Convention of Colorado, 1875 and 1876* (Denver, 1906),
44, 374.

and pressures.''[50] But his own book raises doubts. For example, on the Cache La Poudre River priority has not proven flexible. The three major ditches date from 1865, 1870, and 1878. In spring, when the river carries its largest volume, all three get a full supply of water. But by mid-summer, the "newer" diversions are often cut back. Priority of claim, not efficiency or justice, determines which farmers receive water and which do not. The law does not answer the important question of why a few months or years of prior use should give such a vital advantage over those with equal needs. Moreover, while some communities, such as Phoenix, have been able to buy up agricultural water rights relatively easily, Tucson, Denver, San Francisco, and Los Angeles have all faced expensive court challenges from agricultural interests. Finally, Dunbar acknowledges that by exhausting streams, appropriation often threatens recreational uses of water, particularly sport fishing. Recreational uses have a vast economic potential in certain parts of the West. Although some states now recognize the maintenance of minimum flows as a beneficial use of water, recreational needs still take a back seat to traditional water uses.[51] In 1961 a U.S. senate committee concluded: "The present system of water rights, which provide for diversions first in time to have the most secure rights, provides little stimulus toward more efficient use of water, and, in fact, may promote inefficient and wasteful use of water in order to perfect larger rights. As the demands on the water resources of the West grow, it may well be an economic necessity for some of the Western States to review their water laws with a view to changes which will bring about more efficient use of water, or else accept a ceiling on their potential growth."[52]

In 1839 the Kentucky Supreme Court upheld the right of a railroad to run trains through Louisville even though the noise constituted a public nuisance. "The onward spirit of the age must, to a reasonable extent, have its way," the court noted. "The law is made for the times, and will be made or modified by them. The expanded and still expanding genius of the *common law* should adapt it here, as elsewhere, to the improved and improving conditions of our country and countrymen."[53] In the nineteenth century the courts had to adapt to canals, railroads, steam power, telegraphs, telephones, and a multitude of other technological innovations that had a profound effect on the structure of the American economy. The law exalted personal rights and individualism, defining freedom largely as economic opportunity.

[50] Dunbar, *Forging New Rights in Western Waters*, 209, 217.

[51] See Dunbar's chapter "The Appropriation Right and Its Critics," *Forging New Rights in Western Waters*, 209-217, especially 214-16.

[52] "National Water Resources," 87th Cong., 1st sess., Senate Reports, no. 29 (Washington, DC, 1961), 54.

[53] *Lexington & Ohio Rail Road* v. *Applegate*, 8 Dana 289, 309 (1839).

Western courts tried to balance opportunity against the perceived need to develop resources as rapidly as possible; they attempted to lay a foundation for future settlement in the West as well.[54] The courts often took a broader view of economic development than state legislatures, which were much more susceptible to political and economic pressure. John Guice has called the territorial judges of Colorado, Montana, and Wyoming "the real heroes of the period [1861-1890]" because they were able to assure "maximum economic development . . . through the establishment of order in mining and agriculture, no mean accomplishment."[55] Perhaps so. But the courts were neither omniscient nor omnipotent. Whatever changes occurred in prior appropriation as it spread from mining to agriculture, two principles remained inviolable: that priority of use transcended the value of a use, and that rights to water were exclusive and absolute. In 1902, Frederick Haynes Newell, first director of the United States Reclamation Service (now Bureau), prophesied that "there must come a time when water must be apportioned with justice to all, and a century or more hence we will have it distributed not upon priority rights, but upon technical rights. We cannot have a farmer getting more water than he is entitled to, because his great-grandfather or somebody else happened to secure the water right two months ahead of somebody else. Water must ultimately be conserved in the most just manner for the general welfare of all citizens."[56] That time did not come. The pursuit of wealth took precedence. Enterprise triumphed over equity.

[54] The courts did not simply bend to the needs of the dominant industry or economic activity. For example, Harry Scheiber has shown, in "Public Rights and the Rule of Law in American Legal History," that California courts often gave agriculture preference over the "modern sector." Similarly, the law often favored small businesses over corporate capital. (pp. 240, 251).

[55] Guice, *The Rocky Mountain Bench*, 113.

[56] Los Angeles *Times*, 28 July 1902, p. 8. Also see Frederick Haynes Newell's *Irrigation in the United States* (New York, 1902), 291-92.

THE SAN JOAQUIN GRANT:
WHO OWNED THE COMMON LANDS?
A HISTORICAL-LEGAL PUZZLE

MALCOLM EBRIGHT

No QUESTION HAS SO perplexed both historians and lawyers as the one addressed in this study: under Spanish law who owned the common lands of a community land grant?[1] The United States Supreme Court purportedly applied Spanish law in a landmark case involving the San Joaquín land grant in Rio Arriba County when it determined that the Spanish government owned these lands.[2] The Supreme Court's decision was based on scanty Spanish legal authorities and did not take into account the long history of the Castilian land-owning pueblo.

This study will examine this and other data not brought to the Supreme Court's attention, indicating that the New Mexico community land grant owned its common lands. The problem will be approached using the San Joaquín grant as a case study. Before examining the history and adjudication of the San Joaquín grant, a summary of the antecedents of the New Mexico community land grant should help to put this problem in context.

The New Mexico community land grant was a direct descendant of the Spanish pueblo, which in turn can be traced back to Roman times. The word "pueblo" as used in Spain (and to some extent New Mexico) has multiple meanings. In New Mexico its primary usage was in reference to the villages of sedentary Indians. In Spain, however, the word refers both to a place (a village, together with its outlying lands) and to the people who live at that place. Thus it has both geographical and human connotations. A man born in a pueblo is referred to as a "son of the pueblo" (*hijo del pueblo*).[3]

As Spain regained control of her land from the Moors, the pueblos were of strategic importance, as fortified centers holding the land against the Moors and as colonizing centers from which to plant new settlements. This importance made it possible for the pueblos to gain control, by grant from the king, of areas surrounding the pueblo administered according to local custom rather than by codified law.[4]

These lands of the Spanish pueblo were divided into several classes according to their use. The *monte* (Latin *montis*, mountain), low quality pasture land because it was mountainous and covered with trees and brush, was used primarily for gathering wood and acorns. The *prado* (*pratum*, meadow) was high quality pasture, often irrigated. The *dehesa* (*defensa*, enclosed) was fenced pasture land. The *ejido* (*exitus*, exit) was a multipurpose piece of land just outside the pueblo (at its exit), which was used as a threshing floor, a garbage dump or for keeping stray animals. These lands of the people were called *tierras concegiles* (lands of the council) and were usually used in common.[5]

The tierras concegiles provided the means of maintaining a self-sufficient community; they were the keystone of its economic and social life. When the Americas were colonized, the institution of common lands was transplanted to New Spain.[6] In New Mexico, these lands were often simply called ejidos[7] or—as in the case of the San Joaquín grant—*pastos* (pastures) and *abrevaderos* (watering places).[8] Other New Mexican land grant documents refer to "montes" and "agua" as additional names for the common lands.[9]

Besides the right to use the common lands, the settlers on a community land grant in New Mexico received allotments of land for a house lot and an irrigable garden plot. These were treated as private property and could be sold after the four-year possession requirement was satisfied.[10]

The San Joaquín grant followed the usual pattern of a New Mexico community land grant. The history of this grant, however, is replete with contradictions and controversies.[11] Even the name of the grant is open to question. San Joaquín is used here because those living in the villages on the grant have always referred to it by this name. But on the official records of the U.S. Court of Private Land Claims the grant is called the Cañón de Chama grant. Ironically, this name presaged the fate of the grant, which was held by that court in 1894 to include only the allotted lands in the Chama River canyon, surveyed in 1901 as containing a mere 1,422 acres. (The entire community grant, including the common lands, contained almost half a million acres.)[12]

The confusion as to the name of the grant starts with the original grant documents. When Francisco Salazar petitioned for the grant in 1806—along with thirty other prospective settlers—he referred to it as "el Cañón del Rio de Chama." Alcalde Manuel García de la Mora also used this name in his report to the governor on the propriety of making the grant. But when Governor Joaquín Real Alencaster made the grant, he provided that the first settlement on the grant be called San Joaquín del Rio de Chama, presumably in honor of his name saint. This name stuck, for in 1808 when Alcalde García de la Mora made his report on the ceremony in which he delivered possession of the land to the grantees (whose number had now increased to thirty-nine), he stated: "I proceeded to the Chama River canyon, called San Joaquín."[13]

Governor Alencaster's granting decree made it clear that this was to be a community grant with individual allotments and common lands to be used jointly by the settlers for grazing and watering their animals and for gathering wood, herbs, and other resources of the land. The decree provided that each settler receive a plot of land "capable of being planted with the equivalent of three *cuartillas*[14] of wheat[,] . . . three *almudes*[15] of corn, another three of beans, and of having erected on them a small house with a garden." The remaining lands were designated as common lands. Alférez Salazar[16] received a double allotment of land as *poblador principal*[17] and was appointed justice for the community.

The boundaries were designated as: the Cebolla River on the north, the Capulin (mountain) on the south, the boundary of the Martínezes on the east, and the *cejita blanca* (little white ridge) on the west.[18] The boundary of the Martínezes referred to the Piedra Lumbre grant, a private grant made to Pedro Martín Serrano in 1766,[19] and the boundaries on the north and south were clearly defined natural landmarks, but the western boundary call was not as clear and was destined to cause a great deal of controversy after the United States occupation of New Mexico.

There was never a serious question as to the validity of the San Joaquín grant nor as to its nature as a community grant. The main question that U.S. officials asked in connection with its adjudication was about its size. In 1861, when approximately four hundred of the grantees and their heirs petitioned the surveyor general of New Mexico for confirmation of the grant, it was estimated at 184,320 acres.[20] But when surveyed in 1878, it turned out to contain 472,736 acres.[21]

Surveyor General George Washington Julian[22] rendered the first report recommending rejection of the common lands of the San Joaquín grant in 1886.[23] Before that, the grant had been recommended for confirmation twice, once by Surveyor General James K. Proudfit in 1872, before the grant had been surveyed,[24] and again in 1880 after the official survey showed how much land was encompassed within the grant boundaries.[25]

The latter recommendation for approval was unusual, for prior to the establishment of the Court of Private Land Claims, the only government official authorized to investigate the validity of land grants was the surveyor general. Thereafter, Congress either confirmed, rejected, or failed to act regarding the surveyor general's recommendation. But in the case of the San Joaquín grant the House Committee on Private Land Claims requested more information from the secretary of the interior concerning the grant.[26] Commissioner J. A. Williamson replied in a letter dated 20 May 1880 in which he recommended that the grant be confirmed in its entirety.[27]

The first inkling of the government's position against the confirmation of the common lands is found in Julian's supplemental report of 1886. Until Julian arbitrarily reversed the presumptions that had been in favor of land grant claimants,[28] a community land grant, including its common lands, was presumed to be valid if there was a town or community within the grant as of 1846.[29] In his report on the San Joaquín grant, Julian did not provide any theory to support his opinion regarding the ownership of the common lands, but merely stated that it was not the alcalde's intent to transfer title to the common lands to the grantees.[30] This was contrary to the language used by Alcalde García de la Mora (after reciting the boundaries, he stated that the unallotted land was "for their pastures and watering places, with a view to the coming of other settlers and the increase of families. . .").[31] So Julian probably thought that he needed a more substantial basis to justify the rejection of millions of acres of common lands in New Mexico community grants.[32]

In 1887 the surveyor general set about establishing his theory that the Spanish government retained the title to the common lands. He sent investigators to San Miguel County to search for evidence in the deed books in Las Vegas to support his view about the Las Vegas grant.[33] Although funds for this investigation ran out before Julian's theory could be documented, Matthew Reynolds, the U.S. attorney for the Court of Private Land Claims, picked up the thread when he prosecuted the government's case against the San Joaquín grant before the U.S. Supreme Court.

The government did not assert Julian's theory of retained title to the common lands in the government of Spain, however, until after the Court of Private Land Claims had limited its confirmation of the San Joaquín grant to the allotted lands in the Chama River canyon. Until the appeal to the Supreme Court, the government's attack on the grant was limited to an attack on the boundaries; the Claims Court's rejection of the common lands was not supported by any legal theory.

Even before Julian submitted his report of 1886, a protest against the 1878 survey of the grant was filed in his office by a group that claimed that the survey of the grant had improperly included their lands.[34] The U.S. government was in a delicate position regarding the survey because one of the U.S. attorney's key assistants, Will M. Tipton, was a member of the survey crew. Later Tipton prepared a memorandum stating that he had not agreed with the survey and had refused to sign the required oath although he had supervised the chaining (measuring) of most of the land and had written the rough notes. Tipton then made the shocking statement that the affidavits of the witnesses, which pointed out the landmarks serving as boundaries, were forged.[35]

These witnesses had been furnished by the speculators who

LAS SIETE PARTIDAS

DEL SABIO REY

DON ALONSO EL IX,

GLOSADAS

POR EL LIC. GREGORIO LOPEZ,

del Consejo Real de Indias de S. M.

TOMO II,

QUE CONTIENE LA 3.ª 4.ª Y 5.ª PARTIDA.

MADRID 1829:

EN LA OFICINA DE *D. Leon Amarita,*

CON ESPECIAL PERMISO DE S. M.,

bajo del examen y aprobacion de la Inspeccion General de Instruccion pública.

had purportedly acquired the San Joaquín grant. One wonders whether some of the deeds upon which their claim to ownership was based were not also forgeries. Instead of pursuing this inquiry, however, the government investigators set about procuring witnesses to establish the forgeries relating to the boundaries and witnesses to testify to what they considered to be the true boundaries.[36]

The most questionable boundary was the western one, the cejita blanca. Apparently there were two such landmarks: one was the continental divide, which was used in the survey of 1878; the other was in the Chama River canyon near the San Joaquín settlement of 1808, some fifteen miles to the east of the continental divide. When the San Joaquín grant was adjudicated before the Court of Private Land Claims, most of the testimony at the trial centered on the question of which cejita blanca was called for in the original grant.[37] This point was considered so important by the government that it took the deposition of two witnesses before Chief Justice Wilbur F. Stone prior to trial, a procedure seldom followed before the Claims Court. One of the witnesses, General José María Chávez, testified that the continental divide was the true western boundary and that a monument had been erected upon it.[38] Strangely enough Chávez was not called to testify at the trial for the claimants.

The testimony about the location of the boundaries of the San Joaquín grant is important because the case was argued by the government on the theory that if the grant were valid, its extent should be determined by the locations of these boundaries, not by the location of the allotments, as the court eventually decided. This was how the court understood the issues at the trial, for the only questions the judges asked were about the exterior boundaries. No testimony was taken concerning the location of the allotments; thus, the decision limiting the size of the grant to these individual allotments was entirely an afterthought.[39]

The United States Supreme Court affirmed the decision of the Court of Private Land Claims on two grounds. First, the decision of Justice Fuller reviews the title papers and concludes, in language reminiscent of Surveyor General Julian's report of 1886, that the alcalde did not intend to transfer title to the common lands to the grantees. Fuller writes that "reference is indeed made to the use of the lands within the out-boundaries for pastures and watering places, but this did not put them out of the class of public lands, and . . . no title was conveyed." He then cites the Sandoval case,[40] which was decided on the same day as the San Joaquín grant case, and says that "we have just held . . . that as to all unallotted lands within exterior boundaries where towns or communities were sought to be formed, as in this instance, the title remained in the [Spanish] government for such disposition as it might see proper to make."[41]

The theory of these cases was that if the Spanish—and then the Mexican—government owned the common lands, the United States (and not the heirs of the San Joaquín grant) inherited that ownership as successor sovereign. The question of the ownership of the common lands has both legal and historical implications. The Supreme Court purported to decide this question without all the historical facts before it, so a legal and historical distortion resulted. Subsequent historians like Ralph Emerson Twitchell, writing on questions of Hispanic land tenure, have quoted these and other similar cases instead of engaging in independent research on the ownership of the common lands of a community land grant.[42]

Besides missing the historical fact of the Castilian land-owning pueblo that took root in New Mexico,[43] the Supreme Court was not made aware of additional legal and historical authorities that bear on the question. The lands owned by the Castilian pueblo were generally distinguished from the lands owned by the king. Crown lands that had not been granted to individuals or communities were called *tierras realengas* or *tierras baldías*. In sixteenth-century Castile, the monarchs followed a policy of protecting the lands of the pueblos—the tierras concegiles. Numerous laws were enacted to safeguard the tierras concegiles from usurpation by the nobility, by municipal officials, or by ordinary citizens.[44]

An extremely important point concerning the tierras concegiles was not mentioned in the San Joaquín litigation. While both the tierras baldías and the tierras concegiles fell into the broad classification of public domain, civil law countries like Spain had two classes of public domain: the public domain proper, which was owned by the sovereign, and the private domain which was owned by communities and municipalities. The former was the tierras baldías and the latter was the tierras concegiles. The importance of this distinction is that under international law, which the Claims Court was supposed to follow, the public domain passes to a successor state when there is a change of sovereignty (as when New Mexico was occupied by the United States), but the private domain is retained by the communities and municipalities just as the private property of individuals is retained by its owners.[45] This well-established rule could have disposed of the question of ownership of the common lands of the San Joaquín and other community land grants. But it was overlooked, by the lawyers and by the judges.

Also overlooked were three types of Spanish law germane to the issue: codified law, commentaries on codified law, and Spanish custom. The foremost Spanish code, which was still in effect at the time of the U.S. occupation of New Mexico, was *Las Siete Partidas*. Partida 3, título 28, deals with the Spanish concept of ownership. Título 28, ley 9, spells out the ownership of pueblo lands by the community:

> the things which belong separately to the commons of cities or towns are the *exidos*, the forests and pastures, and all other similar places which have been appropriated and granted for the common use of each city or town.[46]

The Recopilación de Leyes de los Reynos de las Indias dealt with the procedural problems of forming settlements in the Americas, but had little to say about the substantive law concerning ownership of property; these matters were covered in earlier codes like *Las Siete Partidas*, which was specifically made applicable to the Americas.[47] The Mexican Colonization Law of 1824 and the regulations issued under that law in 1828 were the first comprehensive legislation regarding New Mexico land grants. Article 2 of the 1824 law recognized the traditional ownership of the common lands by the pueblo when it stated:

> the object of this law is those lands of the nation, not being private property *nor belonging to any corporation or pueblo*, and can therefore be colonized [emphasis added].[48]

There were numerous Spanish law codes, but none was truly comprehensive. Instead of providing that later ones would super-cede earlier ones, Spanish officials allowed them to overlap and duplicate one another. For this reason it was necessary for legal scholars to synthesize and summarize the authorities on various points of law. Most often cited and considered the leading author-ities are the works of Mariano Galván-Rivera and Joaquín Escriche.

Galván's primary work, *Tierras y Aguas*, which was attached as an appendix to Escriche's authoritative *Diccionario Razonado de Legislación y Jurisprudencia*, aptly summarizes the situation regarding the ownership of the common lands of a community land grant:

> they [the kings] had to cede to the communities of America and to their councils . . . a certain portion of lands, so that people would come for the maintenance and betterment of the land, mak-ing use of the pastures and tillable lands. . . . These lands they im-mediately named according to their kind, ownership and use: *con-cejiles.* . . .[49]

The third type of Hispanic law, custom and usage, is the most important. Since there were few law books or lawyers in New Mexico prior to American occupation, disputes about land owner-ship were settled in traditional ways, which were considered bind-ing and accepted by all sides.[50] Though falling under the classification of customary law, this litigation was usually written down and was characterized by a formality somewhat amazing considering the frontier setting in which it took place. The parties were often adept at the use of argumentation and persuasive tech-niques generally reserved to trained lawyers.[51]

In the case of the San Joaquín grant such a dispute occurred at a time when New Mexico had the closest thing to a formal judicial system prior to the United States occupation.[52] The details of this litigation are of interest historically, showing how the traditional system of customary law operated and shedding light on the his-tory of the San Joaquín grant. Also of interest here is the effect of this lawsuit on the question of ownership of the common lands. For under the international law doctrine of acquired rights, a determination by a former government of the validity and nature of the property rights of its citizens is binding on the successor government (the United States).[53] The Mexican government made such a determination as a result of this litigation.

The dispute began in 1828 when Alcalde José María Ortiz gave a group of settlers possession of allotments along the Gallina River, at its confluence with the Rio Chama. Alcalde Ortiz apparently realized that since the allotments of 1828 on the Gallina were within the boundaries of the San Joaquín grant and were without the sanction of those grantees, they could be justified only by attacking the original allotments made by Alcalde García de la Mora in 1808. This Ortiz did by deciding on his own that a provision in the San Joaquín grant for returning the original title papers to the governor, for deposit in the archives, had not been complied with.[54]

Alcalde Pedro Ignacio Gallegos, who was the head of the ayuntamiento of Abiquiu, sided with the San Joaquín settlers and ordered the Gallina settlers off the land. Then, in 1832, José de Jesús Chacón, leader of the Gallina group (he was the son of one of the original grantees who had sold his interest in the grant),[55] petitioned Governor Santiago Abreu, seeking a declaration that the actions of Alcalde Gallegos were illegal, appealing to the governor as one "who knows the alcaldes of the territories very well and that many times they avail themselves of our ignorance to commit arbitrary acts. . . ." Chacón stated that he and his fellow settlers had raised crops on the land they were claiming, a fact he said he could prove by the tithe collector.[56] The governor referred the petition to the *asesor* (attorney general), Antonio Barreiro, a lawyer who the central government in Mexico City sent to act as a one-man judicial system for the province of New Mexico.[57] Barreiro notified Abreu that he had already been approached by Alcalde Gallegos and had told him to form an *expediente*, as he could not decide the matter on the basis of a simple communication.[58] So the governor conveyed the wishes of the asesor to Alcalde Gallegos for the second time.[59]

Again Gallegos tried to circumvent Barreiro's request. Instead of forming an expediente, he purported to decide the controversy himself, stating: "I declare the possession . . . given by . . . Ortiz of the lands on the Gallina River . . . not legal." This was true, he

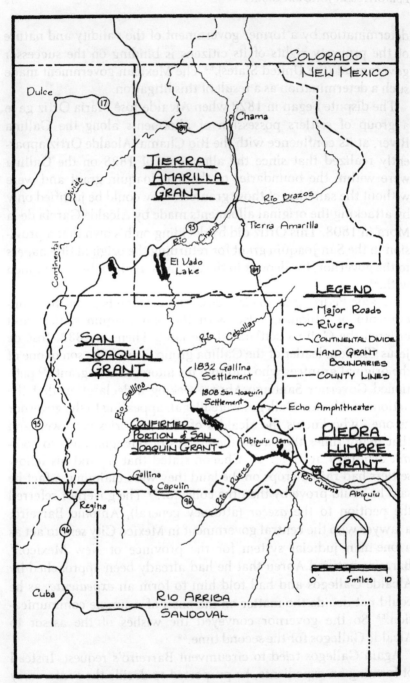

Map labels: COLORADO / NEW MEXICO, Dulce, Chama, 17, 84, TIERRA AMARILLA GRANT, Rio Brazos, Tierra Amarilla, 95, Rio Chama, Continental Divide, El Vado Lake, 84, LEGEND — Major Roads, Rivers, Continental Divide, Land Grant Boundaries, County Lines, SAN JOAQUÍN GRANT, Rio Ceballa, 1832 Gallina Settlement, 1808 San Joaquín Settlement, Rio Gallina, 95, Echo Amphitheater, CONFIRMED PORTION of SAN JOAQUÍN GRANT, Abiquiu Dam, PIEDRA LUMBRE GRANT, Gallina, Capulin, Rio Puerco, Rio Chama, Abiquiu, 96, Regina, 96, 0 5 miles 10, Cuba, RIO ARRIBA, SANDOVAL

The San Joaquin and adjoining grants. Courtesy of the author.

said, because the title papers had not been certified by the alcalde, certified copies given to the parties, and the original returned to the governor in Santa Fe to be deposited in the archives.[60]

Again Barreiro patiently but firmly explained in detail what he meant by his order to Alcalde Gallegos to form an expediente:

> Salazar, Chávez and the other complainants [leaders of the San Joaquín settlers], must present you a written statement in which they should set forth plainly and simply the facts relating to their possession and the right which they believe they have to the lands which they claim; of this statement you will give a copy to Chacón, García, Durán and Contreras [leaders of the Gallina settlers], in order that they also may give an idea of the right which they claim, basing it upon whatever they believe to be right, but they must express it clearly and briefly. . . .

A copy of the Gallina reply statement was to be given to the San Joaquín settlers, who were to respond to it within six days. This statement was to be delivered to the Gallina settlers, who then had another six days to reply. Alcalde Gallegos was then asked to assemble these statements, two from each side, and forward them to Asesor Barreiro for his decision, which ultimately would determine the validity of the San Joaquín grant.[61] Barreiro's minute specificity as to what he required as a proper expediente did not leave room for any further evasions by Alcalde Gallegos.

The first statement of the San Joaquín settlers argues that their possession was legal and that the possession given by Alcalde Ortiz to the Gallina settlers was not legal because it was within the limits of the San Joaquín grant and had not been approved by the Territorial Deputation.[62] The first statement of the Gallina people raises two new points: that the allotments made by Alcalde Ortiz were made with the knowledge of the governor, José Antonio Chávez, and that the San Joaquín grantees should have protested in 1828 when the allotments were made. They close their brief with a bit of overstatement, charging that the San Joaquín settlers "want to enjoy our property without the labor of reclaiming these far off lands which we have improved with our blood . . . notwithstanding that we are so poor that to procure an axe or a hoe we would pledge our persons. . . ."[63]

The second statement of the San Joaquín group focuses on this last remark. It singles out Mateo García as not being as poor as stated but rather owning land in Abiquiu sufficient to support a large family and a tract in El Rito "from which he fills a granery every year." Next it says, as to the work done by the Gallina group on the land, that it is "nothing more than to yoke a pair of oxen and go along planting their seeds." As to the delay in making their protest, it states that two of their group did in fact protest to Alcalde Ortiz at the time of the Gallina allotment of 1828, but he would not hear them. Finally the San Joaquín settlers reveal that their work in making the ditch to obtain water for irrigating the San Joaquín fields, when they were put into possession in 1808, was very great, notwithstanding the fact that their efforts were unsuccessful. This probably explains why some of these settlers joined the settlement on the Gallina.[64]

At this point in the proceedings much of the argument advanced had degenerated into name-calling and flowery rhetoric in spite of Barreiro's admonition to both sides to express themselves plainly, simply, and briefly. The final statement of the Gallina settlers complains that "now we see only rights usurped, justice delayed and ourselves burdened with costs we can ill afford to bear."[65]

Barreiro now had the expediente he had requested. He was acting as a sort of "Supreme Court of New Mexico" when he rendered his decision, which cut through the verbiage of the expediente to the heart of the matter. That the original grant document was not in the archives, he said, did not make the grant invalid. In Barreiro's words, "the possession given at the Cañón de San Joaquín del Rio de Chama is legal, because even if there be any requisite lacking, it is not an essential requisite, but one of pure formality."[66]

The final step in this litigation was taken when Alcalde Gallegos executed this decision on 10 May 1832. He announced that anyone who considered himself to have any right to an allotment of land on the Gallina should appear on that day. Three citizens chose not to: Mateo García, Tomás Chacón, and Tomás Salazar. José María Chávez, senior *regidor* of the ayuntamiento of Abiquiu,[67] was appointed to notify these three that by failing to appear they had forfeited any right to an allotment. Alcalde Gallegos pointed out in his report that neither García nor Chacón would have been entitled to an allotment anyway because García had sold his interest in the grant, and Chacón's father had sold their rights.

Those who did show up at Gallina that day in May received *suertes*[68] of 150 varas—fifty varas of irrigable land and one hundred varas of uncultivated land. Most of the eighteen settlers who received allotments at Gallina in 1832 had also received allotments in 1808 at the village of San Joaquín.[69] Among those receiving allotments in 1832 were the children of the deceased Francisco Salazar.[70]

The allotments in 1832 at Gallina, about five miles from the original village of San Joaquín, demonstrate that the Mexican government viewed the ownership of the San Joaquín grant differently than did the United States Court of Private Land Claims and the Supreme Court, which held that only the allotments of 1808 were valid and that the rest of the land within the grant belonged to the U.S. government.

But the historical as well as the legal facts show that the lands outside the village of San Joaquín were as much a part of the grant as were the allotments of 1808. Alcalde Gallegos's report on the *repartimiento* proceedings makes this conclusion clear:

> I, having caused the grant made by the governor, Don Joaquín de Real Alencaster, to be read in the presence of all, . . . ascertained that the lands of the Gallina River were and are within the limits of the grant, and . . . that the lands that were not partitioned at the time when possession was given[,] remained for the children that might be born to the settlers.[71]

The epilogue to this litigation was a decision by a commission of the Territorial Deputation in 1833, based on a claim by those dispossessed by the 1832 allotments, led by Mateo García. The committee reaffirmed the decision of Asesor Barreiro when it refused to even hear the claim, stating that the land in question had already been the subject of litigation.[72] It is significant that the commission of 1833 found that the lands on the Gallina River, outside the area confirmed by the Court of Private Land Claims, were not public lands, as held by the Claims Court, but were private property. García was not daunted by this second decision upholding the San Joaquín grant in its entirety. In 1834, he arranged a trade with ex-Alcalde Gallegos for the land that Gallegos had received as his fee for performing the repartimiento of 1832.[13]

This litigation indicates that the Mexican government considered the entire San Joaquín grant—not just the allotments of 1808—to be owned by the settlers and not by the government. The common lands, like the Castilian tierras concegiles, belonged to the community, and the fact that the Mexican government still exercised some control over them through the making of additional allotments did not mean that this land was public domain. Even in the case of private land grants, alcaldes often made allotments, for example, dividing the land among heirs upon the death of the owners.[14]

Furthermore, the acquired rights doctrine dictates that Barreiro's decision and that of the commission of 1833 should be conclusive on the question of the ownership of the common lands. These decisions, added to the long history of community land ownership in Spain and in New Mexico, suggest that the traditional view of common land ownership, as expressed by Twitchell, needs to be revised.

NOTES

1. My use of the terms Spanish law and Spanish land grant also includes Mexican law and Mexican land grants.

2. Rio Arriba Land and Cattle Company v. United States, *United States Reports*, vol. 167 (1897), p. 298.

3. J. A. Pitt-Rivers, *The People of the Sierra*, 2nd ed. (Chicago and London: University of Chicago Press, 1971), pp. 14-33.

4. Betty Eakle Dobkins, *The Spanish Element in Texas Water Law* (Austin: University of Texas Press, 1959), p. 71, and David E. Vassberg, "The *Tierras Baldías*: Community Property and Public Lands in 16th Century Castile," *Agricultural History* 48 (July 1974): 383-90.

5. Vassberg, "The *Tierras Baldías*," p. 391.

6. "The municipal community was a landowning democracy. It reached a considerable development, particularly in Castile, where it became a kind of small republic, with its own army and flag. This was the municipal spirit which the Spaniards transferred to the New World, where it struck root . . ." (Salvador

de Madariaga, *Latin America Between the Eagle and the Bear* [New York: Frederick A. Praeger, 1962], p. 60).

7. J. Richard Salazar, "Nuestra Señora del Rosario, San Fernando y Santiago *del Rio de las Truchas: A Brief History"* (Paper presented at the Twenty-second Annual Conference of the Western Social Science Association, Albuquerque, 25 April 1980), p. 8, and Ralph Emerson Twitchell, *The Spanish Archives of New Mexico,* 2 vols. (Cedar Rapids, Iowa: Torch Press, 1914), 1:208-9, item 771. Original documents are housed at the New Mexico State Records Center and Archives (SRCA), Santa Fe.

8. U.S., Bureau of Land Management, New Mexico Land Grants, Records of Private Land Claims Adjudicated by the U.S. Court of Private Land Claims, case no. 107, reel 45, frames 9, 14. Originals are housed at SRCA. These terms were also used in the Tierra Amarilla grant. Malcolm Ebright, *The Tierra Amarilla Grant: A History of Chicanery* (Santa Fe: Center for Land Grant Studies, 1980), pp. 4-5, 40.

9. The Petaca Grant, Court of Private Land Claims, case no. 99, reel 44, frames 21-22.

10. *Recopilación de Leyes de los Reynos de las Indias,* 4 vols. (Madrid: Iulian de Paredes, 1681), 4: título 12, ley 2. This period was sometimes changed in specific grant documents. For example, the period was five years in the Petaca grant (Court of Private Land Claims, case no. 99, reel 44, frames 21-22).

11. In an article of 1 February 1979 in the Santa Fe *New Mexican,* State Historian Dr. Myra Ellen Jenkins was quoted as saying that no title papers to any genuine San Joaquín grant existed and that copies of these records were very suspect. Then in March 1979 she discovered the original title papers for the San Joaquín grant misfiled in another land grant file (*New Mexican,* 27 March 1981). On 9 July 1979, heirs of the original settlers of the grant set up a road-block preventing logging trucks from hauling timber from what is now the Santa Fe National Forest and was once the common lands of the grant (*New Mexican,* 9 July 1979). When land grant activist Reies Tijerina led the occupation of Echo Ampitheater near Ghost Ranch in October 1966, his stated purpose was to force the U.S. government to prove in court its ownership of the land, once part of the San Joaquín grant (*New Mexican,* 1 February 1979). There is now pending before Congress a bill designed to establish a commission to study the San Joa-quín grant and recommend solutions to the many problems that have arisen throughout the grant's history (U.S., Congress, House, Report 5963, 96th Cong., 1st sess., 1980, introduced by Congressman Manuel Lujan).

12. For a summary of the history and adjudication of the San Joaquín grant, see J. J. Bowden, "Private Land Claims in the Southwest," 6 vols. (Master's thesis, Southern Methodist University, 1969), 4:1058-64.

13. The title papers for the San Joaquín grant are found in U.S., Bureau of Land Management, Surveyor General's Report, New Mexico Land Grants, Records of Private Land Claims Adjudicated by the U.S. Surveyor General, 1855-1890, Cañón de Chama Grant, report no. 71, reel 20, frames 1-4.

14. A *cuartilla* was one-fourth of an *arroba* and was equal to 20.6 quarts or 22.7 liters (*Velázquez Spanish and English Dictionary* [Chicago: Follet Publishing Company, 1974], p. 209, and Manuel Carrera Stampa, "The Evolution of Weights and Measures in New Spain," *Hispanic American Historical Review* 29 [February 1949]:15).

15. An *almud* was a measure of grain equaling from three to twenty-three liters in New Mexico, depending on the locality (Marc Simmons, *Spanish Government in New Mexico* [Albuquerque: University of New Mexico (UNM) Press, 1968], p. 219), and equaling 7.5 liters or 6.8 quarts on the average in the rest of New Spain (Stampa, "Weights and Measures," p. 15).

16. Francisco Salazar was an *alférez* in the Abiquiu militia (Court of Private Land Claims, case no. 107, reel 45, frames 8, 13). The alférez was the standard bearer and is often translated as ensign although his functions were closer to those of a second lieutenant (Oakah L. Jones Jr., "Pueblo Indian Auxiliaries and the Spanish Defense of New Mexico, 1692–1974" [Ph.D. diss., University of Oklahoma, 1964], pp. 147–48, no. 112).

17. A *poblador principal* (principal settler) was the leader of the group receiving a community land grant (*Recopilación* 4: título 3, ley 24).

18. Court of Private Land Claims, case no. 107, reel 45, frames 9, 14.

19. For the history of the Piedra Lumbre grant, see Bowden, "Private Land Claims," 4:1077–82, and John R. Van Ness, "The Piedra Lumbre Grant and Hispanic Settlement in the Cañones Region" (Paper presented at the Nineteenth Annual Conference of the Western Social Science Association, Denver, 21 April 1977). For a discussion of the specific geographical meaning of piedra lumbre, see Frank D. Reeve, "Early Navajo Geography," *New Mexico Historical Review* (NMHR) 31 (October 1956): 290–98.

20. Petition for confirmation, Surveyor General's Reports, report no. 71, reel 20, frames 15–16.

21. Court of Private Land Claims, case no. 107, reel 45, frames 18–18a.

22. When Julian was appointed surveyor general of New Mexico in 1885 by President Cleveland, his primary objective was to break up the Santa Fe Ring (George W. Julian, "Land Stealing in New Mexico," *North American Review* 145 [July 1887]:17). He was ordered by his superior, General Land Office Commissioner William A. J. Sparks, to review any questionable cases reported upon by his predecessors (U.S., Congress, Senate, Ex. Doc. 113, 49th Cong., 2d sess., 1887, p. 2, quoted in Bowden, "Private Land Claims," 1:224). As a former chairman of the Committee of Private Land Claims in the House of Representatives, Julian had acquired some knowledge of New Mexico land grants (Bowden, "Private Land Claims," 1:222). He was prejudiced, however, against New Mexico even before he arrived here. Often in his journal he referred to the "stagnation of the natives" and the "prevailing tendency here to degenerate into barbarism" (R. Hal Williams, "George W. Julian and Land Reform in New Mexico, 1885–1889," *Agricultural History* 41 [January 1967]:84). Julian's zeal to correct the real abuses of land grant adjudication led him to an overcritical questioning of all grants.

23. Court of Private Land Claims, case no. 107, reel 45, frames 85–104.

24. Surveyor General's Reports, report no. 71, reel 20, frames 43–45.

25. Bowden, "Private Land Claims," 4:1062.

26. Bowden, "Private Land Claims," 4:1062.

27. U.S., Congress, House, Report No. 131, 47th Cong., 1st sess., 1882, pp. 1–2.

28. Bowden, "Private Land Claims," 1:225.

29. Act of 3 March 1851, Chap. 41, U.S., *Statutes at Large*, vol. 9 (1851), pp. 631–34, section 14.

30. U.S., Congress, Senate, Exec. Doc. No. 21, 50th Cong., 1st sess., 1887, p. 5.

31. Court of Private Land Claims, case no. 107, reel 45, frames 9, 14.

32. The Court of Private Land Claims rejected 32,718,354 acres of the 34,653,340 acres claimed before it. Of the rejected acres, 12,467,456 are represented by the notoriously fraudulent Peralta–Reavis grant. Of the remaining 20,250,898 rejected acres, an estimated 50 percent is comprised of common lands rejected under the doctrine established in the cases of the San Joaquín and San Miguel del Vado grants (*Land Title Study*, prepared by White, Koch, Kelley & McCarthy, Attorneys and Counselors at Law . . . [Santa Fe: State Planning Office, 1972], pp. 228–34).

33. Russell B. Rice, San Miguel County Surveyor, to J. N. Lamoreaux, Commissioner, General Land Office, 8 April 1893, cited in Clark S. Knowlton, "The Town of Las Vegas Community Grant: An Anglo-American Coup d' Etat," *Journal of the West* 19 (July 1980): 18.

34. Surveyor General's Reports, report no. 71, reel 20, frames 77–79, 81–83.

35. Thomas B. Catron Collection, box 22, folder 107(2), Special Collections Department, University of New Mexico Library (UNM-SC), Albuquerque.

36. Catron Collection, box 22, folder 107(2) UNM-SC.

37. Transcript of Trial, Catron Collection, box 22, folder 107(2), UNM-SC.

38. Court of Private Land Claims, case no. 107, reel 45, frame 300.

39. The government did claim in its answer to the claimants' complaint that only the allotted lands should be confirmed, but no mention was made of this contention at the trail.

40. United States v. Sandoval, *United States Reports*, vol. 167 (1897), p. 278.

41. Rio Arriba Land and Cattle Company v. United States, pp. 298, 308.

42. Twitchell's discussion of the ownership of property in a villa or other settlement in the nature of a community grant paraphrases or quotes at length (without quotation marks) from United States v. Santa Fe, *United States Reports*, vol. 165 (1897), pp. 675, 683 ff., which in turn is quoted in United States v. Sandoval, pp. 295–97 (Ralph Emerson Twitchell, *Old Santa Fe* [1925; reprint ed., Chicago: Rio Grande Press, 1963], pp. 37–38).

43. Vassberg, "The *Tierras Baldías*," p. 400. The distinction between the tierras baldías and the tierras concegiles was not always clear in practice. Because of this, sixteenth-century Castilian monarchs were sometimes able to exact payment from municipalities for land used by them. Presumably, however,

the tierras concegiles that had been granted to a municipality were exempt from such payments (Vassberg, "The Sale of *Tierras Baldías* in Sixteenth-Century Castile," *Journal of Modern History* 47 [December 1975]:631-33, 637-38).

44. Vassberg, "The *Tierras Baldías*," p. 400.

45. John L. Walker, "The Treatment of Private Property in International Law After State Succession," pp. 65-68, 74, in "Land, Law and La Raza" (A collection of papers presented for Professor Theodore Parnall's seminar in comparative law, UNM School of Law, Fall Semester, 1972), and Daniel Patrick O'Connell, *State Succession in Municipal Law and International Law*, 2 vols. (London: Cambridge University Press, 1967), 1:200.

46. *Las Siete Partidas del sabio rey don Alfonso el IX*, glosadas por el lic. Gregorio Lopez, 4 vols. (Madrid: Oficina de d. Leon Amarita, 1829-1831), and *Las Siete Partidas*, Samuel Parsons Scott, trans. (Chicago: Commerce Clearing House, 1931).

47. *Recopiliación*, 2: título 1, ley 2.

48. Decreto de 18 de Agosto de 1824, sobre colonizacion, Manuel Dublán and José María Lozano, *Legislacion Mexicana*, 19 vols. (Mexico: Imprenta del comercio, 1876-1890), 1:712, translated in Frederic Hall, *The Laws of Mexico* (San Francisco: A. L. Bancroft, 1885), p. 148.

49. Mariano Galván-Rivera, *Ordenanzas de Tierras y Aguas . . . Dictadas Sobre la Materia y Vigentes hasta el Dia en la Republica Mejicana*, published as a supplement to Joaquín Escriche's *Diccionario Razonado de Legislación y Jurisprudencia* (Paris: Librería Rosa y Bouret, [1863]), p. 187.

50. Simmons, *Spanish Government*, pp. 176-77.

51. For an example of such litigation, see Malcolm Ebright, "Manuel Martínez's Ditch Dispute: A Study in Mexican Period Custom and Justice," NMHR 54 (January 1979): 21-34.

52. In 1828, the Ministry of Justice in Mexico City provided for the first independent judicial system for New Mexico. The following positions and salaries were authorized: district judge—1,000 pesos; *asesor* (attorney general)—500 pesos; clerk of the district judge—500 pesos; and constable of the district judge—500 pesos. None of these positions was filled except that of asesor, which was filled in 1831 by *licenciado* Antonio Barreiro (*Old Santa Fe* 1 [January 1914]: 271).

53. O'Connell, *State Succession*, 1:239-50. For a comprehensive discussion of the acquired rights doctrine and its application to numerous specific situations in international practice, see Walker, "The Treatment of Private Property," pp. 40-73.

54. Pedro Ignacio Gallegos to Licenciado Barreiro, 6 April 1832, Court of Private Land Claims, case no. 107, reel 45, frames 42, 257. A handwritten copy of the original Spanish documents covering this litigation is found beginning at frame 24.

55. Repartimiento de tierra, 10 May 1832, Court of Private Land Claims, case no. 107, reel 45, frames 49, 264.

56. Petition of Juan de Jesus Chacón to Governor Santiago Abreu, 2 April 1832, Court of Private Land Claims, case no. 107, reel 45, frames 40–41, 255–56.

57. Governor Abreu to Licenciado Barreiro, 2 April 1832, Court of Private Land Claims, case no. 107, reel 45, frames 41, 256.

58. Licenciado Barreiro to Governor Abreu, 2 April 1832, Court of Private Land Claims, case no. 107, reel 45, frames 41, 256.

59. Governor Abreu to Alcalde Gallegos, 2 April 1832, Court of Private Land Claims, case no. 107, reel 45, frames 41–42, 256.

60. Alcalde Gallegos to Licenciado Barreiro, 6 April 1832, Court of Private Land Claims, case no. 107, reel 45, frames 42, 257.

61. Licenciado Barreiro to Alcalde Gallegos, 9 April 1832, Court of Private Land Claims, case no. 107, reel 45, frames 43, 257–58.

62. Statement of José María Chávez, José Pablo Salazar, Miguel Velarde, and Santiago Salazar, 11 April 1832, Court of Private Land Claims, case no. 107, reel 45, frames 43–44, 258.

63. Statement of Juan de Jesus Chacón, José Antonio Durán, and Mateo García, 13 April 1832, Court of Private Land Claims, case no. 107, reel 45, frames 44–45, 259.

64. Statement of José María Chávez, José Pablo Salazar, Miguel Velarde, and Santiago Salazar, 17 April 1832, Court of Private Land Claims, case no. 107, reel 45, frames 45–46, 260–61.

65. Statement of Juan de Jesus Chacón, José Antonio Durán, and Mateo García, 22 April 1832, Court of Private Land Claims, case no. 107, reel 45, frames 46–47, 261.

66. Decision of Licenciado Barreiro, 26 April 1832, Court of Private Land Claims, case no. 107, reel 45, frames 48–49, 262–63.

67. The ayuntamiento was the local governing body or town council authorized for villages having a population of at least one thousand. It was composed of two councilmen (regidores), two magistrates (alcaldes constitucionales), a secretary, and an attorney. The latter post was usually omitted as there were few attorneys in New Mexico at this time (Simmons, Spanish Government, pp. 206–7).

68. A suerte was a tract of land so-called because it was drawn by lot (Dobkins, Texas Water Law, p. 97).

69. Nine of the eighteen individuals receiving allotments in 1832 had received allotments in 1808 at San Joaquín.

70. Repartimiento de tierra, 10 May 1832, Court of Private Land Claims, case no. 107, reel 45, frames 49, 264.

71. Repartimiento de tierra, 10 May 1832, Court of Private Land Claims, case no. 107, reel 45, frames 49, 264.

72. Twitchell, Spanish Archives, 1:360, item 1241.

73. Catron Collection, box 22, folder 107, UNM-SC.

74. See the Cristóbal de la Serna Grant, Surveyor General's Report, report no.

158, reel 29, frames 113, 117–18, and the Gijosa Grant, Court of Private Land Claims, case no. 16, reel 34, frames 48–49, 52–53. The Serna grant was actually a quasi-community grant. It began as a private grant, but with the coming of additional settlers using the unallotted lands in common, it came to be treated as a community grant.

Captives of Law:
Judicial Enforcement of the Chinese
Exclusion Laws, 1891–1905

Lucy Salyer

The *Gaelic* sailed into San Francisco harbor on June 11, 1892, completing a routine voyage from Hong Kong. As usual, the ship carried several Chinese passengers. Yeap Shee was journeying to the United States to join her husband, Young Ah Chew, a merchant in San Francisco. Another traveler, Fong Yot Hing, had been born in San Francisco in 1875 but had left to live in China when only six years old. Now, at the behest of his older brother, he was returning to his birthplace in Chinatown to learn the family's goldsmithing business. A third passenger, Fong Sam Toy, was coming back to his general merchandising firm after a visit to China to get married.

When the so-called Chinese inspectors from the Chinese Bureau of the Office of the Collector of Customs boarded the ship, it became clear that the journey of Yeap Shee, Fong Yot Hing, and Fong Sam Toy was not yet over. It would end only after a protracted struggle involving the federal courts. Those passengers, like all other Chinese coming to the United States, had to surmount obstacles created by the federal Chinese exclusion laws to prove they had a right to enter. Though the collector of customs, as supervisor of the Chinese Bureau, allowed several Chinese passengers on the *Gaelic* to land, he refused entry to other passengers, including those three. Rather than accept their exclusion, however, Yeap Shee, Fong Yot Hing, and Fong Sam Toy chose to challenge the collector's decision by petitioning the local federal district court for writs of habeas corpus. It was a wise strategy; District Court Judge William W. Morrow ordered the collector to allow all three to enter and reside in the United States.[1]

Lucy E. Salyer recently received her Ph.D. in jurisprudence and social policy from the University of California, Berkeley, and is now an assistant professor of history at the University of New Hampshire. This essay received the Louis Pelzer Memorial Award for 1988.

I am deeply grateful for the comments and criticisms of my colleagues in the Jurisprudence and Social Policy Program and in the History Department at the University of California, Berkeley. Special thanks are due to my adviser, Harry N. Scheiber, and to Sucheng Chan, Marianne Constable, Pete Daniel, Robert Gordon, Martin Shapiro, Susan Sterett, and David Thelen. Financial assistance for photographs was provided by the United States District Court for the Northern District of California Historical Society.

[1] *In re Yeap Shee*, no. 10357, 1892, U.S. District Court for the Northern District of California, Admiralty Casefiles, RG 21 (National Archives, San Francisco Branch, San Bruno, Cal.); *In re Fong Yot Hing*, no. 10360, 1892, *ibid.*; *In re Fong Sam Toy*, no. 10361, 1892, *ibid.*

Their victory in court was not unusual. Since the passage of the Chinese Exclusion Act in 1882, Chinese had turned repeatedly to the federal district and circuit courts, especially in northern California where the vast majority of Chinese landed. By 1890, Chinese had filed in the federal courts at San Francisco a total of 7,080 petitions to challenge the collector's decisions to deny them entry and had won reversals in approximately 85 to 90 percent of the cases.[2] In the eyes of the public and administrative officials, the courts made effective enforcement of the Chinese exclusion laws impossible.

This Chinese success story runs counter to traditional assumptions about the history of immigrants and courts. Immigration law scholars such as Peter H. Schuck argue that since 1891 courts have rarely intervened in immigration policy, treating the decisions of the immigration agency with unusual deference. The portrayal of a judiciary passive toward non-Chinese immigrants seems true. In 1891 Congress curtailed immigrants' access to the federal courts by making the decisions of the newly created federal immigration office final. In 1892 the United States Supreme Court sanctioned the power of Congress to forbid judicial review, declaring, "It is not within the province of the judiciary to order that foreigners . . . shall be permitted to enter."[3]

Drawing on the unpublished records of cases filed between 1891 and 1905 in the federal district and circuit courts for the Northern District of California, this article reevaluates the relationship between federal courts and immigrants in order to explain why the Chinese prevailed in court so often.[4] The Chinese differed from other immigrants in their response to efforts to keep them out of the United States. Immigrants (primarily European) arriving between 1891 and 1910 at Ellis Island, New York, filed only 273 habeas corpus petitions in the local federal courts to challenge

---

[2] In 1891, 97% of Chinese entering the United States came through San Francisco; by 1901, 64% came through the port. See U.S. Department of the Treasury, *Annual Report of the Secretary of the Treasury for Fiscal Year Ended 1891* (Washington, 1891), 865; U.S. Department of Commerce and Labor, *Annual Report of the Commissioner-General of Immigration for Fiscal Year Ended 1901* (Washington, 1901), 49. Christian G. Fritz, "San Francisco's First Federal Court: Ogden Hoffman and the Northern District of California, 1851–1891" (Ph.D. diss., University of California, Berkeley, 1987), 721n105; U.S. Congress, Select Committee on Immigration and Naturalization, *Chinese Immigration*, 51 Cong., 2 sess., March 2, 1891, p. 412; Hudson N. Janisch, "The Chinese, the Courts, and the Constitution: A Study of the Legal Issues Raised by Chinese Immigration to the United States, 1850–1902" (J.S.D. diss., University of Chicago Law School, 1971), 678–79.

[3] Peter H. Schuck, "The Transformation of Immigration Law," *Columbia Law Review*, 84 (Jan. 1984), 1–90; Act of March 3, 1891, 26 Stat. 1084, sec. 8; *Nishimura Ekiu v. United States*, 142 U.S. 651, 660 (1892).

[4] From 1891 to 1911, both the district and circuit courts were federal trial courts. Petitioners could file for writs of habeas corpus in either court, but they almost always filed in the district court. I obtained data on both courts from two sources. From the courts' docket books, I recorded the disposition (as well as other basic information) for all the Chinese habeas corpus cases (2,657) filed between 1891 and 1905. From these cases, I drew a random sample of 392, choosing 10% or 5 cases, whichever was larger, from each year for an in-depth review of the case files. The files often included the transcripts of the court hearings and the notes and transcripts from the immigration agency's investigation. For the district court docket books, see Admiralty Dockets, vol. 14–18, U.S. District Court for the Northern District of California, 1891–1905 (Archives Room, U.S. District Court, San Francisco, Cal.). For the circuit court docket books, see Common Law and Equity Register, U.S. Circuit Court for the Northern District of California, *ibid*. For the district court casefiles, see U.S. District Court for the Northern District of California, Admiralty Casefiles. For the circuit court casefiles, see U.S. Circuit Court for the Northern District of California, Common Law and Equity Casefiles, RG 21 (National Archives, San Francisco Branch).

their rejection by immigration officers. In a similar period, between 1891 and 1905, Chinese in San Francisco filed 2,657 habeas corpus petitions. Approximately sixty thousand Chinese applied for admission to the United States between 1891 and 1905 while almost six million non-Chinese came to the United States during that period. Thus Chinese arriving on the West Coast filed petitions at a much higher rate than Europeans arriving on the East Coast.[5]

The greater activity on the part of Chinese reflects differences in the laws governing their admission and perhaps in the immigrant communities as well. The Chinese exclusion laws subjected Chinese to much harsher restrictions and excluded them in much greater proportions than the laws governing the admission of non-Chinese immigrants. Under the Chinese exclusion laws, the percentage of Chinese denied entry between 1894 and 1901 varied from a low of 5 percent in 1898 to a high of 34 percent in 1901. In contrast, the Bureau of Immigration during the same period never rejected more than 1.3 percent of non-Chinese applicants. Given their greater ease of entry and the 1891 law making the decisions of immigration officials final in their cases, non-Chinese immigrants probably had less reason to appeal to the courts. Ironically, Chinese retained the right of judicial review after the courts had been closed to other immigrants. The Chinese-American community, drawn together by traditional social ties and by the need to protect itself from the discrimination Chinese encountered in America, provided the resources and impetus for the habeas corpus litigation. Chinese took advantage of the opportunity for judicial review and proved to be tenacious and sophisticated litigators.[6]

The litigants' determination and skill alone did not secure their victory, however. The fate of their cases rested with the federal courts. Fortunately for the Chinese, the courts proved to be an especially receptive forum.

That the federal courts were so favorable to the Chinese is surprising given the backgrounds of the judges and the national political and social climate. A blatant racism pervaded the nation and crept into federal judicial decisions. Black Americans in the 1890s, for example, discovered the federal courts to be unresponsive and, in fact, damaging, to their fight against discriminatory laws. In California

[5] For habeas corpus cases brought by immigrants in New York, see Equity Docket, U.S. District Court for the Southern District of New York, 1897–1910, RG 21 (National Archives, New York Branch, Bayonne, N. J.); Habeas Corpus Docket, U.S. Circuit Court for the Southern District of New York, 1891–1906, *ibid.* For such cases brought by Chinese, see sources cited in note 4, above. For immigration figures, see U.S. Department of Treasury, *Annual Report of the Secretary of the Treasury on the State of the Finances for the Year 1894* (Washington, 1894), 958–59; *Annual Report of the Secretary of the Treasury on the State of the Finances for the Year 1895* (Washington, 1896), 715–16; *Annual Report of the Secretary of the Treasury on the State of the Finances for the Year 1896* (Washington, 1897), 798–99; *Annual Report of the Secretary of the Treasury on the State of the Finances for the Year 1897* (Washington, 1897), LIII; *Annual Report of the Secretary of the Treasury on the State of the Finances for the Year 1898* (Washington, 1898), LVI; *Annual Report of the Secretary of the Treasury on the State of the Finances for the Fiscal Year Ended June 30, 1899* (Washington, 1900), LI; U.S. Department of Treasury, *Annual Report of the Commissioner-General of Immigration for the Fiscal Year Ended June 30, 1901* (Washington, 1901), 49; and U.S. Immigration Commission, *Statistical Review of Immigration, 1820–1910* (Washington, 1911), 38–42.

[6] In addition to the sources cited in note 5, above, see U.S. Immigration Commission, *Statistical Review of Immigration, 1820–1910*, table 42, p. 367. The immigration laws governing non-Chinese excluded certain classes of people, including by 1891, prostitutes, convicts, lunatics, and those unable to care for themselves. The Chinese exclusion laws made much more sweeping restrictions, excluding all Chinese laborers. E. P. Hutchinson, *Legislative History of American Immigration Policy, 1798–1965* (Philadelphia, 1981), 405–42.

Chinese encountered intense hostility from white Americans, who since the 1850s had vented their racism in discriminatory legislation, boycotts, and extralegal intimidation and violence. As a congressman, William W. Morrow, who as judge of the District Court for the Northern District of California freed the *Gaelic* passengers, had spearheaded California's campaign for more stringent Chinese exclusion laws. Other future federal court judges for the same district, Joseph McKenna and John De Haven, were also strong proponents of Chinese exclusion and other nativist legislation in congressional debates.[7]

While the judges agreed with and attempted to facilitate the public policy of excluding Chinese, they were, in a sense, "captured" by law. When judges took the bench, they entered into an institution that had particular procedural rules and practices rooted in Anglo-American common law tradition. Two procedures of the federal trial courts—the writ of habeas corpus and judicial evidentiary rules—were especially important to the success of Chinese. Because of the institutional norms that required them to treat cases individually and to apply general principles in decision making, the judges felt obligated to extend those practices to both Chinese and non-Chinese litigants.

By examining how institutional norms and practices influenced judicial decision making, I hope to expand the prevailing understanding of the nature of courts at the turn of the century. Traditionally, scholars studying courts of that period, such as Arnold M. Paul, Benjamin R. Twiss, Louis B. Boudin, and William F. Swindler, have focused on the Supreme Court and its decisions regarding social and economic regulations. Writing in the legal realist tradition, such scholars, discarding the notion that judges simply identify and apply law in a neutral manner, highlighted the political nature of judicial decisions. They portrayed the Court as a bastion of conservatism, clinging to narrow conceptions of government power to defeat local and national economic legislation while protecting certain business interests. Until recently, that interpretation has dominated the history of courts during the Progressive Era. Recent studies have begun to modify the realists' interpretation of that era, revealing that the Supreme Court was not always a bulwark against Progressive reforms and that principle, as well as politics, guided the justices' decisions. Others have broadened the study of courts to include state appellate and county criminal courts.[8]

[7] For the federal courts' response to black Americans' challenges to discrimination, see C. Vann Woodward, *The Strange Career of Jim Crow* (New York, 1974), 70–72. William W. Morrow served as district court judge for the Northern District of California between 1891 and 1897. He served on the circuit court for the same district between 1897 and 1923. John De Haven sat on the district court bench between 1897 and 1913, and Joseph McKenna served as circuit court judge from 1892 until 1897, when he was appointed to the United States Supreme Court. See *Dictionary of American Biography*, s.v. "Morrow, William W."; *ibid.*, s.v. "McKenna, Joseph"; and on De Haven, J. Edward Johnson, *History of the Supreme Court Justices of California* (2 vols., San Francisco, 1963), I, 175–77.

[8] For the legal realist tradition, see Arnold M. Paul, *The Conservative Crisis and the Rule of Law: Attitudes of Bar and Bench, 1887–1895* (Ithaca, 1960); Benjamin R. Twiss, *Lawyers and the Constitution: How Laissez-Faire Came to the Supreme Court* (Princeton, 1942); Louis B. Boudin, *Government by Judiciary* (New York, 1932); and William F. Swindler, *Court and Constitution in the Twentieth Century* (3 vols., Indianapolis, 1969–1974). For newer studies of the Supreme Court, see John E. Semonche, *Charting the Future: The Supreme Court Responds to a Changing Society, 1890–1920* (Westport, 1978); Charles W. McCurdy, "Justice Field and the Jurisprudence of

William W. Morrow was U.S. District Judge (1891–1897) and
U.S. Circuit Judge (1897–1929) for the Northern District of California.
Courtesy U.S. District Court, San Francisco, California.

This article focuses on federal trial courts, rather than on appellate federal and state courts, and adopts an institutional perspective, paying close attention to judges' actions, as well as to their words. Such an approach does not mean returning to a notion that judges "discover" law nor does it discard the argument that judges' political orientation influences their decisions. Federal judges in northern California allowed their personal anti-Chinese biases to affect their treatment of Chinese litigants. An institutional approach, however, adds a different dimension to the study of courts by suggesting that judges inherit traditions that may constrain their actions.[9]

Government-Business Relations: Some Parameters of Laissez-Faire Constitutionalism, 1863–1897," *Journal of American History*, 61 (March 1975), 970–1005. On state and county courts, see Melvin I. Urofsky, "State Courts and Protective Legislation during the Progressive Era: A Reevaluation," *ibid.*, 63 (June 1985), 63–91, esp. 63–87; Lawrence M. Friedman and Robert V. Percival, *The Roots of Justice: Crime and Punishment in Alameda County, California, 1870–1910* (Chapel Hill, 1981).

[9] My thesis is consistent with the findings of Christian G. Fritz and Hudson N. Janisch, who examine the Chinese habeas corpus cases for different periods and with an approach different from mine. Both focus on the important substantive legal decisions made by the California federal courts in Chinese cases. My study concentrates on the court's *procedures* in handling the run-of-the-mill Chinese cases, which allows an in-depth analysis of institutional practices. Fritz, "San Francisco's First Federal Court," 377–423; Janisch, "The Chinese, the Courts, and the Constitution," 476–519, 654–762, 931–1045.

Three successful challengers
to the Chinese exclusion laws.

Lau Yuen (upper left) was admitted
as an American citizen in 1904.
His western dress was unusual,
given his occupation as cook and launderer.

Jew Gan Yin (upper right) was one of
the few Chinese women who came before
the federal courts. Initially denied
admission (probably on suspicion
of prostitution), she entered as a
citizen in 1892.

Jew Yee Lin (lower left) was declared a
citizen by the court in 1904 because he
was born in San Francisco.

*Courtesy National Archives,
San Francisco Branch.*

Federal trial courts played a major and surprising part in the drama of Chinese immigrants partly because of the body of special laws applied to the Chinese and the administrative structure established to implement those laws in the 1880s. The Chinese were the earliest targets of restrictionist fervor. The United States gained a concession from China in an 1880 amendment to the Burlingame Treaty of 1868, permitting the United States to limit, though not absolutely to prohibit, the future immigration of Chinese laborers whenever American officials judged that such immigration "affects or threatens to affect the interests of that country, or to endanger the good order of the said country." The restriction applied only to Chinese laborers who had not yet immigrated to the United States.

> [Other] Chinese subjects, whether proceeding to the United States as teachers, students, merchants or from curiosity, . . . and Chinese laborers who are now in the United States shall be allowed to go and come of their own free will and accord, and shall be accorded all the rights, privileges, immunities, and exemptions which are accorded to the citizens and subjects of the most favored nation.[10]

Congress proceeded to curtail Chinese immigration to the United States in a series of acts in 1882, 1884, and 1888, jointly known as the Chinese exclusion laws. Only Chinese who were not laborers (including merchants, students, and travelers) and those who had been born in the United States and thus were American citizens were allowed to enter. Chinese laborers residing in California before 1880 were allowed to remain; once they left the United States, however, they could not return.[11] The latter provision clearly contravened the 1880 treaty with China, and in the 1894 treaty, China succeeded in gaining an exception to this rule. A Chinese laborer could leave and return to the United States if he had a "lawful wife, child, or parent" living in the United States, or if he had at least one thousand dollars worth of property or of debts owed him. The statutes did not address explicitly the admissibility of Chinese women and children. The lower federal courts ruled in the 1880s that Chinese women and children would be allowed to enter if they were native-born American citizens. The Supreme Court in 1901 clarified the admissibility of others, holding that the status of the wife and child followed that of the husband. Thus, if the Chinese exclusion laws exempted the husband, the wife and child could also enter. Finally, the laws denied all Chinese the privilege of becoming naturalized United States citizens. Thus, by 1891 the Chinese had the dubious distinction of being the only immigrant group to be specifically excluded from the United States and to be denied the privilege of naturalization.[12]

[10] Treaty between the United States and China concerning Immigration, Nov. 17, 1880, art. I, 22 Stat. 826; *Ibid.*, art. II.
[11] Act of May 6, 1882, 22 Stat. 58; Act of July 5, 1884, 23 Stat. 115; Act of Sept. 13, 1888, 25 Stat. 476; Act of Oct. 1, 1888, 25 Stat. 504. Though Chinese could not become naturalized citizens, the Ninth Circuit in 1884 had recognized the citizenship of Chinese born in the United States. See *In re Look Tin Sing*, 21 25.6 905 (C.C.D. Cal. 1884).
[12] Convention between the United States of America and the Empire of China concerning Emigration, March 17, 1894, 28 Stat. 1210; *In re Look Tin Sing*, 21 F. 905; *Ex parte Chin King*, 35 F. 354 (C.C.D. Or. 1888); *United States v. Mrs. Gue Lim*, 176 U.S. 459 (1900).

When Morrow took the bench as district court judge in 1891, public worries about the Chinese had momentarily subsided and the prospects for a vigorous enforcement of the Chinese exclusion laws appeared promising. The deaths of Judge Ogden Hoffman of the district court and Judge Lorenzo Sawyer of the circuit court in 1891 brought a close to the first era of the northern district court's history. Californians had a new federal court staffed with judges — Morrow in the district court and McKenna in the circuit court — who had demonstrated their loyalty to anti-Chinese forces in Congress. Furthermore, a new collector, Timothy Phelps, had been appointed to enforce the laws regulating Chinese immigration. Several people realized that the tension between the courts and the local administration in the 1880s had resulted in part from the overly rigid interpretation of the laws adopted by Phelps's zealous predecessor, John Hager.[13] With a new, more cautious collector and the new judges, a less combative relationship in the enforcement of the Chinese exclusion laws seemed possible.

By 1891 a new national consensus about the acceptability of exclusion had also developed. The Supreme Court had upheld the constitutionality of the Exclusion Act in 1889. When Congress considered amendments to the exclusion laws in 1892, Sen. William M. Stewart of Nevada claimed: "There was a time when there was great diversity of opinion on the question of Chinese immigration to this country, but I think there is practically none now. The American people are now convinced that the Chinese can not be incorporated among our citizens, can not be amalgamated, can not be absorbed, but that they will remain a distinct element."[14]

Stephen Chase Houghton, a United States commissioner appointed to assist the circuit court with the Chinese habeas corpus cases, commented in 1890 that the Chinese litigation was "really practically over." Because of the success of the legislation restricting Chinese immigration, explained Houghton, the number of Chinese entering the United States had declined and, consequently, very few cases came before the courts anymore.[15] Yet the courts' involvement was not over by any means. Between 1891 and 1905, the district and circuit courts in San Francisco heard 2,657 Chinese habeas corpus cases. And the courts, according to many observers, continued to frustrate the purposes of the Chinese exclusion laws.

That Chinese continued to have access to the courts was an ironic consequence of the administrative structure instituted by the Immigration Act of 1891. The act specifically omitted Chinese from its reach and, in effect, established a dual system of administration, one for the Chinese and another for all other immigrants. The collectors of customs in the various ports remained responsible for enforcing the laws regulating Chinese immigration, while the newly created office of the superintendent of immigration administered the laws governing non-Chinese immigrants.

[13] Select Committee on Immigration and Naturalization, *Chinese Immigration*, 332–33, 344.
[14] *Chae Chan Ping v. United States*, 130 U.S. 581 (1889); *Congressional Record*, 52 Cong., 1 sess., Apr. 23, 1892, p. 3559.
[15] Select Committee on Immigration and Naturalization, *Chinese Immigration*, 323. Stephen Chase Houghton served as referee for the federal courts under Judge Ogden Hoffman, hearing admiralty and Chinese habeas corpus cases until 1892.

It was not until 1903 that the Chinese came under the aegis of that office, the Bureau of Immigration, and became subject to the immigration laws. As a consequence, the 1891 act's prohibition on judicial review of administrative decisions to deny immigrants entry did not apply to Chinese immigrants, and they could use the federal courts to challenge such administrative decisions.[16]

The Chinese in northern California put the opportunity for judicial review to good use. By the time the Chinese restriction laws were passed, Chinese had already proved themselves determined and skillful litigators in their challenges to other discriminatory laws before the federal courts.[17] The success of Chinese in the courts in those matters showed Chinese immigrants how to use the legal system to challenge the decisions of the collector.

Chinese arriving in San Francisco from Kwangtung Province in southeastern China found a network of family and service associations led by members of the elite merchant class. Each Chinese in California belonged to one of several family associations based loosely on lineage. Someone from the family association — an uncle or a distant cousin, for example — would meet the newcomer and help him or her with any immigration difficulties, hiring an attorney if necessary. Once landed, the immigrant could rely on his or her clan to provide aid in getting settled.[18]

In addition to the family organizations, Chinese also belonged to district associations (or *huiguan*), depending on the regions they came from in China. The district associations played an important role in their members' lives. The associations often provided Chinese immigrants with money for their passage to the United States in exchange for the newcomers' labor for a specified time. Once Chinese arrived in the United States, the associations helped their members find employment, housing, and medical care and lent them money if necessary.[19]

Chinese immigrants might also belong to a third type of organization — a secret society (or *tong*). In China the secret societies, being associated with political rebellions and crime, had a subversive character. Similarly, Chinese joined tongs in the United States both to oppose the local merchant leadership and to profit from the organizations' gambling, opium, and prostitution enterprises. The secret societies also provided many of the same services — lodging, medical care, and dispute settlement — as the family and district associations.[20]

---

[16] Act of March 3, 1891, 26 Stat. 1084.

[17] See Charles J. McClain, Jr., "The Chinese Struggle for Civil Rights in Nineteenth-Century America: The First Phase, 1850-1870," *California Law Review*, 72 (July 1984), 529–68; Janisch, "The Chinese, the Courts, and the Constitution," 296–314, 374–98, 581–653; Fritz, "San Francisco's First Federal Court," 343–77; Ralph James Mooney, "Matthew Deady and the Federal Judicial Response to Racism in the Early West," *Oregon Law Review*, 63 (no. 4, 1984), 561–644; John R. Wunder, "The Chinese and the Courts in the Pacific Northwest: Justice Denied?" *Pacific Historical Review*, 52 (May 1893), 191–211.

[18] Victor B. Nee and Brett de Bary Nee, *Long Time Californ': A Documentary Study of an American Chinatown* (New York, 1973), 64–65; Select Committee on Immigration and Naturalization, *Chinese Immigration*, 398.

[19] Stanford M. Lyman, "Conflict and the Web of Group Affiliation in San Francisco's Chinatown, 1850-1910," *Pacific Historical Review*, 43 (Nov. 1974), 473–99, esp. 482; Nee and Nee, *Long Time Californ'*, 67.

[20] Lyman, "Conflict and the Web of Group Affiliation," 484–90.

The Chinese Consolidated Benevolent Association, more commonly known to white Americans as the Chinese Six Companies, acted as the local governing unit in San Francisco's Chinatown. The original purpose of the association, composed of representatives from all the district associations, was to arbitrate disputes within the Chinese community. Eventually, however, the Chinese Six Companies took on a broader role as advocate of the Chinese community in the white world. The organization kept an attorney on retainer to contest anti-Chinese legislation and practices.[21]

Experienced white attorneys were willing to represent Chinese in the habeas corpus cases before the federal courts. Indeed, one of the complaints against the Chinese was that they hired the best legal talent. The Chinese immigration cases became a new specialty; although other attorneys tried to compete with them for this profitable business, a small group of six to eight attorneys handled practically all such cases before the district court. Attorneys could make between seventy-five and one hundred dollars per case, according to estimates sent to the United States attorney-general. Drawn by the profitability of the work and the expertise they had developed in the field, United States district attorneys who had appeared before the district court defending the collector's decisions to exclude Chinese often worked on the side of the Chinese after their terms in office ended. The Chinese litigants' ability to obtain representation was a key to their success in the federal courts.[22]

With the support of their community and attorneys, Chinese people brought their cases to the district court on writs of habeas corpus, claiming that they were being held on ships illegally because the collector refused them their right to land in the United States. In such cases the customs inspectors of the Chinese Bureau, a subdivision of the customs office, had already investigated the Chinese applicants on board and had made recommendations as to whether they fell under the Chinese exclusion laws and should be landed or deported. The collector usually accepted the recommendation of the inspector. Chinese who were denied landing could then appeal to the secretary of the treasury (as could non-Chinese under the 1891 act), but instead almost all went directly to court to challenge the collector's decisions.

When a Chinese man or woman petitioned the federal courts at San Francisco for a writ of habeas corpus, the judges felt bound to issue the writ and to hear the case. The fact that the case came before the court on a writ of habeas corpus had special significance. Literally, habeas corpus means "you have the body." A writ of habeas corpus requires the person detaining the petitioner to demonstrate to the court that the confinement is lawful. For the judges of the court, the writ of habeas corpus had an honored place in Anglo-American jurisprudence; it evoked the basic

[21] Gunther Barth, *Bitter Strength: A History of the Chinese in the United States, 1850–1870* (Cambridge, Mass., 1964), 79–102; Nee and Nee, *Long Time Californ'*, 65–66. On the Six Companies' retaining of attorneys, see Alta California, *The Alta California Commercial Edition* (San Francisco, 1889), 23, 32; and *Who's Who on the Pacific Coast* (1913), s.v. "Stidger, Oliver Perry."

[22] For the complaints, see, for example, Oscar Greenhalge to Walter Chance, March 11, 1899, Central Office Subject Correspondence, 52730/84, Records of the Immigration and Naturalization Service, RG 85 (National Archives). On fees, see Leigh Chalmers to Attorney-General, Dec. 5, 1887, Letters Received, 980/84, Records of the Department of Justice, RG 60, *ibid.*; and Janisch, "The Chinese, the Courts, and the Constitution," 678.

The Chinese habeas corpus cases were so numerous and routine that attorneys for the Chinese developed standard petitions like this one. *Courtesy National Archives, San Francisco Branch.*

principle of the liberty of the individual from the arbitrary acts of government. The Constitution forbade Congress to suspend the privilege of habeas corpus, except in "Cases of Rebellion or Invasion." And the privilege was not limited to citizens. Reconstruction legislation in 1867 expanded the privilege of habeas corpus, giving the federal courts broad powers to issue such writs in cases in which persons (not just citizens) were held in violation of the United States Constitution, laws, or treaties. When Chinese Inspector S. J. Ruddell suggested to the congressional Subcommittee on Immigration in 1890 that the problem of Chinese immigration could be solved by taking away the privilege of habeas corpus from the Chinese, Sen. Watson C. Squire of Washington wryly queried: "That would be a little inimical to the spirit of the Constitution?"[23]

The district court under Judge Hoffman had upheld the right of the Chinese to habeas corpus in an 1888 case, *In re Jung Ah Lung*. In that case the collector of San Francisco, furious at the intervention of the courts, argued that the Chinese were not entitled to the writ of habeas corpus. Judge Hoffman indignantly rejected the collector's arguments, declaring: "The petitioner is a free man, under our flag, and within the protection of our laws." Hoffman went on to celebrate the historic writ: "Such an abrogation of the writ of *habeas corpus*, which has always been considered among English-speaking peoples the most sacred monument of personal freedom, must be unmistakably declared by congress before any court could venture to withhold its benefits from any human being, no matter what his race or color."[24]

More apologetic spokesmen for the court emphasized that it had no choice but to issue the writs. Anxious to deflect the virulent public criticism of the court, United States commissioner for the court, Stephen Houghton, explained that "the courts are utterly powerless, under the law, to do different from what they have done. The Revised Statutes provide that, upon a proper application being made, all parties, except in certain excepted cases, and these cases don't come within the exception, are absolutely entitled to the writ of habeas corpus."[25]

Thus, when a petition was filed, the judges of the district and circuit courts invariably issued a writ of habeas corpus, which entitled the petitioner to a hearing in court as to whether he or she should be admitted into the United States. Although the historic writ of liberty got Chinese into the court, the proceedings before the court fell short of the due process celebrated in Anglo-American jurisprudence. The proceedings in the habeas corpus cases were "novel and strange," as United States Attorney John P. Carey put it in 1890. "There is no criminal that has ever been subjected by order of court to things the Chinese have been subjected to in the enforcement of these acts," he said.[26] Initially, Carey explained, the Chinese person was im-

---

[23] *Black's Law Dictionary*, s.v. "habeas corpus"; U.S. Const., art. I, sec. 9; William F. Duker, *A Constitutional History of Habeas Corpus* (Westport, 1980), 189–94; Select Committee on Immigration and Naturalization, *Chinese Immigration*, 277.

[24] *In re Jung Ah Lung*, 25 F. 141, 142–43 (N.D. Cal. 1885), *aff'd*, *United States v. Jung Ah Lung*, 124 U.S. 621 (1888). On the case, see Janisch, "The Chinese, the Courts, and the Constitution," 673–78; and Fritz, "San Francisco's First Federal Court," 37–38.

[25] Select Committee on Immigration and Naturalization, *Chinese Immigration*, 345. Houghton was referring to 13 Rev. Stat. sec. 755 (1878).

[26] *Ibid.*, 364.

mediately brought before the United States attorney for an examination, without his attorney. Carey's staff took down his statement and then released him on bail. The United States attorney could introduce and use the statement against the Chinese petitioner in court.

Judge Hoffman, who had authorized the procedure, had realized that such an extrajudicial proceeding would probably not stand if challenged. David Fisher, examiner for the Department of Justice, reported to the attorney-general that "Judge Hoffman endeavored to impress very deeply on my mind the fact that he believed this 'Star Chamber' proceeding . . . to be absolutely necessary for the successful carrying out of the provisions of the Restriction Act. He does not attempt, nor seek to defend the proceeding as a legal one, but he thinks that, so long as the Chinamen do not raise the question of the legality of the thing, the Government ought not to, but, to the contrary, ought to give it its sanction and encouragement."[27]

Hoffman and the United States attorney felt the special procedure was a necessary abrogation of due process that enabled the court to get at the truth of the cases. The usual court procedures did not work, government officials thought, for two reasons. One was the lack of documentation for the claims made by the Chinese. For example, petitioners claiming to be born in the United States and exempt from the Chinese exclusion laws had no birth certificates to prove their allegations of citizenship. Nor did laborers have proof of prior residence to establish their exemption from the exclusion acts of 1882 and 1884. They had only witnesses, usually Chinese, to verify their claims.

That led to the second problem for the officials. It was widely believed, especially by exclusionists, that the Chinese and their witnesses lied in the proceedings. "They are all liars and have no regard for an oath so that there is no reliance to be placed in anything they say," complained Carey to the attorney-general in 1888. Commissioner Houghton agreed: "the Chinamen are very adroit people; they are not scrupulous people at all in these matters; even the men who have good cases will swear to lies if they think the lies will help the cases on." Thus the collector and the United States attorney habitually cross-examined petitioners and their witnesses in great detail, trying to find discrepancies in their stories that would jeopardize their claims.[28]

Though it appears that the United States attorney had dropped the preliminary examination by the 1890s, the procedure employed by the court continued to be somewhat "novel and strange." In the 1880s the district and circuit courts had established a special system to handle the overwhelming number of Chinese cases coming before them. To free the judges to attend to the other business of the courts, the judges prescribed that the Chinese cases were to be referred to a United States commissioner, who would try the case *de novo*. That is, the commissioner would come to his own decision about the right of the petitioner to land, independent of the collector's ruling. E. H. Heacock succeeded Houghton as United States commis-

[27] David Fisher to Attorney-General, March 16, 1886, Letters Received, 980/84, Records of the Department of Justice.
[28] John P. Carey to Attorney-General, Sept. 7, 1888, *ibid.*; Select Committee on Immigration and Naturalization, *Chinese Immigration*, 344.

sioner for the courts and served as referee in the Chinese habeas corpus cases between 1892 and 1910. As the referee, Heacock took testimony, made a finding of facts, and recommended that the court either discharge the petitioner, that is, allow him or her to enter the United States, or remand the petitioner to the custody of the collector for deportation.[29]

The customary trial procedures and rules of evidence were not applied strictly in the hearings before Commissioner Heacock. Though both the petitioner and the government were allowed to introduce evidence and to produce and cross-examine witnesses, the hearing was informal in many respects.[30] The commissioner often took an active role in the hearing, requesting, for example, that the attorney for the petitioner obtain further witnesses when the commissioner was not satisfied with the testimony. More striking, however, is the type of evidence Heacock allowed. The district attorney, appearing for the collector, relied on intensive, detailed cross-examination to disprove the petitioner's claim that he was exempt from exclusion as either a merchant or a native-born citizen. In citizenship cases, for example, the petitioner typically claimed that he had been born in San Francisco but had left to live in China when quite young. To prove his claim, the petitioner would present witnesses who remembered his birth in the United States and who could identify the petitioner as the same person who was born here. The witnesses verifying his identity would claim that they had seen him in China with his family and thus could be sure he was the same person.

The district attorney, assuming that the claim was fraudulent and that the witnesses and the petitioner did not actually know each other, would subject them to questioning, often in incredible detail, about their visit in China. He would ask such questions as: How many steps were there out of the petitioner's back door? Where did the petitioner sit in the village schoolhouse? Did the petitioner's mother have bound feet? Who was present when the witness visited the petitioner's home? Did the petitioner accompany the witness to the door, or did he walk outside with him at the end of the visit? The questions were often about visits that had occurred several years earlier, and, not surprisingly, it was difficult to answer them with great accuracy. Furthermore, without the restrictions set by standard trial procedure, there seemed no limit to the type or number of questions the district attorney could ask. Practically any question was fair game.

In general, the petitioners' attorneys accepted the procedure, though attorneys new to the Chinese cases sometimes objected at first. When attorney Waldemar Tuska upset the usual routine of the hearings by objecting to each of the district attorney's questions as immaterial and irrelevant, Commissioner Heacock overruled almost every objection. He explained to the upstart that "in this class of cases the

---

[29] The United States commissioners were given power to hear habeas corpus cases brought by Chinese immigrants in 1888. Stephen Chase Houghton was appointed commissioner in the circuit court, Ward McAllister, Jr., commissioner in the district court. E. H. Heacock, appointed commissioner in 1892, heard such cases for both courts until 1910. Act of Sept. 13, 1888, 25 Stat. 476; Select Committee on Immigration and Naturalization, *Chinese Immigration*, 315, 342–43; *San Francisco Examiner*, March 18, 1910, p. 6.

[30] The observations that follow were obtained from the transcripts of the hearings before the Commissioner Heacock, found in the district court case files, Admiralty Casefiles. See note 4 for details on methodology.

examination is intended to be very full, and the questions are sometimes asked that are immaterial."[31]

The court accepted this departure from normal procedure for the same reason that it had allowed the district attorney a preliminary examination of Chinese in the 1880s. That is, the judges and commissioners shared the belief that Chinese witnesses lied in the hearings. Commissioner Houghton explained the need to take testimony that might appear irrelevant: "It is difficult to get at the truth, particularly so for the reason that there have been so many of these cases running over a long period of time, and the Chinese have learned the routine thoroughly and they have drilled these men who come in here very thoroughly. . . . Now, in attacking the cases, the difficulty is this: If you cross-examine them on the lines they have testified about they are thoroughly fortified. You cannot catch them very well and therefore you must go into collateral matters."[32]

Although the type of evidence allowed in the hearings worked to the Chinese petitioner's disadvantage, Commissioner Heacock often decided in the petitioner's favor, largely because he adhered to the general principles of evidence in making his recommendation. Heacock's decisions hinged on the consistency of the testimony. If there were no discrepancies in the testimony, he followed the "general rule [that] positive testimony as to a particular fact, uncontradicted by any one, should control the decision of the court" and recommended the discharge of the petitioner.[33] Often he was convinced of the veracity of the petitioner's claim. Sometimes, however, he was more dubious but felt bound by the evidence.

Heacock abided by this general rule even though the United States Supreme Court had in 1890 suggested that a lesser standard could be adopted in the Chinese habeas corpus cases. In an appeal from the Circuit Court for the Northern District of California, the Supreme Court ruled in *Quock Ting v. United States* that the court could decide against the petitioner even though his testimony was uncontradicted. Justice Stephen Field reasoned that "there may be such an inherent improbability in the statements of a witness as to induce the court or jury to disregard his evidence, even in the absence of any direct conflicting testimony," especially when the witness has a stake in the outcome of the case. In this case, the Court found the sixteen-year-old petitioner's testimony improbable because he was able to testify about the place of his birth (San Francisco) "with surprising particularity." The Court concluded that he could not have remembered those details on his own as he had not been in San Francisco since he was ten years old, and thus, that his testimony was "coached" and fraudulent.[34]

The Circuit Court of Appeals for the Ninth Circuit addressed the issue again in *Woey Ho v. United States* in 1901 in an appeal from the District Court for the Northern District of California. The case was unusual because the judge, rather than

[31] *In re Wong Yen*, no. 11359, 1897, U.S. District Court for the Northern District of California, Admiralty Casefiles.
[32] Select Committee on Immigration and Naturalization, *Chinese Immigration*, 344.
[33] *Quock Ting v. United States*, 140 U.S. 417, 420 (1891).
[34] *Ibid.*, 418, 420.

Commissioner Heacock, had presided at the hearing. As a consequence, the hearing had taken on a different tone. Though well-known Chinese merchants gave positive, uncontradicted testimony that the petitioner was born in San Francisco, Judge De Haven impatiently refused to allow further testimony as to the reputation and credibility of the merchant witnesses and decided against the petitioner, saying:

> It is not only a very reasonable presumption that a person of her descent coming to this country from China is a person born in China, but the statute makes it the duty of the Court to presume that she was born in China, and to require testimony that is entirely satisfactory to show that she is a native of this country. The Court need not be satisfied beyond a reasonable doubt, but must be satisfied that it is not being made an instrument for the evasion of these exclusion laws. . . . I myself do not believe this testimony, and, not believing it, I do not think the Court should be required to found any judgement on it.

The circuit court of appeals upheld De Haven's decision. The court admitted that De Haven had not elaborated his reasons for disbelieving the testimony; thus the case came "nearer the border line, beyond which courts must not go." But the court held it could not "assume that the court below acted arbitrarily in refusing to believe the testimony of any witness." Before the appellate court reversed the judge, there would have to be clear evidence that the judge erred in some way.[35]

Despite those decisions, however, Heacock continued to make his recommendations based on the general rule that positive, uncontradicted testimony required the release of the petitioner. If there were discrepancies, other factors, such as the seriousness of the discrepancies and the credibility of the witnesses, came into play. Heacock confronted the petitioner with the discrepancies and allowed him an opportunity to resolve them. If the explanation did not completely resolve the discrepancy, Heacock might still discharge the petitioner, citing most often the "manner of testimony" or the "appearance of the witnesses" as reasons. The testimony of respectable members of the "merchant class" or of white witnesses often helped the petitioner's case as well.

Heacock's recommendations carried great weight in the final disposition of the case as the judge routinely confirmed his decisions. Either party could object to Heacock's findings and recommendation, and the judge would then review the transcripts of the commissioner's hearing. But the judge seldom reversed the commissioner, except in the few cases where the judge differed with Heacock on a matter of law. Occasionally, the judge referred the case back to Heacock, asking him to take

[35] *In re Woey Ho*, no. 12099, 1900, U.S. District Court for the Northern District of California, Admiralty Casefiles; *Woey Ho v. United States*, 109 F. 888, 891 (9th Cir. 1901).
[36] The rarity of such a reversal was highlighted in a newspaper article that noted (inaccurately), "This is the first time that Judge Heacock's report in a Chinese case has been disaffirmed." See *San Francisco Call*, Feb. 3, 1898, p. 12.
[37] John Wise to Barry Baldwin, March 13, 1896, Correspondence from the Collector to Other Federal Agencies and the General Public, Records of the Bureau of Customs, Port of San Francisco, RG 36 (National Archives, San Francisco Branch); U.S. Congress, House, *Facts concerning the Enforcement of the Chinese-Exclusion Laws*, 59 Cong., 1 sess., May 25, 1906, pp. 101–2.

Table 1
Disposition of Habeas Corpus Cases Brought by Chinese

	District Court					Circuit Court				
Year	Discharge[a] (%)	Remand[b] (%)	Dismissal[c] (%)	Unknown (%)	N	Discharge[a] (%)	Remand[b] (%)	Dismissal[c] (%)	Unknown (%)	N
1891	73	23	3	—	30	63	27	10	—	206
1892	88	9	3	—	153	68	29	3	—	71
1893	66	33	1	—	308	6	94	—	—	17
1894	80	20	—	—	207	—	—	—	—	0
1895	75	25	—	—	36	—	—	—	—	0
1896	89	11	—	—	35	—	—	—	—	0
1897	60	40	—	—	42	—	—	—	—	0
1898	49	50	.4	—	261	50	50	—	—	2
1899	46	53	.5	.5	182	—	—	—	—	0
1900	46	52	1	.5	177	—	—	—	—	0
1901	52	45	2	.6	162	57	43	—	—	7
1902	63	36	.4	—	242	69	31	—	—	16
1903	60	40	—	—	295	61	39	—	—	23
1904	60	40	—	—	127	77	23	—	—	26
1905	29	68	—	3	31	—	100	—	—	1

[a] Court finds that the petitioner should be allowed to enter the United States, reversing the decision of the collector.

[b] Court upholds the collector's decision to exclude and remands the petitioner for deportation.

[c] Court dismisses the petition because, for example, the petitioner dies before the case comes for a hearing. Sources: Admiralty Dockets, vol. 14–18, U.S. District Court for the Northern District of California, 1891–1905 (Archives Room, U.S. District Court, San Francisco, Cal.); Common Law and Equity Register, U.S. Circuit Court for the Northern District of California, *ibid*.

further testimony and to make a recommendation on the new evidence. In general, however, the judge accepted the commissioner's findings, on the grounds that as the fact finder, the referee was in the best position to evaluate things that did not emerge clearly from the transcripts of hearings, such as the credibility of witnesses.

Chinese generally fared well in the proceedings before Heacock. Until the late 1890s, the commissioner overturned the collector's decision to deny entry in more than 80 percent of the cases. The rate of reversal reached a low of 46 percent in 1899, but otherwise it averaged well over 50 percent until 1905. (See table 1.)

Heacock's method of investigating cases was quite similar to the collector's: both relied on detailed examinations to reveal discrepancies. Yet, as the statistics in table 1 reveal, they frequently came to different conclusions. They differed, claimed the collector and his inspectors, because Chinese immigrants had time to perfect their fraudulent stories by the time they came before the commissioner. Collectors gave accounts of intercepted "coaching letters" and of disreputable attorneys who used their right of counsel to visit their clients and to instruct them on how to testify. Collector John Wise prohibited the detained Chinese in San Francisco from speaking with their friends or attorneys but claimed he could not prevent the coaching altogether, particularly when the United States marshal took the Chinese from his custody to attend their hearings before the court.[37]

There is no doubt that some Chinese made fraudulent claims. When the United States enacted the Chinese exclusion laws, it forced the immigration of Chinese laborers underground. Peasant families in the impoverished Kwangtung Province in China relied heavily on the financial contributions of their kin working in the United States, as well as in other foreign countries. Consequently, many families continued to send their sons to the United States after the passage of the restriction acts, relying on false papers and clan members already in America to help them land. At least eight thousand Chinese have admitted that they originally entered the United States as "paper sons."[38]

But it is impossible to gauge the full extent of illegal entry by Chinese while the restriction laws were in force. The contemporary sources asserting that the vast majority of Chinese, if not all, were in the United States illegally are suspect for their bias. By the time Congress had passed the Chinese restriction acts, Chinese had already been stereotyped as deceitful, cunning, and dishonest.[39] Americans looked to find confirmations of their beliefs that Chinese were corrupt and thus probably exaggerated the extent of fraud. Chinese might possess "coaching papers" as part of an attempt to enter illegally, though even Chinese eligible to enter the United States legally may have used such papers to prepare themselves for the rigorous, detailed questioning by the immigration inspectors and the courts.

Despite the possibility of fraud, however, the difference between the collector's and the commissioner's results was not due simply to coaching. The high reversal rate reflected the different institutional orientation and practices of the court and the collector as well. Of particular importance was the evidentiary standard employed by each.

Although Congress made some stipulations about the evidence Chinese had to present to prove their claims, the secretary of the treasury, as the central administrator of the Chinese laws, and the local collector of customs had the discretion to require other evidence as well. In 1897 the secretary of the treasury required wives and children of merchants to obtain certificates from the Chinese government proving their status, whereas earlier they simply presented witnesses to testify to the fact. In cases in which Chinese alleged that they were born the United States, the secretary also required a higher standard of proof than the court. In contrast to the court's standard of uncontradicted testimony, the secretary instructed the collector that "in no case should the applicant be admitted . . . unless the Collector is *fully satisfied* and the evidence presented is reliable and justifies such admission." Thus

---

[38] See, for example, Wong Yow's account of his entry as a "paper son" in Peter C. Y. Leung, "When a Haircut Was a Luxury: A Chinese Farm Laborer in the Sacramento Delta," *California History*, 64 (Summer 1985), 211–17, esp. 212–13. A 1957 law provided that a Chinese who had entered as a "paper son" could not be deported if he had a parent, spouse, or child who was a United States citizen or a permanent resident alien. Act of Sept. 11, 1957, 71 Stat. 639. In response to this act, 8,000 Chinese had by 1969 confessed that they were paper sons. Thomas W. Chinn, H. Mark Lai, and Philip P. Choy, eds., *A History of the Chinese in California* (San Francisco, 1969), 28.

[39] Stuart Creighton Miller, *The Unwelcome Immigrant: The American Image of the Chinese, 1785–1882* (Berkeley, 1969), 29–31.

the collector could deny entry to a Chinese applicant if he thought his story fraudulent, even though the witnesses' testimony was without discrepancies. The collector of San Francisco imposed further burdens on Chinese in citizenship cases, often requiring the testimony of two white witnesses to prove an applicant's birth in the United States.[40]

Thus the administrators of the Chinese exclusion laws used more stringent standards than the commissioner or the judges. Most Chinese, particularly those with Section 6 certificates from the Chinese government—attesting to their exemption from the exclusion laws as specified in Section 6 of the Chinese Exclusion Act of 1882—succeeded in entering the United States. But those without documentation—wives and children of exempt Chinese, Chinese born in the United States, and merchants returning to their businesses in California—who relied solely on the testimony of witnesses to prove their claims often ended up in the federal court.

In the courts, Chinese found a much more receptive forum. The collector at Port Townsend, Washington, perceived the importance of judicial evidentiary standards to the success of Chinese in the courts.

> The rules of evidence . . . which seem to have been adopted by the courts, are not such as are used by the collector, and as a result, most of the Chinamen are admitted.[41]

In addition to adhering to more favorable evidentiary standards, the court provided Chinese with basic procedural protections that the collector did not, such as the right to representation by an attorney. Attorneys had legal and practical knowledge crucial to the success of their Chinese clients. Well-versed in American legal discourse, attorneys understood how to frame their arguments and how to present evidence in the most favorable light. An extensive working knowledge of the collector's admission procedures, gained either through repeated litigation in the Chinese habeas corpus cases or through previous employment as district attorneys for the federal government, supplemented the attorneys' legal expertise. In contrast, the lack of counsel in the administrative hearings before the collector worked to the disadvantage of Chinese. The secretary of the treasury explicitly forbade Chinese the right to counsel until after the collector had examined and decided to exclude the applicant. Without an attorney to steer the inexperienced applicant through the confusing and detailed questioning, the chances of damaging discrepancies creeping into the testimony greatly increased.[42]

The court drew much attention and criticism from those who thought its deci-

[40] Special Deputy Collector to R. P. Schwerin, Jan. 5, 1897, Correspondence from the Collector to Other Federal Agencies and the General Public, vol. 3, Records of the Bureau of Customs, Port of San Francisco; U.S. Department of the Treasury, *Laws, Treaty, and Regulations relating to the Exclusion of Chinese* (Washington, 1902), paragraph 88, pp. 51–52 (emphasis added); Special Deputy Collector to Henry Hogan, Feb. 4, 1896, Correspondence from the Collector to the General Public, Records of the Bureau of Customs, San Francisco.

[41] J. C. Saunders to the Secretary of the Treasury, Jan. 3, 1894, Letters Received, 980/84, Records of the Department of Justice.

[42] Frederick S. Stratton to the Commissioner-General of Immigration, Dec. 20, 1900, Correspondence from the Collector to Other Federal Agencies and the General Public, Records of the Bureau of Customs, Port of San Francisco.

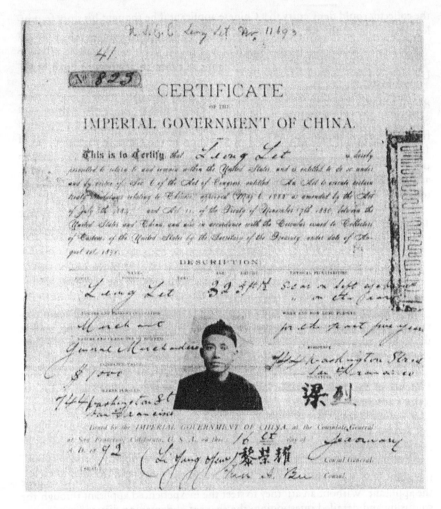

This so-called Section 6 certificate was issued by the Chinese
government to merchants, students, teachers, and diplomats who
claimed exemption from Chinese exclusion laws.
Courtesy National Archives, San Francisco Branch.

sions in the Chinese cases frustrated the purpose of the Chinese exclusion laws. The
San Francisco Call protested, "Why should the Collector keep a force of men at work
questioning and examining Chinese who come to this port if his work can be un-
done by the courts?" Some charged that the federal courts, especially in New York
and Vermont, deliberately released Chinese because they found the Chinese exclusion laws unjust. Others, such as Ed Rosenberg, Secretary of the San Francisco Labor

Council, alleged that federal judges' political connections disposed them to rule in favor of the Chinese.

> The great majority of Federal judges are appointed and advanced through the influence of the trusts and corporations of the country, and these trusts and corporations . . . want cheap and servile labor . . . what more natural than the Federal judges should, wherever and whenever possible, further the interests of those who befriend them?[43]

Most critics, however, hesitated to accuse the court of being intentionally pro-Chinese. Rather, they excused the court's actions on the grounds that a court of law had no choice but to apply objective standards, regardless of the case involved. Such observers tended to portray the court as the "dupe" of the Chinese. They laid the blame on the Chinese and their attorneys who "imposed" upon the dignity of the court by appealing to Anglo-American common law traditions to which, critics seemed to suggest, Chinese had no legitimate claim. One United States senator complained, for example, that any Chinese trying to enter the United States "unhesitatingly commits perjury, [and] is set free, by the 'sacred habeas corpus' writ (a process unknown in Asia)." In a similar vein, the attorney-general warned that "processes of the courts are being abused" by "disingenuous claims and fraudulent devices." Thus, to the anti-Chinese forces and the policy makers, the court, as an institution, appeared a weak and ineffective enforcer of the Chinese exclusion laws. Hampered by legal niceties and traditions, the judiciary seemed unable to protect itself or American society from the intrusion of Chinese.[44]

If "law," as represented by the courts, stood in the way of stringent enforcement of Chinese exclusion, the critics agreed that only one thing could improve the situation: remove the courts' jurisdiction to review the Chinese cases and expand the discretion of administrative officials.

Critics of the courts turned to Congress to obtain legislation, similar to the Immigration Act of 1891, forbidding judicial review in Chinese cases. They attached a rider to the 1894 appropriations bill that achieved their purpose. The new law provided that "in every case where an alien is excluded from admission into the United States under any law or treaty now existing or hereafter made, the decision of the appropriate immigration or customs officers, if adverse to the admission of such alien, shall be final, unless reversed on appeal to the Secretary of the Treasury."[45]

Judge Morrow was only too happy to comply with the law. He dismissed the habeas corpus petition of a Chinese merchant, Lem Moon Sing, on the grounds that

---

[43] *San Francisco Call*, April. 13, 1894, p. 6. For examples of the charge that federal judges thought exclusion unjust, see *ibid*, Jan. 18, 1898, p. 6; and U.S. Department of Commerce and Labor, *Annual Report of the Commissioner-General of Immigration to the Secretary of Commerce and Labor for the Fiscal Year Ended June 30, 1904* (Washington, 1904), 137. *San Francisco Call*, Oct. 24, 1897, p. 16.

[44] *San Francisco Call*, Sept. 26, 1902, p. 1; Charles Garter to Attorney-General, Oct. 25, 1893, Letters Received, 980/84, Records of the Department of Justice; *Congressional Record*, 52 Cong., 1 sess., April 21, 1892, p. 3480; Attorney-General to Judge George Washington Ray, Nov. 23, 1903, Letters Received, 9473/03, Records of the Department of Justice.

[45] Act of Aug. 18, 1894, 28 Stat. 390.

the district court no longer had authority to review such cases.[46] The court immediately felt the effect of the new law. The number of petitions filed dropped dramatically from 207 in 1894 to 36 in 1895 and remained at that low level for the next two years.

But the inactivity did not last long, as Chinese realized that one class of cases—those of Chinese claiming to be born in the United States—was still open to the review of the court. The courts of the northern district of California had long recognized the rights of native-born citizens of Chinese descent. In 1884 the circuit court had ruled that, although Chinese could not become naturalized, Chinese born in the United States of Chinese parents were United States citizens and thus not subject to the Chinese exclusion laws since "no citizen can be excluded from this country except in punishment for crime." The Supreme Court in 1898 adopted the same position and confirmed the rights of Chinese born in the United States.[47]

Not long after his decision in Lem Moon Sing, Morrow held that the 1894 "finality clause" did not apply to cases in which the Chinese person claimed to be a United States citizen. The judge explained: "The determination of the question in the matter now before the court, viz. whether Tom Yum is a citizen, as he claims to be, or is an alien, is the very fact upon which the jurisdiction of the collector depends. If he is an alien, then the collector has undoubted and complete jurisdiction, but, if he is a citizen, the authority vested in him by the provision, in unmistakable terms, does not empower him to finally pass upon the latter's right to come into this country."[48]

The collector of San Francisco deplored Morrow's decision as frustrating the intent of the 1894 law and predicted that there would soon be "a great influx of youngsters from China" claiming to be born in the United States. The collector warned that "the old farce will be re-enacted of the Collector being merely the middle-man between the Chinese and the Courts, without power to enforce the laws of Congress." True to the collector's predictions, in 1898 Chinese again began to resort to the court in large numbers (261 petitions were filed that year), claiming that they were native-born citizens.[49]

Thus, the battle over court jurisdiction was not yet over. Over the next seven years, 1898–1905, the administrative officials tried several strategies to minimize the court's influence in the enforcement of the Chinese exclusion laws. Since the court's evidentiary practices accounted for the decisions favoring Chinese immigrants, one solution was to persuade the court to adopt more stringent evidentiary standards. That approach was not very successful. Congress did not respond to the secretary of the treasury's appeals for legislation requiring the testimony of non-Chinese witnesses in citizenship cases before the court. Furthermore, the court rejected argu-

[46] In re Lem Moon Sing, 158 U.S. 538 (1895).
[47] In re Look Tin Sing, 21 F. at 910–11; United States v. Wong Kim Ark, 169 U.S. 649–75 (1898).
[48] In re Tom Yum, 64 F. 485, 490 (N.D. Cal. 1894).
[49] Wise to Secretary of the Treasury, Nov. 17, 1894, Letters Received, 5306/94, Records of the Department of Justice. For the petitions, see Admiralty Dockets, vol. 16, U.S. District Court for the Northern District of California.

ments made by the United States attorney in San Francisco that the court should consider only evidence taken by the Chinese inspectors.[50]

If the courts would not change their decision-making practices, administrative officials believed that they could gain control over the enforcement of the Chinese exclusion laws only by challenging the power of the courts to hear the citizenship cases. Consequently, they embarked on a program to redefine the roles of the courts and administrative officials.

The first step toward success, officials thought, was to transfer administration of the Chinese exclusion laws to the Bureau of Immigration, headed by the commissioner-general of immigration. The Chinese Bureau was just one part of the Bureau of Customs. The customs collectors supervised large and diverse offices and, officials alleged, could not give the Chinese Bureau the attention and energy necessary to a stringent enforcement of the laws. Thus, in 1903 administration of the Chinese exclusion laws in San Francisco was transferred from the port's collector to the commissioner of immigration there. The commissioner-general of immigration in Washington, D.C., assumed the general supervision of the laws, subject to the review of the secretary of commerce and labor.[51]

This administrative change entrusted enforcement of the Chinese laws to the Bureau of Immigration, an agency accustomed to operating free from court scrutiny. Since the Act of 1891 making the decisions of the bureau on the admission of non-Chinese immigrants final, the district and circuit courts in the Southern District of New York with jurisdiction over Ellis Island had rarely intervened in non-Chinese immigration cases. One New York federal judge commented in 1896, "If the Commissioners [of immigration] wish to order an alien drawn, quartered, and chucked overboard they could do so without interference." Given the bureau's tradition of agency autonomy, it seemed likely that the commissioner-general would resist judicial review of Chinese cases.[52]

With the administration of the Chinese laws under the strong hand of the commissioner-general, Bureau of Immigration officials turned their attention to lessening the power of the courts. They began by insisting that Chinese applicants should exhaust the remedies available through administrative channels before taking their cases to court. Though the statutes provided that Chinese denied entry could take an appeal from the decision of the collector to the secretary of the treasury, and as of 1903 from the commissioner of immigration to the secretary of commerce and labor, Chinese applicants preferred to appeal directly to the court. In the fall of 1903, on the attorney-general's instructions, United States attorneys at all ports requested federal courts to dismiss the habeas corpus cases of Chinese petitioners who had not appealed to the secretary of commerce and labor.[53]

[50] U.S. Secretary of the Treasury, *Annual Report of the Secretary of the Treasury on the State of the Finances for the Year 1896* (Washington, 1897), 798; *San Francisco Chronicle*, Sept. 24, 1904, p. 5.

[51] Act of Feb. 14, 1903, sec. 7, 32 Stat. 825.

[52] Thomas M. Pitkin, *Keepers of the Gate: A History of Ellis Island* (New York, 1975), 23–24.

[53] See, for example, Attorney-General to George B. Curtis, Oct. 8, 1903, Letters Received, 11547/00, Records of the Department of Justice; and *San Francisco Chronicle*, Sept. 24, 1904, p. 5.

A few months later, the attorney-general decided to push for a final resolution of the issue. He instructed the United States attorneys to challenge *all* habeas corpus petitions on the grounds that the decision of the Bureau of Immigration to allow or deny entry, subject to the review of the secretary of commerce and labor, was final and conclusive whether or not the Chinese applicant purported to be a citizen.[54] The attorney-general's argument struck at the heart of the debate; if it was accepted, the courts would no longer review the findings of the administrative officials.

A case from New York in 1904 gave the officials a significant, though not a total, victory. The Supreme Court in *United States v. Sing Tuck* addressed the issue of "exhaustion." Justice Oliver Wendell Holmes, writing for the majority, held that the applicant must go through "the preliminary sifting process provided by the statutes . . . before the courts can be called upon," even if he claimed to be a citizen. Holmes refused to decide whether administrative officers had jurisdiction to decide a Chinese person's citizenship and argued that it did not matter to his decision.[55]

Justice David J. Brewer, with Justice Rufus W. Peckham concurring, rendered an ardent dissent. He argued that the finality clause of the Act of 1894 applied only to aliens, not to citizens. He assailed the majority opinion for allowing an inspector of immigration, "a mere ministerial officer," the power to decide whether a citizen could enter the country. Brewer cut through the arguments of the majority to suggest that racial prejudice lay behind the willingness to subject Chinese-American citizens to such "harsh and arbitrary" proceedings.

> Must an American citizen, seeking to return to this, his native land, be compelled to bring with him two witnesses to prove the place of his birth, or else be denied his right to return and all opportunity of establishing his citizenship in the courts of his country? No such rule is enforced against an American citizen of Anglo-Saxon descent, and if this be, as claimed, a government of laws, and not of men, I do not think it should be enforced against American citizens of Chinese descent.[56]

Justice Holmes explicitly left open the question of what action a court could take *after* the applicant had exhausted his remedies within the agency. Riding high on his successes, the attorney-general was eager to have the remaining question about judicial review settled as quickly as possible, and he pressed District Attorney Marshall B. Woodworth in San Francisco to set up a test case. Woodworth chose the case of Ju Toy, a cook from Oakland, California, who, upon his return from a visit to China, claimed to be born and raised in the United States. The district court, finding the petitioner's evidence of citizenship exceptionally compelling, ordered that Ju Toy be allowed to enter the United States.[57]

---

[54] Attorney-General to Marshall Woodworth, Dec. 22, 1903, Letters Received, 19482/03, Records of the Department of Justice.
[55] *United States v. Sing Tuck*, 194 U.S. 161, 170 (1904).
[56] *Ibid.*, 171, 177, 178.
[57] Attorney-General to Woodworth, Nov. 25, Nov. 28, 1904, Letters Received, 19482/03, Records of the Department of Justice; *In re Ju Toy*, no. 13397, 1905, U.S. District Court for the Northern District of California, Admiralty Casefiles.

In 1905 the government appealed the district court's decision to the Supreme Court in *United States v. Ju Toy* and received a favorable opinion. Justice Holmes, again writing for the majority, disposed of the rights of Chinese-American citizens in a few, brief pages. He held that the decision of the secretary of commerce and labor was final and conclusive even when the petitioner alleged citizenship. "Due process of law does not require a judicial trial" for citizens entering the United States, said Holmes. The courts should abide by the decision of the immigration officials and dismiss all petitions for habeas corpus except those alleging that officials acted unlawfully or abused their authority.[58]

Justice Brewer, again dissenting with Justice Peckham, protested that "such a decision . . . is appalling." Not only did the Court condone the Bureau of Immigration's procedure, "a star chamber proceeding of the most stringent sort," but also, in allowing the bureau to deport Ju Toy, it sanctioned the banishment by ministerial officers of an American "guilty of no crime." Such an action "strips him of all the rights which are given to a citizen."[59]

With the *Ju Toy* opinion, the government succeeded in cutting off the access of the Chinese to the courts. The district court in northern California would no longer investigate the right of a petitioner to enter the United States. When Chinese petitioned for habeas corpus after *Ju Toy*, the court routinely dismissed the petitions on the grounds that the detentions were lawful.

The Supreme Court seemed to open a door for procedural review, however, even while it prohibited the lower courts from a substantive review of the Bureau of Immigration's actions. In 1908 the Court held that the lower courts still had authority to ensure that the bureau maintained certain basic procedures and afforded aliens a fair hearing.[60] The lower courts were then called upon to venture into novel legal territory, to decide what due process was required in the new administrative state. Chinese, quick to pursue the new line of review, argued that due process required the Bureau of Immigration to adopt more courtlike procedures. The federal courts in San Francisco, however, refused to impose judicial procedures on the bureau, generally allowing it to follow its own practices. Though the courts' unwillingness to intervene after 1908 stood in stark contrast to their earlier record, the courts' actions were not necessarily inconsistent. Judges had felt obligated to follow the courts' institutional norms and practices when they had decided the right of Chinese to enter the United States, but they did not believe administrative officials were bound by the same rules. Judges perceived the functions of courts and agencies to be different and to require distinct procedures. Furthermore, the judges in San Francisco had never been anxious to hear the Chinese habeas corpus cases and were probably content to let the Bureau of Immigration assume responsibility for Chinese exclusion.

The courts' abdication in immigration policy made it more difficult for many

[58] *United States v. Ju Toy*, 198 U.S. 253, 261–63 (1905).
[59] *Ibid.*, 269, 268, 279.
[60] *Chin Yow v. United States*, 28 S. Ct. 201 (1908). For an example of cases involving procedural review, see *Low Wah Suey v. Backus*, 225 U.S. 460 (1912).

Chinese to enter the United States, though some found other ways to challenge or evade the bureau's decisions. Chinese learned how to meet the bureau's strict standards for admission or bypassed the inspection process by entering illegally. Bureau of Immigration officials remained frustrated by the persistence of the Chinese, complaining at one point that the law regulating Chinese immigration was "probably the most difficult piece of legislation to enforce ever placed upon the statute books."[61] But, they were quick to admit, enforcement was much easier without the courts' involvement.

In the end, then, Chinese became subject to the same administrative discretion as other immigrants. That they were able to challenge the discretion for so long, and with such success, is largely due to the organization and persistence of the Chinese and their attorneys. They continually brought their cases before the courts, and they fashioned their claims according to Anglo-American legal traditions that courts found difficult to refuse.

The courts' allegiance to those legal traditions in the Chinese habeas corpus cases illustrates the power of the idea of the rule of law in Anglo-American jurisprudence. As E. P. Thompson asserts in *Whigs and Hunters,* "law" presupposes "standards of universality and equality" that can temper the effects of even the most discriminatory laws. But the courts' decisons cannot be adequately explained by such a general notion of the rule of law, for the judges clearly departed from legal norms at certain stages of the Chinese hearings. They broke some procedural rules, allowing the constitutionally questionable *ex parte* examination before the United States attorney and the "novel and strange" hearings before the commissioner. But when it came to other practices—the granting of habeas corpus petitions and the application of judicial evidentiary standards—the judges were less willing to deviate from legal tradition. That leaves the perplexing question of why the judges chose to draw the line where they did.[62]

The answer may be that the judges and the commissioner considered the doctrine of habeas corpus and the principles of evidence closely tied to what it meant to be a court. Their conception of the court, although complex, undoubtedly embraced a key principle in Anglo-American thought, that courts should be independent of personal or political influence.

Certain legal procedures, such as the writ of habeas corpus and judicial evidentiary standards, were more important than others in maintaining judicial independence, or at least its semblance. As Judge Hoffman's vehement defense of the writ suggests, habeas corpus provided a powerful, historic symbol of the supremacy of law over the rulers. It promised that a government could not confine an individual without just cause and that the courts, as the ones responsible for issuing the writs,

[61] U.S. Department of Commerce and Labor, *Annual Report of the Commissioner-General of Immigration for the Fiscal Year Ended June 30, 1909* (Washington, 1909), 127.

[62] E. P. Thompson, *Whigs and Hunters: The Origin of the Black Act* (New York, 1975), 258–69. I am indebted to Robert Gordon for bringing this issue to my attention. My thinking on this issue has been stimulated by the works of Douglas Hay, "Property, Authority, and the Criminal Law," in *Albion's Fatal Tree: Crime and Society in Eighteenth-Century England* (New York, 1975); Martin Shapiro, *Courts: A Comparative and Political Analysis* (Chicago, 1981); and Thompson, *Whigs and Hunters.*

would guard against arbitrary government and preserve law from the influence of politics. So, too, the evidentiary standards were central to the ideal of judicial independence because they committed judges to decide cases on the evidence, not on intuition or personal belief. The judges and commissioner of the federal courts in San Francisco clearly felt a tension between their personal beliefs and judicial evidentiary standards. They all believed that Chinese lied in the proceedings, but judicial norms did not allow them to take that belief into consideration unless there was proof of the perjury. In one rare instance, Judge De Haven allowed his gut instincts to overcome evidentiary requirements. While the circuit court of appeals upheld Judge De Haven's decision in *Woey Ho v. United States*, the appellate court warned that the case "comes nearer the border line, beyond which the courts must not go."[63] By basing his decision on his personal belief rather than the evidence presented, De Haven threatened to cross the line distinguishing judicial independence from arbitrary power. The federal judges and commissioner in San Francisco were not often willing to transgress that line, perhaps because to do so would violate their notion of judicial duty and would undermine the conception of the court as an independent, neutral, and just institution.

Thus, though the judicial officers of the courts approached the Chinese habeas corpus cases with divided loyalties, the logic and the norms of the court as an institution proved stronger than politics. The judges and the commissioner shared their contemporaries' negative, stereotypical view of the Chinese and supported the Chinese exclusion policy. Consequently, they allowed certain procedures that made it more difficult for Chinese to prove their claims. Yet the judges, and particularly the commissioner, also felt bound by judicial rules and norms that called for hearing and weighing evidence in individual cases, regardless of the litigants' Chinese birth or descent. In this instance, institutional obligations triumphed over personal loyalties.

[63] *Woey Ho v. United States*, 109 F. at 891.

Protection of the Family Home
from Seizure by Creditors:
The Sources and Evolution
of a Legal Principle

JOSEPH W. MCKNIGHT*

IN POPULAR AS WELL AS LEGAL PARLANCE, HOMESTEAD MEANS NOT only family home but property that is accorded particular protection because it is the family home. From one American state to another, and elsewhere as well, the most significant protection of the home is that which is accorded it against seizure by the owner's creditors for payment of general, private debts. The term homestead was also once used to refer to a sovereign grant of western lands where the frontiersman and his family made their home. But it is in the sense of a home protected from creditors that the concept of homestead is one of the most significant later contributions to family jurisprudence.

Legal tradition has long acknowledged that this notion of homestead emerged on the Mexican-Texan frontier. But the sources and development of the concept have never been clearly demonstrated. Simply stated, the tradition is that an 1829 act of the Mexican state of Coahuila y Texas recodified Castilian exemption principles and extended them to sovereign grants of land. Carrying this development forward, a Texas act of 1839 defined exempt lands in terms of the family home, and from this model the principle of homestead exemption from the claims of creditors spread throughout the United States and beyond.

Although much has been written about the origin of the Texas homestead law and its Hispano-Mexican antecedents, there are several crucial points in its development that require reexamination.[1] If the

*Joseph W. McKnight is professor of law at Southern Methodist University. He is grateful to his assistants, Robert C. White and Kathleen LaValle, for the aid they have given him in preparing his manuscript for publication.

[1]C. W. Raines, "Enduring Laws of the Republic of Texas," *Quarterly of the Texas State Historical Association*, I (Oct., 1897), 96, 105–107; A. E. Wilkinson, "The Author of the Texas Homestead Exemption Law," *Southwestern Historical Quarterly*, XX (July, 1916), 35; Eugene C. Barker, *The Life of Stephen F. Austin, Founder of Texas, 1793–1836: A Chapter in the Westward Movement of the Anglo-American People* (Nashville,

1829 act of Coahuila y Texas and the 1839 Texas homestead act are
the links that bind modern homestead-exemption law to the Hispanic
past, two points must be established. First, the text of the 1829 act
must perpetuate some aspects of Hispanic debtor-exemption law.
Second, these elements of the 1829 act must be carried forward by the
1839 act.

In Spanish law the principle of property exempt from creditors'
claims (*bienes inembargables*) received its fullest treatment from the
Spanish legal commentators as a part of the law related to the enforcement of judgments, rather than as a part of family law. This principle
of exempt property was rooted in Castilian law and was related to a
larger body of rules related to relief from the stress of debt. As applied
to Spanish colonists, all of these laws can be classified under two basic
heads: (1) relief from public charges as incentives to colonization, and
(2) principles of general application for relief from private debts, including privileges of special classes of citizens that in some cases extended to so many persons as to be regarded as applicable to the
citizenry in general. Under the first head, an inducement to colonization normally took the form of waiver of taxes, tithes, and imposts.[2]
In each instance these privileges were granted by Spanish law for a
fixed number of years, and the Mexican government perpetuated this
policy. Under the second head of laws offering relief to debtors from
private debts generally, there are three further types of rules: moratorium for payment of debts, release from imprisonment for debt, and
property exempt from liability for debt. The most significant of these
principles is the last, by which certain movables and some immovables
were exempt from pledge and seizure for satisfaction of private debts.

The great medieval code, the *Siete Partidas*, compiled in the mid-
thirteenth century and promulgated a century later, protected certain
essential movables from pledge on the part of debtors. These items

---

1925), 221–227; José Uriarte, "Derecho agrario español: propiedad familiar," *Revista
crítica de derecho inmobilario*, XI (1935), 481, 486–488; Agustín Luna Serrano, *El pa-
trimonio familiar: la ley española de 15 de julio de 1952* (Madrid, 1952), 29–30; Gerald
Ashford, "Jacksonian Liberalism and Spanish Law in Early Texas," *Southwestern Historical Quarterly*, LVII (July, 1953), 1, 8–10; Lena London, "The Initial Homestead Exemption in Texas," ibid. (Apr., 1954), 432.

[2]For example, see *Novísima Recopilación* VII. 22.3 for settlers in the Sierra Morena
(1767), no. 10 (lands not subject to pledge or seizure for taxes), no. 56 (colonists not subject to certain tribute and duties for ten years), no. 57 (nor tithes for four years), no. 61
(lands not subject to mortgage). For other peninsular examples, see *Novísima Recopilación* VII. 22.6–9. Waiver of duties was also used as a commercial inducement. See Jack
D. L. Holmes, *Gayoso: The Life of a Spanish Governor in the Mississippi Valley, 1789–
1799* (Baton Rouge, 1965), 141.

included clothing, beds, and other things necessary for daily use, although in the more restricted context of a debtor's assignment of his property to his creditors, it was said that only everyday linen clothing was protected.[3] Apart from the general principle of exemption from pledge, property exempt from creditors' seizure tended to be treated as the privilege of two principal classes: fighting men and farmers.

During the succeeding centuries the protection of property of these two privileged groups was restated and extended. The *Partidas* had exempted the horses and arms of knights, their pay, and the land allotted to their support.[4] In 1435 this protection was extended to the horses and arms of gentry (*hidalgos*), and the protection of knights' property was reiterated. Both were reconfirmed in 1476, and this principle was restated a century later.[5]

The protection offered to the agricultural community was also subject to periodic reassurance. The thirteenth-century *Fuero Real*, as well as the *Partidas*, made special provision for farmers' plow animals and implements. The *Fuero Real* forbade pledging them for debt and prohibited enforcement of any pledges made. Not only were such pledges unenforceable, but a civil penalty was imposed for violation of the law—a penalty to be shared equally by the crown and the pledgor. But if exemption from *seizure* was granted by the *Fuero Real*, it was only by implication. In the *Partidas*, however, exemption from claims was made explicit for plow oxen, but whether the exemption was absolute is not clear.[6] The provisions concerning forbidden pledges were confirmed by the *Ordenamiento de Alcalá* of 1348, and the absolute exemption of a pair of plow oxen was decreed in 1435. Livestock

---

[3]*Siete Partidas* V. 13.5, 15.1. See also *Fuero Viejo* III. 4.2 (1056) with respect to exemption privileges of the gentry. The provision regarding a debtor's assignment of property went on to say that if the debt was incurred in a less-than-arm's-length transaction (for example, owed to one's descendent or business partner), the judge ought to make an allowance of property for the debtor according to his station. Ibid.

[4]*Siete Partidas* III. 27.3. See also ibid., II. 21.23, which is not quite so absolute in its terms.

[5]For the rule generated by Petitions 41 (1435), 23 (1476), and 27 (1593), see *Novísima Recopilación* XI. 31.13. The exempt property of knights and gentry is summarized in Juan de Hevia Bolaños, *Curia Filípica* (Valladolid, 1600), II. 16.7. Hevia makes the further point that arms could not be seized even for debts due to the crown. *Nueva Recopilación* IV. 21.27; *Novísima Recopilación* XI. 31.13.

[6]*Fuero Real* III. 19.5; *Siete Partidas* III. 27.3, V. 13.4. *Siete Partidas* V. 13.4 seems to be in absolute terms, whereas *Siete Partidas* III. 27.3 states that the exemption prevails only as long as other assets are available for satisfaction of the creditor's claim.
The functional and conceptual relationship between voluntary pledge and the involuntary execution process was perfectly clear to the Spanish commentators. It was equally clear to those who enacted the provision forbidding mortgage as well as seizure of the Texas homestead. Texas, *Constitution* (1876), Art. XVI, Sec. 50.

of urban folk, villagers, and the Mesta was given similar treatment in 1462. In 1476 the exemption of plow animals was reiterated, and this protection was confirmed twenty years later. It was further provided that contracts that purported to be secured by such exempt property were declared void, and any creditor who extracted such an agreement lost not only the security but the debt itself.[7] An ordinance of 1594 reenumerated farmers' exemptions: plow animals, tools (*herramientas*), implements, and provisions. Agricultural exemptions were restated in 1619 and 1633, when the exemption of breeding stock of sheepraisers was also provided.[8]

From the sixteenth century special protection was extended to the property of those engaged in a great variety of callings, both in the Indies and on the peninsula.[9] When exemption was finally extended to the tools of trade of artisans and craftsmen in 1786, the exemption of tools of trade became virtually universal.[10] In the lists of exempt property compiled by legal scholars toward the end of the eighteenth century, certain other types of chattels—in addition to class-exemptions and tools of trade—were treated as generally exempt: wearing apparel, beds, and other things necessary for daily use, agricultural implements, and beasts of the plow.[11] By the early nineteenth century both Juan

---

[7]*Ordenamiento de Alcalá* 18.2, *Novísima Recopilación* XI. 31.12; Petition 41 (1435), ibid., 31.13; Petition 17 (1462), reiterated in Petitions 18 and 19 (1473), ibid., 31.9; Petition 25 (1476), ibid., 31.12; Leyes de la Hermandad (1496), ibid., 31.14 (oxen and mules were also protected); Petition 25 (1476), ibid., 31.12. As a national stockmen's (particularly sheepraisers') association, the Mesta was extended special protection.

[8]Francisco de Elizondo, *Practica universal forense de los tribunales superiores é inferiores, de España, y de las Indias* (10 vols.; 3rd ed.; Madrid, 1796), III, 25–26; Hevia Bolaños, *Curia Filípica*, II. 16.9. For the seventeenth-century exemptions, see *Novísima Recopilación* XI. 31.16 (1619; beasts of the plow and tools of trade for farmers); Ch. 1 (1633), ibid., 31.15; ibid., 31.17.

[9]Regarding the Indies, see for example the following: sugar makers, laws of 1529, 1534, 1537, 1557, 1570, 1588, 1605, *Recopilación de Indias* V. 14.4; metalurgists and sugar makers, laws of 1538, 1572, ibid., 14.5; persons engaged in mining, law of 1540, ibid., 14.3; pearl divers, law of 1593, ibid., 14.2; the arms and horses of anyone, laws of 1537, 1554, 1555, 1572, ibid., 14.6. Holmes, *Gayoso*, 21, refers to the decree of 1789 concerning fishermen.

Examples for the peninsula include books of advocates and students, Hevia Bolaños, *Curia Filípica* II. 16.8; salaries of judges, ibid., 16.11; tools of trade of silk makers, *Novísima Recopilación* XI. 31.18.

It is not suggested that all laws of Castile from the seventeenth and eighteenth centuries (on this or any other subject) were applicable to the Indies. *Recopilación de Indias* II. 1.39 (1614, 1626, 1645). But the peninsular development is traced to show the prevailing Castilian law that was reflected in the standard treatises in later use on the peninsula and in New Spain.

[10]*Novísima Recopilación* XI. 31.19.

[11]For compilations of exemption provisions, see Ignacio Asso and Miguel Manuel,

Sala and José María Alvarez had given succinct generalizations of the subject matter of exemption, which theretofore had been dealt with as a compendious exercise in cataloging.[12]

Exemptions of land occurred only in exceptional situations. Among the privileges extended to the nobility and gentry was the assurance that their homes (*casas*) would be inviolate from seizure under execution, except in payment of debts due to the crown. At the other end of the social ladder, plowed and seeded lands were also exempt to farmers.[13]

In addition to the rules of law protecting certain property from liability, there were two further types of laws that gave relief to debtors. First, there was the extraordinary remedy of moratorium, which might be granted by the crown in favor of debtors. But the privilege from imprisonment for debt was far more significant to those classes of debtors to whom it applied. In 1633 farmers were guaranteed freedom from imprisonment for debt from July to December, and by the mid-eighteenth century Castilian law had extended the privilege of exemption from arrest and imprisonment for debt to a number of other groups: nobles (except for delicts), doctors, lawyers, and women.[14] The

Instituciones del derecho civil de Castilla (6th ed.; Madrid, 1805), 306; Josef Febrero, *Librería de escribanos, é instrucción jurídica theorico practica de principiantes* (3rd ed.; 6 vols.; Madrid, 1783–1786), Pt. 2, III, 455–470.

For the exemption of wearing apparel, etc., see Asso and Manuel, *Instituciones del derecho civil*, citing Hevia Bolaños, *Curia Filipica* II. 16.19, relying on *Siete Partidas* V. 13.5; *Nueva Recopilación* I. 12.20; the commentaries of Bartolus and Baldus on Codex VII. 17.1, *Que res pignari obligari possunt*; and Jerónimo Castillo de Bobadilla, *Política para regidores . . .* (Madrid, 1597), III. 15.64. The ultimate source of the clothing exemption may be Biblical. Deut. 24:10, 12, 13 obliquely forbade taking clothing as a pledge. Exodus 22:26, 27 is to the same effect.

A constitution of Emperor Frederick II, *Consuetudines Feudorum* V. 17.11, is similar to *Siete Partidas* V. 13.4 and III. 27.3 with respect to exemptions from seizure of plow animals and farm tools.

12Juan Sala, *Ilustración del derecho real de España* (2 vols.; 2nd ed.; Madrid, 1820), II, 297, 298; José María Alvarez, *Instituciones de derecho real de Castilla y de Indias* (3 vols.; Guatemala City, 1818–1820), III, Appendix 8, pp. 319–320. Alvarez's treatment of the subject is very brief.

13Regarding the nobility and gentry, see *Ordenamiento de Alcalá* 18.4, 32.57, and Petitions 7 and 9 (1348), in *Nueva Recopilación* VI. 1.9, 2.3, and 2.10, and *Novísima Recopilación* VI. 2.1, respectively. See also Petition 44 (1593), in *Nueva Recopilación* VI. 2.13 and *Novísima Recopilación* VI. 2.13; Petition 33 (1593) in *Nueva Recopilación* II. 4.61 and *Novísima Recopilación* VI. 2.14. See also Hevia Bolaños, *Curia Filipica* II. 16.7.

In his edition of Asso and Manuel, Joaquín Palacios noted that homes of the nobility and gentry were in fact available for satisfaction of debts in the absence of other property. [Ignacio Jordan] Asso and [Miguel] Manuel, *Instituciones del derecho civil de Castilla*, ed. Joaquín María Palacios (2 vols.; 7th ed.; Madrid, 1806), II, 319.

Concerning exemptions allowed to farmers, see Pragmatica of Mar. 9, 1594, *Novísima Recopilación* XI. 31.15.1.

14*Novísima Recopilación* XI. 33.1–4 (on moratorium); Decree of 1619, ibid., 31.16, and blanket extension of the privilege to rural laborers, skilled urban workers, and artisans in 1786 virtually eliminated imprisonment for debt as a practical means of debt enforcement.[15] As long as the threat of imprisonment for debt was an effective means of debt enforcement, however, exemptions of property from seizure must have been regarded as of secondary importance for debtors' protection. Finally, under the rules relating to assignments for the benefit of creditors (*cessio bonorum*), judges had long allowed the debtor to retain his clothing, and in some instances further necessaries. The making of an assignment had been a long-standing means of avoiding imprisonment for debt.

The records of the Spanish borderlands during the late eighteenth century show no awareness of property exempt from private debt.[16] But there was little occasion to assert exemption from seizure when civil litigation of any kind was uncommon and disputes involving monetary awards and their enforcement were unusual. At any rate, the early families of New Mexico and Texas, who were otherwise so proud of their lineage, did not assert their privileges as *hidalgos* in response to creditors' claims. Nor are soldiers found to assert the *fuero militar* against creditors.[17] Among the Anglo-American colonists in Mexican

---

Decree of 1633, ch. 2, ibid., 31.15.2 (farmers protected from imprisonment). On the significance of protection from imprisonment, see Francisco Tomas Valiente, "La prisión por deudas en los derechos castellanos y aragones," *Anuario de historia de derecho español*, XXX (1960), 249, 411–421. On other groups exempted from imprisonment, see Asso and Manuel, *Instituciones del derecho civil* (6th ed.), 307. The list given there is somewhat more refined and detailed.

15Pragmatica of May 27, 1786, *Novísima Recopilación* XI. 31.19 (rural laborers, skilled urban workers, and artisans); ibid., VI. 4.14 (1768) (those in military service); ibid., VII. 29.11 (1789) (horse-breeders). See also Valiente, "La prisión por deudas," 419–420.

16If it had been perceived that beds, clothing, and other things necessary for daily use were exempt from execution (Hevia Bolaños, *Curia Filipica* II. 16.19), one would think it unlikely that a man would mortgage all the goods in his home for payment of an existing debt (for 359 pesos). Mortgage by Julian de Arocha to José Antonio de Bustillos y Zavallos, 1790, Bexar Archives (Bexar County Courthouse, San Antonio). In Piernas v. Fernandez, Sept. 9, 1809, Bexar Archives (microfilm; Eugene C. Barker Texas History Center, University of Texas, Austin; cited hereafter as BTHC), a resident of Nacogdoches was allowed to avoid execution of a judgment by undertaking to pay within one year. All of his property was seized and held pending satisfaction. There is no suggestion in the voluminous record that any of the property was treated as exempt.

17A capitulation of Viceroy Luis de Velasco (1595) conferred the status of *hidalgo* on Juan de Oñate's settlers of New Mexico, pursuant to Ordenanzas para nuevos descubrimientos y poblaciones, No. 99 (1573), *Recopilación de Indias* IV. 6.6, which was confirmed by royal *cédula* of July 8, 1802. Pedro Bautista Pino, "Exposición sucinta y sencilla de la provincia del Nuevo Mexico . . . ," H. Bailey Carroll and J. Villasana Haggard (eds. & trans.), *Three New Mexico Chronicles* . . . (Albuquerque, 1942), 8, 9, 154, 156, 157, 209; Angelico Chavez, *Origins of New Mexico Families in the Spanish Colonial Period* . . . (Santa Fe, 1954), xiv–xv. The Canary Islanders of San Antonio were given

Texas in the 1820s, however, suits for debts were numerous, and there was no established tradition of exempt property in Texas to deter creditors from asserting their claims.

Moving West was a frequent early nineteenth-century response to the series of economic crises in the new American nation. A move to Texas where land was cheap was particularly attractive to venturous spirits in the southern United States. The Texas colonists were by no means generally insolvent, but there were some who came to Texas with the hope of leaving debts permanently behind them, and those debts were sometimes large.[18] By the mid-1820s Texas had achieved the reputation as a haven for debtors. First in 1826 and again in 1828 the United States Congress directed questions to the president concerning the obvious irritant to American creditors whose debtors had removed themselves to Mexican territory.[19] The perception of Texas as a refuge for debtors was a consequence of several factors: Texas's primitive judicial system, the difficulty of finding debtors there, and, most particularly, the reluctance of local judges to enforce foreign debts against fellow colonists.[20] From the beginning of the negotiations

the same status. The dignity was conferred on the first settlers of the new town of San Fernando de Béjar in 1731. See Frederick C. Chabot, *With the Makers of San Antonio* (San Antonio, 1937), 144, 165. See also T. R. Fehrenbach, *Lone Star: A History of Texas and the Texans* (New York, 1968), 54–55.

Hidalgos (gentlemen; gentry) were entitled to their houses, arms, and horses. Alvarez, *Instituciones de derecho real*, III, Appendix 8, p. 300; Asso and Manuel, *Instituciones del derecho civil*, 306, citing *Nueva Recopilación* V. 17.6 and IV. 21.27 (later consolidated as *Novísima Recopilación* XI. 31.13) for the same proposition. In his 1806 edition of Asso and Manuel, *Instituciones*, II, 319, Palacios notes that neither of the laws cited prohibited execution against the *home* (la casa de la morada) of a noble or gentleman, though *Nueva Recopilación* II. 4.61 did. See also *Novísima Recopilación* VI. 2.14. For other privileges of *hidalgos* with respect to debts, see Petitions 8 and 9 (1348) and Petition 104 (1545), *Novísima Recopilación* VI. 2.2; Laws of Toro 79, ibid., 2.10.

On the *fuero militar*, see Lyle McAllister, *The Fuero Militar in New Spain, 1764–1800* (Gainesville, Fla., 1957), 8. Hevia Bolaños, *Curia Filipica* II. 16.11 stated that a soldier's pay was exempt. Eugenio de Tapia (ed.), *Febrero novísimo; o, librería de jueces, abogados, escribanos, y medicos legistas . . .* (Valencia, 1829), V. 71 (No. 47), indicated that a soldier's pay was exempt from execution unless no other property was available.

[18]Barker, *Life of Stephen F. Austin*, 154. See also J. Thomas to Stephen F. Austin, Apr. 15, 1824, Eugene C. Barker (ed.), *The Austin Papers* (3 vols.; Vols. I, II, Washington, D.C., 1924–1928; Vol. III, Austin, 1927), I, Pt. 1, 765–766.

[19]Margaret Swett Henson, *Samuel May Williams, Early Texas Entrepreneur* (College Station, Tex., 1976), 3; Mark E. Nackman, "Anglo-American Migrants to the West: Men of Broken Fortunes? The Case of Texas, 1821–46," *Western Historical Quarterly*, V (Oct., 1974), 441, 443, 444, 446; John Quincy Adams to House of Representatives, Dec. 28, 1826, enclosing report by Henry Clay, Dec. 26, 1826, United States, Congress, *American State Papers: Documents, Legislative and Executive of the Congress of the United States . . .,* Class I: Foreign Relations (38 vols.; Washington, D.C., 1832–1861), VI, 366, 822–823 (U.S. Serial 06).

[20]Austin wrote to Lorenzo de Zavala on June 24, 1828, "hasta ahora las autoridades

of the commercial treaty between the United States and Mexico in the mid-1820s until its promulgation in 1832, the proposed solution of this problem was a provision that citizens of each nation should have access to the courts of the other.

The question of enforceability of foreign debts was raised in Stephen F. Austin's colony early in its judicial history. In response to an inquiry from Asa Mitchel, Austin wrote his alcalde Josiah Bell, in September, 1823, that there was no law or custom to preclude the collection of such debts and that Bell should proceed to consider the claim before him. Speculating that Mexican law might be different from that with which he was more familiar, the debtor apparently had convinced the judge that the point against enforcement was worth raising. The problem was of sufficient importance to Austin for him to make a special provision in his local regulations for debts contracted abroad between persons who were not then residents of Texas. Austin's Civil Regulations provided that application for enforcement of foreign debts be made to "the judge of the colony," a position he then held, rather than to an alcalde.[21] After approval of his Regulations by the departmental executive at Béxar, but before their approval by the governor, Austin sent a memorial on the subject to the congress of Coahuila y Texas through Baron de Bastrop, Texas's elected representative at Saltillo. In his memorial Austin suggested a twelve-year moratorium on the enforcement of prior foreign debts of settlers so that they would be free from the harassment of creditors to establish themselves as useful citizens.[22] Austin's suggestion, however, produced no response from the congress.

From the American point of view it is evident that collection of debts from Texans continued to be regarded as a problem. Notes executed by Texan colonists before their migration to Texas apparently were a popular item of merchandise among speculators. At least one

---

no han procedido en estos casos. . . ." Barker (ed.), *The Austin Papers*, II, 47, 49 (*quotation*).

21Austin to Josiah H. Bell, Sept. 5, 1823, Barker (ed.), *The Austin Papers*, I, Pt. 1, 693; Civil Regulations, art. 27, [Stephen F. Austin], *Translation of the Laws, Orders, and Contracts, on Colonization, from January, 1821, up to This Time* (San Filipe [*sic*] de Austin, 1829), 64 (quotation); David B. Gracy (ed.), *Establishing Austin's Colony: The First Book Printed In Texas, with the Laws, Orders, and Contracts of Colonization* (Austin, 1970), 75, 81 (quotation); Dudley G. Wooten (ed.), *A Comprehensive History of Texas, 1685 to 1897* (2 vols.; Dallas, 1898), I, 481, 486.

22Austin's Regulations had been approved by the departmental executive (*jefe politico*) of Texas on May 24, 1824, and by the governor of Coahuila y Texas on Feb. 12, 1825. Barker, *Life of Stephen F. Austin*, 223.

Austin's memorial to the legislature through Baron de Bastrop, Dec. 22, 1824, Barker (ed.), *The Austin Papers*, I, Pt. 1, 996–997, 1,000. Austin's phrase was "old foreign debts." Ibid., 997.

colonist was prompted to post a notice upon his arrival in San Felipe de Austin that all the property he brought with him belonged to his wife, thus discouraging the unwary from purchasing foreign claims against him.[23]

In response to a question from the House of Representatives to President John Quincy Adams, Secretary of State Henry Clay reported on January 14, 1828, that "upon inquiry of the [Mexican] minister . . . , he stated that he was not aware of the existence of any such impediment [to debt collection in Mexican courts], but that, on the contrary, he believed the tribunals of his country were open alike to foreigners and inhabitants for the recovery of their debts. . . ." The secretary further reported that "an instruction has been addressed to the minister of the United States at Mexico to inquire into the true state of the fact and, if necessary, to make such representations or remonstrances as its actual condition may call for." From Mexico Joel Poinsett responded to Secretary Clay's inquiry on March 15, 1828.[24] Poinsett had inquired of the Mexican government and was told that the courts of Mexico were open to the citizens of both nations on an equal basis, and hence to his knowledge there were no problems of debt enforcement in Texas.[25]

By mid-1828 word had reached Texas that the United States and Mexico had entered into a commercial treaty to implement debt enforcement and that the treaty was about to be ratified by the United States Senate. Consequently Austin renewed his efforts for legislation to forestall debt collection. About this time Anthony Butler of Mississippi was pressing Austin for payment of old personal debts of some size.[26] His own debts, therefore, would have made Austin particularly sympathetic as to those of his colonists.

23Gerald Ashford, *Spanish Texas, Yesterday and Today* (Austin, 1971), 238, 239; Peter Ellis Bean to Austin, Mar. 18, 1829, Barker (ed.), *The Austin Papers*, II, 192; "Notice of Ownership of Property," Barker (ed.), *The Austin Papers*, I, Pt. 2, 1,255–1,256.

24Adams to House of Representatives, Jan. 15, 1828, enclosing report by Henry Clay, Jan. 14, 1828, *American State Papers*, Foreign Relations, VI, 822–823; Despatch No. 120, responding to Instruction No. 126, Despatches from United States Ministers to Mexico, 1823–1906, Washington National Archives, 1946–1955 (National Archives Microfilm Publications, Microcopy No. M-97).

25For some insights into the process of negotiation of the terms of the Mexican-American commercial treaty see *American State Papers*, Foreign Relations, VI, 603 (art. 12 of the projet of the treaty of 1826, which became art. 14 of the treaties of 1826, 1828, and 1831), 585 (protocol of the second conference of the plenipotentiaries, Sept. 13, 1825), 594 (protocol of the ninth conference, June 15, 1826), 609 (art. 14 of treaty of 1826), 954 (art. 14 of treaty of 1828).

26See Barker, *Life of Stephen F. Austin*, 286–287. Butler, who had achieved some prominence in Kentucky, was living in Mississippi when commissioned as United States chargé d'affaires in Mexico in October, 1829. His successor presented his credentials in Mexico on May 11, 1836. Eugene C. Barker, "President Jackson and the Texas Revolution," *American Historical Review*, XII (July, 1907), 791.

Austin's approach to the state legislature on this occasion was far better planned than his first attempt. Toward the end of June, 1828, he addressed long letters to Governor José María Viesca, Boundary Commissioner Manuel de Mier y Terán, Departmental Executive Ramón Músquiz, Senator Manuel Ceballos, and Treasury Secretary Lorenzo de Zavala urging a legislative moratorium on the collection of colonists' foreign debts. The theme of Austin's correspondence was that immigrants to Texas were encountering unforeseen difficulties in raising capital and that demands from outside creditors would devastate the already faltering financial condition of the settlers.[27] Austin pointed out that publication of the Mexican minister's remark that there were no impediments to debt collection in Texas had precipitated a rush of claims against the colonists. Austin also related a local rumor that the treaty between Mexico and the United States, once ratified, would guarantee immediate collection of the Texans' foreign debts. Austin feared, therefore, that the creditors' agents would descend upon the legislature in the fall to present their claims. Four of the recipients of Austin's letter responded, and all supported his proposal.[28] Ramón Músquiz at Béxar supported the suggestion but added that he had no official word that the treaty compelled the repayment of foreign debts.

In making this proposal Austin seemed unaware of much of the Anglo-American legal tradition, and even less of the Spanish legal tradition, for the protection of debtors.[29] He concluded that legislation was necessary to authorize postponement of foreign debts owed by the Texan colonists. Austin asserted a precedent for such legislation in the "Laws of the Indies," but even in the absence of such a precedent, he felt that the situation warranted the remedy suggested—just as similar circumstances had justified enactments by American state legislatures for curtailing collection of British debts following the American revolution.[30]

27These letters were virtually identical. See Austin to Zavala, June 24, 1828, Barker (ed.), *The Austin Papers*, II, 47–49, 51.

28Mier y Terán to Austin, July 8, 1828, ibid., II, 70; Músquiz to Austin, July 24, 1828, ibid., 75–76; Zavala to Austin, Aug. 6, 1828, ibid., 87–88; José María Viesca to Austin, Aug. 8, 1828, ibid., 88–89.

29While Austin had some knowledge of law and had been appointed to the bench of Arkansas Territory, he did not consider himself a lawyer. Barker, *Life of Stephen F. Austin*, 24; "Stephen F. Austin's Commission as a Judge," July 10, 1820, Barker (ed.), *The Austin Papers*, I, Pt. 1. 365–366. See also Barker, *Life of Stephen F. Austin*, 32–33, 101, 150–153, 156; Austin to Josiah H. Bell, Apr. 16, 1829, Barker (ed.), *The Austin Papers*, II, 205, 206. For a discussion of Anglo-American debtor law, see pages 389–390 below.

30Austin to Zavala, June 24, 1828, Barker (ed.), *The Austin Papers*, II, 50. He refers to laws of Virginia and South Carolina. For these see Peter J. Coleman, *Debtors and*

Austin's reference to the "Laws of the Indies," as his manner of presenting his argument suggests, seems little more than rhetorical. It would have been difficult for him to find a provision in the collected *Laws of the Indies* to support his assertion. If Austin had heard of the late eighteenth-century moratoria granted to the debtors of Spanish New Orleans or Natchez, however, he might have thought that these were the consequences of particular laws of the Indies allowing the suspension of creditors' claims.[31] But these were instances of *extraordinary* moratoria granted by the governor. There were no ordinary debt-stays under Spanish law apart from those granted by creditors themselves. Thus, if Austin had been familiar with the operation of the Spanish moratorium applicable to private debts, he would have realized that it was not germane to the context of his proposal. If Austin's reference was to specific laws of the Indies affecting colonists' debts, it was to those provisions of the *Novísima Recopilación* encouraging colonization by way of waiver of liability for taxes and tithes, a policy which the Mexican government had carried forward in its colonization laws. While Eugene C. Barker suggests that Austin's reference to the "Laws of the Indies" was a probable allusion to Spanish exemption laws, Austin suggested a postponement of debts, not an exemption from their collection. The Anglo-American practices to which Austin referred were instances of debt-stay laws utilized in Virginia, the Carolinas, Jamaica, and elsewhere for the relief of debtors. [32]

In his reply to Austin on August 8, Governor Viesca said a proposal concerning colonists' debts would be presented to the legislature. Secretary of State Antonio Padilla's letter to Austin on August 9 reiterated this point. Padilla indicated further that he and Viesca would work for its passage. The First Constitutional Congress of Coahuila y Texas convened on August 28, but in the meantime Austin does not appear

---

Creditors in America: Insolvency, Imprisonment for Debt, and Bankruptcy, 1607–1900 (Madison, 1974), 189, 199.

[31]Holmes, *Gayoso*, 96–99, 129, 187, 189. For an earlier instance of extraordinary moratorium on all outstanding debts after the great New Orleans fire of 1788, see Laura L. Porteous, "Index to the Spanish Judicial Records of Louisiana, LXXXII," *Louisiana Historical Quarterly*, XXIX (Jan., 1946), 208, 209.

When the Audiencia of New Galicia had attempted to grant a general debt-moratorium two centuries earlier, the crown forbade it, but allowed the grant of six months' grace to deserving individuals. See J. H. Parry, *The Audiencia of New Galicia in the Sixteenth Century: A Study in Spanish Colonial Government* (Cambridge, 1948), 152. See also *Recopilación de Indias* II. 15.95 (1563, 1575, 1596), VII. 1.73 (1609).

[32]*Novísima Recopilación* XI. 33.1–4; *Recopilación de Indias* VIII. 1.73, 4.17; Tapia *Febrero novísimo*, V, 326–328; Barker, *Life of Stephen F. Austin*, 224–225; London, "The Initial Homestead Exemption in Texas," 432, 438–439; Coleman, *Debtors and Creditors in America*, 54, 131, 163–164, 182, 192–194, 215–216, 233, 242.

to have contacted either of the Texas representatives with respect to his proposal.[33] On September 2 Governor Viesca sent the congress his recommendation for legislation to give protection from prior debts to all lands granted to anyone (Mexican nationals, foreign colonists, and empresarios) under the Colonization Act of March 24, 1825, along with a commentary on each of the four articles of the proposed law. Viesca's message pointed out that article 27 of the Colonization Law of 1825 prevented alienation of land grants by colonists until after they had been fully cultivated, and experience had shown that it would take ten to twenty years before a settler without substantial capital could achieve full cultivation. It was, therefore, recommended that relief from prior claims be granted.[34]

Unaware of the developments in Saltillo, during early September Austin tried his hand at drafting an appropriate law. His proposal, however, did not go beyond his original suggestion of a twelve-year moratorium on the enforcement of foreign debts. Whether Austin's draft ever reached Saltillo is unknown, although it is possible that a copy was enclosed in one of his letters to Padilla. By subserving Austin's initial recommendation for a stay of debts for twelve years to a provision for an absolute exemption of land grants from prior creditors' claims, the draftsman of the first article of the proposed statute provided the basis for a new institution in family law. We are left to conjecture as to why this change of emphasis occurred, but its ultimate impact was momentous. Barker suggests that the draftsman was Antonio Padilla, who had first served in Texas as a Spanish administrator in 1812.[35] The draftsman was certainly passingly familiar with the principal elements of Spanish exemption law. But neither the draftsman—

33Viesca to Austin, Aug. 8, 1828, Barker (ed.), *The Austin Papers*, II, 88–89; Padilla to Austin, Aug. 9, 1828, ibid., 89; Actas del congreso del estado de Coahuila y Texas, Aug. 28, 1828, pp. 911–912 (transcripts; BTHC). At the first, short session of the Constitutional Congress, Texas was represented by José Antonio Navarro (Béxar) and by Miguel Arciniega (Béxar), who was elected as one of the two secretaries of the congress. Ibid., 911, 912.

34Actas del Congreso, Sept. 2, 1828, p. 913; Viesca to the Legislature, Sept. 2, 1828, Barker (ed.), *The Austin Papers*, II, 96–98. Although the commentary accompanying his project remains, the text of the governor's proposal seems to have disappeared. In his letter of October 18 to Austin, Padilla intended to enclose a copy of the legislation already proposed, and in his letter of November 1, he said he enclosed the draft (now lost). Ibid., 132–134, 137.

35Projet of law relative to foreign debts, Sept. 8, 1828, Barker (ed.), *The Austin Papers*, II, 102; Barker, *Life of Stephen F. Austin*, 225; Walter Prescott Webb, H. Bailey Carroll, and Eldon Stephen Branda (eds.), *The Handbook of Texas* (3 vols.; Austin, 1952, 1976), II, 323. Padilla had seen prior service in the Spanish army as an ensign in 1810–1811. See Robert S. Weddle, *The San Sabá Mission: Spanish Pivot in Texas* (Austin, 1964), 199; Josef Arcos to Manuel Salcedo, May 12, 1812, Bexar Archives (BTHC).

ship of the first article nor that of the third, in its reference to exempt movables, suggests that the draftsman referred to any of the standard legal works dealing with that concept. He seems merely to have drawn on his general knowledge of the subject.

By transforming the request for local relief for *foreign* colonists into a measure of general application to all grantees under the colonization laws, the draftsman treated all new settlers alike and provided relief not merely from debts owed to foreign creditors but from all prior debts regardless of source. The draftsman very likely sensed that a law of general application would be more acceptable to the twelve members of the congress, none of whom was Anglo-American, than an act for the relief of foreign settlers in Texas.

The rest of the draft generally followed Austin's suggestions. The second and third articles provided respectively for a moratorium until 1840 and for payment of prior debts after 1840 (with further exemption provisions). The fourth article provided that a tenth part of debts be paid annually thereafter without interest.[36]

The governor's proposal, presented to the legislature on September 2, was referred promptly to the Committee on Legislation, which recommended its adoption in giving it a first reading to the legislature on September 22. The proposal received a second reading in the legislature on the twenty-fifth and was to be given further discussion at the first time available. Although a majority favored article 1, the legislative inclination was to reject or modify the rest. When the session ended on September 30, the entire matter was left pending to be considered by the next congress. The departmental executive, Ramón Músquiz, had been in Saltillo during the September session and commented briefly to Austin that there was resistance to the bill. Vice-governor Victor Blanco wrote to Austin on November 15 that he would handle the bill's passage at the January session.[37]

The Second Constitutional Congress convened on December 28. On January 9, 1829, the recommendation for legislation concerning colonists' debts was read again, and the measure was brought up for a discussion and vote. The record does not indicate, however, whether it

<hr/>

[36]Austin to Zavala, June 24, 1828, Barker (ed.), *The Austin Papers*, II, 51; Viesca to the Legislature, Sept. 2, 1828, ibid., 98. It is assumed that the text of three articles of the bill that came to the floor of Congress in 1829 was the same as that of the first three articles of the governor's recommendation of 1828.

[37]Actas del Congreso, Sept. 2, 1828, p. 913, Sept. 24, 1828, p. 924, Sept. 25, 1828, p. 926, Sept. 30, 1828, p. 930; Músquiz to Austin, Nov. 27, 1828, Barker (ed.), *The Austin Papers*, II, 146–147; Victor Blanco to Austin, ibid., 141–142. The legislative attitude toward the proposal is not noted in Actas del Congreso but is briefly summarized (without date) in Padilla to Austin, Oct. 18, 1828, ibid., 132, 134.

was at this point or later that the original fourth article of the draft was dropped from the proposal. Although consideration of the measure had been long delayed, once the congress began to discuss it, its provisions were given careful attention. The first article was read, and after a full discussion its provisions were approved: sovereign land grants were protected from the enforcement of debts contracted before the acquisition of those lands. Article 2 was then brought up, and the president of the congress, Ramón García Rojas of Monclova, and the secretary, Manuel de Cárdenas of Saltillo, were in the midst of discussing it when time came for adjournment. After further deliberation on January 12, García offered an amended version of article 2, which was discussed and adopted. As passed, article 2 precluded legal action by creditors for recovery of debts for twelve years after the debtor was put in possession of his land grant.[38] Article 3 was then read and discussed. It provided that debts antecedent to land grants would be enforceable after 1840, but even then, land, farming equipment, and tools of trade would not be subject to payment. This provision was in the Hispanic debtor-exemption tradition with respect to the types of chattels protected. The article as drafted went on to provide that the fruits and earnings derived from the exempt property were then subject to payment, *but not to the prejudice of the debtor's family, his farming, or trade.* It was evidently realized that this last, hardship provision was far too broad. García, therefore, moved an amended version of article 3 without the hardship provision, and the amended version was adopted. On January 13 the minutes on the measure were read and approved, and Decree No. 70 was thus enacted.[39]

In sum, the decree (1) protected land grants to colonists from enforcement of any prior debts for twelve years after acquisition of the land, (2) forbade suits for recovery of those debts during that interval, and (3) put those lands, farming equipment, and tools or machinery of trade beyond the reach of prior creditors thereafter. The focus of all three articles was the protection of sovereign land grants. Not only was collection of prior debts postponed for twelve years as Austin had suggested, but both lands for colonization and vital tools of all Coahuil-

---

[38]Actas del Congreso, Dec. 28, 1828, p. 930, Jan. 9, 1829, pp. 935–936, Jan. 10, 1829, pp. 936–937, Jan. 12, 1829, p. 937; Padilla to Austin, Jan. 24, 1829, Barker (ed.), *The Austin Papers*, II, 162.

[39]Actas del Congreso, Jan. 12, 1829, p. 937, Jan. 13, 1829, p. 938. In J. P. Kimball (trans.), *Laws and Decrees of the State of Coahuila and Texas, to Which Is Added the Constitution of Said State* . . . (Houston, 1839), 110, 111, the text of Decree No. 70 includes the hardship provision excised by García's amendment. Misled by the inclusion of this provision in Kimball's text, Barker noted its inordinate scope. Barker, *Life of Stephen F. Austin*, 226.

texan grantees were permanently exempted from the reach of prior creditors. After 1840 such debts would be collectible from other property that the debtor-colonist might then have. This was an enormously generous debtor-protection statute.

Although the decree had been finally enacted on January 13, Congressional Secretary Cárdenas pointed out to the congress on January 28 that fifteen days had passed since the decree had been sent to the governor, but that it had not been published or returned, and he inquired why the governor had failed to perform his constitutional duty to publish the law within the required period.[40] The delay seems to have been occasioned by the language of García's amendment to the third article, which exempted "tools or machinery (*maquinarias*) of trade." In his letter to Austin on January 24, Padilla referred to this "category or absurd idea which the Government found unacceptable." The governor evidently thought that the connotation of "machinery" was too broad. Without going into the governor's objection, García responded to Cárdenas in a spirit of conciliation: it was within his power as a member of the Committee on Correction of Style to repair slight errors of spelling, and the matter would be taken care of immediately. The word "machines" (*máquinas*) was therefore substituted for "machinery," the governor was placated, and publication, which must have occurred very soon thereafter, was back-dated to January 22. A copy arrived in San Felipe de Austin on February 24 and another, in San Antonio on March 1.[41]

Since 1825 the United States and Mexico had pursued a lengthy course of talks concerning a commercial treaty, which was negotiated and signed three times. On each occasion the treaty contained terms requiring its ratification by both parties within a specified period. Since bilateral ratification did not occur within the time period prescribed after the treaty was concluded on July 10, 1826, and on February 14, 1828, it was necessary for it to be concluded again on April 5, 1831. Ratifications were finally exchanged on April 5, 1832. The exemption

---

[40]Actas del Congreso, Jan. 28, 1829, p. 950. Padilla to Austin, Jan. 24, 1829, confirms that the law had not been issued when he wrote. Barker (ed.), *The Austin Papers*, II, 162. For an English translation of the law concerning the governor's approval or rejection of legislation, see "Constitution of the State of Coahuila and Texas," 1827, Sec. V, Art. 102, H. P. N. Gammel (comp.), *The Laws of Texas 1822–1897* . . . (10 vols.; Austin, 1898), I, 437.

[41]Padilla to Austin, Jan. 24, 1829, Barker (ed.), *The Austin Papers*, II, 162; Actas del Congreso, Jan. 12, 1828, p. 937 (first quotation), Jan. 28, 1829, p. 950; Decree No. 70, Bexar Archives (Bexar County Courthouse; this copy was endorsed by Ramón Músquiz as being received on March 1). Austin's favorable reaction to the decree is expressed in Austin to Bell, Feb. 24, 1829, Barker (ed.), *The Austin Papers*, II, 172. Translations in this article are by the author, unless otherwise indicated.

law that was to have such an important impact on later legislation fell as a victim of that treaty. A little more than two years after its adoption—almost immediately after the ultimate conclusion of the commercial treaty with the United States which Decree No. 70 was meant to circumvent—the decree of 1829 was repealed on April 8, 1831.[42] In all drafts of the treaty from 1825 to 1831 the debt-enforcement problem had been dealt with by a clause providing that the citizens of each signatory state would have full access to the courts of the other, and that term was embodied in the treaty as finally concluded in 1831.[43] Although no record has been found of pressure put on the congress of Coahuila y Texas to repeal the decree, its repeal seems closely associated with the negotiation and conclusion of the treaty.

On February 16, 1831, repeal was first mentioned to the congress by the chairman of its Committee on Governmental Affairs, President José I. Canales of Monclova.[44] His reference to the practice of "all nations" suggests that his rhetoric was formulated by the Mexican Ministry of Foreign Affairs, whether or not prompted by suggestions of the American chargé d'affaires:

Decree No. 70 is notoriously favorable to dishonest debtors and works a fraud to the prejudice of creditors. Neither justice nor good sense can allow a rule to stand which neither conforms to general principles adopted by all nations nor can be harmonized with just notions of property. It is a stain on the Legislature of Coahuila that this is allowed to continue, and I therefore make the following proposal: I beg that this Honorable Congress repeal Decree No. 70 passed on January 13, 1829.[45]

The chairman of the legislative and judicial committees, Lic. Jesús González of Saltillo, seconded Canales's proposal at this first reading. The second reading was had on February 19. After discussion the proposal was referred to the Legislative Committee. Nothing more is heard of this measure until March 29, when it was given its first reading as a recommendation of the Legislative Committee. The second reading

---

42Decree No. 173, Actas del Congreso, Apr. 8, 1831, p. 1,466. For the negotiations of the 1826 and 1828 treaties, see *American State Papers*, Foreign Relations, VI, 210, 578–613, 952–962. For further discussion of persons in Mexico indebted to U.S. creditors, see ibid., 366, 822.

43"Treaty of Amity, Commerce, and Navigation, Concluded April 5, 1831," art. 14, John H. Haswell (comp. and ed.), *Treaties and Conventions Concluded between the United States of America and Other Powers since July 4, 1776 . . .* (Washington, D.C., 1889), 664, 667; Hunter Miller (ed.), *Treaties and Other International Acts of the United States of America* (8 vols.; Washington, D.C., 1933), III, 599, 608. See also Luis G. Zorrilla, *Historia de las relaciones entre Mexico y los Estados Unidos de America, 1800–1958* (2 vols.; Mexico City, 1965), I, 111, 112.

44Actas del Congreso, Feb. 7, 1831, pp. 1,400–1,401.

45Ibid., Feb. 16, 1831, p. 1,411.

was on April 2, and at that sitting Austin was recorded as absent because of illness. The proposal was brought up for discussion and vote on April 7. The proposal then read: "Decree No. 70 passed by the Congress on January 13, 1829, is repealed in full." The proposal was explained, the words "in full" were deleted, and the proposal then passed. This action received final approval on the following day and was designated as Decree No. 173.[46] With little recorded discussion, Decree No. 70 was thus repealed. In spite of all the energy he had expended for its enactment, Austin made no murmur of public protest at its repeal, nor does his extant correspondence reveal the fact or circumstances of the repeal. Surviving Texas newspapers are also silent on the subject.

If the relationship of the 1829 act to the proposed treaty had been mentioned, it had not occurred to anyone to assert that exemption laws do not affect access to the courts, although the debt-stay provision of article 2 and the reference to it in article 3 would have fallen to that objection. No one seemed to have perceived the function of exemption laws or even that an exemption was in issue, though this exemption law was not generically different from those that a Mexican creditor would have encountered in every American state at that time. Although its exemption of land made its scope broader, its reference only to debts incurred prior to acquisition of land grants made it less extensive in effect than many American exemption laws. If it had been realized that exemption merely from seizure for debt did not affect access to the courts, much of the statute could have been saved. American creditors could not have legitimately complained in the light of their own similar laws.[47] Further, the genera of exemption doctrine embodied in this law of 1829 were no different from Hispanic principles that had been embodied in Spanish law for centuries, except for the exemption of land grants from debts antedating acquisition. But everyone knew that this law had been passed only two years before to protect American colonists from their existing American creditors. Hence, the whole law was repealed to achieve good-faith compliance with the treaty. At the upper levels of government on both sides, among lawyers and non-lawyers alike, there was a seeming ignorance of exemption laws and their function, although the principle was well established in both legal cultures.

But once Decree No. 70 had been formally repealed, and those con-

---

[46]Ibid., Feb. 16, 1831, p. 1,411, Feb. 19, 1831, p. 1,414, Mar. 29, 1831, p. 1,457, Apr. 2, 1831, p. 1,461, Apr. 7, 1831, 1,465–1,466 (quotations), Apr. 8, 1831, p. 1,466.

[47]For a comment on American exemption laws of the time, see text accompanying notes 57–61.

cerned were presumably satisfied that the terms of the treaty had been complied with by Mexico, perceptions of debtor-creditor law do not appear to have changed on the Texas frontier. Although copies of Decree No. 173 were presumably distributed to the various municipalities, insofar as contemporary sources indicate, Texas colonists never became aware of the repealer.[48] Since the subject matter of the repealing decree was not apparent on its face, the local inhabitants were unaware that any change had occurred. If knowledge of repeal had been meant to be kept as limited as possible, the terse and abstract form of Decree No. 173 could not have been better chosen. The form of repeal was, however, usual and customary.[49] Thus, the failure of communication was mere happenstance. No one seems to have related the numbers of the two decrees, and there was no general collection of decrees to which one might have referred, even if anyone had been curious.

Decree No. 173 can scarcely have been a secret. But David Edward was certainly unaware of its existence when he included Decree No. 70 in an emigrant's guidebook, which he compiled at Gonzales in 1835; indeed, Barker, writing another ninety years later, seems to have been equally unaware of the repealing decree.[50] Another reference to exempt property also appeared in Edward's book. The English text of the Texas Judiciary Act of 1834, as quoted there, included two unenacted sections that itemized exempt property along Castilian lines.[51] These

---

[48]The only suggestion of local awareness of the decree is a comment of an American traveler in Texas during early May, 1831: "about this time a colonist . . . being alarmed at the report that a law had been passed in Mexico, providing for the collection of debts due abroad by residents in the republic, advertised and sold [a large number of slaves] at auction . . . [but] most of them were purchased by one of his family connexions." *Visit to Texas: Being the Journal of a Traveller through Those Parts Most Interesting to American Settlers* (New York, 1834), 210. Word of the passage of Decree No. 173 would have reached Central Texas about this time. It was received in San Antonio on April 28. But it may have been word of the signing of the treaty that alarmed the colonist. One historian is inclined to identify the author of the *Visit* as Asahel Langworthy. Marilyn McAdams Sibley, *Travelers in Texas, 1761–1860* (Austin, 1967), 181. But even if it was Langworthy, it did not occur to him that Decree No. 70 had been repealed, because he included it in his collection of Mexican laws published in 1832. See note 64.

[49]For instances immediately preceding and succeeding the repeal of Decree No. 70 by Decree No. 173, see Decree No. 147 of Apr. 29, 1829, repealing Decrees No. 47 and 88, and Decree No. 182 of February 7, 1832, repealing Decree No. 146. Kimball (trans.), *Laws and Decrees*, 159–160, 184.

[50]David B. Edward, *The History of Texas; or, The Emigrant's, Farmer's, and Politician's Guide to the Character, Climate, Soil and Productions of That Country . . .* (Cincinnati, 1836), 159. Barker's comment that the law of 1829 was in effect for ten years indicates his belief that it was still in effect in 1839 when "renewed" by the Texas act. Barker, *Life of Stephen F. Austin*, 227.

[51]Edward, *History of Texas*, 176 (arts. 141, 142). The draftsman of the act was Thomas Jefferson Chambers. His apparent source was Sala, *Ilustración*, 298, perhaps supplemented

provisions may have heightened the general awareness of the exemption principle, but they do not seem to have affected the formulation of the later law directly.

In popular, and even professional, understanding the effects of the 1829 act seem to have been magnified rather than diminished in the years immediately after its repeal. An Ohio lawyer traveling through the principal towns of Central Texas in 1837 made this observation:

> The laws of Texas most important to the people of the United States . . . [include] that which prohibits the collection of debts contracted in other countries. It is said in defense of this . . . that if Congress had not taken this step to prevent the collection of foreign claims general distress and bankruptcy among the people would [have been] the consequence. The argument, to make the best of it, supposes a general insolvency, and it is a legitimate inference that the importunities of creditors are one of the leading causes which have given a population to Texas.
>
> I . . . will merely add that by a subsequent amendment of this law the rights of creditors are not entirely taken away, but postponed for a period of time.[52]

The folklore of the 1829 act not only was impervious to repeal but had also generated reenactment and amendment. Obviously the Ohio traveler was simply repeating what he had been told concerning current Texas law.

Decree No. 70 of 1829 was composed of three articles. All three were in a very broad sense incentives to colonization, although the third gave less immediate encouragement to immigrants than the other two. Their primary objective was, however, to benefit Texas colonists already in residence, though future colonists might also benefit by them. Article 1 protected sovereign grants of land from seizure for prior indebtedness; article 2 (as Austin had suggested) put a twelve-year moratorium on legal actions to enforce those prior debts. In effect, the first two articles merely put the same proposition twice over with different emphasis, as though the draftsman had given the congress a choice in response to Austin's request, and it had failed to make the selection. Even after the twelve-year period had passed, it was provided in article 3 that prior creditors could not enforce their claims against land grants and particular movables: "farming equipment, or tools or machines of

---

by article 644 of the Louisiana Code of Practice 1825, which was also derived from a Spanish source. See projet of the *Code of Practice in Civil Cases of the State of Louisiana* (New Orleans, 1823), 102.

[52]Andrew Forest Muir (ed.), *Texas in 1837: An Anonymous Contemporary Narrative* (Austin, 1958), xvi, xix, 161 (quotation), 162. The references to Congress are to that of the Republic of Texas. But the Congress had only sat twice, and the second session was still in progress during the author's visit to Texas.

trade" (*aperos de labor, ni instrumentos de su oficio o maquinas*). The term *aperos de labor* in Mexican usage included not only agricultural implements but also the animals used to pull them.[53] The Spanish tradition in favor of this type of exemption was therefore clearly perpetuated in the third article, and its spirit and terms were to be carried forward in the Texas act of 1839.

Austin had merely proposed a stay of debt enforcement. But the draftsman of the 1829 legislation had drawn on the general tradition of Spanish law to implement the suggestion for a debt moratorium with a property exemption law for the protection of land and vital chattels, to shield them from the satisfaction of private indebtedness. With respect to lands, however, the law went much further than existing rules. Prior law had not suggested that anything more than *casas* of nobles and gentry and tilled or seeded lands of farmers were protected from seizure. But as to chattels, the provisions of the 1829 act were somewhat narrower than the list of movables normally protected, in that clothing and household articles of daily use went unmentioned.

Considered apart from the provisions of the Texas act which it inspired, the innovation of the 1829 act must have struck the Coahuiltexan congress as relatively innocuous in its application to Texas in that it put no significant burden on local commerce: lands granted by the sovereign were to be protected mainly from *foreign* creditors. While the act did not refer specifically to foreign creditors, most debts owed by Texas colonists before they established possession of a land grant in Texas would have been owed to foreigners—apart from those owed to the empresarios. But by a modest substitution of terms and a reorientation toward future creditors, the provisions of the third article would be transformed into the initial homestead exemption of 1839, which in turn matured into Texas's general homestead exemption of 1845. Although Austin was cognizant of the principle of debt moratorium, he does not appear to have been familiar with the concept of exempt property in Spanish or in Anglo-American law. The draftsman of the Texas act of 1839 was, however, clearly aware of the 1829 act of Coahuila y Texas, as well as the form and content of current Anglo-American property-exemption statutes.

---

[53]See Sarah T. Hughes, "Development of the Homestead Exemption in Texas," *The Dallas Bar Speaks, 1936* (Dallas, 1937), 397, 399, 400. See also Wooten (ed.), *History of Texas,* 127; J. F. H. Clairborne, *Mississippi as a Province, Territory and State, with Biographical Notices of Eminent Citizens* (Jackson, Miss., 1880), 138. The term *aperos de labor* in Mexican usage included not only agricultural implements, but also the animals that pulled them. Francisco Javier Santamaría, *Diccionario de mejicanismos* (2nd ed.; Mexico City, 1974), 73.

When compared to Spanish law of the eighteenth century, English law of the same period made more modest provisions to ameliorate the hardship of debtors. Since the late thirteenth century, oxen and beasts of the plow had been exempt from creditors' seizure when lands as well as chattels were the object of debt enforcement by the writ of eligit.[54] Certain movables were also exempt from the process of distress by landlords, but English rules for the relief of debtors had not been further developed prior to the sixteenth century.[55] A succession of English statutes (based on continental models) were enacted thereafter to allow insolvent debtors to assign their property (saving essential movables) for the benefit of their creditors. By a statute of 1670, for example, the clothing, bedding, and tools of trade of a debtor released from prison were made exempt from execution. By the end of the eighteenth century, freedom from imprisonment for debt in England was similar to that afforded by Spanish law, but with less solicitude for the farming community.[56]

Though the law of England's American colonies was rooted in English tradition, local enactments from the mid-seventeenth century onward gave debtors protection exceeding that afforded in England.[57]

---

[54]The writ of elegit instituted by the Statute of Westminster II provided that the creditor might *elect* to possess one-half of the lands of the debtor and his movables (apart from the exemptions mentioned) rather than the mere income from lands and the movables. Statute of Westminster II, 13 Edw. I, c. 18 (1285). See also Stefan A. Riesenfeld, *Cases and Materials on Creditors' Remedies and Debtors' Protection* (3rd ed.; St. Paul, 1979), 207; Seymour D. Thompson, *A Treatise on Homestead and Exemption Laws* (St. Louis, 1878), 4.

[55]William Holdsworth, *A History of English Law* (16 vols.; London, 1922–1966), VIII, 229–245, XI, 597–600; F. A. Enever, *History of the Law of Distress for Rent and Damage Feasant* (London, 1931), 92–94; Edward Coke, *Institutes of the Laws of England . . .* (3rd. ed.; London, 1633), 47a–47b. Though many early continental legal systems privileged cattle and certain other animals from seizure, the privilege is not found in English borough customs. Enever, *Law of Distress*, 142. Kent stated that beasts of the plow, instruments of husbandry, and tools of trade were exempted from distress *sub modo*, i.e., "upon the supposition that there was other sufficient distress." James Kent, *Commentaries on American Law*, ed. O. W. Holmes, Jr. (4 vols.; 12th ed.; Boston, 1873), III, 478, 479 (quotation).

[56]22 & 23 Car. 2, c. 20, § 4; William Blackstone, *Commentaries on the Laws of England* (4 vols.; 9th ed.; London, 1783), III, 288–290, 292, 414. For later examples of exemptions, see 2 & 3 Anne, c. 10, § 8 (1703) (up to £10 in value); 4 & 5 Anne, c. 4, § 1 (1705) (his "necessary wearing apparel" and that for his wife and children only); 32 Geo. 2, c. 28, § 13 (1759).

[57]Apparently the first American statute of this sort was enacted in Maryland in 1642. William H. Browne (ed.), *Proceedings and Acts of the General Assembly of Maryland*, Archives of Maryland, vols. 1–2 (Baltimore, 1883), I, 152–154. See Stefan A. Riesenfeld, "Enforcement of Money Judgments in Early American History," *Michigan Law Review*, LXI (Mar., 1973), 691, 715. See also Riesenfeld, *Cases and Materials on Creditors' Remedies and Debtors' Protection*, 308–310.

But how effective these laws were after the English act of 1732, which
made all lands and slaves, as well as ordinary movables in the plantations, subject to debt enforcement, can only be surmised.[58] This legislation of 1732 apparently was meant to negate colonial debt-stay and
exemption statutes that discriminated against any English subject. During the late eighteenth and early nineteenth centuries, however, almost
all of the states of the North American union had enacted exemption
laws as to movables, and these laws would have been familiar to some
who settled in the Hispano-Mexican borderlands. Apart from a few instances of postponement of seizure of land for the satisfaction of debt,
and one statutory provision exempting burial places, these American
statutes did not give favorable treatment to lands in the process of debt
enforcement. But these Anglo-American laws often made very generous
exemptions of movables.[59] The personal-property exemption statutes
varied from providing relatively short lists of exempt property to
enumerating long catalogues of miscellaneous items, catalogues which
had been expanded in some instances at successive legislative sessions.[60]
Most such statutes put monetary limitations on the value of certain
types of property that could be claimed as exempt. Others merely specified certain kinds, numbers, or weights of things that were exempt,
without specifying monetary limitations. But prior to 1839 every jurisdiction except the two territories most recently organized had provided
some sort of statutory list of exempt movables.[61]

58An act for the more easy recovery of debts in His Majesty's plantations and colonies
in America, 5 Geo. 2, c. 7 (1732), particularly § 4. See also London, "The Initial Homestead Exemption in Texas," 432, 438–439, 440; Kent, *Commentaries on American Law*, IV,
443–448. For the far-reaching implications of this act, see Riesenfeld, *Cases and Materials
on Creditors' Remedies and Debtors' Protection*, 6–7.

59Indiana Laws [1824] ch. 40, § 2, p. 188; Mississippi Revised Code [1824] ch. 27,
§ 20, p. 200; Act of Feb. 4, 1809, §6, Michigan Laws [1809]; Ohio Laws [1895] 11, § 1. For
examples of generous exemptions of movables, see Arkansas Revised Statutes [1838] ch.
60, §§ 19–20, pp. 376-377; Connecticut Compiled Laws [1839] tit. 2, § 74, pp. 62–63; 2
New York Revised Statutes [1836] § 22, p. 290; Pennsylvania Laws [1835–1836] No. 191,
§ 26, pp. 765–766.

60One example of a short list is Massachusetts Revised Statutes [1826] ch. 97, § 22, p.
589. For examples of long lists, see Connecticut Compiled Laws [1839] tit. 2, § 74, pp.
62–63, where acts of 1829, 1832, and 1837 are compiled; Indiana Laws [1831] ch. 36, § 1,
as amended by Indiana Laws [1833–1834] ch. 51, §§ 1–2, p. 81, and Indiana Laws [1838–
1839] ch. 21, § 1, pp. 35–36; Michigan Laws [1827] § 25, 2 Michigan Territorial Laws
492 (1874), as amended by Michigan Laws [1828] § 3, 2 Michigan Territorial Laws 704
(1874) and Michigan Laws [1833] §2, 3 Michigan Territorial Laws 1,073 (1874).

61For examples of monetary limitations, see Pennsylvania Laws [1835–1836] No. 191,
§ 26, pp. 765–766; South Carolina Laws [1823] § IV, 6, South Carolina Statutes at Large
[1814–1838] No. 2315, p. 214 (1839). Among those statutes making nonmonetary specifi-
cations in regard to exemptions, see Arkansas Revised Statutes [1838] ch. 60, §§ 19–20,
pp. 376–377; Maryland Laws [1715] ch. 40, § 5, Maryland General Laws [1692–1839] 763

In its general form and substance the Texas act of 1839 was a statute of the Anglo-American type in most of its provisions concerning movables, some of which seem to have been selected at random, while others were subject to a monetary limitation, as was common in the United States. But the Texas exemption act of 1839 also shows significant textual borrowing from the 1829 act of Coahuila y Texas. The provisions of that decree were clearly in the mind of the draftsman.

[F]rom and after the passage of this act, there shall be reserved to every citizen or head of family in this Republic, free and independent of the power of fire [*sic*] facias, or other execution issuing from any court of competent jurisdiction whatever, fifty acres of land or one town lot, including his or her homestead, and improvements not exceeding five hundred dollars in value, all house hold and kitchen furniture, (providing it does not exceed in value two hundred dollars,) all implements of husbandry, (provided they shall not exceed fifty dollars in value,) all tools, apparatus and books belonging to the trade or profession of any citizen, five milch cows, one yoke of work oxen or one horse, twenty hogs, and one year's provisions; and that all laws and parts of laws contravening or opposing the provisions of this act, be and the same are hereby repealed: Provided, The passage of this act shall not interfere with contracts between parties heretofore made.[62]

The provision for "implements of husbandry" is an English rendering of *aperos de labor* in the 1829 act. "Implements of husbandry" is a term that appears nowhere in any Anglo-American exemption statute of the time. The 1838–1839 session of the Texas Congress met at Houston. At the time that the homestead bill was drafted there, Dr. John Kimball had already completed a translation of the laws and decrees of Coahuila y Texas on which he had been engaged since the past summer at the instance of the secretary of state, Dr. Robert Irion. At the end of 1838 Kimball was superintending the printing of his work.[63] In

(1840); Maryland Laws [1814] ch. 135, ibid., 621. But almost all personal property exemption statutes contained some monetary limitations.

Wisconsin Territory, organized in 1836, enacted an exemption law during its 1838–1839 legislative session. Wisconsin Laws [1838–1839] 231, § 42. Iowa Territory was organized in 1838 and promptly enacted an exemption statute on January 25, 1839. Iowa Laws [1838–1839] 197, 198, § 4.

[62]An act to exempt certain property named therein from execution, Texas Laws [1838–1839] 125–126; Gammel (comp.), *Laws of Texas*, II, 125, 126 (quotation).

[63]This was the continuation of a project awarded by the congress of Coahuila y Texas to José María Jesús Carbajal, then a deputy from Béxar and one of the secretaries of the congress. Decree No. 319, May 18, 1835, Kimball (trans.), *Laws and Decrees*, 307. A joint resolution of December, 1837, cited in 2 Texas Laws [1836–1837] 25, and in Gammel (comp.), *Laws of Texas*, I, 1,367, also authorized the payment to "Manuel Carabajal" of up to $1,200 for compiling the laws of Coahuila y Texas. Secretary of State Robert A. Irion reported to the Third Congress that difficulty in finding a translator had delayed the publication of those laws in English, but that he had finally engaged Kimball, "who

his translation of Decree No. 70 Kimball also used the phrase "implements of husbandry" to translate *aperos de labor*. It is, therefore, plausible to conclude that the act's draftsman was either using Kimball's translation, or that he had consulted Kimball, who was living nearby.[64] If the draftsman of the statute had consulted a dictionary identical to that used by Kimball to translate the decree of 1829, the same result would have occurred, but no dictionary giving the terminology of the translation of Decree No. 70 has yet come to light.[65]

The 1839 act's reference to "apparatus" is also virtually unique. This term was not generally used in Anglo-American statutes of the time, but it could have been suggested by *máquinas* in the 1829 act.[66] Thus the draftsman of the Texas act of 1839 used the act of Coahuila y Texas as one of his models, and the reference to "implements of husbandry, . . . tools, apparatus . . . belonging to the trade or profession," as well as the inspiration for the exemption of lands, is drawn from the earlier Coahuiltexan law.

The rest of the exemption provisions are derived from Anglo-American models, and the exemptions are enumerated as exceptions to seizure by the writ of fieri facias.[67] Anglo-American exemption statutes of

---

has labored diligently during the last summer, in translating them, which he has competed and is now superintending their publication." Texas (Republic), Congress, House of Representatives, *Journal of the House of Representatives of the Republic of Texas, Regular Session of Third Congress, Nov. 5, 1838* (Houston, 1839), 21, 22 (quotation), 23. Whether the first parts had yet been printed and distributed by the time the bill was drafted is doubtful. Streeter notes that the Kimball translation was sold in two parts, with the index and title pages attached to the second part. The first part ended with the Spanish text of Decree No. 132 on page 149a. Thomas W. Streeter, *Bibliography of Texas, 1795–1845, Part I: Texas Imprints* (2 vols.; Cambridge, Mass., 1955), II, 263, 264. White, *New Collection*, I, 421–558, reproduces slightly less than half of the English translations from Kimball's book, and all of the English translation is duplicated in Gammel (comp.), *Laws of Texas*, I, 111–473, with the original pagination. White's book, published in 1839, was clearly not available to the draftsman of the act.

64Kimball (trans.), *Laws and Decrees*, 110–111. The conclusion regarding the use of Kimball's translation is reached from the fact that both use the term "implements of husbandry." The translations of Decree No. 70 in [Asahel Langworthy], *The Constitution of the Republic of Mexico, and of the State of Coahuila and Texas* (New York, 1832), borrowed by David Edward for his emigrants' guide (1836), and in the *Texas Gazette* (San Felipe de Austin), Nov. 7, 1829, used the phrase "farming utensils" to render *aperos de labor*.

65A dictionary that Kimball might have used is Mariano Cubí y Soler, *A New Pocket Dictionary of the English and Spanish Languages . . . Compiled from Neuman, Connelly, &c.* (2 vols.; Baltimore, 1823). But the Spanish word meanings it supplies are not reflectd in Kimball's translation of Decree No. 70.

66The only instance of the use of the term "apparatus" is in the Missouri exemption statute: "apparatus, necessary for manufacturing cloth." Missouri Revised Statutes [1835] § 15, p. 255.

67A writ of fieri facias empowered a sheriff to satisfy a claim against the debtor by

the time commonly took that form. Several of the exemptions are defined in terms of monetary values—a form also commonly used in Anglo-American exemption statutes. Although the reference to "head of family" is also found in Anglo-American exemption statutes of the time, no particular Anglo-American provisions can be identified as the model for the language of this statute.[68] The draftsman seems to have been generally familiar with the United States exemption statutes and used that knowledge to formulate the 1839 act. The most notable omission from the 1839 act and the other early Texas exemption acts is that of firearms, although in 1836, while engaged in her revolution against Mexico, Texas had enacted an ordinance making both the person and property of soldiers privileged "from arrest, attachment, execution, embargo and sequestration, in all civil cases."[69] The omission of arms is particularly striking in that most American states then included them in their lists of exempt property or made special provision for them in their militia laws.

The 1839 act exempted the family home as well as chattels from the claims of subsequent creditors and provided specifically that it should not interfere with contracts already binding between parties. Following the Constitution of the United States, the Declaration of Rights of the 1836 Constitution of Texas forbade enactment of "retrospective or ex-post facto law, or laws impairing the obligation of contracts." During the legislative session at which the Texas homestead law was adopted, a select committee of the lower house discussed both constitutional provisions at some length in recommending against the adoption of a bill to allow a stay of execution in particular situations.[70]

The American financial crisis of 1837, which precipitated the movement of so many distressed debtors into Texas, was a likely catalyst to the 1839 Texas enactment.[71] Although there is no legislative history of

seizing the debtor's personal property.

[68]For exemptions defined in terms of monetary values, see Michigan Laws [1839] 10, § 1; Indiana Revised Statutes [1834] 60, § 2; Laws of Pennsylvania [1836] 20, §§ 20 et seq. For references to the "head of family," see Illinois Revised Laws [1833] § 19, p. 376; Missouri Revised Statutes [1835] § 15, p. 255.

[69]Ordinance of Jan. 16, 1836, *Ordinances and Decrees of the Consultation* . . . (Houston, 1838), cited in Gammel (comp.), *Laws of Texas*, I, 1,039, 1,041 (quotation). The mixture of English and Spanish legal terminology is notable.

[70]Texas (Republic), *Constitution*, Declaration of Rights, § 16; *Journal of the House . . . Regular Session of Third Congress*, 385–387.

[71]Willis W. Pratt (ed.), *Galveston Island; or, A Few Months off the Coast of Texas: The Journal of Francis Sheridan, 1839–1840* (Austin, 1954), 105–107; Clarence R. Wharton, *The Republic of Texas* (Houston, 1922), 221; Mark E. Nackman, "Anglo-American Migrants to the West: Men of Broken Fortunes? The Case of Texas, 1821–46," *Western Historical Quarterly*, V (Oct., 1974), 441, 444, 449–454.

the 1839 act by way of committee reports or debates, its course of passage through the Congress is well documented. On December 14, 1838,
a bill exempting certain movables from execution of judgments was
introduced in the upper house of the Texas Congress.[72] Two weeks
later Louis P. Cooke of Brazoria County introduced another bill exempting both lands and chattels from subsequent debts in the lower
house.[73] This is the proposal that was enacted, and the earlier bill ultimately died in Senate committee. Cooke's bill was read, passed by both
houses in the last days of the session without any note of discussion or
amendment, and assented to by the president on January 26, 1839.[74]

In spite of the fact that Cooke introduced the bill, there is some evidence that its author was Emory Rains, who represented Shelby and
Sabine counties in the Senate.[75] The bill was referred to the Senate
Judiciary Committee, of which Rains was chairman, and with the committee's favorable report it was passed. Rains was a Texan of long residence and experience. He had probably settled in Texas in the mid-
1820s and had served as alcalde of the Teneha District in 1830, as head
of the San Augustine municipal council in 1834, and again as judge of
that region during 1835–1836.[76] Although authorship of the bill is uncertain, of all those associated with its passage Rains is the only one
whose background was such that he was likely to have been its draftsman.

There is no indication that this law was regarded at the time as note-

---

72Texas (Republic), Senate, *Journal of the Senate of the Republic of Texas, First Session of the Third Congress, 1838* (Houston, 1839), 54, 58; A. E. Wilkinson, "The Author
of the Texas Homestead Exemption Law," *Southwestern Historical Quarterly*, XX (July,
1916), 35, 36. The bill's sponsor and presumed author was Beden Stroud, a native of
Georgia who had probably come to Texas from Alabama in 1837. See Webb, Carroll,
and Branda (eds.), *Handbook of Texas*, II, 680.

73*Journal of the House . . . Regular Session of the Third Congress*, 238. This bill
was introduced on December 29, 1838. Louis P. Cooke, a native of Tennessee and a student at the United States Military Academy, had arrived in Texas with Morehouse's
New York Battalion just after the battle of San Jacinto in 1836. He was added to the
house judiciary committee, to which his bill was referred. Ibid., 256; Webb, Carroll, and
Branda (eds.), *Handbook of Texas*, I, 406.

74*Journal of the Senate . . . First Session of the Third Congress*, 131; *Journal of the
House . . . Regular Session of Third Congress*, 408, 410; Wilkinson, "The Author of the
Texas Homestead Exemption Law," 35–37.

75"Emory Rains," sketch in general biographical notebook, Louis W. Kemp Papers
(BTHC); Wilkinson, "The Author of the Texas Homestead Exemption Law," 40. It is
said that Emory Rains later asserted authorship of the bill but had introduced it
through a fellow member, Cooke. Raines, "Enduring Laws of the Republic of Texas," 96,
105–107.

76"Emory Rains." Kemp Papers; Nacogdoches Archives, LXXV, 75–80, LXXXII, 61–63
(transcripts, BTHC).

worthy in any respect. The Houston newspaper, which reported transactions of the Texas Congress, made no comment on it whatever. The
passage of the first homestead act apparently was not treated as an event
of any consequence by observers of the daily scene in Texas.[77] Anyone
who thought to consider the matter may have viewed its enactment as
a continuation of existing law. But the law was deemed significant
enough for inclusion in a collection of the most important laws of the
first three congresses, which were translated into Spanish and published
in 1841 for dissemination to Spanish-speaking inhabitants of the
Republic.[78]

Just as its progenitor of 1829 had suffered congressional repeal, the
first homestead exemption law was also the victim of temporary eclipse.
What may have prompted second thoughts about the wisdom of the
1839 enactment cannot be discerned from the meager records that have
survived, but at the next session of the Texas Congress, which convened at the end of 1839, the act of January 26, 1839, was superseded
by an enactment which removed the absolute exemption of the family
home from execution and made it available for satisfaction of debt in
the absence of other property in the county.[79] But the Texas legislators
perceived a continuing need for protecting colonists from foreign
debts, and at the same session the Congress enacted another law providing that land grants of the Republic as well as those of Coahuila y
Texas were exempt from debts of the owner contracted prior to immigration, unless otherwise specifically provided. But just as quickly as
the first homestead law was repealed, it was reinstated at the succeeding
congressional session in December, 1840.[80]

---

[77]But the English barrister Doran Maillard, who visited Houston in 1839, was sufficiently struck by the act to record its principal terms (along with its date of enactment)
as a significant aspect of Texas law. N. Doran Maillard, *The History of the Republic of
Texas, from the Discovery of the Country to the Present Time, and the Course of Her
Separation from the Republic of Mexico* (London, 1842), 394

[78]S[tephen] P. Andrews, *Constitución, leyes jenerales, etc. de la república de Tejas*
(Houston, 1841), 304. Andrews was a lawyer who had arrived in Texas in 1839. Webb,
Carroll, and Branda (eds.), *Handbook of Texas*, I, 48. He was apparently unaware of the
1829 statute on which this provision was partially based. The provision concerning implements of husbandry and tools of trade is retranslated into Spanish as follows: "todas
sus herramientas aparato i libros de su oficio o profesión."

[79]An act concerning executions, Feb. 5, 1840, Texas Laws [1839–1840] 93–94, § 4;
Gammel (comp.), *Laws of Texas*, II, 267–268. See Harriet Smither (ed.), *Journals of the
Fourth Congress of the Republic of Texas, 1839–1840, to Which Are Added the Relief
Laws* (3 vols.; Austin, 1929), I, 253, 348, II, 181, 193–194, 262.

[80]Texas Laws [1839–1840] 173; ibid. [1840–1841] 62–63, § 7; Gammel (comp.), *Laws of
Texas*, II, 347, 525–526. The revival of the act of 1839 was achieved by a senate amend-

The Hispanic and Anglo-American traditions of exempt property thus interacted to produce the lasting concept of protecting the family home and certain movables from the claims of creditors. These ideas came to full flower in the formulation of the homestead and chattel-exemption provision of the Texas Constitution of 1845. Forceful minds, well versed in the Hispanic concepts of exempt property and their further development in the decree of 1829, composed and passed the constitutional provision that would publish the expanded concept of exempt property in louder tones to the rest of the United States. The idea had already spread, on the apparent inspiration of the 1839 act, to Mississippi, Georgia, and Florida; within a few years more, similar provisions were enacted in a number of other states and were added to some state constitutions.[81] Well before the end of the century the family home had been extended protection from creditors in almost every American state.[82]

Though the constitutional homestead provision of 1845 did not purport to affect prior debts, some of which were covered by the statute of 1839, it was a true exemption law in that it applied to all obligations incurred in the future, and hence, by passage of time, it referred to all unsecured debts incurred.[83] By the adoption of this constitutional rule, the Hispanic rule for protection of property from seizure was regenerated and extended. As one of those responsible for its formulation,

ment to a house bill amending the act of February 5, 1840. The congressional journals do not show its author.

[81]Texas, *Consitution* (1845), VII, Sec. 22; Law of Jan. 22, 1841, Mississippi Laws [1841] 113, ch. 15, § 1; Law of Dec. 11, 1841, Georgia Laws [1841] 134-135, § 1, amended by Law of Dec. 22, 1843, Georgia Laws [1843] 121-122, § 1; Law of Feb. 15, 1843, Alabama Laws [1843] 73, § 1; Law of Mar. 11, 1845, Florida Laws [1845] 23-24, § 1. In each instance, however, a specified acreage of land was made exempt without any mention of the family *home* or *homestead*.

Wisconsin, California, Michigan, Indiana, Minnesota, and Maryland adopted constitutional provisions prior to 1860. London, "The Initial Homestead Exemption in Texas," 432. See also George L. Haskins, "Homestead Exemptions," *Harvard Law Review*, LXIII (June, 1950), 1,289; "State Homestead Exemption Laws," *Yale Law Journal*, XLVI (Apr., 1937), 1,026-1,027.

[82]Rufus Waples, *A Treatise on Homestead and Exemption* (Chicago, 1893), 955-975. Forty-two states and territories then had homestead laws. The first treatise on the subject was John H. Smyth, *The Law of Homestead and Exemptions* (San Francisco, 1875), which was followed by Thompson, *A Treatise on Homestead and Exemption Laws*. Today all but six states maintain the principle. Max Rheinstein and Mary Ann Glendon, *The Laws of Decedents' Estates . . .* (3rd ed.; Mineola, N.Y., 1971), 102.

[83]Texas, *Constitution* (1845), Art. VII, Sec. 22. The constitution became effective February 16, 1846; sovereignty was transferred to the United States government on February 19. In Wood v. Wheeler, 7 Tex. 13, 24 (1851), Chief Justice John Hemphill analyzed the categories of debts as affected by existing exemption laws.

Chief Justice John Hemphill related that it was derived from the prototype of 1829, as amplified in favor of the family home by the act of
1839.[84]

Today's Texas exemption statute also bears a family resemblance to
the 1829 act of Coahuila y Texas and the Texas act of 1839, which link
it to the Hispanic prototypes of the eighteenth century. Though the
phrase "implements of husbandry" has been somewhat modernized,
aperos de labor, . . . instrumentos de su oficio o máquinas are still recognizably present in the statute: "implements of farming or ranching;
tools, equipment, apparatus (including a boat), and books used in any
trade or profession. . . ."[85]

In Texas the concept of the protected family home has continued to
grow, and some, but not all, of the principles enunciated there have
spread beyond her borders. The act of 1839 furnished a new general
formula for the protection of the surviving widow in terms of exempt
property, and this concept was widely adopted as the "probate homestead."[86] The provision of the 1845 constitution required joinder of
both spouses to convey the home. This principle has been widely adopted elsewhere.[87] In the Texas Constitution of 1876 it was further provided that the family home would not be subject to encumbrance except for its cost, the cost of its improvements, and taxes. This rule,
which bars mortgaging the home merely to borrow money, has not
been so popular elsewhere, and the Texas concept of an exempt place
of business has not been adopted anywhere else at all. Texas's abiding
concern for the welfare of debtors is also exemplified by her law that
wages owing to a debtor are not subject to seizure in the hands of an
employer.[88] While many other states provide for a partial bar to seizure

---

[84]Coleman v. Cobbs, 14 Tex. 598 (1855). See also A. H. Willie, "Introduction," John
Sayles and Henry Sayles, *Early Laws of Texas: General Laws from 1836 to 1879 . . .* (3
vols.; St. Louis, 1888), I, vi; George C. Butte, "Early Development of Law and Equity in
Texas," *Yale Law Journal,* XXVI (June, 1917), 699.

[85]Texas Revised Statutes art. 3,836, enacted by Texas Laws [1973] 1,628, ch. 588, § 2.

[86]Act of Jan. 9, 1843, Texas Laws [1842–1843] 14, §§ 1–2; Gammel (comp), *Laws of
Texas,* II, 834; William F. Fratcher, "Protection of the Family against Disinheritance in
American Law," *International and Comparative Law Quarterly,* XIV (Jan., 1965), 293,
297. Texas was not, however, the first state to extend the exemption privilege to a surviving spouse. Tennessee had so provided in 1833. Tennessee Laws [1833] ch. 80, §§ 1–2.

[87]Texas, *Constitution* (1845), Art. VII, Sec. 22, derived from Texas Laws [1841] § 1, p.
144; Gammell (comp.), *Laws of Texas,* II, 1,294; Act of Apr. 21, 1851, California Laws
[1851] § 2; Massachusetts Laws [1857] ch. 298, § 6; Michigan, *Constitution* (1850), Art. 16,
Sec. 2; Wisconsin Revised Statutes [1849] ch. 102, § 52.

[88]Texas, *Constitution* (1876), Art. XVI, Secs. 28, 50. The proposal concerning home
mortgage was made to the California Constitutional Convention of 1878 and was defeat-

of unpaid wages for debts, this absolute bar is almost unique in American law.

The homestead principle, of mixed Mexican and Texan ancestry, has also had an impact on American federal law. Prior to 1862 United States land-distribution policy had not been directed primarily to bona fide colonists but rather to buyers in general, which very often meant land speculators. But with the example of Texas land grants before the public, the land-reform and free-soil movements produced federal legislation in favor of settlers, and the principle of protection of the family home was embodied in it.[89] Using the term "homestead" in a somewhat broader sense, the legislation was termed the Homestead Act.

The federal government was equally slow in providing legislation for the relief of debtors through national bankruptcy legislation. Permanent legislation to that end was not enacted until 1898. But acts of short duration, modeled on earlier English statutes, had been enacted on three occasions during the nineteenth century: 1800–1803, 1841–1842, and 1867–1878. In all these instances the ultimate underlying model was the *cessio bonorum* of Roman law, under which a debtor was allowed to retain his necessary clothing.[90] Already somewhat broadened prior to its American reception, the nineteenth-century definition of necessaries that the bankrupt debtor might retain was expanded to include property exempt to the debtor by the law of the state of his domicile. Thus American bankruptcy law came to embrace the concept of protection of the family home and exempt movables to the extent that the law of the bankrupt's domicile offered that protection. It was not until 1902, however, that the United States Supreme Court concluded that the adoption of state practice in the exemption clause of the bankruptcy law did not make the federal law impermissibly nonuniform. In the enactment of the present federal bankruptcy law, adopted in 1978, the concept of exemption had become so generally ac-

ed. Theodore H. Hittell, *History of California* (4 vols.; San Francisco, 1898), IV, 625. Although no other state has exempted places of business, the Texas homestead tax exemption provided by the Texas Constitution, Art. VIII, Sec. 1-a (1932), has been somewhat popular. Over a dozen other states have enacted similar provisions.

89Thomas Le Duc, "History and Appraisal of United States Land Policy to 1862," Howard W. Ottoson (ed.), *Land Use Policy and Problems in the United States* (Lincoln, 1963), 3, 11; Henry W. Farnam, *Chapters in the History of Social Legislation in the United States to 1860* (Washington, D.C., 1938), 127–140; Gracy (ed.), *Establishing Austin's Colony*, vii–viii; Thomas Donaldson, *The Public Domain* (Washington, D.C., 1884), 295–296, 332–350.

90Charles Warren, *Bankruptcy in United States History* (1935; reprint ed., New York, 1972), 12–22, 49–92, 95–128; Louisiana Civil Code 1825 art. 2,179, Louisiana Civil Code 1870 art. 2,183; 32 George 2, c. 28, § 13 (1759).

cepted that a standard federal homestead exemption is now offered to a bankrupt as an alternative to that provided by his state of domicile.[91]

Nor is that quite the end of the story. In 1917 the concept of homestead was incorporated in the Mexican constitution, and in 1907 and 1921, into Spanish law. Thus the Spanish notion of protection of debtors' vital property from creditors, developed and fully matured on the former frontier of Spanish America, returned to the lands of its ultimate sources.[92]

---

[91]Vern Countryman, "A History of American Bankruptcy Law," *Commercial Law Journal*, LXXXI (June–July, 1976), 226–230; U.S. Bankruptcy Act, 1898 § 6; U.S. Bankruptcy Act, 1978 § 552; Hanover National Bank v. Moyses, 186 U.S. 181 (1902). Coleman, *Debtors and Creditors in America*, 25–26; Warren, *Bankruptcy in United States History*, 100, 106, 110–112; 11 U.S.C. § 522(b) (1), (d) (1) or (b) (2) (1978).

[92]*Constitución política de los Estados Mexicanos*, 1917, art. 123, in *Derechos del pueblo mexicano* . . . (8 vols.; Mexico City, 1967), II, following p. 620; Luna Serrano, *El patrimonia familiar*, 55–56.

Law and Legal Tender in California and the West

BY GORDON M. BAKKEN

When Congress passed the Legal Tender Act in 1862 declaring United States notes to be legal tender for debts, it presented a critical question of federalism to our nation's courts. The national government, as part of its effort to deal with our greatest internal emergency, had laid down important new national money-supply policy. The declared public policy was clear. The legal tender acts were specifically part of the national war effort. They were soon followed by national banking legislation which filled out the contours of national money policy. Yet several western states, loyal to the national government otherwise, openly seceded from this important aspect of national policy.

The legal tender issue forced several western supreme courts to grapple with problems involving political, economic, and legal considerations of public policy. The response of these courts varied regionally, but each reflected judicial attitudes on the state of the law during and after the Civil War and the extent of judicial review. Moreover, these decisions reflected a judicial view of the necessities of their respective commercial communities. The legal tender issue, then, demonstrated both the role of the judiciary in defining a proper medium for the conduct of credit transactions and the limits of judicial power.

The public policy issues had several facets. Legal tender forced judges to decide four related questions. First, as greenbacks could be considered simply factors in a money system, judges were concerned with facilitating exchanges and the medium was therefore significant. Second, equity was important; creditor-debtor relations would be radically altered by allowing payment of debts in depreciated paper. Third, courts considered the need to adjust contractual relations to the impact of money value fluctuation. While not major consideration in the period, judges did weigh its impact upon the general course of dealings. Finally, the state courts most carefully weighed the impact of their decisions upon federal relations. Argument and decision often centered upon the authority of sovereigns and the impact on the new national banking system.

California's Specific Contract Act of 1863 represented a reaction to national Republican efforts in the Legal Tender Act to establsh a national currency and finance the war, and to the local merchants' demands for a stable medium of exchange. California merchants feared a possible deluge of greenbacks into the state and a subsequent decline in profits and certainly in transactions. Further, California had had a money supply problem from the 1850s, but stability was more important than money supply to dealers in the marketplace. California legislators reacted with the Specific Contract Act.[1] The statute provided that in an action on a written contract specifyng payment in a specific kind of money, judgment for the plaintiff could follow the contract. The execution of judgment was to specify the kind of money. The law bound the sheriff to satisfy the judgment in the kind of money specified. In sum, lenders, by specifying payment in gold, could avoid payment in depreciated paper money.[2]

Money supply, interest rates, and financial uncertainty had plagued California since statehood. Montgomery Martin reported to Benjamin D. Wilson in 1850 that money was "very scarce" and that "some of the largest houses in San Francisco are now tottering." Martin was even at a loss on how to get money from Sacramento to Los Angeles. He wrote, "I am somewhat at a loss how to remit the money safely, can you suggest any plan?"[3] Thomas A. Hereford wrote from San Pedro in 1851 that money was "as scarce as in any country in the world."[4] Promissory notes became a medium of exchange, but at the extraordinary interest rates of the 1850s and 1860s they were of uncertain value and often required expensive litigation. This was particularly true of debts carrying interest rates of 10 to 15% per month.[5] In the period 1850-1870, barter was often a means of exchange without money. In 1863 Adolph Eberhart of San Francisco described a proposed transaction for a wine press to Benjamin D. Wilson in terms of "the price is $375 payable in wine."[6] In 1866 he was negotiating an exchange of wine for groceries from "a Front street wholesale grocery."[7] To settle a debt, in 1869, a Los Angeles furniture dealer suggested that the transaction be in lumber.[8] The problem of exchange was very real as specie was infrequently available. Charles Robinson Johnson wrote Abel Stearns in 1862 that he could not get a draft cashed until "the steamer arrives."[9] The Specific Contract Act of 1863 was passed with over a decade of uncertainty behind it.

The California Supreme Court upheld the Specific Contract Act in 1864. Justice John Currey speaking for the court in *Carpentier v. Atherton* found that the California act and the federal law were not in conflict.[10] While the national Legislature could issue and make legal tender of a currency, it did not follow that any legal tender could satisfy every contract. Gold and silver were commodities of value relative to paper money on which businessmen agreed a specific value could be determined. However, despite any agreement on specie values operatives in the marketplace could agree that any obligation could only be satisfied by the delivery of a specific commodity. Hence, where such a commodity was specified, it was within a court's traditional powers to decree specific performance where money damages would be an inadequate remedy for breach of contract. Currey stated that:

> If one agrees to pay or deliver to another a given number of dollars, he may perform his contract by the payment of the specified sum in any kind of dollars which are recognized as such and made a legal tender for the purpose by the law of the land; for by doing so he fullfills his engagement according to its letter; but if he contracts to pay his debt in a particular kind of money, his obligation cannot be discharged in accordance with his stipulation by payment in a different kind of money; and though by the unaided rules of the common law he could not be compelled to perform specifically that which he had promised, yet, in morals, his obligation to do so is in no degree diminished.
>
> Courts of equity from an early period have exercised jurisdiction, enforcing the specific performance of contracts, for the reason that the Courts of common law, though recognizing the obligation of the parties to a contract to perform their respective parts of it according to its terms, could not afford this remedy to the party injured by the non-performance of the other. At law the party disappointed by the breach of the contract was compelled to be satisfied with money as a substitute for the thing

for which he had contracted, and to which he was in justice entitled.

The money recovered in such cases, by way of damages, was considered as a substantial equivalent for the injury sustained by the breach of the contract. But upon this subject Judge Story says: "It is against conscience that a party should have a right of election whether he will perform his covenant or only pay damages for the breach of it." (Story on Eq. Jur. 717 a.)

This was especially true, Currey argued, where the paper money's worth relative to the specific commodity could not be correctly estimated. Such was the case with Civil War paper money.

On the constitutional question, Currey maintained that the Legal Tender Act declared the federal notes lawful currency and legal tender for private debts, but it did not follow that legal tender notes could be tendered in satisfaction of every obligation. The California legislature by the Specific Contract Act had merely afforded a statutory remedy for enforcing certain contracts. This right to enforcement was "consistent with good faith" and with the dictates of a "scrupulous and exact justice."[11] Currey with the traditional doctrine of construction that courts should give reasonable interpretation to legislation to save it from the brand of unconstitutionality, Currey ably stacked his logic for validity. He also dredged up the vested rights to support his argument. The right to a remedy was a right to a commodity and must be guarded.[12]

The only limitation was, of course, conflict with federal law, a circumstance requiring that federal law should control. A court, Currey argued, should only strike down state law where the state legislature's act transcended its powers or derogated federal law. But was the Legal Tender Act "paramount law" to justify striking down the state statute?

The federal law was paramount where a debt was payable in money, but a contract which was more specific was within the language of the statute. Manifestly, a contract that called for a specific act to be performed must be enforced according to the intent of the parties, Curry observed. Even more certainly, where a party needed a particular medium of exchange as the payment of duties and debts outside the United States, commercial necessity dictated that gold or silver be used. How could it be logical,

Currey asked, that Congress should require taxes to be paid in specie and not have made exactly the exception to the Legal Tender Act that he advocated. How could the importation of foreign goods, regulated by Congress, be maintained, if merchants were required to accept payment of domestic debts in paper money and to pay foreign debts in specie? Obviously, Currey intimated, Congress must have intended such an exception lest business collapse. By the same reasoning, state law could not discriminate against federal paper currency because "Congress itself has limited the uses to which the notes can be applied."[13] In sum, there was no conflict and the state law must stand.

Justice Lorenzo Sawyer in a concurring opinion added several alternative arguments. He observed that a right or privilege conferred upon an individual by statute could be waived by the party. The only limitation was if the waiver was against public policy. Sawyer maintained that while usury was against public policy in some states a contract "for a sufficient consideration to pay a given sum in gold coin, or any other kind of money" was certainly not immoral. In fact, the federal government expressly recognized contracts for the delivery of gold coin in an 1863 internal revenue statute.[14] Similarly, federal law authorizing the Secretary of Treasury to receive deposits of gold coin and bullion impliedly recognized contracts specifying gold as payment. Sawyer concluded that the federal government made gold clause contracts with its citizens and hence recognized such contracts between its citizens.

Vested rights language also abounded in Sawyers opinion. Sawyer argued, as did Currey, that without a decree of specific performance there was no adequate remedy. Since a court would not inquire into the relative value of monies, there was in theory a remedy, but in reality it was inadequate. Hence, enforcing a gold clause "most nearly" did "substantial justice to all parties"[15] Here again, the state statute only provided a just remedy.

While both justices' opinions emphasized points of construction and interpretation supporting the validity of the State law, both contained contract law reasoning. First, a contract must be enforced according to the intent of the parties unless against public policy. A gold clause, in writing, was such an expression of intent. Second, such enforcement supported another public policy of providing certainty through contract law in marketplace dealings. A fluctuating medium of exchange was not an advisable commercial medium. Greenbacks posed the specter of inflation which decreased the value of an interest held by creditors which, in turn, decreased certainty in the marketplace.[16]

The Specific Contract Act and the *Carpentier* decision received strong public support in California. John Ferris published a supportive tract in 1867 entitled *The Financial Economy of the United States Illustrated and Some of the Causes which Retard the Progress of California Demonstrated.*[17] Dealers in currency and obligations quickly turned to buying gold in 1862. Charles R. Johnson complained to Abel Stearns in August 1862 that there was "actually no money in town (Los Angeles)." Further, "what little money the traders have, they buy gold dust, which pays them a profit."[18] In September 1862, Cave Johnson Couts was dealing in both paper and specie, but the former only at a discount.[19] After the Specific Contract Act merchants turned to specifying the medium for payment. M. W. Childs, a Los Angeles store owner, had "payable in U.S. Gold Coin" printed on his invoices. Corbitt and Barker, also Los Angeles merchants, had the same inscription enblazoned on their invoices. Similarly, A. Portugal, a hat store owner in Los Angeles, wrote "the Buyer agrees to pay this Bill in U.S. Gold Coin at par or its Equivalent" on his invoices.[20] The practice of specifying a medium for payment continued into the 1870s. The firms of Jose Mascarel and Company, S. C. Foy Saddlery, Louis Lewin & Co., Stationer, and M. W. Childs, Farming and Mining Tools all of Los Angeles required "U.S. Gold Coin."[21] Other Los Angeles merchants provided alternatives. H. Newmark and Company rubber stamped "This Bill of Goods is sold for U.S. Gold Coin, Silver, only taken at Current rates of discount" on its invoices. Barrow, Furrey, and Co., Implements had a similar legend printed on its invoices.[22] The reason for the preference was quite clear. Greenbacks were of fluctuating value. As Charles Johnson reported to Abel Stearns in 1865, "Twelve thousand dollars legal tenders will be sold on Tuesday at public auction by the Sheriff on Account of Parrott." They were "brought by Downey . . . at Fifty-four cents."[23] Crane and Brigham of San Francisco in 1864 sold greenbacks at 68¢ on the dollar when they received them.[24] Dealers in money and goods found the Specific Contract Act a means of avoiding uncertainty in their transactions.

The *Carpentier* decision had marked impact in California. Despite the protests of the Secretary of Treasury, Salmon P. Chase, the California legislature refused to modify its stand, emboldened by the war and isolation. As a result national banking did not spread to California until the late 1880s[25] The forty-niner attitude toward paper money coupled with legislative intransigence and judicial enforcement of gold clause contracts[26] resulted in federal bank notes circulating at discount.

The Specific Contract Act found advocates in other western states and territories. The 1863 influx of greenbacks into the Pacific coast resulted in businessmen denying credit to persons who paid in greenbacks.[27] John Wesley North, a justice of the Nevada territorial supreme court, reported to his wife in 1865 that before the Nevada Specific Contract Act, lenders "were careful to loan only to men in who they had confidence that they would not pay in Greenbacks." North also observed that those who pay in paper were subject to either interest rates double the market or being denied loans.[28] But lenders in Nevada and Idaho did get the protection of the California variety Specific Contract Acts.[29] Both acts required judgments to follow the contract where a specified kind of medium was payable. Both required that execution sales be satisfied in specified commodity. Nevada's statute went further in applying its provisions to implied contracts "if satisfactory evidence (were) offered at trial." Similar pressures by businessmen had come to bear, but the reception of the laws was not as favorable in the courts.

The Nevada extension of its statute to implied contracts raised serious questions of federalism. Its potential for conflict with federal control of the money supply was a serious issue. It was one thing to accord enforcement to clear cut, express private agreements for specie, but where the state's official agencies could find implied agreements for specie payment, the state was clearly intervening in an area of national concern. The statute challenged the general presumption of the federal Constitution that the national money supply was in the hands of Congress.

In 1865 the Nevada Supreme Court considered both the federal Legal Tender Act and the State Specific Contract Act. In *Maynard v. Newman* (1865) the Nevada Supreme Court found, as the U.S. Supreme Court later held, that the Legal Tender Act was constitutional and authorized by the necessary and proper clause.[30] The case involved a promissory note for ten thousand dollars; there was no stipulation for payment or any particular commodity, or form of money. The note was assigned to the plaintiff, on which he obtained judgment. After judgment, defendants paid into court the full amount of the debt, interest and costs, in U.S. legal tender notes. Plaintiff refused to accept the notes and appealed for an order to the clerk of court to satisfy judgment. The only question was the constitutionality of the federal law. Justice Henry O. Beatty for a unanimous court found the act constitutional and based on the necessary and proper clause.

The structure of Beatty's argument was similar to Hamilton's debate with Jefferson over the meaning of necessary and proper. Beatty reviewed the "history of the formation of this Government prior to the adoption of the present Constitution" and the Constitutional convention.[31] He then agreed with Hamilton's position that necessary and proper "should have a most liberal construction."[32] Hence, the act was an authorized exercise of power and constitutional because it had a reasonable relationship to another authorized function, coining money.

Even if authorized, counsel argued that the law was "unjust, oppressive and impolitic" and on that ground be struck down. But Beatty disagreed. The Legal Tender Act was also an expedient war measure. It created a circulating medium, saved "the debtor classes" from ruin, and fostered "the universal prosperity of the Eastern States."[33] The act was, in sum, constitutional and wise public policy. In 1865 unionists and Republicans could have reasoned no other way.

Beatty's analysis was curious in its explicit balancing of interests. Instead of a terse application of the presumption of constitutionality, Beatty indulged in a flourish of judicial rhetoric and historical analysis much as the U.S. Supreme Court did in the first legal tender cases. As was somewhat characteristic of state judges, Beatty chose to construe national public policy rather than applying the presumption. The potential for state judicial activism in national affairs was thereby maintained without exercise in the case at bar.

The case of *Burling v. Goodman* (1865) was concurrently submitted to the court with many of the same briefs.[34] The case differed in that a mortgage and promissory notes containing a gold clause were involved. The trial court's decree required payment in gold. However, the supreme court did not hesitate to deny effect to the gold clause. Although the specific Contract Act was on the books, it was not in force at the time of judgment. The judgment was governed by common law. At common law, Justice Cornelius M. Brosnan argued, when an action was brought on a contract for the payment of money, the judgment of the court was only that the plaintiff recover his debt and damages and not how the amount was to be paid or made.[35] Since the constitutionality of the federal act had been decided, the court directed the district court to modify its order so that it allowed payment in paper money.

The Nevada court struck down the Specific Contract Act in *Miliken v. Sloat* (1865).[36] The case involved a promissory note with a gold clause on which judgment had been obtained and execution issued. The defendant had tendered greenbacks in satisfaction of judgment and moved the district court to order satisfaction of judgment. This motion failed and the defendant appealed. In a two-to-one decision the court found the state act in conflict with the Legal Tender Act and void.

The court found that the Specific Contract Act was prospective only. Justice Beatty, speaking for the majority, held that a statute was to have prospective application only unless a retroactive intention was so plainly expressed by the legislature as to leave no doubt in the mind. However, Beatty intimated that there were "vested right(s) as the Legislature had not the power to overthrow."[37] While not deciding the question, Beatty suggested that such rights were those of "contract or property." However, the Nevada court rejected California precedents that found retroactivity in their Specific Contract Act. Similarly, the court rejected counsel's argument for implied retroactivity. By maintaining that the statute could only be construed as operating prospectively, Beatty avoided the grave constitutional issue of conflict with the Legal Tender Act. Further, Beatty noted that the court had already found the Legal Tender Act valid in *Maynard v.*

Newman. He then maintained that "being valid, it (was) supreme."[38]

The Specific Contract Act, Beatty argued, aimed to engraft an exception to the federal law. It was "making the Act to read: except duties on imports, interest on public debt and a class of debts *payable in gold coin*" (emphasis Beatty's).[39] The consequences of upholding the state law would be the emasculation of federal law by state statute.

The court rejected the argument that the Nevada law was merely remedial and that the remedy was just and equittable. Beatty contended that characterizing the statute as remedial in no way lifted the cloak of conflict. The state law was in derogation of federal law no matter what name it was given. Beatty castigated counsel saying

> All such laws stand in direct and brazen antagonism to the policy of the nation, and, practically extended through several States, during the rayless period of the national travail, would have inflicted a wound upon constitutional liberty which the coming ages would not see healed.[40]

The argument for the gold clause, as he saw it, was states' rightism at its "most odious." The Civil War and Republican thought was indelibly branded on this analysis of conflict.

On rehearing, Beatty reiterated his constitutional arguments, and confronted the waiver contention raised in *Carpentier.* Beatty contended that counsel misconstrued the meaning of waiver. Waiver, defined by Beatty, was the relinquishment or refusal to accept a right. In gold clause contracts, a debtor bound himself to pay in gold. If the contract was legal, he never had a right or power to discharge the debt with greenbacks. How then, Beatty inquired, could the debtor waive the right he never possessed. Moreover, the waiver issue was "simply an evasion of the true issue."[41] The true question was the power of a state legislature to license two of its citizens to contract that a positive law of Congress be void regarding their transaction. To Beatty such a proposition "out in plain English would be laughed at."[42] The constitutional question being answered, the state law clearly had to fall. By rejecting the waiver argument, Beatty assumed that the issue was one appropriate for judicial resolution at the state level and decided the question by reference to the war time federal money policy.

Counsel also tried to persuade the court of the wisdom of the Specific Contract and implored the justices to uphold it on the grounds of public policy. Beatty's reply was terse.

> Twelve months ago the money lenders assured the Legislature if they would pass this law the business of the State would be restored to a prosperous condition. The law was passed, and within twelve months the assessed value of property in the State had diminished more than one-third. Nearly the entire population is embarrassed and groaning under debts bearing such a rate of interest as must reduce them to bankruptcy if they cannot get a change of laws and financial policy. We certainly do not see anything so encouraging in the system as to induce us to disregard all legal principle and rules of common sense to sustain it.[43]

So concluding, Beatty found neither constitutional nor financial merit in the Specific Contract Act. It is clear from this excerpt that Beatty hardly had the presumption of constitutionality in mind. The Court explicitly entered into a consideration of factual grounding for policy.

Chief Justice James F. Lewis dissented. The dissent was based on the reasoning of *Carpentier v. Atherton*. While all justices were Republican, the political factor was not overt although Beatty's opinion openly castigated counsel for their use of John C. Calhoun's writings as precedent. However, the division on the court did indicate the potential for reversal. Hence, in a long series of cases counsel continued to raise constitutional and policy arguments against the Legal Tender Act and for the Specific Contract Statute.

The Legal Tender Act applied to the satisfaction of "debts" and counsel came before the court questioning whether money owed a state or local government for taxes was owed on a "debt" within the meaning of the federal law.

In *Rhodes v. O'Farrel* (1866) the Nevada court found that application of the term "debts" to taxes split the *Milliken* majority.[44] The case involved taxes levied on real estate for which the state had obtained judgment. The taxpayer tendered greenbacks. The tax collector refused because judgment called for gold coin. The question was whether a judgment for taxes was a debt within the meaning of the Legal Tender Act. Beatty thought that such judgments were debts and payable in paper money. Justice Brosnan differed with Beatty on what a judgment for taxes was in law.

Beatty relied on the opinion of Stephen J. Field, on circuit in *Perry v. Washburne,* a California case.[45] Field had argued that taxes were not debts within the meaning of the Legal Tender Act. He would later reiterate this view in *Lane Co. v. Oregon* (1869) for the U.S. Supreme Court. But Beatty disagreed with Field in *Perry,* arguing that "debt" referred to a category, broader than obligation, created by contract. A "debt" also included the obligation of a judgment, where that judgment was based on a tax obligation, it was no less a debt. (So utilizing Field, Beatty totally disagreed with his result in Perry.) To Beatty, tax obligations reduced to judgment were debts because judgments for money were debts.

Brosnan disagreed with Beatty's characterization of taxes. A tax was not an implied promise to pay, or anything like a debt. It reflected on non-contractual duty, a pecuniary charge levied by government, without assent by the individual except his representation in the legislation. But the process below forced Brosnan to concur in the result. He concluded:

> It the State will disrobe herself of sovereignty, and enter the forensic arena with her subject, to collect a paltry tax of one dollar by the ordinary process of a suit at law, and at a cost to the delinquent taxpayer of from twenty to thirty dollars, which is of no benefit to the State, as is now the patent fact; and if in doing this the State recovers judgment, I can perceive no satisfactory reason why such judgment may not be satisfied by payment of the amount in legal tender notes of the United States.[46]

While conceding the state's power to tax and collect in gold, Brosnan found that the state was subject to criteria of equity in pursuing its remedy. As *Lane Co. v. Oregon* would later hold, Brosnan's position on the more general question was the more meritorious. While *Lane County* did not go on any such particular ruling of equity as Brosnan would have, it did express, as Brosnan did, a concern that if Congress subjected the state's revenue collecting powers to its power to define legal tender, it might raise a serious constitutional question of invading one of the most important spheres of power reserved to the states via the Tenth Amendment.

Beatty received another setback trying to collect his salary in 1867. In *Nevada v. Beatty* (1867)[47] Justice Lewis, Beatty's antagonist in *Milliken v. Sloat,* for the Nevada court denied Beatty his salary in gold. The state legislature changed its position on the payment of salaries to state officers. Previously the legislature made such salaries payable in coin. Now the state made legal tender the proper medium for salaries. Beatty objected, arguing that the statute was rendered unconstitutional by the section of the state Constitution declaring that salaries of certain officers could not be increased or decreased during their term of office. Lewis rejected this contention, stating that in the payment of a debt, legal tender notes were in contemplation of law equal to coin. In effect, he threw Beatty's reasoning in *Milliken* back at him.

The setback in *Nevada v. Beatty* changed the chief justice's mind about the wisdom of his *Milliken* approach. In *Nevada v. Kruttschnitt* (1868), Beatty, in discussing the taxation of mines, commented on the value of greenbacks. He observed that there seemed "to be some sort of vague notion that because the Government has made paper money a legal tender, it has attempted to make it equal to gold. But this is not so."[48] The consistent position taken by jurists upholding in Legal Tender Act that a court would not inquire into the relative value of monies was thus repudiated in dicta.

The composition of the Nevada court changed. Justice Brosnan died April 21, 1867 and was replaced by another Republican, J. Neely Johnson. Chief Justice Beatty resigned November 9, 1868. B. C. Whitman, a Republican, received appointment to Beatty's unexpired term. Justice Lewis became the court's chief justice.

The Nevada court in 1868 reversed its field on legal tender and overruled *Milliken.* Chief Justice Lewis in *Linn v. Minor*[49] found that Congress had neither prohibited specific contract laws, nor had it required the payment of debts in any particular medium. Further, *Milliken v. Sloat* could not be allowed to stand despite the doctrine of *stare decisis.* It was clearly incorrect and the Nevada business community had repudiated it. The Court's notation of business community distress over its ruling was significant. Law in books had not been law in action; in fact, the opposite had taken place, disregard of law. Whether legally enforceable or otherwise enforceable, money lenders had chosen to follow their version of sound lending policy rather than declared public policy.

On the question of Congressional intent in the Legal Tender Act, Lewis was confident that Congress could never have wanted what the *Milliken* court had claimed. First, there was nothing in the law specifically prohibiting judgments enforcing contracts in accordance with their "strict letter." Secondly, the *Milliken* court was mistaken about the government's interest in having debts paid in legal tender notes. Lewis claimed that the act indicated only that coin and paper notes were legal tender to settle claims in the absence of some legally effective provision to the contrary. The "General Government" indicated no desire to have one medium circulate in preference to the other. "Nothing (was) clearer than the right to discharge a debt in notes (was) simply a privilege given to the individual."[50] The statute prescribed no duty to pay notes in preference to coin. The option lay with the volition of the contracting partner.

Lewis' analysis was based on a vested rights interpretation of contract law. Without a specifically prescribed duty to act otherwise, an individual's options were part of his marketplace rights. Contract rights were paramount in this arena. Lewis also used his judicial power to guard these rights following a tradition of the early 19th century. Lewis' analysis also relied on a strict interpretation of statutory language. This strict interpretation was equally manifest in his view of public policy.

Courts have refused to enforce contracts which contravene public policy. This doctrine recognized that private parties in exercising their contract rights could not undercut a public power. Contract law demands the responsible exercise of power within such areas concerning a public policy. To Lewis, the doctrine was limited to barring contracts for immoral purposes, and those in contravention of explicitly stated public policies. Again, the strict interpretation of the Legal Tender Act revealed no violation. Here Lewis simply relied upon *Carpentier v. Atherton* for authority. In sum, on legal grounds *Milliken* had to fall. Even with the doctrine of *stare decisis*, Lewis thought *Milliken* so "manifestly erroneous" and productive "only of wrong and injustice," that it could not stand.[51]

The business community's reaction to *Milliken* was further proof of its lack of wisdom. Reversing *Milliken* could do no commercial wrong, Lewis argued, because "the moral sense of the community had repudiated it from the moment it was rendered." Only "that class of persons" without moral rightness who could perceive "no wrong in the violation of a deliberate and fair contract" supported *Milliken*. The business community since *Milliken* had conducted affairs with coin based on honor. In sum, "beyond giving legal sanction to the violation of contracts," the defrauding of creditors, and the depriving of labor of 30% of its wages, "the decision has been a dead letter—virtually overrulled by the moral power of the upright portion of the communtiy."[52] In observing this behavior, Lewis, romanticized the lending practices of the era which effectively denied substantial bargaining. 'Deliberate and fair' contracts were drafted by lenders.

Lewis' vested rights analysis was one which related both to substantive due process of law concepts as well as the retroactivity of statute. The former found dramatic application in the late 19th century and basically held that a legislature could not alter a contractual relationship which deprived a party of property without the due process of the judiciary. Where a statute deprived a person of property, the Court had an obligation to declare it unconstitutional. The latter merely held that where contracts were made before the legal tender acts, the creditor's gold clause rested on the contract and the very strong claim that public policy favored freedom of contract. In light of this very strong policy, unless the federal legal tender laws very clearly forbade gold clauses, any doubt in their interpretation should be resolved in favor of the contract language. Lewis strongly supported freedom of contract while asserting the Court's authority to question the wisdom of public policy.

The series of Nevada cases demonstrated both the course of judicial thought and the limits of power. *Linn*, like *Carpentier*, was an assertion of state sovereignty. The state had a right to control its courts, a facet of which was the entry of judgment.

Federal law could create currencies, but it could not intrude into this area of state right. *Linn* also was a manifestation of vested rights philosophy. Operatives in the marketplace had a right in contract law to bargain for an exchange of commodities. If the contract was not immoral, the courts would enforce the bargain. But even with *Milliken*, dealers in the money market refused to alter their behavior. Legal tender worked an economic hardship that lenders would not accept. Moreover, the Nevada court was unable to enforce its public policy declaration.

In Idaho the business community had similar problems, but both the court and the lenders found the Specific Contract Act void. The 1863 influx of greenbacks into the Pacific coast at first had the same result in Idaho as it had had in California and Nevada. Lenders denied credit to those who paid in greenbacks. Business sought and won a Specific Contract Act from the territorial legislature. But mercantile experience demonstrated the need for legal tender notes. The circulating medium in Idaho prior to greenbacks was primarily gold dust. But the counterfeiting of gold dust resulted in consistently higher values for notes in Idaho than in the San Francisco market. Hence Idaho merchants lobbied for a repeal of the Specific Contract Act, and business accepted greenbacks at par to avoid losses due to "bogus dust."[53] In this context, the Idaho court found the Specific Contract Act void. In Idaho the practical business policy question was clearly one of the money supply and certainly of exchange. While California merchants could write contracts for gold coin, Idaho dealers possessed few coins. Gold dust was less reliable because of counterfeiting and federal notes thereby gained value.

In *Betts v. Butler* (1868) the Idaho territorial supreme court struck down the territorial act.[54] In a brief opinion, Justice John Cummins had "no hesitancy in pronouncing (the Idaho Specific Contract Act) in direct conflict" with the Legal Tender Act, and void. The latter act was the "supreme law of the land." Further, based on *Milliken v. Sloat* judgment could not be rendered in dollars.[55] So saying, the court aided the business community without legislative aid.

While the Betts opinion was terse, the Idaho court extensively discussed the Legal Tender Act's impact on state taxing power. In *Haas v. Misner* (1867) the court considered an action by the

Ada county tax assessor.[56] The assessor sought to enforce payment of taxes in gold or silver coin, or their equivalent in gold dust, bullion, or legal tender notes at 2% above the San Francisco market quotations. The question, Justice Cummins recognized, was of an "important and grave character." Further, there were conflicting opinions on the matter in "the highest tribunals of some of our sister states and territories." This division was complicated by "the great dearth of authorities."[57] However, one issue was assumed to be settled. The Legal Tender Act was constitutional. What remained was whether territorial taxes were debts whithin the meaning of the statute. If they were, the territorial law would be in conflict with the federal statute and would be void.

The discussion of the terms "tax" and "debt" was extensive. Counsel urged Justice Cummins to follow *Perry v. Washburn* and find a tax not a debt. While the Idaho justice displayed respect for Field's California opinion, he rejected his arguments. Debts did not have to be founded on a contract. Taxes were legislatively created and assented to, although impliedly, through the representative system of government. Individuals in society impliedly assent to contribute to social needs. The California position did not necessarily lead to a logical conclusion. Moreover, a debt had been broadly defined by Bouvier and Webster to include claims for money and money which a person was bound to pay. A tax could easily fit these definitions and thereby be within the intent of Congress.

Counsel also argued that the states and territories were supreme in matters pertaining to their revenue systems, Cummins rejected the contenton. Cummins maintained then the power of states was only to levy and collect taxes, not to prescribe the medium of payment. To hold otherwise would allow legislative whim to deprive "nine tenths of the taxpayers" of a medium to pay taxes.

Finally, Cummins rejected *Carpentier v. Atherton* on the relative value of gold and notes. "Plainly stated, a dollar in law is precisely the same whether composed of gold or of paper."[58] Unless gold were treated as a commodity, Cummins observed, liability of a contract was based on a promise to pay in lawful money. Taxpayers as well as debtors, Cummins held, could pay in greenbacks. Cummins clearly understood the federalism issues better than the Nevada justices and there put *Haas* on firmer ground.

The Idaho court allowed debts and taxes to be paid in greenbacks, but the legislature revived the 1864 Specific Contract Act a decade later. The eighth session of the territorial legislature revived the statute.[59] The Idaho Supreme Court in *Emery v. Laugley* (1878) casually allowed the jury to decide whether, on well-pleaded facts a contract was for gold or greenbacks.[60] Gold clause contracts continued as part of lending practices throughout the 19th century. While judicial power was exercised in *Betts* with the approval of the merchants, it is equally apparent that lenders maintained terms which they desired despite *Betts*.

The Legal Tender Act had impact in other western states, but the constitutional conflict was absent. Colorado miners, who traditionally distrusted paper money, continued business as usual on a specie basis.[61] Montana's first territorial legislature made the measure of damages in actions on gold contracts the market value of the dust or bullion, but payable in Treasury Notes. The Montana court followed the lead of the legislature by denying enforcement of gold clause contracts.[62] As late as 1884 a Utah statute allowed judgments on contracts to follow the contract and require payment in a specified kind of money or currency.[63] Lending practices varied from state to state, but even after the Legal Tender Cases, some state laws allowed gold clause contracts to remain a part of business transactions.

While state courts across the nation repudiated gold clause contracts,[64] the peculiar circumstances of several western jurisdictions led jurists to defy the national trend. The courts responded to business needs and legal doctrines. But judges also realized the limits of judicial review. Nevada's court waivered on doctrine and business wisdom, but without the business community's support, its holdings went unheeded. Idaho's supreme bench fulfilled a pressing mercantile need at a particular time by striking down the specific Contract Act. However, as times changed, the legislature re-enacted the once unconstitutional law and also fulfilled creditor needs. While vested rights, states' rights, and other doctrines were important in the process of decision, supreme court justices declared a public policy which they felt suited the economic needs of the moment.

The courts also exhibited varying views of their authority and role in a federal system. As noted, the presumption of constitutionality was inconsistently applied. Some courts exhibited a willingness to enter into extensve public policy analysis in resolving the benefit of the doubt for federal authority. While national money supply policy carried with it the authority of Congress and a presumption of constitutionality, several courts found local interests of greater compelling weight.

In broader terms of jurisprudence, these legal tender and specific contract cases demonstrate the vitality of the instrumentalist approach to law. Clearly, the instrumentalists dominated. Their inquiry was into the political and economic expediency of legislative decisions. The courts of the region were attempting to forge law useful in the marketplace while also deciding their proper roles in government.

NOTES

The author acknowledges a grant from the National Endowment for the Humanities in support of this research paper.

[1] California S.L. 1863, p. 687.

[2] On the California Specific Contract Act see Wesley C. Mitchell, *A History of the Greenbacks* (Chicago, 1903), p. 144; William C. Frankhauser, *A Financial History of California, 1849-1910* (Berkeley, 1913), pp. 219-222; Ira B. Cross, *Financing an Empire*, 4 vols. (New York, 1927), 1: 300-360; Joseph W. Ellison, *California and the Nation, 1849-1866* (Berkeley, 1927), pp. 216-227.

[3] Martin to Wilson, January 23, 1850, Benjamin D. Wilson Collection, MSS, Box 1, Huntington Library, San Marino, California.

[4] Hereford to Ester S. Hereford, February 20, 1851, *Ibid.*, Box 2.

[5] See Martin to Wilson, January 23, 1850 (10-15% rates). Also Box 2, see lawsuit of Abel Stearns versus Martin and Wilson on a 90 day note at 2% per month. *Ibid.*

[6] Eberhart to Wilson, July 16, 1863, *Ibid.*, Box 9.

[7] Eberhart to Wilson, May 12, 1866, *Ibid.*, Box 11.

[8] Perry and Woodworth (Los Angeles) to Wilson, December 21, 1869. *Ibid.*, Box 14.

[9] Johnson to Stearns, August 14, 1862, Abel Stearns Collection, MSS, Huntington Library. On Stearns see Doris M. Wright, *A Yankee in Mexican California: Abel Stearns, 1798-1848* (Santa Barbara, 1977); Robert G. Cleland, *The Cattle on a Thousand Hills* (San Marino, 1941). On early California banking see Robert G. Cleland and Frank B. Putnam, *Isaiah W. Hellman and the Farmers and Merchants Bank* (San Marino, 1965).

[10] 25 Cal. 564, 570-71 (1864).

[11] 25 Cal. 564, 572.

[12] Charles M. Bufford, "Inalienable Rights of Property: A Study of Contract Obligations and Other Vested Rights," *California Law Review*, 5 (1917), 209-236.

[13] 25 Cal. 564, 574.

[14] 25 Cal. 564, 578.

[15] 25 Cal. 564, 583.

[16] On the effects of inflation and the gold clause cases nationally see John P. Dawson, "The Gold Clause Decisions," *Michigan Law Review*, 33 (1935), 647-684; John P. Dawson and Frank P. Cooper, "The Effect of Inflation on Private Contracts: United States, 1861-1879," *Michigan Law Review*, 33 (1935), 706-757.

[17] San Francisco, 1867. Huntington Library Rare Book Collection.

[18] Johnson to Stearns, August 14, 19, 21, 1862. Abel Stearns Collection, Huntington Library.

[19] Couts to Stearns, September 17, 1862.

[20] Stearns Collection, Box 85.

[21] Centinela Orchard Receipts and Accounts, 1874-1878, Los Angeles, MSS, Huntington Library. Also see for examples Benjamin D. Wilson Collection, MSS, Huntington Library, Boxes 10, 11, and 15 for similar notices from 1865-1871 invoices.

[22] *Ibid.*

[23] Johnson to Stearns, March 18, 24, 1865. MSS, Stearns Collection, Box 37.

[24] Crane and Bingham to Benjamin D. Wilson, January 5, 1864, Wilson Collection, Box 10.

[25] Gerald D. Nash, *State Government and Economic Development: A History of Administrative Policies in California, 1849-1933* (Berkeley, 1964), p. 89.

[26] The California court followed *Carpentier* in numerous cases. *Gallard v. Lewis*, 26 Cal. 47 (1864); *McKeown v. Beatty*, 1 Cal. Unrep. 190 (1865); *Gryff v. Rohrer*, 1 Cal. Unrep. 192 (1865); *Poett v. Stearns*, 31 Cal. 79 (1866); *Rand v. Hastings*, 1 Cal. Unrep. 307 (1866).

[27] Thomas G. McFadden, "Banking in the Boise Region," *Idaho Yesterdays*, 11 (1967), 8-9.

[28] John Wesley North to Ann, July 23, 1865, North Papers, Box 13, MSS, Huntington Library.

[29] Nevada S.L. 1864-1865, Ch. 4, pp. 84-88; Idaho S.L. 1864, Ch. 21, pp. 419-29.

[30] 1 Nevada 271.

[31] 1 Nevada 271, 273-286.

[32] 1 Nevada 271, 287.

[33] 1 Nevada 271, 292-93.

[34] 1 Nevada 314.

[35] 1 Nevada 314, 317.

[36] 1 Nevada 573.

[37] 1 Nevada 573, 579.

[38] 1 Nevada 573, 581.

[39] 1 Nevada 573, 581.

[40] 1 Nevada 573, 582.

[41] 1 Nevada 573, 592.

[42] 1 Nevada 573, 592.

[43] 1 Nevada 573, 603.

[44] 2 Nevada 60.

[45] 2 Nevada 60, 61-62. Also see Carl B. Swisher, *Stephen J. Field* (1969 Phoenix edition), pp. 170-172.

[46] 2 Nevada 60, 64.

[47] 3 Nevada 240.

[48] 4 Nevada 178, 204.

[49] 4 Nevada 462.

[50] 4 Nevada 462, 464

[51] 4 Nevada 462, 467.

[52] 4 Nevada 462, 468.

[53] McFadden, "Banking," *Idaho Yesterdays*, pp. 9-13. California had a similar Problem in the 1850s. Thomas Jackson reported to Charlotte Prince on June 27, 1851 that "clean gold dust has advanced to $16.50 and $16.75 per ounce, but in trade we have to take very sandy dust to $16.00." William Prince Collection, MSS, Huntington Library.

[54] 1 Idaho 185.

[55] 1 Idaho 185, 189.

[56] 1 Idaho 170.

[57] 1 Idaho 170, 172-173.

[58] 1 Idaho 170, 183.

[59] Idaho S.L. 1874-75, pp. 802-3. Also see *Idaho Rev. Stat.* Title 8, Ch. 9, Sec. 4453, p. 490, Idaho S.L. 1893, pp. 78-79.

[60] 1 Idaho 694.

[61] See Carl Ubbelhode, *A Colorado History* (Boulder, 1965), p. 212. Colo. S.L. 1893, Ch. 114, p. 306.

[62] Mont. S.L. 1864-65, p. 338; *Taylor v. Holter*, 1 Mont. 688 (1872).

[63] *Utah Rev. Stat.*, Part 2, Title 7, Ch. 9, sec. 548.

[64] Dawson, "Gold Clause Decisions," *Michigan Law Review*, 33: 674. It must be noted that gold clause contracts were approved by the U.S. Supreme Court in *Bronson v. Rodes*, 7 Wall, 229 (1869). Also see Charles Fairman, *History of the Supreme Court of the United States*, vol. 6, part 1 (New York, 1971), pp. 692-710; James Willard Hurst, *A Legal History of Money in the United States, 1174-1970* (Lincoln, Nebraska, 1973), pp. 41-44, 183-186, 198-199.

The Development of the Law of Mortgage In Frontier California, 1850-1890

Part I: 1850-1866

BY GORDON M. BAKKEN

The development of the law of mortgage in California, 1850-1866, reflected the tensions of lawmaking amid rapid social and economic change. Mortgage law development was critical for the new state because of the need for investment capital, the security of interests in land, and the stability of investment without mature banking institutions. The legislature and Supreme Court labored to create a mortgage law to enable transactions in a frontier marketplace.

There were several different types of mortgage instruments. The common mortgage was a deed or conveyance of land by a borrower to a lender followed by or preceded by a description of a debt, commonly a promissory note, included in or attached to the mortgage instrument. A second type of mortgage was the trust deed. Here the borrower conveyed the land to a third party, not the lender, in trust for the benefit of the holder of the note that represented the mortgage debt. Finally, an equitable mortgage was any written instrument demonstrating the intent of the parties that real estate be held as security for the payment of a debt.

Not only did California lawmakers have a variety of mortgage instruments to deal with, but they were aware of a substantial history of mortgage law developed amidst the pull and haul of creditor-debtor antagonism. Much of mortgage law has been developed by courts of equity in the colonial period,' and a costly

* The author acknowledges a grant from the American Bar Foundation in support of this research.

and complicated system of equitable foreclosure had evolved giving the debtor a right to redeem his land.[2] Skillful lawyers drafted mortgage instruments around this "equity" and created the trust deed by which the debtor agreed, in advance, that if he defaulted, the trustee could sell his land without going into court. Legislators, however, urged on by debtors caught in the crush of a boom and bust economy enacted statutes to protect debtors. New York passed a statute in 1820 giving debtors a year of grace in response to the Panic of 1819.[3] Illinois legislators passed a one year redemption statute in 1841 spurred on by the Panic of 1837.[4] The Illinois statute applied to existing as well as future mortgages.

The United States Supreme Court struck down the Illinois statute in *Bronson v. Kinzie* (1843).[5] Chief Justice Roger B. Taney held the statute unconstitutional as an impairment of the obligation of contracts, but explained that the legislature could alter the remedy so long as the modification of the legal remedy or the method of enforcing the mortgage did not impair the terms of the mortgage itself.[6] The decision in Bronson, while establishing that a legislature could impose a redemption right on future mortgages, also served notice on legislatures that the courts would intervene to curb legislative excesses favoring debtors.[7]

Again, in the 1850s states tampered with mortgage law amid economic stress. Debtors, particularly farmers, agitated for government loans, cheap mortgage money, tough rules on foreclosure, and easy rules on redemption.[8] Laws such as Wisconsin's 1858 statute stripping the notes and mortgages of negotiability, were struck down by state courts.[9] The tensions between legislators sympathetic to debtor interests and the courts which tended to adhere to constitutional law doctrines was part of California's legal context for lawmaking.

The California Supreme Court's approach to the redemption issues was, in the early cases, to apply rules of construction beneficial to the statute. In *Kent and Cahoon v. Laffan* (1852), Justice Solomon Heydenfeldt applied the rule of construction to the California Practice Act, section 229. The statute provided that upon a sale of real property, when the estate was less than a leasehold of two years unexpired term, the sale should be absolute. In all other cases, the real estate was subject to the redemption. The mortgage in question was made subsequent to the redemption act.

Heydenfeldt found the act "sufficiently comprehensive to include within its design, sales of real estate under decrees of foreclosure of mortgages." Heydenfeldt rejected any technical reading of the act and concluded that "it (was) safest to look to the obvious policy of the law and to maintain such policy against a mere hesitation, caused by the inapt language of the act."[10] Heydenfeldt also had occasion to declare law on redemption in *Benham v. Rowe* (1852). There he concluded that "where a power of sale (was) contained in a mortgage, and under a sale by virtue of such power, the mortgage (became) the purchaser, the equity of redemption still attache(d) to the property in favor of the mortgager."[11]

The problems of the first years of statehood also were the problems of rapid development. The facts of *Woodworth v. Guzman* (1850) illustrate the frenzy of San Francisco in 1849. The defendant Guzman bought city property on June 17, 1849 from Samuel Brannan. Brannan in the haste of the transaction made the deed on property on Montgomery Street instead of Washington Street and gave Guzman a receipt for part payment. Guzman then borrowed $3,000 on the property from Brannan giving him a mortgage on the property. Subsequently, Guzman mortgaged the property again, this time to a Mr. Rynders for $7,000. Foreclosure followed and the trial court gave the Brannan mortgage priority over the Rynders mortgage. On appeal, Justice Nathaniel Bennett rejected Rynder's claim that Brannan's mortgage being unrecorded should not receive priority in foreclosure. Bennett noted that is was "settled in the states, where statutes requiring mortgages to be recorded are in force, that if a subsequent mortgagee has notice of the existence of a prior unrecorded mortgage, he takes his lien subject to the lien of the first mortgage."[12] Rynders had such notice. Further, Bennett declared, "we think the same rules applie(d) under the Mexican system." Even if it did not, "we are not aware that there was any officer in San Francisco, who according to Mexican law, was authorized to record mortgages."[13] The public policy was to prevent imposition upon subsequent purchasers and mortgagees, in good faith, and without notice of prior incumbrance. Here, Rynders had notice and the protection of law was unavailable.

The Court in *Woodworth* set policy in tune with general national legal experience. That policy protected dealers in the marketplace in their expectations, even expectations in the rough and tumble speculation of rapid urbanization amid a gold rush. The legislature aided this policy by providing dealers with a recording statute in 1850. The legislature also provided for conveyances and mortgages of real estate.[14] In 1851 the legislature provided that a judgment debtor could redeem his real property by paying the purchaser the amount of his purchase plus eighteen percent and any taxes, assessment, or creditor's liens within six months after sale.[15]

As Woodworth demonstrated, speculation in land was prevalent, trading sharp, and litigation common. In July 1852 Cave Johnson Couts accurately reported to Abel Stearns in Los Angeles that "speculations in land is rife-plenty of sellers and as many purchasers."[16] Money was dear and mortgages short term. John Center bought a downtown San Francisco lot for $1,000 down, a six-week note for $1,000 at three percent per month, and a five-month note for $2,500 at three percent per month due August 1, 1851.[17] Speculation in Los Angeles city land was fierce, but at moderate prices. Benjamin D. Wilson acquired numerous city lots in 1853 and 1854 for $300 to $4,500 each for interest ranging from two percent to five percent per month, for terms ranging from eighteen days to six months.[18] Phineas Banning, founder of Wilmington, built up substantial interests in wharves, warehouses, and lumber yards through rapid trading in swamp lands, railroad leases, lumber yard leases, and tax title purchases.[19]

Speculation in agricultural land was equally sharp, interest rates were high, and mortgages were short term.[20] Abel Stearns frequently loaned money on southern California land at two percent per month for six months to one year.[21] Frequently, Stearns foreclosed on mortgages and became the owner of numerous ranchos. Litigation also was very much a part of his dealings.[22] In most transactions in the 1850s, time was of the essence in the turbulent dealings in land and money at high interest.[23] But profits were equally high in the first flush years of statehood and dealers were quite willing to assume the risk of unconscionable interest rates, inflated prices, and short-term notes.[24]

The torrid pace of transactions often made dealers less mindful of the formalities of their transactions. Mortgages took a great variety of forms. Some were printed forms with the appropriate blanks completed, others were handwritten. Some were entitled "indentures," others were described as a "contract and deed of mortgage."[25] A deed and promissory note often evidenced a mortgage. Some were two separate documents, others were incorporated in a single paper.[26] In a more formal format, deeds of trust could detail many aspects of a transaction. In an 1864 trust deed Abel Stearns transferred cattle, horses, mines and water rights to Henry Davis Bacon as trustee on a three-year trust deed for several ranches on a $150,000 transaction carrying eighteen percent interest.[27] Complex transactions could also be overly simple, such as "sheep raising, being in liue of interest" or promises to execute notes without simultaneous execution.[28] Some dealers struck out one form of legal action on default on a document and substituted another.[29] Lawmakers had to bring some regularity to preserve the expectations of the parties.

The California Supreme Court had an early and surprisingly prolonged problem of legally defining a mortgage. Justice Heydenfeldt declared in *Godeffory v. Caldwell* (1852) that "mortgages at the present day, are considered as mere securities for the payment of money, and no breach of their conditions can possibly vest the title in the mortgagee."[30] Justice David S. Terry repeated Heydenfeldt in *Sherwood v. Dunbar* (1856).[31] Chief Justice Peter H. Burnett repeated the principle at great length in *Belloc v. Rogers* (1858):

> At common law, a mortgage vested the legal title in the mortgagee, subject to be defeated by the performance of the condition subsequent. But this theory is entirely changed by our system, and the legal title remains with the mortgagor, subject to be divested by a foreclosure and sale. And, when regularly sold, the purchaser obtains whatever title was in the mortgagor at the instance of time when he executed the mortgage.[32]

Justice Stephen J. Field felt compelled in *McMillian v. Richard* (1858) to embark upon a sixteen page disquisition on the subject.[33] Citing *Godeffroy v. Caldwell,* Field declared that

The settled doctrine of equity is, that a mortgage is a mere security for a debt, and passes only a chattel interest; that the debt is the principal, and the land the incident; that the mortgage constitutes simply a lien or incumbrance, and that the equity of redemption is the real and beneficial estate in the land which may be sold and conveyed by the mortgagor, in any of the ordinary modes of assurance, subject only to the lien of the mortgage. This equitable doctrine, established to prevent the hardships springing by the rules of law from a failure in the strict performance of the condition attached to the conveyance, and to give effect to the just intents of the parties.[43]

Field cited Chancellor Kent and concluded that "in truth, the original character of mortgages had undergone a change. They have ceased to be conveyances, except in form."[35] Field's extensive scholarship and detailed declaration of law quieted counsel on the subject, but justices did, from time to time, repeat the Field litany in brief. The legal character of California mortgages was established.

With the legal character of the mortgage established, the California Supreme Court had to deal with whether a mortgage was legally existing in the rough and tumble transactions of frontier speculation. The justices had little sympathy for sloppy draftsmanship and clever argument. As Justice Joseph G. Baldwin warned in 1859, careful research on title and liens was necessary to avoid some subsequent reverse, which he called "one of the unfortunate blunders common to all speculation."[37] Another critical question to determine the legal existence of a mortgage was the admissibility of parol evidence (verbal evidence). The problem arose from the often irregular transactions in property. A deed in the hands of a party would indicate nothing more than fee ownership. A deed and promissory note could evidence a mortgage or unrelated transactions. To clarify the situation, testimony under oath could supply needed information for a judge. However, parol evidence was not always considered desirable or reliable.

Stephen J. Field first approached the issue of the admissibility of parol evidence as an advocate. In *Lee v. Evans* (1857) Field argued for the appellant. He noted that English and American decisions held that such evidence was admissible in cases of fraud, accident, or mistake, but there was a conflict of authority on whether it could be admitted in the absence of special circumstances. Field argued for the admissibility of parol evidence based on Kent's *Commentaries*, opinions by Joseph Story, and numerous other cases.[38]

The Court, by Justice Burnett, rejected Field's argument, Burnett painstakingly reviewed Field's cited cases as well as Kent's *Commentaries*. He distinguished some precedents involving fraud, accident, or mistake as not legally on point and others on the basis of fact. After such review, Burnett concluded that "with the utmost deference for authorities so high, I must confess I could never see the reason upon which these decisions rest."[39] Burnett's vision was clearer on viewing the terms of California statute. The clear language would not permit Field's reasoning. Further, Burnett was concerned about the role of the court.

In statutory interpretation, Burnett rejected what he considered an invitation to make law. To revise statute, Burnett claimed, exceeded the Court's authority:

> The language of the statute is not only clear but *negative*, and not *directory*; and the act itself points out the *exception* to the rule therein laid down. And when a statute is not only *negative* and *restrictive*, but, in addition to these, *assumes itself* to point out certain exceptions, can a Court, by any recognized rule of construction, go further, and say the law-giver forgot exceptions he intended to, but did not specify? Is it not, in essence, a *legislative act*? Are we not saying, the law should have been so made, but was not?
>
> The question is one solely relating to evidence. What shall be competent evidence to prove certain facts? The statute says, *none but written* testimony will do, and the Courts say *oral* testimony is sufficient. Is not this a plain contradiction of the statute?[40]

Burnett concluded on the Court's constitutional authority that any exceptions to the rule that parol should not be received to contradict written evidence would have to be enacted by the legislature.

But Burnett was not satisfied to leave the issue alone. He embarked upon a subterranean undermining of cited authorities reconciling the statutory language and the admission of parol evidence. On a U.S. Supreme Court opinion of Justice John McLean's which had been joined by Joseph Story, Burnett tunneled in and retorted that he could not "understand the force of this explanation."[41] Similarly, Burnett could not "see the reason of the distinction" in an opinion by Chief Justice John Bannister Gibson of Pennsylvania. But dredging up dissents seemingly silted over by time, Burnett declared that "we think the strict rule the true one."[42] Field's argument was seemingly buried under the tailings of Burnett's labors.

Rebuffed on parol evidence, Field nonetheless won the case and ultimately made the rule. After seven pages of argument on Field's position, Burnett acknowledged in two sentences that Field's opposition had failed to deny facts alleged in Field's pleading resulting in a mortgage being admitted as a matter of law. On October 13, 1857 Field joined the Court and set about unearthing his parol evidence rule. In *Pierce v. Robinson* (1859) Field wrote the opinion for the Court overruling *Lee v. Evans* in part holding that parol was admissible in equity to show that a deed, absolute on its face, was intended as a mortgage.[43] Field's opinion clearly established California law. In 1865 Justice Lorenzo Sawyer could safely say that "it is now settled in this State that parol evidence is admissible to show that a deed absolute on its face was intended to be a mortgage."[44] Field's position was California's. It was a position well-suited to California's frontier condition.

The California Supreme Court also decided doctrinal questions of conditional sales contracts and mortgages containing the power of sale. Both types of transactions exhibited both the turbulence of the era and the desire to promote the rapid, certain, and conclusive sale of property upon the default of a debtor. In *Hickox v. Lowe* (1858), Chief Justice Field distinguished the mortgage from a conditional sale in deciding a case involving a conveyance and an agreement to reconvey. Field repeated the well-known fact that a mortgage was mere security for a debt and noted that "the relation of creditor and debtor must exist between . . . (the) parties."[45] If the debt was extinguished by the conveyance, the agreement to reconvey was an independent contract. Where doubt existed, the court would find a mortgage.[46] In *Fogarty v. Sawyer* (1861), Field again stated California law with clarity.

He declared that there was "nothing in the law of mortgages in this State which prevents the mortgagor from investing the mortgagee with a power to sell the premise upon default in the payment of the debt secured."[47] This was a critical holding because it allowed dealers to write mortgage instruments with strong default language and upon default to sell without resort to statutory procedures. Further, when sold in accordance with mortgage contract language, good title would pass to the purchaser.[48] It was only a single step to the trust deed by putting the trustee in the place of the mortgagee.[49] The ingenuity of draftsmen and dealers was directed at avoiding the more cumbersome statutory foreclosure procedures.

In construing the statutory foreclosure procedures and the Statute of Limitations, the Court favored bringing debtor and creditor into the judicial foreclosure proceedings unless the creditor had been sitting on his rights in violation of the Statute of Limitations. In *Guy v. Ide* (1856), Justice Heydenfeldt rejected the English rule providing for the appointment of a receiver of rents and profits. Heydenfeldt declared that the statute forbade the recovery of the mortgaged estate except by foreclosure. The estate remained "that of the mortgagor in the character of the owner, and must continue to remain so, with all the incidents of ownership, until, by foreclosure and sale, a new owner (was) substituted."[50] Despite language in the mortgage instrument, the Court required statutory procedures. In *Cormerias v. Ganella* (1863) Chief Justice Edwin B. Crocker noted that the mortgage instrument contained language vesting a power of sale in the mortgage "according to law." Crocker observed that "the clause (was) evidently copied from some form in a State having laws regulating such sales." In that the California statute required a judicial proceeding, the Court held that the statutory procedure be followed. "In that way," Crocker maintained, "there is no doubt of the right of the mortgagor, or parties holding under him, to redeem the property within six months after the sale."[51] The case evidenced both the frontier nature of legal documents adopted from other jurisdictions rather than drafted for California law and the willingness of the Court to require the statutory procedure. Not only redemption was involved, however, but more fundamental rights were at stake. Due process was a definite consideration. As the Court asserted in *Skinner v. Buck* (1865), the statute "does not propose to relieve mortgagees from the constitutional necessity of giving all persons whose interests they may seek to compromise by foreclosure decrees a chance to be heard."[52] The justices gave the Statute of Limitations similar application. In *Grattan v. Wiggins* (1863), Justice Crocker rejected English statutory applications and declared that California's Statute of Limitations applied to the subject matter of the law suit regardless of the form of action or the type of court in which the suit was being tried.[53] In *Low v. Allen* (1864) the court observed that a mortgage contract was "manifestly one of the written contracts" described by the statute limiting actions for four years from accrual. The Court found the facts presented to be "within the mischiefs against which the Statute of Limitations was intended to guard."[54] The Court was loath to allow untimely law suits in times of rapid frontier transactions.

In accordance with the foreclosure statute, when the trial court had rendered judgment in favor of the creditor, the creditor could have the property sold by the sheriff at auction.[55] The statute required the posting of notice of sale for twenty days and publication in the newspaper for the period of one week "in a newspaper in the county if there be one." The sheriff could be penalized $500 for failure to publish such notice. Sales were at auction to the highest bidder. Upon sale, the sheriff issued a certificate of sale which was to state whether the property was subject to redemption. The sheriff also filed duplicates of the certificates with the county recorder. The property could be redeemed six month after sale by the judgment debtor or a creditor having a judgment against the property or a mortgage. Redemption required payment to the purchaser at the sheriff's sale of the purchase price plus eighteen percent interest plus assessments or taxes plus interest. If the sheriff's sale purchaser was a creditor, redemption required the amount of the prior creditor's lien plus interest. If a creditor redeemed the property, other creditors had sixty days in which to redeem from him with six percent interest added on. This sixty day window could be exercised again and again by all subsequent creditors until the last had redeemed or the sixty day period had passed without a redemption. Notice of these redemptions were to be given to the sheriff when the six month or sixty day term had duly expired, the last redemptioner was entitled to a sheriff's deed. The process was slow and, being subject to redemption for a lengthy period of time, costly.[56] Creditors obtained possession of property, but because of redemption interests were seldom free to rapidly sell their property.

The Supreme Court did provide creditors with assistance in enforcing their rights. The Court ruled that fixtures could pass by sheriff's deed. In arriving at the position Chief Justice Field applied familiar property law concepts and precedents.[57] Where the purchaser had a sheriff's deed in hand, but the occupier of the premises refused to vacate, the Court, by Chief Justice Field, held that a writ of assistance was an appropriate remedy.[58] While providing the creditor with the sheriff's strong arm of the law in sale and dispossession, the Court construed the statute strictly. In *Heyman v. Babcock* (1866) the Court voided a sheriff's sale where both the creditor and sheriff had failed to follow the statute.[56] The Court favored the statutory proceeding and carefully protected creditor and debtor interests within the terms of the law.

Similarly, the Court protected the statutory and equitable rights of debtors to redeem their interest in the real estate. Even where the power of sale was contained in the mortgage, if the creditor became purchaser, the equity of redemption still attached to the property. The Court construed statutory language beneficially considering redemption to be a remedial legislative act. Where interpretative questions arose, the Court attempted to balance interests and retain for the debtor the opportunity to completely fulfill his obligation. This was made difficult by failures of legislative craftsmanship, but the Court construed language to save it and make the statutory system workable.[60] The antagonism frequently experienced in other states was not overtly evident excepting the Court's open distaste for unskillful draftsmanship of early statutes.

While the foreclosure proceedings were available to creditors, the lender had a variety of hurdles to vault to obtain a judgment. Where a woman was involved in a transaction, creditors could easily be hamstrung by common-law doctrines concerning capacity or spiked by a homestead exemption. Where a married woman signed the note and mortgage without her husband, the creditor had no contract. The woman lacked legal capacity to make a contract. The Supreme Court was unwilling to unilaterally alter this doctrine. Justice Heydenfeldt stated in 1855, that a married woman "has no power to make a contract is a doctrine of law which this Court has no power to disturb."[61] The burden of inquiry was upon the creditor or purchaser. As Justice Sawyer pointed out in *Ramsdell v. Fuller and Summers* (1865) the fact of a woman's name on a deed "afforded to all persons seeking to acquire title under it a clue to the title, which they were bound to pursue, or suffer the consequences." The presumption of the law was that she was not married and could pass title, "but she may be married, and her deed may not pass title." The fact of marital status had to be determined by the creditor/purchaser," or omit to do so at their peril."[62] Creditors could be left with a worthless deed and an uncollectable promissory note if not diligent.

Creditors also had to be cognizant of the $5,000 homestead exemption from execution for debt. The Supreme Court construed the statute favorably to debtors to find a homestead. In *Moss v. Wainer and Wife* (1858) Chief Justice Field held that the fact that the debtors were driven from their ranch by Indians, their buildings burned, their cattle stolen, and their lives preserved only by a hasty retreat to San Diego was not an abandonment of their homestead.[63] Similarly, in *Lies v. De Diablar* (1859) Justice Baldwin declared that "adultery or abandonment by the wife did not divest the property of the character of the homestead."[64] But the Court would not brook the deliberate manipulation of creditors to evade a mortgage. Chief Justice Hugh C. Murray forcefully stated that the Court would not "lend its aid to do an injustice and assist a party in escaping from a just liability which he has contracted."[65] Despite the Court's stern warning, the creditor of the family farm or ranch had a particular limitation in getting from the blocks to the finish line without an occasional stumble.

While a creditor could control, to a degree, the problems of married woman's property and the homestead exemption, hard times and bankruptcy were not so easily avoided. Bankruptcy did not release the lien of the mortgage, but did operate to limit the creditor's recovery to the proceeds of the mortgaged premises.[66] A debtor could mortgage property and not have the mortgage be declared an assignment for benefit of creditors to avoid the statutory distribution of assets.[67] Nonetheless, bankruptcy stood as yet another statutory mechanism altering creditor expectations.

Creditors often grounded their expectations in the priority of their interest in real estate. But in the turbulent speculation of frontier transactions, whether a creditor had a first, second, or sixtieth mortgage on a single piece of California terra was often a question only a court could answer. The questions of priority came to the Court with statehood. In *Woodworth v. Guzman* (1850) the Court held that notice to a subsequent creditor of a prior unrecorded mortgage gave priority to the first in time.[66] The legislature's efforts to give creditors notice of mortgages and other liens were insufficient. As Chief Justice Murray lamented in *Rose v. Munie* (1854), "not only is the Mechanics' Lien Law defective, but also the Recording Act itself, and it may be safely said, that no provision is made for recording a numerous class of liens." Without compulsory recording of mortgages, the Court relied upon common law which did not require recording and recording did not impart notice. All had the duty of "ascertaining all outstanding titles or incumbrances against the estate."[69] With knowledge of prior incumbrances, creditors, of course, loaned money at the risk of the value of the property being insufficient to satisfy all debts. With the recording of mortgages, secret liens were less likely and creditor risks reduced by reference to the county recorder's mortgage book.[70]

*   *   *

California mortgage law was primarily the product of the California Supreme Court. The legislature did provide the necessary statutes to provide for conveyances, mortgages, foreclosures, and the like. But judicial output dwarfed the legislature's productivity. The Court's handiwork was significant. The cases provided the vehicle for working out the principles that would guide dealers in the marketplace.

The fact situations of the cases portray the vitality and variety of mortgage transactions of the period. Of the 144 cases studied,

118 of them had identifiable demographic facts set out in the appellate reports. Forty-four percent involved property in urban areas. Nineteen percent concerned commercial properties, while canals represent nine percent and mines seven percent of the cases. Cases concerning the family farm or ranch, and the great ranchos comprised the remainder. The cases coming before the Supreme Court were those of an urban frontier and of an exploitative era. The monetary stakes involved were also significant. Ninety-seven of the cases had monetary values contained in the report. The ranged from $202.65 on a mine to $120,000 on a San Francisco office building. The average values per year indicate that significant economic stakes came before the bench for decision.[71]

The Supreme Court decided fifty-eight percent of its cases in favor of creditors. Had the lender/plaintiffs been more careful in drafting documents, securing a wife's signature, searching title, or prosecuting foreclosure in a timely manner the percentage of creditor holdings would have been much higher. The Court was making an overt effort to protect creditor expectations, preserve statutory procedures, and maintain the debtor's statutory recourse of redemption. The justices attempted to rationalize the legal system to these ends while according the legislature's statutory pronouncements appropriate deference.

The Court's methodology was significant given the turbulent frontier nature of transactions. Where statute would provide a means to resolve creditor-debtor problems, the Court would defer. Where statute was inadequate, the Court would rely upon common law. Where common law was not clearly applicable to California's frontier condition, the Court would make law for the state in tune with its needs. This methodology was instrumentalist in character, and reflected a means-end mode of analysis focusing upon expected consequences.[72] Given the turbulent, sharp, and varied nature of frontier transactions, the judicial style suited the situation. However, the justices, particularly Chief Justice Field, were very careful to extensively review precedents and ground decisions both in law and public policy.[73] The work of the Court in the period laid the foundation for the extensive litigation that would follow in the remainder of the century.

NOTES

Note: The author wishes to acknowledge a grant from the American Bar Association in support of this research.

[1] Lawrence M. Friedman, *A History of American Law* (New York, 1973), p. 216; Morton J. Horwitz, *The Transformation of American Law* (Cambridge, Mass., 1977), pp. 265-66.

[2] Friedman, *History of American Law*, p. 217.

[3] *Ibid.*

[4] *Ibid.*, p. 217-18.

[5] 1 How. 311.

[6] See Carl B. Swisher, *History of the Supreme Court of the United States: The Taney Period* (New York, 1974), pp. 148-51; Charles Warren, *The Supreme Court in United States History* (2 vols., Boston, 1926), 2: 104-5; Gerald T. Dunne, *Justice Joseph Story* (New York, 1970), p. 392. Also see George L. Priest, "Law and Economic Distress," *Journal of Legal Studies*, 2 (June 1973), 469-92, on the Illinois experience.

[7] Friedman, *History of American Law*, p. 218.

[8] *Ibid.*, pp. 374-75.

[9] Lawrence Friedman, *Contract Law in America* (Madison, Wis., 1965), pp. 144-45.

[10] 2 Cal. 595, 596.

[11] 2 Cal. 387, 407.

[12] 1 Cal. 203, 205.

[13] *Ibid.*

[14] *Cal. Stats. 1850-53*, Ch. 122 (April 16, 1850), pp. 513-519.

[15] *Cal. Stats. 1850-53*, Civil Procedure, Title 7, Chapter 1, section 231 (April 29, 1851), p. 562.

[16] Couts to Stearns, July 12, 1852, Cave Johnson Couts Collection, Box 18, MSS, Huntington Library.

[17] John Center Collection, arch 18, 1857 deed and notes, Box 1, MSS, Huntington Library.

[18] Benjamin Davis Wilson Collection, Box 2 and 3, MSS, Huntington Library.

[19] Banning Company Papers, Boxes 2, 5A, 6 and 8, MSS Huntington Library.

[20] See Robert Glass Cleland, *The Cattle on a Thousand Hills* (San Marino, Calif., 1941), pp. 102-16.

[21] See Abel Stearns Collection, Box 85 and 87, MSS, Huntington Library.

[22] See *Ibid.*, Box 84, Los Alamitos Ranch Records.

[23] See Couts to Stearns, Oct. 13, 1852. Couts Collection, Box 18, MSS, Huntington Library.

[24] John Center paid off a $20,000 mortgage in 8 months in San Francisco selling bricks, while Stearns in Los Angeles frequently turned mortgages into real estate ownership within a year. See Center Collection, Box 1, Aug. 3, 1853 Mortgage, Stearns Collection, Box. 85.

[25] See Stearns Collection, Box 85, Indenture of Sept. 2, 1854.

[26] *Ibid.*, Jan. 27, 1854 note and mortgage. Also see Jan. 11, 1854 and Nov. 14, 1854 notes and quit claim deed. Similarly, see Rancho Los Bolsas Collection, MSS, Huntington Library.

[27] Bacon Collection, Dec. 22, 1864 (HM 27622).

[28] See Charles Robinson Johnson to Abel Stearns, Oct. 27, 1862, Stearns Collection, Box 27 and Eagle Mills documents, June 13, 1864, Stearns Collection, Box 88.

[29] See Benjamin D. Wilson, Collection, Drummer-Carrillo Mortgage (1851).

[30] 2 Cal. 489, 492. Also see *Ord v. McKee*, 5 Cal 515, 516 (1855).

[31] 6 Cal 53, 54.

[32] 9 Cal 123, 125.

³³ 9 Cal 365, 405-21.

³⁴ 9 Cal 365, 407-408.

³⁵ 9 Cal 365, 411. On the common law of mortgages, see Theodore F. T. Plucknett, *A Concise History of the Common Law* (Boston, 1956), p. 603-608. Max Radin, *Handbook of Anglo-American Legal History* (St. Paul, Minn., 1936), pp. 404-5. Also see James Kent, *Commentaries on American Law,* volume 4 (New York, 1830); Francis Hilliard, *The Law of Mortgages of Real and Personal Property* (Boston, 1872); Charles T. Boone, *The Law of Mortgages of Real and Personal Property* (San Francisco, 1886).

³⁶ See *Johnson v. Sherman,* 15 Cal 287, 293 (1860); *Goodenow v. Ever,* 16 Cal 461, 467-70 (1860); *Lent v. Morrill,* 25 Cal 492, 500 (1864).

³⁷ *Swift v. Kraemer,* 13 Cal 526, 531 (1859). Also see *Ferguson v. Miller,* 4 Cal 97 (1854) as an example of the rapid sale and resale of property evidenced by careless documentation.

³⁸ 8 Cal 424, 435-6.

³⁹ 8 Cal 424, 430.

⁴⁰ 8 Cal 424, 431.

⁴¹ *Ibid.*

⁴² 8 Cal 424, 432-34.

⁴³ 13 Cal 116.

⁴⁴ *Cunningham v. Hawkins,* 27 Cal 603, 606 (1865). Also see *Johnson v. Sherman,* 15 Cal 291 (1860); *Lodge v. Turman,* 24 Cal 385 (1864); *Hooper v. Jones,* 29 Cal 18 (1865).

⁴⁵ 10 Cal 197, 206. Also see *Ferguson v. Miller* (1856), 4 Cal 97.

⁴⁶ 10 Cal 197, 207.

⁴⁷ 17 Cal 589, 593.

⁴⁸ Also see *Fogarty v. Sawyer* (1863), 23 Cal 570.

⁴⁹ See *Green v. Butler,* (1864), 26 Cal 505.

⁵⁰ 6 Cal 99, 101.

⁵¹ 22 Cal 116, 124.

⁵² 29 Cal 253, 256. Also see *Spring v. Hill and Carr* (1856), 6 Cal 17. *Phelan v. Oleny* (1856), 6 Cal 478; *Montgomery v. Tutt* (1858), 11 Cal 307; *Tyler v. Yreka Water Co.* (1859), 14 Cal 212; *Horn v. Volcano Water Co.* (1861), 18 Cal 141; *Kearsing v. Kilian* (1861), 18 Cal 491; *Cook v. Guerra* (1864), 24 Cal 237; *Doe v. Vallejo* (1866), 29 Cal 385.

⁵³ 23 Cal 16, 31-34.

⁵⁴ 26 Cal 141, 145. Also see *Lent v. Shear* (1864), 26 Cal 361.

⁵⁵ Cal Code of Civil Proceedings (1851), sections 221-237.

⁵⁶ Charles Walter purchased part of Rancho Lupyomi in 1852. On Feb. 17, 1857 he completed his ownership of the rancho by sheriff's deed. David Alexander Collection, MSS, Box 1, Huntington Library. Also see Cleland, *Cattle on A Thousand Hills,* pp. 164-66.

⁵⁷ *Sands v. Pfeiffer and Schleischer* (1858), 10 Cal 258, 246-65.

⁵⁸ *Montgomery v. Tutt, Wilson, et al* (1858), 111 Cal 190. Also see *Skinner v. Beatty* (1860), 16 Cal 156.

⁵⁹ 30 Cal 367. Also see *Brown v. Winter and Sherry* (1859), 14 Cal 31; *The People v. Irwin* (1859), 14 Cal 428; *Boggs v. Fowler and Hargrave* (1860), 16 Cal 559; *Horn v. Jones* (1865), 28 Cal 194; *Thomas v. Vanlieu* (1865), 28 Cal 616.

⁶⁰ *Benham v. Rowe* (1852), 2 Cal 387; *Kent and Cahoon v. Laffan* (1852), 2 Cal 595; *Allen v. Phelps* (1854), 4 Cal 256; *Frink v. Murphy* (1862), 21 Cal 108; *Blockley v. Fowler* (1863), 21 Cal 326; *Daubenspeck v. Platt* (1863), 22 Cal 330; *Green v. Butler* (1864), 26 Cal 595; *Alexander v. Greenwood* (1864), 24 Cal 505.

⁶¹ *Simpers and Craumer v. Sloan and Sloan* (1855), 5 Cal 457. Also see *Pfeiffer and Wife v. Riehn and Scannell* (1859), 13 Cal 643.

[62] 28 Cal 37, 43. Lack of capacity was not limited to married women. One interesting case involved the Pueblo of San Jose and its efforts to become the state capital. To house the legislature, seventeen citizens put up money to buy a facility. The city council or Ayutamiento, purchased the land and building from the citizens' trustees. The city then sold the facility to the County of Santa Clara at a profit and refused to pay the trustees, who sued, purchased at the sheriff's sale, resold and collected. But to their distress, the Court informed them that the city council lacked capacity and they were without effective remedy. *Branham v. Mayor and Common Council of San Jose* (1864), 24 Cal 585.

[63] 10 Cal 296.

[64] 12 Cal 327, 329.

[65] *Dillon v. Byrne and Byrne* (1855), 5 Cal 455, 457; Also see *Rix v. McHenry and Wife* (1857), 7 Cal 89; *Dorsey v. McFarland* (1857), 7 Cal 342; *Revalk v. Kraemer* (1857), 8 Cal 66; *Cook v. Klink* (1857), 8 Cal 347.

[66] *Lunig v. Brady and Gilson* (1858), 10 Cal 265.

[67] *Dana v. Stanfords and Dietz* (1858), 10 Cal 269. The debtor could die creating other problems. See *Belloc v. Rogers* (1858), 9 Cal 123; *Peachaud v. Rinquet* (1862), 21 Cal 76; *Burton v. Lies* (1862), 21 Cal 87; *Willis v. Farley* (1864), 24 Cal 490; *Peck v. Brummagim* (1866), 31 Cal 440.

[68] 1 Cal 203.

[69] 4 Cal 173, 174.

[70] *Furguson v. Miller* (1854), 4 Cal 97; *Peters v. Jamestown Bridge Co.* (1855), 5 Cal 334; *Guy v. Carriere* (1855), 5 Cal 511; *Borrell v. Schie* (1858), 9 Cal 104; *Raun v. Reynolds* (1858), 11 Cal 15; *May v. Borel* (1859), 12 Cal 91; *Houseman v. Chase* (1859), 12 Cal 290; *Daggett v. Rankin and Vischer* (1866), 31 Cal 321. The priority questions were often clouded by the rapid and multiple transactions concerning the same property as well as sloppy legal work. See as examples *Furguson* (1854), *Peters* (1855), *Daggett* (1866). In *Daggett*, Chief Justice Currey caustically commented that "the pleadings in the suit are drawn in an extremely loose and careless manner." 31 Cal 321, 326.

[71] Average values of mortgage cases: 1850, $3,000.00; 1852, $3,675.30; 1853, $1,932.00; 1854, $7,828.55; 1855, $29,600.00; 1856, $2,513.70; 1857, $7,610.30; 1858, $11,211.50; 1859, $9,570.20; 1860, $21,257.40; 1861, $16,733.17, 1862, $4,431.40; 1863, $20,664.00; 1864, $7,402.40; 1865, $5,522.10; 1866, $8,350.00.

[72] On instrumentalism see Morton J. Horwitz, "The Emergence of an Instrumental Conception of American Law, 1780-1820," *Perspectives in American History* (1971), 5: 287-326; Harry N. Scheiber, "Instrumentalism and Property Rights: A Reconsideration of American 'Styles in Judicial Reasoning' in the 19th Century," *Wisconsin Law Review*, 1975 (1975), 1-18; Lynda Sharp Paine, "Instrumentalism v. Formalism: Dissolving the Dichotomy," *Wisconsin Law Review*, 1978 (1978), 997-1025.

[73] See *Johnson v. Sherman* (1860), 15 Cal 287; *Dana v. Stanfords and Deitz* (1858), 10 Cal 269; *Hickox v. Lowe* (1858), 10 Cal 197; Charles W. McCurdy, "Stephen J. Field and Public Land Law Development in California, 1850-1866," *Law and Society Review*, 10 (Winter 1976), 235-266; Charles W. McCurdy, "Justice Field and the Jurisprudence of Government-Business Relations," *Journal of American History*, 61 (1975), 970-1005.

The Development of Mortgage Law in Frontier California, 1850-1890

Part II: 1867-1880

BY GORDON M. BAKKEN

The California Supreme Court in the period 1850-1866 laid the foundation for the mortgage law development of the 1870s. The first decade and one-half witnessed the Court making an overt effort to protect creditor expectations, preserve statutory procedures, and maintain the debtor's statutory recourse of redemption. The period 1867-1880 was one of boom and bust, speculation, monopolies in land and transportation, and the stabilization of financial institutions. It also was a period of constitution-making. In this context the California Supreme Court and legislature continued the efforts to foster the mortgage money market.

The availability of money at interest on real estate became critical to California in this period because of the expansion of wheat production and the first real estate boom in the state's history.[1] Many large land holders subdivided their lands and sold them off to small farmers.[2] Concurrently, Dr. Hugh J. Glenn and Isaac Friedlander bought up huge tracts of land in the Sacramento and San Joaquin valleys and then planted wheat.[3] In the Salinas Valley, David Jacks combined vast holdings in wheat with cattle, sheep, mustard, lumber, cord wood, nursery trees and cashmere goats.[4] The real estate and wheat boom had repercussions in the handling trade, mercantile interests, and the railroad industry. For example, Phineas Banning bought up swamp lands, leased land to railroads, lumber companies, and purchased tax titles to further his interests in the port of Wilmington.[5] David Jacks helped develop the Monterey harbor and promoted a narrow gauge railroad to get his crops to harbor. Economic expansion, of course, impacted other sectors. Demand increased. H. T. Holmes of the Pacific Glassworks, San Francisco, sent a plea to David Jacks in Monterey on May 16, 1866: "You must try and send us more sand as the Glassworks have taken all you have sent . . . and we have a great many outside orders which we have not been able to fill."[6] While the fever of speculation reverberated across the state, the small farmer's desire for a family farm was ever present. D. W. Lawton said it to David Jacks in September 1873 when he asked for a $500 loan on his 40-acre farm: "I feel like making a great effort to secure what I think every family ought to have — a home."[7] Under such conditions, the pressures for land financing would be constant.

The form for the transaction was still less than clear to dealers in the marketplace during this period despite the Supreme Court's efforts, particularly Stephen J. Field's efforts, to clarify the law of mortgage. Printed form deeds and promissory notes avoided some problems.[8] The A. L. Bancroft Company of San Francisco, among others, supplied dealers with form number 1072, "Mortgage" which recited appropriate language and allowed the lender to fill in the details.[9] But dealers did not always have forms and transactions could be relatively informal on small mortgages.[10] Some experienced dealers in land still did not make clear distinctions between mortgages and deeds of trust.[11] However, the vast majority of dealers avoided warranty deeds because of title problems. George Hansen writing to Matthew Keller on May 12, 1877 stated the California situation clearly:

> The purchaser wants a warranty deed: we have a kind of warranty deed from Judge Widney and the title is otherwise perfect and there is no reason, why we should not give a warranty deed except the *general habit* of the country to give bargain and sale deeds, *based on the fear of blackmailing.*[12]

With titles so subject to litigation no dealer in land dared venture liability on the title and while lenders might want greater security of title, it was not generally to be had in the period.

The Supreme Court often reiterated the definition of a mortgage and pondered the intent of parties using a deed as part of a transaction. As Mr. Justice A. L. Rhodes cautioned in *Henley v. Hotaling* (1871) "to convert the deed into a mortgage, the evidence ought to be so clear as to leave no doubt that the real intention . . . was to execute a mortgage."[13] In *Farmer v. Grose* (1871) Mr. Justice B. Crockett restated the familiar rule making a transaction a mortgage. "The fact whether or not, notwithstanding the conveyance, there [was] a subsisting, continuing debt from the grantor to the grantee" rendered the transaction a mortgage.[14] Where the consideration for the conveyance was a pre-existing debt, a mortgage existed. Often the justices looked to the instrument of the transaction. As Mr. Justice Rhodes stated in *Hellman v. Howard* (1872) "the term 'deed' will in its largest sense include a mortgage . . . , but it is manifest from the context, that the term was used in that instrument in a more limited sense."[15] While issues of interpreting the intent of parties would be expected before the California courts, the reiteration of well-known legal rules indicates a degree of uncertainty on the court and more likely in the legal profession.[16] One necessary task, therefore, was the consolidation of legal principles established by the Supreme Court in the preceding fifteen years. But on occasion, the justices could not agree among themselves whether certain basic principles should apply.[17] The uncertainty of the court and legal profession would be a factor in the marketplace.

The legislature attempted to lend a degree of certainty to transactions by statute. One of the first acts of statehood was "an act concerning conveyances" which provided for conveyances of real estate by deed, acknowledgment of the conveyance, the recording of documents, and the discharge of mortgages.[18] The act gave recorded conveyances special status as unrecorded transactions were void against subsequent purchasers. In 1866 the legislature provided for out-of-state acknowledgements.[19] Here the fact of eastern and international investment was specifically recognized. Further, county recorders were required to prepare an index of sales of real estate sold under execution.[20] This segregated the mortgage foreclosure sales and identified the plaintiff and defendant in a convenient and accessible place, the county recorder's office. The legislature also gave purchasers at the sheriff's sale greater certainty by declaring that conveyance recorded after a foreclosure action was commenced did not impart notice.[21] The courts followed the traditional path of enforcing the statute and making careful inquiry of personal knowledge of unrecorded mortgages in deciding cases.[22]

Foreclosure of a mortgage with the subsequent redemption period and Sheriff's sale was not always the result of debtors' default. Refinancing the original debt or continuing it for an additional term of years was a means of avoiding foreclosure. Debtors often asked "What will be the prospects to let the mortgage run another year if I keep the interest paid up?"[23] Others wanted to refinance to make improvements.[24] Large-scale dealers in land and businessmen regularly refinanced to consolidate debts, lower interest, create liquid capital, or speculate further in land.[25] Debtors also made partial payment to avoid foreclosure. As Isaias Hellman told Matthew Keller in 1879, with the creditor having half the mortgage money in hand and a promise of the rest being forthcoming in his ear, "he will not push the balance."[26] Creditors, of course, had the heavy hand of the law if payment was ultimately not forthcoming. In fact, creditors could use the threat of foreclosure to spur fiscal responsibility in debtors. James A. Clayton of San Jose asked his client, David Jacks, to give him such leverage in 1879. "You had better write me a letter *I can show him* — stating that you want the money or more security and ordering me to commence suit if not settled," Clayton wrote.[27] Not surprisingly, Clayton was able to report, two weeks later, that the debtor had obtained the money from an Oakland bank.[26] But when the loan fell through, Clayton ruminated that "if you could spare the money it would be good policy to let them have it at the same rate (10% per year)."[29] Jacks could and did. But where the debtor had not demonstrated a basis for extending further credit or time, foreclosure could result.[30] After the action and the Sheriff's sale, the debtor could redeem his property upon payment to the lender. The creditor was normally forced to rent the premises for the period.[31] While the legal system gave the creditor the force of the law to protect his interests, informal settlement was always available.

Some debtors opted to sell out rather than continuing in their relationship with the creditor. Depression, crop-failures, bad judgment, and a high debt service often combined to motivate the debtor to look for other means of employment. J. M. Soto pondered his situation and wrote to David Jacks in 1870 that he had "been figuring the interest on my debt and I do not feel very encouraged; because what I make with the people that owe me is not even one half of what I pay; therefore I want to offer you all my ranch at $18 per acre with all improvements."[32] The other option for the debtor was bankruptcy. Interestingly, creditors sometimes found that under certain circumstances bankruptcy could yield more than a foreclosure.[33]

The Supreme Court enforced mortgages and their foreclosure attempting to avoid the legal conclusion that the creditor was without remedy. For example, in *Himmelmann v. Fitzpatrick* (1875) the justices avoided the conclusion that the plaintiff was without recourse for refusing the debtor's tender of payment.[34] Himmelman had loaned $1100 on December 1, 1868 for one year at 2% per month. Fitzpatrick and his wife had given him a mortgage on San Francisco real estate. On April 1, 1871 Fitzpatrick made a tender of $1567.20, then due; but Himmelmann refused to take it. Rather he filed an action of foreclosure on May 3, 1873. The trial court found for him in the amount of $2,991.46 including $250 attorney's fees. The mortgage contained a clause requiring 20% of the amount due as attorney's fees. The trial court found the 20% to be a penalty and held that only reasonable attorney fees could be allowed. The Supreme Court agreed. Following a precedent case of nearly sixteen years standing, the Court reiterated that "it would be very harsh to hold that the debt is lost — the general effect of losing the security — by a mere refusal at a particular moment to receive it."[35] The California Civil Code, section 1504 further stopped the running of interest at the time of tender. The attorney's fee issue also was affirmed, but had been dealt with by the legislature. In 1874 the legislature had passed "an act to abolish attorney's fees, and other charges, in foreclosure suits" leaving to the courts rather than the creditor the setting of a reasonable attorney's fee.[36]

The Homestead Act of 1860 continued to be a concern to lenders.[37] Section two of that act declared void any mortgage on the homestead portion of property. In *Sears v. Dixon* (1867) the Supreme Court left the unwary plaintiff with a decision and no money. The defendant had applied to the lender for $1,000. The lender, doing the prudent thing, "referred the matter to his lawyer, who advised him that a mortgage on the homestead ... would be ineffectual to secure the payment of the money."[38] The lender refused the loan. But the defendant proposed and the lender accepted a transaction whereby the defendant conveyed the land by deed, the lender leased-back to the debtor at a "rent" equivalent to interest on the $1,000, the lender covenanted to reconvey upon payment of $1,000 plus "rent," and the defendant-debtor covenanted to pay $1,000 plus "rent" on or before the expiration of the lease. Of course, the debtor stopped the payment of the rent, and the prudent lender conveyed the land to a third party, now the plaintiff. Citing extensive precedent from Massachusetts and California as well as Chief Justice John Marshall, the Court found that a mortgage existed and in that it was on a homestead, the mortgage was void. Lenders and third party purchasers of land clearly heard the signal.[39]

But the naivete of lenders and the ingenuity of debtors was unlimited. In *Barber v. Babel* (1868) the debtors Frederick Babel and his wife executed a note and mortgage to Julia Barber in 1860.[40] In 1861 the Babels filed their homestead declaration. In 1865 Frederick, applying his sly tongue and quick wit, induced Julia to take a new note and mortgage and surrender the first. She did so and entered a discharge and satisfaction on the record. Fred even went so far as to swear that no homestead declaration had been filed. Mrs. Babel uncharacteristically remained mute on the homestead declaration and refused to sign the second note and mortgage. As fate would have it, the debtors stopped paying and the lender sued.

Chief Justice Lorenzo Sawyer met the issues head-on in his analysis. The legislature had clearly stated that a husband could not divest the wife of her homestead interests without her concurrent act. Even more certainly the second mortgage not being executed by the wife was invalid. Unfortunately, for poor Julia any action on the first mortgage was barred by the Statute of Limitations and, Sawyer concluded, "the husband having been discharged in insolvency from the debt in question, there is, and can be no personal judgment against him, and as the action to foreclose the mortgage fails, there is nothing left."[41] Julia was, as Sawyer put it, "not the first in the business world to find herself a victim of misplaced confidence."[42] Perhaps also Julia was not sufficiently suspicious of Babel's many tongues.

Fate occasionally worked in favor of lenders. In *Parry v. Kelley* (1877) the husband's unfortunate demise left the lender with a mortgage lien he otherwise would have been deprived of by law.[43] In 1872 the Kelley's purchased a lot in Oakland with community funds, but solely in the name of the wife, Seraph, a physician. George Parry loaned Mr. Kelley some money and the good doctor gave Parry a mortgage on the lot telling him that the property was "bought with money she had earned in the practice of medicine." In 1875 Mr. Kelley passed away and Mr. Parry bought an action to foreclose the mortgage. To no one's surprise the doctor denied the validity of the mortgage she signed. The trial court agreed with poor Mrs. Kelley, but George Parry appealed.

The Court reasoned around the Civil Code, section 167 language which stated that "the property of the community is not liable for contracts of the wife made after marriage, unless secured by a pledge or mortgage thereof executed by the husband." First, the Civil Code also gave the wife the capacity to give the mortgage. Clearly, the mortgage stood "on the same footing as a mortgage made by any other person on property to which he had, at the time, no title."[44] Second, another Civil Code section provided for after acquired title to inure to the benefit of the mortgagee. Finally, in that the husband died intestate, the wife was entitled to the lot and thereby the mortgagee to his mortgage foreclosure. Had the husband willed his interest to his children or not so conveniently passed on, the lender, Parry, would have been without his security.

Debtors also claimed duress to avoid paying. Duress did not render a deed void, but it did make it voidable. In *Connecticut Life Insurance v. McCormick* (1873) the defendant's wife attempted to set up the defense of duress to have declared void a year old mortgage. The Court found that she had signed the deed over to avoid the criminal prosecution of her husband for embezzlement. The court found no evidence of notice to Connecticut Life "of the alleged compulsion under which the mortgage was executed."[45]

Intrafamily transactions could also make less certain titles to land. In the case of *Bernal v. Gelim* (1867), the husband and wife entered the land in 1846, mortgaged it in 1851, and conveyed it to their children without the wife acknowledging the transfer to pass her separate property. Default and foreclosure followed. Then the sheriff sold the property in 1852. Twelve years later the children reached the age of majority and dutifully conveyed to their beloved mother in 1865. To no one's surprise she sued and the court found the sheriff's sale void and put dear mother into possession under the 1865 conveyance.[46]

Lenders on land had to proceed with great care whenever a married couple were involved in the transaction. As the cases demonstrated, without a careful and professional search of the title and a transaction of some exactitude, the lender had some concern for an actual return on his money. The certainty law should lend to transactions was existent, but creditors had to proceed only after close scrutiny of the title to land and the transaction itself.

Another unsettling case was *Simpson v. Castle* (1878).[47] The Court struck at the heart of one of Stephen J. Field's significant pronouncements on mortgage law, *McMillian v. Richards* (1858). The facts of the case were not unusual; the legal background was complex. The defendant, creditor, had loaned money on land and had received a mortgage. The debtor defaulted. The creditor foreclosed. Castle bought the premises at the sheriff's foreclosure sale for less than the amount of the judgment. The sheriff issued the usual certificate to Castle and reported the deficiency to the court. A judgment was duly docketed. The six month term for redemption began to run and during this term the debtor conveyed the premises to Simpson. Being careful of his rights, Simpson made the redemption payment to the sheriff and the sheriff issued a certificate of redemption to Simpson. Castle then sued out an execution on the judgment for the deficiency on the property and the sheriff stood poised to sell it again for the deficiency. Here the saga took a new twist. To the dismay of the creditor, Simpson sued to enjoin the sale. The trial court sustained the defendant's demurrer and ordered the sale. So it had been for twenty years in California.

The law for twenty years had been based on *McMillian* and statute. The Practice Act of 1851 had provided for the six month term of redemption in which a judgment debtor or a redemptioner could pay the purchaser the amount of the purchase plus 18% interest "and if the purchaser be also a creditor, having a lien prior to that of the redemptioner, the amount with interest." Stephen J. Field interpreted the language to mean that neither the judgment-debtor or a redemptioner could redeem without paying the deficiency. In reaction to Field's holding in *McMillian,* the legislature embarked on anti-deficiency legislating. First in 1859, the legislature amended the Practice Act by adding "after the sale of any real estate, the judgment under which such sale was had shall cease to be a lien on such real estate." Then in 1860, the legislators honed their language to greater sharpness. They added that if the purchaser be also a creditor having a prior lien to that of the redemptioner other than the judgment under which such purchase was made," the amount of such lien, with interest, shall also be paid. The legislative intent was simply to cut off creditors from continuing liens against property and to practically free debtors from their incumbrances. The public policy interests were similar to those of bankruptcy legislation. The Supreme Court in *Simpson* recognized this policy grounding, struck *McMillian's* effect, and denied Castle his execution sale. Simpson "took title free from the pretended lien of the judgment for the deficiency."[48]

The impact of the decision on creditors was multiple. First, the redemption period rendered most land useful only for tenants during the six month period. As W. H. Clark informed David Jacks in 1879, with the default of the debtor and the contemplation of foreclosure only tenancy was functional.

> The workingmen have a written lease from Jolly to cover all the time of redemption at $3 per month. The proper way to get at it if it can be done now, will be to have a receiver appointed by the Court to take charge of the property and rents.[49]

With deficiency judgments unavailable against the property, lenders had to be sure of sufficient security resulting in a lower percent of the property being financed and at higher interest rates. While interest rates had been higher in the 1850s and 1860s, the interest of the late 1870s was greater cause for concern as economic distress befell many. Bankruptcy as well as deficiency resulted. But some creditors like David Jacks allowed late payments and even extended the time of redemption.[50] California's experience was not one exclusively of rapacious creditors and pitiful debtors caught in the vice of low prices, drought, and debt.

But depression and high interest forced many into insolvency. Speculation was clearly a factor. As Henry D. Bacon complained to Samuel Barlow in 1879, "the loan is for a year and in the meantime sales must be made of property to meet it. The mortgage is for $27,000. How soon I am fast come to grief."[51] Bankruptcy proceedings and assignments for the benefit of creditors closely followed over-extension, depression, or drought.[52] Bankruptcy was another alternative to foreclosure of a mortgage. In 1878 David Jacks received such an option from T. Wood, the assignee in bankruptcy for Peter Herron. Wood told Jacks that he knew of "no objections to Peter Herron getting his discharge [in bankruptcy] and presume he will sometime in January. If you wish the mortgaged property to be sold I can go on and it will not cost as much as for you to foreclose the mortgage."[53] While the costs might be less, the creditor could generally receive only his proportional share of the debtor's assets.

While creditor and debtor struggled to protect their respective interests under California law, the California Supreme Court had a concurrent struggle with statutory construction. *Odd Fellows Savings Bank v. Banton* (1873) sorely tested judicial analysis.[54] On the 13th of January 1873, the defendant Banton executed and delivered a mortgage to another defendant named Hammett. The mortgage was recorded on February 15th in the San Francisco County Recorders Office. On February 7, 1873 Banton executed and delivered another mortgage to another defendant, Kingsbury. This mortgage was recorded on February 12th. On February 10, 1873, the industrious Banton executed a third mortgage to the Odd Fellows Savings Bank. The mortgage was recorded on the same day. Hammett was a resident of Portland, Kingsbury of Sacramento, and the bank a local. All these creditors took mortgages in good faith and without notice of the other mortgages. The whole affair became a case, of course, when Mr. Mortgagor, Banton, failed to pay. The sole question for the court was the priority of the three mortgages.

The statutory scheme of things was less than clear. One section of the Civil Code provided that every conveyance of real estate from the time filed gave constructive notice of its contents to subsequent purchasers. Another section held that first recorded conveyances voided subsequent conveyances of the same property. It was apparent "that the Legislature intended that all ... conveyances ... should be filed for record in the proper Recorder's office, and until so filed should be void as against all persons who subsequently without notice, in good faith and for valuable conisderation, might acquire any interest therein either as purchasers or incumbrances."⁵⁵ Elsewhere in the Civil Code, the legislature provided that mortgages be recorded in books kept exclusively for real estate mortgages. Further, the mortgagee was allowed one day for every 20 miles of distance between his residence and the County Recorder's office to record. More importantly, during this period of time, the mortgage was legally considered recorded. This time allowance acknowledged the problems of frontier transportation and attempted to protect non-resident investors. Here Hammett was 683 miles away and Kingsbury 117 miles distant. Naturally all claimed to have priority.

The Court recognized that a statutory conflict existed. Mr. Justice Isaac S. Belcher went directly to the California Political Code, section 4480 and 4481 which provided that the statutes must be construed as though they were parts of the same statute and that the provision of each Title in the code must prevail for all matters arising from the subject matter of the title. Hence, in that one title covered "transfers," another liens, and another "mortgages of real property," the matter of recording mortgages of real estate would fall under transfers rather than liens, and more clearly mortgages of real estate than mortgages in general. The only result possible, then, was that former statutes prevail against the mileage statutes and Odd Fellows' filing first had the first priority. To creditors the ruling was clear. The rush to the Recorder's Office was imperative. For the Court, the decision was one to make the system workable and more certain, although certain by judicial opinion.

Legislative waffling also confused a mortgagee's rights when the mortgagor passed away. In *Hibernia Savings and Loan Society v. Hayes* (1880) statute made three different procedural provisions between the time the mortgage was executed in 1872 and the time the banks started foreclosure proceedings in 1875.⁵⁶ When the mortgage was executed in March 1872, the presentation of all claims for allowance to the representative of the estate of the deceased mortgagor was necessary. The mortgagor died in December 1872. In January 1873 the legislature changed the law so that a mortgage claim need not be presented where recourse against all other than the mortgaged property was expressly waived. The next month the administrator of the estate published notice to all creditors. In July 1874 the legislature again changed the law. Now a claim must be presented. If a claim arising upon a contract made before July 1874 was not presented within the time limits, the claim was "barred forever." The bank filed its foreclosure suit in 1877.

Mr. Justice E. M. Ross for the court acknowledged all the legislative tinkering and found for the bank. Ross could find no legislative intent to apply the 1874 legislation retroactively. Absent retroactivity, the notice of February 1873 could not affect the banks' right to foreclose under the January 1873 statute. The majority viewed the right to a remedy as frozen in time in January 1873 regardless of the 1874 statutory change, the mortgage's maturity in March 1875, and the bank's foreclose in 1877.

Mr. Justice Samuel B. McKee caustically dissented.[57] The California Codes went into effect on January 1, 1873, McKee pointed out, and required the presentation of a claim within the 10-month period of publication of notice to creditors or if the debt was not then due, ten months after it was due. Thereafter the claim was lost, forever barred by statute. The 1873 law gave the mortgagee the options of presentation of a claim against the estate or foreclosure after the debt was due but before barred by the Statute of Limitations. When the latter option was repealed by the 1874 amendment of the Code, the remedy was repealed as well. Here McKee parted company with the majority heaping corrosive precedents on Ross's opinion attempting to burn holes in his reasoning. Most tellingly, he decanted *Ogden v. Saunders* (1827) and poured the Marshall Court's weighty language into the fray. "The right to a particular remedy [was] not a vested right." McKee declared citing *Ogden*.[58] If the remedy was repealed, the right no longer existed, he continued. In the situation facing the Court, the remedy had been repealed by the legislature. McKee concluded that the creditor's failure to avail himself of the remedy in a timely manner barred him forever.[59] Mr. Justice John R. Sharpstein concurred in McKee's dissent, but the bank had its foreclosure. The year before the Supreme Court had denied the Hibernia Savings and Loan a remedy because it had waited too long to foreclose and was barred by the Statute of Limitations.[60] Creditors had to be diligent to enforce their rights.

The California Supreme Court had early established and continued to maintain that the mortgage contract was "manifestly one of the written contracts" described by the statute limiting actions to four years from accrual.[61] If the instrument did not contain a due date, the Court presumed that it was due immediately or on demand, starting the running of the four year limitation.[62] The exception to the running of the term was the creditor leaving the state. The Court made it clear in *Wood v. Goodfellow* (1872) that it did not favor devices prolonging the payment of a debt and forestalling actions. The law favored quiet title and releasing the energy of private property, not silent and stagnant interests. Wood's administrator attempted in the case to resurrect a sleeping interest. Goodfellow had made a mortgage in June 1860 on his interest in the Keystone mine and mill. In October 1860 and May 1862 Goodfellow and other joint owners made two other mortgages. These mortgages were assigned to Harris and McCarthy who foreclosed, but failed to make Wood, the holder of the June 1860 mortgage, a party to the suit. Harris and McCarthy obtained their decree and then a sheriff's deed. On March 30, 1864 they conveyed the whole of the property to the Keystone Quartz Mining Company. Our mysterious Goodfellow then dropped out of sight leaving the state and never returning. Wood, who had notice of the two subsequent mortgages, the foreclosure sale, and subsequent possession by Harris and McCarthy, died on March 4, 1868. The administrator of his estate pounced on the Keystone Company one week later with a foreclosure suit.

Keystone defended its interests with the Statute of Limitations, but the plaintiff raised Goodfellow's departure from the state in 1862 as an argument extending the four year term of the statute. Mr. Justice Joseph B. Crockett found plaintiff's argument "very able and ingenious."[63] Unfortunately for Wood's estate, it was wrong. Crockett slashed through the plaintiff's printed brief and shredded it in two pages of searing language. "This Court has repeatedly decided," Crockett proclaimed, "that as against subsequent incumbrances, or a subsequent holder of the equity of redemption, the mortgagor had no power, by stipulation, to prolong the time of payment, or in any manner increase the burdens on the mortgage premises."[64] On plaintiff's argument distinguishing a mortgage as collateral security rather than the debt, Crockett similarly belittled the argument stating that the Court had clearly and uniformly adhered to a position which found mortgages to fall within the statute. In sum, the Court favored quiet title and certainty in transactions rather than dormant interests.

While counsel's argument in *Wood* was "very able and ingenious," the Court displayed overt distress over counsel's actions in other cases. In *Christy v. Dana and Natoma Water and Mining Co.* (1868), Mr. Justice Crockett angrily pointed out that the argument made by the defendant was "no longer an open question in this Court." Further, the Court was "strongly inclined to treat the appeal as frivolous and taken only for delay."[65] Chief Justice William T. Wallace echoed Crockett's concern four years later in *Wilber v. Sanderson* (1872). No briefs were filed. The defendant's appeal was "without merit" and Wallace tersely affirmed the judgment "with 20% damages."[66] Sloppy representation could also delay the process. Plaintiff's counsel in *Carpentier v. Brenham* (1875) had failed to properly file the complaint fifteen years earlier and when finally adjudicated the plaintiff was dead and fortunately did not live to see the demise of his claim.[67] The pitfalls of the marketplace were only one hazard for creditors. Experienced and competent counsel was necessary to the process.

While the legislature, the Court, and counsel gave some creditors reason for pause in the period, the rise of the Workingmen's Party and the Constitution of 1879 gave most visions of disaster. The Workmingmen's Party began in the fall or 1877 in San Francisco. Made up of the unemployed and the landless, the party grew dramatically under the leadership of Denis Kearney. Kearney aimed his inflammatory rhetoric against the railroads, the landed, the wealthy, and the Chinese. The Workingmen demanded the dismemberment of the railroad, land, and water monopolies. They wanted national control of the banks. Taxation required reform. Finally, the Chinese needed to be driven from the workplace and the land. To achieve these goals, the Workingmen sought and obtained the calling of a constitutional convention. In a frenzy, the conservative elements of both parties united against the Workingmen and prevented their domination of the convention.[68]

One convention proposal that sent shock waves through the financial community was the taxation mortgages. The banks in 1878 and 1879 were emerging from the depression of 1876 with renewed confidence. The San Francisco Evening Bulletin reported on April 19, 1878 that "San Francisco has been measurably fortunate in her Savings Banks. Some of the earliest established still continue, notwithstanding all the violent fluctuations in values to which they have been exposed, and the senseless runs which have been made upon them."[69] But the confident optimism in the financial community was quickly shattered by the passage of a section in the taxation article taxing mortgages. Isaias Hellman wrote to Matthew Keller on April 22, 1879 that

> Business is very dull here, the question whether the new Constitution is going to be adopted or rejected is the topic with everyone. If adopted business of all kinds will be paralyzed. The banks all over California are preparing for the worst and are calling in mature loans.[70]

The clear intent of the convention delegates to shift the burden of taxation was cause for concern.[71] The San Luis Obispo *Tribune* saw the provision as a blow to debtors and a deterrent to capital:

> Before voting in favor of the new constitution, men who are likely to be in the market as borrowers of money during the next year, should stop and consider the probable effect that the constitution will have on capital. It is well known to those who have ever attempted to negotiate a loan that the money lender is shy even under the most favorable circumstances. Not only must the security be ample, but the requirements of the law must be complied with in every particular. What will be the condition of affairs supposing the new constitution is adopted. There is certain to be an interim of nearly a year when there will be no law. That is to say, men with money will not know what restrictions will be imposed upon their capital by the Legislature. In such a condition of doubt and uncertainty will they be likely to risk their money by making loans which may be declared illegal and void? Not much. Is it not more reasonable to expect that they would adopt this

plan: Notify their debtors that they must settle as soon as their debts are due. If these debts are secured by mortgages as fast as they fall due they must be paid or foreclosure proceedings will be instituted. There will be no renewals. Capital will withdraw from sight and await the issue. Capital can afford to wait — it can afford to remain idle. Are men who are doing business and borrowing capital prepared to face a result like this?[72]

The Santa Barbara *Daily Press* not only saw the provisions driving away capital, [73] but also as a windfall for the railroads. A May 5, 1879 editorial declared that "under the specious pretext of taxing mortgages, they have exempted every railroad in the state."[74] Many echoed this observation because the railroads were heavily mortgaged with New York creditors not subject to the tax. But it was uncertainty that troubled many. Matthew Keller wrote Isaias Hellman from New York on April 30, 1879:

> I see the new Constitution is agitating the whole state. It appears that it affects banking stocks, railroads, and mortgages. I hope the results will be for the general good.[75]

This view from New York was mirrored in a San Luis Obispo editorial stating that "the adoption of the new Constitution may so unsettle values that the savings banks and others loaning money may be compelled to foreclose mortgages."[76] Despite all the fears and trepidation, the Constitution passed 77,959 to 67,134.[77]

For mortgage lenders the period started as it had ended. They were emerging from depression and uncertainty, but again the law and now the Constitution itself created some uncertainty. The banking institutions of the state were more stable, more regulated. California was poised for the boom of the 80s in which the ingenuity of counsel and the flexibility and craftsmanship of the judiciary would facilitate economic expansion despite the predictions of doom.

Frontier California, 1850-1890

NOTES

[1] Walton Bean, *California, An Interpretative History* (New York, 1973), pp. 271-276. Also see Hubert Howe Bancroft, *History of California* (7 vols., San Francisco, 1890), 7: 1-37, and Gerald D. Nash, "Stages of California's Economic Growth, 1870-1970: An Interpretation" in George H. Knoles, *Essays and Assays: California History Reappraised* (Los Angeles, 1973), pp. 41-43.

[2] Bean, *California*, p. 276; Robert Glass Cleland, *The Cattle on a Thousand Hills* (San Marino, Ca., 1941), pp. 172-73. See Abel Stearns Collection, MSS, Huntington Library, Box 85 for some of the major transactions including one for 55,523 acres.

[3] Bean, *California*, pp. 271-72; Warren Beck and David Williams, *California* (Garden City, N.Y., 1972), pp. 278-79; David Lavender, *California* (New York, 1972), pp. 292-94.

[4] See the David Jacks Collection, MSS, Huntington Library.

[5] Banning Co. Papers, MSS Huntington, Boxes 2, 5A, 6, and 8. Also see Maymie Krythe, *Port Admiral, Phineas Banning, 1830-1885* (San Francisco, 1957).

[6] Holmes to Jacks, May 16, 1866, Jacks MSS, Box C (1).

[7] Lawton to Jacks, Sept. 20, 1873, Jacks, MSS, Box C (2).

[8] Compare, for example, the handwritten deeds of the 1850s and 1860s with the printed form deeds of the 1870s. See Gideon J. Carpenter Collection, MSS, Bancroft Library deeds of Nov. 29, 1853, April 14, 1855, April 16, 1856, and April 23, 1861 (bargain and sale deed language). Campodonico Family Collection, MSS, California State Library, Sacramento, Box 146, deeds of June 15, 1872, December 8, 1877 (Quitclaim). George McKinstry, Jr. Collection, MSS, Cal State Library, Box 236, John A. Sutter deed of June 1, 1849 (bargain and sale). For form deeds of period see John W. Snowball Collection, Cal State Library, Box 490, deeds of September 10, 1877 and October 10, 1885.

[9] Matthew Keller Collection, MSS, Huntington Library, Box 3, Lemmert mortgage of January 29, 1877 is a good example.

[10] See J. Downey to Benjamin D. Wilson, July 20, 1866, B.D. Wilson Collection, MSS, Huntington Library, Box 11. A deed was dropped off with two notes. Dealers in small transactions but high volume like David Jacks had several real estate agents and a bevy of attorneys to superintend the loaning of money on land.

[11] For example, see Henry D. Bacon to Samuel L. M. Barlow, May 16, 1873, Barlow Collection, MSS, Huntington Library, Box 83. Also see William Perry to Matthew Keller, May 18, 1868, bond for deed to portion of Rancho San Francisquito, William Wolfskill Collection, MSS, Huntington Library.

[12] Matthew Keller Collection, MSS, Huntington Library, Box 1.

[13] 41 Cal. 22, 27.

[14] 42 Cal. 169, 172.

[15] 44 Cal. 100, 104.

[16]. Also see *Purdy v. Bullard* (1871), 41 Cal. 444. *Hall v. Yoell* (1873), 45 Cal. 584. *Hill v. Eldred* (1874), 49 Cal. 398.

[17] See *Patterson v. Donner*, 48 Cal. 369; particularly Rhodes' dissent, p. 380-82.

[18] *California Compiled Laws* (1853), ch. 122, pp. 513-519 (April 16, 1850). Also see Lawrence M. Friedman, *A History of American Law* (New York, 1973), p. 55.

[19] *Cal. Laws* (1856-66), ch. 349, p. 429 (1866).

[20] *Cal. Laws* (1865-66), ch. 636, p. 813 (1866).

[21] *Cal. Laws* (1865-66), ch. 620, p. 848 (1866).

[22] See *Pio Pico v. Gallardo* (1877), 52 Cal. 206. *Frey v. Clifford* (1872), 44 Cal. 335.

[23] John Reynolds to David Jacks, August 9, 1878 (also June 4, 1979), Jacks Collection, MSS, Box C (2).

[24] James A. Clayton to Jacks, February 14, 23, 1878; January 10, 1879, Jacks Collection, MSS, Box C (2) and C (3).

[25] See Henry D. Bacon to Samuel L. M. Barlow correspondence, July-December, 1869, Barlow Collection, Box 69, Huntington. Isaias Hellman to Matthew Keller, April 3, September 11, 1878, Keller Collection, Box 1, Huntington.

[26] Hellman to Keller, August 12, 1879, Keller Collection, Box 1, Huntington.

[27] Clayton to Jacks, January 10, 1879, Jacks Collection, Box C (3), Huntington.

[28] Clayton to Jacks, January 25, 1879, Jacks Collection, Box C (3), Huntington.

[29] Clayton to Jacks, May 10, 1879, Jacks Collection, Box C (3), Huntington.

[30] Debtors often expressed personal regret that the action was necessary. For example, William Robson told Jacks in 1878 that his whole family was sick with the "idea of being attached." William Robson to Jacks, December 28, 1878, Jacks Collection, Box C (3), Huntington.

[31] Jacks would lease property for six months to keep it up and obtain some cash from the property. See W. H. Clark to Jacks, April 2, 1879, July 30, 1879, Jacks Collection, Box C (3), Huntington. Jacks even extended redemption beyond 6 months. John Markley to Jacks, May 14, 1879, Jacks Collection, Box C (3), Huntington.

[32] Soto to Jacks, December 30, 1879, Jacks Collection, Box C (1), Huntington.

[33] T. Wood to Jacks, December 17, 1878, Jacks Collection. Box C (2), Huntington. Also see Notice of Warrant in Bankruptcy of Peter Heron, August 8, 1878, Jacks Collection, Box C (2). Memorandum of Agreement of June 4, 1879 of creditors of W. B. Wells, Jacks Collection, Box B (V) (I) (10). Charles Langley to Jacks, June 24, 1879, Jacks Collection, Box C (3).

[34] 59 Cal. 650.

[35] 50 Cal. 650, 651.

[36] *Cal. Laws* (1873-74), ch. 474, p. 707 (1874).

[37] *Cal. Laws* (1860), p. 311.

[38] 33 Cal. 326, 331.

[39] Also see *McLaughlin v. Hart* (1873), 46 Cal. 638.

[40] 36 Cal. 11.

[42] 36 Cal. 11, 23.

[43] 52 Cal. 334.

[44] 52 Cal. 334, 335.

[45] 45 Cal. 580, 583-84. Also see *Perkins v. Center* (1868), 35 Cal. 713.

[46] 33 Cal. 668. Also see *Remington v. Higgins* (1880), 54 Cal. 620.

[47] 52 Cal. 644.

[48] 52 Cal. 644, 650. Also see *Bludworth v. Lake* (1867), 33 Cal. 255. Joining all parties was also necessary to avoid losing part of an investment.

[49] Clark to Jacks, April 2, 1879, Jacks Collection, Box C (3), Huntington. The workingmen paid six months in advance. Clarks to Jacks, July 30, 1879.

[50] Jacks frequently carried debtors from year to year. See Soto to Jacks, December 28, 1870, Jacks Collection, Box C (1), Huntington. Albon to Jacks, July 27, 1878, Box C (2). Abbott to Jacks, April 23, 1878, Box C (2). Jacks even extended to statutory time of redemption. John Markley to Jacks, May 14, 1879, Box C (3). See generally on the late 1870s Robert Glass Cleland, *A History of*

California: The American Period (N.Y., 1922), pp. 402-423. David Lavender, *California: Land of New Beginnings* (N.Y., 1972), pp. 295-310.

[51] Bacon to Barlow, August 30, 1879, Barlow Collection, Box 125, Huntington.

[52] See Notice of Warrant of Bankruptcy of Peter Heron, August 8, 1878, Jacks Collection, Box C (2), Huntington. Memorandum Agreement of Creditors of W. B. Wells, June 4, 1879, Jacks Collection, Box B (V) (I) (10). Charles Langley to Jacks, June 24, 1879, Box C (3).

[53] Wood to Jacks, December 17, 1878, Box C (2).

[54] 46 Cal. 603.

[55] 46 Cal. 603, 607.

[56] 56 Cal. 297.

[57] 56 Cal. 297, 300-307.

[58] 56 Cal. 297, 303. On *Ogden* see Carl B. Swisher, *The History of the Supreme Court of the United States, The Taney Period, 1836-1864* (New York, 1974), pp. 152.-154.

[59] Also see *Pitte v. Shipley* (1873). Chief Justice Addison C. Niles declared similarly that "the failure to present the mortgage to the executrix and the Probate Judge in the manner required by the Probate Act, was fatal to plaintiff's recovery." 46 Cal. 154, 161. Statute of Limitations cases often presented similar problems. See *Wells v. Harter* (1880), 56 Cal. 342. *Biddel v. Brizzolara* (1880), 56 Cal.

[60] *Hibernia Savings and Loan v. Herbert* (1879), 53 Cal. 375.

[62] *Espinosa v. Gregory* (1870), 40 Cal. 58, 62.

[64] 43 Cal. 185, 187-88.

[63] 43 Cal. 185, 187.

[65] 34 Cal. 548, 553-54.

[66] 43 Cal. 496, 497.

[67] 50 Cal. 549.

[68] See Beck and Williams, *California*, pp. 260-65. Bean, *California*, pp. 304-305, Zoeth Skinner Eldredge, *History of California* (5 vol.), (New York, 1915), vol. 4, pp. 341-72.

[69] First National Gold Bank Scrap Book, MSS, Santa Barbara Historical Society.

[70] Hellman to Keller, April 22, 1879, Matthew Keller Collection, MSS, Huntington Library, Box 1.

[71] See Carl B. Swisher, *Motivation and Political Technique in the California Constitutional Convention, 1878-79* (Claremont, Cal., 1930), pp. 84-85.

[72] SLO Tribune, April 19, 1879, p. 4, col. 2.

[73] May 6, 1879, p. 1. col. 3. April 29, 1879, p. 4, col. 4.

[74] Santa Barbara *Daily Press*, May 5, 1879, p. 3, col. 3.

[75] Keller to Hellman, April 30, 1879, Huntington, Box 1.

[76] SLO Tribune, April 28, 1879, p. 2, col. 1.

[77] Bean, *California*, p. 305.

The Development of Mortgage Law in Frontier California, 1850-1890

Part III: 1880-1890

BY GORDON M. BAKKEN

California's mortgage law and practice in the decade of the 1880s reflected the uncertainty of a boom and bust real estate market, the problems of living with a new state constitution, and the eccentricities of the State Supreme Court. With the uncertainty of the marketplace and the growing complexity of law, lawyers came to play a greater role in the mortgage field. With the professionalization of dealers in mortgage money, California's mortgage law matured to meet the needs of the marketplace.

During the 1880s, California experienced a real estate boom as well as the increased commercialization of agriculture. Southern California land values skyrocketed in the period.[1] Like wheat in the 1870s, crops like walnuts expanded to commercial proportions.[2] Railroad promotions brought thousands to California resulting in Los Angeles' eight-fold growth in the period.[3] A key ingredient in the boom was, of course, the mortgage money that fueled the boom and ultimately snuffed it out.

As California entered the decade, the 1879 Constitution loomed as a formidable barrier to expansive mortgage lending. The new organic act placed a tax on mortgages.[4] In anticipation of the constitution's ratification by the people in 1879, California banks severely curtailed lending. As Frank Clough, a young San Francisco attorney reported to his mother in August of 1879, "Nobody has any money here now. The banks won't lend money on the best kind of real estate as security."[5] After the people ratified the constitution, lawyers and lenders turned their immediate attention to avoiding the Constitution's provisions and maintaining the burden of taxation with the borrower. Some merely increased the interest rate to provide for the taxes. Jackson A. Graves, a Los Angeles attorney and one of the founders of the powerful O'Melveny firm, wrote to Simon Wallace in 1881 that "we will make the note 11½% which will give you ten percent and will allow 1½% for taxes."[6] Others were direct and explicit. David Jacks, a Monterey County farmer and mortgage lender, merely inserted the mortgage tax directly into the mortgage instrument and if not paid, charged the debtor interest.[7] If the tax assessor visited, John Reynolds, one of Jacks' real estate agents "did not say anything about the mortgage . . . as our contract was made before the new constitution."[8] Lenders converted the mortgage tax from a threat into a mere nuisance through artful drafting.

However, in the period 1867-1880, the California Supreme Court's record on mortgage cases gave creditors greater reason for pause. Lenders won only two of every three appellate decisions in the period.[9] Given the existing value and potential appreciation of property, large sums of money were at stake.[10] The state of the law in the decade of the seventies caused enough concern for David Jacks that he bought a personal law library and kept several lawyers in business.[11] Professionals, such as Graves, O'Melveny and Shankland of Los Angeles found the California Supreme Court "eccentric" and proceeded cautiously in real estate foreclosures.[12]

One element of uncertainty, the mortgage tax, loomed large, and the California Supreme Court gave lenders some indications of its reach early in the decade. In *Beckman v Skaggs* (1881) the court made an ex cathedra statement on the contract clause and mortgage taxation.[13] Applying the long-standing federal constitutional doctrine of *Sturges v Crowninshield*[14] without ever citing it or any other case, the court declared that contracts made before the Constitution were valid. Hence, an agreement whereby the debtor paid any and all taxes must stand. John Reynolds' restraint in 1880 was constitutionally correct. But would he be right in 1882? *McCoppin v McCartney* (1882) took another position. As appellant's attorney, Edward J. Pringle, observed, "the Constitution of 1880 made a revolution in the revenue system of the State."[15] Amid the chaos of revolution, the court, again without citing a single case for precedent, announced that "a mortgagee, prior to the adoption of the new Constitution, did not have a vested right or exemption from taxation." As to this 1872 mortgage, "the plain intent of the new Constitution [was] to subject to taxation classes of property previously exempt."[16] The state constitution apparently, in California at least, could wipe out precedent contractual expectations. Here the purchaser found to his pocketbook discomfort that a satisfied mortgage made before the Constitution could not only be assessed for taxation, but also that he must now pay again to maintain title.

In *Hay v Hill* (1884) the constitutionality of the mortgage taxation provision again became a question. An 1879 mortgage for three years contained no covenants for the payment of taxes. In January, 1883 the mortgagor paid off the note plus all interest excepting $395.00 he had paid in taxes on the mortgage interest. To Hill's surprise, George Hay foreclosed apparently wanting his extra bale of $395.00. The Supreme Court, citing *McCoppin*, rejected windrows of precedents and tersely stated that "the mortgagor having paid an amount due from the mortgage to the third party — the State — is entitled to recover the amount so paid."[17] While rejecting any unjust enrichment for Hay, the Court clearly identified the creditor as liable for the taxes.

While Hay foraged for hundreds of dollars, the Sutter Street Railroad Company gang plowed for thousands in 1884. As corporations often found, they were in need of capital. To keep debt a profitable venture, the faceless company often turned to its directors for mutual benefit. So too here, as Julius Baum, corporate director, and Henry Shrier, his business partner, offered to advance capital to further the worthy goals of the Sutter Street while collecting interest as well as dividends. But this was California in 1879, so with the specter of the constitution confounding profit, Baum's lawyer and the corporation's lawyer held a conclave. They drafted new corporate board resolutions and a new mortgage instrument. Before the constitution they had a $125,000 mortgage due in five years at 10%. After the conclave but before January 1, 1880 the effective date of the new constitution, the corporation had $125,000 in hand and Baum had corporate notes for $137,000. But all was not bliss on the board as the corporation filed suit on June 26, 1880.[18]

Baum's attorney argued against the application of the constitution and unjust enrichment. The mortgage and notes predated the constitution. The constitution should not impair the agreement. Even if it did, Baum had paid out $5,436.43 in taxes and should be compensated. So went the litany.

Neither the trial court nor the Supreme Court were sympathetic. Not only was the mortgage found to be for $125,000 only, but also at the reasonable rate of 9% less 158.00 expended in making and acknowledging the mortgage. While the Supreme Court used corporation law for guidance, the locus of responsibility for taxes remained clear and creditor Baum's attorney had not struck on any magic language.

The counselor's pen was without success until 1888 when in *Marye v Hart*, the Court discovered that the "taxes may be paid by either party."[19] The Court also uncovered the perfect exemption arrangement provided for by the Constitution itself. In *People v Board of Supervisors of the City and County of San Francisco* (1888), Mrs. C. L. Tams of San Francisco had a $63,000 mortgage on her property. The mortgage belonged to the Regents of the University of California. The tax collector, knowing he could not get a cent from the Regents, assessed Mrs. Tams for the full value of $142,845 refusing to deduct the $63,000. Mrs. Tams appealed to the supervisors, sitting as a board of equalization. The board agreed with Tams, but the Attorney General intervened to overturn the board claiming in lurid detail how the state's coffers would be depleted. Mr. Justice Thomas B. McFarland caustically reminded the Attorney General that "the state should not expect to collect taxes on her own property — much less should she expect someone else to pay them." Finally, regarding the expected revenue shortfall, McFarland quipped that "the anticipated losses of the state will therefore simply be like the fancied losses of other people who fail to get what they ought not to have."[20] In sum, the Court left little room for legal maneuvering.[21] What creditors did in fact, of course, was to take the advice of Jackson A. Graves and "allow 1½% for taxes" when setting an interest rate.

While the 1979 constitution posed a new challenge to lenders, many older problems plagued expectations. Transactions as well as the documents that evidenced the intent of the parties were not always clear despite the increased use of form mortgages and deeds. California's homestead law exempting $5,000 in value from execution for debt snared the casual lender. Statutes also protected the property rights of married women and the courts were firm in that protection even if a lender's expectations were dashed. Fraud as always was part of the risk. But mistakes were part of the legal record as well as the human condition. Lenders made mistakes failing to check for a homestead or a senior mortgage, forgetting to have the wife sign and acknowledge the mortgage, and trusting the representations of debtors. Lawyers made mistakes costing lenders their all, but this was the 1880s before malpractice suits were entertained, and lenders could only shop for better practitioners of the trade. The system made mistakes. Trial court judges erred on occasion. Delay was a part of the system. Fate could strike the debtor down before his time (payment in full), and the lender or his lawyers could mistakenly interpret the probate code. Finally, as old and as chronic a problem as the boom and bust economy of the century, insolvency could intervene to deflate a lender's expectations. While California law on these matters was relatively clear, the practice of lenders and their counselors-at-law did not avoid the age-old pitfalls.

While the availability of form legal instruments was widespread in the decade, lenders and their lawyers still made mistakes. H. H. Bancroft and Company of San Francisco, among others; offered an extensive line of forms including mortgage, deed, lease, power of attorney, bond, bill of sale, assignment, and acknowledgement.[22] However, the boom of the 1880s made people scramble for property and pens went awry in the process. "The people are getting the Los Angeles fever," William Warner reported in 1887, in fact, "Billy Minner was down 3 or 4 weeks and in that short time he made $5,000.00 speculating in property."[23] While "some of the wildcat outside schemes, to wit: lots in the desert have fallen through," Jackson A. Graves reported that same year, Los Angeles property "will double in value in 12 months."[24] When the pen slipped in haste, some blots were caught before resort to law. John D. Goodwin wrote to his "Friend Smith" in 1884 about a note and mortgage, "the former [being] all right but the latter [being] all wrong." It seems that the clerk "failed to copy either of the notes into the mortgage correctly. Nor did he copy your names to the notes."[25] William Pyburn wrote to David Jacks in 1887 that "in that mortgage made by

Ford to you the other day you made yourself "party of the first part" and Ford "party of the second part" and it should be just the reverse."[26]

Lenders also failed to describe adequately the property in the mortgage. John Markey, Monterey County undersheriff and former county clerk, wrote David Jacks in 1881 that "it is hard to tell what is included in your descriptions, if anything. After some tracing back of original titles, I am almost certain that the lot on Alvarado St. known as the "Zuick House" is in Wither's mortgage but not yours."[27] As often was the case, courts became the interpreters of the documents. The courts worked out doctrines and applied rules of construction that required a description sufficiently definite to identify the land, but allowed judges to interpret where doubt remained.[28] For example, the number of acres was an essential part of the description.[29] Land described in metes and bounds or with specific references to records was sufficiently definite.[30] Sometimes boundaries were lines between "an oak standing on the east and in contact with rocks forming the first rocky point on the south side of the Meadow Valley" and "the Rocky Hall at the San Jose Indian Village."[31] Despite the willingness of the court to find a definite description, some instruments were "too indefinite and uncertain to support a judgment for specific performance." In *Burnett v Kullak* (1888) the court found a mortgage for $2,500 with no stated term, no rate of interest, and no default language.[32] The haste of transactions as well as the geography made description of the property a problem for some California lenders.

Lenders also neglected to check the homestead books before advancing funds secured by a mortgage on real estate. The result under statute was that $5,000 was exempt from execution for debt. As late as 1888 such an experienced lender as David Jacks still needed to inquire regarding the effect of a homestead declaration. William Pyburn told Jacks that

A mortgage given or made *subsequent* to the filing of a declaration of a Homestead by a single person, does away with such declaration only so far as the mortgage is concerned. When the mortgage has been satisfied and satisfaction recorded, the declaration of Homestead before filed holds good. In a declaration of homestead by a married person, a mortgage if made must then be signed by both husband and wife. The effect of a satisfaction of mortgage is the same.

In other words a Homestead declaration is to save the property from execution and unless it is encumbered afterwards it cannot be levied on only for the encumbrance placed upon it after homestead declaration."[33]

Other lenders inquired too late. The law firm of Graves and Chapman, Los Angeles, tersely replied to J. H. Elwood in 1884: "Enclosed find Br...'s note. We can't collect it. He... has a house and lot, but when we came to look it up found a homestead on it."[34] Similarly, when the firm of Graves and O'Melveny requested an investigation, "the first question issuing [was] is that property subject to a homestead?"[35] If it was, only the excess over $5,000 could be obtained. For the small farmer, merchant, and entrepreneur, this gave the debtor great leverage. As Graves, O'Melveny and Shankland reported to a client in 1889, "if we hadn't accepted this settlement, he would undoubtedly have gone into insolvency and none of you would have gotten anything... the real estate not covered by the homestead would not bring $50, so it looked very much as if we would have gotten nothing if we hadn't accepted his proposition."[36] In this particular case, the creditor happily accepted 32 cents on the dollar.

The defense of a statutory homestead was a potent one, but the court occasionally found that the declaration itself was invalid. In *Booth v Galt* (1881) the court found that the "declaration of homestead was clearly invalid" because the married woman failed to state that her husband had not made a homestead declaration when filing alone."[37] Further, Pyburn related to David Jacks and the Supreme Court declared in 1881, a subsequent declaration of homestead could have no effect on a precedent mortgage."[38] But in the main, the homestead declaration was an effective tool to preserve the $5,000 in value of the debtor's property and a stumbling block to the careless lender."[39] The law presumed that the lender knew of the homestead when the declaration had been properly filed."[40] Lending on such property was clearly at great risk. Fraud was a greater risk, but the court would not allow it to stand defeating creditor interests. In *Shinn v Macpherson* (1881) the defendant attempted to use the homestead act for diabolical purposes, but to no avail. John Macpherson and Howard Shinn were business partners. Macpherson had a $1,700 mortgage on his property. Eight days before the partnership was mutually dissolved, Macpherson's wife, Ester, filed her homestead declarations. The next day John withdrew $2,400 from the partnership assets, paid off the mortgage, and pocketed $700. Shinn, discovering the scheme, filed suit and obtained a lien against Macpherson's house and lot. On appeal, Ester claimed the homestead, but the court would not hear of it. The statute "was enacted for beneficent purposes," not as a cloak for fraud.[41] Equity would not allow the debtor to reap the fruits of his fraud.

When a lender was dealing with a married woman, special care was needed as well. While statute had eliminated the capacity problem of married women to make mortgages so prevalent in the 1850s and 60s, the lender of the 80s had to obtain a proper acknowledgement of the mortgage.[42] In 1850 the legislature passed a statute providing for the execution, acknowledgement, and certification of the acknowledgement of a conveyance of a married woman. Her acknowledgement had to made to an officer qualified to take it and who personally knew the woman. The Supreme Court strictly construed the statute to provide the sole means for lawful conveyances. Reacting to the Court's construction, the legislature provided in 1860 that a county judge could correct defective acknowledgements made in good faith by husband and wife. On January 1, 1873 California adopted its civil code. The code changed the certification procedure making execution, acknowledgement, *and* certification no longer necessary for the validity of a conveyance. Now execution and acknowledgement in accordance with the code was sufficient. Certification was simply a record proof of acknowledgement. Once obtained the wife was bound by the contents of the deed on mortgage.[43] In sum, the legislature made the lender's task easier while continuing to protect the property interests of married women. The lender who failed to obtain the acknowledgement of the married woman to a mortgage had a mortgage that was "void."[44] But for the lender who proceeded carefully obtaining the proper execution and acknowledgement, the court would not later hear complaints about capacity or injustice.[45] It was the prudent lender, like David Jacks, who asked his lawyers in San Francisco, "Can a married woman living with her husband make a promissory note with mortgage to it acknowledging the mortgage before a notary public?" *before* he loaned money.[46]

Both lender and borrower had to be wary of sharp dealing. In *Hendy v Kier* (1881) the lender induced the debtor to sign over a first mortgage in return for $400 and the release of a second mortgage. The lender then tried to foreclose the second mortgage, but the court would hear none of it.[47] In *Rosenberg v Ford* (1890) the court used the doctrine of consideration to foil a foul machination grinding down the poor widow Ford. It seems that Jacob Rosenberg held a mortgage on the Ford homestead, but when the good Mr. Ford passed from this life, Jacob failed to present his claim to the widow Ford, administrix, as required by statute. Jacob then went to widow Ford and obtained a second mortgage and notes, the poor widow not knowing that Jacob's tardiness had cut him off from ever collecting his money. When she learned of her ignorance of the law, she lost a degree of moral duty to pay and went to "Judge" Goodwin for advice. "Stop paying," said the judge and after trial and appeal the Supreme Court agreed with the judge, the transaction lacked consideration and Jack Rosenberg lost his mortgage.[48]

A specter far more poignant appeared in *Randall v Duff* (1889) with a widow and orphan pleading for justice. In 1863 William Duff departed California leaving a power of attorney with his father, Richard. Dad fraudulently and without consideration conveyed the land to brother Robert Duff. Robert quickly mortgaged one parcel to William Ritchie and another to Charles Fiebig. William passed away in 1875. Suddenly in 1881 William's widow and orphan learned of grandfather's dastardly deed and they sued Robert and Frank Duff. Neither Ritchie or Fiebig had any inkling that William had any interest in the property when they loaned out their money, but both foreclosed after William's untimely demise. A. W. Randall bought the parcel Ritchie loaned money on and happily received a sheriff's deed. Fiebig bought the other parcel and received his sheriff's deed. But, the widow, Julia Duff, had filed her suit against Robert and Frank *before* the mortgages were foreclosed. *Duff v Duff* resulted in a judgment for Julia, reversed on appeal, and remanded for new trial.

Meanwhile, *Randall v Duff* was in trial. The trial court ruled for the plaintiff and Julia appealed. In 1888 the Supreme Court reversed and remanded for a new trial. In 1889 the Court reheard the case. After sorting out all the litigational details, the Court simply stated that Robert acquired no title from William, Ritchie was an innocent mortgagee and acquired a valid lien by estoppel. Importantly, the Court applied equitable principles in arriving at its decision to avoid gross "injustice." The appellate cases dealing with fraud clearly established the Court's willingness to apply equity to avoid loss to an innocent lender.

Lenders had to be precise in following statutory provisions for foreclosure and redemption. Moreover, the interpretations of the Supreme Court could have impact upon practice. Witness Graves, O'Melveny and Shankland's March 19, 1890 opinion to another law firm:

> As to the necessity of including the description of the mortgaged premises in the foreclosure summons, we refer you to People v. Greene, 52 Ca., p. 577. This was an action to foreclose the interest of the purchaser of lands from the State of California, holding under a certificate of purchase, and, while the point was not directly decided, still we think there is enough in the case to justify a Court as eccentric as the present Supreme Court of this State is in holding it to be conclusive of the proposition. However, as we agree that it is well to avoid all possible chances, we will insert description in the summons, irrespective of the law of the case.[50]

Not only did the Supreme Court's opinion sway practice, but the legal system's grindingly slow process impacted practice. Witness David Jacks writing to C. W. Gates on December 15, 1886:

> It is more than five years since judgment of foreclosure was rendered as you will see by the papers in the case.
>
> But Judge Webb told me that Mr. Beeman made an application for a new trial in the case and that it was more than two years from that time until Judge Belden rendered a decision refusing to allow a new trial.
>
> Judge Webb says that it will be all right to make an application to Judge Alexander for an order of sale to sell the property and that he will grant it on a reasonable showing. . . . If Beeman thinks that he can take advantage, of the delay in getting the order of sale, he will be apt to do it.

If a deed from Mrs. Johnson will carry the legal title to the property by paying her some money to obtain it that will be the easiest and quickest way to end the matter.[51]

After foreclosure and sale, a sheriff's deed was issued to the purchaser.[52] The debtor was then allowed six months to redeem the property by settling up, under statute, with the purchaser.[53] The effect of the redemption period was, of course, to reduce the immediate marketability of the property.

When lenders blundered in their transactions, the Court was not always sympathetic. In *Hibernia Savings and Loan Society v Moore* (1885) the Court chided the lending institution for its failure to investigate the scope of a power of attorney. In this case, $57,000 was a hard lesson to learn, but clearly, the lender had limited recourse given its cavalier effusion of money.[54] The Court did come to the aid of the stumbling lender in *Weyant v Murphy* (1889). In a sheriff's sale pursuant to a decree of foreclosure, the defendant failed, by what the Supreme Court characterized as "a stupid blunder," to bid the full amount of the judgment. He later increased his bid which was accepted by the receiver. Weyant then tendered the original bid to Murphy. Murphy refused it and Weyant sued. The Court would hear none of Weyant's argument and "assist him to profit by the defendant's mistake."[55] Again the Court applied equitable principles, avoided "the strict legal rights of the parties," and rendered "justice."[56]

The Supreme Court was not as charitable with the California bar. In 19th century California, the creditor often put his interests at risk when he engaged legal counsel. As in most of the affairs of mankind, men were not perfect. Unfortunately for some lenders, their lawyers were sloppy, tardy, or incompetent. Lawyers were even critical of their brethren in the bar. For example, Creed Hammond, a successful Sacramento trial attorney, wrote to John D. Goodwin, a Quincy attorney in February 1869:

> When I received the papers in *Madden v Reynolds* I felt like murdering you — how did you expect the sheriff of this county to make an arrest on an order directed to the Sheriff of Plumas County. You must be more careful my boy when you proceed under "the statute." See sec. 77, Pr[actice] Act for form of order. We of course could do nothing in the premises. You may tell your client that we raised heaven and earth, pursued the defendant

with a vigilance worthy of the cause, charged you $100 for expenses, but could not capture him.[57]

While the debtor was lost, the fee was seldom forgotten.

The lender's attorney sometimes failed to bring all the parties before the bench. In *Brown v Willis* (1885) the Supreme Court used the words of Chancellor Kent to remind the lender that "every person is bound to take care of his own rights, and to vindicate them in due season, and in proper order. This a sound and salutary principle of law. Accordingly, if a defendant having the means of defense in his power, neglects to use them, and suffers a recovery to be had against him in a competent tribunal, he is forever precluded."[58] In *Brown* the lender's attorney failed in his original suit to include all the proper parties and the litigation foreclosed any further opportunity to collect.

In the rough and tumble real estate market, a lawyer's mistake could be costly. David Jacks got involved in prolonged litigation over two lots in Monterey. Lots worth only $5.00 per acre seldom inspired lengthy litigation, but when Jacks constructed a narrow gauge railroad from Monterey to Salinas City, the lots soared to $50,000 each and lawsuits began to fly. Three of the law suits ultimately reached the California Supreme Court.[59] Milton Little and his wife Mary borrowed money from David Jacks in 1874 and from James Withers in 1875. But the 70s were hard times and the lenders foreclosed. At the foreclosure sale Withers purchased lots 1 and 2 and Jacks bought lots 3, 4, 5, and 6. Jacks appealed from the trial court decree adjudging Withers' mortgage to be prior in right to Jacks' on the ground of the date of the filing of the mortgages.[60] However, in the notice of appeal dated July 21, 1879, Jacks attorneys failed to stay the execution of the decree of foreclosure. Hence, the sheriff's sale was held, the property sold, and certificates issued. In 1887 the Supreme Court decided *Little v Superior Court* holding that when the Littles consented to judgment against them, fixing the amount due to Jacks, it would be an injustice to open the judgment, sell the property again, or grant a personal judgment against the Littles.[61] Soon after the decision, Jacks wrote to his Los Angeles attorney inquiring about a rehearing.[62] Jacks complained that he was out the $5,000 loan made over a decade ago excepting two quarters interest payments. Further, Withers knew of the mortgage to Jacks before he subsequently loaned money on Little's property.[63] Jacks also sought a second opinion on getting a rehearing, but a San Jose attorney gave him little hope.[64] The second shoe dropped in *Withers v Jacks* (1889). When Jacks' attorneys failed to request the stay of execution of the foreclosure decree and subsquent sheriff's sale, the purchaser's title was final. Withers owned the land and Jacks was a wiser man for the experience, although no richer.[65] Hopefully, the firm of Houghton and Reynolds, Los Angeles, learned an equally useful lesson about California procedure.

On occasion the Court was disposed to give a creditor a second chance before the bench. The Bank of Sonoma loaned George W. Charles and J. M. Charles $42,250 in 1886. Unfortunately, George passed away in 1889 leaving $38,069.58 in principal and $5,979.07 interest unpaid. The Bank made a presentation of the promissory note, but not the mortgage of the administrix. The probate judge rendered judgment foreclosing the mortgage, awarding $500 in attorneys fees, but refusing any deficiency judgment against the estate. On appeal in 1890 the Supreme Court found that the Bank had failed to comply with the statutes providing for the presentation of mortgages. Hence, the demurrer refused at trial should have been sustained and the Bank thrown out of court. On appeal, the Bank argued that another section of the California Civil Code allowed a holder of a mortgage to enforce the mortgage against a particular parcel of property "when all recourse against any other property of the estate is expressly waived in the complaint; but no counsel fees shall be recovered..."[66] But the complaint contained "no such waiver, and such a plain statutory provision cannot be disregarded or explained away," Mr. Justice Thomas B. McFarland declared. But with the sweep of the pen, McFarland proceeded to disregard the statute because "we do not think that the consequences of plaintiff's carelessness are so ruinous as to utterly preclude it from the benefit of the mortgage lien."[67] Further, McFarland stated, "the plaintiff certainly did not intend to waive or abandon its mortgage." Hence, to avoid injustice or inequity, the Court held that the Bank could amend its complaint, waive all recovery against any property except the mortgaged parcel, and, of course, forego counsel fees so richly undeserved. Here equity was applied to provide counsel opportunity to amend sloppy pleadings and practice, and the bank a foreclosure sale.

The Court was not sympathetic to the blatantly sloppy pleader. In *Bunnel v Stockton* (1890) the trial court had decided a case against a homestead claimant for failure to comply with statute. It was discovered, subsequently, that at the time the homestead was declared, the statute did not require a statement of value of the property. Hence, the first trial was concluded on a present statute not in force at the time of the accrual of the homestead interest and a new trial was held. Bunnel's motion for a new trial was then denied after one extension for thirty days, another of twenty days, and then another twenty days. Statute provided for extensions of not longer than thirty days without the consent of the adverse party which was not obtained for the final extension. The Court tersely held that the statement was filed "too late" and the last extension was "unauthorized."[68] As Mr. Justice John D. Works concisely stated "the one extension of time beyond the thirty days did not give the judge any additional authority."[69] The case pointed out several imperfections in the legal system. The first trial in Lassen County, a rural jurisdiction, proceeded on a statutory theory that was incorrect. Neither lawyers nor the judge knew of their error. None of them had done their homework. On the motion for new trial, the judge exceeded his authority and the respondent's lawyer was delinquent in making a timely filing.

The lender was often at the mercy of his attorney. In *Johnston v McDuffee* (1890) the Court in rendering judgment against him commented that "though McDuffee's rights as a mortgagee might have been protected by taking the proper steps to bring them before the court, the record before us is not in a shape that presents them."[70] Other cases contain pleading error after pleading error.[71] Some cases were presented without documentary evidence; hence, the appellate court judges could collectively scratch their heads and observe that "it is somewhat uncertain who purchased at this foreclosure sale. No documents were introduced in evidence."[72] Still others evidenced the failure to serve the proper parties with required documents.[73] Competent counsel was clearly a factor in successful mortgage lending.

Even with effective representation, California's judicial system was far from perfect. Some trial court judges were far from precise in their findings of fact and conclusions of law. As the Supreme Court commented in *Bettis v Townsend* (1882), "the decision of the Court below was somewhat informal."[74] On occasion, a trial court judge would order more land sold than was mortgaged.[75] On another, the trial judge would erroneously order a new trial such as *Santa Marina v Connolly* (1889) on "wholly immaterial" grounds.[76] Oftentimes, the errors led to considerable delay.

As was true across the country in the 19th century, the legal system could be used to delay foreclosure. Litigation could save clients money. Appeals could stop the legal process of foreclosure sale in its tracks. Sometimes it was a blatant practice. The Supreme Court was openly annoyed with counsel's stratagems. In *Durkin v Burr* (1882) the Court dismissed the suit for the third time in one sentence.[77] The Court often assessed costs or damages when appeals were brought for the obvious purpose of delay. In *Montgomery v Robinson* (1888) the Court tersely dismissed the appeal as one "without merit" and assessed five percent damages.[78] Mr. Justice Thomas B. McFarland analyzed *Whitby v Rowell* (1890) in two paragraphs, observing that "the appeal was evidently for delay," and assessed the debtor with $200 damages plus court costs.[79] While debtors could use delay as an important tool to frustrate process, lenders who failed to exercise their right could lose their investment under the Statute of Limitations.[80] Regardless of whether one party or another used or failed to use the judicial system, the process was slow. John Wise loaned money in March 1876, reecived a judgment in August 1877, was forced to file an amended complaint in July of 1880, and received finality in an affirmation of the decree of foreclosure by the Supreme Court in January 1889.[81] Collecting on a mortgage, where the debtor resisted the process, could be a long and complex process.

Even more complex was the collection of a mortgage after the debtor or spouse passed from this earth. The problem was complex because questions of homestead were often commingled with probate issues. The legislature attempted to preserve the homestead by having it set aside by the Probate Court (1860) and by having it vest absolutely in the survivor (1862).[82] However, debts acquired subsequent to the death of a spouse were not protected by the homestead declaration.[83] Clearly, those mortgages made after the declaration of a homestead had to be presented to the administrator of the estate and could not operate to dissolve the homestead exemption. The legislature had undoubtedly intended "to preserve the homestead if possible."[84] If the mortgage was not an incumbrance on a homestead, the lender could foreclose without presentment to the administrator if all recourse against all other property of the estate was expressly waived.[85] The key analytical question for the attorney was statutory construction, but the California Supreme Court attempted to make clear that the presentment was necessary where a homestead was involved. Unfortunately, the lender and his counsel often read the statute book rather than the *Reports of the California Supreme Court,* and procedural error abounded.[86] Further, counsel often failed to bring the proper parties before the bench or the trial courts confused statutory issues opening cases for appeal.[87] The process created confusion and delay. As Jackson A. Graves wrote to a client in 1880, "The mortgage has been foreclosed *properly*. At the sale the property bid in the name of yourself and the church as representatives of the estate of your husband and the deed was issued. This is *bad* for the reason that you *individually* own half of it."[88] Because of the blunder, the wife had to go to probate to liquidate her interests. To prevent procedural catastrophes, lenders had to be particularly aware of the obituary columns. David Jacks hurriedly telegraphed James A. Clayton in 1890, "If they are probating Shedaker estate, file sworn claim amount my note, mortgage immediately to prevent any bar of foreclosure. See recent decision Supreme Court."[89] Foreclosure was crucial to the lender to provide for the first mortgage gaining priority over other claims and avoiding a proportional distribution of estate assets where debts exceeded assets. The death of a debtor could signal the race to the courthouse. Significantly, David Jacks was reading the advance sheets of the California Supreme Court as well as the obituary columns.[90] Law was not the exclusive province of lawyers in California in the 19th century nor could it be given the uncertainty of mortgage law and practice.

While death was more certain than law, bankruptcy certainly followed drought, credit constriction, or eastern financial panic.

Here again the lender was caught up in the intricate web of procedure, practice, and practicality. Collecting debts was a specialty of the lawyer's craft. Massillon Marsteller of Susanville
told the world on his letterhead, "Collection of Debts a Specialty."[91] It must have been true. One thing that was true was
that collecting was a high stakes game. For example, Graves and
O'Melveny took great pains to map out a game plan for D. N. and
E. Walter and Company in collecting on their mortgage. Their
mortgage was "good against the assignment recently made by
them (Barnhart and Kelly, debtors) for the benefit of their
creditors." But if the other five creditors should "file a petition
in insolvency against Barnhart and Kelly or should they volun-
tarily go into insolvency within thirty days after the date of your
mortgage, there [was] some question as to whether your mortgage would have the preference." It was best to wait and let the
thirty days run. If after thirty days, Barnhart and Kelly had failed
to pay the interest due, then "immediately foreclose and sell the
mortgaged property." Meanwhile, the creditor was not to sue on
two small promissory notes then due because it might stampede
the other creditors into filing insolvency proceedings. To make
the point absolutely clear, Graves and O'Melveny pointed out
that "you have too much at stake in the mortgage to risk for so
small a consideration."[92] In other cases, the creditor would have
to take what he could get to avoid insolvency. In 1889 Graves,
O'Melveny and Shankland reported that "the best terms of settlement we could get out of him was that he would turn over the
liquor and give his note for $135 payable ten months after date
with interest at one percent per month. If we hadn't accepted this
settlement, he would have undoubtedly gone into insolvency and
none of you would have gotten anything."[93] Whether the settlement was a better shake than insolvency was sometimes questionable. As Jackson A. Graves reported to a client in 1881:
"Enclosed you will find a deed from that bitch of a Johan Roberts
to 500 acres in Rancho El Mission of San Diego. ... I do not
know whether the interest is worth a tinker's d. or not."[94] But
the worst possible situation was, of course, the judgment proof
debtor. Such a person was one "Mr. Smart of Downey City,"
according to Graves. In fact, "he will promise payment with the
same good grace that a worthy Friar does absolution and fail to

pay on time with equal grace. To sue him comes to folly. If we can even catch him."[95]

On occasion, insolvency proceedings were advantageous to the creditor, but more often than not the problems outweighed the advantages. Where inter-spousal transactions were raised as a defense to creditor interests, insolvency was a means of negating such stratagems.[96] If the assignee could be controlled, prior interests could be advantaged.[97] But if the assignee failed in his duties, interests could be tied up for years. As George E. Bates, a San Francisco attorney, reported to David Jacks in 1890:

> (Peter) Heron filed his petition in bankruptcy July 12th, 1878. He was adjudicated a bankrupt July 13, 1878. Townsend Wood of Castroville was appointed assignee and a deed of assignment was made to him by the Register in Bankruptcy on March 8, 1879.
>
> The assignee has never filed any account, nor has the bankrupt ever applied for any discharge from his debts.
>
> These proceedings can not be dismissed, but they can be terminated. The debtor can apply for and obtain his discharge and (if necessary) the assignee can be required to account and thereupon the assignee can be discharged and the proceedings closed. The matter can be terminated in no other way.[98]

Insolvency proceedings clearly advantaged debtors and continued as a consideration in lending money in the decade.

° ° ° ° ° ° ° °

While lenders and borrowers operated in the marketplace, the California Supreme Court struggled with fact situations springing from the frenzied speculation of the decade. One continuing function of the Court was interpreting transactions to determine whether a mortgage had been intended. Here the work of Stephen J. Field had played a significant role.

One of Field's major contributions of the 1850s, the parol evidence rule application to mortgages, was accepted as controlling in the 1880s. Field's opinion in *Pierce v Robinson* (1859) and expanded upon in *Cunningham v Hawkins* (1865) established that parol evidence (oral testimony) was admissible to show that a deed absolute on its face was intended as a mortgage.[99] When California adopted its Civil Code in 1873, the Code Commissioners declared their intent, in two sections, to be to restore the rule of *Cunningham*.[100] With Field on the United States Supreme Court bench, the California Court also cited his similar holding in federal court.[101] The Court in the 80s had continuing need to apply the rule. For example, in *J. S. Manasse v Lazarus Dinkelspiel* (1886) the parties made an oral agreement to exchange a deed for property held by Manasse for an evidence of indebtedness held by Dinkelspiel of $1,800. In that Manasse's property might not bring at sale the $1,800 owed to Dinkelspiel, Manasse gave Lazarus a note for $500 to cover any deficiency. However, if the sale netted $1,800, Lazarus was to return any surplus land and the note. All seemed settled. Then the land boom shattered expectations and Manasse wanted to raise up a mortgage from the deed, to pay it off, and reap a profit. But the Court simply went back to Field's test of "if there is no debt, there is no mortgage," and found that the $1,800 debt was satisfied by the deed and that no debt existed. In that Manasse could not raise a mortgage from the deed, Lazarus Dinkelspiel was left with the land to reap his harvest.[102]

The California Supreme Court also spent a great deal of energy exercising its equitable jurisdiction superintending mortgages. This had become a substantial and a mainstream function of American state courts in the late 19th century.[103] Equity was a system of jurisprudence that focused upon the fairness or justice of dealings rather than strict legal rules. Naturally, equity gave courts greater latitude for decision and the California experience was little different.

In *Wilhelmina Rumpp v Jacob Gerkens* (1881) the Court applied equitable principles to decide the case. The plaintiff, Rumpp, had a mortgage from Gerkens and wife, Isadora, dated July 18, 1876. Another defendant, Miguel Leonis, had a mortgage from the Gerkens dated July 1, 1875. Leonis foreclosed on May 28, 1878, but did not make Rumpp a party as Leonis had no idea that the Gerkens had mortgaged the place twice. The trial court granted the petition, entered a decree of foreclosure, and authorized the sale of the property. Leonis purchased at sale and received a sheriff's deed. But on December 19, 1878 Jacob and Isadora struck a bargain with Miguel to give him their deed in return for $3,973.25 and the cancellation of all debts Miguel held. For Miguel, it was a worthwhile bargain because the tyranny of the redemption period was thus slashed away from the execution sale and sheriff's deed. But all was not so clear in the brine in which transactions cured in Los Angeles in the period. Suddenly, Wilhelmina appeared and a trial court found that the Gerkens owed her $1,039.32 in gold and that she now had the right of redemption which Miguel had just paid dear dollars to avoid. Parenthetically, the trial court ordered the Gerkenses to pay Wilhelmina $1,185.92 immediately or suffer a 7% per year penalty. The Supreme Court placed its stamp of approval on the holding citing equity. Equity protected Leonis by finding that he did not intend to give up his security by taking the deed or that his lien should be extinguished as against subsequent incumbrances.[104] Whether such a holding comforted a lender who had spent money to foreclose, paid out more money to avoid redemption, disbursed more to counsel to defend at trial and on appeal, and now faced an unknown creditor who could redeem for $2,800 is doubtful. Equity as well as debtors, litigation, and lawyers could leave lenders in a pickle.

While equity and law could result in ironic holdings for creditors, its use was generally beneficial to lenders' interests. Equity would not aid those that sat idly on their rights.[105] Debtors could not complain of a lender's lack of authority to loan money with the lucre in their hands attempting to avoid their obligation to pay.[106] Affirmatively, courts in equity could settle all accounts and grant damages for waste on rents and profits.[107] Clearly, the principles of equity fávored the creditor. For example, as stated in *Booth v Hoskins* (1888) denying affiirmative relief to the plaintiff until the money due the defendant was paid:

> Common honesty required a debtor to pay his just debts if he is able to do so, and the courts, when called upon, always enforce such payments if they can. The fact that a debt is barred by the statute of limitations in no way releases the debtor from his moral obligation to pay it. Moreover, one of the maxims which courts of equity should always act upon is...that he who seeks equity must do equity.[106]

It was that "common honesty" that bound debtors to pay by whatever means that cemented the marketplace relations of many together on a continuing basis. David Jacks carried Jim Kee, a

Salinas Valley farmer, for years extending debts, signing new notes and mortgages, and taking crops in lieu of cash.[109] The great bulk of debtors paid on time and received the signed satisfaction of mortgage document whether they paid in cash, kind, or land.[110] The principles of common honesty were very much a part of the marketplace.

Another institutional obligation of the California Supreme Court was considering the developing mortgage law of other states in formulating mortgage law for the state.[111] Generally, the Supreme Court looked to New York cases for guidance.[112] The Court's reliance upon New York was not particularly surprising given the state's adoption of the Field Code of New York and the influence of New York on law in the century in general.[113] Equally expected, California jurists and lawyers found some New York precedent not on point.[114] Unexpectedly, the California Court also ridiculed the New York court. In *Brickell v Batchelder* (1882) Mr. Justice James D. Thornton tore a New York opinios to shreds. After reciting the opinion of the New York court, Thornton, attacking the ability of the New York court to read plain English, asserted that given the mortgage language: "If such language does not authorize a party to proceed for a statutory foreclosure on failure to pay taxes by the mortgagor, it would be difficult to find any sufficient reason why." Thornton looking at the same language then declared that the "words could not make it plainer." How then could the New York judge make such a stupid reading of plain English? Thornton had the politic answer. "The Judge was surely mistaken." Even if he had not made a mistake, clearly the rule was "peculiar to the jurisprudence of New York."[115] The *Batchelder* opinion was critical of the New York court without jurisprudential cause because the mortgages could have been distinguished. However, the California court, here as elsewhere, asserted its uniqueness and the rightness of its declarations as means of identification. Some found this eccentric. For the Court it was part of a more general process of asserting its judicial leadership in the developing law of the land.[116]

∗ ∘ ∘ ∘ ∘ ∘ ∘ ∘ ∘

Despite the uncertainties of law in California, mortgage practice matured in the 1880s seeking greater certainty, but con-

tinuing to seek more opportunity for creative financing. Creditors
and debtors alike sought creative draftsmanship and found it to
circumvent taxation as well as court rulings.

Entrepreneurs sought money in every corner. Many borrowed
from banks. Others borrowed from family. Prospective debtors
deluged private lenders with requests for money on "good security."[117] Since many mortgages were short-term, many debtors
sought refinancing,[118] Other debtors requested extensions of existing loans.[119] Construction loans became a part of financing the
expansion of rural enterprise.[120] Lenders adjusted interest rates
to deal with the 1879 Constitution's tax on mortgages.[121] As the
economy changed, they also adjusted interest rates to market conditions even if downward.[122] With flush times, lenders introduced
a prepayment penalty to assure their return.[123] The prepayment
penalty clause quickly became part of mortgage boilerplate. As
James A. Clayton explained to David Jacks in 1890:

> The 3 months clause in the Welborn note is the customary method
> of making a note payable before due. This is found to be quite
> just as there are as many chances that it will be paid late in the
> year as it will be about the time of taxes — but it is figured that if
> it is paid shortly after the tax assessment the 3 months bonus will
> more than cover the amount of taxes . . .
> . . . as a whole you will find the rule of making a mortgagor pay
> 3 months bonus for paying before due a very satisfactory one to
> lender and borrower.[124]

Lenders also drafted around the deficiency judgment holdings of
the Court. Debtors simply guaranteed by contract that they
would pay any deficiency in a foreclosure sale.[125] The creditor as
well as the debtor attempted to adjust practice to the market as
best they could.

One such adjustment was the use of the deed of trust. The
trust deed was a three-party transaction, the debtor being the
trustor, the creditor being the beneficiary, and a third party being
the trustee holding legal title to the land with the power to sell
or reconvey if the debtor defaulted. The trust deed provided
expedited sale and cut off the redemption period. In the 20th
century the deed of trust became virtually the sole instrument
for security transactions in real estate.[126] In the decade of the
1880s the California Court scrutinized such trust deeds care-

fully and required that debtors be treated equitably.[127] Further, although the redemption period was cut off, the purchaser had a difficult time dispossessing the debtor because the legal status of the trust deed and the debtor was uncertain.[128] In the next forty years the California court and the legislature would enhance the trust deed's utility and make it the most desirable instrument.

* * * * * * * * * * * *

The development of mortgage law in the period, 1850-1890, evidenced a sometimes sketchy record of formal law fostering security and certainty in mortgage transactions. Clearly, the main thread of law encouraging the release of energy inherent in real estate transactions existed as Willard Hurst has often told us. But in California there was more. Legal development followed social and economic change. But practitioners often found the law poorly suited to their goals. They drafted around problems where they could. However, as the California Court entered the 1870s without Stephen J. Field, the holdings oftentimes confounded the policies laid down in the 1850s and 60s. Further, practitioners were not always certain of what the law was. This chief element of uncertainty was both due to the court and to the practitioners.[129] Clearly, the Court was not always helpful in guiding entrepreneurs and their counsel, but equally clear, lawyers and lenders made egregious errors of omission and commission. The frontier nature of much of the marketplace as well as the frenzied bargaining in a boom and bust economy made mortgage law in California a challenge for jurists, legislators, lawyers, and lenders. As the law of mortgage developed, California's frontier economy and society made imprints in law and practice.

NOTES

Acknowledgment. The author acknowledges a grant from the American Bar Association in support of this research.

¹ See Glenn S. Dumke, *The Boom of the Eighties in Southern California* (San Marino, 1944).

² Warren A. Beck and David A. Williams, *California* (New York, 1972), p. 290.

³ *Ibid.*, pp. 299-303.

⁴ Carl B. Swisher, *Motivation and Political Technique in the California Constitutional Convention, 1878-79* (Claremont, CA., 1930), pp. 66-79.

⁵ Clough to Mother, August 18, 1879, Clough Collection, California State Library, California Section, MSS, Box 157.

⁶ Graves to Wallace, February 22, 1881, Graves Collection, Huntington Library, MSS, 1881-83 Letterbook.

⁷ Memorandum of McCarthy Loan, February 23, 1881 and April 19, 1881 entries, Jacks Collection, Huntington Library, MSS, Box B(II)(4).

⁸ Reynolds to Jacks, May 10, 1880, Jacks Collection, Huntington Library, MSS, Box C(3).

⁹ Ninety-one cases were studied:

Year	Creditors won:
1867	71%
1868	60%
1869	50%
1870	43%
1871	90%
1872	71%
1873	67%
1874	67%
1875	75%
1876	100%
1877	100%
1878	60%
1879	40%
1880	62%
Total	67%

¹⁰ Average by year of amount in controversy where noted in appellate case report.

1867	$24,732.50	1874	$ 8,646.38
1868	2,166.67	1875	17,927.67
1869	9,581.79	1876	no data
1870	16,493.19	1877	$ 1,150 (single case with data)
1871	3,040.14	1878	$ 3,293.00
1872	24,229.00	1879	17,833.33
1873	2,950.67	1880	34,628.13

Range = $225,000 to $145.00

¹¹ For example, see March 8, 1888 receipt for the W. A. Keaney law library. Jacks Collection, Huntington Library, MSS, Box B(V)(10). See James A. Clayton-Jacks correspondence, 1879-80, *Ibid.*, Box C (3).

¹² Graves, O'Melveny and Shankland to Jarboe, Harrison and Goodfellow, March 19, 1890, Graves Collection, Huntington Library, MSS, 1890-91 Letterbook.

¹³ 59 Cal. 541.

¹⁴ 4 Wheaton 122.

¹⁵ 60 Cal. 367, 368.

[16] 60 Cal. 367, 371.

[17] 65 Cal. 383, 384.

[18] 66 Cal. 44, 45-46. For other corporation cases see *Granger v Original Empire Mill and Mining Co.* (1881), 59 Cal. 678. *McLane v Placerville and Sacramento Valley RR Co.* (1885), 66 Cal. 606. *Alta Silver Mining Co. v Alta Placer Mining Co.* (1889), 78 Cal. 629. Mining companies were also in court. *Cornell v Corbin* (1883), 64 Cal. 197. *Montgomery v Keppeland Spring Valley Mining & Irrigating Co.* (1880), 75 Cal. 128. *McPherson v Weston* (1890), 85 Cal. 90.

[19] 76 Cal. 291. As late as 1887, the Court remained reluctant to so decide. See *Doland v Mooney* (1887), 72 Cal. 34.

[20] 77 Cal. 136, 139.

[21] The Court did uphold the *Mayre v Harte* rule in *Brown v Clark* (1891), 89 Cal. 196. The issue did not go away until Nov. 8, 1910 when the section was repealed. See *Knott v Peden* (1890), 84 Cal. 299. *San Gabriel Co. v Witmer Co.* (1892), 96 Cal. 623. *Mackay v San Francisco* (1896), 113 Cal. 392. *Hibernia Savings & Loan Society v Behnke* (1898), 121 Cal. 339. *Canadian Co. v Boas* (1902), 136 Cal. 419. *Matthew v Ormed* (1903), 140 Cal. 578. *William Ede Co. v Heywood* (1908), 153 Cal. 615. *Bank of Willows v County of Glenn* (1909), 155 Cal. 352.

[22] H. H. Bancroft and Company to John D. Goodwin, September 15, 1869, Goodwin Collection, California State Library, California Section, MSS, Box 727. Also see Cave Johnson Couts Collection, Huntington Library, MSS Box 75. Blue Lake Water Company, Huntington Library, MSS, BC 338. Bancroft Blank No. 398-Declaration of Abandonment in David Jacks Collection, Huntington Library, MSS, Box B(III)(8). Barclay Collection, Rancho Mascupiabe Section, Huntington Library, MSS, Box 4.

[23] Warner to Geo., Allice, and Elsie Warner, October 23, 1887, Warner Collection, California State Library, California Section, Box 327.

[24] Graves to F. A. Hihn, November 10, 1887, Graves Collection, Huntington Library, MSS, 1885-88 Letterbook.

[25] Goodwin to Smith, November 2, 1884, Goodwin Collection, California State Library, California Section, MSS, Box 730.

[26] Pyburn to Jacks, December 15, 1887, Jacks Collection, Huntington Library, MSS, Box C(6).

[27] Markey to Jacks, April 13, 1881, Jacks Collection, Huntington Library, MSS, Box C(4).

[28] Arthur G. Bowman, *Ogden's Revised California Real Property Law*, vol. 1 (Berkeley, 1974), pp. 587-588. Also see Laurence M. Friedman, *A History of American Law* (New York, 1973), pp. 212-213.

[29] *Hall v Shotwell* (1885), 66 Cal. 379. Also see *Pellier v Gillespie* (1885), 67 Cal. 582.

[30] *Supulveda v Baugh* (1887), 74 Cal. 468.

[31] *Gage v Downey* (1889), 79 Cal. 140.

[32] 76 Cal. 535, 536-37. Also see *Borel v Donahue* (1884), 64 Cal. 447.

[33] Pyburn to Jacks, March 13, 1888, Jacks Collection, Huntington Library, MSS, Box C(7).

[34] January 21, 1884, Graves Collection, Huntington Library, MSS, 1883-85 Letterbook.

[35] Graves and O'Melveny to Klauber and Live, May 26, 1885, Graves Collection, Huntington Library, MSS, 1883-85 Letterbook.

[36] Graves to Dalleman and Company, October 26, 1889, Graves Collection, Huntington Library, MSS, 1889-90 Letterbook.

[37] 58 Cal. 254. Also see *Grogan v Thrift* (1881), 58 Cal. 378. *Fitzgerald v Fernandez* (1886), 71 Cal. 504.

[38] *Graham v Oviatt* (1881), 58 Cal. 428.

[39] See *Marbury v. Ruiz* (1881), 58 Cal. 11. *Orr v Stewart* (1885), 67 Cal. 275.

[40] *Grupe v Byers* (1887), 73 Cal. 271. *Gleason v Spray* (1889), 81 Cal. 217.

[41] *Shinn v Macpherson* (1881), 58 Cal. 596, 599.

[42] See *Simpers and Craumer v Sloan and Sloan* (1855), 5 Cal. 457. *Pfeiffer and Wife v Riehn and Schannell* (1859), 13 Cal. 643. *Ramsdell v Fuller and Summer* (1865), 28 Cal. 37.

[43] *DeArnaz v Escandon* (1881), 59 Cal. 486. *Joseph v Dougherty* (1882), 60 Cal. 358. *California Civil Code* (1873), Sections 158, 1093, 1186, 1187, 1187, 1191, 1202.

[44] *Tolman v Smith* (1887), 74 Cal. 345.

[45] *Burkle v Levy* (1886), 70 Cal. 250. *Bull v Coe* (1888), 77 Cal. 54.

[46] Jacks to Freeman and Bates, June 21, 1889, Jacks Collection, Huntington, MSS, Box C(7).

[47] 59 Cal. 138.

[48] 85 Cal. 610.

[49] 79 Cal. 115, 119.

[50] Graves, *et al.* to Jarboe, Harrison & Goodfellow, March 19, 1890, Graves Collection, Huntington, MSS, 1890-91 Letterbook.

[51] Jacks Collection, Huntington, MSS, Box C(5). Also see Jacks to S. O. Houghton (L.A.), May 31, December 11, 12, 14, 1887, Box C(6) and April 26, 1888, Box C(6) and April 26, 1888, Box C(7) for numerous complaints about delay and expense in foreclosure.

[52] David Jacks had an agent in Salinas City dealing in sheriff's deeds for him. See J. F. Birlem to Jacks, January 7, 1888, Jacks Collection, Huntington, MSS, Box C(6).

[53] See *Calkins v Steinbach* (1884), 66 Cal. 117. *Watt v Wright* (1884), 66 Cal. 202. *Hall v Arnott* (1889), 80 Cal. 348.

[54] 68 Cal. 156.

[55] 78 Cal. 278, 282.

[56] 78 Cal. 278, 283.

[57] Hammond to Goodwin, February 28, 1869, Goodwin Collection, MSS, California State Library, California Section, Box 731. On attorney's fees see *Dean v Applegarth* (1884), 65 Cal. 391. *Monroe v Fohl* (1887), 72 Cal. 568.

[58] 67 Cal. 235, 236.

[59] *Withers v Little* (1880), 56 Cal. 219. *Little v Superior Court* (1887), 74 Cal. 219. *Withers v Jacks* (1889), 79 Cal. 297. Also see *Little v Jacks* (1885), 67 Cal. 165 and *Little v Jacks* (1886), 68 Cal 343. Jacks was often in court. See *Jacks v Buell* (1873), 47 Cal. 162, *Jacks v Baldez* (1892), 97 Cal. 91, *Jacks v Estee* (1903), 139 Cal. 507, *Jacks v Deering* (1907), 150 Cal. 272, *Jacks v Johnston* (1890), 86 Cal. 384, *Swain v Jacks* (1899), 125 Cal. 215 (on an 1877 foreclosure). Jacks went all the way to the U.S. Supreme Court to have title to lands he purchased on Feb. 9, 1859 confirmed. *City of Monterey v Jacks* (1906), 203 US 360.

[60] Jacks filed on June 2, 1876; Withers filed on December 12, 1875.

[61] 74 Cal. 219.

[62] Jacks to S. O. Houghton, December 11, 1887, Jacks Collection, Huntington, MSS, Box C(6).

[63] Jacks to Houghton, December 12, 1887 and December 14, 1887, Jacks Collection, Huntington, MSS, Box C(6).

[64] S. F. Leib to Jacks, December 10, 1887, Jacks Collection, Huntington, MSS, Box C(6).

[65] 79 Cal. 297, 299-300.

[66] *Bank of Sonoma v Charles* (1890), 86 Cal. 322, 327.

[67] 86 Cal. 322, 327.

[68] 83 Cal. 319, 320-21.

[69] 83 Cal. 319, 321. On Works see Leland G. Stanford, *Footprints of Justice in San Diego* (San Diego, 1960), pp. 38-40.

[70] 83 Cal. 30, 32.

[71] See *Glide v Dwyer* (1890), 83 Cal. 477, *Campbell v West* (1890), 86 Cal. 197, *McGurren v Garrity* (1886), 68 Cal. 566, *Eaton v Rocca* (1888), 75 Cal. 93.

[72] *Wilson v White* (1890), 84 Cal. 239, 241. Also see *Leviston v Henninger* (1888), 77 Cal. 461 where the plaintiff's attorney failed to introduce the judgment upon which the execution issued.

[73] *White v Patton* (1890), 87 Cal. 151.

[74] 61 Cal. 333, 334.

[75] *Schwartz v Palm* (1884), 65 Cal. 54.

[76] 79 Cal. 517, 523. Also see *Schrivener v Dietz* (1885), 68 Cal. 1 granting new trial for trial court error. For a case without substantial legal questions on appeal, see *Phelan v DeMartin* (1890) 85 Cal. 365.

[77] 60 Cal. 360. Also see *Hamilton v Jones* (1882), 62 Cal. 473. On *Burr* also see *Grant v Burr* (1880), 54 Cal. 298 and *Bateman v Burr* (1881), 57 Cal 480.

[78] 76 Cal. 229.

[79] 82 Cal. 635.

[80] See *Biddel v Brizzolara* (1883), 64 Cal. 354, *Barnard v Wilson* (1884), 66 Cal. 251, *Hibernia Savings & Loan Society v Conlin* (1885), 67 Cal. 178.

[81] *Wise v Griffith* (1889), 78 Cal. 152.

[82] *California Statutes* (1860), p. 311 fourth section amending the 10th section of the 1851 Homestead Act. *California Statutes* (1862), p. 319. See *Herrold v Rene* (1881), 58 Cal. 443.

[83] *Watson v His Creditors* (1881), 58 Cal. 556.

[84] *Camp v Grider* (1882), 62 Cal. 20, 27.

[85] *Ibid.*, p. 26. *Security Savings Bank v Connell* (1884), 65 Cal. 574. *Barnard v Wilson* (1887), 74 Cal. 512. *Moran v Gardemeyer* (1889), 82 Cal. 96.

[86] See *Harn v Kennedy* (1890), 85 Cal. 55, *Perkins v Onyett* (1890), 86 Cal. 348, *Building and Loan Association v King* (1890), 83 Cal. 440.

[87] See *Murdock v Clarke* (1881), 59 Cal. 683, *Crosby v Dowd* (1882) 61 Cal. 557, *Johnston v San Francisco Savings Union* (1883), 63 Cal. 554, *Chambers v Stockton Building and Loan Society* (1883), 64 Cal. 77, *Bayly v Muehe* (1884), 65 Cal. 345, *Goldtree v McAlister* (1890), 86 Cal. 93.

[88] Graves to Mrs. Kellogg, January 5, 1880, Graves Collection, Huntington, MSS, 1879-80 Letterbook.

[89] Jacks to Clayton, March 22, 1980, Jacks Collection, Huntington, MSS, Box C(8).

[90] In 1888, Jacks purchased W. A. Kearney's law library for $200 and moved his prior collection including "Judge Cutter's library" into Kearney's office. See bill of sale *Ibid.*, Box B(V)(10).

[91] Marsteller to Goodwin, May 21, 1883, Goodwin Collection, California State Library, California Section, MSS, Box 733.

[92] Graves and O'Melveny to D. N. & E. Walter & Co., March 16, 1888 and May 10, 1888, Graves Collection, Huntington, MSS 1885-88 Letterbook.

[93] Graves, O'Melveny and Shankland to Dalleman and Company, Oct. 26, 1889, Graves Collection, Huntington, MSS, 1889-90 Letterbook.

[94] Graves to Leach, November 19, 1881, Graves Collection, Huntington, MSS, 1881-83 Letterbook.

[95] Graves to Lilienthal and Company, December 27, 1881, Graves Collection, Huntington Library, MSS, 1881-83 Letterbook.

⁹⁶ Graves and O'Melveny to Klauber and Live (law firm), May 26, 1885, Graves Collection, Huntington Library, MSS, 1883-85 Letterbook.

⁹⁷ Graves to J. Naphtely, February 24 and March 1, 1880, Graves Collection, Huntington Library, MSS, 1879-80 Letterbook.

⁹⁸ Bates to Jacks, April 15, 1890, Jacks Collection, Hunington Library, MSS, Box C(8).

⁹⁹ 13 Cal. 116; 27 Cal. 604.

¹⁰⁰ See Laurence M. Friedman, *A History of American Law* (New York, 1973), p. 353. *Taylor v McLain* (1884), 64 Cal. 513.

¹⁰¹ See *Husheon v Husheon* (1886), 71 Cal. 407, 411-12.

¹⁰² 68 Cal. 404. Also see *Scranton v Begol* (1882), 60 Cal. 642. *Ross v Brusie* (1886) 70 Cal. 465. *Dalton v Leahey* (1889), 80 Cal. 446. *Smith v Smith* (1889), 80 Cal. 323.

¹⁰³ Friedman, *History of American Law*, pp. 374-75. Morton J. Horwitz, *The Transformation of American Law* (Cambridge, Mass., 1977), pp. 265-66. James Willard Hurst, *Law and Economic Growth* (Cambridge, Mass., 1964), pp. 285-88. Edwin G. Gager, "Mortgages of Real Property" in *Two Centuries' Growth of American Law* (New York, 1901), pp. 153-66.

¹⁰⁴ 59 Cal. 496, 501-2. Also see *Boughton v Vasquez* (1887), 73 Cal. 325 where equity is applied giving the creditor a mortgage interest in the property of an insolvent debtor.

¹⁰⁵ *Persons v Shaeffer* (1884), 65 Cal. 79. *Matzen v Shaeffer* (1884), 65 Cal. 81.

¹⁰⁶ *Grangers' Business Association of California v Clark* (1885), 67 Cal. 634.

¹⁰⁷ *Wise v Walker* (1889), 81 Cal. 11. *Montgomery v Merrill* (1884), 65 Cal. 432 (a 25-page opinion).

¹⁰⁸ 75 Cal. 271. Also see *Cazara v Orena* (1889), 80 Cal. 132. *Rhorer v Bila* (1890), 83 Cal. 51.

¹⁰⁹ As F. Blackie (Castroville) reported to Jacks on August 26, 1890, "Jim Kee promises verbally to bring all or nearly all of his crop here (Morocojo Warehouse) and instructs me to send you net proceeds thereof to be applied in paying off his mortgage. He seems to be quite honest in his intentions, but as his promise to haul his crop here is only verbal, I would suggest the better to secure yourself that you have some written agreement whereby to bind him to deliver all here on your account or until such time as the mortgage is paid." Jacks Collection, Huntington Library, MSS, Box C(8). The prevalent felt need to have a written contract was clearly evidenced here as well as the developing use of warehousemen as third party receivers of goods to pay outstanding debts. Jacks used the warehousemen and warehouse receipts as part of his lending and collection system throughout the decade. See W. P. L. Winham to Jacks, November 11, 1880, Jacks Collection, Huntington Library, MSS, Box C(3).

¹¹⁰ For example, see James A. Clayton to Jacks, June 2, 1887, October 13, 1887, Jacks Collection, Huntington Library, MSS, Box C(6). John Markey to Jacks, October 19, 1881, *Ibid.*, Box C(4). John Chase Hall to John Goodwin, May 30, 1883, June 16, 1883, Goodwin Collection, California State Library, California Section, MSS, Box 731. "Deeds and Mortgages given by W. B. Couts . . . 1887," Cave Johnson Couts Collection, Huntington Library, MSS, Box 75.

¹¹¹ The California court was quite willing to follow its own precedent as well as to overthrow it and make new law. The parol evidence rule cases of earlier decades of the 1860s and the deficiency judgment cases of the 1870s were examples of creating new precedents. In the 1880s the Court avoided creating new law by deference to the legislature or the code where convenient. See *Bollinger v Manning* (1889), 79 Cal. 7. *Barbieri v Ramelli* (1890), 84 Cal. 154, 158 in

which Mr. Justice Thomas B. McFarland tersely stated the general proposition where "there is no sufficient reason for overturning the line of decisions on the subject," they should stand. However, "if the question were an open one, I would come to a different conclusion." The court's reputation as eccentric stemmed from viewing too many questions as "open ones."

¹¹² See *Tapia v Demartini* (1888), 77 Cal. 383. *Lavenson v Standard Soap* (1889), 80 Cal. 245. *Staples v May* (1890), 87 Cal. 178. *Downing v LeDu* (1890), 82 Cal. 471. *Wilson v White* (1890), 84 Cal. 239.

¹¹³ See Friedman, *History of American Law*, pp. 343-45. Also see on the adoption of English common law, Edwin W. Young, "The Adoption of Common Law in California," *American Journal of Legal History*, 4 (1960), 355-63. Leon R. Yankwich, "Social Attitudes as Reflected in Early California Law," *Hastings Law Review*, 10 (1959), 250-70.

¹¹⁴ See John C. Hall to John D. Goodwin, May 5, 1883, Goodwin Collection, MSS, California Section, California State Library, Box 731. *Brickell v Batchelder* (1882), 62 Cal. 623. The Court also found a Pennsylvania precedent not to be helpful. *Kelly v Matlock* (1890), 85 Cal. 122.

¹¹⁵ 62 Cal. 623, 633-37.

¹¹⁶ Also see Gordon M. Bakken, "Admiralty Law in Nineteenth Century California," *Southern California Quarterly*, 58 (Winter 1976), 499-513.

¹¹⁷ See Deeds and Mortgages listing in Cave Johnson Couts Collection, Huntington Library, MSS, Box 75. William H. Patterson (San Francisco) to David Jacks, April 26, 1880, Jacks Collection, Huntington Library, MSS, Box C(3). James A. Clayton to Jacks, September 12, 1883, *Ibid.*, Box C(4). J. S. Raine to John Goodwin, August 20, 1881, Goodwin Collection, California State Library, MSS, Box 735. There are dozens of solicitations in the Jacks Collection for every year 1880-88. For 1879-80, see Box C(3) especially James A. Clayton and R. D. McElroy correspondence.

¹¹⁸ For example, see Benjamin F. Jones (Buffalo, N.Y.) to David Jacks, Dec. 18, 1889, January 18, 1890, February 10, 1890, February 20, 1890, Jacks Collection, Huntington Library, MSS, Boxes C(7) and C(8). H. S. Dunn to John Goodwin, March 25, 1882, Goodwin Collection, California State Library, MSS, Box 729.

¹¹⁹ See Mary S. Salisbury to David Jacks, March 22, 1886, Jacks Collection, Huntington Library, MSS, Box C(5). Lizzie L. Suedaker to Jacks, Dec. 9, 1889, Jacks to Suedaker, December 13, 1889, *Ibid.*, Box C(7). J. A. Riley to Jacks, Jan. 7, 1890, *Ibid.*, Box C(8).

¹²⁰ For example, L. W. Pollard increased his mortgage indebtedness to David Jacks to finance the construction of ranch buildings. James A. Clayton to Jacks, April 3, 1888 and May 3, 1888, *Ibid.*, Box C(6).

¹²² Jacks adjusted his rates downward in the mid-1880s. See N. A. Dorn to Jacks, March 15, 1883, *Ibid.*, Box C(4). James A. Clayton to Jacks, June 28, 1884, *Ibid.*, Box C(5). William P. Hook to Jacks, July 21, 26, 28, 1887, *Ibid.*, Box C(6).

¹²³ James A. Clayton to Jacks, Oct. 29, 1888, *Ibid.*, Box C(6).

¹²⁴ Clayton to Jacks, June 6, 1890. *Ibid.*, Box C(8).

¹²⁵ Contract of Guarantee to Henry Cowell, December 31, 1875, Jacks Collection, Huntington Library, MSS, Box (V)(I)(10).

¹²⁶ John R. Hetland, *California Real Estate Secured Transactions* (Berkeley, 1970), p. 11.

¹²⁷ *More v Calkins* (1890), 85 Cal. 177.

¹²⁸ A. M. Kidd, "Trust Deeds and Mortgages in California," *California Law Review*, 3 (1915), 381, 390.

[129] The appellate win-loss record for the decade was little different from the decade of the 1870s.

Year	Creditors won	Average value (number of cases studied)
1881	66.00%	$ 3,807.30 (10)
1882	87.00%	$ 8,874.68 (10)
1883	53.00%	$ 18,389.40 (5)
1884	72.00%	$ 16,662.14 (10)
1885	66.00%	$ 23,051.99 (8)
1886	73.00%	$ 7,781.63 (10)
1887	71.00%	$ 3,087.91 (7)
1888	57.00%	$116,006.22 (9)
1889	47.50%	$ 16,543.52 (10)
1890	78.00%	$ 11,608.07 (19)
Total	68.47%	average for period based on 97
176 cases studied		cases = $11,332.79 excluding
		one $1,000,000 case.

COMMUNITY PROPERTY LAW AND THE POLITICS OF MARRIED WOMEN'S RIGHTS IN NINETEENTH-CENTURY CALIFORNIA

DONNA C. SCHUELE

$\mathbf{A}$merican marital property law has always been the province of the individual states. During the nineteenth century, this became a particularly volatile issue across the nation, and no two jurisdictions treated the subject identically. Nevertheless, marital property schemes did divide into two general categories: those based in the common law, and those situated within the French and Spanish civil law tradition. These schemes generally separated geographically; states east of the Mississippi were common law jurisdictions, while community property states and territories were west of the Mississippi.[1]

In connection with the increased attention given to women's history, American legal historians have undertaken studies of the development and changes in nineteenth-century marital

Donna C. Schuele is a doctoral candidate in the Jurisprudence and Social Policy Program at the University of California, Berkeley. Research funding for this article was provided by the Huntington Library, the American Historical Association, the Woodrow Wilson Foundation, and the Sourriseau Academy. The author would like to thank Harry Scheiber, Joseph Mc-Knight, Kermit Hall, David Langum, John Reid, Barbara Babcock, Sara Alpern, Reva Siegel, Amy Bridges, Michael Strine, Sally Merry, and Michael Grossberg for their helpful comments on earlier versions of this article.

[1]The following states and territories operated under the community property system during the nineteenth century: Arizona, California, Idaho, Louisiana, Nevada, New Mexico, Texas, and Washington. William Q. de Funiak, *Principles of Community Property* (Chicago, 1943), 1:72 [hereafter cited as de Funiak, *Community Property*].

property law, thereby elucidating transformations in women's legal status and changes in domestic relations. Such studies have properly focused on individual jurisdictions, but by and large it is the eastern common law states that have garnered scholars' interest.[2] And, when historians sought to generalize from their individual case studies, community property states were marginalized or ignored.[3] Yet the history of the nineteenth-century West suggests that the evolution of marital property law there was distinctive enough to warrant separate study. This, in turn, would more fully inform our understanding of women's legal status and domestic relations in nineteenth-century America.[4]

[2]Peggy Rabkin, *Fathers to Daughters: The Legal Foundations of Female Emancipation* (Westport, Conn., 1980); Norma Basch, *In the Eyes of the Law: Women, Marriage, and Property in Nineteenth-Century New York* (Ithaca, 1982) [hereafter cited as Basch, *Eyes of the Law*]; Richard Chused, "Married Women's Property Law," *Georgetown Law Journal* 71 (1983), 1359-1425; Marylynn Salmon, *Women and the Law of Property in Early America* (Chapel Hill, 1986) [hereafter cited as Salmon, *Women and the Law of Property*].

[3]Even when a community property state has been the subject of a study, the focus has remained on the common law, with historians seeking to explain the development of marital property law in that jurisdiction as a product of common law influence. Kathleen E. Lazarou undertook a study of marital property law in Texas from 1840 to 1913, primarily focusing on doctrine in order to discern the continuity between Texan developments and the national experience. She did not search for potential regional differences in legal or political cultures, which may have been unique to Texas. Idem, *Concealed Under Petticoats: Married Women's Property and the Law of Texas, 1840-1913* (New York, 1986). Meanwhile, Susan Westerberg Prager's study of California led her to conclude that California's system operated no differently from a common law marital property regime modified by married women's property acts. "The Persistence of Separate Property Concepts in California's Community Property System, 1849-1975," *UCLA Law Review* 24 (1976), 1-82 [hereafter cited as Prager, "Persistence of Separate Property Concepts"]. Other recent work has concluded that the retention or adoption of community property systems in the American West can be traced to the growing interest in reforming married women's property rights in the common law states. See Ray August, "The Spread of Community-Property Law to the Far West," *Western Legal History* 3:1 (1990), 35, 63 [hereafter cited as August, "Community-Property Law"]; Carol Shammas, Marylynn Salmon, and Michael Dahlin, *Inheritance in America from Colonial Times to the Present* (New Brunswick, N.J., 1987), 291-92, n. 2 [hereafter cited as Shammas, *Inheritance*].

[4]Mari Matsuda, "The West and the Legal State of Women: Explanations of Frontier Feminism," *Journal of the West* 24 (January 1985), 47-56. If nothing else, the gender-neutral notion of common property could lead one to hypothesize that there was no need for reform of property rights specifically targeted at wives. See also Gloria Ricci Lothrop, "Rancheras and the Land: Women and Property Rights in Hispanic California," *Southern California Quarterly* 76:1 (1994), 59, 79 [hereafter cited as Lothrop, "Rancheras and the Land"]. Nevertheless, the national trend toward married women's property acts as a means of providing either family protection or female independence swept over the West in the nineteenth century. But it would be unwarranted to

Such a full understanding can only be achieved by placing marital property law within American legal, political, economic, and social history, as was ably recognized by Norma Basch in her path-breaking study, *In the Eyes of the Law*. While Basch described the doctrinal changes in the mid-nineteenth century in New York's marital property law, focusing on early instances of what was to become a nationwide trend of enacting married women's property acts, she went further by incorporating accounts of the leadership played by women (such as Elizabeth Cady Stanton) in the political maneuverings resulting in these statutes, which altered the common law.[5] Previous accounts of women as political reformers in the nineteenth century focused mostly on the suffrage movement, showing women as outsiders agitating for an avenue into politics.[6] Basch's work reminded us that the woman suffrage movement was born of a broader-based women's rights movement, in which increased property rights for married women were an important part. In addition, Basch portrayed women in the pre-suffrage era, moving successfully within the political realm to bring about self-interested reform.[7]

This article attempts to correct the overwhelming focus on eastern common law states in the history of nineteenth-century marital property law in America, while examining the role of woman's rights activists in the political system as they worked to effect an increase in women's legal status and changes in family relationships. In particular, it homes in on middle-class Anglo women in the young state of California during the 1870s, as they worked to reform the community property, probate, and divorce statutes that had been instituted only twenty years previously at the meeting of California's first legislature.

---

assume that community property states' experience with marital property reform was identical to that of eastern common law states. To that end, studies of community property jurisdictions, which set out to discover continuities and commonalities with common law jurisdictions, are not framed so as to permit us to uncover the regionality of nineteenth-century marital property developments.

[5]Basch, *Eyes of the Law*, supra note 2, esp. ch. 6.

[6]Some writers, notably Ellen Carol DuBois, acknowledged the tremendous value of the abolitionist experience for many suffragists, yet DuBois focused on the tactical adjustments the experience required of female suffrage workers as they became political actors in their own right later in the century. Ellen Carol DuBois, *Feminism and Suffrage: The Emergence of an Independent Women's Movement in America, 1848-1869* (Ithaca, 1978), 22, 182-84.

[7]See also Paula Baker, "The Domestication of Politics: Women and American Political Society, 1780-1920," *American Historical Review* 89 (June 1984), 620-47.

FOUNDATIONS OF COMMUNITY PROPERTY LAW
IN THE STATE OF CALIFORNIA

Fixing the point at which California "became" a community property jurisdiction is not as straightforward a task as it might seem. Examining the formation of California's state government reveals a more complex story. To some appearances, California retained the community property system introduced by Spain and continued by Mexico; alternatively, the state seemed to be adopting a community property system; yet it is fair to say that the state of California in the nineteenth century failed to operate within a true community property framework.[8] Throughout the period, the question was, at the least, complicated by the difficulty of merging just one portion of the civil law into the common law jurisprudence adopted by California at statehood. The issues arising from that arrangement were closely intertwined with the place of women in society. Even before Anglo women became demographically significant in California, their presence was felt in the initial formal considerations of marital property law,[9] which provided a forum for debating crucial questions of family protection and individual female independence. The issues of both formal law and the role of women were issues of culture, and they were played out during a period of upheaval and change, when the state's legal and political systems became increasingly dominated by Anglo-Americans steeped in common law culture, and when women's legal and political status was coming under critical scrutiny not just in California but throughout the United States.

During the Spanish and Mexican periods, the territory of

[8]De Funiak noted that commentators before him often mistakenly believed that California had "adopted" the community property system, in the sense that they believed that the acts of the first legislature gave force to the system. De Funiak pointed out that both theoretically, under international law, and actually, based on the actions of United States military governors, the community property system continued in force from the Mexican period to the time of statehood. "Thus, even the absence of any action by the legislature would not have affected the existence of the community property system. . . . Legislative action could only have the effect, so far as permitted by constitutional limitations, of defining certain provisions of the existing community property system." *Community Property*, supra note 1 at 110 n. 33. Notwithstanding the force of this reasoning, it does not describe the consciousness of participants in nineteenth-century law and politics.

[9]While native-born women were not ignored in the 1849 Constitutional Convention debates on marital property law, monopolization of the debate by Anglo delegates marginalized the concerns of women and their families native to the state. J. Ross Browne, *Report of the Debates in the Convention of California, on the Formation of the State Constitution* (Washington, 1850), 257-69 [hereafter cited as Browne, *Debates*].

California operated, at least formally, under a civil law system that included a community property regime.[10] Under this system, marriage was said to create a partnership in which economic benefits and burdens were shared equally by the spouses, who retained their individual identities under the law.[11] Accordingly, what mattered in determining the rights of each spouse to property was the time, the method, and the type of acquisition; title—always crucial under the common law—was not determinative.[12] Common property consisted of "acquests and gains by the spouses during the marriage while they are living as husband and wife,"[13] with each spouse holding equal ownership rights.[14] Thus the system acknowledged economically the wife's contribution to the marriage and valued it equally with the husband's contribution.[15] Anything not part of the community was designated as separate property, leaving gifts, legacies and inheritances in this category.[16]

[10]De Funiak, *Community Property*, supra note 1 at 40. The community property system was derived from Germanic law, but early commentators, believing that the system had Roman roots, subsumed the Spanish marital property system under the rubric of civil law. Ibid. at 23-24. In giving voice to the Anglo-American lawmakers, I will sometimes refer to the Spanish system as being part of the civil law.

De Funiak's treatise was unique in its treatment of the subject. While its stated goal was to provide the bench and bar with information regarding the Spanish sources of community property law, the author adopted a critical stance toward the Anglocentric attitudes of judges and lawyers trained in the common law, which had served to warp the development of community property law. Ibid. at iv. When his position met with skepticism, he then asserted that these judges and lawyers even went so far as "to deny that the Spanish law and its principles have anything to do with the present day community property system." Ibid. (1948 Supplement) at 5. His treatise is thus a valuable resource for a cultural inquiry into the subject.

[11]De Funiak observed that "this recognition of the wife as a person in her own right is one of the outstanding principles of the civil law and is one of those in which it diverges sharply from the common law." Ibid. at 6.

[12]Ibid. at 3. Later, de Funiak commented, "Indeed, the civil law generally has given primary consideration to the question of ownership, in contradistinction to the English common law which developed to such an extent the technical importance of title that it had to be offset by the development of equitable principles." Ibid. at 142.

[13]Ibid. at 136-37.

[14]Ibid. at 159.

[15]Ibid. at 167. De Funiak reasoned that this result could be justified even when the wife herself acquired no earnings or similar gains, by recognizing that such acquisition was made "at the expense of the community in that the one making the earnings or gains is furthered therein by the use of community property or by the joint efforts of the other spouse, [which] may consist, as in the case of the wife, in maintaining the home and rearing the children, for that is a sharing of the burdens of the marital partnership and a contribution to the community effort." Ibid. at 146-47.

[16]Ibid. at 137, 136-37 n. 4.

While the husband was given full control of the common property during the marriage, he was required to operate within limits to protect the wife's ownership interest.[17] Yet, for the vast majority of marriages, the community property system probably mattered most as an instrument of succession.[18] Both spouses were entitled to make testamentary disposition of their respective properties, including each one's share of the common property.[19] Intestate succession also operated in a gender-neutral fashion to pass both common and separate property to the deceased's heirs.[20] Upon the death of either spouse, the surviving spouse was treated the same, whether husband or wife,[21] and there is no evidence that the regime failed to

[17]Ibid. at 284-85. According to de Funiak, "even during the marriage [the wife's] ownership [of the common property] was so full and complete that she might vigorously oppose and seek to correct any administration by the husband that was in fraud or prejudicial to her interest, and upon occasion the administration of the entire community property might be shifted to her." Actions "in fraud or prejudicial to her interest" included any acts of management "which deprived or tended to deprive her of the benefit and enjoyment of half the community property or to deprive her of such half without adequate consideration." Ibid. at 298-99. However, after statehood, Anglos in California would wrongly attempt to equate these management rights with the rights of control that the husband held under the common law. The difference between the two systems arises from differing notions of possession and ownership under each system. De Funiak complained that "Many lawyers trained in the common law . . . seem to fail to comprehend . . . that the management of the common property placed in the husband was an administrative duty only . . . and not in any sense the equivalent of the common law 'control' by the husband of the wife's property which made him virtual owner and gave him the right to appropriate its use to his own enjoyment and benefit." Ibid. at 298.

[18]In Spanish and Mexican California, marriages appear to have ended only with death. Consistent with those countries' Catholic heritage, legal divorce did not exist, and few, if any, couples even sought a legally sanctioned permanent separation. David Langum, *Law and Community on the Mexican Frontier: Anglo-American Expatriates and the Clash of Legal Traditions, 1821-1846* (Norman, 1987), 232-67 [hereafter cited as Langum, *Law and Community*]; de Funiak, *Community Property*, supra note 1 at 623-25.

[19]De Funiak, *Community Property*, supra note 1 at 554. However, Spanish law placed restrictions on this disposition, so that four-fifths of the property had to be bequeathed to blood relatives, if any. This restriction also applied to limit bequests to spouses, although the surviving spouse could be bequeathed a usufructuary interest in the property otherwise required to be given to the children of the marriage. The law made it clear that a bequest to the wife in no way affected her ownership of her half of the common property. Ibid. at 557-58.

[20]Ibid. at 558-59. The spouse succeeded to the deceased's property only if there were no descendants or ascendants. Lest this all sound too harsh for the surviving spouse, the law provided that he or she have a usufructuary interest in the property inherited by the children, which was retained until death or remarriage. Ibid. at 560-61.

[21]Ibid. at 554. On the other hand, traditional common law rules governing marital property and devise and descent were highly gendered. Once a woman married, her legal identity merged with that of her husband. He took ownership

achieve its purpose of providing for the surviving spouse. In fact, it appears that some widows made out quite well, amassing large landholdings.[22]

After the signing of the Treaty of Guadalupe Hidalgo in 1848, United States military governors initially maintained the status quo as far as the legal system was concerned. However, this displeased many Americans.[23] During the 1840s, and particularly following the discovery of gold, California experienced a huge influx of fortune-seeking Americans who were not interested in adapting to the local culture.[24] The newcomers brought with them a strong allegiance to Anglo-American common law culture that was quite at odds with the prevailing legal culture.[25]

This eventually contributed to the calling of a state constitutional convention in 1849.[26] While the rise in American influence corresponded with declining local power, the delegates elected to the convention nevertheless consisted of a mix of native Californios, longer-time Anglos, and new arrivals drawn by the gold rush.[27] In resolving one of the first orders of business, delegates agreed that proposed constitutional provisions would be issued from the standing committee on the

---

of any personal property she brought into the marriage, as well as any acquired thereafter, and gained management control of her real property. For the wife to gain assets from the marriage upon the husband's death, title to the property would have had to be transferred to her, under the guise of dower rights or by virtue of the terms of the husband's will. Dower rights were meant to protect a wife from the husband's inter vivos and testamentary caprices, but the extent of these rights did not depend on when the husband's property was acquired or the length of the marriage. The status of wife could give her significant rights in the property of an already wealthy husband. In addition, under traditional common law, dower rights could not be defeated by a husband's acting alone during the marriage. Dower rights did not restore property a wife had brought to the marriage, nor were they nearly as generous or as autonomous as the one-half full ownership provided by the Spanish system. Life estates in land, as well as the lack of dower rights in personal property, functioned to keep widows dependent, usually on their grown children. Salmon, *Women and the Law of Property*, supra note 2 at 142-47.

[22]Lothrop, "Rancheras and the Land," supra note 4 at 68-70.

[23]Leonard Pitt, *Decline of the Californios: A Social History of the Spanish-Speaking Californians, 1846-1890* (Berkeley, 1966), 35-39, 42 [hereafter cited as Pitt, *Decline of the Californios*].

[24]Langum, *Law and Community*, supra note 18 at 21-24; Pitt, *Decline of the Californios*, supra note 23 at 52.

[25]John Phillip Reid, *Law for the Elephant: Property and Social Behavior on the Overland Trail* (San Marino, 1980), 11; Langum, *Law and Community*, supra note 18 at 271, 275.

[26]Pitt, *Decline of the Californios*, supra note 23 at 42.

[27]Browne, *Debates*, supra note 9 at 478-79.

Constitution. Yet the standards adopted for determining membership on the committee led to its underrepresentation of the newcomers.[28]

CALIFORNIA'S FIRST CONSTITUTION AND COMMUNITY PROPERTY LAW

The issue of a marital property regime was first hashed out at the Constitutional Convention.[29] Notwithstanding the lack of Anglo women and children in California,[30] issues of female independence and family protection swirled through the debate amongst the Anglo delegates, following the standing committee's presentation of Section 13 to the delegation. It read:

> Section 13. All property, both real and personal, of the wife, owned or claimed by her before marriage, and that acquired afterwards by gift, devise, or descent, shall be her separate property, and laws shall be passed more clearly defining the rights of the wife, in relation as well to her separate property as that held *in common* with her husband. Laws shall also be passed providing for the registration of the wife's separate property.[31]

[28]The standing committee consisted of two delegates from each district appointed by the president of the convention, and was charged with "report[ing] the plan or any portion of the plan of a State Constitution for the action of this body." Ibid. at 19, 29. The number of delegates seated from each district depended on the relative population of that district. Ibid. at 11. The Anglo delegates, especially the newcomers, tended to come from the more populous, and more Anglo-populated, northern section, while the Californios and old-time Anglos represented the southern section. David Alan Johnson, *Founding the Far West: California, Oregon and Nevada, 1840-1890* (Berkeley, 1992), 104-8; Pitt, *Decline of the Californios*, supra note 23 at 43-44.

[29]The proposal nearly replicated a provision of Texas's constitution, adopted almost five years previously. It appears that none but the scrivener realized the source of the standing committee's proposal. De Funiak, *Community Property*, supra note 1 at 96-97; Orrin K. McMurray, "The Beginnings of the Community Property System in California and the Adoption of the Common Law," *California Law Review* 3 (1915), 359, 369 [hereafter cited as McMurray, "Beginnings of the Community Property System"].

[30]Hubert Howe Bancroft, *History of California* (San Francisco, 1884-90), 6:221.

[31]Browne, *Debates*, supra note 9 at 257 (emphasis added). No records of the internal workings of the standing committee survive to explain why it proposed this provision. In the debates among the delegation as a whole (conducted in English), the Californios often proved reticent even though translators were provided. They may have wielded much more influence at the committee level. Nevertheless, Henry Halleck, a member of the standing committee whose bid for president of the convention was thwarted by a

Apparently, during an earlier break in the convention proceedings, delegates had been tipped off to the standing committee's proposal, and concern was raised among some Anglo
delegates as to whether "this was an attempt to insert in our
Constitution a provision of the civil law."[32] Thus a counterpro-
posal had been prepared by Francis J. Lippitt, a lawyer from
New York who had settled in California in 1847.[33] It stated:

> Section 13. Laws shall be passed more effectually se-
> curing to the wife the benefit of all property owned by
> her at her marriage, or acquired by her afterwards, by
> gift, demise [sic], or bequest, or otherwise than from
> her husband.[34]

Taken together, both versions of Section 13 indicated a
widely held interest by the delegates in securing married
women's property rights in California. The difference between
the two, however, was the reference in the committee's version
to property "held in common" by the husband and wife. "Common property" within marriage had a specific, essential meaning in Spanish law, none in the common law.[35] Furthermore,

---

widespread belief that he had come to ram through a facsimile of the New
York Constitution, later recalled that he had formulated most first drafts of the
articles, which were then submitted to the committee for consideration. H.W.
Halleck to Dr. Francis Lieber, July 5, 1867, in Prager, "Persistence of Separate
Property Concepts," supra note 3 at 9 n. 41. Noteworthy for this study is the
fact that the alternative to Section 13 more closely resembles New York's
marital property statute, raising doubts about Halleck's influence over the
formulation of the standing committee's version.

[32]Browne, *Debates*, supra note 9 at 258.

[33]Ibid. at 478-79.

[34]Ibid. at 257. Inasmuch as elevating marital property law to constitutional
status was outside the Anglo-American legal tradition, it is not surprising that
discussion first centered on the concern that the committee's version would
institute an "experimental" marital property system: "The relative rights of
property of husband and wife, I think, are matters involving laws that can more
safely be entrusted to the action of the Legislature, than introduced at once
into one Constitution, and form part of the fundamental irrepealable law of the
land. . . . I do not say that the experiment is not worth trying; . . . what I con-
tend against is, trying the experiment in our Constitution." 257-58. That the
alternative version of Section 13, which itself accorded with legislative reforms,
would do the same was lost on its proponent.

[35]Common property was not simply what was left over after the designation
of certain property as separate. With their common law bias, however, "Some
American writers have remarked that it is easier to define separate than community property and that the difficulty of defining the latter is avoided by
saying that all that is not separate is community property. . . . Indeed, the
practice of the Spanish law . . . was to define the community property first."
De Funiak, *Community Property*, supra note 1 at 136-37. Failure to define the
term "common property," argued de Funiak, was irrelevant to a determination

within the civil law, the category of separate property contained no characteristics of gender. The concern was with distinguishing separate property from what was otherwise presumed to be common, and not (as in the common law) in fencing off the wife's separate property from the rest, which was the husband's.[36] Thus the committee's version appeared to be neither a clear call for retention of the existing community property regime, nor a requirement that California should adopt the progressive reforms of a state such as New York in married women's property.[37]

If the standing committee's intent had been to retain the marital property system in place, framing the section in terms of married women and their separate property rights (hardly central to a community property regime) at least obscured the lurking concept of common property. Moreover, in distracting attention from the notion of joint ownership of property within marriage, the section's language hinted at the contemporary Anglo-American controversy over married women's property rights under the common law.[38] The non-native delegates seem

---

of whether a jurisdiction meant to continue the recognition of the community of marital acquests and gains. He noted that "since our community property law is that developed in Spain, which clearly and sufficiently defines what is community property . . . , there is in fact no necessity that our American statutes should have to define what is community property, for that is already clearly established." Ibid. at 137.

[36]De Funiak concluded that Anglo-American definitional problems over common property were actually motivated by concerns over what constituted separate property, and, more specifically, what constituted the wife's separate property. Furthermore, he recognized that the jurisdictions had been "most careful" about defining the wife's, and only the wife's, separate property, even though these definitions merely repeated well-settled principles of the Spanish system. He attributed this to "training in the English common law," which caused a fixation on the wife's separate property. Yet he did not discuss whether the concern was to separate the wife's separate property clearly apart from the husband's, or clearly apart from the community's. Ibid. at 145-46, 173.

[37]In his eagerness to demonstrate that later legislative tinkering with the marital property system was often unconstitutional, de Funiak reasoned that "It is obvious . . . that the constitutional provision providing for community of property must mean a community of property according to some system with established principles, and it is equally obvious that the system provided for was the continuation of the system already in force and effect . . . at that time. That is to say, the Spanish community property system." Ibid. at 72-73. This formalistic objective blinded him to the ambiguities and ignorance under which the delegates actually labored, both in constructing Section 13 and in debating its merits.

[38]Reva Siegel demonstrates that notions of joint ownership of marital property were beginning to seep into American consciousness about this time. "Home As Work: The First Woman's Rights Claims Concerning Wives' Household Labor, 1850-1880," *Yale Law Journal* 103 (1994), 1073, 1091-1146 [hereafter cited as Siegel, "Home as Work"].

Colton Hall, Monterey, was the site of California's first Constitutional Convention. (City of Monterey Collection, Colton Hall Museum Archives)

to have known of this means of using the wife's separate property to mitigate the harsh effects of the common law,[39] but were probably unaware of the subtle but radical difference between a system based on common property with ungendered notions of separate property, and a system, always gender-based, that was just beginning to carve out distinct property rights for women.[40] In short, the American delegates may have been caught off guard by use of the same term, "separate property," to describe two very different concepts.

Nevertheless, these delegates realized that the committee's version of Section 13 embodied something more than simply the establishment of married women's property rights, and that it was rooted in Spanish law. Inasmuch as the constitutional provision itself did not define "common" property (while it did define separate property), some discussion was held as to whether the proposal actually constituted a new order, or simply a retention of the Californios' law.[41] But before that issue could be resolved, delegates were distracted over a larger debate

[39]Joan Hoff, Law, Gender, and Injustice (New York, 1991), 122 [hereafter cited as Hoff, Law, Gender, and Injustice].

[40]Contributing to this singular fixation on the wife's property rights, one delegate, a young bachelor lawyer from Louisiana presumably well versed in the civil law of that jurisdiction, asserted the superior treatment of women there. Browne, Debates, supra note 9 at 263-65, 478-79.

[41]Ibid. at 258-60.

on the merits of the civil and common law systems, although it was put off as being outside the scope of the convention.[42]

Lippitt, who had introduced the alternate version, was the only delegate to come close to acknowledging the potentially radical difference between the two systems, as he argued:

> I have lived some years in countries where the civil law prevails, and where such a separate right of property is given to the wife. . . . If there is any country in the world which presents the spectacle of domestic disunion more than another, it is France. . . . There the husband and wife are partners in business . . . raising [the wife] from head clerk to partner. The very principle . . . is contrary to nature and contrary to the interest of the married state.[43]

Other delegates missed the oblique reference to the nature of common property. Instead, they responded to Lippitt's Anglocentric reference to the wife's separate property as a general attack on married women's property rights.[44] Again an opportunity to explore the true ramifications of the standing committee's proposal was bypassed.

It has been argued that, had the delegates really understood the philosophies behind the community property system, they would have opted instead for the common law system, enhanced by reforms in married women's property.[45] To them,

---

[42]Ibid. at 258-61, 265-67. The issue of choosing between the common and civil law was left for the first legislature to decide. "Report of Mr. Crosby on the Civil and Common Law, Senate Committee on the Judiciary," *Journal of the California Senate* (Sacramento, 1850), Appendix O [hereafter cited as "Report on the Civil and Common Law"].

[43]Browne, *Debates,* supra note 9 at 261.

[44]Ibid. at 262-68.

[45]Prager, "Persistence of Separate Property Concepts," supra note 3 at 10-11. It will probably never be clear why the majority of the delegates favored the standing committee's version of Section 13, as apparently no roll-call vote was taken on the issue, nor do the debates reveal vote totals. Among recent commentators, Shammas et al. reject out of hand any explanations based on ethnic and cultural traditions, finding that the pre-existing Spanish system was a necessary, but not sufficient, condition. Instead, they argue simply that "the debates on married women's property were what swung legislators over to acceptance of the community property system," while assuming that legislators were initially disinclined to support the system. Shammas, *Inheritance,* supra note 3 at 291-92, n. 2. The basis for this conclusion is unclear, and it apparently does not include Prager's nuanced analysis. In addition, this conclusion is unsupported, at least in California, by actions in the first legislature that made women worse off than if they had lived in a common law jurisdiction with married women's property statutes. Meanwhile, August documented the correlation suggested by Shammas between the growing interest in married

however, the two different systems appeared to lead to similar enough ends, in whatever way that might be characterized.[46] It was only later, when legislation to implement Section 13 was enacted, that the lurking word "common" could not be ignored, as lawmakers were required to face head-on the issue of whether California would retain the Spanish marital property system or adopt a modified common law scheme.

The Anglo delegates' focus on married women's property rights really involved two concerns, sometimes overlapping, but more often conflicting: whether women ought to be empowered by the law, and whether families ought to be protected by the law. As noted above, both versions of Section 13 offered property rights to married women. From this angle, the debate is best characterized as being over whether any form of Section 13 ought to be included in the Constitution, rather than over which version.

Some delegates actually argued for increased legal power for women,[47] one of them quaintly admitting,

> Having some hopes that some time or another I may be wedded . . . I shall advocate this section in the Constitution, and I would call upon all the bachelors in this Convention to vote for it. I do not think we can offer a greater inducement for women of fortune to come to California. It is the very best provision to get us wives that we can introduce into the Constitution.[48]

---

women's property rights in the common law states and the increasing number of community property states. According to him, initial common law reform, which took place in Mississippi, can be traced to the Louisiana community property system. In turn, the Mississippi reforms influenced Texas's formulation of a marital property system. "Community-Property Law," supra note 3 at 49, 57. However, August does not refer to Prager's work, either here or in his doctoral dissertation ("Law in the American West: A History of Its Origins and Its Dissemination" [Ph.D. diss., University of Idaho, 1987]).

This focus on a connection between married women's property acts and the community property system causes these authors to conflate the two very different concepts of separate property operating under each, and thus to fail to notice those points where the nineteenth-century lawmakers were doing the same. Prager falls into the same pattern in concluding that "*the* separate property concept was not simply dependent on a civil law ancestry; rather it reflected concern for married women's property rights substantially similar to social policies voiced in reform common law states [emphasis added]." Prager, 32.

[46]One delegate argued that if California were to become a common law state, the committee's proposal was imperative for the just treatment of married women. Browne, *Debates*, supra note 9 at 265-67.

[47]Ibid. at 258, 259; 263; 265.

[48]Ibid. at 259.

This position engendered vociferous opposition.[49] Another delegate railed in response:

> I believe this plan by which you propose to make the wife independent of the husband, is contrary to the laws and provisions of nature. . . . This doctrine of women's rights, is the doctrine of those mental hermaphrodites, Abby Folsom, Fanny Wright, and the rest of that tribe. . . . It is often the case that the union takes place between a man of little or no property, and a woman of immense landed estate. But do you mean to say that, under such circumstances, the husband must remain a dependent upon his wife? a dependent upon her bounty? Would you, in short, make Prince Albert's [sic] of us all?[50]

Later, he added:

> If [woman] had a masculine arm and a strong beard, who would love her? She had just as well have them as a strong purse; she is rendered just as independent by the one as the other, and as little lovable.[51]

On the other hand, the delegates knew that California was a place where fortunes could be made and lost in a day, and that the new state would be in no position to provide for the welfare of its inhabitants. Trying to protect the wife and family from the misfortunes of an unlucky or unscrupulous husband seemed a laudable goal. One delegate remarked,

> Any cool, dispassionate man, who looks forward to California, as she will be in five years to come, who does not see that wildness of speculation will be the characteristic of her citizens, as it has been for some time past, is not, I think, gifted with the power of prophecy. I claim that it is due to every wife, and to the children of every family, that the wife's property should be protected.[52]

While a counterpoint was attempted, defending husbands from this peremptory charge of bad faith, the vagaries of economic bad luck, which certainly did not suggest a husband's

---

[49]Ibid. at 259-60, 268; 261.

[50]Ibid. at 259-60.

[51]Ibid. at 268.

[52]Ibid. at 258.

culpability, could not reasonably be denied.[53] Probably more important was the realization that full exposure to liability for the husband's ventures could leave a family with "no other means of subsistence," the implication being that dependence on the state would result. To avoid this, it was imperative for family protection to be constitutionally mandated.[54]

Protection of some family property was thus in the interests of all married men, and in the interests of the state as well. At the same time, protecting that which was defined as the wife's separate property was fast becoming the conventional way to protect the American family.[55] One other method of family protection coming into vogue in the mid-nineteenth century permitted the set-aside of a homestead; tellingly, this option was considered and enacted by the delegates immediately following the vote on Section 13.[56]

The inclusion of Section 13 in California's first Constitution should not, therefore, be seen as an indication of the convention's support for the legal empowerment of women;

[53]Botts certainly took a hard line against granting the wife property rights for any reason: "I say, sir, that the husband will take better care of the wife, provide for her better and protect her better, than the law. He who would not let the winds of heaven too rudely touch her, is her best protector. When she trusts him with her happiness, she may trust him with her gold." Tefft remarked that opposition to the protection of the wife's property was, he believed, due to false pride on the part of men, who wrongly believed that protection of women's property necessarily implicated husbands in unscrupulousness. Ibid. at 259.

[54]Ibid. Another delegate pointed to the limitation of such a provision in attempting to shield the state from welfare responsibilities: "You may give the right and control of separate property to the wife—but every wife who habitually yields to her husband, will yield to him in all cases relative to the disposition of that property, and the husband will have control of it, just as if no such enactment existed." Ibid. at 261.

[55]Anglo-American legal culture made room for the notion of sequestering a wife's property from the debts of the husband (even when these debts were contracted for the benefit of the family), beginning with equitable marriage settlements and moving on to married women's property legislation. Implied throughout this evolution appear to be three correlative beliefs: first, that a wife would be less likely to waste property to the detriment of her family, and that protecting her property would thus achieve the goal of family protection; second, that it was somewhat acceptable for a husband to waste property he brought to, or acquired during, the marriage, or that it was at least acceptable (even laudable) for him to speculate with this property to improve his family's finances; and third, that it was contrary to the accepted norm to permit men to be paternalistically protected. Hoff, *Law, Gender, and Injustice,* supra note 39 at 119-24.

[56]Browne, *Debates,* supra note 9 at 269-271; Paul Goodman, "The Emergence of Homestead Exemptions in the United States: Accommodation and Resistance to the Market Revolution, 1840-1880," *Journal of American History* 80 (1993), 470-98.

paternalistic impulses appear to have been much more strongly at work.[57] Furthermore, such impulses continued to influence the later development of California's law of marital property. Yet, by choosing the committee's version over the "New York" alternative, the delegates, ultimately although unwittingly, provided later woman's rights activists with the advantage of having the already established category of common and separate property.

Section 13 in Practice

Although California's voters approved the Constitution, which contained the standing committee's version of Section 13, the marital property provision required enabling legislation to give it meaning and force. With its inherent textual ambiguities and the unfocused nature of the debate that followed its introduction in the convention, the section did not clearly mandate a community property system.[58] Although the first legislature met less than three months after the Constitutional Convention, the unprecedented gold rush immigration of Americans among other conditions guaranteed that the balance of legislative power would tip clearly toward the newcomers

[57]August, "Community-Property Law," supra note 3 at 50-51, 52-53, 56. This is consistent with the national mood of the time, according to Hoff, who argues that "The Married Women's Property Acts before the Civil War represented a necessary afterthought in the ensuing codification process that was based on protecting, not granting, equality to females." Law, Gender, and Injustice, supra note 39 at 120. Having concluded that Texas delegates were persuaded by the protective, rather than the enabling, strand of debate, August asserts that California delegates, on the other hand, were more interested in providing an advantageous climate for women. "Community-Property Law," supra note 3 at 56. Although there was a scarcity of marriageable Anglo women in California at the time, this position gives undue emphasis to Halleck's above-quoted comment, which August himself notes was derided when made as a "light and trivial argument." Browne, Debates, supra note 9 at 259.

[58]De Funiak argued that "The language of [Section 13] as well as the views expressed in the debates in the Constitutional Convention of 1849 show conclusively that it was the intention to place in the framework of the constitution itself the Spanish system of community property; and to place it therein beyond the reach of the legislature." Community Property, supra note 1 at 109. However, it is difficult to make a case for ascribing any particular intention to the delegation as a whole, inasmuch as the debates on Section 13 skipped from issue to issue without resolution. Further, such an exercise somewhat misses the point of discerning the process by which California's marital property system evolved during the nineteenth century. Material to that inquiry is the question of the degree to which the first and subsequent legislatures, as well as the judiciary, believed that a mandate for a community property regime based on Spanish-Mexican law had emerged from the 1849 convention, as well as the ways in which that belief was or was not expressed.

and away from the Californios.[59] It would not have been at all
surprising if the first legislature had ignored the use of the word
"common" in Section 13, focused instead on the gendered language, and gone on to enact a statutory scheme creating a modified common law marital property system.

Yet the legislature first took up the task of deciding whether
the state's jurisprudence generally would be based in civil or
common law, and it found surprisingly strong support for the
civil law among certain influential Anglo settlers.[60] Resolving
this overarching issue in favor of civil law would have determined the interpretation Section 13 would be given. Fueling
the debate was a report issued by the Senate Committee on the
Judiciary that provided a scathing indictment of both the legal
system of territorial California and the civil law in its "pure"
form. The report included a telling discussion of marital property law under each mode of jurisprudence that was far more
balanced.[61] Although the committee appeared to view the systems as containing somewhat comparable tradeoffs of rights
and duties, it accused the civil law of treating marriage as a

---

[59]Pitt, *Decline of the Californios*, supra note 23 at 46-47; Prager, "Persistence
of Separate Property Concepts," supra note 3 at 30. Prager notes that the gold
rush, occurring in the months surrounding the convention, had boosted the
number of Americans in California more than 900 percent, so that by January
1850 they outnumbered native Californians by more than four to one. Ibid. at
29 n. 143. She also notes that "Fear created by ignorance of the Californians
and their customs, disregard for non-democratic institutions and a typically
American arrogance all combined to produce an intensely antagonistic
climate." Ibid. at 29-30.

[60]Support for the civil law came from somewhat unexpected sources. First, in
an address to the new legislature, Governor Peter H. Burnett recommended
the adoption of the Civil Code and the Code of Practice of Louisiana, while
suggesting that crimes, evidence, and commercial transactions be controlled by
the common law. This drew howls of protest from most of the members of the
San Francisco bar, who then met to enact a resolution recommending the full-
scale adoption of the common law. Their action in turn encouraged a splinter
group (about one-fifth of the members) to file a formal petition with the state
Senate praying that the civil law be substantially retained. This group was led
by John W. Dwinelle, who had written an early history of San Francisco based
on his role in pre-statehood litigation. McMurray, "Beginnings of the Community Property System," supra note 29 at 373, 374. Some advocated the civil law
as a retention of the status quo, but others, who maintained that territorial
California had been virtually lawless, believed that, as compared with the civil
law, the common law would provide an enlightened reform.

[61]In an effort to show that the first legislature behaved in a manner consistent
with an understanding of the community property system as constitutionally
mandated, de Funiak claimed that the debate over the adoption of the civil and
common law dealt with matters other than marital property rights. However,
this is not supported by the evidence in the final report from the Senate, inasmuch as the report contains a comparison of marital property law under each
system of jurisprudence. De Funiak, *Community Property*, supra note 1 at 109;
"Report on the Civil and Common Law," supra note 42 at 588, 596.

partnership "no more intimate than an ordinary partnership in
... commercial business." It also indirectly acknowledged the
value of the common property arrangement for women by conceding that dower rights and the shifting of the wife's debts to
the husband provided "ample equivalent for the communion
of goods allowed her by the Civil Law."[62] Nowhere else was
the report arranged in a way that required the common law to
measure up to the civil law.

In the end, the common law was made the basis of jurisprudence in California, while at the same time the first legislature
interpreted Section 13 of the Constitution as requiring the continuation of the pre-existing marital property regime. Not only
was legislation permitting registration of the wife's separate
property to be introduced, but a bill covering the whole subject
of marital property was put forward that included the establishment of the two categories of separate and common property
and otherwise accorded with the Spanish system.[63]

Legislators appear to have been unable to ignore their common-law heritage and may even have been hostile toward the
property rights of married women.[64] Contrary to the spirit of
Section 13, women were given no management rights over
their separate property, much less over the common property.[65]

---

[62]"Report on the Civil and Common Law," supra note 42 at 588, 596.

[63]Act of April 17, 1850, ch. 103, *California Statutes* at 254-55.

[64]Circumstances suggest that common law attitudes ruled the legislature
generally as it set about the task of designing a code of laws to govern the new
state. While a convention delegate had urged that a committee be formed to
draft a code to be considered by the first legislature, this was rejected in favor of
hammering out a scheme within the give-and-take of the legislative process.
J.M. Jones to his mother, October 1, 1849, in Prager, "Persistence of Separate
Property Concepts," supra note 3 at 33 n. 160. Given the short time the
legislature had for formulating a code, the body resorted to a "cut-and-paste"
method of lifting statutes wholesale from other jurisdictions, notably common
law states. As a result, laws were imported that disabled married women in
ways wholly antithetical to the Spanish community property scheme. Ibid.
at 28, 32-33. De Funiak noted continuing hostility toward community property
law and speculated that its sources lay in "the mistaken belief that the
community property system substitutes some sort of cold blooded partnership
for marriage as a sacrament," or in "injured male vanity which resents anything recognizing woman as a person in her own right and which would seem
to threaten or question male dominance of all conjugal affairs." *Community
Property,* supra note 1 at 8-9.

[65]Act of April 17, 1850, ch. 103, sec. 6, *California Statutes* at 254. See also
Prager, "Persistence of Separate Property Concepts," supra note 3 at 26. De
Funiak indicated that common law attitudes of early legislators led them to
believe that Spanish law accorded with English common law in granting
management control of the wife's separate property to the husband. In fact,
Spanish law made no distinction between the spouses in the management
rights of separate property. *Community Property,* supra note 1 at 316.

More important, in a society and legal system that permitted divorce and separation, the language of the statutory scheme failed to indicate that the wife had any interest in the common property during the marriage.[66] It appeared that women's legal status was by that time worse in California than in common law states with married woman's property acts.[67] The resulting superimposition of this portion of civil law on a common law regime thus created a variety of anomalies and contradictions that were largely unfair to wives.[68] Only later would the woman's rights movement bring this to light.

THE POLITICS OF PROPERTY RIGHTS IN CALIFORNIA'S WOMAN'S RIGHTS MOVEMENT

Over the remainder of the nineteenth century, legislative and judicial machinations led California's marital property regime to function more like a common law scheme modified by married women's property acts. A husband's reach over community property became indistinguishable from his rights to his separate property, while on her husband's death a widow in California was treated similarly to a widow in the East.[69] California's law not only failed to deliver what it purported to in the way of rights to married women, but in some ways offered less than a modified common law system would have.[70] Would this arrangement be protested, and, if so, by whom, on what basis, and to what end?

During marriage, most wives (East or West) would have

Common law attitudes were also reflected in the remedies available to a wife for the husband's mismanagement of her separate property—remedies involving the assignment of power over property to a trusted third party— rather than any transfer of power to the owner-wife. Prager, "Persistence of Separate Property Concepts," supra note 3 at 26, discussing Act of April 17, 1850, ch. 103, sec. 8, *California Statutes* at 254.

[66]Ibid. at 35.

[67]Ibid. at 28.

[68]An intestacy scheme was enacted without regard to the community-property regime, while the community-property statute also provided for descent, albeit of only the common property. Further, the common-law tradition of requiring the husband's consent to the wife's testation was carried over by statute, thus removing control of the wife over her separate property even at her death. Prager, "Persistence of Separate Property Concepts," supra note 3 at 33 n. 161.

[69]Ibid. at 46-47; de Funiak, *Community Property*, supra note 1 at 7-11.

[70]Initially, the husband was given sole management rights over the wife's separate property. Act of April 17, 1850, ch. 103, sec. 6, *California Statutes* at 254, discussed in Prager, "Persistence of Separate Property Concepts," supra note 3 at 26.

had little opportunity to experience the workings of marital property law. The reaction of women in California to the state's marital property scheme would have depended first of all on their legal awareness,[71] and many of them, having reached adulthood in the East, might not have realized that California's marital property laws supposedly differed from those in much of the rest of the nation. Even if women had been aware of the laws, they might have lobbied for an elimination of the warped community property system in favor of a system that recognized property rights simply in the individual husband and wife—especially considering their eastern, common law roots. However, the notion of common property appeared to hold particular promise for women's equality, and would certainly have been lost in a switch to a reformed common law system.[72] By the 1870s this "foreign" marital property regime fitted well with important aspects of Victorian legal and popular cultures, and with a strain of marital property rhetoric that had been developing in the woman's rights movement for about twenty years. Activists thus focused from the start on making the system gender-neutral as the way to give women the same rights men enjoyed.

By the 1870s, women in California who were crucial to the movement had become aware not only that the state operated under the community property scheme, but that the scheme had been skewed in ways unfair to them. The nascent woman suffrage movement in California, which early considered the goals of political equality and legal equality as being inextricable, offered these women a forum for addressing marital property reform. Most of them were married, and many of them had experienced the force of marital property law, whether in California or elsewhere, while supporting themselves and their families, sometimes because their marriages had ended (by separation, divorce, desertion, or widowhood), or sometimes because of their husbands' disabilities.[73]

[71]Basch noted the difficulty with assessing lay understanding of common-law principles affecting the marital relationship, but found "considerable evidence . . . that the parroting of common law classifications and designations for married women went beyond legal abridgments to popular books and magazines." Eyes of the Law, supra note 2 at 67. In a related vein, Ronald Schaffer raises the issue of the development of political consciousness in California's woman-suffrage movement in the early twentieth century in "The Problem of Consciousness in the Woman Suffrage Movement: A California Perspective," Pacific Historical Review 45 (1976), 469. Schaffer implies that historians have paid insufficient attention to the issue of consciousness in studying the early woman's rights movement. Ibid. at 470 n. 2.

[72]See Siegel, "Home as Work," supra note 38 at 1091-1146.

[73]See Elizabeth Cady Stanton, Susan B. Anthony, and Matilda J. Gage, eds., History of Woman Suffrage (Rochester, 1881), 3:740-66 [hereafter cited as

These women's experiences with the law may have been personal, but their reaction to it was organized and political. Linking marital property reform to suffrage no doubt seemed natural to them, given that California's marital property law was firmly based in statute, born of the legislative process, rather than (as was the case in the East) in judicially determined common law. The connection between the political and the legal processes was therefore far clearer. Although the lack of any legal training at first hindered the women themselves in arguing for specific changes in the property laws, they were helped by some dedicated male lawyers, judges, and legislators.[74]

In the fall of 1869, individuals interested in pressing the cause for equal rights formed the San Francisco Woman Suffrage Association. This group immediately pushed for a statewide organization while encouraging other counties to form local affiliates, and undertook a petition drive for an amendment of the state Constitution giving women the vote. A few months later the California Woman Suffrage Association was inaugurated, and the association presented the suffrage petition to the California Senate on March 2, 1870. The roster of signers extended to thirty-one pages and represented a wide geographic range.[75]

Meanwhile, the concerns of California's suffragists were broadening to include legal as well as political equality, particularly in regard to the law's treatment of married women's rights in both separate and common property. At the inaugural meeting of the Suffrage Association, Judge Addison M. Crane, who was already active with the San Francisco group, gave a detailed exposition of the laws affecting married women in California.[76] Before recounting the probate laws and their differing

Stanton, *History of Woman Suffrage*]; Reda Davis, *Woman's Republic* (San Francisco, 1967), 201-32, for discussions of the woman suffrage movement in California during the 1870s [hereafter cited as Davis, *Woman's Republic*].

[74]Not too many years later, two women who were mainstays in California's woman's rights movement, Clara Shortridge Foltz and Laura deForce Gordon, fought for the right of women to be admitted to the bar and themselves gained admission after a period of private study. Barbara Allen Babcock, "Clara Shortridge Foltz: Constitution-Maker," *Indiana Law Journal* 66:4 (1991), 849-940 [hereafter cited as Babcock, "Constitution-Maker"] and idem, "Clara Shortridge Foltz: 'First Woman,'" *Arizona Law Review* 30:4 (1988), 673-717 [hereafter cited as Babcock, "First Woman"]. Babcock connects the relative ease with which women were admitted to the practice of law in the West with the fact that woman suffrage was first adopted there. "Western Women Lawyers," *Stanford Law Review* 45 (July 1993), 2181-82.

[75]Davis, *Woman's Republic*, supra note 73 at 201, 206-7, 212; "Petition for Woman's Suffrage. In the Senate, March 2, 1870," in Woman's Rights Pamphlets, Bancroft Library.

[76]Crane "was never too busy to explain California law to women, including property law, which he considered most unjust." Davis, *Woman's Republic*, supra note 73 at 228.

effects on husband and wife, he began with an assertion that was consistent with the theory of community property and the convictions of woman's rights advocates: "A man and a woman without property marry, and gain it mutually."[77]

With California remaining at least nominally a community property state, Crane could more advantageously advocate gender-neutral treatment in the realm of marital property. The idea of marriage as a partnership, rather than as the individual domination of separate spheres, could be authoritatively expressed in this jurisdiction. The same could not be said for women living in common law states with the modified common law, where any discussion of equal treatment had to proceed from that system's gendered, individualistic notions.[78]

This speech, with other convention activities, was carefully reported in the Pioneer by its editor and proprietor, Emily Pitts Stevens, a founding force in San Francisco for women's political and legal equality. Her weekly publication—the only one of its kind on the Pacific slope—was devoted to reporting the activities of California woman suffrage societies, and to raising the consciousness of her readers regarding the unfairnesses women faced in politics, law, and labor.[79] Pitts Stevens followed the publication of Crane's speech with a lengthy article, which included case and statutory authority proposing changes to remedy the inequities in California's laws.[80]

The exposition concluded as follows:

> The fact is that husbands are better than the law. They do not, with rare exception, avail themselves of the power, and the unjust advantages which the law gives them. They do, on the contrary, very generally respect the wife's property interests, beyond and above what the law requires. . . . The changes proposed here would

---

[77]Pioneer, February 5, 1870, 2. While Crane was loath to base woman's deprivations on man's animosity, suggesting instead that man simply failed to understand the matter, he predicted that reform of the laws would occur only when women gained suffrage rights.

[78]Siegel documents the complexities involved with making claims based on a partnership notion of marriage in common law jurisdictions. "Home as Work," supra note 38 at 1114-18.

[79]Sherilyn Cox Bennion, Equal to the Occasion (Reno, 1990), 57-62. See also Roger Levenson, Women in Printing: Northern California, 1857-1890 (Santa Barbara, 1994), 89-113. Levenson notes the persistent misspellings of Pitts Stevens' name, both then (e.g., San Francisco newspapers used "Pitt"), and now (e.g., Bennion's Pitts-Stevens). Ibid. at 89, 91, 89 n. 3.

[80]Pioneer, February 12, 1870, 2. This piece was probably written by Crane, as it echoes the opinions he expressed in his speech to the California Woman Suffrage Association, and no evidence suggests that Pitts Stevens possessed the legal training required to produce such an article.

Emily Pitts Stevens, a founding force in San Francisco for women's
legal and political equality (Detail of a drawing from the Huntington
Library, San Marino, California)

merely conform the law to what is now the higher and
better moral sense of both husband and wife. . . .
[They] will then become equal before the law. . . . The
enfranchisement of woman will place in her hands the
power to make these needed reforms in the law. The
ballot and nothing short of this, will secure to her
justice and equality.[81]

Presaging rhetorical tactics used later, this call was at the same
time conservative in its assessment of the problem, that most
men were not to blame and that the law needed to be "conformed" rather than reformed, and radical in its proposed
solution, that only women could be relied on to correct the
injustice.[82]

[81]Ibid.

[82]Crane, who regularly attended the weekly San Francisco Woman Suffrage
Association meetings, spoke again on the law at the end of March, and this
time a Mrs. Barber followed with her own comments on the subject. *Pioneer*,
March 26, 1870, 1. Two months later, Judge Tweed, another ardent supporter of
the cause, explained a recent amendment to the state's divorce statute to the
San Francisco group. *Pioneer*, May 21, 1870, 1.

THE PRESSURE FOR LEGAL REFORM

When disagreements within the California Woman Suffrage Association caused an offshoot to be formed in 1871, the new group, the Pacific Coast Woman Suffrage Association, adopted educative and reform missions regarding married women's legal rights that were similar to those of the original group.[83] Plans were made for a publication that would show "just what the laws are which bear unjustly on women. . . . Lawyers and lawmakers feel terribly hit by being held up to the gaze of the world as a little less gallant than they have professed to be."[84] To that end, at the group's Fourth of July picnic, C.C. Stephens,[85] a lawyer from San Jose, read a paper on the subject that was later reprinted.[86] At the same time, "a resolution was introduced, and unanimously carried, to the effect that there be a form of amendments prepared, by which these laws should be made equal, and that such should be referred to the commissioners now engaged in revising the laws of the State. This will bring a direct issue before the people, and will show how far it is true that men are ready to make and administer law equitably."[87]

As a result of this new prodding, woman's rights activists began to lobby legislators directly for reform of the community property system, with the biennial legislative session for the 1871-72 term opening in only a few months. Their strategy was to link legal and political rights instrumentally by arguing that the legal system would operate fairly toward women only when women secured the right to vote. This position did not prevent them from working immediately for reform of California's marital property system. In 1872 the California Woman Suffrage Association presented the legislature with a petition that called for an amendment to the state Constitution granting women suffrage and that generally requested changes in statutes so as to equalize marital property rights. The petition was officially

[83]These disagreements appeared to mirror those on the East Coast, which caused a split resulting in the formation of the National Woman Suffrage Association and the American Woman Suffrage Association. Babcock, "First Woman," supra note 74 at 677 n. 15.

[84]H.M. Tracy-Cutler, "Letter from California," *Woman's Journal*, April 1, 1871, 104 [hereafter cited as Tracy-Cutler, "Letter from California"].

[85]Later in the decade, Stephens tutored Clara Shortridge Foltz, in her quest to be admitted to the California bar. Babcock, "First Woman," supra note 74 at 685.

[86]Tracy-Cutler, "Letter from California," supra note 84 at 232.

[87]Ibid.

presented by Leland Stanford, the former governor, and bore more than five thousand signatures.[88]

Although it was not spelled out in the petition, a significant concern of the activists was inheritance inequalities. Upon the death of a wife, her husband automatically succeeded to the common property, while a widow's succession to the common property was subjected to estate administration, inasmuch as she was not viewed as having had ownership in the property during the marriage.[89] This meant that more of a widow's assets would be subject to statutorily prescribed administration fees, resulting in a consumption of assets sorely needed to support the widow and children. The fact that these fees were set by male legislators, were enforced by male probate judges, and lined the pockets of male executors and administrators, while the process required the widow to hire a male attorney, was not lost on woman's rights agitators. This arrangement seemed patently unfair, and even rigged. Although many statutes needed to be changed in order to fulfill the mandate of the petition, activists concentrated particularly on the law's differing treatment of surviving spouses.[90] This appears to have been a

---

[88]State of California, "Report of Special Committee in Relation to Granting Women Political Equality," in *Appendix to Journals of the Senate and Assembly*, 19th sess., 1871-72, 3:7, 3 [hereafter cited as "Report of Special Committee"].

[89]Under common law, the probate process played a necessary role in enforcing the dower rights of widows by overseeing the transfer of property rights through a transfer of title. Under Spanish law no similar judicial function was necessary, as widows (and widowers) used the estate administration process chiefly to obtain division of the community property. Otherwise, they simply took control of property they had always owned. In Mexican California, estate administration appears to have been very informal, with much of the process involving property division and debt payment taken care of by the surviving spouse and the decedent's heirs. No formal process was required for title to the decedent's property to pass to the heirs. De Funiak, *Community Property*, supra note 1 at 580-83.

Thus Anglo-American legal culture led legislators to construct an estate administration scheme and to do so without questioning its necessity or purpose vis-a-vis the marital relationship. The first legislature borrowed the wills statute and the intestacy scheme from traditional common law, so that there was no distinction between separate and common property. Meanwhile, the community property statute dealt with the passage of common property at death. Neither statute referred to the other. According to Prager, "It is highly doubtful that . . . legislators considered the interrelationship of the basic community property statute with these other essential elements." "Persistence of Separate Property Concepts," supra note 3 at 33 n. 161.

[90]A legislative committee report, responding later to the petition, noted that there were too many laws "which in their operations work severe hardships upon wives." Thus the committee decided to pay "particular attention to the very great hardships which the existing probate laws work upon widows and orphans." "Report of Special Committee," supra note 88 at 9.

good strategy; not only did the law work hardships on many women, but men would be more inclined to support such a change, since they certainly would not want what they might view as "their" assets to be eaten away by the legal system.[91]

Nettie C. Tator, a suffragist from the Santa Cruz area who had studied law in an unsuccessful attempt to become California's first woman lawyer, was sent to address the legislature on behalf of the petition.[92] Her address first pointed to the wife's claim on common property: "When a man and his wife commence life poor, and struggle along together in the acquirement of property, by good right half of that property and whatever income accrues from it, is hers. But does she get it? No!"[93] The nature of the "good right" was unclear, and her argument seemed more ideological than formalistic.

This position highlighted the dissonance between California's community property law and the law that had developed through Spanish-Mexican jurisprudence. Two aspects of Anglo-American legal culture during the last third of the nineteenth century should have served to sensitize Californians to this dissonance. First was the increasing characterization of the common law, by courts and legalists, as a "science" striving for internal consistency.[94] Second, and not unconnected, was the codification movement, with its greatest successes in the West, particularly in California, beginning with the adoption of a civil code during this same legislative session considering

[91]As the committee noted later regarding probate judges and other public officers who did not directly gain from statutory fees, "The great hardships and cruelties which this system imposes are familiar. . . .The great injuries it inflicts are matters of almost daily observation and experience." The members believed that, but for "custom," which had desensitized the "public mind," "there would be a general outcry against its continuance." Ibid. at 10.

[92]Tator made the attempt in the few months before this appearance in the legislature. After examining her qualifications, a local committee unanimously recommended her admission. When it was determined that the state barred women from the legal profession, Tator made an unsuccessful attempt to change the law. Stanton, History of Woman Suffrage, supra note 73 at 757; Babcock, "First Woman," supra note 74 at 686 n. 65; Carolyn Swift and Judith Steen, eds., Georgiana: Feminist Reformer of the West (Santa Cruz, 1987), 45-46. This last source refers to "Nellie" Tator, as does Babcock. All other sources consulted for this study designate her as "Nettie" Tator.

[93]"Address of Mrs. Nettie C. Tator before the Joint Committees of the Senate and Assembly of the State of California on the subject of Extending the Right of Suffrage to Women, Sacramento, March 13, 1872," 8 [hereafter cited as "Address of Mrs. Tator"].

[94]This view, which, according to Lawrence M. Friedman, was "in the air" in the late 1860s, can be connected to the ideas of Christopher Columbus Langdell, whose educational reforms at Harvard Law School most notably treated common law as a science. Idem, History of American Law, 2d ed. (New York, 1985), 405 [hereafter cited as Friedman, History].

community property issues.[95] According to Lawrence Friedman, law reformers of the time embraced the theory that a legal system is at its best when it "conforms to the ideal of legal rationality—the legal order which is most clear, orderly, systematic (in its formal parts), which has the most structural beauty."[96]

Tator might have been appealing to these essentially conservative, hegemonic cultural threads to win support for a legal change whose effect would actually be quite radical—increased legal status and power for women.[97] However, if indeed this was her strategy, it was not transparent: in her argument for gender-neutral treatment, she did not appear to be holding lawmakers to the internal logic of the community property system. Calling attention to inconsistencies within the system could just as easily have led to solving that problem by jettisoning the Spanish-based system altogether.[98]

Instead, Tator seemed to be appealing to a more widely accepted notion of joint property rights. By that time the ideal of companionate marriage was firmly fixed in American culture, and, as one scholar has argued, it "provided a powerful counterbalance to male dominance in nineteenth-century male-female relationships."[99] Consistent with this, from the start, the eastern-based woman's rights movement called for a partnership vision of marriage that included the idea of joint ownership interests in property acquired during the marriage. According to Reva Siegel, who has documented the development of this claim, antebellum rights advocates sought recognition of the wife's concrete contributions to the family's well-being by creating a legal right to share in the wealth resulting from that contribution.[100]

[95]Ibid. at 394-95, 405-6. Friedman specifically mentions the civil law tradition of the western states as an explanatory factor for this success.

[96]Ibid. at 407.

[97]Siegel has analyzed the advocates of joint-property rights. "In their view," she writes, "marital property reform was not about protecting economically dependent women from men, but instead was about empowering economically productive women to participate equally with men in managing assets both had helped to accumulate." "Home as Work," supra note 38 at 1116.

[98]However, two years later, Laura deForce Gordon reported that Senator Laine, representing Santa Clara County, was considering introducing a bill that would "re-establish the Common Law in California, or . . . repeal all ordinances and statutes pertaining to women that are modifications thereof." Stockton Weekly Leader, March 7, 1874, 2. Suffice it to say that Laine was sorely misinformed as to the history of the state's jurisprudence regarding marital property law, both in its inception and its subsequent modifications.

[99]Karen Lystra, Searching the Heart (New York, 1989), 233; Carl N. Degler, At Odds (New York, 1980), 50.

[100]Siegel, "Home as Work," supra note 38 at 1112-35.

However, when suffrage issues moved to the foreground of the woman's rights movement, joint property claims took on a decidedly different cast. According to Siegel, "Joint property conversations began to revolve around questions of social roles rather than legal rights. . . . The joint property concept appeared as a species of marital therapy, rather than a claim of right."[101] Yet she also found that the antebellum approach to joint property appeared to survive on the western frontier, as the emphasis remained on the wife's actual contribution to the family maintenance.[102] No doubt the fact that the community property system formed part of the legal framework of California, and that other jurisdictions helped keep the stronger rights-based rhetoric alive, enabled Tator to inject an urgency into her argument that would have been taken less seriously in the East.

Tator also focused legislators' attention on the differential treatment of the marital estate depending on whether the decedent was the husband or the wife. She challenged this arrangement: "You say this is necessary to protect the interest of her children. Who, I ask, looks after the interest of children more closely than mothers do?"[103]

The Legislature Considers Reform in Married Women's Property Rights

The Special Committee in Relation to Granting Women Political Equality was then formed to consider both the suffrage and the property rights matters, and issued an exceedingly favorable report two weeks after Nettie Tator's appearance. The committee came out in favor of granting women suffrage, and in doing so adopted two rhetorical tactics, playing down the radical nature of this stance while portraying the call for woman suffrage as yet another aspect of California's superior

[101]Ibid. at 1166.

[102]Ibid. at 1165. Californian farm wives provide an interesting study of the vitality of the position of valuing wives' actual contributions to the marriage. The California Grange developed at the same time as the woman's rights movement in the 1870s. The organization not only decreased the isolation of farm wives, but was ostensibly dedicated to equality of the sexes in recognition of the farm wife's necessary and significant contribution to the family economy. The group's newspaper, the *California Patron*, contained a women's section called "The Matron," which published contributions regularly from a member in San Diego, Flora M. Kimball, who became known as a leading suffragist. In September 1878 she offered a fable for farm wives on the concept of common property, but also pointed out the theoretical inconsistency in women's lack of ownership and control over that property. *California Patron*, September 7, 1878, 2.

[103]"Address of Mrs. Tator," supra note 93 at 8.

brand of progressiveness.[104] Following this line, the committee asserted that the equalization of property rights, "being within the province of ordinary legislation, [could] be granted without delay."[105] It would be an almost matter-of-fact realignment of law "which has survived its usefulness."[106]

The committee echoed Tator's assertion that it was the mother who best looked after the interests of the children upon the death of their father;[107] more importantly, it recognized the wife's contribution to the marriage. At first the committee fell into a quite traditional "separate spheres" analysis. Though it did not characterize the wife's activities as adding to the family's financial wealth, it did assert that her contribution, made within the home, was no less important than her husband's, made outside the home, and thus should be equally valued.[108] Having reached this conclusion, the committee could easily assert that the method for valuing the wife's contribution was to treat her survivorship interest in the common property of the marriage no differently from that of her husband.[109]

[104]The committee asserted that "there is nothing in the proposed [woman suffrage] amendment which is either of a revolutionary character or in opposition to the spirit and genius of the Government." "Report of Special Committee," supra note 88 at 5.

[105]Ibid. at 3.

[106]Ibid. at 10.

[107]"Who is prepared to toil harder, or to economize more rigidly, or willing to make greater sacrifices for their good than she?" Ibid. at 11.

[108]According to the committee, a wife "gratif[ies] the family pride by the embellishment of the home," and, through "the cultivation of her mind, the refinement of her taste, and the protection of her health," places herself in a condition "to bear . . . well formed and beautiful and healthy children, and to intelligently surround them with improving and refining conditions that will tend to give them a noble direction in life, and thus honoring [her husband's] name, transmit it to the future untarnished." The committee concluded, "Unless money is more valuable than the mind of man, and coin than character, the business qualifications of the husband may be fairly and equitably offset by the home duties of the wife." Ibid. at 10. This position was more consistent with the eastern postbellum developments in joint-property rhetoric. Siegel notes that, for the first time, "advocates began to talk about the joint property claim as compensation to keep woman in her 'sphere.'" "Home as Work," supra note 38 at 1165.

This argument was in response to the claim that the widow should not be permitted to succeed to the husband's estate because "he earned it by virtue of his own personal foresight, enterprise, perseverance and business energy, and that therefore it belongs to him," a claim the committee characterized as "one of the most plausible and forcible objections that has been and probably that can be urged against the proposed change." "Report of Special Committee," supra note 88 at 10. That this was really an absurd objection in a community property regime seems to have been lost on the committee.

[109]"Report of Special Committee," supra note 88 at 11. While the committee was sensitive to the fact that this was a rough calculation, it seemed to recognize that marital property rights involved something more than a

The committee then explored less charted but more realistic territory as it acknowledged the experiences of many married women:

> Facts are numerous showing that wives during years of wedded life experience great hardships, arising from the inability of their husbands to provide for their wants, but who, on becoming widows, supported themselves, educated their orphan children, and accumulated property. Instances are numerous where wives . . . have rescued and brought out incumbered estates, involved by the unfortunate speculations or business incapacities of their husbands.[110]

The committee attributed the achievements of these women simply to a transference of skills learned in running a household: "These once learned, it is an easy matter to transfer them from one system of arrangements or business to another. The skill necessary to manage a large household with success would be useful when directed to the control of any ordinary business."[111] And, even more, "it is notorious that woman has a natural tact for business. They [sic] are great contrivers and economists. Their watchful care and industrious habits are proverbial."[112]

Finally, the committee believed that giving the wife survivorship interest in the common property of the marriage would positively influence the interactions between husbands and wives:

> If . . . husbands knew that their widows would succeed to their business, this would necessarily operate as a powerful stimulus to induce them to instruct their wives not only in business matters generally, but also to enlighten them as to their own pecuniary condition and manner of conducting their affairs. It would stimulate wives to fit themselves for the proper discharge of the new responsibilities and duties which the changed order of things would impose upon them.[113]

---

contractual agreement when it asserted, "If either partner of the matrimonial firm fails to perform a full share of the labor assumed or assigned that is a misfortune, but it should not be allowed to vitiate the personal or property right of either partner." Ibid. at 10.

[110]Ibid. at 11.

[111]Ibid.

[112]Ibid.

[113]Ibid.

For all of its enlightened attitudes toward the capabilities and place of women, the committee did not acknowledge that such a change in the law would, for the most part, simply bring California's community property law back to its Spanish-Mexican form.[114]

At the time the committee submitted its report to the legislature, one of its members offered a bill in the Assembly that would invest the widow "with the ownership and management of the family estate on the decease of her husband."[115] The bill was voted on two days later, with thirty-six legislators in favor and twenty-seven opposed.[116] Its passage occurred late enough in the session for the Senate to avoid acting on the measure.[117]

When the legislature convened for the 1874 session, the California Woman Suffrage Association again presented a petition "for legal and political equality with men," signed only by the officers of the organization. The petition set forth specific "grievances," asking that they "be repealed and the Constitution amended so that women may vote." Five of the grievances pointed out the different treatment accorded wives regarding both common and separate property.[118] The petition was presented to both the Assembly and the Senate by sympathetic legislators, and, rather than mounting a show of support in Sacramento, the association formed a special committee to lobby individual legislators before the start of the session in December 1873.[119]

Although the reformers were unable to change the probate law, issues arose during the session that brought success in another area of married women's rights. In the previous session, California had adopted a civil code, its own version of the Field Code. Code Section 162 returned to wives a right that constituted a crucial part of the community property system: the right of each spouse to manage his or her separate

[114]In states such as California where the community property system was provided for constitutionally, de Funiak pointed out, "the state legislature [or the courts, for that matter] cannot constitutionally abrogate the community property system so incorporated in the constitutional framework or alter the principles of such system. . . . It is probable, indeed, that many of the present legislative enactments in these states are in fact unconstitutional and invalid." *Community Property*, supra note 1 at 73.

[115]State of California, *Journal of the Assembly*, 19th sess., 1871-72, March 23, 1872, 883. At the same time, a bill was introduced permitting women to hold management offices in public schools, and a constitutional amendment was proposed granting women suffrage.

[116]Ibid. at 880.

[117]*Woman's Journal*, January 24, 1874, 32.

[118]*Woman's Journal*, January 10, 1874, 11.

[119]*Woman's Journal*, June 6, 1874, 179.

property.[120] The legislature was now on the verge of enacting contradictory amendments to the code that would effectively have obliterated this right. Key members of the organized suffrage movement rushed to Sacramento and, after two weeks of vigorous lobbying, were able to procure a harmonization of various code sections affecting married women's property rights, thereby salvaging the rights accorded under Section 162.[121]

The reformers did not give up on the probate law. In the 1875-76 legislative session, Sarah Wallis presented the Senate with a bill to equalize the probate law, this time regarding the ability of the wife to devise or bequest her portion of common property.[122] Wallis, thrice-married (lastly to Judge Joseph B. Wallis, who served as a state senator in the early 1860s), was one of the founding mothers of the California woman suffrage movement.[123] Of all the women associated with the organized movement, she made the most sustained efforts toward securing equal treatment for women within community property and probate law. Unsuccessful in 1876, five years later she could be found circulating a petition to the legislature for passage of "an Act to confer upon the wife the right to succeed to the community property on the death of the husband."[124]

[120]Codes and Statutes of California (Sacramento, 1876), 1:595, §5162.

[121]M. Louise Willson, "State Woman Suffrage Society: Reports Showing the Origin of the Amendments to the Code Concerning Woman's Property Rights," Common Sense, July 11, 1874, 108. Willson was serving as secretary of the California Woman Suffrage Association. Indicative of disagreements continually plaguing the suffrage cause in California, her letter to the editor was prompted by an "extraordinary misunderstanding that ha[d] arisen in regard to the agencies concerned in the passage of the very important amendment to the Code concerning the property rights of married women." She went on to say that "we are not willing that any misrepresentation should cover or distort the fact that Mrs. [Sarah] Wallis, aided by Mrs. L[aura] deForce Gordon [as well as the writer] and the delegated authority of the Society, procured the amendment to the Code giving to women the right to control and manage their separate estate." Ibid.

While Prager may be correct in her assessment that the right of married women to manage their separate property came about because of the adoption of the Field Code, her observation that this, "ironically," was not "the product of specific reform-minded activity in behalf of married women," seems conclusive. Prager, "Persistence of Separate Property Concepts," supra note 3 at 41.

[122]Stockton Weekly Leader, January 22, 1876, 2.

[123]Dorothy Regnery, "Portraits of Sarah," The Californian 8 (1986), 8.

[124]Wallis to Gordon, January 25, 1881, on printed petition form entitled "Petition for Equal Rights." Laura deForce Gordon Collection, Bancroft Library. However, by then Wallis was complaining to Gordon that the organized movement had inexplicably removed her from the task of lobbying "my bill." Ibid.

ONE LAST ATTEMPT AT REFORM

By 1876 those working through organized channels had to share the stage with a recently widowed San Franciscan, Marietta Stow.[125] Unlike other woman's rights activists, Stow conducted her crusade as a personal one, motivated by the belief that she had been severely wronged by San Francisco's male-dominated probate system and California's marital property laws, which she claimed had robbed her of a two-hundred-thousand-dollar estate.[126] Backed by some separate property of her own and by her experience as a lecturer before her marriage (often speaking in favor of women's economic rights), Stow was able to fight back with a vengeance. She published an account of her travails, entitled *Probate Confiscation*, which also served as a manifesto calling for reform of California's marital property law. Inasmuch as her voice was never subjected to the modulating influence of an organization, it was far more strident than those of the suffrage activists.[127]

Early in 1876, Stow herself drafted legislation entitled "A Bill for the Protection of Widows and Orphans."[128] The proposed

---

[125]Stow was one of the original members of the San Francisco suffrage society in 1869, even serving as vice-president, but she left the organization late in that year over a disagreement regarding tactics. She remained aloof from woman's rights causes until 1876, and after that operated on the fringe of the organized movement in the 1880s. Donna C. Schuele, "Marietta Stow, the Widow's Widow: Reform in the Nineteenth Century," presented at the annual meeting of the Pacific Coast Branch of the American Historical Association, Corvallis, Oregon, August 1992 [hereafter cited as Schuele, "Marietta Stow"].

[126]Marietta Stow, *Probate Confiscation* (reprint, New York, 1974) [hereafter cited as Stow, *Probate Confiscation*].

[127]Like the organized suffragists, Stow strove to raise the consciousness of women in California regarding marital property and probate law by educating them to the actual shortcomings of the community property scheme when measured against its theoretical framework of spousal equality. She promoted the sale of her book assiduously, and was quite successful in the number of reviews (mostly positive) she garnered in newspapers across the country. In her book, she chided women for remaining ignorant about the laws that governed them, and warned that, with exclusive rights of management and control, during the marriage a husband could "with almost his last breath, . . . convey away the community property so deftly that no known law can reach it." Ibid. at 65. She also wrote scathingly of those widows who would refuse to challenge a husband's will and secure what belonged to them for fear of being "anathematized . . . as a woman's-righter, crusader, or any kind of rebel." Ibid. at 80-81.

[128]Ibid. at 13-20; "The Intestate Laws: Text of a New Bill to be Presented to the Legislature," *San Francisco Chronicle*, January 8, 1876, clipping in Marietta L. Stow scrapbook [hereafter cited as MLS scrapbook], Special Collections, University of San Francisco. Although the *Chronicle* considered her proposal "radical," her crusade met with approval from others. The *Evening Express* (Los Angeles), June 8, 1876; *San Francisco Evening Post*, December 30, 1876;

law would have equalized the rules governing property distribution upon the death of a spouse and given the survivor broad administrative rights. Further, it called for exempting half the common property, as well as the family home and its contents, from estate administration. The decedent's half of the common property would descend to the children of the marriage, or to the surviving spouse if there were no children; nor could an executor exercise any control over this half of the common property. The surviving spouse would be responsible for disposing of common property necessary to pay the debts of the deceased.[129]

Although her legislative proposal was more narrowly drawn than that of the organized reformers, Stow argued for broad changes in the probate and marital property systems. Much of her criticism of California's system was based on her understanding of marriage as a partnership and on the concept of common property.[130] She assailed the notion that a wife lacked any tangible interest in the common property during the marriage as being inconsistent with the partnership philosophy.

and *Sacramento Daily Bee*, March 31, 1877, clippings in MLS scrapbook. Stow appears not to have worked within any organization in her attempts to get her probate bill passed, and never acknowledged any significant support by other women activists. The title of this bill was probably a bit of political legerdemain. Stow resisted mightily the notion that women needed to be protected, either by men or the legal system. According to her, equality of treatment under the law was the best form of protection. *Probate Confiscation*, supra note 126 at 97-98.

[129]Stow, *Probate Confiscation*, supra note 126 at 13-14. The law would have injected theoretical consistency into California's community property system by negating provisions applying only to the wife. Broadening the rights of estate administration was meant to support the partnership notion of marriage. The bill likened the surviving spouse's administrative control to that of "a surviving partner [who] has the sole power to settle the affairs of a copartnership at the death of one of the partners." Ibid. at 13.

[130]The condition of California's community property scheme caused Stow to conclude that "there is no such thing as a partnership relation in the marriage union . . . .The rights of the married woman are still nearly all suspended during coverture. . . . In spite of our boasted progress and civilization, in wedlock woman is still a slave, because she is not a free agent. She cannot use a dollar of the common property which she has helped to earn, without the husband's consent. . . . You may say that making the wife a legal partner will embarrass and cripple the business transactions of the husband. . . . Nothing but recognition of the importance of the wife's consent will lift her out of the position of a legal nonentity." Ibid. at 232-33.

Stow traced the oppressive treatment of widows in California to English law, claiming that "in many of the Continental countries the wife is as free—as regards her own property and industry—in wedlock as out of it." Ibid. at 353. It is unclear whether she was unaware of the roots of California's marital property law, or whether she simply recognized the effect of the vagaries of a common law consciousness upon it.

"A thorough knowledge of the financial condition of the marriage-firm is quite as important to the wife as to the husband. . . . A true partnership has no secrets."[131] She also pointed out the inconsistency and unfairness of subjecting the widow's own portion of the common property to the probate process (while a widower avoided such), again arguing that the arrangement "sets at nought the true relation of husband and wife as business partners."[132] Based on her own experiences, she recognized the difficulty faced by women who married late, after their husbands had acquired their assets as separate property. She believed that the absence of common property permitted men who owned such property to keep their wives hostage to their testamentary whims and encouraged secrecy in the marriage, which again was contrary to the notion of marriage as a partnership.[133]

[131]Ibid. at 72.

[132]Ibid. at 16. She asked: "Why are not widowers probated? Why these one-sided laws which refuse their vulture protection to men? Would that they . . . be obliged to plead . . . for . . . the allowance money . . . taken out of their hard earnings, and be refused even that! I think this charming probate business would sink down low . . . into the seething, boiling caldron beneath this crust of earth where it belongs, never to rear its hydra head again." Ibid. at 39.

[133]Ibid. at 223-25. Under traditional Spanish law, the fruits and profits of separate property would have been considered common property, while intrinsic increases in value remained separate property. De Funiak, *Community Property*, supra note 1 at 180, 187. However, in *George v. Ransom*, 15 Cal 322 (1860), the California Supreme Court invalidated a portion of the 1850 enabling legislation, which had properly designated income from separate property as common property. In its decision, the Court was purporting to be upholding the constitutional guarantee of married women's separate property. *George v. Ransom* at 323-24.

De Funiak saw this case as an example of the court's thinking on common law: "The court was constitutionally bound to determine what was community and what was separate property, not by the common law, but by principles of the Spanish community property system which had been incorporated into the framework of the state constitution." *Community Property*, supra note 1 at 183-84.

However, Stow's proposals went even further than the theories of community property would allow. First, they called for categorizing intrinsic increases in the value of separate property as common. More radically, they suggested that "the moment a man marries, the half of his entire possessions should belong to his wife." On the other hand, Stow believed that men should not have an automatic half-interest in the wife's separate property. She based this conclusion on social realities: that women ususally abandoned self-supporting work when they married, that it was difficult to resume this work upon widowhood, especially if there were children to care for, and that women's wages were far below men's. Stow also believed that widows facing an insolvent estate ought to have a claim against it for "services . . . rendered as wife, domestic, nurse, and housekeeper," thus proposing a method for recouping the wife's contribution where the husband's management of the common property had dissipated it. Stow, *Probate Confiscation*, supra note 126 at 26, 223-26.

In most of her arguments against California's probate and marital property

Stow lobbied this bill to no successful end in 1876, and then set off on a cross-country campaign to reform the probate laws in the eastern common law states. On her return to California in the early 1880s, she tried again to get her proposal passed, but by that time she was giving much of her attention to other reforms.[134] Furthermore, the organized woman's rights movement in the state had fallen into the doldrums, ceasing for the time to be a force in Sacramento politics.

California never strenuously resisted the national, common law-based trend of carving out special individual property rights for married women, and by the 1890s the state's scheme operated much like a modified common law system.[135] With no one championing the potential of common property for women's equality, the focus turned to the category of separate property, more specifically a wife's separate property, as a way to provide women with additional rights, short of suffrage. Nationally, earnings statutes that lodged the title in wives' earnings with the wives gained popularity, while undercutting the force of joint-property rhetoric. In California the same trend was occurring, even as reformists worked unsuccessfully to shore up women's rights to common property. This was the nature of the legacy left to California's women.[136]

CONCLUSION

Although the agitation for marital property rights in California in the 1870s hardly represents a success, it does show that the agitation and arguments were made on a different basis from those in the East. Reformers in the West began from the

---

systems, Stow was in touch with the basic philosophies of the community property system and indicated where the state's laws were inconsistent with the notion of marriage as a partnership that required a gender-neutral treatment of spouses. However, these three ideas exhibited a certain confusion. While the first proposal may simply have displayed an ignorance of the finer points of the community property system, the second, based on status, was more consistent with the common law system. The third suggestion, based on quasi-contract principles, ignored the fact that the marital community was based on sharing in gains and losses, and was inconsistent with Stow's own view of marriage as a partnership.

It is not surprising that Stow succumbed to the gendered, status-based notions of the common law. Seemingly unconscious of the contradictions, like her contemporaries in the woman's rights movement she fought for equal treatment of women while arguing for special, protective treatment based on the ideology of separate spheres.

[134]Schuele, "Marietta Stow," supra note 125 at 14, 22.

[135]Prager, "Persistence of Separate Property Concepts," supra note 3 at 46.

[136]Ibid. at 47; Siegel, "Home as Work," supra note 38 at 1179.

point that marriage was a partnership, not simply because they believed it to be so, but because the marital property system chosen by male lawmakers was based on that notion. While those who gathered at the Constitutional Convention in 1849 may have intended to enact a marital property system that would protect wives and families from the fluctuations of the state's economy, they left women with a powerful tool in the form of common property.

Although California's marital property law may quickly have functioned like a modified common law system, the nominal designation of common property was a politically valuable asset that eastern woman's rights agitators lacked. Reva Siegel has noted of advocates of joint-property rights, "In their view, marital property reform was not about protecting economically dependent women from men, but instead was about empowering economically productive women to participate equally with men in managing assets both had helped to accumulate."[137] The recognition of joint property in California's law thus gave woman's rights activists in the state a critical advantage over their eastern sisters. While these women by the 1870s were focusing their efforts on seeking the ballot as well as gender-based marital property rights, in the Golden State, advocacy of joint property remained a politically potent force for much longer, and with it attempts to use marital property law to empower women rather than simply to protect them.

[137]Siegel, "Home as Work," supra note 38 at 1116.

SEND THE BIRD AND CAGE: THE DEVELOPMENT OF DIVORCE LAW IN WYOMING, 1868-1900

PAULA PETRIK

O n September 14, 1876, Ruthina deMars wrote to her husband that she was enjoying herself "first class" and hoped "to continue to do the same without [his] assistance. I am very much obliged to you for past favors," she added, "but should much rather our intercourse should cease from this time. Please send me my bird and cage and wax flowers" by express.[1] Whether the bird and cage arrived via the Union Pacific in Evanston, Wyoming, is unclear; it was clear to the court, however, that Ruthina deMars, like many others in Wyoming between 1868 and 1900, had sundered the bond between husband and wife by deserting her spouse. In consequence, the Albany County court awarded her husband, a town soda-water manufacturer, a divorce.

Only one of several hundred divorce suits in Albany County, the deMars case serves as the simplest example of desertion, but, as in the adjacent Laramie County, the interpretation of divorce law, especially desertion, was much more complex and masked more serious causes for marital breakup. Later, the use

Paula Petrik is professor of history and associate dean of the College of Arts and Humanities, University of Maine.

[1]Civil Case No. 864, Albany County, Wyoming State Archives, Cheyenne, Wyoming. Data analysis is based on 237/245 completed divorce cases from Albany County, Wyoming, and 258/275 *available* completed divorce suits from Laramie County, Wyoming, by computer. In Albany County, few files were absent from the archive, but in Laramie County the clerk of the court did not index divorce cases among the civil suits between 1881 and 1885. The entries simply record the granting of a divorce but not the particulars of the case. Defective and missing cases also complicated analysis of the Laramie County material. Nonetheless, it is reasonable to assume that the absence of some fifty cases from 1881 to 1885 and approximately twenty missing files would not substantially alter the results of the statistical research for Laramie County. Spelling and punctuation have been regularized throughout.

of mental cruelty as a reason for divorce proved even more problematic. The ideal of the companionate marriage, mutually affectionate, cooperative, and reciprocal, in short, was slow to arrive in Wyoming, and was in part the result of rising expectations as working-class people aspired to the middle ranks.

Recognizably similar circumstances, although they differed in degree, contributed to the two counties' understanding of divorce laws. The largest city in Laramie County was Cheyenne. By virtue of its role as the territorial capital (and, after 1890, the state capital) and the division point for the Union Pacific Railroad, it harbored a variety of social groups: skilled, unskilled, and professional rail employees; state and federal bureaucrats; several bands of merchants and artisans; and a bevy of western capitalists. Despite the sizable population of single males within its precincts, soldiers posted nearby to Fort D.A. Russell, and single men from cattle ranches in the area, Cheyenne was predominantly a city of families. Laramie, the main population center of Albany County, was smaller, and was also a product of the Union Pacific, which designated the town as its section point. Whereas middling business people dominated Cheyenne's social structure, Laramie was a working-class town, populated by Union Pacific rail and shop workers, rolling mill laborers, and roustabouts from the cattle operations. Like Cheyenne, Laramie was the home of a number of single men, but determined middle- and working-class families set the tone for the town.[2]

Although Ruthina deMars took the easiest route out of her marriage, Wyoming law provided a number of grounds for divorce: desertion for one year, adultery, cruelty, indignities rendering a spouse's condition intolerable, a husband's neglect or failure to provide for one year, intemperance, a husband's vagrancy, physical incompetency, prenuptial pregnancy of the wife by another man, and conviction of felony before the marriage.[3] While Wyoming's canon was a lengthy one, Albany and Laramie County courts initially reduced the list to desertion, cruelty, adultery, and intemperance; only after 1885 did the courts regularly recognize a husband's willful neglect and indignities rendering a spouse's condition intolerable, and even then plaintiffs and their lawyers seldom availed themselves of these

[2]Beginning with 1,450 residents in 1870, Cheyenne experienced sustained growth, reaching a population of 14,087 by 1900. In 1870 Laramie's population numbered 854, increasing to over 8,000 by 1900 with the growth of area ranching and the addition of the university.

[3]Carroll D. Wright, *A Report on Marriage and Divorce in the United States* (Washington, D.C., 1891), 112-13; Special Reports, *Marriage and Divorce 1867-1906, Part 1* (Washington, D.C., 1909), 327. Later, the canon allowed divorce for conviction of a felony after a marriage.

provisions. "Indignities" (often interpreted as forms of mental harassment or meanness) were, moreover, subsumed under the general heading of "cruelty" (usually defined as physical violence) and, again, only after 1885 did the courts allow cruelty specified as "indignities" to be sufficient for a divorce. This informal concatenation of the divorce statute also extended to desertion, which accounted for the largest number of divorces in Wyoming as well as elsewhere.

As in other areas of the United States, desertion in Albany and Laramie counties was most often a case of a husband's and, to a much lesser extent, a wife's slipping away.[4] Although the trend in desertion eventually declined, between 1869 and 1900 roughly two-thirds of all divorces recorded in Albany County involved desertion; in 60 percent of them a husband simply left his wife and often his children. Laramie County duplicated this pattern; desertion declined over time but accounted on the average for 44 percent of the divorces. Men were the more likely to depart; in 53 percent of the Laramie County desertions a husband left his family (Figures 1A and B). Although several men sent their wives to relatives before they disappeared,[5] in other cases wives refused to leave their families to pioneer in Wyoming or to follow their railroading husbands.[6] Still others were unwilling to endure the isolation of ranch life. Luther Randall, for example, testified that his wife "did not like the country."[7] And Samuel Slaymaker said that his wife, Ella, thought "a ranch was too dull a place to live" and that "she wanted to live in a place where she could see somebody."[8] Ella Slaymaker left to open a hotel at Fort Fetterman, from which she realized $500 a year. When the court asked John Skinner why his wife had left, he replied, "She merely did not want to live here in this country. That was all I got out of her." For Morris Idelman's wife, the life of a prosperous merchant in Cheyenne with the city's numerous social possibilities was not enough. In 1880 she announced that she was "dissatisfied with the country" and returned to Europe.[9] Some women were

[4]Civil Cases 598, 603, 675, 727, 756, 829, 864, 880, 893, 910, 917, 934, 939, 961, 970, 992, 996, 999, 1043, 1048, 1106, 1142, 1286, 1356, 1467, 1454, 1489, 1604, 1630, 1645, 1656, 1679, 1703, 1728, 1757, 1882, 1909, 1934, 1999, 2030, 2072, 2107, 2112, 2137, 2149, 2157, 2264, 2279, 2292, 2304, 2317, 2323, 2355, 2359, 2373, 2383, 2391, 2394, 2395, 2403, 2404, 2423, 2424, 2429, 2461, 2466, 1470, 2485, 2521, 2534, 2566, Albany County.

[5]Civil Cases 230, 438, 1044, 1904, 948, Albany County.

[6]Civil Cases 752, 936, 1069, 1985, 1466, 2387, Albany County; 2-162, Laramie County.

[7]Civil Case 231, Albany County.

[8]Civil Case 1324, Albany County.

[9]Civil Case 2141, Albany County; 3-255, Laramie County.

FIGURE 1A
ALBANY COUNTY, WYOMING—DESERTION

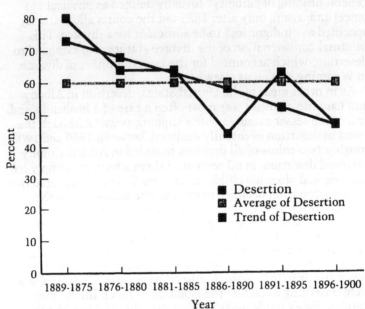

forced out of their homes and told to make their own way.[10] Mary Knabe's husband put her and her child out on the street in Council Bluffs, Iowa, on a Sunday afternoon in November 1869; Mary went west until she arrived in Laramie, where she supported herself and her son by washing and sewing. For Mary Knabe, being ejected from her house was tantamount to her husband's desertion.[11]

Petitions pleading desertion (much more common in Albany than in Laramie County) also masked other unacceptable marital behaviors—adultery, cruelty, or drunkenness, or an emotionally comatose marriage. Often such charges could not be substantiated, yet they were acceptable to the court. Hearsay or confessed reports of extramarital affairs, drinking that did not incapacitate a partner, mental or physical cruelty, or general marital malaise were in some instances resolved informally by a husband's or wife's leave-taking and then formalized by a divorce. Besides abrogating the one-year requirement necessary to a charge of desertion, these complex desertion suits also

[10]Civil Case 1162, 1969, 2227, Albany County; 2-432, Laramie County.
[11]Civil Case 213, Albany County.

FIGURE 1B
LARAMIE COUNTY, WYOMING—DESERTION

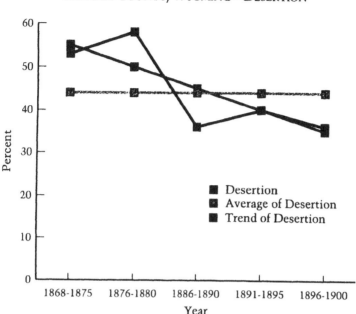

illustrate some of the pressures attendant on nineteenth-century marriage.

Whether from a charitable impulse or the inability to garner evidence for the more serious charge of infidelity, the desertion provision could be used to end a marriage in which unwitnessed adultery had occurred. William Crout, who would be divorced three times in Albany County, charged his wife, Melissa, with desertion; the court records showed that she had deserted Crout to live with Charles Stansberry. In letters attached to the case, Melissa Crout, who "would not give Stanberry's shirt stuffed with satin for Crout," and Stansberry confessed that they had eloped. Stansberry wrote that Melissa had taken sick and that he had paid a visit to her room. He admitted:

> From that time I was in love with a married woman. After some time I thought it was folly to think any more about it until one evening being unwell retired to my room very early. I had not been in bed but a short [time] when I overheard a conversation between Melissa and Crout charging him of being a thief and everything that is bad and asked him for money to go

home which he denied and said that she would live
with him for she had no friends to send for money.
Little did he know that she had a friend in the next
room that would give the money as free as the water
that runs. After this conversation I heard her ask him
for a divorce which he denied, and he consented and
then went for a lawyer to make out the papers. I saw
in a moment that there was a chance for me and I
improved the opportunities and I won the case.[12]

A few months after his divorce, William Crout remarried, but
his luck was no better. Rebecca Crout deserted him. When the
chancery commissioner quizzed him about her reasons for leaving, Crout claimed that she had left because he "did not pet her
as much as he should" and because he had given a horse to his
daughter rather than to his wife.[13]

In a similar case, John Webb charged his wife with desertion,
although she had obviously been living in an adulterous relationship with Webb's brother in Colorado. Instead of returning
to Iowa to visit her parents in 1876, Sena Webb decamped with
her brother-in-law, by whom she had a child. In a candid letter,
Joe Webb acknowledged that they had "yielded to a hot, unbri-
dled passion," and outlined the circumstances of their affair in
order to exonerate Sena:

She acknowledged her heart mine but her hand and
honor yours. She said she would rather die than be
untrue to you. She begged and entreated me from her
knees to leave her forever, ere she fell from the high
pillars of honor she had ever rested upon. She begged
me if I respected her, [by] all I revere on earth by the
memory of all those near and dear to me to leave her
whilst yet we were guiltless in the eyes of God and
our conscience. But no. With a persistency seldom
equaled, I continued my entreaties until the 4th of
September, 1876, Saturday when you were in town.
She yielded all to me that very night, the first of our
intercourse she became impregnated. Hence, Lillian.[14]

---

[12]Civil Case 234, Albany County. How these letters from Melissa Crout and
Charles Stansberry, written to a sister and sister-in-law, found their way into
the docket remains a mystery. Perhaps Melissa's sister agreed to pass the letters
on to Crout to speed the process.

[13]Civil Case 607, Albany County.

[14]Civil Case 989, Albany County.

Whether out of remorse, duty, or trouble with her adulterous relationship, Sena Webb returned to her husband in 1877 or 1878. He agreed to support her and *all* of her children, but declined to live with her. Meantime, against her wishes, Joe Webb resumed his correspondence in February 1878, begging her to return to him in Colorado. By April that year, Sena had decided that her attempt at reconciliation had failed and agreed to join her lover, who admitted that without her he was "drifting toward recklessness fast." Despite the obvious evidence, John Webb chose "desertion" rather than "adultery" when he approached the court.[15]

In 1888 Myra Allen elected to prosecute her husband, Arthur, on the grounds of desertion, although she had letters to prove and witnesses to testify that he had engineered a train wreck at Missoula, Montana, in order to leave his wife. The most damning evidence, however, was a letter in which Myra Allen's lover explained the obstacles to their reunion, not the least of which was Myra's revealing letter in which she wondered why "Hallie" ran after her husband and "could not attract a single man."[16] Similarly, Margaret Aiken concluded that her husband had deserted her when he left for the Black Hills "with a lot of prostitutes" and Tom Miller's Variety Show, although a charge of adultery might well have carried the day.[17] Gaylord Bell, too, charged desertion, but his petition clearly stated that his wife had left him to "live in the company of Jacob Ryan," with whom he believed his wife had committed adultery.[18]

Although desertion cases in Albany County also masked situations in which physical cruelty and drink forced one partner from the home, more numerous were those that indicated emotional dissatisfaction with the relationship or complaints more in tune with Wyoming's indignities provision.[19] In 1869 Emma Cutler refused to follow her husband farther west and returned to her mother's home in Waltham, Massachusetts. Despite an impassioned letter from husband's attorney, reminding her of her marriage vows and her husband's apparent willingness to reconcile with his wife, Eliza balked. "I was a girl not seventeen years old, thought I loved him, and it is his fault that my feelings were changed. I have long since made up my mind that I should not ever live with him again as I have neither love nor respect for him. . . . I am better off with my

[15]Ibid.

[16]Civil Case 1894, Albany County; see also 958, 1438, 1468, Albany County, for other suits involving adultery and desertion.

[17]Civil Case 3-104, Laramie County.

[18]Civil Case 2-562, Laramie County.

[19]For examples, see Civil Cases 1119, 2318, 675, Albany County.

mother and my children than I was with him. Years of experience have taught me there is no friend to be depended upon in sickness and health like a mother."[20] Julia Ford did not travel across country to desert her husband; she simply abandoned him within the couple's home by refusing sexual companionship and children. The court was especially sensitive to the latter charge and questioned James Ford closely on his wife's birth-control program, which apparently included measures other than abstinence.[21] Olive Sheldon waited until her children were grown to leave a marriage evidently long since hopeless. "If I was dead it would then be all right," she wrote in her parting note. "I am just as dead to you as though you had closed my eyes and seen me lowered in the ground. There will be no going back. The world is wide, wide enough for you and me. Let there be peace. As to the next life, I will have what I have earned, nothing more."[22] Similarly, Anah and Henry Whittemore fought over money and conduct. Henry claimed that, besides her refusal to prepare his meals, Anah, "instead of being a companion to him . . . absented herself from his company and home until late hours of the night . . . [and] that she has repeatedly told plaintiff that she married him for his money and as soon as she got all of his money that she intended to leave him."[23]

The situation was much the same in Laramie County: plaintiffs often cited desertion when vague disappointments or incompatibility were at the root of one partner's departure. Isabella Pyper apparently referred to general disillusionment with her marriage, stating that "she did not consider herself James' wife." With that she decamped, leaving her two children behind.[24] Elizabeth Wilkins vowed that she could not make her home anywhere near any of her husband's relatives, and George Wallace voiced his unmanly disappointment in his wife's refusal to work. She testified that her husband "wouldn't live with a woman who wouldn't support him and knew women who would."[25] And William Mater's wife claimed that he "did not make money fast enough, did not support her in the style she wished to live [and] that she could do better."[26]

[20]Civil Case 38, Albany County.
[21]Civil Case 1121, Albany County.
[22]Civil Case 1817, Albany County.
[23]Civil Case 2399, Albany County.
[24]Civil Case 2-255, Laramie County.
[25]Civil Case 2-254; 2-253, Laramie County; see also 2-78, 3-7, Laramie County.
[26]Civil Case 2-478, Laramie County.

When divorcing women went to court, they enteed a profoundly male world. Early in its history, Wyoming's women won the right to sit on juries, as this photograph from about 1890 shows, but they seldom sat on juries in divorce cases. (Wyoming State Museum)

The Elastic Nature of Desertion

Clearly, desertion encompassed any number of marital failures; emotional dissatisfaction with a marriage, a partner's failure to fulfill the role of breadwinner or helpmate, suspicion of infidelity, and drinking proved successful in court under the rubric of desertion. Two cases from Albany County, in particular, illustrate the elastic nature of desertion as a legal definition in nineteenth-century Wyoming. Distinguished by the detail of their testimony and the complexity of the financial and emotional relationships that bound and finally broke their marriages, *Kellogg v. Kellogg* and *Fein v. Fein* demonstrate how courts could stretch desertion to incorporate a number of unhappy circumstances not covered by statute.

The Feins initially went to court over John Fein's alleged desertion of his wife on December 10, 1883. Married in 1874 to her former husband's partner, Barbara Fein successively ran a saloon, a boarding house, and a restaurant, where both she and her two children worked. The Feins moved onto a ranch in May 1875 to "prove up," returning to Laramie in July 1876. All apparently went well until December 1883, when Barbara's daughter sickened from the effects of a botched criminal abor-

tion late in her pregnancy. The culprit: one of the Feins' boarders. When the effects of the misconduct came to light, according to Barbara Fein, "[Fein] had a fuss with the girl and because
I would not send her away, and because I would not give him
any more money, he left."[27] While making other living arrangements, Fein suggested that his wife should move to a remodeled house on the creek. Barbara Fein agreed, on condition that
she would receive the rent from the restaurant; she discovered,
however, that both the property her husband owned and the
$10,000 she had contributed to their joint ventures had disap-
peared. At that point, her efforts centered on securing her interest in the property, long since mortgaged and passed into other
hands.

John Fein admitted that, although he could not stand living
with his wife, he was perfectly willing to come to some domestic agreement. His wife could either return to him on the ranch
or take up residence in the house by the creek. Far more critical
for him was to resist her charges of his defrauding her of any
claim to his property. In his defense, he claimed that his wife
had contributed no money or labor to their various ventures,
and had no interest in the property in question—either homestead or city property, or property from their marriage or from
her previous marriage. As for the loss of his own fortune and
property, he attributed his ruin to "[m]isfortune, bad management and bad luck."[28]

John and Martha Kellogg were married in August 1872 in
Laramie. Two years later, having amassed enough capital from
John's trade as a blacksmith, the couple moved to a homestead
on the Little Laramie River, where they lived for fifteen years.
Their next move took them to a coal mine on Mill Creek and
eventually, like many other financially ruined homesteaders,
back to the town and to any work at hand. From John Kellogg's
perspective, his wife deserted him in March 1889 when she
refused to sleep with him. Under cross-examination, he admitted that perhaps he had denied her because "he got vexed at her
for going with another man. Her own daughter," he said,
"caught her in the park with another man [at] ten o'clock at
night. It would make anybody mad." Asked if he had ever ordered her to leave, he replied, "I never ordered her to leave the
house; but after she got in with this man I told her that if she

[27]Coroner's Inquest 41, Albany County, Wyoming State Archives; Wyoming
Supreme Court Docket No. 2, Case No. 31, Wyoming State Archives. As it
was, Mary Roth died from the effects of a septic abortion, having delivered a
nearly full-term child. The event was aggravated by her admission of
infanticide before her death and her paramour's timely flight from the town.
[28]Ibid.

loved him better to go with him, but she still kept him. She is living with him now."[29]

Predictably, Martha Kellogg had a different version of events. According to her, in March 1889, her husband had returned home drunk, had abused her and her daughter, and had ordered her to leave: "Well, I heard him say that he would do so much better by the children if I was away."[30] Instead of leaving physically, Martha admitted to denying him conjugal companionship, but stayed on in the house until August 1890, when she went to sew for a woman near Cheyenne and from there to live with her sister. In contrast to her husband's protestations of support, Martha claimed that her parents had been responsible for feeding both her and the children. In addition, her husband had squandered his money on drink. For Martha, her final departure had been only one in a long line of separations. She told the court that she could no longer live with him: "I tried for it for seventeen years; I left him several times and went back, but it was just the same."[31]

The critical issue for the court in both cases was whether Martha Kellogg or John Fein had *reasonable cause* to abandon their spouses, households, and children, despite the fact that *reasonable cause* was nowhere a part of the desertion statute. To determine this, the officers of the court concentrated on John Kellogg's drinking, asking him to describe his habits. "Well," he answered, "I have been here since 1869. I am an old timer in this county and we all take our sprees sometimes; after that I would work as two men to get over it. I could do more work than any two men; I could do more work with machinery because I understood it."[32] Even an appeal to pioneer brotherhood and claims against his wife's chastity went for naught. The court understood that his intemperance threatened family life and allowed that Martha Kellogg had reasonable cause to leave her home in granting her a divorce on the grounds of desertion. Similarly, the court questioned John Fein about his heartless behavior and bad business practices and decided that he had no bona fide reason for leaving. For Barbara Fein and Martha Kellogg, their decrees were pyrrhic victories: they had prevailed but were without means.

[29]Civil Case 2048, Albany County.
[30]Ibid.
[31]Ibid.
[32]Ibid.

FIGURE 2A
ALBANY COUNTY, WYOMING—ADULTERY

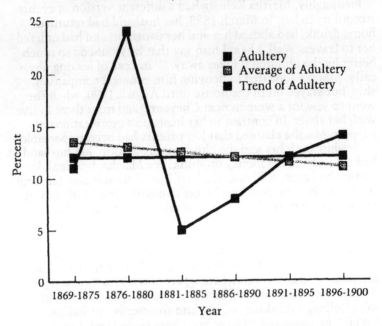

■ Adultery
▨ Average of Adultery
■ Trend of Adultery

ADULTERY REQUIRES CLOSER SCRUTINY

If Albany and Laramie County courts were flexible in their interpretation of desertion, they were more stringent in their interpretation of adultery, demanding witnesses or other incontrovertible proof of illicit intercourse. Hence judges listened to hotel managers, hostelry guests, detectives, whorehouse cronies, and remorseful paramours, and took account of venereal disease in gathering evidence of adultery. Accounting for roughly 12 percent of the divorces in the period, adultery showed signs of diminishing as a cause for marital dissolution (Figures 2A and B). Nonetheless, for one segment of the divorcing couples, infidelity remained an option, and the discussions surrounding sexual transgression shed light on another aspect of life in nineteenth-century marriage in Wyoming.

Following the national trend, men were far more likely to complain of their wives' infidelity or questionable misconduct. Because women had no institutionalized places of assignation or the financial means to follow their errant mates, their husbands could more easily catch their spouses in compromising

FIGURE 2B
LARAMIE COUNTY, WYOMING—ADULTERY

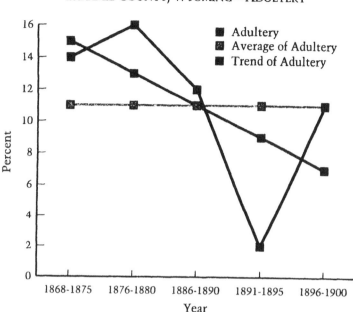

circumstances at home, in the countryside, in hotels on the Union Pacific route, or across the nation, if need be. Isaac Menke provided convincing evidence that his wife, Elizabeth, had "fled to the arms and lustful embraces of one Sidney LaStrange" and that the pair had traveled to a boardinghouse in a town along the railroad line.[33] In *Hall v. Hall*, William Clark testified that he saw Hall's wife having intercourse beside the road near the rolling mills in Topeka, Kansas.[34] In another case, Charles Clark obtained convincing testimony from a hotel manager and a guest in Eldorado, Kansas, that his wife, her lover, and another couple had engaged in criminal intercourse in 1881.[35] Charles Harden resorted to employing detectives to track down his wife in Los Angeles, where the investigators reported that they espied his wife and Clarence Rodgers through a crack in the door of an adjoining room. With some wonder, they commented that Rodgers "came into the room holding his penis in *both* hands," and noted Cordelia Harden's

[33]Civil Case 83, Albany County; see also 3-356, 6-39, 7-13, Laramie County.
[34]Civil Case 604, Albany County.
[35]Civil Case 1006, Albany County.

Photographs entered into the court record suggest the pathos of marital dissolution. Eleanor Clark's picture was lovingly inscribed on the back to her two sons, whose custody she lost as a consequence of a menage à trois or quatre witnessed by a hotel clerk spying through a transom. (Wyoming State Museum)

douching both before and after their "connection."[36]

Because of the bordellos near Laramie's railyard and Cheyenne's Chicago district, men could more easily conceal their sexual escapades from their wives. Yet in several instances Albany and Laramie County wives did not hesitate to cross into the tenderloin to get the goods on their husbands. In 1883 Laura Crawford discovered that her husband had been intimate with three prostitutes in Armdale, Kansas. Accordingly, she traveled to Kansas and obtained the women's corroborated testimony that her husband had been unfaithful numerous times.[37] In 1893 Ella Cobb confronted her rival at a house of ill fame, reporting in her deposition:

> I thereafter went to the house of Monte Grover and asked to see the girl, Little Ella, whereupon she came out, and I asked her to give me the ring which my husband had given her, whereupon she pulled the same from her finger and handed it to me; she then told me that my husband was [a] regular visitor at this house. Where-

[36]Civil Case 2565, Albany County. Cordelia Harden's fling with Clarence Rodgers was not her only transgression. She had reportedly had a series of lovers: one Crum, who had been convicted of stealing horses; Fred Williams; and one Hill—all of whom worked for her husband on their ranch. Despite her adultery, her husband still felt friendly toward her but wanted the divorce.

[37]Civil Case 1151, Albany County.

Husbands resorted to hiring detectives and other agents to collect the evidence many courts demanded for proof of adultery by erring wives. Pinkerton detectives peered through a knothole in the door of an adjoining room to catch Cordelia Harden with her lover. (Wyoming State Museum)

> upon I asked her to forego him; in answer to which she said she would be willing to let him come back to me if he wanted to.[38]

Although Ella Cobb's chief complaint against her husband, Samuel, was an economic one (their farm was "conducted on the communistic plan," and he compelled her to contribute her teacher's wages to the collective against her wishes), she traveled to Wichita, Kansas, to obtain more serious information about his sexual misconduct and received her divorce on the grounds of adultery.[39] In 1895 Helen Barnes persuaded both the housekeeper and the landlord at a bordello, Monte Hall's, to testify that her physician husband had been intimate with an

[38]Civil Case 2143, Albany County. Charles Cobb had brought "Little Ella" along from Cheyenne as he and his wife made their wedding trip.
[39]Civil Case 2544, Albany County.

inmate, Ada Robinson.[40] To ferret out her husband's activities, Mary Alice Scott went to Belle Williams's brothel in Cheyenne, where she found that it mattered little to her husband's inamorata that he was married "as long as she got his money."[41]

Men and women often admitted their peccadilloes in letters to friends, in conversation with others, or even in court—sometimes with remorse and sometimes without. "When my wife was in the States," wrote William Burnham to his associate, "I went to San Francisco to meet her. There I was tempted by a she devil and let my foot slip." Subsequent letters from his "she devil," another visit to a house of ill repute, and his deceit in business affairs caused his wife to separate from him.[42] Burnham pleaded with his friend to shield his wife from any hurtful talk and admitted that his weakness had cost him the best of wives. In the same vein, Perry Newell, a boarder and hand on the Vail ranch in Albany County, admitted in court that he and Maggie Vail were caught in the act on the Vails' sofa by her husband.[43] In *Barker v. Barker*, two men testified that they had been intimate with Barker's wife, which the latter confirmed in contrite letters to her husband and her lovers.[44] On a less remorseful note, Isaac Davis admitted his adultery with Lizzie "Pawnee Liz" Stevens to his father-in-law, and boasted that he got "a damn sight better fucking over here than I ever did at your house."[45] Henry Jones, in *Schoonmaker v. Schoonmaker*, also confessed to his involvement with Schoonmaker's wife and obliquely referred to his own sexual prowess, claiming that "the only reason for Mrs. Schoonmaker drawing a six-shooter on Mrs. Wardell was I was sleeping with Mrs. Wardell more than Mrs. Schoonmaker. Therefore she was jealous."[46] In Arthur Smith's suit against his wife, Mary, he reported that Shady Hall coyly hinted at sexual involvement with Smith's wife when Hall said, "You don't suppose I have women come here without I have something to do with them, do you."[47]

[40]Civil Case 2356, Albany County. Leroy Barnes initially had a legitimate reason for his presence at Monte Hall's: he was attending Hall's final illness.

[41]Civil Case, 2-182, Laramie County; see also 4-370, Laramie County.

[42]Civil Case 137, Albany County.

[42]Civil Case 1946, Albany County.

[44]Civil Case 2-568, Laramie County.

[45]Civil Case 706, Albany County.

[46]Civil Case 962, Albany County.

[47]Civil Case 1736, Albany County. *Smith v. Smith* is also notable for a woman's electing to enter prostitution. "I am going to turn out," Mary Smith is reported to have said, and later her husband, looking through a window at Fannie Cook's bawdy house, heard her say in response to Tom Ferguson's

Other men simply saw a liaison outside marriage as more unin-
hibited or economically advantageous; they thought they could
do better on their own and did not wish to support wives or
children. Stephen Mills, for example, simply said that he was
sorry he married his wife, Alice, "as he wanted to be free and
easy and go and stay or sleep with as many women as he saw
fit."[48]

CRUELTY, BOTH PHYSICAL AND MENTAL, GAINS GROUND

In addition to adultery, Albany County courts also recognized—albeit slowly—cruelty as permissible grounds for divorce. Cruelty accounted for approximately 10 percent of the
divorces in the period, and the chancery commissioner recommended dissolution in only two cases before 1880, in one of
which a husband petitioned the court because of his wife's
attempt to kill him (Figures 3A and B).[49] Even after 1880 Albany
County judges did not hear many divorces predicated on cruelty, and when magistrates did hear such a suit, the complain-
ant most often offered evidence of unambiguous battering,
choking, pinching, or assault with weapons and household
wares, although Wyoming law made provision for mental harm
under its "indignities" clause.[50] In a handful of cases in the
1880s, the court began to accept failure to perform the traditional roles of husband or wife as sufficient for divorce. Asa
Clark, for example, won a divorce from his wife, Vashti, on the
grounds of cruelty in 1883, claiming that she would not prepare
his meals, keep the house neat, or care for the children properly, and Ezra Flemming and Susan Tracy successfully charged
their spouses with publicly impugning their chastity.[51] Fred
Munn, too, was able to obtain a divorce when he provided convincing evidence that his wife associated with lewd women
and visited beer gardens alone.[52]

After 1890 and increasingly toward the end of the century,
complainants in Albany County succeeded in their divorce
petitions on the grounds of mental cruelty under both the cru-

---

invitation to go to bed, "This is the last night I will stay with you for five
dollars." Arthur Smith tried to summon the police, but the lawman proved
reluctant to go into an establishment that paid its monthly fine.

[48]Civil Case 3-229, Laramie County; see also 2385, 2472, Albany County.

[49]Civil Case 67, 480, Albany County.

[50]Civil Cases 995, 1031, 1516, 1666, 1873, 2441, 2448, 2458, Albany County.

[51]Civil Case 1138, 1236, 1350, Albany County.

[52]Civil Case 1544, Albany County.

FIGURE 3A
ALBANY COUNTY, WYOMING—CRUELTY

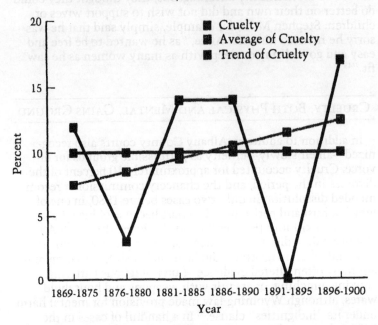

elty and indignities clauses. Although Kate Bennett testified that her husband "was guilty of extreme cruelty toward me in every way possible except by actual blows," his constant fault finding, name calling, and taunts about his illicit affairs in local bawdy houses made her life unbearable.[53] Otto Gramm, the president of the rolling mill, also claimed that his wife's mental abuse interfered with his work and contributed to his skin rash. Catherine Gramm, he testified, moved his library and office to the barn, spied on him through the windows of his factory, and threatened townspeople with the loss of their mill jobs if they crossed her.[54] Winnie and Franklin Bevans accused one another of extreme cruelty and indignities. Winnie averred that Frank, a Union Pacific conductor, would come off the road drunk and would abuse her, both physically and mentally; while Frank testified that Winnie vexed him by her refusal to cook, keep him company at home, or care for their daughter, and by her

[53]Civil Case 1977, Albany County.
[54]Civil Case 2514, Albany County.

Figure 3b
Laramie County, Wyoming—Cruelty

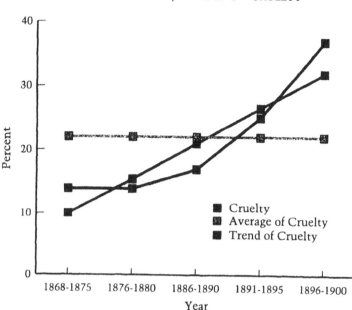

■ Cruelty
▧ Average of Cruelty
■ Trend of Cruelty

assaults with shears, teacups, plates, pokers, and a bicycle pump.[55]

In Laramie County judicial interpretation and behavior regarding cruelty developed differently. As in Albany County, most cruelty suits listed incidences of physical violence or assault with handy tools and housewares. (One case recorded a threat to do away with a wife with a Union Pacific ticket punch.[56]) Laramie County differed from its neighbor in that suits predicated on cruelty appeared with some frequency from the beginning, and in greater proportions. While cruelty accounted for roughly 10 percent of the divorces during any quinquennial period in Albany County, it was the cause of 22 percent of divorces in the same periods in Laramie County (Figure 3). Of more importance is that suits in Laramie County succeeded regularly on the basis of mental cruelty or indignities before the practice became commonplace in Albany

[55]Civil Case 2473, Albany County.
[56]Civil Case 6-195, Laramie County.

County. As early as 1878, Viola McGregor claimed that her husband had abused her in every way except striking her, and between 1886 and 1890, 53 percent of Laramie County divorces cited instances of mental cruelty or indignities.[57]

Essentially, charges of mental cruelty fell into three distinct groups: unwifely or unhusbandly conduct, verbal abuse, and emotional neglect. The Sissons' marriage dissolved because of William Sisson's late hours, visits to bordellos, and correspondence with another woman, while the Downeys parted because the husband simply ignored his wife and generally denied his marriage.[58] Nora and Ben Van Dyke eventually divorced for other reasons, but their earlier petitions arrayed a host of unbecoming spousal behaviors.[59] In the same fashion Lillie Hunter escaped her marriage by citing her husband's "frenzies" and general rudeness.[60] Although husbands sometimes laid claims against their wives' conduct, most plaintiffs charging cruelty were women. Among the exceptions was May Gilman, who vilified her husband to her neighbors and embarrassed him on a number of occasions, including stripping to the buff and parading around the yard under a full moon.[61] Between 1895 and 1900, more husbands than wives in Laramie County accused their partners of various persecutions, tyrannies, vulgarities, and unspouse-like behavior. Mental cruelty, once almost solely a women's prerogative, became a powerful weapon for husbands.

The Furniss divorce suggests how men, especially railroaders, may have used charges of mental cruelty to end their marriages as well as to preserve their social standing, counting on their wives' reluctance or lack of money to bring a cross-petition. John Furniss, a railroad engineer, initially charged his wife with the usual catalog of indignities: blackening his reputation among the neighbors; unwarranted ejection from the couple's

[57]Civil Case 3-218, Laramie County. The absence of any cases for analysis from 1881 to 1885 is especially vexing with regard to the development of interpretations of cruelty, although it seems reasonable to assume from the frequency of cases citing cruelty—both mental and physical—between 1886 and 1890 that 1881-1885 marked the acceptance of "indignities" by the two counties' courts.

[58]Civil Case 4-586; 5-393, Laramie County.

[59]Civil Case 2-253, Laramie County. Finally divorced in 1896, the Van Dykes had already appeared in court on other occasions. This particular petition was one of the few instances in which the court denied a divorce. From the list of charges and counter-charges, some of which appear ludicrous, the court may have decided that the Van Dykes deserved one another.

[60]Civil Case 5-202, Laramie County; see also 4-398, 6-221, 5-63, 5-58, Laramie County.

[61]Civil Case 4-247, Laramie County; see also 5-63, Laramie County.

home; a quarrelsome, insulting, and abusive temperament; threats against his life; and mismanagement of the children and household. In the absence of a cross-petition, this list would have convinced the Laramie County Court of Ella Furniss's marital missteps and won her husband a speedy divorce.[62]

But Ella Furniss fought back. In her cross-petition, she denied all his allegations; the fault, she maintained lay with her husband. Far from besmirching his reputation in the neighborhood, she had disclosed his shortcomings only to those who needed to know: the county commissioners (to obtain public aid) and her minister (to get advice on her husband's venereal disease). Ella Furniss admitted that she had thrown her husband out of the house, but for good reason: she charged him with leaving the secretions of his venereal disease in the household wash-bowls, endangering the children's health and disgusting the roomers. As for her neglect of the children, she claimed the opposite: her husband had contributed little financially to their support, even begrudging them schooling. What she earned from music lessons, book canvassing, and boardinghouse keeping, moreover, he converted to his own use, spending the money in whorehouses and on riotous living. As if that were not enough, she said he disrupted her boardinghouse by spying in the pantries and kitchens and complaining that "there was too much fuel burned, that there were too many vegetables on the table, and [that] there was too much flour wasted." The court agreed with Ella's version of her husband's conduct and awarded her a divorce on the grounds of neglect.[63]

INTEMPERANCE AND NEGLECT AS DISRUPTIVE FORCES

From the outset both county courts recognized drink, which accounted for approximately 10 percent of the divorces in both counties, as a reason for divorce (Figures 4A and B). Intemperance, the court understood, undermined a man's ability to provide for his family by interfering with his capacity to work and leading him into other immoralities. The problem for the courts in a society in which male sociability centered on the saloon was to determine when a defendant drank to excess. In a petition for divorce in 1872, when Emilie Waldschmidt accused

[62]Civil Case 5-391, Laramie County. It is interesting to note that the majority of men initiating mental-cruelty suits against their wives were associated with the Union Pacific Railroad.

[63]Ibid. Although Ella Furniss was aware that her husband probably had extramarital relationships and that such a charge was not useful after she had thrown him out, in the end she confronted her husband and his lover, Lillian Hunter, in their love nest.

FIGURE 4A
ALBANY COUNTY, WYOMING—INTEMPERANCE

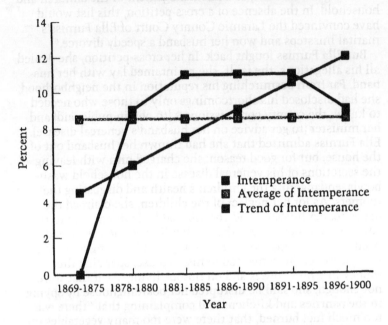

her husband, Albert, of habitual drunkenness, the Laramie
County bench had to struggle to define "intemperance."
Numerous witnesses for the plaintiff testified that he drank
enough to keep him from work of any kind, although one
claimed that he did not stagger when he drank and did as much
work in several months as the witness did in a day. Others
saw his drinking as intermittent—drunk one day and sober the
next—or as merely social. Witnesses who had dealings with
Emilie, however, tended to the view that Albert was so drunk
that Emilie had to keep the boardinghouse going and the family
afloat. Their evidence convinced the court, whose members
thereafter settled on gauging drunkenness by the degree to
which liquor undermined a husband's capacity to work and the
extent to which a woman assumed the support of the family.[64]

Drink forced more than one Wyoming woman to assume the
role of breadwinner. Tom Tutton's, James Baillie's, and John

[64]Civil Case 2-148, Laramie County; see also 4-617, Laramie County. The
Waldschmidt case also describes the geographical movement typical of
westerners, their ready acceptance of separation from family for greater
opportunity or work, and the range of people's acquaintances across time and
distance. Besides those in Laramie, several witnesses in St. Louis, Omaha, and
St. Joseph knew the Waldschmidts.

Figure 4b
Laramie County, Wyoming—Intemperance

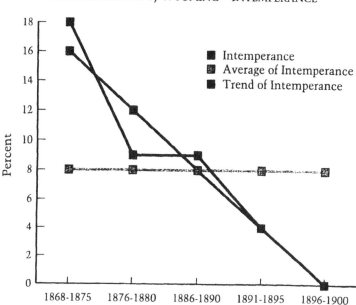

Wright's need for drink led them to saloons, gambling tables, and brothels, and Ida Devereaux, Mary Washburn, Louisa Feulner, and Louisa Wright joined the Laramie workforce to support themselves and their children in the face of their husbands' alcoholism.[65] Martha Bramel, the wife of a divorce lawyer, Charles Bramel, testified that his drinking had incapacitated him to such an extent that she could no longer trust him as her agent. "I managed my own business," she declared. "What he did, he did at my direction and most it was wrong in a measure." The cashier at the bank corroborated her estimate of her husband's ability; he was allowed to perform "the required slight attention" to her affairs but nothing that demanded "good judgment."[66]

Just as the proportion of cases naming cruelty rose in the two counties, so did neglect, accounting for 10 percent of the cases in Albany and 13 percent in Laramie, as the courts after 1882 accepted women's disenchantment with their husbands' performance as familial providers (Figures 5a and b). Desertion forced many women to rely on their own resources, but judges

[65]Civil Case 1731, 1082, 1990, 1045, 1102, 1114, Albany County.
[66]Civil Case 1978, Albany County.

FIGURE 5A
ALBANY COUNTY, WYOMING—NEGLECT

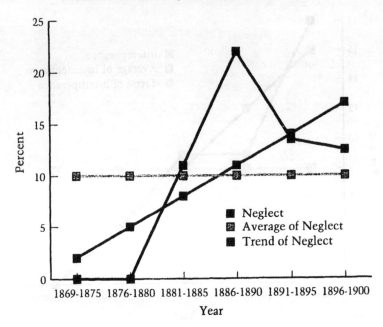

increasingly accepted a woman's complaint that her husband had failed to provide the necessities of life even though he was still present in the household.[67] In Laramie County neglect apparently served to speed a desertion proceeding that might have stretched over a year.[68] Some men evidently expected their wives to fund their ease. Miriam Brown testified that her husband had supported her for a few weeks after their marriage and then refused to work. "He laughed," she claimed, "and said that was what he got a wife for—to earn money for him to sport on."[69] Richard Sowden vowed that he "would rather starve than grub sage brush," and Charles Knadler said he "didn't want to be employed."[70] Adolph Helmer simply filched his wife's earnings and her loan repayments and used them for his own pleasure.[71]

[67]Civil Cases 1118, 1305, 1773, 1819, 1837, 1838, 2003, 2061, 2071, 2139, 2392, 2454, 2462, 2474, 2561, Albany County; 2-253, 2-261, Laramie County.

[68]Civil Cases 5-257; 5-285; 6-217-11; 7-128; 7-174; 7-257, Laramie County.

[69]Civil Case 1115, Albany County.

[70]Civil Cases 1707, 2520, Albany County; see also 2-253, 2-343, Laramie County.

[71]Civil Case 2510, Albany County.

Figure 5b
Laramie County, Wyoming—Neglect

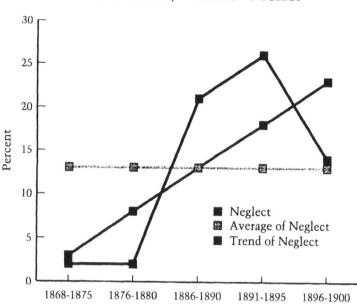

Almost all the cases indicate to some degree the involvement of neighbors, relatives, boarders, and lawyers in marriages in the two counties. Newspapers listed divorce cases, providing a schedule for those wanting to attend the legal theater, and commented on them for public delectation. A former roomer in the Bevans household, W.S. McDowell, testified that Winnie Bevans had admitted that she could live happily with her husband if she cared to, while another witness said that Winnie was far more interested in her own social life and in spending her husband's money than in her marriage.[72] When Minnie McRae implored her husband's ranch foreman, Peter Mordhorst, to stay at the house for her protection, he brushed her off. A few weeks later, after a particularly violent episode between the McRaes, Mordhorst decided to leave, but not before he had a conversation with his boss:

> After a little while he came in and wanted to know if I wanted to take the woman's part. If I did, I could pitch in. I said I don't want to take your wife['s] or no other woman's part, but I won't see any of them abused.

[72]Civil Case 2473, Albany County.

Then on the next morning I got ready to leave, and he
came out and said you had better have your say. You
get more excited over a little thing like that than I do
myself. Then he said, "That woman, I will break her
to mind me, or I will lick her regular."[73]

For Mordhorst, that was enough, and he testified for Minnie
McRae before the chancery commissioner. On several occasions, adjacent roomers, partygoers, and passersby aided Minnie
Moorland when her husband beat her.[74] Townspeople intervened in 1887, horsewhipped James Cooke, and ran him out
of town for his public wife-beating. Lawyers, too, acted as marriage counselors when they attempted to effect reconciliations
or recommended that parents remove a daughter from a potentially lethal situation.[75]

In 1889, in an odd enclosure in *Wilder v. Wilder*, Robert
Morris recorded the dicta of the presiding judge, M.C. Sanfley.
Sanfley had said:

I have a prejudice against divorces, and I am free to
confess it. I view them with a feeling almost akin to
horror. It is not my place to say anything about the
laws of this territory upon that subject, I nevertheless,
desire to take this occasion to say that they seem to be
extremely lax. The interest of society is not promoted,
as a rule, by granting divorces; like homicide, they
should be resorted to only in cases of extreme necessity. What interest does society now have in perpetu-
ating any relation between these two people? Shall the
holy estate of matrimony be further contaminated by
having these people as a living illustration and expo-
nent of that relation? I don't see that it does; this case
seems to be an exception to the rule.[76]

[73]Civil Case 1873, Albany County.

[74]Civil Case 2-442, Laramie County.

[75]Civil Cases 995, 1666, 2362, Albany County. The last case in the foregoing
list represents an instance in which lawyers were successful in reuniting a
couple by acting as mediators in their marital dispute. John Symons, John Hill's
counsel, wrote to Hill, "It appears that Mr. Corthell has advised Mrs. H. to
remain a little longer until the late storm in your domestic affairs has blown
over, or until both of you feel in a better frame of mind than you do at present,
and Mr. Corthell thinks she will be willing to return home. Under these
circumstances I don't think that it would be good policy for you to push the
matter, and it is my opinion that Mrs. H. will come around all right." Clearly,
both lawyers were operating under certain time-honored maxims governing
conflict resolution.

[76]Civil Case 4-551, Laramie County.

Unfortunately for Sanfley, there were a good many exceptions to the rule in Wyoming. His rhetoric perhaps summed up legal attitudes toward divorce. Besides suggesting a basic conservatism in combination with a reluctant pragmatism, the judge's remarks stressed an overweening concern with public perceptions. In many ways, they help us understand what influenced the application of statutes to specific cases and, in turn, why divorce developed as it did in Wyoming.

By and large Wyoming replicated regional and national trends: a diminution in desertion and adultery and a corresponding increase in cruelty and neglect, with two major variations (Figures 6A and B). The first of these was the counties' early tendency to subsume the more serious marital difficulties under the heading of desertion; the second, their comparatively slow recognition of mental cruelty under the state's indignities clause. While Montana's Lewis and Clark County began to grant divorces on the basis of mental cruelty after 1880 wholly in the absence of any statute authorizing such dissolutions, the phenomenon appeared routinely in Laramie County only after 1890, although a serviceable clause was on the books. In both Montana counties, desertion rarely included other grounds for divorce.[77] The explanation may lie in the social expectations and self-consciousness associated with rail towns and their populations' aspirations toward middle-class membership.[78]

Railroad corporate policy affected a community's economic health and, less visibly, its social mores. The railroad permeated all aspects of community life in Laramie and Albany counties. Their businesses depended on the railroad's commerce and contracts; their service industries catered to travelers and railroad workers in transit; and their citizens moved in and out of the line's employ or allied enterprises. The railroad, too, provided an avenue into the middle class for first-generation, native-born men as operatives (engineers, clerks, conductors), and employment security for immigrants in its maintenance jobs (wipers, tenders, mechanics).

---

[77]Paula Petrik, "If She Be Content: The Development of Montana Divorce Law, 1865-1907," *Western Historical Quarterly* 28 (July 1987), 261-91. Lewis and Clark County's Silver Bow courts often used desertion in combination with cruelty, but the divorce was granted on the grounds of cruelty. Addition of cruelty to a desertion petition was apparently a means to circumvent the one-year-absence condition and speed a proceeding, rather than to disguise a more severe form of marital breakdown.

[78]Kathleen Underwood, *Town Building on the Colorado Frontier* (Albuquerque, 1987), 109, 113. Although the author does not specifically address the railroad's influence in Grand Junction, Colorado, on attitudes toward the family and marriage, she does indicate that the workforce included more white-collar operatives over time and that the family increasingly made its presence felt in the community.

FIGURE 6A
ALBANY COUNTY, WYOMING—DIVORCE TRENDS

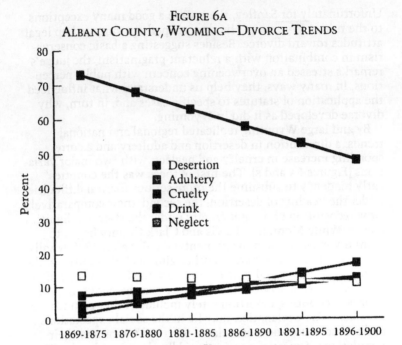

By its nature, the railroad required a certain sort of worker: punctual, dependable, temperate, and settled—qualities associated with the middle-class family. Drunken switchmen or engineers could cause train wrecks; tardy workers brought about delays; and larcenous conductors cut into company profits. Employees who deviated from the standard both on and off the job faced dismissal or stymied their own promotion, and those who depended on the railroad's business might see their custom and contracts go to others. Respectability, therefore, ranked high on the residents' list of social requirements, and divorce petitions in Albany County and, to a lesser extent, Laramie County, although they often mentioned incidents of adultery or cruelty, were granted on the basis of desertion even when it was clear that one spouse had not deserted the other. In this fashion, aspirants to the middle class cloaked marital breakdown with the unfortunate (and easily explicable) absence of a spouse and avoided the social stigma associated with drink, domestic violence, and sexual misconduct. In short, a flexible use of desertion allowed middle-class hopefuls to preserve their credentials.

That there was a discrepancy between the use of desertion between Albany and Laramie counties supports this observa-

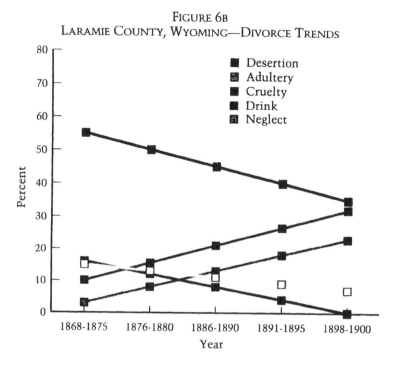

FIGURE 6B
LARAMIE COUNTY, WYOMING—DIVORCE TRENDS

tion. Such concepts as the companionate marriage were familiar to Cheyenne's veteran middle class, and couples demanded
that the law conform to their marital expectations. Thus mental cruelty came more quickly into legal usage in Cheyenne. In
contrast, Laramie was home to those who looked forward to
middle-class membership or those who had recently arrived
among the bourgeoisie. New concepts of marriage and family
life were unfamiliar to them, and the use of mental cruelty
was, therefore, slower to take hold. Both counties' laggard implementation of mental cruelty can be traced to the different
rates at which candidates for the middle class felt comfortable
enough to take their new habits of the heart to court.

FIGURE 68
LARAMIE COUNTY, WYOMING—DIVORCE TRENDS

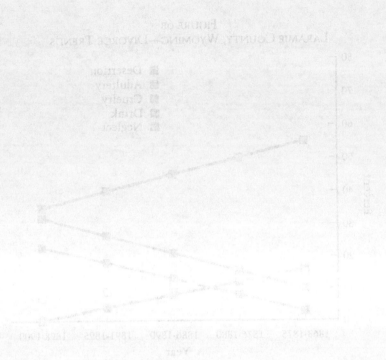

face, such concepts as the companionate marriage were born so far removed. Those were a certain middle class, and couples demanded that the law conform to their marital expectations. This particular change came more quickly into legal usage in Cheyenne, in certain affluent residential areas who had taken to court to middle-class memberships, those who had recently arrived among the bourgeoisie. New concepts of marriage and family life were unfamiliar to them, and the use of mental cruelty was therefore slower to take hold. Both countries, largest implementation of mental cruelty can be traced to the different rates at which candidates for the middle class felt comfortable enough to take their new beliefs of the heart to court.

Acknowledgments

Wunder, John R. "What's Old About the New Western History? Part 3: Law," *Western Legal History* 10 (1997): 85–116. Reprinted with the permission of the Ninth Judicial Circuit Historical Society.

Reid, John Phillip. "Some Lessons of Western Legal History," *Western Legal History* 1 (1988): 3–21. Reprinted with the permission of the Ninth Judicial Circuit Historical Society.

White, Richard. "Outlaw Gangs of the Middle Border: American Social Bandits," *Western Historical Quarterly* 12 (1981): 387–408. Reprinted with the permission of *Western Historical Quarterly*.

Wunder, John R. "Chinese in Trouble: Criminal Law and Race on the Trans-Mississippi West Frontier," *Western Historical Quarterly* 17 (1986): 25–41. Reprinted with the permission of *Western Historical Quarterly*.

Fritz, Christian G. "Popular Sovereignty, Vigilantism, and the Constitutional Right of Revolution," *Pacific Historical Review* 63 (1994): 39–66. Reprinted with the permission of the University of California Press. Copyright by the Pacific Coast Branch, American Historical Society.

Woolsey, Ronald C. "Crime and Punishment: Los Angeles County, 1850–1856," *Southern California Quarterly* 61 (1979): 79–98. Reprinted with the permission of the Historical Society of Southern California.

Dale, Lyle A. "Rough Justice: Felony Crime and the Superior Court in San Luis Obispo County, 1880–1910," *Southern California Quarterly* 76 (1994): 195–216. Reprinted with the permission of the Historical Society of Southern California.

Stanley, John J. "Bearers of the Burden: Justices of the Peace, Their Courts and the Law, in Orange County, California, 1870–1907," *Western Legal History* 5 (1992): 37–67. Reprinted with the permission of the Ninth Judicial Circuit Historical Society.

Wunder, John R. "The Chinese and the Courts in the Pacific Northwest: Justice Denied?" *Pacific Historical Review* 52 (1983): 191–211. Reprinted with the permission of the University of California Press. Copyright by the Pacific Coast Branch, American Historical Society.

Pisani, Donald J. "Enterprise and Equity: A Critique of Western Water Law in the

Nineteenth Century," *Western Historical Quarterly* 18 (1982): 15–37.
Reprinted with the permission of *Western Historical Quarterly.*

Ebright, Malcolm. "The San Joaquin Grant: Who Owned the Common Lands?: A
Historical-Legal Puzzle," *New Mexico Historical Review* 57 (1982): 5–26.
Reprinted with the permission of the University of New Mexico.

Salyer, Lucy. "Captives of Law: Judicial Enforcement of the Chinese Exclusion Laws,
1891–1905," *Journal of American History* 76 (1989): 91–117. Reprinted with
the permission of the Organization of American Historians.

McKnight, Joseph W. "Protection of the Family Home from Seizure by Creditors: The
Sources and Evolution of a Legal Principle," *Southwestern Historical Quarterly*
86 (1983): 369–99. Reprinted with the permission of The Texas State
Historical Association. All rights reserved.

Bakken, Gorden M. "Law and Legal Tender in California and the West," *Southern
California Quarterly* 62 (1980): 239–59. Reprinted with the permission of the
Historical Society of Southern California.

Bakken, Gordon M. "The Development of the Law of Mortgage in Frontier
California, 1850–1890, Part I: 1850–1866," *Southern California Quarterly* 63
(1981): 45–61. Reprinted with the permission of the Historical Society of
Southern California.

Bakken, Gordon M. "The Development of Mortgage Law in Frontier California,
1850–1890, Part II: 1867–1880," *Southern California Quarterly* 63 (1981):
137–55. Reprinted with the permission of the Historical Society of Southern
California.

Bakken, Gordon M. "The Development of Mortgage Law in Frontier California,
1850–1890, Part III: 1880–1890," *Southern California Quarterly* 63 (1981):
232–61. Reprinted with the permission of the Historical Society of Southern
California.

Schuele, Donna C. "Community Property Law and the Politics of Married Women's
Rights in Nineteenth-Century California," *Western Legal History* 7 (1994):
245–81. Reprinted with the permission of the Ninth Judicial Circuit
Historical Society.

Petrik, Paula. "'Send the Bird and Cage': The Development of Divorce Law in
Wyoming, 1868–1900," *Western Legal History* 6 (1993): 153–81. Reprinted
with the permission of the Ninth Judicial Circuit Historical Society.

For Product Safety Concerns and Information please contact our EU
representative GPSR@taylorandfrancis.com Taylor & Francis Verlag GmbH,
Kaufingerstraße 24, 80331 München, Germany

Printed and bound by CPI Group (UK) Ltd, Croydon, CR0 4YY
08/06/2025
01896977-0017